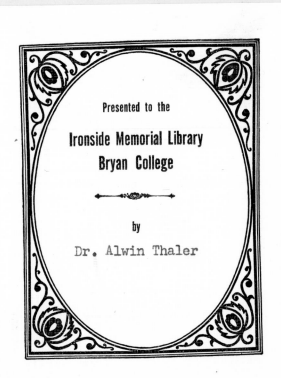

THE CHIEF MIDDLE ENGLISH POETS

THE CHIEF
MIDDLE ENGLISH POETS
Selected Poems

NEWLY RENDERED AND EDITED, WITH NOTES
AND BIBLIOGRAPHICAL REFERENCES

BY

JESSIE L. WESTON

BOSTON NEW YORK CHICAGO
HOUGHTON MIFFLIN COMPANY
The Riverside Press Cambridge

The Riverside Press
CAMBRIDGE . MASSACHUSETTS
U . S . A

PREFACE

THE selection of texts to be included in this volume has been a matter of much careful consideration. I already possessed a list of works of the period, drawn up for my guidance by Professor Schofield; a questionnaire, circulated by Messrs. Houghton Mifflin Company among the leading professors of English literature in America, brought forth numerous valuable additional suggestions; finally, I referred the list of translations, then practically completed, to Professor W. P. Ker, who, on his part, suggested other additions. The collection may thus claim to be fairly representative of the best American and English opinion, and as such will, it is hoped, meet the requirements of the majority of students of our common literature.

But if I have been guided by others in the choice of the texts, for the manner in which they are presented I am myself responsible. It has seemed to me desirable to give the poems as much as possible in their entirety, or, that being impracticable, in complete and representative episodes. I am, and always have been, strongly of opinion that to compile such a manual as the present on the lines of short extracts only results in inflicting injustice alike on the student and on the author. I have at present before me a work designed for the use of students of English literature, where *Amis and Amiloun* and *Sir Tristrem* are represented by five and a half stanzas allotted to each, *Sir Gawain and the Green Knight* and *Pearl* by three and a few lines, breaking off in the midst of a section; in one case not even at a full stop! Is it possible for any student to form an opinion of the style and merits of an author from such a collection of " shreds and patches"? Or is it fair to such poets as, for example, Layamon, or the author of *Pearl*, to present them in such a mutilated form? On the other hand, the continued utility of such compilations as those of Ritson and Weber, which, in spite of their age (both have been published for more than a century) and many critical imperfections, are still consulted by scholars, seems to me an argument in favor of printing the complete texts.

So far as possible the collection has been arranged to include all the principal branches of English mediæval literature; in the "Chronicles" section special attention has been given to Layamon, both on account of the real poetical merit of his work, and also for its critical interest. As is well known, his account of the founding of the Round Table is unique, and of extreme value as throwing light upon the character of Arthurian tradition before it came under the influence of the ideals of chivalric romance. Again, Arthur's dream as related here should be compared with the version of the Thornton *Morte Arthure*, given in my volume entitled *Romance, Vision, and Satire* (Boston, 1912). Layamon's version is distinctly the more vigorous and dramatic. It is interesting, too, to compare his account of the closing scenes of Arthur's life, and his testimony to the persistent belief of the folk in the hero's return, with the more polished version of the same themes given in the Harleian *M. A.*; both are fine, but there is a note of poignant reality and regret in Layamon's lines which seem to place the writer in a closer and more intimate relation with his theme; we may suspect that the Saxon priest of the twelfth century was not altogether disinclined to share the belief of the folk among whom he lived, while to the unknown poet of the fourteenth century Arthur was a poetic tradition, and no more.

The "Introduction," given from each of the "Chronicles," throws an interesting light on the aim and purpose (indirectly also on the personality) of the writers, and the sources they employed.

The "Legendaries" form so important a section of our mediæval literature, and were so active a factor in the instruction and edification of our forefathers, that it seemed well they should be fully represented. *Saint Dunstan* and *Saint Thomas* were included in my original scheme; they are of historical interest, and, in the case of the latter, of decided literary merit. On the advice of Professor Ker I have added *Saint Brandan*, which affords a notable example of the *Wonder-Voyage*, a favorite theme in all literatures; examples of the Northern Legendary, and *Lives of the Saints* in their earlier and independent form. Of the "Romances" here given, *Amis and Amiloun* and *Arthur and Merlin* were added as the result of the question- naire, and *Syr Percyvelle* on the suggestion of Professor Ker; this romance is so inter- esting a factor in the criticism of the evolution of an important romantic cycle that it is as well to render it more easily accessible than it is at present.

To the section devoted to works of edification I have added the *Bestiary*, on my own initiative, as its quaint lore has so strongly colored mediæval art and teaching.

The "Lyrical and Religious" section has grown with the progress of the work; in looking up isolated texts, I frequently, in the same volume, came across poems which seemed to me too good to be omitted from our collection. As it stands now I hope it may be found fairly representative of the different branches of a singularly rich and varied literature, and as such receive the kindly welcome of scholars.

In conclusion, my thanks are due to all those scholars who, by advice and sugges- tion, have contributed towards the formation and completion of the work; I only trust that, in the form it has finally assumed, it may prove to them of enduring inter- est and utility.

J. L. W.

Paris, December, 1913.

CONTENTS

HISTORICAL

TALES

PROVERBIAL AND DIDACTIC

RELIGIOUS AND LYRICAL

CONTENTS

THE CHIEF MIDDLE ENGLISH POETS

HISTORICAL

CHIEF MIDDLE ENGLISH POETS

LAYAMON

INTRODUCTION

There was a priest of yore,
Layamon, the name he bore;
The son of Leuca he —
God to him gracious be —
At Ernley that priest did dwell
Where the churches be builded well;
There, upon Severn's flood,
The place, it seemed him good,
To Radestone was it nigh —
There he read books, verily,   10
And the thought upon him fell,
In his mind he pondered well,
How folk might by him be told
Of the noble deeds of old;
How men those folk did call,
Whence they had come withal,
Who first did England hold
As their own, in days of old,
After that flood was spent
Which God on the world had sent,   20
When every soul was drowned,
And no man alive was found
Save Noah, I trow, and Shem,
And Japhet and Ham with them;
These four, each one with his wife,
In the ark, they kept in life.
Layamon, as I understand,
He journeyed far thro' the land,
And sought for each noble book,
Which he as his model took;   30
The English book, to wit,
Which erst by Saint Bede was writ;
And one of Latin lore,
By Saint Albin made of yore,
And eke by fair Austin wrought
Who Baptism hither brought.

And a third book he took alway
Which he 'twixt the twain did lay —
('T was a French clerk made that same,
Wace, did men call his name,   40
And well did he write, I wis!
And he offered that book of his
To Eleanor, Henry's queen —
A high king was he, I ween.)
He laid those books adown,
That priest, hight Layamon,
He turned the leaves carefully,
And looked on them lovingly,
(God be gracious to him, I pray!)
Then a pen he took that day   50
And he wrote upon parchment fair
The true words together there,
And of these three books, anon,
For our use hath he made but one.
Now Layamon doth beseech
That good men, all and each,
For the love of God on high,
Who this book read verily,
And learn its runes alway,
That in soothfast words they pray   60
That his soul, who did him beget,
May in endless bliss be set,
And his mother's soul also,
Who bare him, such bliss may know;
And for Layamon pray that he
May hereafter the better be!

KING LEIR [1]

After Bladud came Leir
His son, whom he held full dear;
He held this lordly land
Long time in his own hand,

[1] Ed. Madden, vol. i, p. 123.

Sixty winters past —
So long did his life-days last.
A goodly burg he wrought
Through the counsel his wise men brought,
And he called that castle fair
E'en by the name he bare;   10
Kaer-Leir he the burg did call,
('T was dear to his heart withal,)
But when men speak thereof to-day
Leirchestre do they say.
Of yore, in the olden days,
'T was a burg right fair to praise,
Since then much woe hath it seen,
Mickle sorrow its lot hath been,
For 't was all destroyed and undone,
And its folk they were slain, each
      one.   20
Thus sixty winters all told
Leir did his kingdom hold.
The queen, his wife, she bore
Three daughters, and no child more;
The king he had ne'er a son,
(Sorrow therefrom he won,)
Who heir to his honour should be
He had but these daughters three.
And thus were they hight; Gornoille,
Then Regau, the third Cordoille;   30
The youngest sister was she
And fairest of all the three,
To her father's heart was she near,
E'en as his life was dear.
The king, he waxed old in days,
And feeble in strength always,
And much did he vex his mind
What counsel 't were best to find,
And who should the kingdom hold
When he should be under mould.   40
And thus he himself bethought,
(Evil thereby he wrought,)
"My realm in three will I share
Betwixt these my daughters fair;
To my children I'll give my land
To have, and to hold in their hand.
But first will I search and see
The which of them best loves me,
And she shall have largest measure
Of my goodly lands and treasure."   50

In this manner, the king, he thought,
And even thereafter wrought,
For he bade Gornoille come near,
The first of his daughters dear,
And forth she came from her bower
To her father the self-same hour.
And these words did the old king say
As he sat on his throne that day:
"Gornoille, hearken and speak,
Soothfast words do I seek,   60
Very dear art thou to me,
Say, am I dear to thee?
What worth dost thou set this hour
On me, and my kingly power?"
Wary was Gornoille there,
As women be everywhere,
And she answered a fair leasing
Unto her father the king:
"Hearken, dear father and lord,
By the god I have aye adored,   70
(So help me Apollin to-day,
For my trust is in him alway,)
I wot that I love thee more
Than this world and its treasure store;
Yet more would I say to thee,
Thou art dearer than life to me!
This do I say thee for sooth,
Thou shalt hold it for very truth."
And Leir, the king, hearkened and heard,
He believed his daughter's word,   80
And this was the answer told
From the lips of that father old:
"I say to thee, Gornoille, here,
Gentle daughter and dear,
Right goodly shall be thy meed
As fitting for goodly deed:
I am old and feeble grown,
Great love to me thou hast shown,
I am dearer than life to thee —
Now this land will I deal in three,   90
And thine be the larger part,
Daughter dear to my heart!
And for lord will I give thine hand
To the highest thane in my land."
The old king, he spake thereafter
With Regau, his second daughter:
"Regau, my daughter dear,

Rede me thy counsel here,
Before all my folk say to me
How dear to thy heart I be!"   100
Then wisely she played her part,
And made answer, with mouth, not with
          heart:
"One limb of thine do I love
All on this earth above,
Yea, dearer than life it were" —
But no word of truth spake she there
No more than her sister had done.
Yet the lies they spake, each one,
Their father for truth did hold:
Then he answered, King Leir the old,110
For his daughter pleased him well —
"The third part of my land will I tell
To thine hand, and at my behest
Choose thy lord where thou likest best."
Yet the king he was not content,
On his folly he still was bent;
To come to his presence he bade
Cordoille, the third fair maid,
(The youngest was she in sooth,
And the wisest in words of truth,   120
And the king he loved her more
Than the twain who had come before).
Cordoille, who had hearkened and heard,
Knew that false was her sisters' word,
And she sware upon oath that day
That never a lie would she say,
Nor the truth from her father hide
Were he lief, were he loth, that tide.
In this wise spake Leir, the king,
(Ill rede was he following,)   130
"Now from thy lips will I hear,
Cordoille my daughter dear,
(Apollin be good to thee!)
How dear is my life to thee?"
Then answered Cordoille the daughter,
With mirth, and aye with laughter,
"My father is dear to me
As thy daughter is dear to thee,
Soothfast my love, I ween,
For the kinship us twain between.   140
As I hope for mercy alway
This more I to thee will say;
Thou art worth as much, I trow,

As that which thou holdest now,
And methinks the tale of thy treasure
Shall be e'en of men's love the measure;
For right soon are they loathed of all
Whom misfortune doth aye befall."
Thus, the maiden, she spake her will,
And afterward held her still.   150
The king, he was wroth at her word,
It pleased him ill what he heard,
For aye in his heart he thought
That to shame him the maiden sought;
He thought that she held him light,
And less dear he was in her sight
Than he was to her sisters twain —
But to leasing they aye were fain!
Then King Leir, he waxed black withal,
Black as a funeral pall,   160
So changed his skin and his hue
As the anger within him grew,
And he fell aback in a swoon —
But he lifted him up full soon.
The maiden feared when he spake,
With ill words his wrath out-brake:
"Hearken, Cordoille, to me,
My will here I tell to thee;
My dearest daughter wast thou,
I count thee most hateful now!   170
Never a foot of my land
Shall be given into thine hand!
In two portions my realm shall fall
And thy sisters shall hold it all.
But care shall thy portion be,
And thy dwelling with misery,
For ne'er had I dreamt this thing
That thou shame upon me should'st
          bring!
Henceforth art thou dead to me,
From my sight do I bid thee flee: 180
To thy sisters my land I give,
For such is my will, while I live,
Cornwall's duke, he with Regau shall
          share,
And the Scotch king wed Gornoille fair,
All mine shall be their's evermore,
Yea, all that I ruled afore!"
And thus the old king he wrought
In such wise as he had thought;

Oft was that maiden sad,
But never more cause she had!   190
She was heavy at heart and sore
For the anger her father bore;
She gat her into her bower,
Where she hid her many an hour,
But never a lie would she tell
Though she loved her father well.
Shamefast that gentle maid,
From her father she shrank afraid;
Wise rede she found at that tide,
In her bower did she still abide,   200
And wept, and lamented her sore
For the sorrow of heart she bore.
Thus one day after another
It passed, each like to the other.

In France was a king, I ween,
A rich man, and warrior keen,
Aganippus was he hight,
Chief of the folk, that knight.
Young was the king at that tide,
Nor as yet had he found a bride.   210
He sent messengers at this same,
And unto Britain they came,
Even to Leir, the king.
Fair greeting they here did bring
From their chief, — Would Leir hearken
      his prayer
And give him Cordoille the fair,
He would have her to crown her as queen,
And do all that should best to her seem,
Even all she desired at her word.
From wayfaring men had he heard   220
How men spake of that maiden fair,
Of the fairness and fame she bare
E'en before the French king's throne —
Of the beauty that was her own,
Of her honour and patient mind,
Of her courteous ways and kind,
In all the land of King Leir
Was there none men might call her peer.
In this wise Aganippus, the king,
To King Leir did greeting bring.   230
King Leir, he himself bethought,
And fitting answer he sought;
He bade his scribes to write

And a letter right well indite,
And he sent it forthwith by hand
Into the French king's land;
Thus ran King Leir, his writ, —
Wide spread the news of it —
"To Aganippus, France's chief,
Leir of Britain, this brief —   240
All honour I wish to thee still
For thy good deed, and right good will,
And the message so fair and meet
With which thou myself didst greet.
But I do thee well to wit,
Here, by my royal writ,
That my lordly land and fair
I have given, in equal share,
To my daughters, each a part,
For the twain are dear to my heart.   250
A third daughter I have, I trow,
But her dwelling I know not now,
For she hath despiséd me
And angered me bitterly;
For a wretch she doth me hold,
And because I be waxen old
Hath she put me to open shame,
The greater shall be her blame!
Of all my folk or my land   259
Which I hold, or may hold, in my hand
No whit, so I swear to thee,
Of this shall her portion be.
But an if thou desire that maid,
(She is very fair be it said,)
I herewith yield ye consent;
In a ship shall the maid be sent,
With the clothes that she with her bore,
Of me shall she have no more.
If thou wilt take her alway
I will do even this that I say.   270
Now thou know'st of my wrath the
      ground —
I pray thou abide whole and sound."
This writing to France they bring,
Straight to that noble king,
He bade them open and read,
Dear were its runes, indeed.
The king he deemed awhile
That the words were but words of guile;
That King Leir, her father old,

The maiden would fain withhold,   280
And the madder grew his desire,
And the flame of his love waxed higher,
And he spake to his barons thus,
The folk-king, Aganippus:
"A rich man enow I be,
I care not for lands or fee,
Never shall it be said
That King Leir refused me the maid;
But I will have her, I ween,
For consort, and noble queen.   290
Her father his lands may hold
And keep all his silver and gold,
I ask no treasure of his,
Mine own be enow, I wis!
I ask but the maid Cordoille,
With her shall I have my will."
With writ and with word once more
His folk he sent to this shore,
And again to King Leir made prayer
To send him his daughter fair,   300
And he would receive her well
In honour, as queen, to dwell.
The old king, he no whit stayed,
He took that noble maid
But with the clothes she ware,
And he bade her hence to fare
O'er the sea, that maiden good;
Stern was her father's mood!
But the French king, of heart so mild,
He welcomed the maiden child;   310
His folk, they deemed it right,
And they crowned her queen forth-right.
Thus Cordoille must with them dwell,
And the people loved her well.
But her father, Leir, the king,
In this land had his harbouring,
And had given his daughters dear
All his land, and all his gear.
He gave first Gornoille's hand
To the king of the Scottish land,   320
Maglaunus the prince was hight,
Great was his power and his might!
And Cornwall's duke thereafter
Did he wed to Regau his daughter.
But soon there chanced this thing
That the duke and the Scottish king

In secret together spake,
And thus did they counsel take,
That they would rule all the land
And have it in their own hand;   330
And to Leir, the king, they would give,
For the while that he yet might live,
Food for his days and his nights,
With forty hired knights.
And further there should be found
What was fitting in hawk and hound,
That through the land he might ride
And ever in bliss abide
The while that his life should last —
This counsel made they fast;   340
But e'en as their word they spake
Thereafter that word they brake;
And erstwhile it pleased the king,
And thereafter did sorrow bring.

King Leir, he deemed it well
With the Scottish folk to dwell,
With Maglaunus the king, his son,
Since the elder daughter he won.
Right welcome the king was made
And many fair words were said;   350
They furnished him there forth-right
With forty household knights,
With horses, and eke with hounds,
All that was meet they found.
But soon after it so befell
That Gornoille bethought her well
As to what were the wiser rede,
For evil it seemed, indeed,
That her father maintained these
        knights —
And she spake to her lord by night   360
As the twain in bed they lay,
And thus she began to say —
"My lord give me counsel now,
(Dearest of men art thou!)
Of my father would I complain;
Methinks that he be not sane,
For honour is he unfit
For now hath he lost his wit;
Methinks that so old he be
He doteth full speedily.   370
Now here hath he forty knights,

He keepeth them days and nights;
Here doth he hold these thanes
And with them their serving swains,
Their hounds and their hawks, I trow,
Thereof cometh harm enow!
For never elsewhere do they wend,
And ever the more do they spend,
But blithe of heart do they live
And take the good that we give.　380
Well-doing ever we sow,
And naught but unthank do we know!
Mischief they do evermore,
For they beat our men full sore,
My father he hath in his maisnie
Of idle men too many.
Now thus doth it seem me just,
The fourth part we forth will thrust,
Of thirty he'll yet be lord
Enow to serve at the board.　390
Ourselves we have cooks enow
For the kitchen service, I trow!
Ourselves we have butlers still
And cup-bearers at our will;
Let some of this folk forth fare
As it pleaseth them, otherwhere,
As mercy I hope and implore
I will suffer it never more!"
When he heard, King Maglaunus,
That his queen she spake to him thus,400
He answered the lady there
In noble speech and fair;
"Lady, thou doest ill,
Hast thou not treasure at will?
But keep thou thy father in bliss,
He liveth not long, I wis.
For it may be that foreign kings
Should hear of us evil things,
That we had dealt with him thus
And shame should it bring upon us.　410
But let him keep them still,
All his folk, at his will.
And this, forsooth, is my rede,
For right soon shall he be dead,
And then shall we have in our hand
The better half of his land!"
But Gornoille would have her will,
And she said, "My lord, hold thee still,

Leave it all in my hand
And I will dismiss this band."　420
She sent them all with guile
To their hostelry the while;
Thence she bade them depart with speed,
Since she would them no longer feed —
Many, I ween, of the thanes,
And many too of the swains
Who were servants to Leir, the king,
And whom he did hither bring.
And when the king heard thereof
In sooth he waxed very wroth,　430
Sadly the old king spake,
Bitter complaint did he make;
Thus said the old king good,
(Sorrowful was his mood!)
"Now woe to that man betide
Who hath honour, and lands so wide,
And all to his child doth give
The while that he still doth live
And may rule, for ere life be spent
Methinks he may sore repent!　440
But now will I take my way
To Cornwall without delay,
Counsel I think to hear
From Regau, my daughter dear,
Duke Hemeri hath her hand
And half of my goodly land."
Forth did King Leir wend
To Britain's southernmost end,
To Regau his daughter fair,
For counsel failed him there.　450
When the king to Cornwall came,
They welcomed him at the same;
There a full half year did he dwell
With his knights, and thought it well.
Then Regau spake craftily
To her lord, Duke Hemeri,
"My lord, hearken thou to me,
In good sooth I say to thee
We have done but a foolish thing
In receiving Leir, the king,　460
And these thirty knights of his,
It displeaseth me sore, I wis!
Send we twenty away,
Ten knights may serve him alway,
For ever they drink and they eat,

I find in them naught that is meet!"
Hemeri, the duke, he said,
(His old father he there betrayed,)
"So sure as I be alive
Of knights shall he have but five,   470
With them hath he folk enow,
He doeth naught, I trow;
And if that his will be so
Right soon shall he from us go!"
And as they had planned withal
Even so did the matter fall;
They took from the king his knights
And the folk that was his by rights,
But five of his men they left,
Of the others was he bereft.   480
When King Leir of this was ware,
Woe was his portion there;
Troubled at heart was he,
He lamented him bitterly.
Thus did he speak that day,
And with sorrowful mien did say —
"Weal, Weal, Weal, Weal,
With men dost thou falsely deal,
When on thee most their trust is laid
By thee are they most betrayed!   490
Two years, they have scarcely flown
Since, a rich king, I held mine own;
Many knights were under my sway;
Now I live to see the day
That I sit here stripped and bare;
Bereft of all must I fare!
Woe is me that I saw this land!
I were better in Gornoille's hand,
My goodly daughter and fair;
With her folk I tarried there,   500
Thirty knights would she give,
In some wise I might fitly live;
From her country I needs must go,
I deemed it were better so,
But the worse hath been my share!
To Scotland again will I fare,
With my daughter again to speak,
At her hand will I pity seek
If honour she will not give —
Yet let her once more receive   510
Me, and these five, my knights,
I will dwell with her days and nights,

And a short while endure this strife,
No whit long shall last my life!"
Thus Leir, the king, fared forth
To his daughter who dwelt in the North;
She harboured him full three nights,
Her father, and these his knights;
The fourth day an oath she sware,
By all the Powers that were,   520
That no more should he have of right
Than but one serving knight,
An he liked it not he might fare
And seek harbourage other-where.
Full oft Leir had woeful been,
Never worse than then, I ween!
Thus spake Leir, the king, —
Sorrow his heart did wring, —
"Alas, Death, where art thou?
Why dost thou not slay me now?   530
I wot Cordoille spake sooth,
Now do I know it for truth —
My youngest daughter was she
And very dear to me,
Yet thereafter she was to me loth
For these the words she quoth —
'The man who hath little, I deem,
Shall be held in light esteem,
And methinks of men's love the measure
Is even the tale of thy treasure!'   540
Well spake that maiden young,
Wisdom lay on her tongue!
The while I my kingdom held
My face men with joy beheld;
For my land, and for my fee,
My earls they fell to my knee.
Now am I wretched enow
And beloved of no man, I trow!
My daughter spake truth to me
I believe her verily!   550
And these, her sisters twain,
To lie were they ever fain
When they said they held me near,
Their own life was not so dear.
But Cordoille, my daughter young,
She said with truthful tongue,
That she loved me e'en as a daughter
Were bound to love her father;
What more were I fain to hear

From the lips of a daughter dear?   560
I will fare hence speedily
And get me across the sea;
To Cordoille I think to turn,
Her will I am fain to learn.
Her truthful speech did I blame,
Therefrom I won mickle shame,
For now all my succour lies
In the one I did erst despise.
I look for no worse at her hand
Than that she forbid me her land."   570

King Leir, he fared to the sea —
But a single servant had he —
To a ship he went straightway,
Never man knew him that day.
Over the sea they won
To a haven they came anon,
Forth went Leir, the king,
But one swain in his following;
He asked where the queen might lie,
They were fain to come her nigh?   580
And the folk, forthwith they showed
Where the queen of that land abode.
A field the king had found;
There he rested upon the ground.
His swain he alone would send,
(He was e'en a trusty friend,)
Cordoille, the queen, to seek
And in secret with her to speak.
Thus he said: "Queen, all hail to thee!
Thy father's swain I be;   590
Thy father the sea hath crossed,
For all his land hath he lost;
Thy sisters the realm have ta'en,
Foresworn, I ween, are the twain.
He cometh, in truth and in deed,
To this land, of very need;
Help him now in thy might,
As thy father, it is but right!"
Then the queen, fair Cordoille,
For a while, she sat very still.   600
Then the red to her cheek did flow
As if from the wine draught's glow —
(The swain he sat at her feet,
Right soon he found counsel meet.)
At length all her heart out-brake,

'T was very good that she spake —
"Apollin, fair thanks to thee,
That my father hath come to me.
Tidings right glad I hear
That he liveth, my father dear!   610
Of me shall he have good rede
An I be not afore that dead!
Now, good swain, hearken to me,
Hear what I say to thee:
I will give now unto thy care,
A coffer rich and fair;
Pennies therein be found,
I wot, to a hundred pound.
I give unto thee a steed
Right good, and strong at need   620
To carry this treasure here
E'en to my father dear.
Say that from me ye bear
A goodly greeting, and fair,
And bid him without delay
To some fair burg to find his way,
And in some rich town, or street,
To take him a lodging meet.
There shall ye buy for him first
That which may please him most,   630
What he needeth to drink and to eat,
And vesture fitting and meet.
Hawks and hounds as he needs
And the very best of steeds.
And be to his household told
Forty good knights and bold,
In garments rich and fair —
Then shall ye a bath prepare,
And a couch, and bed him soft,
And bleed him little and oft.   640
If silver be lacking thee,
Then ask it again of me,
And he shall have at my hand
Enough from this my land.
Of his old land never again
Shall he speak to knight or thane.
When forty days be gone
Ye shall make it known, anon,
To this, my lord so dear,
That Leir the king be here,   650
He hath crossed the water to me
My land and kingdom to see.

And I, I will take it so
As if naught thereof did I know;
With my lord I'll towards him ride
And rejoice that we meet that tide;
So shall it be known of none
That he be not newly come.
But thus shalt thou writing bring
Unto my lord the king.   660
Take thou this money from me
And see that well-spent it be;
And if thou dost wisely deal
It shall be to thy good and weal!"
The swain took the money there
And swift to his lord did fare,
Even to Leir, the king,
And the tidings did truly bring
To where on the field he lay
Resting for grief that day.   670
When all to the king was told
Of good comfort was Leir the old;
Truly he spake with voice
In these words did he there rejoice —
"Thus Good after Evil betides,
Well is he who its coming abides!"
To a fair burg his way he made
Right so as the queen him bade,
There he did right wisely and well
All things, e'en as she did tell.   680
And when it came at last
That the forty days were past,
Then took to him King Leir
The knights he held most dear,
To the French king they greeting bore,
(He was his son-in-law,)
And sent word to him by their hand
That King Leir had come to his land
And speech with his daughter prayed, —
She was dear to him, he said.   690
Aganippus, he was fain
That Leir had crossed the main;
Toward him he went forth-right,
And led with him many a knight,
And his fair queen, Cordoille.
Then had King Leir his will;
Together they met in bliss
With many a clasp and kiss,
To the burg they took their way —

Joy was with them that day —   700
They bade the trumpets blow,
And the pipes sound loud and low,
Throughout the castle hall
Were hangings of silken pall;
The boards that were spread for food
Glittered with gold so good;
Gold rings, and golden bands
Each man ware on arms and hands.
Fiddle and harp were strung
And men to their music sung.   710
The king set men on the wall
And bade them proclaim over all
And declare that Leir, the king,
In this land now made sojourning —
"And thus saith Aganippus,
He that is chief over us,
That now unto Leir the king
Ye all shall obedience bring;
Lord shall he be in this land
And have it all in his hand   720
Even as many year
As it please him to tarry here.
And Aganippus, our king,
He shall be but Leir's underling.
He who would live and thrive
Hold this peace while he be alive!
And if any this covenant break
Swift vengeance the king will take.
And he chargeth all who have heard
To hearken, and keep his word!"   730
And the folk they quoth: "We will
Keep the king's peace, loud and still!"
And thus for that same year
They did, even as ye hear,
In peace and loyalty,
And with mickle fealty.
When another year was come,
Then would King Leir fare home.
He was fain to see this land,
And prayed leave at the French king's
          hand.   740
Then the king Aganippus
Answered his father thus:
"Thou shalt never leave my coast
Save with a mickle host.
Of my folk I will thee lend;

Five hundred ships will I send
Filled with the best of my knights
And all they may need for the fight.
And thy daughter Cordoille, I ween,
Who is of this kingdom queen,　750
She, too, shall sail with thee
With an army, across the sea.
Now haste to that land amain
Where thou didst aforetime reign,
And if there be any still
Fain to withstand thy will
And take from thee thy right
And thy kingdom, then shalt thou fight,
And slay them, and take the land,
And set it in Cordoille's hand,　760
That it be hers to have and to hold
Whenever thy days be told."
These words said Aganippus,
And Leir, he did even thus,
In everything he wrought
E'en as his friend had taught.
O'er the sea he gat him here
With Cordoille his daughter dear,
Peace did he swear alway
With those who would own his sway,770
And he felled with his great might
All who would with him fight.
Thus all the kingdom and land
He won again to his hand
And freely to Cordoille gave
Who was queen from across the wave.
Thus was the wrong made good —
And so for a while it stood,
Leir the king this land
For three years held in his hand.　780
Then came the end of his day,
The king, he lifeless lay;
In Leicestre, so 't is said,
His daughter the body laid,
In the temple of Janus, to wit,
In the book may ye read of it.
And Cordoille, she held the land,
With high strength, five years in her
　　hand,
Five years as queen did she reign —
Then tidings came o'er the main　790
That the French king was dead, I ween,

And widowed was Cordoille, the queen.
So men did the tidings bring
Unto the Scottish king,
That dead the French king lay,
And Leir, too, was dead alway;
Through Britain then did he send,
To Cornwall, at its south end,
The strong duke did he command
To harry the Southern land,　800
And he would sally forth
And conquer again the North.
For he deemed it a mickle shame
And held it to them for blame,
That a queen should have all in her
　　hand
And rule as king in the land,
While their sons should landless be
Who in sooth were better than she,
Since their mothers the elder were
And their's was the greater share.　810
"No more will we suffer this wrong,
But the land shall to us belong,
For our sons we the realm will win." —
Thus did they the war begin.
Mischief came swift thereon;
Of their men, her sisters' sons
Led an army against her there —
These were the names they bare,
Morgan, and Cunddegis —
Oft they led their folk, I wis,　820
Oft they fought, oft they won the
　　day,
Oft they lost — so it went alway,
Till at last the Britons were slain,
And Cordoille was captive ta'en.
Their aunt they in prison cast,
In a torture house full fast.
Wrathful the woman's mood,
They vexed her more than was good,
Until she became so wroth,
To her very self was she loth,　830
And she took a long sharp knife
And therewith did she end her life.
But this was an evil rede
That she slew herself, indeed,
And thus the kingdom and land
Fell to her nephews' hand.

THE FOUNDING OF THE ROUND TABLE [1]

IT chanced on a Yule-tide day
That King Arthur in London lay;
There had come to him at that tide
Vassals from far and wide;
From Scotland, and Britain bold,
From Ireland, and Iceland cold,
From every folk and land
That had bowed them to Arthur's hand.
They had sent their highest thanes,
With their horses and serving swains: 10
And beside the folk that, still,
Bowed them to Arthur's will,
Came seven kings' sons, I ween,
With seven hundred knights so keen.

Now each man thought in his heart
That to him fell the higher part,
And each man deemed that he were
Better than this, his peer;
The folk came from diverse lands
And envy came with their bands — 20
This one held him of high degree,
This other, much higher than he!
Then they blew the trumpets' blast,
And they set the boards full fast,
And bare water to young and old
In basons of good red gold.
Soft were the cloths in the hall,
Of white silk woven all.
There Arthur sat in his pride,
With Wenhavere, the queen, at his side,
And the guests in order right, 31
First earl, then baron, then knight,
Each found his appointed seat
As the king's men deemed it meet.
There were men right nobly born
Who did service that Yule-tide morn,
And bare the meat forth-right
To each gay and gallant knight.
Then they turned them toward the thanes,
And below those still, the swains, 40
Thus served they, one and all,
The folk in King Arthur's hall.

[1] Ed. Madden, vol. II, p. 532.

Thus all for a space went well —
But after, a change befell,
For the folk, they fell to strife,
And blows were among them rife.
First they threw the loaves of bread,
And then, when the last was sped,
The bowls of silver-shine
Filled with the good red wine. 50
Thereafter with fists they fought
Each the neck of his foeman sought.
Then sprang forth a young man there, —
(From Winet land did he fare
As hostage to Arthur's hand,
The king's son of Winet land,
Rumaret was his father hight —)
And out spake that gallant knight,
And cried on the king that hour;
"Lord Arthur, get to thy bower, 60
And take with thee Wenhavere,
And the kinsmen thou holdest dear,
And we shall fight out this fray
With the foreign folk to-day!"
And e'en as he spake the word
He leapt to the royal board
Where lay the sharp knives keen,
For the service of king and queen;
Three knives he grasped in his hand,
And he smote the chief of the band 70
And clave the neck of the knight
Who first began the fight,
With a blow so swift and sore
That his head rolled e'en to the floor.
Thereafter he slew another,
Even that first thane's brother,
Ere the swords might come to the hall
Seven men had he slain in all.
'T was a grim and a grisly fight,
Each man would the other smite, 80
Blood gushed forth at every stroke,
Bale was upon the folk.

Then forth from the king's bower strode
Arthur in wrathful mood,
And with him a hundred knights
In helmet and burnie bright;
Each bare in his strong right hand
A gleaming white steel brand.

Then Arthur, king most dear,
Cried so that all might hear: 90
"Sit ye down, sit ye down, each one,
As ye love your lives, sit down!
He that will not while yet he may
I doom him to death straightway!
Now take me that self-same man
Who first this fight began;
Round his neck put a withy stout,
And draw him the hall without
To the moorland and marsh hard by;
There shall ye let him lie!   100
Then seek out his next of kin,
All such as be here within,
And with your broad swords keen
Shall ye strike off their heads, I ween!
Then take ye his women-folk,
And with swift, and with cunning, stroke
Carve off their noses there
That they be no longer fair.
And thus will I bring to shame
The kindred of which he came!   110
And if it be brought to my ear,
Or I otherwise chance to hear,
That one of my house or hold,
High or low, or young or old,
Shall hereafter awaken strife
For this slaughter, I swear on my life,
Neither gold, nor goodly steed,
Nor treasure, nor warlike weed,
Shall be ransom for that man's head
That he be not swiftly dead,   120
Or horses his limbs shall draw —
So speak I the traitor's law!
Bring me the hallows here,
On them will I soothly swear,
And so shall ye too, my knights,
And all who were at this fight."

First Arthur, the noblest of kings,
He swore by the holy things;
Then earls, and barons, and thanes,
And last of them all, the swains,   130
A solemn oath they swore
To wake that strife never more.
Then the dead men, one and all,
They bare them from out the hall,

And laid them low in the earth —
Then the trumpets they blew with mirth.
Each of them, were he lief or loth,
Must needs take water and cloth,
And they sat them, at one accord
Once more, adown to the board,   140
For they feared King Arthur's hand,
Noblest of kings on land!
The cupbearers went their round,
The harpers made merry sound,
The glee-men sang songs so good,
The folk were in gladsome mood;
Thus for full seven days all told
King Arthur his feast did hold.

Thereafter I'ld have ye know,
To Cornwall the king would go,   150
And there cometh to him anon
A crafty and skilful man,
And he met the king in the way,
And in greeting fair did say:
"Arthur, all hail to thee now!
Noblest of kings art thou,
I am thine own true man,
To serve thee as well I can.
I have journeyed in many a land,
Right skilful is this, mine hand,   160
In craft of wood, or of tree, —
But now it was told to me
The slaughter thy knights had wrought,
When of late at thy board they fought,
And how, on mid-winter's day,
Mickle pride wrought murderous play;
For that each man by right of kin,
And high lineage, would sit within.
Now I will for thee, lord, prepare
A board exceeding fair,   170
Where sixteen hundred may sit,
And more, if it seem thee fit.
And all they shall turn about,
So that no man shall be without,
But without and within shall they be,
Man against man, verily!
And when thou to ride art fain,
Thou shalt carry it in thy train;
And when thou shalt hold thee still,
Thou shalt stablish it at thy will;   180

And never shalt thou fear more,
So long as the world endure,
That for envy a moody knight
Shall raise at thy board a fight,
Of high or of low degree
All men there shall equal be!"

Then they bade men timber win
That he might the board begin;
For the space of four weeks he wrought
Ere the work to an end he brought. 190
Then when a high day was come
The folk he called, every one;
And Arthur himself, the lord,
Sat him down at the new-wrought board,
And he bade every gallant knight
Take his place at his side forth-right,
And when each had found his seat,
And all were sat down to meat,
Then each man spake with the other
In such wise as he were his brother. 200
In order they sat about,
And no man was left without;
No knight, whatsoe'er his race,
But found there a fitting place,
Were he high, were he low, in that hall
Was a place for each and all.
And each man, he quaffed at the board
The drink that was there outpoured,
Nor thought he might call for other
Than the draught that would serve his
        brother. 210

Now this was that very Round Table
Of which Britons oft-times fable;
And many a lie shall ye hear
Of Arthur that king so dear;
But I think me 't is ever so
That the custom of men doth go,
He that loveth his friend, I ween,
For his honour is over-keen,
Nor shall deem it a shame to lie
If he win him more praise thereby! 220

The songs that the songmen sing
Of Arthur, the noble king,
All lies are they not, nor all sooth,
But this do I hold for the truth,
There was never such other lord
So mighty in deed and in word,
For so ye may find it writ
In his history, every whit,
From the first to the last, how things
Fell out for Arthur, the king. 230
Neither more nor less may ye read,
But all these, his acts, and his deeds.
The Britons, they loved him well,
And many a tale they tell,
And many a wondrous thing
Concerning Arthur, the king,
Such as never were wrought by man
Since ever the world began!
Yet he who would speak but the truth
He may find, in very sooth, 240
Enough to shape goodly rhymes
Of Arthur, the king, and his times.

THE PASSING OF ARTHUR[1]

A-HORSE to the king's host drew
A knight, both good and true,
Tidings he thought to bring
To Arthur, the Britons' king,
Of Modred his sister's son —
A welcome glad he won
From the king, who thought to hear
That which should bring him cheer.
Arthur lay long that night
And spake with that youthful knight, 10
But never a word did he say
Of that which had chanced alway.

When it came to the morrow's morn,
And the folk, they stirred with the dawn,
Then Arthur arose from his bed;
He stretched his arms over his head,
Then he stood, and he sat again,
E'en as one for misease is fain.
Then asked him that goodly knight,
"Lord, how hast thou passed the night?"
And Arthur, the king so good, 21
Made answer in troubled mood:
"Last night, as I lay on sleep

[1] Ed. Madden, vol. III, p. 117.

In my tent, and slumbered deep,
There came such a dream to me
As hath vexed me right bitterly —
Methought men lifted me there,
And raised me high in air,
Until that the roof-tree tall
I bestrode, of a lofty hall,   30
I sat there as I would ride, —
And below me, stretched out wide,
I saw all my goodly land;
Before me, sword in hand,
Sat Walwain, my kinsman true.
Then Modred towards us drew,
With him came a goodly throng;
In his hand was an axe so strong
And with mighty strokes he felled
The posts that the hall upheld.   40
And then I saw Wenhavere,
(Woman to me most dear,)
With her hands the roof she tare
Of that hall, so great and fair,
Till the building rocked and swayed,
And I fell to the ground dismayed;
And there my right arm I brake —
'Take that!' so Modred spake.
Then in ruins fell that hall,
And it bare Walwain in its fall   50
From the roof-tree e'en to the ground,
And he brake both arms at that stound.
Then I gripped my sword so good
In my left hand, as best I could,
And smote off Modred's head,
On the wold he fell down dead.
In pieces I hewed the queen
With my sword blade, good and keen,
And, methought, her corse at last
In a deep black pit I cast.   60
My folk, they had fled away,
And I knew not, by Christ, that day
Whither they all had gone —
But methought I stood alone
On a moor-land bleak and cold;
I wandered afar on the wold,
Gryphons I saw, I trow,
And grisley fowls enow!
Then over the down to me
Came a beast, most fair to see,   70

A golden lion, methought
'T was a work that God's hand had
    wrought!
The beast came to me forthright,
By the middle it gripped me tight,
And carried me o'er the land
Till we came to the salt sea strand,
And I saw the waves of the sea
How they drave right heavily.
Then the lion the flood would swim,
Bearing me ever with him,   80
But scarce were we come in the sea
Ere the waves bare him far from me.
Then a great fish came in my need,
And bare me to land with speed;
I was wet and weary, I trow,
For sorrow, and sick enow!
And then must I needs awake,
My heart did within me quake.
Then a heat and a trembling fell,
And I burned as with fires of Hell!   90
Thus all night long have I lain
And dreamed that dream o'er again,
'T is a token true, I wis,
That vanished is all my bliss,
And, while life be left to me,
Grief shall my portion be!
Alas! that I have not here
Wenhavere my queen so dear."
Then out spake that youthful knight:
"My lord, thou doest not right,   100
No man should so read a dream
As to turn it to sorrow, I ween!
For of all kings, I know full well,
Who under the welkin dwell,
To whose rule the people bow,
The richest and wisest art thou!
And if it should chance to be,
(May Christ keep it far from thee!)
That Modred, thy sister's son,
The heart of thy queen had won,   110
And had taken thy wife and thy land,
And had set them all in his hand,
(All thou didst leave in his care
When thou thoughtest afar to fare,)
And were thus for a traitor shown, —
Still mightest thou hold thine own,

And avenge thyself by war,
And rule thy folk as before,
And the men who this wrong had done
Thou could'st slay them every one,   120
Yea, and sweep them clean from the
     ground,
So that none should alive be found!"
Arthur, he answered then:
(Noblest was he of men,)
"So long as 'ever' may be
Ne'er do I think to see
The day that my kinsman dear,
The man to my heart most near,
Hath ever such treason planned
As to seize my crown and my land;   130
Or Wenhavere, my queen and love,
Shall other than steadfast prove!
Such work they would ne'er begin,
Tho' they thought thus the world to
     win!"
As he spake the word, forthright
There answered that gallant knight:
"I speak but the truth, my King,
For I am thine underling,
Even thus hath Modred done,
The heart of thy queen hath he won,   140
And all Britain, and thy fair land,
Hath he taken in his own hand.
As king and queen do they reign
Nor deem thou shalt come again,
'T is a far cry to the Roman shore,
From thence shalt thou come no more!
But I am thy man O King!
And I saw this evil thing,
To thyself have I brought this word,
And the truth, e'en as thou hast heard,
My head in pledge will I lay,   151
'T is sooth and no lie, that I say,
But even thus have they done,
Thy queen and thy sister's son,
Modred hath taken thy throne,
Thy land, and thy wife, for his own!"

Then never man stirred of all
Those knights in King Arthur's hall,
Right sorrowful was their mood
For the grief of their king so good.   160

Downcast and sad of mien
Were the British men, I ween!
'T was thus for a space, and then
Rose a clamour of angry men,
Till all far and wide might know
Of the Britons' wrath and woe!
In sooth might ye there have heard
Full many a threatening word,
Doom to the faithless pair,
Modred and the queen, they sware,   170
And the men who held with the twain
They all should be swiftly slain.
Then Arthur cried thro' the hall,
Fairest of Britons all,
"Sit ye down, and hold ye still
My knights, and hearken my will,
Strange words do I think to say,
To-morrow, when it be day,
By Christ, His power, and His grace,
Will I get me forth from this place.   180
To Britain I take my way,
And there will I Modred slay,
And the queen with fire will I burn;
And to loss and to ruin turn
All that have joined their hand
With them, and this treason planned.
But here will I leave in my place
Hoel, the fair of face,
(The first of my kinsmen he,
And dearest of men to me,)   190
With half of my army bold
That this kingdom he keep and hold,
And all this goodly land
That I late have set in mine hand.
And when I have vengeance ta'en
I will turn me to Rome again,
And my lands so wide and fair
Will I give into Walwain's care.
No empty threat do I make
But my life on my word I stake,   200
I will fell my foes every one,
Who this treason and wrong have done!"
Then Walwain arose in the ring,
He was kinsman unto the king,
Wrathful and stern his mood,
And he spake, "O almighty God,
Who dost judgment and doom award,

And this middle earth dost guard,
How did this thing begin?
Why hath Modred wrought this sin? 210
Now ye folk, lend to me the ear;
This day I forsake him here,
I myself will his Doomsman be,
(So the Lord grant it unto me!)
Higher than e'er another
With this hand will I hang my brother!
And the queen I will judge by God's law,
Wild horses her limbs shall draw.
For never shall I be blithe
The while that I be alive   220
Till I right mine uncle and lord
To the best of my hand and sword!"
The Britons made answer then
With one voice, as valiant men:
"Our weapons are keen and bright,
To-morrow we march forthright!"

Then, since the Lord willed it so,
To-morrow they forth would go,
Arthur moved with the dawning light,
And with him his valiant knights,   230
One half of the folk must stay,
And one half marched with him alway.
Thus he led his men through the land
Till they came at the last to Whitsand;
Ships, full many and good,
Ready in harbour stood,
But a fortnight full his host
It lay becalmed on that coast,
Till the weather changed once more, 239
And the wind blew fresh from the shore.

Now in Arthur's host that day
Was one who would traitor play,
And when he heard men speak
Of the vengeance they thought to wreak,
Forthwith he took his swain,
And he bade him haste amain,
And bear to Wenhavere the word
Of how Arthur the tale had heard,
And how he would come ere long,
With a mickle host, and strong;   250
And how he had sworn an oath
To take vengeance upon them both.

The queen came to Modred then,
(Dearest to her of men,)
And told to him everything
Concerning Arthur the king,
How he would act in that day,
And how he the twain would slay.
Then Modred sent speedily
To Saxland across the sea,   260
And he prayed that Childerich,
A monarch exceeding rich,
Would swiftly to Britain fare,
(Of the land should he have his share —)
And he prayed of the king that tide
To send messengers far and wide,
East, West, and South, and North,
And bid all his knights fare forth,
Even all they met on their way, —
And to get them without delay   270
To Britain, and part of the land
Would he give into Childerich's hand;
North of the Humber all
Should be his without recall,
If he men to his aid would bring
Against Arthur his lord and king.
Childerich helped him in need,
To Britain he came with speed;
And Modred called on his men
To gather for battle then,   280
There were sixty thousand all told,
Hardy warriors and bold,
Who were come out of Heathennesse
For King Arthur's sore distress,
For Modred they came to fight,
That evil and traitorous knight!
And when all were come to the place,
Of every folk and race,
Rank upon rank did they press,
One hundred thousand, no less,   290
Of heathen, or Christian, that morn
Were with Modred the false and fore-
    sworn.
Now Arthur and all his host,
At Whitsand they lay, on the coast,
Too long seemed those fourteen days —
And Modred he knew always
What Arthur he planned and he wrought,
For tidings each day were brought

From the army that lay by the sea —
Then the rain, it rained steadily,   300
And the wind, it shifted at last,
And blew from the east full blast,
And Arthur gat him aboard
With every knight and lord;
And he bade his shipmen steer
For Romney, and have no fear,
There he thought him to land, and then
March inland with all his men.
When they came to the haven and shore
Modred was there before,   310
And ere ever the dawn grew bright
The hosts they had fallen to fight,
And they fought through the live-long
          day,
Full many there lifeless lay!
Some of them fought on the land,
And some on the salt sea strand,
Some from the ships' deck cast
Sharp spears, which flew full fast.
Walwain, he went before,
And cleared their path to the shore,   320
Eleven thanes did he slay
With Childerich's son, that day,
Whom his father had hither brought —
When the sun his rest had sought
Bowed was each British head
For Walwain lay there dead
And robbed of his life-days all —
(Through a Saxon earl did he fall,
Sorry be that man's soul!)
To Arthur 't was bitter dole,   330
Full sorrowful was his mood,
And he spake, that chieftain good,
(Mightiest of Britons he —)
"I have lost, ah, woe is me!
Walwain whom I loved so well,
E'en so did my dream foretell,
I deemed it would sorrow bring!
Now slain is Angel the king,
Who was mine own darling, and thane,
And my sister's son, Walwain,   340
Ah, woe is me for this morn,
I would I had ne'er been born!
Now up from your ships, and fight
As ye ne'er yet have fought, my knights!"

Then, even at his command,
His warriors leapt to the land,
Sixty thousand all told,
Stalwart Britons and bold,
And they brake through Modred's host,
Well nigh he himself was lost!   350
Then Modred, he 'gan to flee
And his men followed speedily,
'T was a marvel to see how they fled,
The fields rocked beneath their tread,
And the stones in the river course
Jarred 'neath the blood-streams' force!
Full well had they ended that fight
Were it not for the coming of night,
Had the darkness but made delay
All their foes had been slain that day. 360

The night fell between the twain —
O'er the hills Modred fled amain,
He fled so far and so fast
That to London he came at last,
But they knew, the burghers stout,
How the matter had fallen out,
And bade him and his followers all
Abide there, without the wall.
Modred, he might not stay,
But to Winchester took his way,   370
And they gave him shelter there
And all that with him did fare.
But Arthur, with all his might,
Pursued after him forth-right,
And to Winchester came ere long
With a mickle host and strong;
With his army he sat him down,
And shut Modred within the town.
When Modred saw him so nigh
He bethought him craftily,   380
And oft he turned in his mind
What counsel he there might find.
And there, on that self-same night,
He called unto him his knights,
And bade them to arm them straight
And march out of the city gate,
For there would he make a stand
And fight for the crown and the land.
And unto the burghers he swore
Free law for evermore   390

Would they stand by him at his need
And help him with act and deed.
And thus, when it waxed to light,
All ordered they stood for fight.
Arthur beheld this thing,
Wroth was the Britons' king:
Then the trumpet blast rang clear,
And his men came together there,
And he prayed of his thanes forth-right,
And of every noble knight,   400
To help him, and fight right well,
That he might all his foemen fell;
And to level the city wall,
And to hang the burghers all.
Together they marched, as one man,
And sternly the fight began.
Then Modred, again he thought
In his heart, and counsel sought,
And he did in his danger there
E'en as he did elsewhere,   410
With the best could he traitor play
For treason he wrought alway!
He worked a betrayal grim
On the comrades who fought for him;
For he called from among the rest
The knights whom he loved the best,
And the friends whom he held most
    dear
Of the folk who were with him there,
And he stole from the fight away —
The Devil led him that day!   420
And left his good folk on the land,
To be slain there by Arthur's hand.
Thus all day long they fought,
That their lord was nigh they thought,
And they deemed that he took good heed
To succour them in their need.
But Modred, he went his way
On the road that toward Hampton lay,
And made for the haven then —
(Wickedest he of men! —)   430
Of the ships he took speedily
All that were fitted for sea,
And the steersmen, one and all,
That no harm should his ships befall;
Thus Modred, that traitorous king,
Did they safe into Cornwall bring.

And Arthur his army cast
Round Winchester, fair and fast,
And all the folk did he slay —
Sorrow was their's that day! —   440
He spared no soul that drew breath,
Young or old, all he put to death.
Thus the people to loss he turned,
And the city with fire he burned.
And then he bade them withal
To break down the city wall;
And thus was fulfilled the word,
Aforetime from Merlin heard:
"Winchester, woe unto thee,
For swallowed of earth shalt thou be!"
Thus Merlin the seer foretold,   451
Wisest wizard of old!

In York the queen abode,
Right sorrowful was her mood,
Saddest of women, I ween,
Was Wenhavere, Arthur's queen!
For she heard men say for sooth,
And knew them for words of truth,
How that Modred, he ever fled,
And Arthur behind him sped,   460
Woe was upon her that morn
That ever she had been born!
From York did she take her flight,
In secret, by shades of night,
And to Caerleon made her way
Swiftly, without delay,
Not for all this world's treasure-store
Would she look upon Arthur more.
Thus with but two knights in her train
At Caerleon she drew rein,   470
To the city she came by night,
And they hooded her there forth-right,
And a nun must she henceforth be,
Saddest of women she!
Then men of the queen knew naught,
Where she went, or what fate she sought;
E'en when many years had flown
The truth might by none be known.
And never a book may tell
In what wise her death befell,   480
And if in the water's flow
She cast herself, none may know.

In Cornwall was Modred then,
And he gathered to him his men;
To Ireland he sent with speed
Messengers in his need,
To Scotland, to Saxland, too,
Help from them all he drew.
He bade them come to his land,
All who would win to their hand   490
Silver, or gold, or fee —
Thus he guarded him prudently,
As a wise man will ever do
When need forceth him thereto.
Tidings to Arthur they bring,
(Was never so wroth a king!)
How Modred in Cornwall sped, —
That a mighty host he led,
And there he thought to abide
Till Arthur should 'gainst him ride.   500
Then messengers Arthur sent,
Through the breadth of his land they
                    went,
And they bade every living knight
In the land, who had strength to fight,
To arm him, and come straightway. —
But if he would traitor play,
And hold with Modred, then
The king would have none of such
                    men.
And whoever should take no heed
To do Arthur's will with speed   510
Should be burnt alive on the land,
Or slain, at the king's command.
Then towards the army sped
A folk unnumberéd,
A-horse and afoot they came,
Thick as the falling rain.
To Cornwall marched Arthur the king,
With a mighty following.
And when Modred the tidings knew
Toward him he swiftly drew —   520
Countless the folk that day,
O'er many of them were fey!
To the Tamar their face they set,
By the river those armies met,
Camelford, did they call that shore,
And the name dureth ever more!
Arthur, he reckoned then

On his side, sixty thousand men,
But more by thousands were they
Who stood by Modred that day!   530
No longer would Arthur abide
But thitherward would he ride;
Bold were his knights and fleet,
They hasted their fate to meet!
On the banks of the Tamar river
The armies they came together,
The banners above them flew,
The ranks together drew,
Their long swords flash in the light,
Hard on the helms they smite;   540
The sparks sprang beneath the stroke,
The spears, they shivered and broke;
Cloven each goodly shield,
The shafts they splinter and yield;
The folk they fought passing well,
Their number no man might tell;
Tamar, it ran on flood
Swollen with streams of blood.
Never might man in the fight
Know one from the other knight,   550
Who did better, or who did worse,
So mingled the battle's course,
For each, as he might, would slay,
Were he swain, were he knight, that
                    day!
There was Modred of life-days reft,
On the field was he lifeless left,
And with him all of his knights
Were slain in that fearsome fight.
There too were slain, I ween,
Full many good knights and keen,   560
King Arthur's warriors brave
High and low, all found there their
                    grave,
With every British lord
Who sat at Arthur's board,
And the men who bowed to his hand
Of every kin and land.
And Arthur was smitten sore,
Of spear wounds that day he bore
Fifteen, so deep, and so wide,
In the least gash two gloves might ye
                    hide!   570
When it came to the end of the strife

Nor more were there left on life,
Of two hundred thousand men
Who lay hewn in pieces then,
Save only Arthur, the king,
And two knights of his following.
And Arthur was smitten sore,
Wondrous the wounds he bore!
Then a young knight came to the king,
He was one of his kith and kin, —　580
Son to Cador the keen,
Who earl of Cornwall had been,
Constantine was he hight,
Arthur he loved that knight —
The king looked his face toward
As he lay on the bloody sward,
And thus he spake to the lad
With sorrowful heart and sad:
"Constantine, thou art welcome now,
Cador's son wert thou,　590
I leave thee my kingdom here,
Guard thou my Britons dear
So long as thy life shall last —
And see that they still hold fast
The laws that in my day stood,
And King Uther's laws so good.
But to Avalon will I fare,
A maiden, she ruleth there,
By name Arganté the queen,
Fairest of elves I ween!　600
My wounds shall she handle and heal,
Turning my woe to weal,
For sound is he who hath quaffed
At her hand a healing draught!
And then will I come again

And once more o'er my kingdom reign,
And dwell with my Britons dear
In great joy, and mickle cheer!"
And e'en as the words he said
Swift o'er the sea there sped　610
A little boat, and low,
That came with the wavelets' flow.
Within were two women fair
Who a wondrous semblance bare;
They took up Arthur the king,
And swift to the boat did bring,
Soft they laid down his head,
And swiftly from thence they sped.
Ah! then was fulfilled the word
From Merlin the prophet heard　620
That sorrow and woe should spring
From the passing of Arthur the king.

But the British folk, they say
That Arthur, he lives alway,
That held by a fairy spell,
In Avalon doth he dwell;
And each Briton's hope is strong
That he cometh again ere long!
And there liveth no mother's son
Who desire of women hath won,　630
Who knoweth a better lore
Or of Arthur can tell ye more.
But whilom was a wizard wight,
Merlin that man was hight,
And he said in words of truth,
(For ever his sayings were sooth,)
That Arthur shall come again,
And once more o'er the Britons reign!

ROBERT OF GLOUCESTER'S CHRONICLE

INTRODUCTION

ENGLAND, it is a right good land, I ween of lands the best,
'T is set in one end of the world, and lieth toward the West;
The sea, it girts it all about, it stands as doth an isle,
Thus of their foes they have less doubt, save that they come thro' guile
The people of that self-same land — as hath been seen of old.
From South to North the land is long, eight hundred miles full told,

He who would cross from East to West two hundred miles must wend,
So is the mid-land measure told, 't is less toward the end.
And here in England all good things in plenty may ye see
Save thro' wrong-doing of the folk the years the worser be.   10
For England, it is full enow of fruit, and trees so green,
Of woodland, and of parks so fair, joyful to see, I ween;
And birds and beasts, both wild and tame, ye sure shall find them there
With fishes too, both salt and fresh, and many a river fair!
And wells of water, sweet and cold, pastures and meads wide-spread,
And mines of silver and of gold, of tin, and eke of lead,
Of steel, of iron, and of brass; garners of good corn full,
And wheat have they, and therewithal the very best of wool.
And waters have they there enow, above all others three
(Across the land to sea they run, e'en as its arms they be,)   20
Whereon the ships may safely sail, and from the sea may wend
To land with merchandise enow, and reach to either end.
Two be the Severn and the Thames, Humber the third they call,
And these, e'en as I said to ye, run thro' the land withal.
The Humber runneth to the North, a goodly stream and wide,
South-West, I trow, the Severn's course, the Thames, on the East side,
So that enow of merchandise from distant lands, I wis,
Is borne by them thro' England, the folk, they nothing miss.
And many a smaller isle there be that lieth off this land
But three there be above them all, so do I understand.   30
That which they call the Isle of Man lies in the Irish sea,
And the great Isle of Orkney shall North of Scotland be,
South, toward Normandy, the third the Isle of Wight they call,
These be the three best islands, and the best known of all.
The earliest lords and masters who dwelt within that land
They reared the towns and cities that chief in England stand;
London, and York, and Lincoln. Leicester, the names they bore,
Colchester, Canterbury, Bristol, and Worcester, four,
And Chichester, and Cambridge, with Cirencester, these three
With Dorchester, and Winchester, and Gloucester, next shall be.   40
Other great towns be found there, in Wales, the sooth to say,
And thus it was in England when Britons there held sway.
Men have made war on England, thither as conquerors come,
First, mighty lords they ruled it, the Emperors of Rome,
They fought, and eke they won it, and held it at that same;
The Picts and Scots thereafter, from North to England came,
They warred, and wide they wasted, yet won not all they sought;
Then Angles came, and Saxons, by Britons hither brought
Against these foes to help them — they gained the upper hand
Against these self-same Britons, and took from them their land.   50
And since that time in England the warfare scarce may cease,
First, thro' the folk of Denmark, who be not yet at peace,
England oft-times they won it, and held by mastery —

Fifthly, the land was conquered by folk from Normandy
And still they dwell among us, and shall for evermore —
The book hereafter telleth of all this woe so sore.
The Britons were the first folk who landed on this shore,
The kingdom they divided, and gave to rulers four;
The kings of Kent, and Wessex, and of Northumberland,
And of the March, this last king, he ruled the middle land.   60
The Saxons, and the English, when they the land had won
In shires five and thirty they parted it anon,
Sussex, I trow, and Surrey, Essex, and Kent they be,
And Berkshire next, and Hampshire, and Middlesex, these three.
Then Dorsetshire, and Wiltshire, and Somerset, also,
And Devonshire and Cornwall, with Gloucestershire ye know.
Then Shropshire nigh to Worcester, thereafter Hereford,
With Warwickshire, and Cheshire, Derby, and eke Stafford;
And Lincolnshire, and Bedford, and also Huntingdon,
Buckingham, and Northampton, and Oxenford, anon.   70
Norfolk there is, and Suffolk, and Cambridge-shire also,
And Hertfordshire, and Leicester, and Nottingham thereto.
York and Carlisle, Northumberland, these three complete the tale —
These shires be all in England, without the March of Wales.
With that there be in England Bishoprics seventeen,
Carlisle they be, and Durham, and York, so do I ween,
Ely, and Canterbury, Norwich, and Rochester,
With London, too, and Salisbury, Chichester, Winchester,
Of Lincoln, and of Chester, and Worcester, last there be
Bath, Hereford, and Exeter — these be the final three.   80
With that, Wales too, hath bishops, but three alone, no more,
Saint David first, then Landaff, the third is of Bangor.
But York and Canterbury, Archbishoprics are they,
They of Carlisle, and Durham, must York's decrees obey;
The others all of England with those of Wales, the three,
They all shall owe allegiance to Canterbury's see.

When Saxons ruled in England, tho' they in power did thrive,
But seven kings they made here, and afterward but five;
Northumbria, and East Anglia, these be the names of two,
The kings of Kent, and Wessex, and of the March also.   90
Who ruled the March, I think me, at that time had the best, —
The greater part of England, that lieth toward the West,
Both Worcestershire and Warwick, with Gloucester to him fell,
('T was well nigh all one Bishopric, of Worcester, so men tell.)
And Derbyshire, and Cheshire, and Staffordshire, those three
Again be held together, and make one Bishop's see,
The Bishopric of Chester, yet more to him was told,
Since Shropshire, and the half share of Warwick did he hold.
And this king, too, had Hereford, one bishopric it is,

(But Shropshire forms the half part of that same see, I wis.   100
Of Gloucester part, and Warwick) nor this, I trow, was all,
For still more land as portion unto the March did fall;
Northamptonshire, and Buckingham, and Oxfordshire also,
With Leicestershire, and Lincoln, and Hertford, shall ye know.
One Bishopric 't is counted, of Lincoln is the see,
Whilom it was of Dorchester, that shall by Oxford be.
And Nottinghamshire also fell to that same king's share —
(Unto York's see 't is reckoned, altho' it be not there —)
And thereto Wales was added, 't is a great land I ween,
And all this, of aforetime, the March of Wales hath been.   110
But for the land 'twixt Humber and Thames, that land, I wis,
Is reckoned unto Lincoln, within that see it is.
The Bishopric of Lincoln, and West of all that land,
Who ruled the March, that monarch had all that in his hand.
The King of Wessex, Wiltshire he held beneath his sway
With Dorsetshire and Berkshire, one Bishopric are they
By Salisbury's Bishop holden — and Sussex, too, was his,
The Weald, and with it Chichester, a Bishopric it is.
Southamptonshire and Surrey be 'neath one Bishop's power,
The Bishopric of Winchester — it standeth to this hour.   120
With Somerset, that erstwhile belonged to Wells, I trow,
Of Bath too, is that Bishop, ye know it well enow.
Yet had the King of Wessex all Devonshire, I wis,
And Cornwall, in the bishopric of Exeter it is.
The King of Kent, he ruled then o'er all the Kentish land
Two Bishoprics they had then, and still the same they stand,
The one is Canterbury, that ranks the first of all,
The next place on the West side to Rochester doth fall.
The King of the East Angles, o'er Norfolk did he reign,
The Bishopric is Norwich; Suffolk was his again,   130
Thereto the see of Ely, in Ely's isle it is,
And Cambridgeshire was reckoned unto his land, I wis.
Northumbria's king was ruler, so do I understand,
Of all beyond the Humber, up to the Scottish land.
All these were kings aforetime where now one bears the crown
For that the King of Wessex put all the others down,
Sithen, alone he ruled there, as doth our King indeed,
Here in this book 't is written, and men the tale may read.
In Canterbury's country most fish be found, I wis;
Round Salisbury most hunting of the wild beasts there is;   140
Most ships be found at London; at Winchester, most wine;
Most sheep and kine in Hereford; and Worcester's fruit is fine;
From Coventry the soap comes; in Gloucester iron is found;
And lead and tin in Exeter, and all that country round.
The fairest woods hath Yorkshire; Lincoln, the fairest men;
And Huntingdon and Cambridge, the most of marsh and fen.

Ely, of places fairest; best to sight, Rochester;
Facing toward France there standeth the land of Chichester;
Norwich doth face toward Denmark; Chester, the Irish shore;
And Durham looks toward Norway; so doth it run, my lore.   150

Three Wonders be in England, and three alone, I wot,
The one be the Bath waters, that evermore are hot,
And ever freshly springing, be the chill ne'er so great,
Of such baths there be many, alike in house and street.
On Salisbury's plain it standeth, the second, strange it is,
Stonehenge its name, no marvel shall greater be, I wis;
Upright and high it standeth, 't is wondrous all to see,
The stones they be so mighty, that greater none may be,
Others lie high above them, that men may sorely fear,
And in their hearts may wonder who did them first uprear?   160
For neither strength nor cunning, I trow, that work might do;
And men shall speak hereafter of these same wonders two
How that they first were fashioned — The other wonder is
Upon a hill, they call it the Peak, the wind, I wis,
Up from the earth it cometh, e'en as thro' holes it were,
And thro' these holes it bloweth so that it taketh there
Great cloths, aloft it bears them, if so they be anigh,
And here and there it blows them, up in the air on high.
And of fair roads full many there be throughout that land   170
But four above all others, so do I understand,
The Kings of old, they made them, and by them men may wend
From the one end of England right to the other end.
From South to North it runneth, the first, 't is Erning Street;
From East to West who travels must go by Ykenilde Street;
From Dover up to Chester by Watling Street men fare
From South-east unto North-west, a long road, and a fair;
The fourth, it is the longest, it starteth from Totness,
From the one end of Cornwall, and goeth to Caithness,
From South-west to the North-east, even to England's end,
By many good towns the Fossway, so is it called, doth wend.   180

So clean a land is England, and from all whoredom free
The fairest men in all the world in England born shall be;
So clean they be midst others, so fair and pure, I ween,
In every land men know them, where'er they may be seen.
So clean be all that country, so pure men's blood, that ne'er
The evil men call "*Holy Fire*" may find an entrance there;
That ill men's limbs devoureth, e'en as tho' burned by flame,
But men of France in such case may rid them of that same,
If they be brought to England — whereby they well may see
That England is the best land, e'en as I tell to ye.   190

ROBERT OF BRUNNE'S CHRONICLE

INTRODUCTION

LORDINGS all who now be here
Lend to this, my tale, an ear,
England's story, hearken it,
As Robert Mannynge found it writ,
Into English, as 't is spoke,
Turned it, for the simple folk
(Who in this land were not few,
And nor French nor Latin knew)
For their solace and their glee
When in fellowship they be.   10
For 't is wise that of their land
Men should read and understand,
Know what folk that land first won,
From what race it was begun.
Good it is for many things
Men should hear the deeds of kings,
Who were fools, and who were wise,
Who most cunning in devise,
Who did wrong, and who did right,
Kept the peace, or strove in fight.   20
Of their deeds shall be my saw —
Of what time, and of what law,
I from step to step will say
Even from Sir Noah's day;
From Noah unto Æneas,
And the folk that 'twixt them was;
From Æneas until Brutus came
(From whom Britain took its name) —
Till Cadwallader we see,
Last of British princes he!   30
All the race, and all the fruit
Sprung from Brutus is the *Brut*,
The right *Brut* is told no more
When the Britons' rule is o'er.
After them the English band
Won the lordship of this land,
North and South, and East and West,
That men call the English *Geste*.
When they first to Britain came
Saxons did they call their name,   40
Saxons, English, differ naught, —

Sandwich the first land they sought,
Vortigern, who then held sway
Suffered them to land alway,
Brothers twain led them in fight,
Hengist, Horsa, were they hight,
These the heads, to whom we trace
This, our English folk and race.
And as heathen dwelt they here
Well nigh for two hundred year   50
Ere the christian Faith they knew
From the lips of Austin true,
Mid the Britons in much woe,
Slaughter, slander, threat, and throe.
Ye these deeds may hear right well
E'en as Piers the tale doth tell;
Master Wace in French, to wit,
Turned the *Brut*, in Latin writ,
From Æneas, till there came
Cadwallader, there left the same.   60
I, what Master Wace doth say
Tell in English, that same way.
Wace doth all the Latin rhyme,
Piers, he skipped it many a time;
Wace, the *Brut* throughout he reads,
Piers, tells all the English deeds;
And where Master Wace doth fail
Piers, he oft begins his tale,
Tells the English history,
As he says then, so say I.   70
So, as they have writ and said,
Have I all in English laid,
Even in such simple speech
As be easiest for each,
Not for those my care alway
Who can speak, or harp a lay,
But for love of simple men
Who strange English may not ken.
Many hear good English rhymes
Who their sense know not oft-times,   80
Save they know what here is meant
All my pains were but ill-spent;
Yet for praise I wrote it not,
But for layman's use, I wot!

Were it made in rhyme *couvé*,
Rhymes alternate, strange, since they
Who read English yet be few
Who can turn a couplet true,
This, in *couvé*, or *baston*,
Had been past the wit of some,   90
So that many who should hear
Should not read my meaning clear.
I have seen, in song, and tale,
Of Ercildoun, and of Kendale,
None be told as they were wrought,
In the saying they seem naught.
In *Sir Tristrem* ye may see,
Of all Gestes the best it be,
Of all tales that e'er were made
If men say what Thomas said;   100
None I hear thus tell the tale,
Of the couplets, some, they fail,
So, for all their cunning speech,
Of his labour faileth each.
But for pride the tale they say
Deeming none be such as they;
That which they desire withal
That same fame shall perish all,
'T is in such strange speech, I wis,
Many know not what it is.   110
Thus it irketh me the more
In strange rhymes to travail sore,
All too dull my wit to learn
In strange speech my rhymes to turn,

And forsooth, I knew it naught,
This strange English that they wrought,
And men prayed me many a time
I would write in easy rhyme,
Saying: "If strange words ye use
Many shall to hear refuse,"   120
(For the names be strange, I trow,
Such as men they use not now.)
Thus, for folk who simple be,
And would gladly hearken me,
I in simple speech began
For love of the unlearnéd man,
Telling of the chances bold
That were said and done of old;
For my toll I ask no meed   129
Save your prayers when ye shall read.
Therefore, all ye lordings lay,
For whose sake I wrought alway,
Pray to God He shew me grace.
I have worked for your solace,
Should men blame, of Brunne I came,
Robert Mannynge is my name,
God in Heaven bless him still
Who doth name me with good-will.
In Third Edward's time was I
When I wrote this history,   140
In Sixille's house dwelt anon —
Then Dan Robert, of Malton,
Bade me, for my comrade's sake,
Write, that we might solace make.

BARBOUR'S BRUCE

INTRODUCTION

STORIES we read right willingly,
Altho' they naught but fables be,
So should a truthful tale of old,
An it were well and fitly told,
Be doubly good to hear, I trow —
Pleasant the telling were enow,
Twofold that pleasure, if right well
Ye tell the thing as it befell;
And truth, when it shall please the ear
Is found by men right good to hear.   10

Therefore I fain would set my will,
If so my wit suffice me still,
To write a story true of old
That men may aye in memory hold,
So that it live in this, my rhyme,
Nor be forgot thro' length of time.
For such old tales, to him who reads,
Do represent the valiant deeds
Of stalwart folk, who lived of yore,   19
E'en as they chanced their face before;
And we their memory sure should prize
Who in their days were brave and wise,

And in great travail passed their life —
In battle oft, and sternest strife
Did win of chivalry the praise
Avoiding false and cowardly ways.
For such was our King Robert's part,
Hardy was he of hand and heart,
And good Sir James of Douglas, who
Was in his time a knight so true, 30
So valiant, and so free of hand,
Men sang his praise in many a land.
Of them this book I fain would write,
God give me Grace that I, aright
May treat my theme that ne'er thro' me
Aught but the truth therein shall be.

IN PRAISE OF FREEDOM

ALAS! that folk who once were free,
And wont in freedom aye to be,
Thro' their mischance and folly great
Were fallen on such woeful state,
Had made him judge who erst was foe —
What greater sorrow might man know?
Ah, Freedom is a noble thing!
Freedom a man to joy doth bring,
Freedom to man sweet solace gives,
He lives at ease who freely lives! 10
A noble heart may find no ease,
In life is naught that shall him please,
If Freedom fails, for to be free
Above all things desired shall be.
Only the man who lived before
In Freedom, knows the anguish sore,
The wrath, the wretchedness and pain
That 's coupled with foul thralldom's
    chain.
But let him once have tested it
And then I trow he well shall wit, 20
And Freedom prize, and dearer hold
Than all of this world's wealth in gold;
Thus evermore things opposite
The worth of each doth bring to light.
And naught the thrall his own may call
For that he has abandoned all
Unto his lord, whoe'er he be —
Yet is he still in no wise free
To live as pleaseth him, or do

That which his heart inclines him to. 30
Hereof do clerks a question take
And often disputation make,
That, if a man shall bid his thrall
Do aught, and that his wife, withal,
Doth come, her right of him to pray,
Shall he his lord's command let stay,
First pay his debt, ere that he go
His lord's commandment for to do?
Or shall he leave his wife unpaid
Till that his lord's will be obeyed? 40
I trow that question they may try
Who be more skilled in subtlety,
But since they think there lieth strife
Betwixt the rights of wedded life
And a lord's bidding to his thrall,
Ye need no words from me withal
The ills of thralldom well to see —
For men may know, who wedded be,
That marriage is the hardest band
That any man may take on hand. 50
But thralldom shall be worse than
    death —
For while a thrall may draw his breath
It mars his life in flesh and bone,
Death vexeth him but once alone.
In short, it passeth telling all
The sore condition of a thrall!

JAMES OF DOUGLAS

THUS Douglas to Saint Andrews came,
The Bishop, courteous, at that same
Received him, gave unto his care
His knives, to carve before him there.
He clad him well, in raiment fit,
And gave him lodging fair to wit.
There many days did Douglas dwell;
Men for his bounty loved him well
For he was in his ways most fair,
Courteous and wise and debonaire, 10
True and large-hearted aye was he,
And o'er all things loved loyalty.
'T is well if men their love thus give,
By loyalty men righteous live;
A man, if he but loyal be
Of virtue hath sufficiency,

Without it, none his worth shall prize,
Altho' he valiant be and wise,
For nothing else where that doth fail
May be of value, nor avail   20
To make a man so good that he
Shall for "*a good man*" holden be.
But Douglas was in all things leal,
At all times he disdained to deal
In treachery, or falsehood's part,
But on high honour set his heart,
And bare him in such wise that dear
Was he to all who came him near.
Yet was he not so fair to see
That he for beauty praised might be, 30
In visage was he somewhat gray,
And had black hair, as I heard say;
But in his limbs well-shapen all,
Large-boned, broad-shouldered, he,
          withal:
Lean was his body, shapen well
As those who saw him love to tell;
When he was blithe, then gracious he,
Gentle and meek in companie,
On battlefield, his folk declare
Another countenance he ware!   40
And in his speech he lisped somewhat,
But that became him well, I wot,
With Hector good, of Troy, might he
In many things well likened be;
For Hector's hair was black, I trow,
Strong-limbed was he, well made enow,
And Hector lisped, e'en as did he,
And was fulfilled of loyaltie,
And was a wise and courteous knight
Of manhood true, and mickle might. 50
Yet none who lived on earth I dare
With Hector, truly, to compare
For in his days the deeds he wrought
Much love and honour to him brought.

HOW THE BRUCE CROSSED LOCH LOMOND [1]

THE king, he would no longer stay,
But to Loch Lomond took his way,
The third day to their goal they came,

1 Book IV, 405.

But found no vessel at that same,
Which might them o'er the waters bear
I trow right woeful then they were.
The loch was broad they well must
          know,
At heart they feared them much, also,
To meet their foes, who spread full wide;
Therefore, along the water's side,   10
Full eagerly about they cast,
Till James of Douglas, at the last,
A little boat, half-sunken, found,
And drew it with all speed to ground.
But 't was so small, that boat, that ne'er
More than three men at once 't would
          bear.
They tell the king thereof, and he,
I trow, was glad exceedingly;
He first into the boat hath gone,
Douglas with him, the third was one   20
Who rowed them swift that water o'er,
And set them dry upon the shore.
He rowed so often to and fro
Fetching them over, two by two,
That in the space of night and day
Safely across the loch were they;
For some of them could swim full fair,
And on their back a burden bear,
By force of swimming, and of oar,
They and their goods across they bore.
The king, the while, right merrily,   31
Read to his men, who sat him nigh,
The tale of valiant Fierabras,
How that in strife vanquished he was,
In doughty wise, by Olivere;
And how, one while, the douze peres,
Were fast besieged in Egrimore —
When King Lavyne, the walls before,
With many thousands round them lay —
And but eleven then were they,   40
One woman with them — Sore bestead,
They wist not where to look for bread,
Save what they from their foes might
          take,
And yet such brave defence did make
That they the tower held manfully,
Until Richard of Normandy,
Maugre his foes, might warn the king,

Who was right joyful of this thing,
For that he deemed they had been slain —
Wherefore he turned him back again, 50
Won Mantrybill, passed Flagote's flood,
Lavyne and all his host withstood,
And vanquished them right manfully!
And in this wise his knights set free,
And won the Nails, and eke the Spear,
And Crown of Thorns, as ye may hear;
And of the Cross, a portion fair
He won him by his valour there.
In this wise did the Scottish king, 59
To his men's hearts, fresh courage bring
With knightly game, and solace good,
Till all had safely passed the flood.

HOW AYMER DE VALENCE, AND JOHN OF LORN CHASED THE BRUCE WITH HOUND AND HORN [1]

SIR AYMER had great companie
Of noble men of high degree,
From England, and from Lothian;
And he had also with him then
John of Lorn, with all his might
Of valiant men, and good in fight,
More than eight hundred with him go —
A sleuth-hound had he there, also,
Which no man from a trail might bring —
And some men say, I trow, the king 10
For coursing once that dog had had,
And aye so mickle of him made,
He 'ld feed the hound with his own hand,
Take him where'er he went on land —
And that the dog he loved him so,
That he would never from him go —
How John of Lorn, he gat that hound,
Thereof I never mention found,
But this men say of certainty,
The dog should in his keeping be. 20
He thought thro' him to take the king —
The dog loved him o'er everything,
And ne'er for chance that him befell,
The Bruce's scent, he knew right well,

Would that dog ever change or miss.
This John of Lorn did hate, I wis,
The king, for John of Comyn's sake,
His uncle, — Fain the king to take,
He valued not his life a straw
So that he fitting vengeance saw. 30
The Warden, then, Sir Aymery,
With John of Lorn in company,
And many another goodly knight,
(One of them Thomas Randolph hight, —)
In Cumnok came to seek the king —
The Bruce had knowledge of that thing;
His force had greater waxed by then,
He had with him three hundred men.
His brother too, with him did fare,
And James of Douglas, he was there. 40
Sir Aymer's army well he saw,
The plain they held, and eke the lawe,
For battle all, in fair array —
At the king's heart small doubt there lay
That all his foemen he saw there,
For none beside them had he care;
Wherein he wrought right foolishly,
For John of Lorn, with subtlety,
Thought from behind to seize the king —
Therefore, with all his gathering, 50
Behind a hill he took his way
Holding himself in ambush aye.
Thus came he to the king full nigh;
Ere he his coming did espy,
Well nigh upon the king he fell —
Sir Aymer, with his men, right well,
Pressed on their foes so hardily
The king, he was in jeopardy,
Beset he was on either side,
By foes, who hard to slay him tried; 60
And e'en the lesser force, that day,
More than sufficed his men to slay.
Seeing how strait they on him pressed,
He thought him well what course were best,
And quoth: "My Lords, we have no might
To-day to hold our own in fight,
Divide we now, in parties three,
Thus all will not assailéd be,

And in three parties go our way."
Further, he did his council say　　70
Betwixt them there, full privily,
Where their next hiding-place should be.
With that, they gat them on their way,
In parties three they fled that day.
But John of Lorn, he came full fain,
There, whence the Bruce his flight had
　　ta'en,
The hound set on his track straightway,
That lingered not, nor made delay,
But held the track where he fled fast,
E'en as by sight — The dog, he cast　　80
About, tracks twain, he left them there,
Knowing the path whereon to fare —
The king, he saw the hound that tide,
He kept the line, nor swerved aside,
And knew what dog that same should be,
Therefore he bade his companie
In the three bands to make their way,
And this they did without delay,
Holding their road in parties three —
The hound, he showed his mastery,　　90
For ne'er he swerved aside, but led
Straight on the track where Bruce, he
　　fled.
The king perceivéd at that same,
His foemen still behind him came,
'T was him they followed, not his men —
He gat to him assurance then
That he was known — for that cause, he
Now bade his men, right hastily,
To scatter, and to go his way
Each man alone — and so did they,　　100
Each on his several way has gone —
The king, he had with him but one,
His foster-brother, no man more,
The twain, they fled their foes before;
The hound, he still pursued the king,
And swerved not, for their severing,
But followed on the track full fast,
Knowing right well which way he past.
When John of Lorn thus surely saw
The hound his course thus straight to
　　draw,　　110
And follow hard the twain, he knew
One was the king, by tokens true.

He chose five of his soldiers then,
Who hardy were, and valiant men,
And who right swift of foot should be,
Swiftest of all his companie,
Bade them pursue the Bruce, "That so
He may in no wise pass ye fro' —"
Swift as they heard that counselling
They followed hard upon the king,　　120
So speedily their way they make
That soon they did their foes o'ertake;
The king, he saw them draw anear,
Methinks, he deemed it sorry cheer,
He thought, an they were men of might,
They would in such wise stay his flight,
Force him to make so long a stand,
He were o'er-ta'en by all the band;
But might he dread no other foe
Than five, then do I surely know　　130
Of them were he in little dread —
Then to his fellow, as they fled,
He said: "Yon five come speedily,
Well nigh o'er-taken now are we,
Say, canst thou give me help in fight?
Assailéd shall we be forthright!"
"Yea, Sire," he said, "as best I may" —
The king quoth: "'T is well, by my fay,
I see they draw to us full near,
No further will I, but right here　　140
I'll make my stand, while breath doth
　　last,
And try their valour fair and fast."
The king, he stood there sturdily,
And the five foemen, speedily,
Came with great clamour, menacing;
Three of them set upon the king,
While t'ward his man the other two,
With sword in hand, they swiftly go.
The king, these foemen who him sought
Hath met, on one his vengeance wrought
In such wise that he shore away　　151
Cheek, ear, and shoulder on that day.
So swift he smote, so dizzily,
The twain who saw, thus suddenly,
Their fellow fall, for very fear
They held them back, nor drew so near.
The king, with that he glanced aside,
And saw the other twain, that tide,

'Gainst his man sturdily to fight — 159
With that, he left his two, forthright,
And t'ward those who his man would slay
Full swift and light he leapt that day,
The head of one he off hath ta'en,
Then turned him to his foes again,
Who set on him right hardily —
He met the first so eagerly,
That with his sword, that sharply shore,
The arm he from the body tore.
What strokes they smote I cannot tell,
But to the king it chanced so well 170
That, tho' he travail had, and pain,
Four of his foemen hath he slain.
His foster-brother true, that day,
The fifth from life hath reft away;
And when the king saw of that five
Not one was left on ground alive,
To his companion did he say:
"Well hast thou helped me now, i-fay!"
"To say so pleasures ye," quoth he,
"Too great a share ye took to ye 180
Who slew five, where I slew but one!"
The king quoth: "So the game did run,
Better than thou I here might do,
Of leisure more had I thereto;
Those fellows twain, who dealt with thee,
When they saw me assailed by three
No more of me they went in dread,
Deeming I were too sore bestead, 188
And e'en because they feared me not,
Could I harm them the more, I wot."
With that, the king, he looked near by,
Saw John of Lorn, his company,
That with the hound came on full fast;
Straightway into the wood they passed,
There, with his comrade would he lie,
God save them for His great Mercie!

HOW KING ROBERT WAS HUNTED BY THE SLEUTH-HOUND[1]

THE king hath sought the wood withal,
Covered with sweat, and redeless all,
Straight thro' the wood, and without
        fail,

[1] Book VII, 78.

He held him downward to a vale,
Where thro' the wood a stream doth
        flow —
Thither in haste the king doth go,
Full fain was he to rest him there,
He said he might no further fare —
His man quoth: "Sire, that may not be,
Abide ye here ye soon shall see 10
Five hundred, yearning ye to slay,
'Gainst two, I trow too many they!
Since we may aid us not with might
Help that we get us hence by sleight."
The king quoth: "Since wilt have it so,
Go on, and I will with thee go;
But I have oft-times heard men say
Would one thro' water take his way,
Wading a bow-shot long, that he
Could from a sleuth-hound shake him
        free, 20
For dog and leader should him lose —
I rede that we this sleight now choose,
For were yon Devil's hound away
I 'ld care not for the rest, i-fay!"

As he devised have they done;
Straight to the water have they gone,
Along the stream their way they make,
Then, once again, to woodland take,
And flee, as aye before that day. —
Then John of Lorn, with great array, 30
Hath come unto that place, I trow,
Wherein his men were slain but now,
And when he saw them lying dead,
He sware with mickle grief that stead,
He would have vengeance for their blood,
In other ways take payment good.
He thought to dwell no longer there,
But on the king's track straight would
        fare.
They follow true, until at last
They find the water where he passed, 40
The sleuth-hound might no further go —
Long time he wavered to and fro,
Nor led them truly here nor there.
Then John of Lorn was well aware
Of how the hound had lost the trail —
He quoth: "This shall us naught avail,

The wood, it is both broad and wide,
And he hath gone far by this tide,
Therefore I rede we turn again,
And weary us no more in vain."   50
With that he called his companie,
Back to the host his way took he.

Thus he escaped, the noble king;
But other-wise some tell this thing,
And say that his escape befell
Not thro' his wading, for they tell
How the king had an archer true,
Who, when he his lord's peril knew,
How he was left with ne'er a man,
Ever on foot beside him ran   60
Till he into the wood was gone —
Then said he to himself alone,

That he would there behind him stay,
And see if he the hound might slay.
For, an that dog should live, he knew
Full well he'ld follow, fast and true,
The king's track, till they found him
        fair —
Full well he wist they'ld slay him there;
And, since his lord he fain would aid,
His life he on the venture laid.   70
Hidden within a bush he lay
Until the sleuth-hound passed his way,
Then, with an arrow, he him slew,
And forthwith to the wood withdrew.
But whether his escape befell
As first I said, or as these tell,
I wot not, but I know one thing,
At that stream he escaped, the king.

LAMENT FOR KING EDWARD I

ALL men that be of heart full true
Hearken awhile to this my song
Of dole, that Death has dealt anew,
(I needs must sigh and sorrow long —)
I sing a knight, so brave and strong,
Of whom God now hath done His Will,
Methinks that Death hath wrought us
        wrong
That he so soon lies cold and still.

I trow all England well doth know
Of whom that song is which I sing,   10
Edward our king, now lieth low,
Thro' all the world his name doth ring!
The truest man in everything,
Wary in war was he, and wise,
For him our hands we needs must wring,
Of Christendom he bare the prize!

Before that this, our king, was dead,
He spake as one oppressed with care:
"Clerks, knights, and barons," so he
        said,
"I charge ye by the oath ye sware   20
That ye to England now be true;

I die, my life is well nigh done,
Aid ye my son, crown him anew,
For he is nighest to the throne."

"Here I bequeath my heart aright
That it be ta'en, as I devise,
Across the sea; let Hugh be dight
With fourscore knights, all men of prize,
Who wary be in war, and wise
Against the Paynim for to fight: 30
To raise the Cross, that lowly lies,
Myself I'd given, an I might."

O! King of France, thou workedst ill
When to such deed didst set thy hand
To hinder thus King Edward's will
To go unto the Holy Land.
Our king, he fain had given command
All England so to rule, I wis,
That, faring to the Holy Land,
We thus had won us Heavenly Bliss.   40

A messenger, the Pope he sought,
And told him that our king was dead,
The letter that he there had brought,

The Pope himself he took, and read.
I trow his heart became as lead —
He spake a word of honour there:
"Alas!" he said, "is Edward dead?
Of Christendom the flower he bare!"

The Pope, he to his chamber went,
For sorrow he might speak no more,   50
Straight for his Cardinals he sent
Who well were versed in Holy lore,
And both the less, and eke the more,
He bade them both to read and sing —
Then might ye see a dole full sore,
How many a man his hands did wring.

Saint Peter's Pope, he stood at Mass,
And there, with great solemnity,
The soul departed did he bless;
"King Edward, honoured shalt thou
       be!   60
God grant that thy son after thee
May end what thou hast well begun,
The Holy Cross, once wrought of tree,
Full fain thou hadst Its freedom
       won!"

"Jerusalem, thou here hast lost
The Flower of all chivalrie,

King Edward from this life hath passt
Alas, that he so soon must die!
He would have raised again on high
Our banners brought unto the ground,70
Full long we needs must call and cry
Ere such a king again be found!"

Now Edward of Carnarvon, he,
The king of England shall be hight,
God grant that he no worse man be
Than was his sire, nor less of might
To see the poor man hath his right,
And counsel good to understand;
He shall not fail for faithful knights
To help him rule our English land.   80

But tho' my tongue were made of steel,
And this, my heart, of molten brass,
The goodness I might ne'er reveal
That did with our King Edward pass.
King, whom men hailed as conqueror
In every fight thou fought, I wis,
God bringeth thee to that honour
That ever was, and ever is,
And lasteth aye without an end —
To God, and this, Our Lady, pray   90
That he to Jesu's Bliss us send
Amen, Amen, for Charité!

LEGENDARY

THE LIFE OF SAINT DUNSTAN

SAINT DUNSTAN was of English blood, and born on English earth;
Our Lord a wonder wrought for him ere yet he came to birth;
While he was in his mother's womb, all on a Candlemas,
When folk enow were in the church, for so the manner was,
And as they stood there with their lights, as men are wont to now,
The tapers went out every one, and none wist why, or how.
The lights one while they burnt right well — and then the lights were out, —
The folk they stood in wonder great, and also in great doubt,
And each to other spake, and asked, what might the meaning be
That thus the light that each one bare was quenched so suddenly?   10
And as they stood and spake thereof, in marvel great, each one,
Saint Dunstan's mother's taper burst forth into flame anon,
The while she held it in her hand, and wist not whence the flame!
The folk, they stood, and gazed thereon, and wondered at that same,
And none knew whence it came, that light, but deemed 't was of God's Grace,
Therefrom they kindled all anew their lights throughout that place.
And wherefore did Our Lord and God the light from Heaven send,
And all the folk that stood around their tapers therefrom tend,
Save to foretell of that fair child, ere yet he came to birth,
How that his saintly name should shed a light on English earth?   20
Nine hundred years and twenty-five, whenas this child was born,
Had passed since Our Dear Lord saw light on Holy Christmas morn,
It was the coronation year of our King Athelstan,
His mother's name was Cymfath, his father's Héorstan;
And when the child was born, I wot, his parents took good heed,
They gave him to the good monks' care, to nourish, and to feed.
At Glastonbury was he taught his Credo, and for prayer
The Pater Noster, — there he waxed a goodly child and fair;
Small care had he for worldly things, for righteousness he yearned,
And all men who heard tell of him, for joy, their hearts, they burned.   30
When he to man's estate had come, at Canterbury's throne
He sought Saint Aldhelm, who the lad as nephew fain would own,
Great joy he had of him, I trow, his gladness waxed the more
The more he of his goodness knew, and of his wisdom's lore.
For very pride and love, the youth he speedily did bring
Unto the lord of all the land, to Athelstan the king;
Thereof the king had joy enow, and granted him this boon,
Of anything that he might ask it should be done right soon.
He prayed of him an Abbey there, e'en where he first was brought,
Beside the town of Glastonbury — the king refused him naught,   40

But granted him forthwith that boon, and after him also
Edmund, his brother, who was king, and had the power thereto.
To Glastonbury soon he went, Saint Dunstan, that good man,
Since both the kings they gave him leave, Edmund, and Athelstan.
His house at Glastonbury soon in order fair he set,
For much he made of law and rule, which ne'er had been as yet.
That Abbey fair was founded first four hundred years, they say,
And fifty three, ere Dunstan good had seen the light of day;
For monks were there, or so folk say, ere yet Saint Patrick came,
Or Austin upon English earth had lit the sacred flame.   50
Two hundred years and fifty two, had passed since that glad morn,
(At Patrick's death,) when Our Dear Lord of Virgin Maid was born, —
But all the monks who first were there dwelt each one separately,
As men before the foes of Christ must to the desert flee. —
Saint Dunstan, and Saint Adelwold, God willed it so alway,
Received the gift of priesthood both upon the self-same day;
To Glastonbury, speedily, Dunstan his way did wend,
And Abbot did they make him there — His life he fain would mend,
And since he would not with his will a moment idle be,
A smithy there beside his cell he made him privily,   60
And when his orisons he needs must leave for weariness
With hand he fain would labour there, to flee from idleness.
The while his life-time might endure he served the poor alway,
And all day long, for love of God, he took of them no pay.
And while he sat there at his work, his hands wrought at his trade,
His heart was aye with Jesus Christ, his lips they ever prayed,
So that his labour was, I ween, but one, and yet threefold,
His hands at work, his heart with God, his lips, his bedes they told.
Therefore the Devil had of him envy and hatred great, —
One time he to the smithy came, whenas the day waxed late,   70
E'en as the sun was going down, and there, in woman's guise,
He spake to him about his work, in gay and gladsome wise.
And told him how she had with him much work that must be done —
Trifling, she changed her theme, and spake another tale anon.
That holy man, he marvelled, as her words flew here and there,
He sat him still, and wondered much what meaning this might bear.
Then he bethought him how it was, and for his tongs did reach,
And laid them in the furnace hot, and spake with gentle speech
Until the tongs were all red-hot, then, ere she was aware,
He gripped the Devil by the nose, and held her fast and fair!   80
He held and shook her by the nose, until the fire out-sprung,
The Devil wriggled here and there, yet fast Saint Dunstan clung,
She yelled and hopped, and tugged amain, and made full grisley cheer,
(Had he but known, for all his wealth he had not come anear!)
So with his tongs he blew her nose, and vexed the fiend full sore —
But now the dusk had come, 't was night, and he could see no more,
The fiend was glad and blithe enow to 'scape from out his hand,

He flew, and cried the welkin thro', men heard o'er all the land:
"Out! Out! What hath the bald-head done? What hath the bald-head done?"
Thro' all the land the foul fiend's cry, men heard it every one!   90
But since the Saint he found at home, who blew his nose so sore,
Thither, to cure him of his cold, he hied him never more!

Dunstan, the holy Abbot, he had great fame and power,
The while King Edmund lived and reigned he was his counsellor;
But when, after King Edmund's death, the years had come and gone,
And Edwyn, he was crownéd king, then it fell out anon
That Edwyn hearkened evil rede, and evil ways would go,
With holy Dunstan he was wroth, which wrought him mickle woe;
He drave him from his Abbey forth, and did him shame the while,
But aye the more he did him wrong the more the good man smiled.   100
He drave him forth from English earth, as outlaw must he fare,
The good man, he went forth with joy, he took but little care,
To Saint Amand, beyond the sea, he gat him then, I trow,
And in the Abbey long time dwelt, with ease and peace enow.
But when King Edwyn's life was done, Edgar the crown must win,
For that he was his brother born, and therefore next of kin;
A man of holy life was he, who well loved Holy Kirk,
And when men gave him counsel good thereafter would he work.
Men told him of Saint Dunstan whom the king drave from the land
Unjustly, for his righteousness — thereto he set his hand,   110
And sent his messengers anon, and bade him come again,
For of his counsel and his rede, he, Edgar, was full fain.
Saint Dunstan, he came home again, the king received him well,
And gave him back his Abbey fair, wherein in peace to dwell.
The King, he shewed him favour great, his rede would gladly hear,
And much of Dunstan's goodness spake the folk, both far and near.
It chanced that Worcester's bishop soon thereafter came to die,
Archbishop Odo, and the King, held counsel privily,
Dunstan, the holy Abbot, a bishop made they there,
To raise him higher in God's law, tho' 'gainst his will it were.   120
Some of Archbishop Odo the reason fain would know
Wherefore he made him Bishop, and did such favour shew?
"'T is fitting" quoth Sir Odo, "because that after me
Dunstan shall be Archbishop, as men shall surely see."
"What meanest thou," quoth the other, "dost know what shall befall?
Thou mayest not see beyond thy foot, 't is God Who ruleth all!"
"Dear Friend" the good man answered him, "thou chidest me for naught,
For well I know what my Lord Christ within my mouth hath brought,
And thus He saith about this thing, and by His leave I say
What shall befall in Holy Church when I be passed away."   130
Thereafter unto Dunstan the see of London fell,
Worcester and London both he ruled as Bishop, passing well.
Ere long Archbishop Odo died, in Canterbury's need

King Edgar and the Pope of Rome together sought good rede,
And that good man Saint Dunstan, Archbishop made they there,
And all the folk who were his friends right glad of it they were.
The Christian Faith on English earth he built it up anew,
The laws and rites of Holy Church he 'stablished fast and true;
He set it fast through England that every priest must choose
To free himself from taint of lust, or else his church to lose.   140
The story saith that Oswald, bishop of Worcester then,
And Adelwold of Rochester, who both were holy men,
These bishops twain, and Dunstan, they all were of one rede,
Of one mind with King Edgar to do this goodly deed.
These bishops three, they journeyed throughout the English land,
And each light priest, they cast him out, none might their will withstand,
Their churches, and their worldly goods, they took them there and then,
And thro' the Pope's grant these, their goods, bestowed on poorer men.
And eight and forty Abbeys, for monk and eke for nun,
They 'stablished throughout England with this, the treasure won.   150
So all was better ordered than e'er it was of old,
For when good men be masters good deeds ye may behold!
And good were these three bishops who ruled in days of yore,
England is better for their lives, and shall be evermore.

Our Lord, He gave Saint Dunstan on earth such special grace
That one time as he was in prayer, all in a lonely place,
His father, and his mother both, in Heavenly joy and bliss,
Altho' the twain were dead, he saw right openly, I wis!
No greater love Our Lord and God to any man might shew
Than thus to grant him, while in life, His hidden things to know!   160
For as he lay another time upon his bed, at night,
The joy of Heaven he beheld, and Heavenly mansions bright;
He heard the angels sing a song, the gate of Heaven within,
Even as when in Holy Church the choir doth Mass begin;
"Kyrie Eleison," so it rang, the wondrous note and song,
The holy man who hearkened this he deemed the time not long!
And well might he to Heaven come, whenas his life should end,
To whom, while he was yet on earth, God did such visions send!
The harp, methinks, he loved right well, and well thereon he played, —
One day he sat in solace, and a goodly lay he made;   170
The harp he hung upon the wall, when it was time to eat,
And when it was in safety brought, he sat him down to meat.
Of Heaven he 'gan think anon, the joys that we shall share,
The gladsome bliss of Paradise, the Saints who wait us there.
He sat as he were in a trance, and from the flesh were brought —
The harp which hung upon the wall, whereon he little thought,
Took knowledge of his holy dreams — dead tree it was alway —
And by God's Will 't was as it heard what never tongue might say,
For by itself it 'gan to harp a joyous strain, I wis,

Which men yet sing in Holy Church, whereof the English is: 180
"Rejoice all holy souls to-day who have in Heaven your seat,
Who followed on Our Dear Lord's way, and for His Love so sweet
Have shed your blood, for thereby ye your crown in Heaven have won,
And reign as Kings for evermore with Christ, God's Only Son!"
This Antiphon, that gladsome is, the folk they heard it all,
Whenas the harp sang by itself, there, hanging on the wall.
Great grace Our Lord He shewed him then, when e'en the lifeless tree
Sang of the joys that waited him when he in Heaven should be!
Lord! Praised for evermore Thy Grace, and praised Thy Might also,
Who for Thy Saint, while yet on earth, such miracles didst shew!   190

Now when this holy man had lived on earth full many a day,
And nigh unto his death had come, as well he knew alway,
On Holy Thursday he fell sick, as it fell in that year,
He called unto him all his friends, the men to him most dear,
And those who did him service too, he called them every one,
And there forgave them any wrong that they to him had done.
And there assoiled them of their sins — So in God's Hands he lay
Throughout the Holy Thursday, and eke through the next day.
Then on the Saturday he called to him the brethren all
And bade them all "Farewell," and said what should them next befall;   200
And bade them give him the last rites, and Corpus Domini,
Therewith his soul this world forsook, and passed to Heaven high.
Nine hundred years and eighty eight, I ween, had passed on earth,
Since Our Dear Lord from Mary Maid took Human Flesh, and Birth.
Now sweet our lord, Saint Dunstan, grant us with thee to fare
In Heaven's bliss, where Angel bands thy ransomed spirit bare!

THE DEATH OF SAINT THOMAS À BECKET

SAINT THOMAS, then, he sighed full sore, for he did understand
That he for all too long had been out of the English land,
And, tho' it were against his will, it seemed him an ill deed
That thus his Bishopric had lacked for rule, and eke for rede.
Unto the King of France he went, and to good men and fair,
And from them all his leave he took, to England would he fare.
He thanked them for the honour all that they to him had done,
And so with love, and escort fair, he went his way anon.
With honour great he leaveth France, England to seek withal,
And at a haven did abide, that men shall Whitsand call.   10
The letters that he bare from Rome to England did he send
To spread the sentence far and wide ere that he thither wend;
Of York th' Archbishop was condemned, and so, I trow, should be
The Bishops twain, of London town and him of Salisbury.

He excommunicated them in that they wrong had done
Crowning the young King in the See that was Saint Thomas' own.
But when those tidings came to them they waxed full wroth, I trow,
Heaped threats upon this holy man, and woe to him did vow.
Saint Thomas turned him to the ship, to England would he fare
When that a man from out that land of goodwill met him there: 20
"Ah Sire!" he cried, "for love of God, pass not the sea, I pray,
In England there be many knights full ready thee to slay,
In every haven lie in wait against thee many a one,
And if thou com'st among them now thou shalt be slain anon!"
"Nay, certes," quoth Saint Thomas then, "I will no longer bide,
But get me back to England now, betide what may betide,
And tho' they tear me limb from limb tarry will I no more,
Too long have I been absent now, and that doth rue me sore!
The souls committed to my care, six years and more, I wis,
Have been without my watch and ward, Alas, too long it is!   30
Right well I know I shall be slain, nor long the time shall be,
And, for the sake of Holy Church, I'll take death joyfully.
Now pray for me to Jesu Christ, this do for charitie,
But above all, one thing alone I bid thee pray for me,
That God doth me, of His good Grace, to Canterbury send,
That, quick or dead, to mine own church once more my way I wend;
If that I come not there alive, ere that I martyred be
My body dead be thither brought, pray God to grant it me!"
Then dolefully his leave he took, to ship he there hath gone
Thanking them for the honour all that they to him had done;   40
Commending France to Jesu Christ, he blessed it ere he passed,
The folk there made a dole enow, long did their sorrow last.
At Dover were there knights who heard how that he came again
And made them ready that when he should land, he might be slain;
Sir Renald de Warenne was one, with him Randolf de Broke,
And Gervase too, the sherriff there, much folk with him he took,
At Dover they, this holy man, on landing from the sea
Would take, save he should do their will slain should he surely be.
But unto Sandwich drave the ship, and there to harbour came,
His foes at Dover lay in wait with threatening at that same.   50
On the ship's sail, this holy man, he bade them set on high
A Cross, sown fast unto the sail, that men from far might spy,
That of his banner was the sign, for other had he none —
The men who stood on Sandwich beach beheld the cross anon:
"Our Bishop Thomas hither-ward doth sail, as well we see!"
Altho' the ship was far from land they wist who it should be.
The cry, it spreadeth far and wide, the folk together ran,
And ere the ship had gained the shore there met him many a man.
They cried their thanks on Jesu Christ that they him living see
And welcomed him with joy enow, nor greater bliss might be.   60
'T was the third day of Advent, the Christmas Feast before,

That this good man, Saint Thomas, did land upon our shore;
The seventh year since that he first had left the English land,
Banished for six years and one month, was he, I understand.
Eleven hundred years it was, and sixty more, and ten,
Since that God, from His mother's womb, was born on earth mid men.
Tidings to Dover do they bear unto the knightly band
That Thomas, holy man, had now at Sandwich come to land;
Then swift to Sandwich did they go, Saint Thomas found anon
And with a threatening mien, I trow, they welcomed him each one;   70
And said: "Why hast thou thus thy way once more to England ta'en
In that thou dost disturb the land soon as thou com'st again?
Yea, and upsetteth Holy Church, as all men well may see,
Would'st Bishops excommunicate who thine own fellows be.
Thou should'st by all law love the peace, and cherish and hold dear,
Yet peace was never in this land since thou wast Bishop here!
Would'st thou do well, undo this deed, we counsel thee, right soon,
Or men, I trow, shall do to thee as should to such be done!"
"My dear friends," quoth Saint Thomas then, "the sooth it is to say
That judgment did I give of right, and not of wrong alway,   80
By leave of this my lord the King, that each man have his right,
And who such trespass great hath done should make amends forthright.
For, an it were so soon condoned, against all right and law,
'T would prejudice full sore my church this judgment to withdraw."
Then when the knights they heard him say the King agreed thereto
They did forsake their angry mood, and threatenings great also,
And did beseech him courteously to cancel his decree,
And 'twixt his fellows and the King to cherish charitie;
And respite now, of this their prayer, they granted at that same
So that Saint Thomas with the morn to Canterbury came.   90
Then, with the morn, Saint Thomas doth to Canterbury fare
The country all with joy and bliss came out to greet him there,
For every priest, his parish all, he summoned, end to end,
That they should in procession fair to meet th' Archbishop wend.
In many a procession then, I trow, all fairly found,
With Cross and lighted tapers fair to meet him are they bound,
With cross, and tapers all alight, as many as might be,
And thanks they gave to Jesu Christ that they him, living, see.
Then loud they chimed, the bells, I trow, whenas to town he came
And loudly, to their instruments, their song rose at that same.   100
Yea, men might hear no other thing, the noise it was so loud,
No greater joy, I trow, was made afore by any crowd.
As on Palm Sunday Christ, our Lord, was met with honour high
When to Jerusalem He rode, and to His Death drew nigh,
So was Saint Thomas, as methinks, men might hereafter see
For that Our Lord had willed his death like to His Own should be.
Then, ere Saint Thomas, holy man, came to his church that day,
The monks in fit procession there they met him on the way.

He from his palfrey lighted down, and then the monks each one,
To the High Altar, fittingly, they led him up anon,   110
And when he in the church had done all that was there to do
Then with his men, so courteously, he to his inn did go.
Now ere Saint Thomas long had been within his palace hall
These self-same knights they came again answer to crave withal;
They did beseech him, as before, to loose the ban that day,
And these three Bishops to absolve, who 'neath the judgment lay.
Then quoth Saint Thomas: "Nay, *Beau frère*, herein I can do naught,
For that the doom wherein they lie the Pope on them hath brought,
And I may not undo his deed, ye wot, in any place;
But none the less, in that I have such trust in this, his grace,   120
I will absolve them in this form, to wit, that henceforth they
Assurance give to Holy Church they will her laws obey,
Submit to Holy Church's Head — this form, I trow, or none!"
The Knights who hearkened well his words, to chiding fell anon,
As they none other answer found in wrath they hence did wend
That message to the Bishops bare who did them thither send.
The Bishops, they were wroth enow, their threats they fell full fast,
Natheless, the twain of them withdrew, and yielded at the last,
The Bishops both of Salisbury and London sware that they
Would yield themselves to Holy Church, and all her law obey.   130
But York's Archbishop, he withstood, with word and eke with deed,
And quoth: "Now shame his portion be who giveth us such rede,
That we should put us in his grace who was our foe of yore
For he hath done us many a shame, and now would do us more.
Altho' he may have power o'er you, yet hath he none o'er me
In that I too Archbishop am, ye wot, as well as he!
And I, I have a coffer good, that standeth whole and sound,
Therein shall be, as I think well, at least eight hundred pound,
That am I ready now to spend, nor much it seemeth me,
That we may lower this, his pride, of him avenged may be.   140
Now go we to the King anon, and tell him of this deed,
That if he peace be fain to have he find some other rede."
Then these three Bishops, hastily, across the sea they hied,
And came in safety to the King, ere it was Christmas-tide,
They found him there in Normandy, they knelt low on their knee,
Prayed him his honour to maintain, and their good lord to be,
They told him how that this good man, since that to land he came,
Disturbance wrought, alike in Church, and Kingdom, at that same,
And that he had, with mickle pride, his doom upon them laid,
Who, with his own consent, his son as King afore had made;   150
And how he, in despite of him, had done such evil deed,
That of the land he did outright refuse the laws to heed.
The King, whenas he heard the tale, for wrath was well nigh wood,
Awhile strode up and down the hall, awhile in thought he stood;
"If he doth excommunicate those who made my son King

The doom, it falleth first on me who did ordain this thing,
Now who would in such misery for long time lead his life?
This traitor, he doth ruin my realm, and brings me woe and strife!"
And oft-times did he curse those men he had to honour brought
That of the priest who was his foe they would avenge him naught,   160
The priest, who had his land disturbed, and sorrow on it laid —
As thus the King strode up and down, and as these words he said,
The knights, who hearkened all his words, they stood, and held them still,
And silent, in themselves they thought to do their master's will.
Then four of them, the fiercest there, they thought what they might do,
Sir Rainald de Fitzurse was one, Sir Hugh de Morville two,
Sir William Tracy was the third, the fourth, Richard de Brut,
Their names, for this, their wickedness, they ne'er shall be forgot.
They held their counsel secretly, o'er sea to take their way,
And, to fulfil the royal will, Saint Thomas would they slay.   170
Then, secretly, they gat them forth, that no man saw them go
And well nigh came unto the sea ere that the King did know;
But when the King, he understood, after them did he send,
And bade them leave their folly there, and back to him to wend;
But with no toil this messenger unto the knights hath won
For, ere he came unto the sea, they were far out thereon.
This wrought to Henry dole enow, that thus their way they went,
And spake not with the messenger whom after them he sent.
At Canterbury, Thomas good, upon midwinter's day,
He stood, and preached unto the folk as many a man doth say,   180
And in his sermon, suddenly, began to sigh full sore,
And made such dole and sorrow there that never man made more;
And weeping, he beheld his tears, how fast they ran adown,
I trow that many an eye was wet that day throughout the town!
"My dear Friends:" quoth Saint Thomas, the while he wept full sore
"Your priest I now somewhile have been, but I shall be no more,
For that my end is well nigh come, nor long I here shall be,
But suffer death for Holy Church I must, right speedily.
For love of God, now pray for me, and Holy Church also
That now is well nigh brought to ground save God His Mercy show.   190
Yet would I fain be put to death, when so God's Will shall be,
For this, the right of Holy Church, ere that she ruined be."
Candle and book he took anon, and banned them then and there
Who on the rights of Holy Church made war, her foemen were,
Namely Sir Randolf, he of Broke, Robert of Broke also,
Who this, his See and Bishopric did wrongfully misdo.
For that, the while he was away, of wrong King Henry took
The Bishopric, and gave its lands to Randolf, he of Broke,
Who made Robert de Broke his clerk, for him to come and go,
And Warden under him to be, he wrought the land much woe,   200
And did destroy the Bishopric, and took to him its gold,
And of these goods, won wrongfully, had built to him a hold;

And therein, on that Christmas Day, when Thomas laid the ban,
He sat at meat, in noble state, and with him many a man.
Unto his hounds he threw the bread, that there before him lay,
But every hound, he turned aside, the folk who saw it say.
Then took he to him other bread, and with it mixed anew
Bread from another's trencher, which to the dogs he threw,
And every bit he handled there the dogs, they let it lie,
The other bread, they chose it out, and ate it greedily!   210
The Curse, I trow, was on him seen, upon the self-same day,
The rightful vengeance of Our God, as all the folk must say,
When that the dogs the bread forsook that lay to them anear —
And Christmas-Day, methinks, it fell on Friday, in that year,
When these four wicked knights of whom the deed I tell to-day
Their way to England thus had ta'en Saint Thomas for to slay.
And on Saint Stephen's Day, those four to Saltwood Castle came
Six miles from Canterbury, there they 'lighted, at that same;
And unto them Randolf de Broke, he made his way anon,
That night they counsel took, I trow, how best the deed were done.   220
The morrow, ('t was on Child-Mass Day) as God the grace did send,
To Canterbury speedily, Randolf de Broke did wend,
(For of Saint Thomas he would know where he should be that tide
That he might flee them not, that day, nor might in safety hide.)
Those knights, I trow, when Tuesday came, they would no longer stay,
To Canterbury did they ride before the close of day,
About the time of Evensong they to Saint Thomas came
And boldly to his chamber they betook them at that same.
They came, and found him peacefully, there, in his chamber, stand,
With him his privy clerks, for they a council had on hand.   230
Then grimly, Sir Rainald Fitzurse, he did toward him wend,
And: "Sire:" he saith, "our lord, the king, doth us in message send,
And here, from him in Normandy, we this command have brought,
That thou should'st here his bidding do, and should'st delay thee naught,
And that thou go unto his son, for crownéd king he is,
And should'st amend to him what thou his sire hast done amiss,
And swear thou wilt be true to him, and loyally wilt do
What, for the lands thou hold'st from him in chief thou needs must do;
The clerks, whom thou dost bring with thee, with thee in this must stand,
Swear to be true unto the king, or they must flee the land."   240
"*Beau Sire,*" then answered this good man, "I think to tell no lie,
I'll do my homage to the king for this, my baronie,
But God wills not that Holy Church 'neath foot be trodden so
That I, or other of my clerks, should this thy bidding do.
Thou knowest well the laymen all who be within this land
They take upon them no such oath as here I understand,
By this thou thinkest Holy Church in servitude to bring
More than the lot of laity, nay, I swear no such thing!"
"I think me well," Sir Rainald quoth, "thou wilt obey in naught

This same behest, which unto thee we from the king have brought.   250
And now we bid, on his behalf, that thou absolve straightway
Those Bishops, whom beneath thy ban thou didst but lately lay."
"*Beau Sire*," he quoth, Saint Thomas, "'t was not my deed, I trow,
From his own mouth the Pope himself he hath condemned them now,
And thou know'st well that I may not the Pope's own deed undo —"
"The Pope's deed?" quoth Sir Rainald, "Nay, 't is thy deed also!"
"Sooth" said Saint Thomas, "if the Pope those men to judgment brought
Who this my church have so misdone, it doth displease me naught!"
Sir Rainald made swift answer there: "By all thine acts dost shew
Thou would'st annoy our lord, the king, and that thou art his foe,   260
And 't is thy will to work him harm, that do we clearly see,
Thou fain would'st take from him his crown, but that shall never be!
And king thou would'st be in his stead, but that thou shalt be ne'er!"
"Certes, Sire," quoth Saint Thomas, "that thought I cherished ne'er,
But rather would I be his friend and helper, an I may,
For him, and for his honour do I pray both night and day,
For there is no man on the earth whom I love more, I wis,
Than him, save but his father, who still my liege lord is.
Feast of Saint Mary Magdalene, in sooth I tell to thee,
A full accord was made betwixt my lord the King and me,   270
He gave me leave to ban all those who did in aught misdo
The Church that is his Mother, and naught else did I do!"
"Avaunt thee, priest," quoth Rainald, "too much, I trow, dost say
Thou would'st thine own lord slander, too clever thou alway!
Would'st say that he, my lord the king, would ban them, and disown
Those who had crowned his son as king? Was not the deed his own?
Was it not with his own consent, by no man's rede or lore?
Avaunt, Sir Priest, bethink thee, and say thou so no more!"
"Sir," said Saint Thomas, "thou know'st well that others had a share,
For thou wert present there thyself, as many others were,   280
Archbishops, Bishops, too, I ween, other great men and high,
Yea, well five hundred men and more, as thou didst see with eye!"
"Be still," then quoth that wicked knight "and hold thy tongue to-day,
Thou foully dost belie thy lord, woe him who thus doth say!
Who should such slander suffer, and not avenge the deed?
Nay, by the faith I owe to God I'll teach thee other rede!"
With one consent, his fellows, their arms about they cast,
And fared as men who were nigh mad, their threats they fell full fast.
Then to the monks he turned anon, "Come forth!" he then did cry,
"'T is the King's foe ye have in hold, he knows it verily,   290
To the King's will his body yield, or here do I declare
He taketh to him all your lands, your manors layeth bare!"
"Sir Rainald," quoth Saint Thomas, "dost think that I will flee?
Nay, *pardé*, I'll not stir a foot, nor for the king nor thee!"
"By God, Sir Priest," quoth Rainald, "thou soon wast at a stay,
Thy flight, I trow, it were but short, nor far should'st go alway!"

Those knights, they wrathful were enow, they gat them forth anon,
And then, when they were fully armed they came again, each one,
With swords, and eke with axes, and other weapons more;
Robert of Broke, that wicked clerk, he went them all before, 300
To Canterbury's cloisters they came with all their might,
The monks were singing Compline, for now 't was nigh to night;
Then some, for the great noise they heard, they fell adown for fear,
And some began to run about, as tho' they witless were.
Saint Thomas took his Cross in hand, of other arms had none,
And therewith, with all boldness, towards his foes hath gone,
The monks, they cried upon him there: "Now, Mercy, Sire," they say,
" For God's Sake, bide thee here, Our Lord may give thee rede alway,
Suffer us here to aid thee, or else with thee to die!"
And some, they would shut fast the door, when they their foes espy. 310
"Nay, leave that," quoth this holy man, "therein shall ye do wrong,
Sing on the service of Our Lord, and this, your Evensong,
No man of Holy Church should make a castle 'gainst his foe,
He leaveth fools to rave a stound, and in their folly go."
With that, on folly bent, the knights they rushed in speedily,
"Where is" they quoth, "that Bishop false, that traitor, where is he?"
Saint Thomas took the Cross in hand, and answer made anon:
"Behold me here, God's Priest am I, but traitor am I none!
Look ye for them who think to flee, or do your threatenings dread,
For not more ready are your swords here now to smite me dead 320
Than this, my heart, is ready here death from your hand to take,
And ne'er the rights of Holy Church for death will I forsake!"
The knights, they rushed on him anon, his cap from off his head,
His mantle from his back, they tare, reviling him that stead,
Sir Rainald de Fitzurse, I trow, doth close beside him go —
"Sir Rainald," quoth Saint Thomas there, "what thinkest thou to do?
For oft have I done good to thee, and others too, I trow!"
The other quoth: "What I may do, thou learnest soon enow
Traitor! This will I do to thee, right swiftly shalt thou die!"
"In sooth," then quoth that holy man, "ready thereto am I, 330
Now for the rights of Holy Church to die were I full fain
If so that after this, my death, she should in peace remain.
But if, in sooth, 't is me ye seek, I pray ye, in Christ's Name
That ye come nigh no other man to work upon him shame,
In that none other guilty is of what ye put on me,
Blameless are all, save I alone, of that ye sure may be,
And therefore, since they blameless be, unharmed now let them wend —"
The good man knelt down on his knee, he saw it was his end,
And to receive his martyrdom he bowed his head adown,
And soft and low, as some men heard, he spake his orisoun; 340
"Now to Our Lord, and Saint Marie, and eke Saint Dionis,
And all the patrons of this church where I be slain, I wis,
I here in death commend my soul, and Holy Church's right —"

While yet he prayed for Holy Church, he had none other might,
Sir Rainald de Fitzurse, of all the fiercest there was he,
Drew forth his sword, that holy man to smite right speedily,
But Edward Grim, of Grantboro', who was his clerk, they say
Stretched out his arm, for he was fain to help his lord that day;
The stroke his arm hath wounded sore, the blood it ran adown,
And with that self-same blow he smote Saint Thomas on the crown,   350
So that the blood adown his face, on the right side, did flow,
Then loud he cried, this wicked knight, "Now shall ye smite them low!"
Then Edward Grim, and all the men who stood the Bishop near
To the side altars then they ran, fleeing for very fear —
For e'en as with Our Lord it fared, when the Jews seized Him there,
All His disciples fled away, He wist not where they were —
For in the Gospels it is writ, Christ spake it verily,
"When men shall smite the Shepherd, then the sheep shall scattered be —"
And Christ for His disciples prayed that no man harm should do
To them, and so Saint Thomas, he, prayed for his monks also.   360
Another smote Saint Thomas, in that same wound I trow,
And made him look toward the ground, and his face downward bow;
In the same place, the third knight, a blow he smote anon
And prone he fell, the Bishop, his face upon the stone.
The fourth knight, then he smote him, in that same place again
And on the marble of the floor his sword point brake in twain,
For honour of the holy man who thus his death there met
That point, at Canterbury, the monks they keep it yet.
That stroke hath smitten off the skull, the crown from off the head,
So that, upon the pavement, the brains abroad were spread,   370
White brain, with red blood mingled, lay on the pavement there
And tho' 't was pity great to see, the colour, it was fair!
And it ran all around his head, e'en as a diadem,
And lay, in sooth for all to see, a marvel seemed it them!
For men, when they would paint a saint, I trow, forget it ne'er
But ever paint around his head a circle fit and fair
A diadem, or halo, and so men well might see
By this, the diadem of blood, that he a Saint should be.
Then, when the holy man was slain, the knights, they cried each one:
"This traitor now to death is brought, now go we hence anon,   380
This shall they see, the king's men, and all who with him be,
We on this traitor be avenged, as all men now may see,
He would be higher than the king, and fain had worn the crown,
And all the land have brought to naught, and now is he cast down!"
E'en so the Jews spake of Our Lord, when Him they fain would slay,
That He would make Himself a King, and Son of God alway.
Then when these wicked knights a space had from Saint Thomas gone
Robert de Broke bethought himself, and turned him back anon,
And thro' the skull he smote his sword, right far the head within
So that the skull was empty, no brain was left therein,   390

E'en as the Jews they smote Our Lord, after His Death did take
A spear, and thro' His very Heart a fifth Wound there did make,
Those wicked men did in that stead Saint Thomas smite, I ween,
So that the skull was spread abroad, e'en as the crown had been.
For he was ne'er a man who deigned his head to turn aside,
Nor yield a foot unto his foe, but would the stroke abide,
Nor made he cry, nor uttered groan, but, gracious, bowed his head,
And held it steady, tho' his foes would smite it off that stead.
Those wicked knights, they wend anon unto his treasury,
The doors and coffers there they brake, and wreaked foul robbery.   400
They took his clothes, and eke his horse, and treasure, too, that day,
Charters, and private writings, in coffer locked away;
Randolf de Broke, he took them then, to the king now would wend
To Normandie, and say these knights they did the writings send,
Praying him deal as was his will, if there were any there
Against his royal right and will he should them straightway tear.
Among his treasures did they find two hair shirts rough that day
And vilely did they handle them, as worthless, cast away,
Yet, natheless, they bethought them there, and were afeared, I ween,
And softly spake between themselves, a good man had he been.   410
William of Tracy later told of this good man and true
To Exeter's good Bishop, when he was shrived anew,
That when Saint Thomas had been slain, and they from hence would go,
Well nigh they had waxed mad for fear, such horror did they know,
It seemed them, as they gat them hence, that, swift as they might fare,
The earth, it gaped to swallow them, all living as they were.
Then when Saint Thomas, he was slain, and hence the knights had gone,
Thro' Canterbury town, I trow, 't was known by all anon,
The folk, with cries so doleful, to church they ran, I wis,
Honoured that holy body, and ofttimes did it kiss.   420
The monks, they hasten thither, the holy body take,
On a fair bier they laid it, before the altar wake,
The face was white and clear enow, no blood was there within,
From the left half of his forehead to the left half of his chin
A little streak there was of blood, that o'er his nose did flow,
But no more blood was in his neck as well the folk did know.
The wound, it bled the long night thro', men took thereof, I ween,
To-day, in Canterbury church that blood may still be seen.
Yet he in no-wise changed his hue, for all that he bled there
Clear was he, of good colour, as tho' alive he were,   430
And, somewhat smiling with his mouth, lay as he were asleep —
The folk, they gathered thick around, the blood were fain to keep,
And gather up the drops that there had fallen to the ground,
And of that earth all soaked in blood, glad was he who it found.
That would no man deny them, and much they took away,
Who touched that holy body, a glad man he, that day.
Then, with the morn, those wicked knights, they arm themselves eftsoon,

Without the town took counsel, what now might best be done,
Fain had they ta'en that body, with horses drawn it there,
High on a gibbet hanged it, and said the law it were, 440
Unworthy he within a kirk or kirkyard for to lie —
The monks o'er much believed this, and feared them mightily,
And swift that body buried, in a place near beside,
With little pomp or ritual, they durst no longer bide.
But in Christ's Minster buried the body there anon,
Before Saint Austin's altar, and that of Baptist John.
The monks durst wait no longer, nor wash that body dear
But all unready, laid it low, and fled away for fear.
But, as they stript him of his clothes, the vesture, it did show
The clothing that beseemed a clerk, and other garb below, 450
For a monk's habit was beneath, e'en as they found it there
The cowl, and woollen robe, I trow, above the shirt of hair;
So that within he was a monk, tho' secular without,
And no man knew his secret who was with him about.
Next to his flesh his girdle bare of knots full many a one
That deep into his flesh they ate, some even to the bone.
Tho' shirt and breeches he might wear he little ease might feel
So tightly was he bound therein from shoulder e'en to heel,
Uneasily he needs must sit, uneasily must ride,
Uneasy would he lie at night, or turn on either side. 460
And all his flesh was full of worms, to add to other woe,
Never another creature so many worms might show,
For everywhere within his flesh they were so thickly set
That scarce the large ones for the small unto their meat might get,
But one upon the other crept, and twined them all about,
The small, they clave close to the flesh, the larger were without.
He died, eleven hundred years, and seventy and one
After Our Lord came down to earth, and took our flesh and bone;
And three and fifty years of age were counted to him there
And many a fair day had he lived, in woe, and eke in care. 470
The king was aye in Normandy, and of the deed knew naught,
But dole and sorrow made enow, whenas the news was brought,
In the castle of Argenteyne, he heard the tidings sore
And came not forth from out the gate for forty days and more;
In privacy he kept him, with weeping, and with woe,
And for no need that men might urge without the door would go,
Recked naught of this world's doings, while spare his food should be,
Such dole and grief as there he made no man I trow, might see.
To Canterbury sent anon, all for this doleful deed,
And prayed the monks full piteously for him to intercede, 480
He sent them word assuring them that naught of this he bade,
The knights had gone forth secretly, and nothing to him said,
He sent a message bidding them turn again speedily
But ere the man might come to them they were far out at sea.

And, as 't was good, unto the Pope, the king, he sent right soon
And prayed his counsel piteously, what now might best be done?
And for the love of God besought, in this his anguish, rede,
That he be shriven and absolved of this right wicked deed.
The Pope, I trow, had pity great in that he thus did send
And great joy, too, that he, his life was willing to amend,   490
Two cardinals he sent him, wise men they were, those two,
That he be shriven of this sin, and be absolved also,
And to absolve those bishops, who 'neath the ban yet lay —
Right welcome were those cardinals unto the king alway!
Then, dolefully, he prayed them absolve him of this deed,
That he would stable stand, and swear to follow all their rede.
And there upon the Hallows sware that he therein did naught,
Not by his will, nor his behest, Thomas to death was brought.
Nay, never for his father's death had he such sorrow sore,
Nor for his mother had he felt such grief as now he bore.   500
And that he would, with willing heart, the penance take and bear
That they should lay upon him, however hard it were.
For he was cause of this, his death, and of his woes also,
In that his knights, to please him, had brought him thereunto.
Then, when the cardinals, they saw he did repent that wrong
They shrived him there, and laid on him a penance stern and strong,
But all in secret, as 't was right that no man of it spoke
But this that I now tell ye was known to all the folk.
That he should send to Holy Land two hundred knights, to fight
A year long with the Templars, for Holy Church's right.   510
The Statutes, too, of Clarendon, he should revoke them all
'T was for their sake that holy man did thus, a martyr, fall.
And that, to Canterbury's See he wholly yield again
That which, wroth with Saint Thomas, he erst from it had ta'en.
And that those men should freely, and wholly, be forgiven
Whom of ill-will, for Thomas' sake, he from the land had driven.
The king, he granted all their will, the while he wept full sore
And said it was too little, prayed they 'ld lay on him more;
And saith: "Now here, of my good will my body may ye take
Give me a penance sharp enow, I will it not forsake."   520
Unto the church door did he go, to be absolved, I ween,
Holding himself unworthy within it to be seen.
Without the church door, piteous, he knelt him on his knee,
The cardinals, they willed not his body stript should be
But in some wise, above his clothes, they did absolve him there,
I trow, full many wept for grief of those who round him were.
Upon his son he laid behest with sorry cheer, that he
Fulfil his father's penance, if that unfit he be;
That, should he fall on feeble state, ere to the end he came,
He take the penance on himself, of good will, at that same.   530
Thus that good man, Saint Thomas, to martyrdom was brought

And since then many a marvel for his sake hath been wrought.
Men wist in far Jerusalem that he to death was done
Within a fortnight of the day his earthly race was run,
For that a monk of that same land in his death-struggle lay
His abbot came unto him, ere yet he passed away,
Conjured him solemnly, that dead, he should, without debate,
Return again to him, and say what there should be his state.
The monk, he died soon after, e'en as it was God's Will,
And to the abbot came again, his bidding to fulfil,   540
And told him that, among the saved, in Heaven's joy was he,
And spake much of the gladness that he in Heaven did see,
And told him, in that self-same time that he to Heaven did come
Of Canterbury th' Archbishop had suffered martyrdom,
And that his soul, that self-same hour, to Heaven did ascend
And fair was the procession that did to greet him wend;
Of Patriarchs, of Angels, Apostles, too, also,
Martyrs, Confessors, Virgins, they did to meet him go,
They met and brought his holy soul unto Our Lord, anon,
With great rejoicing as He sat upon the Great White Throne.   550
His crown, it all was smitten off, and bloody was his head,
No brain was left within it, all with his blood was shed.
"Ah, Thomas, Thomas!" quoth Our Lord, "this lot is fallen to thee
To come thus to thy Lord's own Court, and in such guise to Me!
For thy good service will I give to thee such joy and bliss
As I gave to Saint Peter, who mine own Apostle is."
He set upon his head a crown, of gold so bright and good,
And well it showed, the gleaming gold, upon the crimson blood!
And greater joy there ne'er might be than was in Heaven withal
For Canterbury's Archbishop, whom men Saint Thomas call.   560
The Tuesday after Christ's Own Mass, the next as it did come,
That holy man, Saint Thomas, he suffered Martyrdom.
And when thou hearest of his death from English men, in sooth,
Thou shalt remember this my tale, and know 't was very truth!"
The abbot, on the morrow he of Saint Thomas thought,
The tale unto the Patriarch of Jerusalem he brought,
So that they, later in the year, right well did understand
Whenas the pilgrims thither came out of the English land,
And that these pilgrims told as truth all that the monk had seen
The very manner of his death, and when he slain had been.   570
Thus, in Jerusalem, I trow, Saint Thomas' death was known
Within a fortnight of the day that he to death was done.
When five years he had martyred been, so doth the story tell,
Between King Henry and his son a contest great befell,
The son waxed proud of this, his power, since he as king did reign
But lightly held his father, to war with him was fain.
Of England all the greater part they with the son did hold,
The kings of France and Scotland too, so in the tale 't was told,

Then this old man and feeble, much pain and grief he knew,
And laid it on his wicked deed, that men Saint Thomas slew.   580
From Normandy to England he gat him at that tide,
Ere he to Canterbury came nowhere would he abide.
When he was far without the wall from horse he 'lighted down
And all afoot, and barefoot, did wend him to the town,
And with his kirtle all ungirt, as folk might see that day,
He took his way unto the place wherein Saint Thomas lay.
His hands outstretched in sorrow, mercy did aye implore
And at his tomb he knelt adown with sighs and weeping sore,
In Orisons, with weeping, and fasting, there he lay
And thus beside that good man's tomb abode a night and day.   590
And each monk of the Minster he prayed to scourge him there
Each with a rod, and yet he thought the pain too little were.
And dolefully he prayed them, each one, for him to pray,
The evil laws that he had made he sware to put away;
And then he bade them sing a Mass, ere that he thence might wend,
In honour of Saint Thomas, that grace to him he send.
And even while this Mass was sung, as God did grant it so,
The King of Scotland, he was ta'en, who was his fiercest foe,
And many another too with him, who were his foes anon,
And they who thus were captive ta'en power against him had none.   600
So this king old and feeble, who had the lower place,
Was raised again to honour all by Saint Thomas' grace.
His son was put beneath him, little he won that tide
By warring 'gainst his father thro' this, his sorry pride.
By this a man may warning take that never, hastily,
He give his lands unto his son, while yet in life he be!
King Henry's son, thereafter, much evil hath he wrought,
And long before his father died he to his death was brought,
Full sore he pined in sickness, his life it seemed him long,
And died at last a doleful death, in bitter pains and strong.   610
His brother too, Sir Geoffrey, the Earl of Brittany,
He fell in the same sickness, the self-same death had he,
So when he died, King Henry, of heir remained there none
Save this, their brother Richard, and after him was John.
But yet, Sir Geoffrey's children, by rightful law of land,
Were heirs unto the kingdom, so do I understand;
Of Brittany the maiden, his only daughter, she,
For this cause all her lifetime a prisoner must be.
And all four of those wicked knights, who did Saint Thomas slay
Died an ill death, and painful, small wonder 't was alway!   620
They were each one repentant, nay, never men were more,
For mercy on Saint Thomas, I trow, they cried full sore.
Soon after they had done this deed they from their goods did wend
To Holy Land betook them, their lives they would amend.
But William Tracy fared not forth with these his fellows three,
Deeming that he, in England, a penitent might be.

But very soon thereafter in sickness sore he fell
His flesh, it rotted on him, and evil did it smell;
So foul the stench, I trow me, that dole it was to see,
And for its very foulness no man might nigh him be.   630
His flesh, it rotted on him, each day it fell away,
Till that his bones were waxen bare, his joy was all away.
His flesh, with his own hands he tare from off him at the last,
And piece by piece he took it, and far from him he cast.
He tare, I trow, his hands and arms, till there was left thereon
No trace of flesh, but nothing more save sinews, and bare bone.
And many men, they deemed in truth he bare it willingly
To pay sin's debt, that so his soul in lesser peril be.
At last in bitter pain his soul did from his body wend
And, as it were God's Will alway, he made a godly end.   640
Thus, for their wicked deed, these knights, full soon they died each one
And in the third year after there was left living none.
For even as the Psalter saith, the men who treacherous be
They shall not live out half their days, and so we surely see;
E'en tho' they be repentant, as these knights were, I ween,
They shall not live out half their life, on them this well was seen.
Saint Thomas, now, that holy man, in earth he buried lay
Ere men might lay him in a shrine, I trow, for many a day;
For forty years therein he lay, and half a year should be
With eight days added thereunto ere brought from earth was he.   650
For God would wait a fitting time for such a holy thing
Till to a good archbishop was joined a godly king.
The king who came before him, and wicked was also,
He little thought within his day such godly deed to do;
But his young son, King Henry, he would not long delay,
Tho' young he was when made a king, the saint in shrine to lay.
Scarce thirteen years, I trow, had he, when that he did this thing
And in the fourth year this befell since that they made him king.
The good Archbishop, Stephen, he counselled him thereto
So it was by the rede of both that they this deed did do.   660
Honorious, he was Pope then, and thither would he send
From Rome, the Legate Pandolf, to bring this thing to end.
The Pope decreed a pardon to all who there would go
That for long years in England men no such pardon know.
To honour this, his body, the folk they came ere long
Of bishops, and of abbots, full many thither throng,
Of priors, and of parsons, and many a clerk also,
And many an earl and baron with knights did thither go;
The squires and serjants flocked there, and husbandmen enow,
And of the simple land folk, so many came, I trow,   670
That all the land about there, the country far and wide,
Might scarce contain the people who flocked from every side.
So these high men, and noble, elect this deed to do,
Were much in care, lest, for the press, they come not thereunto;

So the Archbishop, Stephen, of whom but now I told,
And Salisbury's Bishop, Richard, they did a council hold,
E'en with the Prior Walter, head of the Convent he,
And thus they took their counsel to do it privilie;
So as men lay and slept by night, thereof had little thought,
They took those holy bones up, and in a coffin brought,   680
And set them in a secret place until the day they see
That it was cried throughout the land the grave should opened be.
July, the month, I think me, upon the seventh day,
It fell upon a Tuesday, so all the folk they say,
On that day to the Minster in order have they gone
With the young child, King Henry, the high men, every one.
And on that day, at underne, they to the body come,
And Pandolf, he hath gone the first, the Legate he, from Rome.
And the Archbishop Stephen, and from beyond the sea
From Rheims came the Archbishop, to this solemnitie.   690
Hubert de Brom, he followed, High Justice was he then
And four great lords came with him, all wise and noble men.
And they, upon their shoulders, the body take anon,
Of bishops, and of abbots, have many with them gone.
And thus to the High Altar of the Trinity they bare
The holy bones, and laid the chest in stately shrine and fair.
He was so young, King Henry, that there he durst do naught,
Nor help them bear the body lest that it hurt him aught,
The holy bones, they raised them on Tuesday, as men tell,
And all his life's chief happenings, on Tuesdays all they fell.   700
For on a Tuesday was he born, from mother's womb he came;
And even as men bring a thief, so was he brought with shame
On Tuesday to Northampton, to stand before the king,
And to receive his judgment — they say, who saw the thing,
That even worse than any thief the folk they served him there —
Banished was he on Tuesday, from England forth must fare;
At Ponteney, on a Tuesday, Our Lord to him did come
And to him spake a gracious word of this, his Martyrdom:
Saith Our Dear Lord: "Now Thomas, thro' shedding of thy blood
Shall all my Church be honoured!" Methinks these words be good.   710
Then back again to England on Tuesday did he come,
After he had been banished, to take his Martyrdom.
And thus at Canterbury, on Tuesday was he slain,
At last, upon a Tuesday, enshrined within that fane.
Thus seven things on Tuesday befell from first to last,
And therefore on a Tuesday doth many a man keep fast
And eat no flesh on Tuesday, others but one meal eat,
And go to Canterbury, to do him honour meet.
Now Jesu, for that great Love, on which Saint Thomas thought
Bring us unto those self-same joys that he so dearly bought!   720

                                                        Amen.

SAINT BRANDAN

SAINT BRANDAN, that same holy man, he lived in this, our land,
A monk he was of strictest life, so do I understand,
In fasting and in penance lived, and Abbot was he there,
Over a thousand monks held rule, who all beneath him were.
And as it fell upon a day, by God's will and decree,
Another abbot came to him, Beryn by name was he;
Saint Brandan prayed of him anon that he would say that tide
What things soe'er he might have seen in other countries wide.
Then the good man, on hearing this, began to sigh eftsoon,
For heavy thought began to weep, and fell adown in swoon.   10
Between his arms Saint Brandan took that good man, at that same,
And kissed him oft, and called on him, till to himself he came.
"Father" he said, "for charity thou other rede must take,
Here for our solace art thou come, and not such dole to make;
Tell us the things that thou hast seen, as thou afar didst wend
Upon the seas of Ocean wide, where Our Lord did thee send." —
(Now is the sea of Ocean the greatest sea of all
The world it doth encircle, and all waters to it fall —)
With that Beryn, the agéd man, e'en from his heart so deep,
He told them all that he had found, the while he needs must weep.   20
He said he had a right good son, and Mernok was his name,
"A monk he was, e'en as we be, therewith a man of fame;
His heart, it urged him forth to wend, to privy place and still,
Wherein he might dwell all alone, and thus might serve God's Will.
Thus by my will did he go forth, e'en as I tell ye now,
To a far island in the sea, that pleasant was enow,
It lies beside the Mount of Stones, the which is known full wide,
And that same monk, he liked it well, and there did long abide;
And in that time full many a monk he had beneath him there,
And I, when I heard tell thereof, I thither thought to fare.   30
And then a vision Our Sweet Lord unto that monk did send
Bidding him go to meet me, a three days' journey wend.
To ship, I trow, we went right soon, Eastward our way did trace
On the far sea of Ocean, as Our Lord sent us Grace.
Toward the East so far we sailed that we were come, at last,
To a place dim and dusky, with clouds all over-cast;
There we abode in darkness, for well nigh all the day,
Until it pleased Our Lord at last to speed us on our way.
A new land we beheld then, and thither turned our prow,
Brighter it was than sunshine, and joy there was enow;   40
The trees and herbs, so thickly they grew on either side,
And stones so fair and precious lay gleaming far and wide;
Each bush was full of blossom, and full of fruit each tree.

Save that it were in Heaven, such perfume ne'er might be!
Therein, with joy and gladness, a long time did we spend,
Yet but short while it seemed us — Nor might we find the end, —
We came unto a water, so clear and bright to see,
From Eastward ever springing, Westward it floweth free.
We stood and looked about us, nor crossing might we find,
A woman came toward us, so young, and fair, and kind,   50
And bade us each one welcome in gentle words and sweet,
Each by his right name hailing, gracious she did us greet,
And said that Our Lord Jesus we now should thank aright —
'Who sheweth you His secrets, and therewithal His might;
This is the land He giveth, whenas the world shall end,
To those on earth He loveth, hither His dear ones wend.
One half on this shore lieth, ye see it is full wide,
And half beyond the water, upon the further side.
Ye may not pass that water, the other half to see,
A year long have ye been here, and meat-less all ye be;   60
Ye ate not, and ye drank not, nor sleep hath closed your eye,
Nor cold nor heat hath grieved you, or be ye low or high.
This is Our Lord's own Country, 't is He Who gives it light,
Thus day for aye endureth, and ne'er shall wane to night.
Had Adam 'gainst God's bidding transgressed not, then I ween
Herein had been his dwelling, here had his offspring been;
But now ye needs must turn again, ye may not linger here,
Tho' a short while ye deem it, here have ye dwelt a year.'
Then to our ship she brought us, and bade us there 'Farewell' —
The sea, it homeward bare us, her way we might not tell.   70
Against our will she left us, I trow it grieved us sore —
Back to the monks, our brethren, swiftly the ship us bore,
The monks, they came to meet us, when they our barque had seen,
And grieved were they, and wrathful, that we so long had been.
We said, in joy and gladness we for awhile did stand,
Before the gates of Paradise, in this, the Promised Land,
Which our Dear Lord hath promised to those He loveth here,
Where it is never night-fall, but ever daylight clear.
'Certes,' the monks, they answered, 'this we right well have seen,
By the sweet smell upon you, there have ye surely been.' "   80
Saint Brandan, when he heard this, awhile in thought stood still,
And in himself he pondered what now might be God's Will.
Then to his monks he turned him, and twelve he took that day,
Those unto whom he trusted, if need upon them lay.
The twelve he took to counsel, and privily he spake:
"A secret thing I purpose, whereof your rede I'ld take:
To seek the Land of Promise, an God will thither lead,
Now say, what is your counsel? Say, shall we do this deed?"
"Dear Father," spake the others, "our own will did we leave,
Our friends, and all our riches, and unto thee did cleave,   90

We do as thou desirest; if so thy will shall be
With thee we'll blithely journey, the Grace of God to see."
Then forty days they fasted, and penance sore they bare,
This, Our Lord's Grace, beseeching their voyage to prosper fair.
A great ship did they dight there, and then above it cast
A strong hood for a covering, and thereto nailed it fast.
And all without they pitched it, to keep it dry and fair,
Then went they to their brethren, and leave they prayed them there.
Sithen, in this, Our Lord's Name, forth to their ship they go,
The brethren left behind them, each one must sorrow know.   100
When they the ship had boarded, after them came there two
And straitly they besought them that they with them might go.
"That may ye," quoth Saint Brandan, "yet one shall at the end,
Repent of this, his coming, to Hell shall, living, wend."
This holy man, he went forth whither Our Lord should guide,
And these two monks, who came last, went with them at that tide.
On the great sea of Ocean forth do they row full fast,
In God's good guidance trusting, for naught are they aghast.
The sea, it drave their ship at will, the wind was strong and high,
And as the breeze it bare them, the ship sailed steadily,   110
Ever toward sun-rising, on a mid-summer day,
No man of them wist where he was, or where the land, it lay.
And thus, forthright, for forty days, the wind, it bare them fast,
Till that, upon the North-side, a great isle rose at last.
Of hard rock was it, great enow, and from the sea rose high,
Three days they sailed about it, ere that they might come nigh.
A little haven there they found, to land they get them there,
They went ashore as 'mazéd men, who wist not where they were.
Then came to them a goodly hound, as guide he drew them near,
And fell down at Saint Brandan's feet, and made of him good cheer.   120
"Beaux Fréres," then quoth Saint Brandan, "to fear have ye no need,
I trow this be a messenger, who will us rightly lead."
The hound, it led this holy man to a fair hall that day,
Noble it was, and high, and strong, within he leads the way;
The monks, they found within the hall a board, with cloths o'erspread,
Thereon was bread, with fish enow, they deemed they were well sped.
They sat them down, and ate full fast, much need had they each one,
And beds were there, all ready made, ere that their meal was done.
Then supper o'er, to bed they went, to rest them as was wise,
And tho' they weary were enow, full soon they 'gan arise,   130
And gat them to their ship again, where they afore had been,
And long time on the sea they were ere land again was seen.
They saw it, on the other side, rise fair from out the wave,
An island green, with pastures fair, thither their barque it drave.
Whenas they came to this fair land, and round about them spied,
The fairest sheep that e'er might be they saw on every side.
Each sheep was greater than an ox, and whiter none might be,

Great joy, it waxed within them, that they this sight might see.
Then came to them a goodly man, greeting he gave them fair,
And said: "The land where ye be come, ye saw aforetime ne'er,   140
It is y'clept '*The Land of Sheep*,' for here fair sheep they be
Mickle, and white, and great enow, as ye full well may see;
And fairer far than are your sheep, greater beyond compare,
The weather here is good enow, the pastures rich and rare;
For never winter vexeth us, nor here shall hay be found,
But each doth crop the herbage new as it doth spring from ground.
And men, they take not of their milk, that they the worser be,
For this and many another thing, they profit verilie.
From hence ye to a land shall fare, by this, Our Lord's good Grace,
That is '*The Paradise of Birds*,' and a right joyous place,   150
And there this Easter shall ye be, and Whitsuntide shall spend;
Now go ye forth in God's good Name, to bring this voyage to end."
Saint Brandan, and his brethren then, to ship they go anon,
And fast they row forth on the sea, with tempests many a one,
Till on the other side they saw an island great up-stand,
Their ship, I trow, by grace of God, it drew toward that land,
So that it almost came thereto, but on the rock did ride,
And came not close unto the isle, but lay the land beside.
Saint Brandan stayed within the ship, the monks, they wade to shore,
They thought to make them here a meal of what they had in store.   160
A fire they made, and boiled them fish all in a cauldron fast,
But ere the fish was cooked enow, somewhat were they aghast,
For as the fire, it burned right thro', the isle, it quaked anon,
And as in wrath it rose up there, the monks took fright each one,
Each after other to the ship they fled, as at that same,
He deemed himself best loved of God who soonest thither came!
And then they saw how this same isle fared thro' the sea full fast,
As a live thing leapt up and down, and fire from off him cast,
More than a two-mile distance swam while that it burned, the fire,
The monks, they saw the flame from far, and were in terror dire.   170
They cried upon Saint Brandan, what should this marvel be?
"Bide still," then quoth this holy man, "fear not for what ye see,
Ye deem it be an island, therein ye think amiss,
It is a fish of this great sea, the greatest that there is,
Jastoni, is he naméd, and seeketh, night and day,
To take his tail within his mouth, for size doth fail alway."
Then forth they rowed upon the sea, and Westward swift they fare
Three days, ere land it came in sight, somewhat they feared them there.
A right fair land they see then, where thick the flowers grow,
And much the sight rejoiced them, their barque they thither row.   180
Thro' this fair land they wandered, longer than I may tell,
A place they found within it, a very goodly well,
There stood a tree beside it, 't was broad and wide enow,
And white and fair the birdlings that sat on every bough;

So thick they perched upon it, ye scarce a leaf might see,
'T was joy and bliss sufficing to look on such a tree!
For joy he wept, Saint Brandan, and on his knee bent low
Praying that God the meaning of this strange sight would show.
A small bird fluttered upward, and as he took his flight,
His wings were as a cithole, toward him came aright,   190
(Than instrument of music sweeter his wings they were —)
He looked upon Saint Brandan with goodly cheer and fair;
"I bid ye," quoth Saint Brandan, "an messenger ye be,
Tell me of these, your doings, your nature show to me!"
Altho' it seemed a marvel, this bird he spake anon,
And quoth: "We were aforetime angels in heaven, each one,
But e'en as we were fashioned, for this, his beauty's pride,
He, Lucifer, our master, full soon was put outside;
And many another with him the self-same doom did win;
And we, adown we fell then, yet not for any sin,   200
And not that we assented to what he did 'gainst right,
But only to bear witness to this, Our Sweet Lord's might.
Nor here in pain we're holden, in joy enow we be,
And somewhat of Our Dear Lord, His might and power, we see.
And on the earth we fly now, and thro' the air also,
As angels good or evil, methinks, may rightly do.
The good aid men to goodness, the evil, evil make —
Our day of rest is Sunday, and then such form we take
As white birds are we fashioned, as here ye well may see,
And honour God our Maker, here, on this spreading tree.   210
A twelvemonth hath passed over, since that ye forth did wend,
Six years more must ye journey ere this, your toil, may end.
When seven years ye've voyaged, Our Lord shall send to ye
The sight that ye full long have sought, yet passed those years must be.
And each year shall ye here with us the Feast of Easter hold
As now ye do, till ye at last the Promised Land behold."
Now it was on an Easter-day that they this venture knew,
The bird, he took his leave of them, and to his fellows flew.
The birds, when it was eventide, began their evensong,
And sweeter song there might not be, were God their ranks among!   220
The monks, they went to bed and sleep, when they had supper ta'en,
And when 't was time for Mattins, then they rose up again.
The birds, they sang their Mattins, they knew the fitting time,
The verses of the Psalter too, and sithen sang they Prime,
At Underne, and at Midday, at Nones, so sang they then,
At all the Hours throughout the day as fitting Christian men.
The monks, they in that land abode until eight weeks had flown,
And they the Feasts of Easter and Whitsuntide had known.
With Trinity there cometh that good man to them there
Who met them in the Land of Sheep, and showed its marvels fair;   230
Their ship he well had loaded, of meat and drink, a store,

Bade them Farewell right gently, and turned them from that shore.
When with his monks, Saint Brandan, once more a-ship was he,
The bird that erst spake with them, it sought them presently,
And spake: "Ye have been with us thro' this high Feast, I ween,
Great travail doth await ye ere land once more be seen,
Ye shall, full seven months ended, behold a goodly isle,
By name 't is calléd Abbey, it lies hence many a mile;
There with good men, and holy, Midwinter shall ye spend,
Your Easter shall be holden, as ye this year did wend,   240
On that great Fish's back-bone, whereof your monks had fear,
The Feast with us be ended, e'en as it was this year."
Then, in God's Name, Saint Brandan, and these his monks, each one,
On the great sea of Ocean they sailéd forth anon;
The wind, it tossed them up and down, they many a peril knew,
And of their lives waxed weary, nor wist they where to go.
For months they were upon the sea, which did them much torment,
Since they saw naught but water, and eke the firmament.
Then saw they land afar from them, as if an isle it were,
And strait they cried on Jesu Christ that He would bring them there. 250
Yet after that Saint Brandan the isle might first espy
For forty days they sailed about ere that they might come nigh,
So that they deemed their life was lost, the monks were much in fear,
And loud they cried on Jesu, that He would help them here.
A haven small and narrow they found there at the last,
Their ship, it scarce might come therein that they might anchor cast.
These monks to shore betook them, too long they'd haven sought,
And looked all round about them, 't was joyous to their thought;
Then two fair wells they see there, the one was very clear,
Troubled and thick the other — The monks they went anear   260
To drink of that clear water, Saint Brandan spake straightway:
"Without the leave of others ye go not nigh to-day,
The leave of old men ancient, who be here thro' God's Will,
For they will share it with us, and therefore hold ye still."
A fair old man, and hoary, toward them came, I wis,
And gave them gracious greeting, and did Saint Brandan kiss;
Then forth with him he led them, by a fair way, and good,
Thro' many a pleasant pasture, to where an Abbey stood.
Saint Brandan looked about him, and asked what place it were?
What men should dwell within it? And how they had come there?   270
The old man held him silent, and answered not his prayer —
Then came a fair procession, a Cross before them bare,
With tapers lit beside it, monks were they, every one,
In choir-copes fairly vested, toward them came anon —
And fair was the procession, the abbot closed the band,
Gracious, he kissed Saint Brandan, and took him by the hand.
He and his monks he led them into a noble hall,
There in a row he set them, their feet he washed withal

In this, the troubled water, that they did first espy;
To the refectory led them, and set them down on high, 280
With these, his own monks, mingled, when each was in his seat,
Then one there came who served them, and brought to each his meat.
A fair white loaf he set there betwixt each two and two,
A white mess, as of herbs 't were, before them set also,
And sweeter food might none be, 't was known afore to none —
Of that clear well the waters, the monks have drunk each one.
"Be glad now:" quoth the abbot, "and take deep draughts and long
In love of this same water ye fain had ta'en with wrong;
Better it is to drink it in love, as now 't is brought,
Than as a thief to steal it, as was at first your thought. 290
This bread that here we eat of, we know not what it is,
Each day a strange man brings it unto our store, I wis,
We trow by God's Grace only this food to us is brought,
Whoso in Jesu trusteth, methinks shall fail for naught.
We be Friars, four and twenty, when thus we take our seat
Twelve manchets white they bring us each day to this, our meat.
And on each holy Feast day, and Sundays too, I wis,
They bring us four and twenty, that every man hath his;
And what each brother leaveth that shall his supper be,
To-day for ye 't is doubled, as ye right well may see; 300
Nor here is all our Convent, there be who do not eat,
But by His Grace Our Dear Lord hath sent to all his meat.
From out Saint Patrick's Abbey, in Ireland, so I ween,
For four-score years we dwell here, no man hath nigh us been,
Yet thro' His Grace, our Dear Lord hath fed us, every one,
And aye have we fine weather, and sickness is there none.
When we should do His Service, Our Lord, He sends us light,
Our tapers be not lessened, tho' burnt by day and night!"
They rose, and forth they gat them to church, thus after meat,
Twelve other Friars they met then, who thither go to eat; 310
"How is this?" quoth Saint Brandan. "Why were they not with us?"
"Dear Father:" quoth the Abbot, "of needs it must be thus,
For four and twenty only, hath our Refectory space,
Whenas that ye were with us then these might find no place,
While Evensong we're singing, then shall they sit and eat,
And after sing their office, when they have had their meat."
Saint Brandan saw that Altar, it seeméd to him here,
With Chalice, and with cruets, all wrought of crystal clear;
The choir had seven tapers, nor more nor less, to wit,
The stalls were four and twenty wherein the monks should sit; 320
For four and twenty brethren there were, and each had his,
Midst of the choir the Abbot, he had his seat, I wis.
Saint Brandan asked the Abbot, "Now tell me, dear my brother,
Why do ye keep such silence that none speaks with the other?"
"Our Lord knows," quoth the Abbot, "that here we now have been

For years four-score, and leading such life as ye have seen,
Nor was there one among us who spake, before to-day,
A word, save what was needed his Office well to say,
And none of us waxed feeble, and sickness fell on none —"
Saint Brandan, when he heard this, for joy he wept anon,   330
"Dear Father" thus he answered, "here may we bide with ye?"
"Ye wot well: " quoth the Abbot, "that may in no wise be,
Hath not our Lord well shown thee that which thou needs must do?
Thou needs must go to Ireland, thy brethren twelve also;
And at the Isle of Ankres, the thirteenth from thee wend,
To Hell alive, the fourteenth, and be there without end."
With that, a fiery arrow in at the window flew,
As tho' it were from Heaven, and trimmed the tapers true,
And then thro' that same window it passed, e'en as it came,
Long enow burned the tapers, nor wasted in the flame.   340
"Lord Christ," then quoth Saint Brandan, "I wonder in my thought,
How thus they burn, these tapers, and how they waste for naught?"
"Hast thou not," quoth the Abbot, "in Holy Scripture found
How Moses saw a thorn burn, from topmost twig to ground,
Yet aye the more it burned there, greener the leaves they were,
Dost thou not deem Our Lord be as mighty here as there?"
Those monks they were together till Christmas-tide was o'er,
Yea, e'en till after Twelfth-day, ere they set forth once more.
Then on the Feast of Hilary, Saint Brandan forth did wend
With his monks on the Ocean, tho' grace that God did send;   350
In grief enow they floated, tossed up and down they be,
Till Lent was well nigh ended, nor sign of land might see,
Till that, about Palm-Sunday, their glance around they cast,
And saw, in the dim distance as 't were a cloud at last.
The monks, thereof they wondered, what that same cloud, it were —
"Bide still" then quoth Saint Brandan, "aforetime were ye there,
There is our procurator, who did us good of yore,
Both in the Paradise of Birds, and Isle of Sheep, afore,"
So that, at last, their vessel came to that Isle, I ween,
Upon the Maunday Thursday, in travail great they'd been.   360
The old man came toward them, and welcomed them anon,
Saint Brandan's feet, he kissed them, and then the monks', each one;
Sithen set them at supper, as fitting for the day,
Then all their feet he washed there, the Maund he would obey.
Thus Maunday did they keep there, and rested at that same
Throughout the whole Good Friday, till Easter Eve, it came;
On Easter Eve that old man bade them take ship anon,
Their Easter Mass to hold it that Fish's back upon.
After the Resurrection he bade them go once more
Unto the Paradise of Birds, where they had been afore.   370
These holy men, they sailed forth, God's Grace did guide their way
To this great Fish, in safety, they came the self-same day.

It stood still, as an island, their cauldron found they here,
As on its back they'd left it, e'en in that bye-gone year;
Lord Christ, to think such monster should in this wise stay still
And suffer men upon it to come and go at will!
There, on its back, the holy men, abode throughout the night,
Sang Evensong, and Mattins, and then, with morning light,
Their Easter Mass they sang there, upon its back, each one,
And that great Fish, it stayed there as still as any stone.   380
Then, when their Resurrection they'd kept with honour due,
And all the monks had sung there their Mass in order true,
About the time of Underne, to ship they took their way,
And to the Paradise of Birds they came the self-same day.
When the birds saw them coming, each one brake into song
With melody to greet them, as doth to Nones belong.
The Bird that erst spake with them, toward them winged his way,
His wings, they beat sweet music, greeting he gave that day,
And quoth: "Ye ought to thank Him, Our Lord Christ, with the best,
Who thus prepared four places whereon ye now may rest,   390
With our good Procurator your Maunday well to do,
Sithen, your Resurrection on that great fish, also,
And here with us full eight weeks, till Whitsuntide, to pass,
And in the Isle of Abbey Christmas to Candlemas.
But on the sea of Ocean in peril must ye wend
These other days, in travail, till seven years shall end.
And then the Land of Promise by God's Will shall ye see,
And forty days within it in bliss and joy shall be.
Thence, to the land ye came from ye shall thereafter wend,
In ease, and without travail, and there your lives shall end."   400
These holy men abode there, even to Trinitie,
The old man, their provider, he fed them plenteouslie,
And meat and drink he brought them, as he afore had done,
Therewith, their barque he loaded, and bade them sail anon.
These holy men, they went forth as God would send them there,
The Grace of God was with them, so might they better fare.
As thus one time they journeyed before a tempest's blast,
A great Fish, and a grisley, the ship it followed fast,
And burning foam he spued forth from out his jaws so wide,
Each time it rose, the water, high o'er the vessel's side,   410
E'en as a house he wallowed, pursuing them so fast,
So fierce, I trow, his threatening, the monks were sore aghast.
They cried upon Saint Brandan, and on Our Lord also,
So swift he did pursue them well nigh he came thereto,
Well nigh did he o'ertake them, their lives for lost they hold,
When, swimming from the West-ward, a great Fish they behold,
This evil fish it met with, and smote upon it fast
Till the foul back was cloven in three parts at the last.
Then the same way he came from, thither he turned again, —

The monks gave thanks to Jesu, they of His aid were fain!   420
Long time these good men wandered upon the Ocean wide,
Till they were sore a-hungered, no meat had they that tide.
Then came a small bird flying, a great bough with him brought
Laden with ripe grapes, ruddy, their ship he straightway sought.
Thereon for days full fourteen, they lived, and lacked for naught.
Then, when these grapes were finished, hunger, it vexed them sore,
An isle they saw beside them, therein of meat a store,
Full of fair trees that island, laden each bough they found
E'en with those grapes I spake of, they trailed upon the ground.
From ship he went, Saint Brandan, the grapes, he plucked them fast,   430
Aboard for food he bare them, for forty days they last.
Soon came a Gryphon flying, pursued them on their way,
And in their ship assailed them, and fain he would them slay;
In dole these monks, they cried out, they deemed their life was o'er —
They saw that small bird flying toward them as before
With whom they oft had spoken, in the Bird's Paradise,
Whenas Saint Brandan saw him the sight rejoiced his eyes;
This small bird smote the gryphon, and aimed his blow so high,
That with the first blow only he smote out either eye.
That evil beast, he slew it, dead in the sea it fell,   440
For none may harm the creature to whom God wisheth well!
These monks on sea they wandered, and sailed now here, now there,
In one of these four places at each high Feast they were.
And one Feast of Saint Peter they joyful spake with tongue,
In honour of Saint Peter on sea they merry sung.
And in that place, it chanced then, so clear the sea they found
On either side about them they saw e'en to the ground,
They deemed the ground on each side with fish was all on heap
And all so still they lay there, as they had been asleep.
The monks beseech Saint Brandan from loud speech to refrain   450
Lest that the fish, awakened, should break the ship in twain.
"Why fear ye?" quoth Saint Brandan. "Whereof are ye in dread?
The Master of the Fishes, on him ye were well sped,
Fire on his back ye kindled, and come there year by year."
Then, louder than aforetime, his song rang sweet and clear,
They started up, the fishes, as wakened from their sleep,
About the ship came thronging, as it were on an heap,
Thick on each side they floated, no water might ye see,
Beset the ship all round about, — from water were they free.
Around the barque lay thickly, and did it close pursue   460
Until his Mass Saint Brandan, had sung it fair and true;
Each on its way departed e'en as the Mass did end —
Yea, man may see great wonders who wide in world doth wend!
The wind, it was both strong and stiff, and drave their ship so fast,
While seven nights they sailéd did that clear water last,
So that, as clear as it were land, they saw beneath the wave,

These good monks, much they wondered, and thanks to God they gave.
With that there came a South wind, and Northward fast they drew,
And long that wind was with them, for full eight days it blew;
Far, in the North, they saw it, a dismal land and dark,   470
It smoked as doth a smithy, thitherward drave their barque.
With that, they heard a blowing of many bellows there,
And beating great, and noise enow, e'en as it thunder were.
Sore vexed was then Saint Brandan, and crossed himself full fast,
With that came forth a wicked wight, full swiftly at the last,
All black was he, and burning, he looked upon the men,
Anon, he turned him back again, the monks were 'frighted then;
That evil wight gave forth a cry, that men might hear him wide,
Then of his like came many more, they thronged on either side,
With tongs, and eke with hammers, and all afire each one,   480
And swiftly to the water's edge, after the ship they run.
Then, since they might not come anigh, they 'gan to yell full fast,
Their hammers all a-burning, after the monks they cast,
That naught but flame about them, those men may hear or see,
The sea all round was burning, as tho' afire it be!
Their casts came each on other, some missiles threw on high,
Thus threw they all around the ship, yet never came they nigh.
At last aback they turn them, since they might profit naught, —
And all the land they dwelt in, it was afire, they thought;
And all the sea around it, it burned and smoked full fast,   490
The smoke was thick, and stinking, and long time did it last,
Altho' that smoke was some part flame — When they could see no more,
Yet still they heard their yelling, the thieves, they wept full sore.
"What think ye?" quoth Saint Brandan: "Was this a merry pass?"
No more we'll come anigh there, one end of Hell it was,
The fiends, they deemed they had here, a good catch, so I wot,
But praiséd be Sweet Jesu, they drew a blank for lot!"
But still the South wind lasted, and still it drave them forth,
Until a hole they saw there, afar, toward the North,
Of glowing smoke, and burning, and strong the stench withal,   500
The lowe thereof, it reached on high, as tho' it were a wall;
If in the other place was much, there was, I trow, much more!
One of the monks he then began to weep and wail full sore
For that his time, it now was come, nor might it be delayed,
Straightway he leapt from out the ship, amid the sea 'gan wade,
Ran fast upon the water, toward that fire drew near,
With dismal yells and doleful, great dole it was to hear:
"Alas!" he cried, "my wretched life, for now I see mine end,
In joy have I been with ye, but back I may not wend,
Accurst be she who bare me, the hour that I was born,   510
The father who begat me, for now am I forlorn!"
The fiends they came toward him, they held that wretch full fast,
And strongly did they bind him, and 'mid the furnace cast;

'T was sooth he said, Saint Brandan, when that he forth would wend
That Grace should surely fail him, his sinful life to mend.
So fast it burned the mountain, that naught of it they know,
For that they still were distant, naught but the fiery glow.
The wind, to North it turned then, Southward it drave them **fast,**
On each side did it strongly blow till seven nights were past.
So long they sailéd Southward until at last they see   520
A rugged rock in Ocean, washed over by the sea;
By water oft-times covered, and oft-times was it bare,
And as they drew anigh it they of a ghost were 'ware.
They saw, on that rock seated, when the wave backward drew,
A wretched ghost all naked, and sore mis-ease he knew;
A cloth was spread above him, with two clasps, made full fast
Beneath his chin at one end, the wind it wide did cast,
That ever when the water withdrew, the cloth from high
Beat downward as the wind blew, and smote him in the eye.
The waves, they beat him also, before, and eke behind,   530
I trow a ghost more wretched a man might hardly find.
Then, in God's Name Saint Brandan conjured him, that he tell
His name, and his misdoing, and why this doom befell?
He quoth: "My name is Judas, a doleful ghost am I,
Who sold Our Lord for silver, with Him on earth was I,
But this is not my dwelling, Our Lord doth me this Grace,
Somewhat to ease my suffering He sets me in this place;
'T is not for good I did erst, but of His Mercy's store,
For never pain I suffer but I were worthy more!
For in that Hell that burneth, there, where ye saw it aye,   540
Therein have I my portion, to burn by night and day,
And there was I but lately when this, your brother, came,
And there was led to torment, and doom of endless flame.
And therefore Hell was joyful, and burned with such a glow,
For that he was come thither, it is their custom so
When any soul, it cometh at first within their thrall,
But I, thro' God's great Mercy from out their clutches fall;
Here am I every Sunday, from Saturday at eve
To Evensong on Sunday, and here they must me leave.
And at Midwinter also, till Twelfth Day, I may know   550
This ease, from dawn of Easter to Whitsunday, also.
And on Our Lady's Feast days, so full of Grace He is,
At other times my portion is cast in Hell, I wis,
With Pilate, and Herodias, Annas, and Caiaphas,
Now may the hour be curséd that born on earth I was!
For love of God I pray ye, now deal ye on this wise,
This night abide ye near me till that the sun shall rise,
And from the fiends protect me, who soon will come for me!"
"By God's Grace." quoth Saint Brandan, "thy shield we sure shall be,
But say, what may that cloth be, that hangeth o'er thee there?"   560

"The while that I on earth was, and Our Lord's silver bare,
This cloth I gave a leper, and yet mine own 't was naught,
With pence of this my Master, and comrades, was it bought.
Since for God's Love I gave it, from me it is not ta'en,
The least man doeth for Him shall be repaid again.
Yet since the cost was others', so have I understood,
Altho' it hangs before me, it doth more harm than good,
For in mine eyes it beateth, and doth them hurt, I wis —
To give at cost of others man may be warned by this,
As many a rich man doeth, who oft with wrong doth take   570
Their goods from many a poor man, and alms thereof doth make.
That for God's Love they do it, it shall not be forgot,
Yet to their pain be turnéd, as they shall surely wot.
These clasps, also:" quoth Judas, "that o'er my head ye see,
To two priests did I give them, and therefore here they be,
Each man shall find that surely which he hath done for love —
The stone that here I sit on, lifted the waves above,
Once on a road I found it, where it was useless all,
Into a ditch I cast it, lest men should o'er it fall.
But few have been the good deeds whereof I now may tell,   580
The smallest one is garnered, either in Heaven or Hell!"
Now, since 't was eve of Sunday, the fiends came on the blast,
That ghost, to Hell to lead it, they howled and yelled full fast;
"Go hence," they said, "thou good man, here may'st thou nothing speed,
But let us take our comrade, to Hell we will him lead,
We dare not face our Master ere that we him have brought,
'T is time thou turnéd'st from him, thou shalt us hinder naught."
"Ye shall not," quoth Saint Brandan, "here do your Master's will,
Our Lord Christ doth forbid it, Who is more powerful still."
The fiends they quoth: "How dar'st thou before him name that Name?   590
Betrayed he did, and sold Him, to death with mickle shame."
Saint Brandan quoth: "In His Name I bid ye, as I may,
To lay no hand upon him ere dawns to-morrow's day."
Rueful, the fiends they yelled then, and homeward 'gan to flee,
Judas, he sadly thanked him, and dole it was to see.
The morrow, with the daylight, the fiends they thither hied,
With grisley yell, and weeping, full fast began to chide:
"Away," they said, "thou good man, acccurséd be the stound,
That thou drew nigh unto us, and that we thee here found,
Our Master, he hath plagued us right bitterly this night   600
With strong pains, since we brought not, with us this sorry wight,
But for these coming six days we'll double all his woe,
And so will we avenge us, to his own count 't will go!"
Sore quaked that ghost so wretched, 't were dole to see, or tell,
The fiends, with them they took him, and led him into Hell.
Saint Brandan there forbade them, in this, Our Dear Lord's, Name,
That for this night of respite they do him greater shame.

Then with his monks, Saint Brandan, he put forth on the sea,
And by Our Lord's Grace journeyed Southward for days full three,
The fourth day, to the Southward they saw an isle rise high, 610
And when Saint Brandan saw it, full sorely did he sigh;
"I trow that Paul, the Hermit, is in that isle I see,
For forty years he dwells here, and never meat hath he."
Whenas they reached the island ashore they went, each one,
That agéd man, the Hermit, toward them came anon,
Down to his feet flowed thickly the hair of beard and head,
Hidden was all his body, that naught was bare that stead;
Naught else had he for raiment, his limbs for age were hoar —
Saint Brandan he beheld him, and there he wept full sore:
"Now living as an angel, a mortal man I see!" 620
"Be still," then quoth the Hermit, "for God doth well by thee,
And shows, as to none other what these, His Secrets, be!
A monk by his own labour, and toil, I trow, doth live,
But thou, by God's Grace only, what He to thee doth give!
In th' Abbey of Saint Patrick a monk was I, I wis,
And of his church a warden, where Purgatory is;
One day a man came to me, I asked who he might be?
He quoth, 'I am thine Abbot, have thou no fear of me!'
'No man save holy Patrick mine Abbot is,' I said;
'I am that man' he answered, 'be not for that afraid, 630
To-morrow, with the daylight,' quoth he 'to sea must wend,
There doth a ship await thee, that God to thee will send,
And in that ship shalt set forth, upon the sea so wide,
It to the place will lead thee, wherein thou shalt abide.'
Early next morn I rose up, to do his will was bound,
And to the sea-shore coming, full soon the ship I found.
I bade that ship sail with me, and straight we forth did wend,
In seven days to this island, Our Lord, He did me send.
Whenas from ship I landed, then, guided by God's Grace,
The way, aright I found it, that led me to this place. 640
Sick, and alone, I came here, and comfort had I none —
On his hind feet an Otter, he came to me anon,
Betwixt his fore-feet brought me fire-iron, and flint, I trow,
Wherewith a fire to kindle, and good fish, too, enow.
He went his way, the Otter, and fire I made me there,
And cooked me fish, in God's Name, I had for three days fare.
And ever since, the third day, that Otter comes to me,
And brings me meat sufficient to last for days full three.
From out this hard rock, water springs at Our Lord's command,
Each day enough there floweth to drink and wash my hands. 650
But here, for thirty winters, I such a life had led
Ere first the well, it sprang forth, as ye see at this stead.
By this well have I lived now, a forty years, full told,
And ere that I came hither, full fifty was I old;

So that of years, one hundred, and twenty more, to-day
May to my lot be counted, God's Will be done, alway!
Here I my death await now, when God the day shall send,
And bid me come unto Him, and from this world to wend.
But take now of this water, for thou hast need anon,
And wend forth on the Ocean, thy journey is not done,   660
For on the sea thou further for forty days must fare,
Thine Easter Mass be holden, as it was holden ere;
Thence, to the Land of Promise, believe me, shalt thou go,
For forty days abiding, its pleasures shalt thou know,
And, leaving it, shalt journey to thine own land again —"
With dole enow, those good men departed them in twain.
These holy men, they sailed forth, a tempest bare them fast,
For forty days to Southward the while that Lent did last,
To their good procurator, on Easter Eve, them bore
And joy enow he made them as he had done afore.   670
To the great Fish he led them, e'en as the evening fell,
All night, till Easter morning, they on its back did dwell.
There did they sing their Mattins, and Easter Mass anon —
The Fish began to move there, e'en as the Mass was done;
Bearing the monks forth with him, he swam forth very fast,
Cleaving the sea so strongly, the monks were sore aghast;
I trow it was a marvel, an one were there to see,
So great a beast forth faring, as 't were a great countrie!
Straight to the Paradise of Birds he bare the monks that day,
There whole and sound he left them, and went upon his way.   680
These monks, when they came thither, so glad and blithe they were —
Till Trinity was over, the while they stayed them there,
For their good procurator brought meat and drink enow,
As he had done aforetime, their ship he stored, I trow,
And also went forth with them where God should think to send —
Toward the east they sailéd, and forty days they wend,
And when those days were finished, it 'gan to hail full fast,
And a thick mist enwrapped them, for long time did it last;
"Rejoice!" he quoth, their guide, then, "and make ye right good cheer,
This is the Land of Promise, I trow that we be here!"   690
When from this mist they came forth, and well might look around,
The land, it was the fairest that ever yet was found,
So clear it was, and sun-lit, it wrought them joy enow,
The trees with fruit were laden, that clustered on each bough;
With trees 't was set full thickly, and each was very fair,
And with ripe apples laden, as harvest-time it were.
And forty days they dwelt there, and did about it wend,
Nor of the land might find there, on either side, the end.
And evermore 't was daylight, and nevermore 't was night,
Nowhere where they had journeyed had they found so much light.   700
The air was ever tempered, nor hot, nor yet too cold,

The joy they found within it, it may by none be told.
They came to a fair water, nor might they further go,
But all the land beyond it for very fair they know.
A young man came toward them, goodly, and fair to see,
'T was God Who sent him to them, fairer no man might be,
Each one by name he welcomed, and kissed them one by one,
Did honour to Saint Brandan, and took his hand anon.
"Lo! here," he said, "the country, that ye have sought so wide,
But yet Our Lord, He wills not that ye for long abide;   710
Now ye have seen His Secrets, ye shall again to sea,
But load your barque with fruit now, since here ye may not be."
Then courteous, to Saint Brandan that young man spake: "Fair Friend,
To thine own land returning thou on thy way must wend,
This world, thou soon must leave it, thy life is near its end.
The water that thou seest, divides this land in two,
This half, right fair ye deem it, beyond, 't is even so —
Ye may not pass the bounds now, for that it is not right;
This fruit aye ripe abideth, this land is ever light,
And when, Our Lord, He willeth a man to Him to draw,   720
So that he well doth know Him, and understand His law,
* That land to him He showeth, and when the world shall end,
The souls that be His chosen, they all shall thither wend."
Saint Brandan and his monks there, of this fruit plucked full fast,
And precious stones took also, into their ship did cast;
Fair leave they then have taken, and when they this had done,
With weeping, grief, and dole enow, they did depart, anon,
And wended homeward on the sea, e'en as Our Lord did send,
And sooner came they home again than they did outward wend.
Their brethren, when they saw them, joyful were they indeed,   730
Saint Brandan, he, that holy man, full soon to death must speed,
For never after this same time, for this world cared he aught,
But as one of another world, he fared as aye in thought.
And soon he died in Ireland, after that self-same stound,
And sithen, many a miracle for his sake hath been found.
A right fair Abbey men have reared, where he was buried low —
God bring us to that self-same joy that this, His saint, doth know!

                                                        Amen.

SAINT CECILIA

CHRIST JESUS, pitiful is He,
And to mankind of mercy free,
And showeth forth His power and might
Oft-times, as men may see with sight,
So that we may his marvels ken
Alike in women as in men.

But most in maidens we behold
Who to His bidding faithful hold,
As an ensample we may see
In Saint Cecilia, maiden free.   10
That maid was born of gentle blood,
Holy was she, and mild of mood,

And in her heart full well she knew
The lore of her dear Lord, Jesu,
And unto Him did ever pray
And ceaséd not, by night or day.
Urban, the Pope, hath her baptized
In the true Faith of Jesus Christ.
Unto her friends right dear was she,
And all who should her comrades be   20
Because she was both fair and good,
And to all folk of gracious mood.
Her friends would wed her with a man
Who hight by name, Valerian,
A young man he, and fair of face,
And sprung from a right noble race,
Heathen he was, and unbaptized,
And knew naught of the law of Christ,
Nor other durst Cecilia do   29
Save what her friends, they told her to.
The day was set, they should be wed,
In cloth of gold fair robed that stead,
Therein Cecilia took no pride,
A cere-cloth 'neath it did she hide;
To outward show, rich raiment ware
Such as her friends for her prepare.
Thus on this wise, when they were wed,
Full many folk, their friends, they fed.
Whenas the bridal came to end,   39
And each man on his way would wend,
Cecilia to her chamber went,
Calling on God with good intent,
A sound they heard, that was full near,
Of Angels' song, and organs clear,
Music she made, their song among,
And in this wise Cecilia sung:
"*Fiat cor meum, et corpus meum immaculatum, ut non confundar.*"
And this, I trow, the words shall mean:
"My heart, O Lord! do thou make clean,
My body keep unstained within,   50
So that I be not lost thro' sin."
When in this wise she'd made her prayer
To God, with good intent, and fair,
She with her husband went to bed
As the law would, since she was wed,
But in her heart she purposed right
To keep her clean, if so she might.
So by her lord when she was laid

In this wise unto him she said:
"Sir, if it so thy will might be   60
A counsel would I give to thee,
That must be said now, with thy leave,
And, good my lord, in no wise grieve.
An Angel, Sir, of heaven bright,
My guardian is, by day and night,
A servant unto God is he —
I love him well, so doth he me,
And if he should be 'ware, this while,
That thou my body should'st defile,
Or carnal love should'st offer me,   70
For this will he be wroth with thee,
And vengeance will upon thee take
That thou all solace shalt forsake,
And lose of this, thy youth, the flower,
'T were well my lord, to dread his
    power!'"
Valerian, he waxed wroth that stead,
Nor durst her touch, for very dread,
Her words he deemed but sorry pay,
And in this wise he spake alway:
"Woman, if thou wilt that I trow   80
The words that thou did'st speak but
    now,
Betwixt us twain here let me see
Him, who thou say'st so loveth thee,
So that I of myself may see
Whether in truth he angel be,
And servant unto Heaven's will.
If so, I'll do thy bidding still;
But if thou dost another love
Thy bane that bargain sure shall prove,
Nor he, nor thou, shall 'scape my wrath,
But I myself will slay ye both,   91
With mickle shame thy deed repay —"
An answer soft she gave alway,
"Good Sir," she said, "ne'er grievéd be
If thou may'st not God's angel see,
For ne'er to man such vision fell
Save he believe, as I shall tell,
In God Who made all things below —
Himself did ne'er beginning know,
But is, and evermore shall be,   100
The most of might, of mercy free —
And in His dear Son, Jesus Christ —
Wilt thou believe, and be baptized,

Then say I, Sir, that thou shalt see
The angel, that I promise thee!
Now Sir, if thou wilt this essay
To Bishop Urban take thy way,
To tell him all these words be bold,
Recite the tale as I have told;
Tell him thy life from end to end,　110
What is amiss shall he amend.
Then when thy troth is plighted true
He'll clothe thee all in clothing new,
Robes white and clean he'll give to
　　thee —
Then shalt thou in my chamber see
That angel bright from heaven, I trow,
Who loves me, as I said but now,
And from him shalt thou surely have
Whatever thing thy heart doth crave."
Then thro' the Spirit's Grace, he rose,
And in all haste he swiftly goes　121
To the good Bishop Urban there,
And doth his tale straightway declare,
How with him, and his wife it stood —
When Urban this had understood,
He raised his hands to heaven's height,
And called on God, the most in might:
"Lord Jesu Christ, loved may'st Thou be
Who sowest seeds of chastity,
And counsel chaste to men dost give　130
Whereby their souls may ever live.
Take Thou the fruit now, as Thine own,
Of seed once in Cecilia sown,
It waxeth now, and multiplies,
As man may see in this same wise;
A spouse she took, with her to dwell,
Who, as a lion, was fierce and fell,
A rebel both by day and night
Who aye against Thy law did fight.
Thy servant now, she maketh him　140
Meek as a lamb, in soul and limb,
For were he not thus waxen meek
Salving of me he would not seek,
And since he hath salvation sought
Lord, save him, and deny him naught!"
Then, when his prayer had come to end,
Before them both they saw descend
An old man, clad in linen clean
And white, who stood the twain between,

Who in his hand a book did hold　150
All written o'er with letters gold.
Valerian when he saw that sight
Was vanquished by excess of light;
For dread he fell adown that stead
And lay as still as he were dead.
The old man then his right hand took
And raised him up, and bade him look
What writing this same book should
　　bear
Which he had brought unto him there.
Valerian did the letters trace,　160
And thus 't was written in that place:
"*Unus Dominus, Una Fides, Unum
　　Baptisma.*"
And this is what the letters mean,
"One God is over all, I ween;
All folk shall to one Faith belong;
One Baptism cleanse all souls from
　　wrong."
Whenas Valerian this had read
The old man asked him, in that stead,
"What now thou readest, trow'st thou
　　well,　169
Or doubt within thy soul doth dwell?"
Then answered him Valerian:
"What more befitteth mortal man
Thro' book, or word of mouth indeed,
Then to believe a Heavenly rede?
And with my mind I now believe,
All that is written here receive."
Whenas Valerian this did say
The old man, he hath gone his way,
But how, they might no way devise —
Urban, Valerian doth baptize,　180
Bade him believe, with conscience clean,
All things that he had heard and seen.
Valerian promised with good will
That he his bidding would fulfil;
Then was he bade go, at that same,
Unto his wife, from whom he came,
And comfort her, as best he might —
Thus, to his wife he went forthright,
Into Cecilia's chamber went
To thank her that she had him sent　190
To get salvation from his sin
That he a new life might begin.

Kneeling in prayer his wife he found,
And soon before her, at that stound,
He saw God's angel, shining bright,
That all the house it beamed with light,
And in his hand two crowns he brought
So fair, as ne'er on earth were wrought,
Gave one unto Cecilia, then
The other to Valerian,   200
And swift he set them on their head,
And spake unto them in that stead:
"Keep these, your crowns, ye twain be-
        tween,
With body chaste, heart pure and clean,
From Paradise I have them brought,
For in that same place were they
        wrought,
My Lord for you did them prepare."
Then to Valerian spake he there:
"Since that thou here consent dost give
By laws of Chastity to live,   210
Jesus, my Lord, of mercy free,
A message hath He sent by me,
Whate'er from Him dost crave as boon,
Ask, and the same shalt have right soon,
What thing thou wilt — yet understood
That it shall be for thy soul's good."
Valerian then this boon besought:
"Of other thing now reck I naught,
This, above all, were sweet to me,
My brother dear from bale to free,   220
That He should help, my Lord Jesus,
My brother, that Tyburcius,
Shall this, His law, henceforth obey,
And be baptized, as I to-day,
That we may both uprightly live,
Our spirits wholly to Him give."
Whenas the angel this had heard
He to Valerian spake this word,
And said: "Thy will, it shall be done,
For that thou askest as thy boon   230
That which thy Lord likes better now
To give, than thou to ask, I trow!
For as my Lord, He hath won thee
Thro' this, thy wife, His servant free,
So, through thy prayer, He now shall
        win
Thy brother from the bands of sin,

And thou and he together come
Unto the meed of Martyrdom."
When this was said, he went, I wis,
In glowing light, to heaven's bliss.   240
And then Valerian and his wife,
In holy wise they led their life;
And after this, as God deemed well,
Tyburcius, of whom I tell,
Valerian's brother, as I say,
He came to him upon a day,
To know how fared his brother dear,
He of his holiness did hear.
And as he entered this, their house,
He kissed his brother, and his spouse,   250
He kissed Cecilia, and spake thus:
"A perfume sweet there is 'midst us,
As rose and lily 't were, I trow,
I ne'er have smelt the like ere now,
Nor scent so sweet was known of man."
Then answered him Valerian:
"Brother, since God doth think it meet
To send to thee this perfume sweet,
Herewith I boldly promise thee
If thou in Faith wilt steadfast be,   260
And Our Lord Jesus Christ adore,
As we who turn us to His lore,
Then shall be granted unto thee
God's angel both to hear and see,
And save thy soul, as now I say."
Tyburcius answered him straightway:
"If so I might God's angel see
No truer token might there be,
And this, His law, as guide I'ld take."
Cecilia heard that thus he spake,   270
And fell adown, and kissed his feet,
Answering him with words so sweet:
"Now will I thee, where'er I wend,
Own as my cousin, and my friend,
For as the love of Jesu free
Did make thy brother yield to me,
So shall He turn thee, that thou take
His might, idolatry forsake.
And Sir, since thou be ready now   279
To plight thy troth, His truth to trow,
Now shalt thou with thy brother go
Unto the Bishop whom we know,
And all his bidding shalt obey."

As she deemed right they did straight-
way;
The Bishop he baptized him then,
And he became a holy man,
So that God granted him such grace
That he might see, in every place,
At will, God's angels come and go,
And all his pleasure to them show,   290
And aye from them might ask, and have,
What thing soe'er his soul might crave.
These brothers then, of whom ye hear,
Cecilia, whom they both held dear,
The three, in love they lived aright,
And honoured God with all their might.
Tyburcius and Valerian there,
Since now the twain baptizéd were,
To serve their God they held them
bound,
In field and town they preached that
stound,   300
Against the idols, less and more,
In which they put their trust of yore.
It were too long their life to tell,
The marvels all that to them fell,
This treatise, it shall show withal
What things did at their death befall,
What wonders God, for them, He
wrought,
When they to martyrdom were brought.
There lived a prince in that same land
Wherein they preached, I understand,
Whose faith was in idolatry,   311
And bare to them great enmity;
He said, with dole the twain he'ld slay
Save they should change their rede
straightway.
He sent to fetch them at that same;
And when they to his presence came,
The law of Christ they preached that
day
So that the prince had naught to say,
Nor had he power to do them ill,   319
But gave them leave to work their will.
A Christian he himself became,
And all his mesnie at that same,
And all those men were turned also
Who to the brethren harm would do.

Soon as Cecilia heard them tell
Of this same chance, how it befell,
Then unto them she soon hath sought,
And thither priests with her she brought,
Who there baptized them every one,
That they should keep Christ's law alone.
When this same prince, Maximius,   331
And all his men baptized were thus,
Cecilia words of comfort spake,
And bade them every way forsake
The idols they believed ere now,
And unto Jesu humbly bow;
She bade them leave the works of night,
In heavenly armour clothe them bright,
She said: "Your course ye have fulfilled
Full worthily, as Christ hath willed,   340
Victors in a great fight are ye,
And therefore shall ye crownéd be
With crowns which Christ Himself shall
give,
In bliss eternal aye shall live;
Therefore be not dismayed to take
Your martyrdom, for Christ's dear
sake."
They promised they would do Christ's
Will,
And all His bidding would fulfil.
Almachius then, this curséd king,
Whenas he heard of this same thing   350
Bade them to sacrifice each one,
Or else they should to death be done.
And since they would not work his will
With bitter pains he plagued them still,
And at the last, without delay,
Bade them smite off their heads that
day.
Thus he their bodies did torment,
But swift their souls to heaven they
went,
And many a man must see, I wis,
How angels led them into bliss,   360
And many folk, for that same sight
Turned Christian, and believed aright.
Maximius, that convert good,
He spake, as 'midst them all he stood,
He said: "I see their souls take flight
With angels, into Heaven's height,

Borne up with wings, lest that they fall,
And like clean virgins are they all!"
Almachius, the king, heard tell,
Of all this marvel, how it fell,   370
And what Maximius had said,
And how his folk were sore afraid,
So with the morn he bade, the king,
Maximius, 'fore him to bring,
And torments sore on him he wrought
Until he too, to death was brought,
His soul, it went to heaven straightway
With solace more than I may say.
Almachius, that wicked king,
Whenas that he had done this thing, 380
And saw thus that Valerian,
And other saints were slain, each man,
Straightway bethought him, in his mood,
To take unto him all their good;
Sent to Valerian's house withal,
Since he was richest of them all,
And of Cecilia his wife,
They, with loud voice, and mickle strife,
Command she bring forth all the store
That was her husband's less and more;
"As traitor done to death is he,   391
And all his goods the king's shall be."
Cecilia did great mourning make,
And in such wise to them she spake
That all those men were turned to Christ,
And in His Name they were baptized,
Their idols all they there did leave,
And did on Jesus Christ believe,
As wise men worshipped Him that tide,
And in His service lived and died.   400
Whenas Almachius heard of this
For wrath nigh mad was he, I wis,
He bade Cecilia should be sought,
And in all haste before him brought,
And all her house commanded he
That burned with fire it straight should
    be.
But first he asked in eager mood,
Where now was all Valerian's good?
She said, his riches did she take
To feed the poor, for Jesu's sake.   410
Then at her words so wroth waxed he
He bade that burned they all should be,

Her house and chattells, more and less,
And she herself, in that same stress.
And soon, at this, the king's desire,
Her dwelling did they set on fire.
And she herself in midst did stand,
And all about was fiery brand,
But all who looked on her, I ween,   419
Had deemed she in a bower had been,
A garden fair, with blossoms bright, —
So stood she thro' a day and night,
And ne'er her heart-felt prayers did
    fail —
Whenas Almachius heard that tale,
He bade the messengers straightway
Smite off her head, nor make delay.
His doomsman to Cecilia went,
There as she stood, with good intent,
Then unto God her prayer she made,
And bowed her neck before the blade.
The custom was, in that countrie,   431
That but three strokes should smitten be,
But when three strokes he smote that
    day
Her neck was not cut thro' alway,
Untouched some sinews were, and veins —
He left her thus, in bitter pains,
The law was, as I said afore,
He might give three strokes, and no
    more.
And thus upon her knees she sat,
And lived for three days after that,   440
And maidens who with her had been
Straightway they came to her, I ween,
And all those days to them she spake
Bidding them all to comfort take.
Unto Pope Urban then she sent,
And told unto him her intent,
She quoth: "Sir, God hath granted me
Here, in this world, to live days three,
As I have prayed Him, this befell
That I my will to thee might tell.   450
My maidens all to thee I give
To guard them well, the while they live,
And teach them that they wisely work —
Now in my name build thou a kirk
Where these, my maidens, aye may
    dwell,

With will and voice, to serve God well."
When this was said, with no delay
To God her spirit passed away;
And Urban, when she thus was dead,
He buried her in that same stead,   460

And made a kirk at great expense,
For worship great, and reverence
Of Jesus Christ, Our Saviour true,
To whom be honour ever due.
                    Amen, Amen.

PLACIDAS (SAINT EUSTACE)

ALL who love God's holy lore,
Old and young, and less and more,
Hearken now this stound,
Of a knight of heathen-ness,
Who had much of earthly bliss,
Many a golden pound.

And this knight, named Placidas,
With the Emperor Trajan was,
A wise man of rede;
With the rich that knight was good,   10
With the poor, of generous mood,
Righteous in his deed.

He of hunting knew enow,
In thick wood, 'neath forest bough,
On wild field and wold;
Thus, while hunting on a day
He a hart found, as he lay,
Right fair to behold.

Fairest of his kind was he,
There in wood, 'neath linden tree,   20
Great was he and tall;
Many a hart and hind also,
Great and small, did with him go,
Stateliest he of all.

That great hart, he fled away;
Placidas, by night and day,
Followed him alone,
To another monarch's land,
There the hart did, waiting, stand
On a rock of stone.   30

High his horns he holdeth now,
There, beneath the woodland bough,

And spake: "Placidas,
Art a knight who huntest free,
Dost me chase, I fly from thee,
Ride a gentler pace!

"If betwixt my horns wilt look
Fairest sight aye writ in book
Thou forthright shalt see,
'T is the Cross of Christ I wis,   40
That shall bring thee unto bliss,
Christ, He hunteth thee!"

Of the light of Heaven, a gleam,
Brighter than the sunshine's beam,
O'er that hart was poured,
Spake that hart with tongue forthright
To that good and gentle knight,
Trow me, 't was Our Lord.

"Placidas, I tell thee now
Changed shall be thy name, and thou   50
Shalt a Christian be;
Jesus Christ, of Heaven, He is
Who with thee doth speak, I wis,
Tarry not from Me.

"Take thy children, and thy wife,
Get thee forth withouten strife,
Swift baptizéd be;
And for ye I'll henceforth care,
Thou and she must sorrow bear
All for love of Me."   60

Bairns and wife he took straightway,
Gat him forth without delay
To the font of stone,
There to be baptized was fain,

With his wife and children twain,
He was not alone.

Placidas, of old he hight,
Eustace, they baptized that knight —
"So I heard Christ say!"
To the woodland forth they fare, 70
All about they wander there,
Thank Our Lord alway.

As the knight, with comrades three,
Sat beneath a linden tree,
Fain to rest that stound,
There, beneath the greenwood bough
Tidings good he heard, I trow,
Brought from heaven to ground.

Spake to him an Angel bright: 79
"Hearken, Eustace, God's own knight,
Blessèd may'st thou be,
These thy children and thy wife,
They shall each one win to life,
Endless bliss shall see.

"Tho' from land and folk did'st fly,
Hall and bower, and station high,
For that, sorrow not,
Since to Christendom hast ta'en
Oft the Fiend will seek full fain
This thy harm, I wot." 99

Quoth the Angel: "Wend God's way,
Watch thy soul by night and day,
And my rede believe,
One and all shall suffer thus,
For the love of Christ Jesus
Martyrdom receive."

To his house I trow, anon,
Swift as may be, hath he gone,
Wife and bairns also,
All his sheep to death were bitten, 100
And his steed by thunder smitten,
He afoot must go.

All he loved, they went him fro'
Save his wife and children two,

They from land must wend;
Ere had dawned the light of day
Silent, went they on their way
By a woodland end.

Thus toward Egypt did they fare,
Sorely were they bowed with care, 110
Love and sorrow bore
For the Christ Who all things made,
Who on earth was lowly laid,
With spear smitten sore.

To the sea-shore have they gone,
And a ship they found anon,
Would the water brave;
He aboard the ship would go
With his wife and children two.
Dark and stern the wave; 120

Saw the shipman that good knight
And his gentle lady bright,
Saw her fair and sheen,
Straightway saith unto him there:
"Whence had'st thou this woman
  fair?
She 'll be mine, I ween!"

From the ship the knight he threw,
And with him his children two,
Woe for that he bore;
Loudly cried the lady there, 130
From her lord full loath to fare,
Wept and sorrowed sore.

Sat the knight down on a stone,
Saw his wife from him was gone,
Ta'en from him with wrong,
Quoth: "Alas that I was born!"
Deemed himself well nigh forlorn,
He had lived too long!

On the ship his eyes he cast, 139
When from out his sight 't was passed,
Saw his children two,
Quoth: "Methinks my heart will bleed,
Motherless, how may I feed
Ye? full sore my woe!"

So long fared he at that same
That he to a water came
Must thereover fare;
Wade he must, the stream was cold,
Wild, on either side, the wold,
Greater was his care.   150

Thus one child he takes on arm,
Wot ye well, it took no harm,
Bare it to the strand;
To himself in grateful mood
Saith: "God's help is ever good,
That I understand!

"Sit thee still, my son so dear,
I will fetch thy brother here,
Give thee meed this stead;
I will come to thee alway   160
E'en as quickly as I may,
Be thou not in dread."

He to wade the stream was fain,
To deep water came again,
Saw the further side;
How a lion fierce there came
Seized his young son at that same
With jaws gaping wide.

Thus the child away with him
Bare the lion, gaunt and grim,   170
Nigh he swoonéd there!
There was he in water deep,
'T was no wonder he must weep,
Had enow of care!

When he came from out his swoon
Looked he up, and then right soon
Back to land turned he,
And a wonder saw he there,
For a wolf his child forth bare,
Down he fell on knee.   180

When he from his swoon uprose,
Looking up, he forward goes,
Nigh of wit forlorn,
Ever thought he of Christ's Pain,
How He died, and rose again,
Who for us was born.

"God of Might, my grief Thou know'st,
Father, Son, and Holy Ghost,
Here I make my moan,
Of my wife who was so true,   190
Fair and gracious, bright of hue —
Now am I alone!

"Of my children twain forlorn,
Whom wild beasts away have borne
None with me may bide!
To what land now shall I go?
How long must I live in woe?
Where my head may hide?

"I of Job must think, I ween,
Who in bliss long time had been,   200
Sithen fell in care,
Lord, I pray, for love of Thee
Let me ne'er too sorry be,
Howsoe'er I fare.

"Soul, now hast thou wept thy fill,
Weep no more, but hold thee still,
God's Help is full nigh."
With that came an Angel bright,
With soft voice unto the knight
Spake of God on high: 210

"Be thou still and glad, Eustace,
God in Heaven prepares thy place,
Joyful shalt thou be;
These thy children and thy wife
They shall have eternal life,
Heaven's Bliss shall see."

So long hath he gone his way
Saying prayers both night and day
Till a town he found,
Toil and travail knew anon   220
Since his money all was gone
This his task that stound.

With his arrows, bow, and horn,
Was he guardian of the corn
Eke by day and night,
Toll to take, and cattle mind;
Little knew he of that kind,
Hayward he, and knight!

Fifteen years abode he there
Ere that men wist who he were,   230
Sought had he been long;
Those the Emperor sent to seek
Were wise men, who well could speak,
Knights both stern and strong.

Thro' the corn one day came three
Riding, men alike to see,
There he did them meet;
Rode those knights on horses tall,
Mild their words and fair withal,
They the hayward greet.   240

Then the hayward blew his horn,
He was warden of the corn,
Toll he bade them yield,
Asked them what had brought them there?
What they sought? And why they fare
Over that wide field?

"Sir, three knights are we, and ride
On a quest both far and wide
After one we seek;
Emperor's counsellor, I ween,   250
Far and near he sought hath been,
None of him can speak.

"Of us all the wisest knight,
Placidas, by name he hight,
Hunting did he go,
Never since his home hath sought,
Ne'er were tidings of him brought,
None his fate might know.

"Here, methinks, he found shall be,
We deem surely thou art he,   260
By thy goodly cheer,
And thy nose a scar doth show
By the which we rightly know
Thee for comrade dear!"

"Nay," quoth he, "how may that be?
How may I be mate to ye
Who of goods have none?"
"To the Emperor must thou fare
And again that honour bear
Which was thine anon."   270

Eustace took his leave that tide,
With his comrades doth he ride,
To the court again;
Joy and bliss were his that while,
Trajan doth upon him smile
With knight, groom, and swain.

To his lord he told his care,
His hard life, his scanty fare,
Even to the end;
Of the ventures he must meet,   280
Whether they were sad or sweet,
That God did him send.

Afterward, ere it was long,
War brake out both fierce and strong,
'Gainst that Emperor brave,
Thither went full many a knight,
Right well arméd for the fight,
Fain his realm to save.

Thither came two knights that day,
Very good in fight were they,   290
Had good horse and brand;
There was no man on the field
Who with either spear or shield
Durst their dints withstand.

Thro' the day they valiant fought,
'T was well done, so each one thought,
To their inn they went,
Comrades good became that tide,
In one house would they abide
Without ill intent.   300

Eat together of one dish,
Were it flesh, or were it fish,
Mickle mirth they make;
After meat they tales would tell,
Of adventures that befell
In their lives they spake.

Then the younger of the twain
Of his comrade asked again
What his kin might be?
Still he sat, and sighed full sore,   310
Little spake, but thought the more,
Dismal cheer made he:

"Sir, wilt keep my secret well
If I of my welfare tell
And my woe this tide?
Of a rich man's race I came,
Placidas, my father's name,
Who had journeyed wide.

"He, my sire, was goodly knight,
And my mother, lady bright,   320
Dwelling fair did own,
Children twain they had, none other,
I, and but one younger brother,
Dwelt in tower of stone.

"Taken by my sire were we,
Mother, brother, yea, all three,
Thro' God's Grace one day,
To the font he hath us led,
There were we baptized that stead,
In God's Name alway.   330

"Sithen, so it seemeth me,
We fell into poverty,
Went from out that land,
O'er a water broad and deep
Sailed, my mother sore did weep,
Wailed and wrung her hands.

"Very fair my mother, she
In that land should fairest be
Both of skin and hue,
And the shipman in that day   340
Bare her from us all away,
Waxed our grief anew;

"We went thro' the wilderness
Weeping sore, in heaviness,
To a river came,
O'er the stream my father bare
Me, and left my brother there
Till again he came.

"Came a lion fierce that tide
Caught me in its jaws so wide,   350
Bare me in its mouth;
Shepherds did the beast espy,
Scared him with their horn blasts high
Eke by North and South.

"Gently took they me that stead,
Bare me softly to a bed,
Blesséd be God's Might!
And a rich man of that land
All I needed, free of hand
Gave, and dubbed me knight."   360

"Brother, hearken now to me,
Came a wolf, and seizéd me,
Forth in mouth he bare,
Ploughmen did the same espy,
Blew their horns both loud and high,
Very strong they were.

"Took me softly in that stead,
And a lady hath me fed,
And hath dubbed me knight,
Palfrey gave she me, and steed,   370
Helm and birnie, other weed,
Sword and spear so bright."

She, their mother, heard that tide
In an orchard there beside,
Wept for very bliss,
To her bower she fain had gone
Swiftly as she might, anon,
Glad was she, I wis.

Riding then Sir Eustace came
Where his wife dwelt at that same,   380
Fain those knights to see;
She beheld that goodly knight,
He, that lady fair and bright,
Blithe of cheer was she.

Quoth he: "Lady, tell to me
What men in that inn may be,
Here, in this next house?"
"Sir," she said: "two knights there be,
Who should be well known to thee,
Welcome, dear, my spouse!"   390

"Ah, my lord, art known to me
By the scar that well I see
On thy nose, I ween;
Love, I must full hardly fare,
Passed my life in mickle care,
As may well be seen."

"He who did me from thee take
Fain would me his leman make,
Pagan he, alway;
In that ship there was a knight,   400
Freed me from the shipman's might,
Bare me safe away.

"True love, without more delay
To this next house go our way,
For our sons be there,
And with joy and mickle bliss
Give we thanks to Christ, I wis,
Who hath cured our care."

Thither then the twain have gone,
Swiftly as they might, anon,   410
Found a welcome fair;
Bade them sit, and drink there wine
In gold cups, with spices fine,
Good cheer made they there.

Spake Sir Eustace of his care,
His hard life, his scanty fare,
Wept the knights for bliss,
Never one with other spake,
From their lips no word might break,
Could but clasp and kiss.   420

To the Emperor news they bare
How with joy and bliss they fare,
Christians were that stound;
Then he sendeth knights anon
For to fetch them every one,
All whom there they found.

Shut them all in prison strong,
Lions and leopards fierce among,
And beasts fierce and fell;
Yet those beasts so strong and wild   430
Glad of them they were, and mild,
Would them no wise quell.

Then, in bowls of brass that day,
One in each, ('t is sooth I say
Fire was made below,)
One and all to death they burn,
But their souls to Heaven they turn,
And no pain they know.

Pray we all to Saint Eustace,
That he gain for us such grace   440
That to heaven we wend,
And when we its bliss have won
With Sweet Jesu, Mary's Son,
Dwell there, without end.

                                    Amen.

OWAIN MILES

OWAIN'S VISIT TO PARADISE

THE fiends, with them the knight they
          bear,
To a foul-smelling water fare,
Such as he ne'er had seen;
Fouler it smelt than any hound,
And deep for many a mile its ground,
And black as pitch, I ween.

Sir Owain saw across it lie
A narrow bridge, both strong and high,
The fiends they spake also;
"Behold, Sir Knight, before thee lies   10
The bridge that leads to Paradise,
Across it must thou go.

"And after thee we stones shall throw,
And strong winds shall upon thee
          blow,
And work thee mickle ill;
Scarce shalt thou go half-way, withal,
But if midway thou chance to fall,
Thou fallest to our will.

"And when thou thus adown shalt
          fall
Thou comest 'midst our comrades
          all,   20
With hooks they shall thee speed;
A new play teach to thee alway,
For thou hast served us many a day,
To Hell they shall thee lead."

Owain beheld that bridge uplift,
The water 'neath it, black and swift,
And dread, it vexed him sore,
And of one thing he took good note,
Thick as the motes in sunbeam float,
The fiends, they were yet more!   30

High as a tower that bridge should be,
And sharp as razor, verilie,
Narrow it was, also,
With that, the stream that ran there-
          under,
It gleamed as lightning, roared like
          thunder,
That did he hold for woe!

There is no clerk may write with ink,
And never man in heart may think,
Nor master may attain,
Diviner's skill may naught devise   40
Beneath that bridge of Paradise
To tell one half the pain.

So the Dominical doth tell,
There is the entrance gate of Hell,
Saint Paul, he witness bore,
Who from that bridge doth fall so low,
Redemption may he never know,
Or less, I trow, or more!

The fiends, the knight they threaten
          there,   49
"Across this bridge thou may'st not fare,
How sore soe'er thy need,
Flee thou this peril, grief, and woe,
And to that place thou comest fro'
Right gladly we'll thee lead."

Sir Owain, he bethought him there
How oft, from out the foul fiends' snare,
God had him safely sped,
He set his foot upon the bridge,
Felt of the razor no sharp ridge,
Nor aught to cause him woe.   60

But when the fiends they saw that he
Half-way across the bridge should be

Loudly they cry and call:
"Alas! that e'er he saw the light,
For now we sure have lost this knight,
He hath escaped our thrall!"

Thus Owain, o'er the bridge he went,
Gave thanks to God Omnipotent,
And Mary, full of grace,   69
Who thus had deigned his way to speed,
And, from the foul fiends' torment freed,
Brought to a better place.

A cloth of gold to him was brought,
But of its coming saw he naught,
Save God had sent that same;
That cloth he did on him that stound,
And whole and healed the wounds he
          found
Wrought by the fire's fierce flame.

Then thanked he God in Trinitie,
And, looking further, thought to see   80
E'en as it were a wall;
He looked about him far and nigh,
But never end he might espy,
Of gold it shone withal.

And further — more he needs must see,
A gate, none fairer might there be
In all this world, well wrought;
Of wood or iron there was none,
'T was all red gold, and precious stone,
And all God made of naught!   90

Of Jasper, Coral, Topaz bright,
Of Pearls so pure and Crystal white,
And of rich Sapphire stone,
Ruby and Onyx might he see,
Chrysoprase, and Chalcedony,
And Diamonds brightly shone.

In tabernacles were they wrought,
Richer, I trow, had ye found naught,
Slender the pillars small;
Curved arches of carbuncle stone,   100
And red-gold bosses wrought thereon,
Turrets of crystal all.

E'en as Our Lord surpasseth still
Of goldsmith, or of artist's skill,
Seek where ye will in land;
So are the gates of Paradise
Fairer than mortal may devise
As ye may understand.

E'en as the gates themselves unclose
So sweet a perfume forth there flows
As precious balm and dear,   111
The knight was of that sweetness fain,
And drew such strength from it again
As ye shall forthwith hear.

It seemed such strength to him were
    told
He well might bear a thousand-fold
More of such woe and pain;
That he, against the fiends to fight,
Might well have turned him back forth-
    right
The road he came again.   120

The knight, he drew the gate anear,
And see, there came with goodly cheer,
Processions fair anon,
Tapers, and candlesticks of gold,
Fairer no man might see on mold,
With Cross, and Gonfanon.

And Popes, in dignity they go,
And many Cardinals also,
And Kings and Queens were there,
And Knights, and Abbots, many Priors,
With Canons, Monks, and preaching
    Friars,   131
Bishops, who croziers bare.

Friars Minor, and Friars Jacobin,
And Carmelites, and Friars Austin,
And Nuns, both black and white,
All manner of religious there
Did in that great procession fare
Who Orders took aright.

There Wedlock's order did he see;
Of men and women many be   140

Who thanked God for His Grace,
Who sent the knight the aid he sought,
And from the foul fiends' torment
    brought
A live man, to this place.

When they had made this melody
There came two from the company
And palms of gold they bare,
And straightway to the knight they hied,
And took him, one on either side,
Archbishops both they were;   150

And up and down they led that knight
And many a joy they shewed to sight
And mickle melody;
Merry the carols he must hear,
Nor songs of folly met his ear
But joy and minstrelsy.

They danced in carols all a-row,
Their joy, I trow, may no man know,
Of God they spake, and sung,
And angels set the measure free   160
With cithole, harp, and psaltery,
And bells that merry rung.

And none may carol there within
Save that he be all clean of sin
And from all folly free;
Now God, for these, Thy Five Wounds
    all,
Grant us to carol in that hall
Thro' Thy Mother, Marie!

And this same joy, as ye may see,
It is for love and charitie,   170
Towards God, and towards man's kin,
Whoso forsaketh earthly love
For love of God, Who reigns above,
May carol there within.

And other joys he saw enow;
Perched on high trees, with many a
    bough,
The birds of Heaven rejoice;
Their notes ring out with merry glee,

In many a changeful melody
On high they lift their voice!   180

And, hearkening to the birds' sweet song,
He deemed he might abide there long,
Yea, till the world should end;
There he beheld that Tree of Life
Whereby both Adam and his wife
To Hell they needs must wend.

Gardens with flowers of diverse hue,
The rose, the lily, there he knew
Primrose and periwink;
Mint, fetherfoy, and eglantine,   190
'Mid other flowers, and columbine,
More than a man may think.

And herbs be there of other kind
Than here on earth a man may find
And e'en the least of price
For ever waxeth green, I wot,
With changing season, changeth not,
Sweeter than liquorice!

And many a well he there must know,
Sweeter than mead their waters flow,
But one above them all,   201
E'en as Saint Owain did behold,
From thence, the stream it runs four-fold,
From Paradise doth fall.

And Dison, so men call one stream,
Its waters flow with brightest gleam,
And gold therein is found;
Fison, the second named shall be,
And of more value, verilie,
The stones within its ground.   210

The third stream shall Euphrates be —
Without a lie I say to ye
Its course it runs aright;
The fourth stream, it is hight Tigris,
Nor hath the world the like, I wis,
Of these, its stones so bright.

Who lives in purity below
This bliss he shall as portion know

And see that seemly sight;
Yet more did Owain see with eye   220
Beneath God's Glory, there on high,
Blessèd shall be His Might!

Some souls, he saw, dwelt by themselves,
Others by ten, or e'en by twelve,
But each one knew the other,
When they together came, I wis,
Then they rejoiced in mickle bliss,
As sister doth with brother.

And some, they were in scarlet clad,
Fair robes of purple others had,   230
And some in ciclaton,
E'en as the priest at Mass doth wear
Thus alb and tunicle they bare,
Some, cloth of gold had on.

And thus, I trow, full well the knight
By this, their clothing, knew aright
E'en in what state they were,
And what the deeds they erst did do,
(By that he saw them clothèd so)
While they 'midst men did fare.   240

Here will I a resemblance tell,
The same, in truth, accordeth well,
E'en by the stars so bright,
As one star brighter is to see
Than others, yea, perchance, than three,
And is of greater might,

So God, He dealeth in this wise
E'en with the Bliss of Paradise,
Deals not the same to all,
The Soul who hath the least, I wot   250
Doth think the greater is his lot,
Doth hold him rich withal!

The Bishops came to him again,
They took the knight betwixt them
          twain,
And led him up and down,
Said: "Brother, God be praised by thee,
This, thy desire fulfilled shall be,
Hearken our words anon,

"Now thou, with these, thine eyes, hast
    seen
Alike the joys and pains, I ween,   260
For that, praise God, His Grace,
We'll tell thee here the common doom,
The way that thou hast hither come
Ere yet thou leave this place.

"That land thou sawest full of sorrow,
Alike to-day, and eke to-morrow,
The which thou passed'st by,
Wherein didst suffer pain and woe,
With many another soul also,
Men call it Purgatory.   270

"And this same land so fair and wide,
That mickle is on every side
And is so full of bliss,
Wherein thou even now shalt be,
And where thou many a joy dost see,
'T is Paradise I wis!

"And never man may hither win
Save that he first be purged of sin,
And be well cleanséd then,
Then come they here —" the Bishop
    said,   280
"By us unto these joys they're led
At times, by twelve or ten.

"But some, they be so straitly bound,
That men know not how long a stound
They suffer in that heat,
Save that their friends on earth who
    be
Sing Mass for them — of charitie
Shall give the poor to eat;

"Or other wise shall do alms-deed,   289
By which they may the better speed,
And these, their torments, cease,
And come to Paradise, I wis,
Wherein is ever joy and bliss,
And there abide in peace.

"And as from Purgatory's pain
We pass, so do we rise again

To God, in Glory's height,
That is the Heavenly Paradise,
Beheld by none but Christian eyes,
No joy is like that sight!   300

"And when we passed from out the
    flame
Of Purgatory, here we came,
We may not scale that height,
(Till that we here long time have been
God's Face by us may not be seen —)
Nor in that place alight!

"The child who was but born last night
Ere his soul hither shall be dight
Those pains shall over flee;
Heavy and strong the torment told   310
To that man who is waxen old
And long in sin shall be."

Forth went they till, before their eye,
There rose a mountain fair and high
And full of game and glee;
So long upon their way they passed
They came unto its top at last
Where they these joys might see.

There diverse songs the birdlings sung,
Great joy they made themselves among,
As ye may understand,   321
More joy in these birds' trill shall be
Than cithole, harp, or psaltery,
Heard here, on sea or land.

That land that is so good withal
'T is Paradise terrestrial,
On earth it lieth fair;
The Heavenly Paradise, I wis,
No bliss is like unto its bliss,
That is above the air.   330

In that which hath on earth its place
Therein was Owain for a space,
'T was that which Adam lost,
Had Adam there but held him still
And wrought according to God's Will,
Ne'er His commandment crost,

He, nor his offspring, trow me, ne'er
From out that bliss were forced to
 fare,
But, since that same he brake,
With pick and spade in ditch to delve,
To help his wife, and eke himself, 341
Much toil God made him take.

God was, I trow, with him so wroth,
He left unto him ne'er a cloth,
But leaf of a fig-tree,
All naked there he went, and stood,
I trow a man might well nigh wood
At such a counsel be.

An Angel there unto him came
With aspect stern, and sword of flame,
Fear in his soul had birth, 351
That they should toil and sorrow know,
The while that they must live below
Drave them to middle-earth.

And when he died he went to Hell, —
To him and his this portion fell
Till God's own Son was born,
And by His Pain and Passion sore
Hath opened wide that prison door,
Else were we all forlorn. 360

. . . .

(Lacuna, in MS.)

The Bishops then the knight did pray
To tell them there without delay
If Heaven were grey or white,
Or blue, or yellow, red or green?
The knight, he answered them, I ween,
"That shall I say forthright.

"Methinks, it be a thousand-fold
Brighter than e'er was any gold
That man with eye might see!" 369
Then quoth the Bishops to the knight:
"That self-same place ye deem so bright
Shall but the entrance be.

"And each day it doth so befall
A meal, to make us glad withal,

Doth come for this, our need;
E'en a sweet smell, as of all good
That to our soul is fitting food,
Stay, and with us shalt feed."

Anon, he saw right well, the knight,
A flame of fire that sprang so bright, 380
From Heaven's gate it fell,
It seemed him there that, far and nigh,
O'er Paradise that flame did fly
And gave so sweet a smell;

The Holy Ghost, as flame so bright,
Did there upon Sir Owain light,
And in that self-same place,
By Virtue of that flame alway
The might of earth was purged away —
He thanked God for His Grace. 390

Then quoth the Bishops in that stead:
"God feeds us daily with His Bread
Yet we be not so nigh
Nor have such foretaste of His Grace
Nor such a sight of this, His Face,
As those that be on high.

"The souls who to God's Feast have
 passed
Their joy, it shall for ever last,
And never know an end; 399
Now must thou dree the common doom,
And by the road that thou didst come
Again thou needs must wend.

"Now keep thee well from deadly sin,
That thou shalt never fall therein
Whate'er shall be thy need;
Then at thy death-day shalt thou wend
Unto the joy that hath no end,
Angels shall thither lead."

Then sore he wept, Sir Owain, there,
And for God's Mercy prayed them fair
That he with them might dwell, 411
And that he might behold no more
That sight that he had seen before,
The bitter pains of Hell.

But this, his prayer, was all in vain, —
He took his leave, and turned again,
His heart was full of woe,
Ten thousand fiends he saw that stead,
But from before his face they fled
As bolt from a cross-bow.   420

No nearer than a bolt might fly
I trow, the fiends might come anigh
Tho' they the world would win,
And when he came unto the hall
The thirty men he found withal
Awaiting him therein.

Each held his hand up in that place,
Gave thanks to Christ for this, His
     Grace,
More than a thousand-fold,
Bade him make no delaying there   430
But back again to Ireland fare,
Swift on his way to hold.

So I find writ in history,
The Prior of Patrick's Purgatory,
To him came word that night,
That Owain had o'ercome his pain,
And with the morrow came again
Thro' grace of God's great Might.

Then with his monks, the Prior anon,
With Crosses, and with Gonfanon,   440
Went to that hole forthright,
Thro' which knight Owain went below,
There, as of burning fire the glow,
They saw a gleam of light;

And right amidst that beam of light
He came up, Owain, God's own knight,
By this knew every man
That he in Paradise had been,
And Purgatory's pains had seen,
And was a holy man.   450

To Holy Church they take their way
To work the works of God that day
There he his prayer doth make,
And on the fifteenth day, at end,
The knight upon his way would wend,
And staff and scrip did take;

And then the Holy places sought
Where Jesus Christ us dearly bought
Upon the Rood's rough Tree;
Where from the grave He rose alive   460
By Virtue of these same Wounds Five,
Yea, blesséd may He be!

And Bethlehem, where Christ was
     born
Of Mary Maid, as flower from thorn,
And where He rose to Heaven;
Sithen to Ireland came anon,
There a monk's habit did he on,
And lived for years full seven.

And when he died he went, I wis,
To Paradise, with joy and bliss,   470
Thro' help of God's good Grace;
Now God, for good Saint Owain's love
Grant us in bliss of Heaven above
To stand before Thy Face!
                              Amen.

ROMANCES

KING HORN

I BID ye all be gay
Who list to this my lay!
A song I now will sing
Of Murry, crownéd king;
He reignéd in the West
While he with life was blest.
Godhild she hight, his queen,
None fairer e'er was seen.
He had a son hight Horn,
A goodlier ne'er was born   10
On whom the rain fell light,
On whom the sun shone bright.
None might his fairness pass;
Brighter was he than glass,
White as the lily flower,
Red as the rose in bower;
Nor near nor far on ground
Might one his peer have found.
Twelve were his comrades gay
Who fared with him alway,   20
Rich men their fathers were
And all were children fair,
Each at his beck and call —
But two he loved o'er all,
The one hight Hathulf Child,
The other Fikenhild;
Hathulf was good, I trow,
Fikenhild, false enow.

E'en as the tale I say
'T was on a summer's day   30
That Murry, the good king,
Rode forth a-pleasuring,
E'en by the salt sea side
As he was wont to ride;
He found upon the strand,
There, where they came to land,
Of ships, I trow, fifteen,
With Saracens so keen,

And asked what there they sought?
What had them thither brought?   40

A Paynim heard the king
And thus made answering:
"Thy folk we think to slay
With all to Christ who pray,
Yea, and thyself, this tide:
Think not thou hence shalt ride!"
He sprang from off his steed
For thereto had he need,
(Two knights both good and true
Had he, they were too few;)   50
They grasp their sword hilts tight,
And all together smite,
By force of sword and shield
They fell their foes on field,
Yet all too few were they
Against their foes that day,
With ease the Paynim might
Hath slain those three in fight.

The Paynims came to land,
They took it in their hand,   60
The folk they smote and slew,
The churches down they threw,
All were of life forlorn,
Stranger or landsman born,
Save they forsook Christ's lore
And Paynim gods adore.

Saddest of women there
I trow was Godhild fair;
For Murry she wept sore
And for her son yet more,   70
She fled forth from her hall
And from her maidens all;
Beneath a rock of stone
The queen abode alone,

And there to God she prayed,
(By Paynim law forbade)
To Christ did service true,
(Thereof no Paynim knew)
Ever for Horn would pray,
Christ be his strength and stay.   80

Horn was in Paynim hands,
He and his folk, and lands;
Full fair was he to see,
Christ wrought him verily.
The Paynims would him slay,
Or would him living flay,
An he less fair had been
All had been slain I ween.
Then spake an Emir old
In words was he full bold: 90
"Horn, thou art quick and keen,
As may be lightly seen,
Thereto art thou full tall
And fair and strong withal,
Nor shalt thou be full grown
Ere seven years be flown;
An we thy life should spare,
Thine, and thy comrades fair,
Methinks it so might fall
That ye should slay us all.   100
Therefore shalt thou to sea,
Thou, and thy mates with thee,
A-ship, 'twixt wave and wind,
Thy death thou 'lt surely find;
Thou in the sea shalt sink,
No more of thee we 'll think.
But an thou wert on life,
With sword, or e'en with knife,
We at thine hand were sped
For this, thy father, dead!"   110

The bairns they brought to strand
Wringing for woe their hands,
And set them all aboard
At bidding of their lord.
Horn had been sad, I trow,
Yet ne'er so sad as now!
The tide began to flow,
Horn Child began to row,
So fast o'er wave they sped

The bairns were sore adread,   120
Full well they deemed, I ween,
Their life had forfeit been.
They drifted day and night
Till dawned the morning light,
And Horn beheld the land
And folk upon the strand;
"My comrades young," quoth he,
"Good news I have for ye,
I hear the sweet birds sing,
I see the green grass spring,   130
Blithe shall be now our band
For here we be at land!"

The ship a haven found,
They set their foot to ground,
There on the flowing tide
They left their ship to ride.
Then spake aloud Child Horn,
(In Suddene was he born,)
"Ship, on the salt sea flood
Make thou a voyage good,   140
Ride gaily on the wave
Nor find therein a grave.
If thou to Suddene fare
Greet well my kinsfolk there,
And well I bid thee greet
Godhild my mother sweet.
And bid that Paynim know,
(Of Christ is he the foe)
That I, both hale and sound,
Have safely come to ground,   150
And say, he yet shall feel
How Horn a blow can deal!"

The children sought the town
By dale and e'en by down;
They met Almair the king,
(Of Christ have he blessing)
King he, of Westerness,
(Christ give him mickle bliss,)
Thus spake he to Horn Child
With courteous speech and mild: 160
"Whence come ye, children dear,
Who thus have landed here?
I see ye all thirteen
Of body strong and keen,

By God Who made us all
Such chance did ne'er befall
That I so fair a band
Should greet in this my land,
Your errand to me tell!"
Horn knew their speech full well   170
And answered for them all
Since so it did befall;
(Fairest was he of face,
And dowered with speech of grace:)
"In Suddene were we born,
From noble kinsfolk torn,
Men of true Christian blood,
Of royal race and good.
But Paynims on our shore
Have wrought a slaughter sore,   180
In pieces did they hew
Full many a Christian true,
As Christ shall give me rede,
Us children did they lead
Unto a ship, and gave
As sport to wind and wave,
Two days hence, without fail;
Rudder had we, nor sail,
Our ship drave with the tide
E'en to this country's side.   190
Thou can'st us beat, and bind
Our hands our back behind,
Or, an it be thy will,
Can'st bring us out of ill!"
Out spake the good king then,
No niggard he midst men,
"Tell me thy name, fair boy,
Here shalt thou find but joy!"

The child made answer clear
As he those words might hear: 200
"Horn, it shall be my name,
Hither by boat I came,
Drifted by wave of sea
In good hour unto thee!"
Swift the king's answer came:
"Have joy of this thy name,
Horn, it shall echo shrill
O'er holt, I ween, and hill,
Horn shall ring up and down
Thro' dale and over down,   210

Thy name and fame shall spring
From knight, I ween, to king,
And this, thy goodliness,
Bring joy to Westerness.
The strength of thy right hand
Be felt thro' every land!
Horn, thou art fair and sweet,
None may thee ill entreat!"
Homeward rode Aylmar there
With him his foundling fair   220
And all his comrades good
Who to his heart nigh stood.

The king came to his hall,
And his knights one and all,
His steward he called forthright,
(Athelbrus was he hight:)
"Now steward to thy care
I give my foundling fair,
Teach him thy craft so good,
Of water and of wood;   230
Teach him the harp to play
With finger deft alway;
To carve in fashion fair;
The wine-cup fitting bear;
To him all craft be shown
That thou hast ever known.
(His comrades otherwise
Bestow in fitting guise,)
Horn shall to thee belong,
Teach him of harp and song."   240

Athelbrus took in care
Horn, and his comrades fair;
Horn, he held fast in heart
The rede he did impart,
All men the court about
Within, and e'en without,
Bare love unto Horn Child —
But chiefly Rimenild,
The king's own daughter fair,
Such love to Horn she bare,   250
So fast on him her thought,
The maid was nigh distraught;
For that at royal board
With him she spake no word,
Nor might she in the hall

Among the courtiers all:
Speak could she in no stead,
Since she of folk had dread,
By night and e'en by day,
No word to him durst say.   260
Sore pain of heart and mind
She bare, nor cure might find.
Thus sad and sorry, she
Bethought her warily,
By messenger straightway
She Athelbrus did pray
To make no tarrying
But Horn Child with him bring
And seek her in her bower —   269
With guile she wrought that hour —
Yea, and the message said
That sick she lay, the maid,
And bade him come with speed
To comfort her at need.
The steward at heart was woe,
He wist not what to do,
What Rimenild besought
A marvel great he thought,
That Horn, at her bidding,
He to her bower should bring.   280
He deemed in thoughtful mood,
Such act were scarce for good,
He called to him Horn's peer,
Athulf, his comrade dear.
"Athulf, now come with me
To bower speedily,
For Rimenild, she will
Speak with us, soft and still,
As Horn be thou arrayed,
And thus deceive the maid,   290
My mind misgives me sore
She hath some guile in store!"
Athulf and Athelbrus
They sought her bower thus,
And Rimenild, the fair,
She deemed that Horn it were;
On her bed must he sit,
She wooed him well, to wit —
Her arms round him she cast,
Athulf she held full fast,   300
And quoth: "Horn, hearken me,
Great love I bear to thee,

Troth with me shalt thou plight,
Here on my hand forthright,
To hold me as thy wife,
As I thee lord, for life!"

Athulf spake in her ear
Softly, as she might hear:
"Speak thou no more of this,
Horn is not here, I wis,   310
Unlike we twain shall be,
Fairer and richer he,
Fairer by measure Horn
Than any man yet born,
Tho' he were under mould,
Or wandering far on wold,
Distant full many a mile,
I would not him beguile!"

Then Rimenild, the maid,
Did Athelbrus upbraid;   320
"Thou traitor, get thee gone,
Mine hatred hast thou won,
Go forth from out my bower,
May ill o'er thee have power!
I would thy shame be sung,
And thou on gallows hung!
This is not Horn, I ween,
More courteous had he been,
And fairer far to see,
A shameful death on thee!"   330

Athelbrus at that stound
Fell low upon the ground:
"Lady I prithee grace,
Hearken a little space,
Hear why I dare not bring
Horn at thy summoning;
For Horn is rich and fair,
None may with him compare,
And Aylmar, my good king,
Gave him to my keeping;   340
If Horn were hereabout
I sorely me misdoubt
Since thou of him art fain,
That were betwixt ye twain
Should make my lord wax wroth —
So think I, on my troth —

Rimenild, lady sweet,
Forgive me, as is meet,
And Horn I 'll bring to thee
Whate'er the forfeit be!"   350

Then Rimenild, her speech
A gentler tone would teach,
Her heart waxed glad and gay,
Blithe was the maid that day.
"Then go," she quoth, "right soon,
And send him after noon,
Whenas the king shall rise
And fare in simple wise
With hound and horn to play,
None shall us then betray;   360
And here till eventide
He may with me abide,
After, for good or ill,
Let folk say what they will!"

The steward went at that stound,
Horn in the hall he found,
On daïs sat the king,
Horn did the wine-cup bring; —
"Horn," quoth he, "for my sake
Thy way in secret take   370
After meat, unafraid,
To Rimenild, the maid,
And words both true and bold
In heart I bid thee hold,
Be thou to me but true
And thou shalt never rue."
Then Horn, to heart he laid
What Athelbrus had said,
He went his way forthright
Unto that maiden bright,   380
Then kneeling, as was meet,
He proffered greeting sweet,
His fairness in that hour
I wot, made light her bower.
He spake with gracious speech
Such as no man may teach:
"Full soft thou sittest there,
Maid Rimenild, the fair,
Thou, and thy maids twice three
Who sit the nighest thee.   390
Thy father's steward, I trow,

He sent me here but now,
Since thou would'st speak with me
Say what thy will shall be,
Speak Lady, without fear,
Since I am fain to hear!"

Rimenild bade him stand,
She took him by the hand,
Set him on silken pall
And gave him wine withal.   400
She made him goodly cheer —
Her arms the maiden dear
Cast round his neck, I wis,
And gave him many a kiss.
"Horn," quoth she, "without strife,
Thou shalt take me to wife,
Have of my sorrow ruth,
Plight me thy troth in truth!"

Horn thought him well that day
What it were best to say: 410
"Christ be thy Help in this,
And give thee mickle bliss
Of him who wins thy hand
Where'er he be on land.
But I be born too low
Such maid as wife to know —
For I am come of thrall,
A foundling too withal,
It were not fit for thee
To wed thyself with me.   420
'T is no fit match, I ween,
For thrall to mate with queen!"

Then Rimenild, the maid,
She sighed, full sore dismayed,
Her arms she loosed full soon,
Adown she sank in swoon.

Horn was to comfort fain,
He raised her up again
Within his arms, I wis,
And gave her many a kiss.   430
He quoth: "My Lady dear,
Now take thou courage here,
Help me that I be knight —
Pray thou, with all thy might,

My lord the king so free
Knighthood to grant to me.
For then, when my thralldom
Hath once knighthood become,
Honour shall wax the more
And I may do thy lore!"   440

Then Rimenild eftsoon
She wakened from her swoon:
"Horn," quoth the maid, "thy rede
It shall be done with speed,
The king shall dub thee knight
Within this seven-night.
This cup I bid thee bring,
And with it, too, this ring,
To Athelbrus the bold,
Covenant bid him hold;   450
Tell him that I beseech
In fit and courteous speech,
That he shall lowly fall
Before the king in hall,
And pray that thou, forthright,
Of him be made a knight;
Silver, I ween, and gold,
Be his in payment told,
Christ speed him well, I pray,
My bidding to obey."   460

Then Horn must take his leave,
The day it waxed to eve;
Athelbrus straight he sought,
And gave him what he brought,
The truth he told him there,
How he in bower did fare,
And told him all his need,
Proffering goodly meed.

The steward, with no delay,
To hall he made his way,   470
"Lord King, now hearken me,
Good rede I bring to thee:
Thou shalt bear royal crown
To-morrow in this town,
To-morrow is high-day,
When men must needs be gay,
Methinks 't were well the morn
If thou should'st knight Child Horn,

If arms he bear for thee
Good knight he'll surely be!"   480
The king, he quoth anon:
"Methinks that were well done,
Of Horn 't is sooth to tell
Knighthood became him well,
That shall he have from me —
My darling shall he be —
And they, his goodly band
Of comrades, at his hand
Shall knighted be forthright
Before me, that same night."   490

Athelbrus deemed alway
'T were long till dawn of day,
When night at last was sped
Horn to the king he led,
With comrades twelve, I trow
Evil were some enow!
There Horn he was dubbed knight
With sword and spurs so bright,
On milk-white steed so fair,
None might with him compare.   500
The king, a blow so light
Dealt, bidding him be knight.

Before King Aylmar free
Athulf, he bent his knee,
And quoth: "O! King, so brave,
A boon from thee I crave.
Now hast thou knighted Horn
Who in Suddene was born,
Lord is he of that land
O'er us who by him stand.   510
Thine arms hath he, and shield,
To fight for thee on field,
Now bid him make us knight
For that is sure our right."
Then Aylmar straightway spake:
"Thy will I bid thee take."
Forthwith did Horn alight,
He dubbed his comrades knight.
Merry the feast and gay,
Mirthful their jest and play.   520
But Rimenild, in her bower,
Seven years she deemed the hour;
A word to Horn she sent,

He to her presence went,
But not alone he sped,
Athulf with him he led.
Rimenild waiting stood,
His coming she deemed good;
"Sir Horn, art welcome here
With Athulf, knight so dear,   530
Sir Knight, 't is fit and meet
By me to take thy seat,
Do that whereof we spake
Me for thy true wife take,
If thou in deeds be true
Yield me what is my due,
Thou hast what thou didst crave,
Me from my sorrow save."

"Maiden," quoth Horn, "be still,
I promise thee thy will,   540
But thus it must betide
With spear I first must ride,
And thus my knighthood prove
Ere yet I think of love.
As knights we be but young —
But since this day were sprung —
And ever of knighthood
This is the custom good,
Each, with some other knight,
Must for his lady fight   550
Or yet a wife he take —
Thus speed I needs must make —
With Christ's good aid, straightway,
Prowess I'll shew to-day
For thy love, in the field,
With spear and eke with shield;
If I come forth with life
Thee will I take to wife."

Quoth she: "Sir Knight, i-sooth
I think thou speakest truth;   560
Take thou this golden ring,
Fair is its fashioning,
Graven upon the gold
My name shalt thou behold;
Far as the sun shall shine
Is none so fair and fine;
This for my love now wear,
Upon thy finger bear,

The stones, they have such grace,
That ne'er in any place   570
Of dints shalt thou have dread,
Tho' ne'er so sore bestead,
If thou in battle see
This ring and think of me.
Sir Athulf, too, thy brother,
I'll give to him another,
And Horn, I here beseech
In love, with gentle speech,
Christ give thee furthering
And back in safety bring."   580

The knight he kissed the maid,
Blessing on him she prayed,
He took leave at the same
And to the hall he came.
The knights, they went to meat,
Horn sped with footsteps fleet,
In stable sought his foal,
(Black was he, e'en as coal,)
His byrnie shook amain,
The court, it rang again,   590
The steed, it gave a spring,
Merrily Horn 'gan sing —
The twain in little while
Had ridden o'er a mile.
A ship he found on strand,
By Paynims was it manned,
He asked them what they sought,
What had them hither brought?
One did Sir Horn behold
Who spake in words so bold: 600
"This land we think to win
And slay the folk therein."
Horn gripped his sword with power,
And wiped it clean that hour;
The Saracen, I wot,
He smote, his blood was hot,
Methinks at every blow
A Paynim head fell low.
The heathen hounds came on,
Horn, he was all alone,   610
His glance the gold ring sought,
On Rimenild he thought,
He slew there in that press
One hundred men, no less,

The tale might no man tell
Of those who 'fore him fell,
They who were left alive
I trow might little thrive.

Horn took the chieftain's head,
In sooth a trophy dread,   620
High on his sword point bright
'T was set, a grisley sight!
He fared him home to hall
Among the knights withal;
"Well dost thou sit, and free,
King, and thy knights with thee!
To-day didst dub me knight,
I gat me hence forthright,
A ship did hither row,
E'en as the flood did flow,   630
Filled with a Paynim band
Men of another land,
Full well they thought to-day
Thee and thy folk to slay.
With force did they assail,
My sword it did not fail,
Some, have I felled to ground,
Some, deathly wounds have found,
The head I hither bring
Of one, their chief and king,   640
Now is thy guerdon paid
Lord, who me knight hast made!"

Next morn, as day might spring,
A-hunting rode the king,
Fikenild stayed behind,
(Worst son of woman-kind,)
He sought the maidens' bower
For venture, in that hour.
He saw fair Rimenild
As one with sorrow filled;   650
She sat there in the sun,
Swiftly her tears did run —
Horn quoth: "Sweet love, give o'er,
Why weepest thou so sore?"
She spake: "I needs must weep,
E'en as I lay asleep
My net in sea I cast,
And, ere long time had past,
I caught a fish full fair —

But thro' my net he tare —   660
Methinks that I shall lose
The prize my heart would choose!"
Quoth Horn: "By Christ I deem
Right foolish is thy dream,
Ne'er will I thee betray
But do thy will alway,
I give myself to thee
In steadfast fealty,
As all may know forthright —
Thereto my troth I plight!"   670
I wot with mickle ruth
They sware that pledge of truth.
Rimenild wept alway
Tho' Horn her tears would stay;
He quoth: "My Lady dear,
Further I bid thee hear;
God shall thy dream fulfil
Or some man means us ill;
The fish that brake the net
I wis, may harm us yet;   680
An it mean ill, I ween,
That shall be swiftly seen."

Aylmar a-hunting rode,
Horn in the bower abode,
Ill words spake Fikenild,
His heart with envy filled —
"Aylmar I would thee warn,
Now be thou ware of Horn,
I heard the words he said;
He drew his good sword blade   690
And sware to take thy life
And win thy child to wife.
By Rimenild in bower
He lieth in this hour,
'Neath covering fair and soft,
And so he doth full oft.
Now hie thee there forthright
And thou shalt see with sight,
Bid him get hence straightway
Else will he thee betray!"   700

Aylmar, he turned him then,
(Saddest was he of men)
Horn he found, taking rest
On his fair daughter's breast;

He cried: "Foul thief, away!
Forfeit my love for aye,
Get thee hence speedily,
Ill fortune go with thee,
Haste thee, or by my word,
I'll smite thee with my sword;   710
Save that my land thou flee
Shame shall thy portion be!"
Horn saddled his good steed,
His arms he sought with speed,
His byrnie swiftly laced,
His harness fitly placed,
His sword he girt straightway
Nor longer thought to stay.
Blithely he sought that tide
Fair Rimenild, his bride;   720
He quoth: "Darling, I deem
Thou findest here thy dream,
The fish that thy net rent
Thy love from thee hath sent.
Rimenild, fare thee well,
No longer here I dwell,
To stranger lands straightway
Needs must I make my way;
There shall my lot be cast
Till seven long years be past,   730
And at the seven years' end,
If I come not, nor send,
A husband may'st thou take
Nor tarry for my sake.
Now hold me close and fast
For one long kiss, our last!"

She kissed him in that stound,
Then, swooning, fell to ground —
Child Horn, he went his way,
No longer might he stay;   740
Athulf, his comrade fair,
He clasped, and kissed him there:
"With true knight's fealty
Guard thou my love for me,
Faith hast thou aye fulfilled,
Now keep well Rimenild!"

His steed he would bestride,
From thence he fain would ride,
To haven did he fare,
A ship he hired him there,   750
That should from out this land
Bear him to Western strand.
Fast Athulf's tears down fall,
Sore weep the people all —
Horn safe in haven rode,
His steed forthwith bestrode;
Two knights upon his way
He found, king's sons were they,
Harold, was named one brother,
And Berold hight the other.   760
Berold, he prayed straightway
That he his name would say,
Whither he thought to fare,
And what had brought him there?
"Cuthbert," he quoth, "my name,
Hither by boat I came,
In West-land to fulfil
My fate, for good or ill."
Berold drew nigh, full fain,
He took his bridle rein,   770
"Knight, thou shalt welcome be,
A while abide with me,
For by my life, I swear
The king's badge shalt thou wear,
So fair a knight before
Ne'er came unto this shore."
Cuthbert he led to hall —
The knight on knee did fall
Greeting he gave, kneeling,
Unto the noble king: 780
Quoth Berold, the king's son:
"Sire, here a prize hast won,
Set him to guard thy land —
Thou wrongest no man's hand,
For 't is the fairest knight
That on our shores did light."
Then quoth the king so dear:
"Knight, thou art welcome here;
Berold, go thou straightway
And make him blithe and gay,   790
But wouldst thou wooing go
Then send him from thee fro',
Hadst thou a mind to wive
Away he should thee drive!
For such his beauty's meed
That thou shouldst never speed."

The Yuletide feast, at last
Had come, nor yet was past,
But, e'en as 't was high noon,
There came a giant full soon   800
All armed in Paynim guise
And spake upon this wise:
"Now bide thee still, Sir King,
And hear the news I bring:
Paynims be come to shore
Full five, I wot, and more,
They stay them on the strand,
Sir King, in this thy land.
One of them fain would fight
Against a three-fold might —   810
If one by three be slain
Take thou thy land again,
But if one vanquish three
This kingdom ours shall be —
To-morrow will we fight
E'en as day conquers night."
Out quoth the King Thurston:
"Cuthbert, thou shalt be one,
Berold shall be the other,
The third Harold, his brother,   820
For of my knights ye three
The best in arms shall be.
But little boots this rede
Since death shall be our meed!"
Then Cuthbert, at the board,
He spake a valiant word:
"Sir King, it were not right
For one with three to fight,
That 'gainst one Paynim hound
Three Christian men be found.   830
Sire, all alone, would I
My fate against him try,
Full lightly shall my sword
Death's portion him award."

The king rose on the morrow,
Mickle, I ween, his sorrow;
Cuthbert must needs awake,
His arms he thought to take,
Child Horn his byrnie cast
Upon him, laced full fast,   840
Swift to the king he sped
E'en as he rose from bed,

He quoth: "King, seek the field,
See how, with sword and shield,
Together we shall fight
And test each other's might."
Right as it were prime tide
Forth from the town they ride,
And found upon the green
A giant, cool and keen;   850
His comrades at his side,
Ready their blow to bide.
The giant, without fail,
Cuthbert he did assail,
Their dints they dealt full well,
Many a-swooning fell;
The giant to rest was fain
For he was well nigh slain —
He quoth: "Knight, bide thee
        still
Awhile, an so ye will, —"   860
He quoth, that blows so sore
He ne'er had felt before
Save once from Murry's hand
Who reigned in Suddene land;
Kinsman was he to Horn
Who was in Suddene born.
Horn waxed wroth at the word,
His blood within him stirred,
He saw before him stand
The folk who took his land,   870
They, who his father slew,
'Gainst them his sword he drew.
The ring his eyes have sought,
On Rimenild he thought,
She smote him to the heart
That must full sorely smart:
His foes, once keen for fight,
Before him turn to flight,
Horn, and his company,
They follow speedily,   880
They slew the Paynim hounds
Ere they their ships had found,
In death they low were laid,
His sire's blood well they paid.
But of King Thurston's knights
Not one escaped that fight,
Not the king's son — the twain
Before his eyes were slain.

The king, he wept withal,
Fast did his tears down fall, 890
A bier they fashioned there,
The bodies homeward bare;
The king, in hall he stood
Amid his knights so good,
And quoth: "Horn, hearken me,
Do as I say to thee,
Slain are my sons in fight,
And thou art valorous knight,
Of body fair and tall
And strong of hand withal, 900
Have thou my lands for life,
And take to thee for wife
Reynild, my daughter fair,
Who sitteth thronéd there."
"Nay, nay, my Sire, 't were ill
Did I such wish fulfil,
Thy daughter and thy land
To take unto mine hand,
Such service, verily,
I'll yield thee ere thou die 910
Thy sorrow shall be sped
Ere seven years' term be fled.
When grief be passed away
Then, Sire, give me my pay;
When I reward have won
Then take me for thy son!"

For seven years long, I ween,
Cuthbert, he there hath been,
Nor Rimenild sweet, he sought,
Nor word to her was brought. 920
She dwelt in Westerness
In grief and heaviness;
A king, he sought that land,
Who prayed the maiden's hand,
Her father gave consent —
The twain, on marriage bent,
But short shrift gave the maid,
Rimenild, sore dismayed,
Their will dare not gainsay —
Message she sent straightway, 930
Athulf the words did write,
He loved well Horn the knight,
And bade him who should bear
The script, with speed to fare

Thro' every land and shore
Till Horn he stood before.
Of this Child Horn knew naught,
Until one day he sought
The wood, in search of game —
A lad towards him came; 940
Horn spake: "My comrade good,
What seek'st thou in this wood?"
"Knight, an it be thy will
I'll tell thee loud and still,
From West I seek, in stress,
Child Horn, of Westerness,
For maiden Rimenild
Who is with sorrow filled;
A king that maid will wed,
And bring her to his bed, 950
Mody of Reynes, he,
Who was Horn's enemy.
I've wandered far and wide
By land and waterside,
And found him not alway.
Alas, woe worth the day!
Alas, woe worth the maid!
Now is she sore betrayed."

Horn hearkened with his ears,
And spake with bitter tears: 960
"Good fortune thee betide,
Horn standeth at thy side;
Back to thy lady go,
And bid her cease her woe
For I shall come in time
Ere Sunday wax to prime."
The lad was glad and gay,
He hied him on his way;
The wind waxed high withal —
Beneath her castle wall 970
The lad lay drowned on shore;
(The maid repented sore.)
Maid Rimenild that tide
Her door she opened wide
To gaze with longing eye
If Horn perchance be nigh.
Of life she found him spent
Whom she for Horn had sent,
Hither her love to bring —
Her hands she 'gan to wring. 980

Now Horn had Thurston sought,
To him his tidings brought,
By what name he was known,
How Rimenild was his own,
And of his kinship fair
Who rule in Suddene bare —
How those he slew in strife
Had ta'en his father's life —
And quoth "Now, good my Lord,
I pray of thee reward,   990
Help me, nor spare thy pain,
To win my love again.
Thy daughter shall espouse
One of a goodly house,
For husband shall she have
Athulf, my comrade brave,
The best of knights is he,
And truest, verily!"
The king quoth loud and still,
"Child Horn, have now thy will."   1000
He sent by his command
Writing to Ireland's strand
To summon many a knight
Irishmen, good at fight,
Enow had Horn of men —
To ship they gat them then,
Horn set forth ere 't was long
On galley stout and strong,
The wind blew fresh and free
Ere they were long at sea,   1010
The waves with storm and stress
Bare them to Westerness;
They hauled down sail and mast
And anchored them full fast.
But ere the dawn of day
The bells rang glad and gay,
And word to them was borne
'T was e'en the wedding morn.
Horn did thro' water wade
Nor closer landing made,   1020
His ship lay off the strand,
He gat him to the land
And bade his folk abide
Hidden, the wood beside.
He gat him forth alone
O'er stock, and over stone,
A palmer did he meet

And forthwith courteous greet:
"Good Palmer, without fail
Now tell me here thy tale."   1030
Then quoth the palmer keen:
"A bridal have I seen,
The bride, that lady bright,
Maid Rimenild was hight,
Her weird she might not dree
But wept right bitterly,
And vowed full steadfastly
Wedded she would not be —
A lord had she alway
Tho' he were far away.   1040
There, by the fortress hall,
Within the castle wall,
Vainly I needs must wait,
I might not pass the gate;
At Mody's word, that tide,
To burg they led the bride —
I turned me on my way,
Small heart had I to stay,
The bride, she weepeth sore,
And that be sorry lore!"   1050
Quoth Horn: "So Christ me rede
We two will change our weed,
My habit hast thou here,
Give me thy palmer's gear;
A draught I'll drink to-day
That some shall dearly pay!"
His staff he laid aside,
And doffed his robe that tide,
Horn's clothes he took straightway,
Nor loth was he that day!   1060
The staff and scrip took Horn,
And made a face forlorn,
Twisted his mouth awry,
And blacked him swarthily,
Uncomely was he then
And strange to all men's ken.
The warden of the gate
Made answer stern and straight,
Horn prayed him, once and oft,
To ope, in accents soft,   1070
But nothing might he win
Nor come a step within.
Then Horn no more would wait
He forced the wicket gate,

The guard o'er bridge he threw,
Horn's coming must he rue!
His ribs he brake withal.
Horn gat him to the hall
And sat him, still and low,
Down in the beggars' row.   1080
He cast around his eyes,
Safe in his foul disguise,
There sat maid Rimenild,
Distraught, with sorrow filled,
Full sore she wept alway,
No man her tears might stay.
Each corner did he spy
But might not see with eye
Athulf, his comrade true —
That he his presence knew.   1090
Athulf, I ween, that hour
Had gat him to the tower
To see if Horn, the brave,
Came sailing o'er the wave;
He saw on every side
Naught but the salt sea tide,
And thus he made his song:
"Horn, thou dost tarry long;
Thou gav'st thy love so fair
Unto my faithful care,   1100
Loyal have I been ever —
Come now, or come thou never!
My charge I may not keep
Longer, so must I weep."

Then rose fair Rimenild —
The cup must needs be filled
When meat was done, in hall,
With wine and ale withal.
One horn she bare in hand
(As meet in this her land),   1110
And knight and squire they quaffed
Therefrom of beer a draught.
All drank save Horn alone,
Thereof would he have none.
Horn sat upon the ground
As he in thought were bound,
And spake: "Queen, graciously,
I pray thee turn to me
And serve us with the first,
We beggars be athirst."   1120

Then turned fair Rimenild
And to the brim she filled
His bowl, a gallon fair,
Glutton she deemed him there:
She quoth "Now take this cup
And swiftly drink it up,
Ne'er saw I, so I ween,
Beggar for drink so keen."
Horn to his comrades bare,
And quoth: "My queen so fair   1130
Wine pleaseth not my sight
Save that the cup be white;
Beggar am I to see,
Fisherman, verily,
I came from the far East
To fish, at this thy feast,
My net lies here at hand
Upon a full fair strand;
I ween it hath lain here
For now full seven year.   1140
Now am I come to see
What fish therein may be,
Here have I come to fish —
Now drink from this my dish,
And quaff a horn to Horn —
From far I fare this morn."

She gazed, fair Rimenild,
Her heart within her chilled,
His word she read not right,
She knew not Horn with sight,   1150
Right strange she needs must think
His prayer, to Horn to drink.
She poured of wine a draught
And to the pilgrim quaffed,
And said: "Now drink thy fill
And tell me, soft and still,
If thou hast seen with sight
Child Horn, that goodly knight?"
The wine, Horn drank it up,
His ring dropped in the cup —   1160
The queen, she sought her bower
With maidens four that hour,
She found there what she sought,
The ring of red gold wrought
That once she gave to Horn —
Heavy her heart that morn,

For sore she feared the ring
Of death were tokening.

The palmer, in that hour,
She bade unto her bower,   1170
And spake: "Palmer, I know
The ring that thou didst throw;
Say now, who gave it thee,
And why art come to me?"
He quoth: "Now, by Saint Giles,
I've wandered many a mile,
Far hence, unto the West,
I ween hath been my quest;
And there Child Horn I found,
On ship-board was he bound,   1180
He said thro' storm and stress
He must to Westerness;
Upon the salt sea flood
I sailed with Horn the good,
But he fell sick and died,
And, dying, on me cried:
'This ring fail not to bear
To Rimenild the fair.'
Oft-times the ring he'ld kiss —
God bring his soul to bliss."   1190

Then out the maiden spake:
"My heart, now must thou break
For thou shalt see no more
Him thou hast mourned so sore."
On her couch fell the maid —
There had she hid a blade
Wherewith, methinks, the twain
Mody and she, were slain
Before the morning light
If Horn came not ere night.   1200
The point to heart she set,
But Horn her deed would let,
He wiped his face from stain,
Quoth: "Sweet, now look again,
I am Child Horn, I trow,
Dost thou not know me now?
In thine arms hold me fast
For Horn is come at last."
The twain they clasp and kiss
With joy and mickle bliss,   1210
He quoth: "Now love, I wend

Down to the woodland's end,
There have I many a knight
Ready, and armed for fight;
Armed are they under cloth
This folk we'll make full wroth,
Yea, all they whom the king
Did to his feasting bring,
I'll teach to them such lore
As they shall rue full sore."   1220

Horn hasted from the hall,
His palmer's weed let fall;
The queen went from her bower
To Athulf in his tower,
"Athulf," she quoth " be gay,
Go seek thou Horn straightway,
Beneath the woodland bough
There hath he knights enow."
Athulf, he made good speed,
Such news were joyful rede,   1230
Horn did he follow there
Swift as his steed might fare,
He did him overtake,
Much bliss the twain did make.
Horn hearkened to his prayer
And bid him with him fare,
Full soon they came to hall,
The gates were open all,
His men were, in that stead,
Well armed, from foot to head,   1240
All whom he found he slew
Save his twelve comrades true
And Aylmar, the land's king —
To death he did them bring,
The wedding guests were left
Each one, of life bereft.
But Horn no vengeance wrung
From Fikenhild's false tongue.
Then all they sware an oath
That never, on their troth,   1250
Would they Child Horn betray
Tho' he on death-bed lay.

Forthwith the bells were rung,
The wedding Mass was sung,
Horn went his way withal
To Aylmar's palace hall,

Bread was there and sweet ale,
Nor of rich guests did fail;
And none might tell with tongue
What gladsome songs were sung. 1260
Horn sat high on his chair
And bade them hearken there:
"King, listen now to me,
A tale I tell to thee,
I say it not for blame:
Child Horn shall be my name,
Thou madest me a knight
Proven am I in fight.
But men in secret said
That I had thee betrayed; 1270
Forthwith from out this land
I fled, at thy command,
Thou deemest that I wrought
What ne'er was in my thought,
By Rimenild did lie —
That do I here deny;
Nor will I so, I ween,
Till I have won Suddene.
I'll trust her to thy care
The while I hence shall fare 1280
Into mine heritage
And to my baronage;
My land I'll win again,
Avenge my father slain,
Rule as a king in town
And wear the royal crown,
Then Rimenild my bride
She shall lie at my side."

Horn sought his ship forthright,
With him each Irish knight; 1290
Athulf he took, his brother,
And saving him, none other.
Forward the ship did sail
Nor favouring wind did fail,
And ere five days were o'er
They came to Suddene's shore.
Then, even at midnight,
Horn went his way forthright,
Took Athulf by the hand,
And gat him there to land. 1300
He found, beneath his shield,
A knight full famed in field,

Right there, beside the way,
That knight in slumber lay.
Child Horn his arm did take
And quoth: "Sir Knight, awake,
And say, a watch dost keep?
Or wherefore here dost sleep?
A shining cross dost bear, 1309
Christ's arms, methinks, dost wear;
Save that thou shew the way
I shall thee straightway slay!"
Uprose that knight so brave,
Answer to Horn he gave:
He quoth: "Against my will
I serve these Paynims still,
Christian was I erst-while —
Then came I to this isle,
And the black Paynims there
Made me my faith forswear; 1320
In Christ would I believe —
Here have they made me reeve,
This way 'gainst Horn to hold
Now waxed to manhood bold;
Eastward his home shall be —
A valiant knight is he,
He slew with his right hand
The ruler of this land,
With many a hundred men —
Right strange I deem it then 1330
He comes not here to fight;
God help him to his right
And give him favouring wind
That these their death may find.
Murry the king they slew
Who was Horn's father true,
And Horn adrift they sent.
Twelve comrades with him went,
Athulf, I trow, was one,
Mine own child he, my son, 1340
If Horn were whole and sound,
And Athulf safe on ground,
(He loved him well, I ween,
And sure hath faithful been,)
And I might see with eye
The twain, for joy I'ld die."

"Knight be thou joyful then
And blithe above all men,

Athulf, and Horn, I trow
They stand before thee now!"   1350
To Horn he gat him there
And gave him greeting fair,
Much joy they make that tide
While they together bide.
"How fared ye, children, tell?
That ye be come 't is well,
Think ye this land to win
And slay the folk therein?"
He quoth: "Now Child Horn, hear,
Godhild, thy mother dear,   1360
Yet lives, she well might speed
Knew she this joyful rede."
Child Horn, he quoth straightway:
"Now blesséd be the day
I came unto Suddenne
With these, my Irish men;
These Paynim hounds we 'll teach
To speak in this our speech,
The folk we swift shalt slay
And living, will them flay."   1370
Child Horn his horn loud blew,
His men the summons knew,
On shore they gat them there
Beneath Horn's banner fair,
They fight and e'en they slay
Till night had waxed to day,
Till of that Paynim kin
No man was left therein.
Horn bade the folk straightway
In church and chapel pray,   1380
The bells he bade them ring
And many a Mass to sing,
He sought his mother's bower
In rock-hewn cave that hour,
Corn for the feast bid bear
And all make merry there,
With gladness there he wrought —
Which Rimenild dear bought.

Now Fikenhild, at heart,
Sore for his shame must smart,   1390
He gave, to young and old,
Gifts, that with him they hold,
Great stones together brought
(Thus for his profit wrought)

A castle strong he made,
The sea around it played,
That none might there alight
Save with the sea-bird's flight;
But when the tide was low
Then men the way might know.   1400
He set him, Fikenhild,
To woo fair Rimenild,
The king, her sire, that day
He durst not say him nay,
The maid was sad of mood,
She wept with tears of blood.
That night Horn restless lay
And dreamed sad dreams alway,
That on a ship that tide
Men bare his maiden bride;   1410
The ship, it sank adown,
And she was like to drown,
Then as, with upraised hand,
She won her way to land,
With sword-hilt, Fikenhild,
He thrust down Rimenild.
Horn, he awakened there
As one in sudden fear;
"Athulf, make no delay,
To ship we must straightway,   1420
Fikenhild, ill hath wrought,
My love to sorrow brought;
Christ, by Thy Five Wounds' Might,
Bring me to her to-night!"
Thus Horn to ship would ride,
His comrades at his side.
Fikenhild, as day did spring,
Betook him to the king,
Rimenild, fair and bright,
He thought to wed ere night.   1430
Before the dawning hour
He led her to his tower.
The feast they had begun
Ere yet uprose the sun;
Horn knew it not alway,
But, with the dawning day
His ship stood neath the tower
Before his lady's bower.
(The maid, small hope had she,
That Horn alive should be —)   1440
Strange to their eyes, and new,

The castle no man knew;
Of Athulf's kin a knight,
Arnoldin was he hight,
They found, who at that tide
Horn's coming would abide;
He quoth "King's son, Child Horn,
Welcome be thou this morn,
To-day false Fikenhild
Doth wed with Rimenild,   1450
No lie I speak, i-troth,
He hath beguiled ye both.
This tower he bade them make
Even as for thy sake,
Enter I ween, none can,
By any wile of man,
An Christ aid not, Child Horn,
Of love art thou forlorn."

Now Horn knew every wile
Wherewith man may beguile,   1460
His harp he took in hand
With certain of his band,
Good knights who, at his will,
Clothed them as harpers still.
They gat them o'er the sand
Towards the tower on strand,
Gaily the harpers sang,
Joyful their music rang,
Rimenild hearkened there
And questioned who they were?   1470
They said "The harp we play,
The viol and lute alway."
Without they need not wait,
Men oped the castle gate,
Set Horn on bench straightway,
His harp they bade him play.
A lay, the bride before,
He harped, she mourned full sore,
Swooning she fell awhile
Never a guest did smile,   1480
It smote Horn to the heart,
Right bitter was love's smart;
His glance the ring hath sought,
On Rimenild he thought,
Bared was his goodly sword,
He strode up to the board,

Fikenhild fell adown,
Cloven the traitor's crown,
His knights who sat a-row
To ground they swiftly throw,   1490
Slain were they all forthright,
And drawn that traitor knight.
Where Aylmar rule did bear
Arnoldin crown shall wear
And rule o'er Westerness
For this, his faithfulness;
The king, and all his men,
They sware him fealty then.

Horn took his bride by hand
And led her to the strand,   1500
And with her Athelbrus,
The steward of his house.
The tide full fast did flow,
Horn Child began to row,
He came unto the shore
Where Mody ruled of yore,
Athelbrus made he king
For his good fostering,
Mercy he shewed that day
As knighthood's fitting pay.   1510
Horn o'er the waves did ride
Blown o'er the waters wide,
He came to Irish ground
Where he had shelter found,
Athulf he wedded there
To Reynild, maiden fair.
Thence fared he to Suddene
Amidst his kinsmen keen,
There crowned his maiden bride,
And set her at his side.   1520
The folk, they loved them true,
Their death they needs must
    rue —
Now are they dead indeed,
Christ give their souls good speed.
Here ends the tale of Horn,
Fair knight, to honour born;
Glad may we be, I wis,
That thus he won to bliss;
And Jesus, Heaven's King,
Us to like ending bring.   1530

HAVELOK THE DANE

(After the death of Havelok's father, Godard seizes the kingdom, kills Havelok's sisters, and orders Havelok himself to be drowned.)

GODARD took the maids that day,
As it were with them to play,
As his mood had sportive been —
(Hunger made them black and green)
Of the twain the throat he slits,
Hacked them both, I trow, to bits;
Sorrowful the sight that day
By the wall the children lay
Dead, and weltering in their blood.
Havelok saw, as nigh he stood,   10
Sorrowful was he that stead,
Well might he know mickle dread,
At his heart he saw a knife
Raised to rob him of his life.
Knelt the little lad that day
To that Judas quoth straightway:
"Lord, now mercy show to me,
Homage here I offer free,
I will Denmark to ye give
If so be ye let me live,   20
Here, on book, I'll freely swear
That I never more will bear
'Gainst ye, lord, nor shield nor arm,
Spear nor sword that may ye harm;
Lord, have mercy now on me
This day Denmark will I flee,
Never to return again —
And I'll swear that Birkabeyne
Ne'er in life begat a son!"
When the devil heard, anon,   30
He his deed did somewhat rue,
And the dripping knife withdrew
Wet with guileless children's blood —
'T was a miracle right good
That the lad he did not slay
But for ruth withheld that day;
Tho' he were full fain that stead
The child Havelok had been dead,
Yet since, foul fiend tho' he were,
He was loth such deed to dare,   40

He thought then, as Havelok stood
Staring, as one well nigh wood:
"If alive I let him go
He may work me mickle woe,
Peace with me he ne'er will make
But will watch my life to take.
An he were no more alive,
And my bairns should live and
    thrive,
Lord and sovereign after me
Of all Denmark should they be.   50
So God help me he shall die
For no better rede have I,
Men shall cast him in the sea
In its wave he drowned shall be,
Round his neck an anchor good
That he float not on the flood."
Then straightway he bade them go
Fetch a fisher, who should do
All his will, and when he came
Spake he to him at that same: 60
"Grim, thou know'st thou art my
    thrall,
An thou doest my will withal,
That which I demand of thee,
On the morn I'll make thee free,
And with goods will wealthy make —
Now this boy I bid thee take,
Lead him forth with thee to-night,
When the moon doth give her light,
On the sea, — drown him therein,
On my head shall be the sin."   70
Grim the child hath bound full fast,
Tightly that the bonds might last,
For of full strong line were made;
Then was Havelok sore dismayed,
Never had he known such woe!
Christ, Who made the lame to go,
And the dumb hath caused to speak
Vengeance now on Godard wreak!

Grim the boy full fast hath bound,   79
With an old cloth wrapped him round,
Took of filthy rags a clout,
Gagged him that he ne'er cry out
Wheresoe'er he should him lead —
Then, when he had done that deed,
As the traitor to him spake
Bidding him the boy to take,
And to drown him in the sea,
This he promised faithfully.
In a sack so foul and black
Soon he took him on his back,   90
To his hut the boy he bare,
Gave him to Dame Levé's care;
Quoth: "This boy guard well, my wife,
E'en as thou wouldst guard my life,
I must drown him in the sea,
And for that freedman shall be,
Gold and fee we'll have enow,
Thus my lord hath sworn, I trow."
When his wife she heard, straightway,
From her seat she rose that day,   100
Threw the boy so hard adown
That well nigh he cracked his crown
'Gainst a stone that lay full nigh —
"Wellaway!" might Havelok cry:
"That King's son I be to-day,
Better had I been their prey
Eagle, Griffin, Wolf, or Bear,
Lion, or She-wolf, beasts that tear!"
There he lay till middle night —   109
Then Grim bade them bring him light,
He would clothe him, little loath —
"Now bethink thee of the oath
That I sware unto my lord,
Never will I break my word,
I will bear him to the sea,
Well dost know it so must be,
Drownéd shall he be therein —
Now rise up, and go within,
Blow the fire, a candle take."
As the clothes she'ld ready make   120
For his use, the embers blow,
Lo! therein a light did glow,
E'en as bright as it were day
Round the boy, who sleeping lay;
From his mouth it forth did stream

Bright it was as sunlight beam,
And the dwelling did it light
E'en as taper, burning bright.
"Jesu Christ!" Leve cried in fear,   129
"What this light? How came it here?
Stir up, Grim, and look and see,
What dost think the light can be?"

To the boy he straight did go,
Right good will had he thereto,
Loosed the gag, the lad unbound,
And right soon on him they found,
As his shirt they turned down there,
On his neck the king's mark fair,
Very bright and fair to see —
Quoth Grim: "Godwot, this is he   140
To whom Denmark shall belong,
He shall be a ruler strong,
He shall hold one day in hand
All Denmark and Engelland,
Godard shall he harm that day,
Hang him high, or, living, flay,
Or alive, burn him anon,
Mercy shall he show him none!"
Thus quoth Grim, and sore did greet,
Down he fell at Havelok's feet,   150
Praying: "Lord, have mercy here,
On me, and my wife so dear;
Lord, we own us bound to thee,
Thralls, and servants both are we.
Lord, we'll cherish thee, and feed,
Till that thou canst ride on steed,
Till the day that thou canst wield
Knightly helm, and spear and shield,
That foul traitor Godard, he
Naught shall know, I swear it thee,   160
And none other, lord, save thou
Makest me free man, I trow,
Thro' thee, lord, will I be free —
I will watch and care for thee,
And by thee be freed alway —"

Havelok, he was glad that day,
Up he sat, and craved for bread,
Quoth: "Now am I well nigh dead,
What with hunger, and the bands
Thou did'st fasten on my hands,   170

And the gag, which, at the last
In my mouth thou madest fast,
Therewith was I squeezed so tight,
Thou hadst strangled me outright!"
"Godwot," quoth Leve, "it pleaseth me
Thou wouldst eat, I'll fetch for thee
Milk and butter, cheese, and bread,
Pasties, pancakes, for thee spread,
With such food we shall thee feed
Lord, in this thy mickle need.   180
Sooth 't is, as men say and swear,
Whom God helps, is harméd ne'er!"

When the dame had brought the meat,
Havelok, he began to eat
Greedily, tho' blithe that tide
He might not his hunger hide;
A whole loaf he ate, and more,
For he needs must hunger sore,
Since for full three days, I ween,
Never meat the lad had seen.   190
Then, when he was fully fed,
Grim, he made a right fair bed,
Did his clothes off, laid him low,
Quoth: "Sleep, Son, 't is better so,
Sleep thou sound, and dread thee naught,
Thou from bale to bliss art brought."
Soon as dawned the light of day
Grim, he went upon his way,
To that traitor, false Godard,
Who of Denmark was the steward,   200
Quoth to him: "Lord, I have done
All thou badest me anon,
Drowned the boy in salt sea flood,
Round his neck an anchor good.
Verily, that boy is dead,
Never more he eateth bread,
He lies drownéd in the sea —
Give me gold and other fee,
That henceforth I rich may be,
With thy charter make me free.   210
Such the promise thou didst make
When I lately with thee spake."
Godard stood, and looked at him
With a piercing glance and grim,
Quoth: "Thou fain wouldst be an Earl?
Get thee home, thou dirty churl,

Go thy way, and evermore
Be the thrall thou wast before.
Other meed thou shalt have none —
With but little thou hadst gone   220
To the gallows, God me speed
Thou hast done a wicked deed,
Here too long thou well mayst stay,
Get thee quickly hence away!"

With all haste then, Grim, he ran
From that wicked, traitorous man,
Thought: "What were it best to do?
An he knew, he'll take us two
Hang us high on gallows-tree,
Better 't were the land to flee   230
So we both may save our life,
And my children, and my wife."
Grim, he sold his corn, I trow,
Fleecy sheep, and hornéd cow,
Horse, and swine, and goat withal,
Geese, and hens, he sold them all;
All that he of worth might hold
And could sell, that same he sold,
Turned it into money there —
Then his ship he fits with care,   240
Tarred and pitched it so that she
Safe on sand or creek might be;
Fixed therein a goodly mast,
Cables strong to hold it fast,
Right good oars, and right good sail,
The ship lacked for ne'er a nail
Nor for aught a man might do —
When he had prepared it so
Havelok on board led he
With his wife, and his sons three,   250
And his daughters, maidens fair —
To the oar he bent him there,
Drew him out on the high sea
Where he deemed he best might flee.
But within a little while,
When he scarce had rowed a mile
Rose a wind from out the North,
Bise men call it, drave them forth,
Drave them to the English land
Which was later in his hand,   260
Havelok, as men call his name —
But he first must suffer shame,

Mickle grief and care, I wis,
But at last it all was his
E'en as I will tell ye here
An ye lend to me your ear.
Grim the Humber did ascend,
E'en to Lindesey, the North end,
There his ship ground on the sand,
Grim, he drave it to the land.   270
There he made a little cote
For himself, and for his boat;
There the land he thought to take
A small house of earth to make,
So that they therein might dwell
In that haven harbour well.
And since Grim that place did own
By his name it soon was known,
Grimsby, men the town do call
Who speak of it, one and all,   280
And so men shall call it aye
Betwixt now and Judgment Day.

Grim, he was a fisher good,
Skilful he upon the flood,
Many fish therein he took
Both with net, and eke with hook,
Sturgeon did he catch, and whale,
Turbot, salmon, without fail,
Soles and eels, the sooth to tell —
Oftentimes he sped full well,   290
Cod and porpoise took he there,
Herrings too, and mackerel fair,
Plaice, and halibut, and thornback.
Baskets good he did not lack,
Four, I trow, he made him there
That he and his sons might bear
Fish for sale or for exchange —
There was never town or grange
Where he went not with his ware;
And he came back never bare,   300
But of bread or victuals, store
In his shirt or cloak he bore,
In his sack were beans or corn,
Ne'er his toil was vainly borne.
When 't was lampreys he had ta'en
Well he knew the way again
To Lincoln town, that borough true,
Oft he passed it thro' and thro'

Till his fish he all had sold
And the pence for it was told.   310
Then his home he gladsome sought,
For ofttimes with him he brought
Cakes and simnels, shaped as horn,
Full his bags with meat and corn,
Flesh of neat, and sheep, and swine,
Hemp wherewith to twist his line,
And strong rope to fix the net
Which in sea full oft he set.

Thus hath Grim a fair life led,
With his folk right well he fed,   320
Winters twelve, I trow, and more —
Havelok knew he laboured sore
For his meat, while still he lay,
Thought: "No child am I to-day,
But well-grown, and I could eat
More than ever Grim may get;
I eat more, by God alive,
Than Grim and his children five!
It may not for long be so,
Godwot, I with them will go,   330
I will learn to get some good,
I will toil for this, my food,
'T is no shame to toil alway, —
Eat and drink that man well may
Who for all has toiled full long;
Thus to lie at home were wrong,
God reward him, I ne'er may,
Who hath fed me to this day,
Glad I'll bear a basket now,
It shall harm me naught, I trow,   340
E'en tho' great the burden be
As a net, yea, verily,
No more will I idle stay
But to-morrow go my way."

On the morn, with light of day,
Up he gat, nor longer lay,
Did a basket on his back
With fish piled up in a stack,
Yea, as much alone he bare
As the four, mine oath I'll swear!   350
Well he bare it, sold it well,
All the silver down did tell,
Of the monies he brought back

Not a farthing there did lack;
Thus he gat him forth each day
And no longer idle lay.
So his trade he learned full well —
On the land a famine fell
Both of corn and bread also;
Grim, he wist not what to do,   360
How his house-hold might be fed —
He for Havelok was in dread,
Strong he was, and much he ate,
More than ever Grim might get.
On the sea no fish he caught,
Ling nor hornback home he brought,
Nay, nor other fish to feed
This his household in their need.
Havelok wrought him mickle care
Pondering how he might fare,   370
These, his children vexed him naught,
Havelok was all his thought.
Grim quoth: "Havelok, son so dear,
Death, I think me, draweth near,
Hunger presseth us too strong,
Food hath failed us over long,
Better now to go thy way
Than with us o'er-long to stay,
Till it were too late to go —
Thou right well the road dost know   380
Unto Lincoln, that good town,
Oft hast paced it up and down;
My life is but worth a sloe,
It were well thou thither go,
Many good men dwell therein,
With them thou thy bread mayst win,
Woe is me! too naked thou,
Of my sail I'll make, I trow,
Coat that thou mayst round thee fold
Son, that thou mayst take no cold."

Shears he taketh from the nail,   391
Made a garment of the sail,
Havelok wrapped it round him there;
Neither hose nor shoes he ware,
Other weed had none that day,
Barefoot did he go his way.
In the town he was full woe,
Had no friend to whom to go,
Two days, fasting, went his way

None his work with food would pay.
The third day he heard men call: 401
"Porters, Porters, come ye all!"
All the poor men at that cry
Swift as sparks from embers fly,
Havelok smote down nine or ten,
In the dust he laid them then,
Came he straightway to the cook
Meat for the Earl's table took,
That he at the bridge did buy,
Let the porters lowly lie,   410
And the meat to castle bare —
Farthing cake they gave him there.

The next day good heed he took,
Lay in wait for the Earl's cook,
On the bridge he stood that tide,
Fishes many lay beside,
For the Earl of Cornwall
Bought he meat, and loud did call:
"Porters, Porters, hither hie!"
Havelok hearkened joyfully,   420
When he "Porters!" heard him call
Down he smote the others all,
Who that day betwixt them stood,
Sixteen lads, so stout and good;
To the cook he made a leap
Thrust them down all in a heap,
With his basket reached his side
Gathered up the fish that tide.
Well a cart-load did he bear,
Sounds, and salmon, plaices fair,   430
Lampreys great he took and eels,
Spared he neither toes nor heels.
To the castle came again
Where his burden men have ta'en.
Then when men had helped him down,
Ta'en the load from off his crown,
The cook eyed him well, I trow,
Thought him stalwart man enow,
Quoth: "Now wilt thou stay with me?
I will feed thee willingly,   440
Well art worth thy hire alway
And the food I'll to thee pay!"
"Godwot," quoth he, "gentle sire
Here I pray none other hire,
Food enow give thou to me,

Water, Fire, I'll fetch for thee,
Blow the fire, and right well make,
Sticks I know well how to break,
And a fire to kindle here
That shall burn both bright and clear.
I can cleave wood passing well;   451
How to skin an eel can tell;
Dishes can I wash also,
All you will I well may do."
Quoth the cook: "'T is well, anon,
Go thou yonder, sit thou down,
And good bread I'll give thee free,
Broth in kettle make for thee,
Sit thee down, thy fill mayst eat,
Woe to those who grudge thee meat!"

Havelok sat him down anon,   461
Stayed as still as any stone
Till meat was before him set;
A fair meal did Havelok get.
When he ate his will that day
To the well he went straightway,
Drew a tub of water there,
Bade no man to help him bear,
But with his own hands alone
In the kitchen set it down.   470
He could carry water there,
He the meat from bridge would bear;
Turf and peat he carried all,
Bare the wood from bridge withal;
All that ever men might use
Havelok carries, draws, or hews,
No more rest he takes than he
Should a beast of burden be.
Of all men was he most meek,
Ever smiling, blithe did speak,   480
Glad and joyous he that tide
Knew full well his grief to hide.
Never was there child so small,
Who was fain to sport withal,
But with him would Havelok play;
Bairns he met upon his way
Readily he did their will,
Gave them all of sport their fill.
All men loved him, quiet and bold,
Knights and children, young and old,
Well-beloved of all was he   491

Both of high and low degree.
Far and wide of him they speak
How he was both strong, and meek;
"God ne'er wrought a man more fair,
Yet he goeth well nigh bare!"
For of clothing naught had he
But a loose robe, ill to see,
Soiled it was, and all unclean,
Not a fir-twig worth, I ween.   500
But his plight the cook did rue,
Clothes he bought him, all brand new,
Hose and shoes he bought anon,
Bade him swiftly put them on,
When new clad, and hosed, and shod,
None so fair was made by God!
Of all men who trod the earth
And of women had their birth,
Never man had ruled, to wit,
Over kingdom, who so fit   510
King or Kaiser for to be,
To all seeming, than was he!
For when all together came
There, at Lincoln, for their game,
And the Earl's men stood him by,
Havelok, by the shoulder high,
Towered above the tallest there —
If to wrestle one would dare
Havelok him to ground soon cast,
Stood above him like a mast;   520
And as he was broad and long
So was he both stout and strong,
None in England was his peer
Or for strength could come him near.
Gentle was he too, as strong,
Tho' a man oft did him wrong
Ill for ill he ne'er repaid
Nor a hand upon him laid.
As a maiden pure and clean,
Ne'er in game or woodland green   530
Would he with a woman play,
Cast such things, as straw, away.
In that time the English land
All lay in Earl Godrich's hand,
To the town he bade them fare,
Many an Earl and baron there,
And all men, who at that tide
Lived in England far and wide,

To all men he summons sent
To attend this parliament.   540
Nor of champions was there lack
With their men, both brown and black,
And it fell out that these men,
Some among them, nine or ten,
Midst themselves began to play —
Strong and weak were there that
        day,
Less and more together fell,
All who in the burg did dwell;
Champions, and lads so strong,
Bondsmen with their goads so long,   550
As they gat them from the plough,
'T was a gathering great, I trow.
Never stable-knave should be,
Tho' his horse in hand had he,
But he came to see that play.
At their feet a tree, it lay,
They began to put the stone
Those strong lads, yea, many a one,
Mickle was that stone and great,
Even as a neat its weight,   560
He a stalwart man should be
Who should lift it to his knee;
There was neither clerk nor priest
Who could raise it to his breast.
The champions the test they dare,
With the barons came they there,
And that man whose throw went past
By an inch another's cast,
Were he young, or were he old,
Men did him for champion hold.   570
Staring, there they stood around;
Lords and champions, on that ground
Make a great debate, I wot,
Which shall be the better shot.
Havelok stood and watched the sport,
But of putting knew he naught,
Never yet he saw them play
"Put the Stone" before that day.
Then his master bade him go
See what he therein might do,   580
Tho' his master had him bade
Of the task was he afraid;
Thither goeth he anon,
Catcheth up the heavy stone,

Wherewith he should put that day —
At the first put did it lay
Over all that came before
A good twelve-foot cast, and more.
The champions who saw that throw
Shoved each other, laughing low,   590
No more would they put that day,
Quoth: "Now all too long we stay."
Men might not this marvel hide,
Loud thereof they spake that tide
How that Havelok threw the stone
Far beyond them, everyone;
How that he was fair and tall,
Very strong, and white withal.
Thro' the land of him they speak
How he was both strong and meek;   600
In the castle, high in hall,
Thereof spake the nobles all,
So that Godrich right well heard
Tales of Havelok, every word;
How he tall and strong should be,
Strong of hand, and fair and free.
Then thought Godrich: "Thro' this
        knave
England in my power I'll have,
I, and my son after me,
So I will that it shall be.   610
Athelwold, he made me swear,
On the Holy Mass-gear there,
That I would his daughter give
To the tallest who should live,
Best and fairest, strongest aye,
That I soothly sware that day.
Where shall I find one so tall
As this Havelok? Skilled withal —
Tho' I sent to search thro' Ynde
One so strong I may not find,   620
Yea, with him my quest is sped
With Goldboro shall he wed."
This he thought of treachery,
Of treason, and of felony,
For he deemed that Havelok, he,
Naught but a churl's son should be,
Ne'er should hold of English land
E'en a furrow in his hand
Tho' he wed the rightful heir
Who was good as she was fair.   630

Havelok he deemed a thrall,
Therefore thought he should have all
England, that the maid's should be —
Worse than Sathanas was he,
He, whose power on earth Christ
    shook —
Well might he be hanged on hook!

Goldboro he hither bade —
(Very fair and sweet that maid)
And to Lincoln did her bring;
All the bells for her did ring,   640
Mickle joy he made that day —
Natheless, traitor he, alway!
Said, for lord he 'ld give her there
One who was of men most fair;
Then she answered him anon,
Sware by Christ, and by Saint John,
That with no man would she wed,
None should bring her to his bed,
Save a king, or a king's heir
Tho' he were of men most fair.   650

Godrich Earl, he waxed full wroth
When he heard her swear such oath,
Quoth: "What, Maiden, wouldst thou be
Queen and Lady over me?
With a vagabond shalt wive
And no other King alive!
Thou shalt wed with my cook's knave,
Ne'er another lord shalt have;
Woe to him who other lot
Gives thee while I live, I wot,   660
With the morn I shall thee wed
Willy-nilly, to his bed!"
Goldboro wept sore that stead,
Fain were she she had been dead;
On the morn, at dawning hour
Rang the bell from the church tower,
Judas sent for Havelok — (he
Worse than Sathanas should be)
Quoth: "Say, Master, wilt a wife?"
"Nay," quoth Havelok, "by my life!
With a wife I naught may do,   671
Find her food, nor clothes, nor shoe,
Where should I a woman bring?
Of mine own I have no thing,

Neither house nor hut have I,
Stick nor twig, or green or dry,
Neither bread nor victuals own,
But an old coat, that alone,
For these clothes that cover me
Are the cook's, his knave I be!"   680
Up sprang Godrich, beat him well,
Hard and strong the blows they fell,
Quoth: "Save thou that maiden take
Whom I think thy wife to make,
Thou shalt hang on gallows high,
Or I will put out thine eye!"
Havelok was adread that day,
Quoth, he would his word obey;
For the maid he sent full soon,
Fairest woman 'neath the moon,   690
Swift he spake to her withal,
That foul traitor, wicked thrall:
"Save that thou take this man's hand
I will drive thee from the land,
Or shalt haste to gallows tree,
In a fire thou burnt shall be!"
Much she feared his threats that day,
Durst not say the spousals nay,
For altho' she liked it ill
Yet she deemed it were God's Will,   700
For that God, Who grows the corn,
Willed her to be woman born.
Then when he for dread did swear
He would wed and feed her there,
And she sware she would him hold,
Then were pence in plenty told,
Mickle monies on the book —
Thus he gave, and thus she took.
They were wedded fast that day —
And the Marriage Mass did say,   710
All pertaining to a Clerk,
The Archbishop good, of York,
For the parliament he came
Sent by God, as at that same.

By God's law they wed have been,
And the folk the deed have seen —
Sore dismay doth Havelok know,
Wist not what they best might do,
Should they bide, or go their way?
There, he would no long-time stay,   720

Godrich hated them he saw —
(Food he, for the Devil's maw)
And if he to dwell there sought,
(This, I trow, was Havelok's thought)
To his wife men might do shame,
Or else bring upon him blame,
Liever he if dead he were —
Other rede he took him there,
That from thence they both would flee,
Seek to Grim and his sons three,   730
There he deemed they best might speed,
Both to clothe them and to feed.
Foot to ground they set straightway,
Other rede had none that day,
Took the right road at that same
Till they safe to Grimsby came.
When he came there, Grim was dead,
Nor with him might speak that stead,
But his children were alive,
Sons and daughters, all the five,   740
And to welcome him were fain
When they knew he came again;
Greeted him with gladness mickle,
Ne'er, I trow, he found them fickle!
On their knees fell speedily,
Greeting Havelok heartily,
Quoth: "Dear Lord, art welcome here,
Welcome too thy Lady dear,
Blesséd be the day ye both
Each to other sware your troth,   750
Well is us that now we live,
Thine we are, to sell or give,
Thine we are, to give or sell,
So that thou wilt with us dwell.
Lord, we here possess much good,
Horses, cattle, ships on flood,
Gold and silver, mickle store
That was Grim's, our sire, of yore;
Gold and silver, other fee
He hath bid us hold for thee;   760
We have sheep, and we have swine,
Dwell here, Lord, and all is thine!
Thou art lord and thou art sire,
We thy servants at thine hire.
These, our sisters, will fulfil
All that is thy Lady's will,

They her clothes will wash and wring,
Water for her hands will bring,
Spread the couch for her and thee,
For our lady shall she be!"   770
Thus rejoicing do they make,
Fetch the sticks, and swiftly break,
Make the fire to burn so bright,
Goose nor hen they spare that night,
Neither duck, nor yet the drake,
Food in plenty ready make.
For good meat they did not fail,
Wine they drew for them, and ale,
Of good heart did they rejoice,   779
"*Wassail*" bade, with gladsome voice.

On that night Goldboro lay
Sad at heart, and sorrowing aye,
Deemed she was betrayed by Fate
With a low-born man to mate.
Thro' the dark she saw a light
Very fair, and very bright,
Yea, so bright it shone, I ween,
As a blazing fire had been.
Looked she North, and looked she
        South,
Lo! it came from out his mouth,   790
Who beside her lay in bed —
'T was no wonder she had dread,
Thought: "What may this marvel
        mean?
He is high-born, so I ween,
He is high-born, or is dead!"
On his neck, in gold so red,
Lo! a Cross, and in her ear
She an angel's voice doth hear.

"Goldboro, let thy mourning be,
Havelok, who hath wedded thee,   800
Is a King's son, and King's heir
As that Cross betokens fair.
More it showeth, in his thrall
Denmark, yea, and England all;
Sovereign he, both strong and true
O'er England, and Denmark too,
With thine eyes this shalt thou see,
With him Queen, and Lady be!"

ARTHUR AND MERLIN

THE CHOOSING OF ARTHUR

At Yule the Bishop Bricius, he
Gave proof that he no fool should be,
There stood he forth amid them all,
In this wise did upon them call:
"Lordings, since ye may not accord
To choose unto ye here a lord,
I pray, for love of Christ so dear,
Ye work by wile and wisdom here;
For such a choice the time is right —
Now go we all to church to-night   10
And pray to Christ, so good and free,
A king to send us, who shall be
Strong for the right against the wrong,
Whom He shall choose our ranks among;
Pray that to us He token send
When the morn's Mass be brought to
      end."
That in such wise it might be done,
To this, they say, "Amen," each one.
Thus they betake them, more or less,
That night to church, with morn to
      Mass,   20
In prayer their cause to God commend
That He a rightful king should send.
And thus, when at the end of Mass,
From out the church the folk would pass,
Before the church door, there they
      found
A great stone standing on the ground,
'T was long and high, the sooth to say,
Therein a right fair sword, it lay.
Then king and duke, baron, and knight,
Were filled with wonder at that sight;
The Bishop, he beheld with eye,   31
And rendered thanks to Christ on high,
And here I rede ye all to wit
That on the pommel fair 't was writ:
"Excalibur, the name I bear,
For a king's treasure fashioned fair."
In English writing there displayed,
In steel 't was graven on the blade.

The Bishop quoth to them anon:
"Who draws this sword from out the
      stone   40
That same shall be our king indeed,
By God's Will, and by this, our rede."
Thereto they give consent alway, —
King Lot, his hand to hilt did lay,
Thinking to draw it out forthright,
But stirred it not, for all his might;
King Nanters, nor King Clarion,
Might not withdraw it from the stone,
Nor gentle man, whoe'er he be,
Was there might stir it, verily.   50
Thither came all of noble blood,
And there till Candlemas it stood;
All who were born in English land
Each to this stone he set his hand,
For life or death, I trow, was none
Might stir that sword from out the
      stone.
There did it stand till Easter-tide;
Thither came men from far and wide,
From this shore, from beyond the sea,
But prospered not, 't was God's decree!
The stone stood there till Pentecost;   61
And thither came a goodly host,
For tournament at that same tide
E'en as it were the stone beside.
Sir Antour did his son then, Kay,
With honour make a knight, that day,
This Kay was ta'en, so saith the Geste,
Away from this, his mother's breast,
For Arthur's sake, she nursed that child
Who grew up courteous, meek, and mild.
Kay was a noble knight, I trow,   71
Save that he stammered somewhat now,
Thro' nurture did he win that same,
They say that from his nurse it came;
And Arthur, he had served King Lot
For this long time, so do I wot.

When thus, Sir Kay, he was made knight,
Sir Antour counselled him forthright

Arthur to fetch to him again
And there to make of him his swain,   80
For he was hardy, true to test,
Thro' all the land of youths the best.
Therewith Kay, he was right well paid —
Then all was done as Antour said,
Arthur came home, and was with Kay,
To tourney went with him alway;
There Kay, he shewed himself in fight
To be a very valiant knight,
O'er all the field, at end, by side,
Full many did he fell that tide.   90

Then, as he came amid the throng,
He laid about with strokes so strong
That this, his sword, asunder brake —
Anon, to Arthur thus he spake:
"Now to my lady swiftly wend,
Pray her another sword to send."
And so he did, nor thought to bide,
But swiftly home again did ride,
His lady found he not that day
So turned him back upon his way.   100

Then to that sword within the stone
I trow me, he hath swiftly gone,
(And never man was there to see
Since all should at the Tourney be,)
Arthur, he took the hilt in hand
Towards himself he drew the brand,
Light from the stone it came away —
He took it in his hand straightway
And leapt upon his horse anon,
Back to the Tourney hath he gone   110
And said: "Have here this sword, Sir Kay,
Thy lady found I not to-day."
Right well Kay knew the sword, I wis,
To Arthur spake "Whence had'st thou this?"
"Certes" quoth Arthur, "that same brand
There, in a stone, I saw it stand."
(Arthur, he saw it ne'er before
Nor wist the meaning that it bore.)
With that, to Arthur spake Sir Kay,
"Par amour, now to no man say   120

Whence thou didst take this sword, I trow,
And riches shalt thou have enow."
Arthur he answered, "Certes, nay!"
With that he gat him forth, Sir Kay,
And led his father, Sir Antour
Straight to the church of Saint Saviour,
And saith: "The sword I forth did draw,
Now am I king, by right and law!"
Sir Antour, he beheld that sword,
Answered again with ready word   130
"'T is but a boast, by God above!
An sooth it be, that must thou prove
Before these nobles everyone,
Must thrust this sword back in the stone;
Save thou again canst draw it free
Then shame upon thy head shall be!"

With that, they get them to the stone,
And Kay thrust back the sword anon,
But tho' a knight both stiff and stout
He had no strength to draw it out.   140
With that besought him Sir Antour,
"Now tell me son, here, par amour,
Who was it drew this sword so good?"
Sir Kay, he laughed as there he stood,
And sware: "By God, as here I stand,
Arthur, he brought it in his hand!"
Antour, he calléd Arthur there
And to the stone he bade him fare
And there, I trow me, swift and soft,
Both in and out he drew it oft.   150
Antour was blithe and glad that day,
Arthur he took to church straightway
And saith to him full secretly,
"Arthur, I prithee, hearken me,
Since thou wast born, 't is true, I ween,
In my house nourished hast thou been."
With that he told him all that morn
How he begotten was, and born;
How that King Uther was his sire,
And how, at that same king's desire,   160
"A nurse I took for my son Kay,
And thee at my wife's breast did lay."
Then Antour quoth: "Now list to me,
Thro' nurture thou my son shalt be,

It were not right didst thou gainsay
A boon that I should rightful pray,
So I beseech, grant me a boon
Which I will ask of thee full soon,
And Arthur, son, I will thee aid   169
That king with honour thou be made."
Then Arthur answered, fair and free:
"Now Christ in Heaven forbid it me
That I deny thee anything
When thou to me a prayer dost bring."
Quoth Antour: "God thee well repay;
Now I for love this boon will pray,
To Kay my son the stewardship give
For all the years that thou mayst live;
In weal, in woe, I pray thee fair,
In every stead, protection swear,   180
And I shall aid, in this, thy need,
That thro' God's Help thou surely
      speed."

With that Sir Arthur spake full soon;
"Sir Antour, take thou this, thy boon,
Kay shall be steward in my land,
For weal or woe I'll by him stand,
And if I ever fail Sir Kay
Then Christ forget me, that same day!"
With that Sir Antour, he forthright
Took Arthur, and hath dubbed him
      knight,   190
First gave him cloth and fitting weed,
Then found him harness for his steed,
Helmet, and byrnie, coat of mail,
Nor plate for arm or thigh did fail;
With collar, shield, and sword to smite,
And shaft with blade that well could bite.
Anon, of knights he gave him there
Forty, to do him service fair.
With morn to tournament they go,   199
And so they dealt, I'ld have ye know,
That here Sir Arthur, day by day,
Honour and praise he bare away.
At morn Sir Antour, who should be
No fool, to Bishop Brice went he,
And saith to him, a knight he knew
Both fair and noble, good and true,
"Who shall be king, by this our law,
For that the sword he forth may draw."

With that, the Bishop, well content,
After Sir Arthur straightway sent,   210
Before the nobles of that land
Arthur, he took the sword in hand,
He drew it out, he thrust it in —
Then many a man must wonder win,
For none might stir it from that stone
I plight my word, save he alone!
Then kings and earls, without a doubt,
They crowded there, the lad about,
Thinking to prove his knowledge here —
Ever he was of gracious cheer,   220
Nor better could a man devise
Than this, his speech, in every wise.
With that, Sir Antour help did bring
So that he there was chosen king,
And to his crowning there withal
Full many a prince and king they call,
All who would come, they pray them
      well
To gather, as Saint John's-tide fell.

.   .   .   .

'T is merry in the June-tide fair
When fennel hangeth everywhere,   230
And violets and rose in flower
Be found in every maiden's bower;
The sun is hot, the day is long,
And merry sounds the birdling's song;
Then first King Arthur bare the crown
Within Cardoil, that noble town.
King Lot, who wedded Belisent,
He to the coronation went,
The King of Lyoneis was he,
A strong man, of great courtesie.   240
Five hundred knights were in his train,
Hardy and strong, for fighting fain.
King Nanters came, as I am told,
Who did the land of Garlot hold,
A noble man, a valiant wight,
Strong to defend himself in fight.
The same had wedded with Blasine,
King Arthur's sister, fair and fine,
Full seven hundred knights, the king
Did with him, as his mesnie, bring,   250
And many a charger, many a steed,
That should be found right good at need.

And thither too, King Urien sped,
Who did with the third sister wed,
'T was from the land of Gorre he came,
A young man he, of noble fame,
With twenty thousand men, and five,
No better knights were there alive.

King Carados, he too, was there,
The crown of Strangore did he bear, 260
A mighty man, and well renowned,
Knight was he of the Table Round,
From far, unto Cardoil he sought,
Six hundred knights with him he
    brought,
Who well knew how to joust in field,
With stiff lance, 'neath the sheltering
    shield.
Thither came Ider in that hour,
King of the Marches, of great power,
And with him brought full thirty score
Of knights who rode his face before. 270

King Anguisant did thither ride,
The King of Scotland at that tide,
The richest he, among them all,
Youngest, and of great power withal,
Five hundred knights he brought, I wot,
Both stout and strong, each man a Scot;
And many more, from South and East,
Thither have come, to that high feast.
Then king and baron, as I tell, 279
Nobly they welcomed them, and well,
And Bishop Brice, the court among,
Crowned Arthur, and the office sung.
And when the service came to end,
Unto the feast their way they wend;
They found all ready, cloth and board,
And first hath gone the highest lord;
Men serve them then with plenteous
    fare,
With meat and drink, and dainties rare,
With venison of hart and boar, 289
Swan, peacock, bustard, to them bore;
Of pheasant, partridge, crane, that day
Great plenty and no lack had they.
Piment and claret served they free
To high lords, and their companie,

Serving them in such noble wise
As any man might well devise.
And when the guests had eaten all,
Both high and low, within that hall,
His gifts to give did Arthur rise,
To noble men, of high emprise, 300
Their homage they should straightway
    plight
E'en as the custom was, and right.
But e'en as this he did, I trow,
King Lot, King Nanters, men enow,
Of these his gifts they had despite,
And to the crown denied his right.

Up from the board they spring with
    boast,
Each king of them, with all his host,
Swearing that ne'er for anything
They'ld own a bastard for their king, 310
Thus, with dishonour great they fare,
Thinking to slay King Arthur there.
But Arthur's men, they came between,
And Merlin, in that strife, I ween,
Stood forth, and spake, no bastard he,
But nobler than them all should be,
And there he told them all that morn
How Arthur was begat, and born.
The wise men of that country, they
Gave thanks to Jesu Christ, alway, 320
In that their king, thro' this, His Grace,
Was come of royal Pendragon's race.
The barons, they to Merlin say:
"Thy witchcraft wrought his birth
    alway,
Thou traitor, know that verily,
For all enchantments known to thee,
No child born in adultery
The king and lord o'er us shall be,
But he shall starve here, now anon —"
Towards King Arthur have they gone,
The king was armed, from head to heel,
And all his friends, in iron and steel, 332
Resistance made they, strong, and stout,
And of a surety, drave them out,
With swords and knives full speedily,
From hall, who Arthur's foes should
    be.

Those same six kings, they were right
    wroth,
And all their barons sware an oath,
That never they two meals should eat
Till they had taken vengeance meet; 340
With that they pitch their tents that
    day
Without the town, a little way.

. . . .

List, tho' ye many be or few,
In May the sun doth slay the dew,
The day is merry, waxing long,
The lark doth, soaring, pour his song,
The meads they seek, the maidens
    fair,
And many a floweret gather there.   ¹

. . . .

'T is merry in the month of May,
Birds in the woodland groves be gay, 350
In every land ariseth song —
Christ Jesu, be Thy folk among!

. . . .

Merry it is in summer-tide
When birds sing in the forest wide,
On jousting bent, the squires they ride,
And maidens deck them in their pride.

. . . .

Merry is June, when flowers blow fair,
And meadows sweet perfume the air,
Lily and rose be bright to see,
The rivers clear from mire be free,   360
Both knight, I trow, and vavassour,
Their demoiselles love *par amour.*

RICHARD CŒUR DE LION

I

HIS PARENTAGE

Lord Jesus, King of Victory,
Who did such grace, and such glory,
Send unto our King Richard,
Who was never proven coward,
Good it is in Geste to read
Of his conquests, and his deeds!
Many tales men weave anew
Of good knights, so strong and true,
Men their deeds read in romance
Both in England, and in France;   10
Of Roland, and of Oliver,
And of every dosiper;
Alexander, Charlemagne,
Of King Arthur and Gawain, —
Courteous knights and good, they
    were —
Of Turpin, and the Dane Ogier.
And of Troy men read in rhyme,
How they warred in olden time,
Of Hector and Achilles true
And the folk whom there they slew.   20

In French books this rhyme is wrought,
Laymen of the tale know naught,
'Mid hundred laymen there be none
Who know French, save, perchance,
    one!
None the less, with gladsome cheer
There be many fain to hear
Noble jousts, I understand,
Wrought by knights of Engelland;
Therefore I, *par foi,* will read
Of a king of doughty deed,   30
Richard, king and warrior best
Men may find in any Geste;
All who to my tale attend
May God grant them right good end!

Lordings, hearken first of all
How King Richard's birth did fall —
Henry, was his father hight;
In his time, to tell aright,
As I find it writ again
Was Saint Thomas foully slain   40
At Canterbury's altar stone
Where be many marvels shown.

Twenty years to him were told,
Then was he a king full bold,
But of wife would he hear naught
Tho' she treasure with her brought.
But to wed they pressed him still
Till he yielded to their will,
Sent of messengers a band
Into many a diverse land,   50
That the fairest maid on life
They should bring their king as wife.
Swift those messengers were dight —
Ship they took the self-same night,
Hoisted up the sail, I trow,
For the wind was good enow.
When they were well out at sea
Then the breeze failed suddenly —
This hath wrought them woe, I ween —
They another ship have seen,   60
Ne'er had they seen such an one,
White it was, of whalës bone,
Every nail was gold engraved,
Of pure gold the rudder-stave,
Ivory the mast *sans* fail,
And of samite all the sail;
And the ropes were twined of silk,
Every one as white as milk.
All the vessel they behold
Hung about with cloth of gold,   70
Loof and windlass, fair to view,
All were bright in azure blue.

In that ship, I trow, there were
Valiant knights, and ladies fair,
And one maiden 'midst them all,
Bright as sun thro' glass doth fall.
Swift, her men aboard they stand,
Seize those others by the hand,
Pray them there with them to dwell
And their tidings swiftly tell.   80
And they answer, they would show
All they might desire to know;
"To far lands our way we went,
For King Henry us hath sent
That the fairest maid on life
We may bring to him for wife!"
As the words were spoken fair
Rose a king from off his chair —

(Of carbuncle was that throne,
Never they its like had known.)   90
Two dukes stood that king beside,
Noble men, of mickle pride,
Welcome fair they gave that day,
Bade them come aboard straightway;
Thirty knights, I speak no lie,
Were they, in that companie,
Straight aboard that barque they went
Who as messengers were sent.
Knights there were, and maids enow —
Seven score, and more, I trow,   100
Welcomed them with one accord,
Set up trestles, laid a board,
Cloth of gold was spread thereon,
And the king, he bade, anon,
That his daughter speedily
Set before his face should be.
Then, with sound of trumpet blast,
Lo! that maid before them passed,
In her train, of knights a score,
And of ladies, many more,   110
Knelt before that maiden free,
Asked her what her will might be?

Thus they feasted and made gay
As the king himself did pray,
And when they had eaten well
Their adventures would they tell.
Then the king, he straightway said,
How in vision he was bade
From his land to take his way
And to England go straightway,   120
And his daughter dear also
With him on the ship should go —
"So, in fitting fashion dight
We would seek that land forthright."
Straight there spake a messenger —
(That man's name was Berenger —)
"To seek further is no need,
Bring her to our king with speed,
When his eyes behold the maid
He will deem him well repaid."   130
From the north-east blew the wind,
Better breeze they might not find,
At the Tower they land straightway
And to London take their way.

Soon the knights their lord have told
Of that lady, fair and bold,
How a ship lay off the Tower
With a maiden white as flower.
Then King Henry did him dight,
Earls and barons, many a knight,   140
Rode with him that maid to meet,
Courteously he would her greet. —
Soon that maid to land they led,
Cloth of gold before her spread,
And her father walked before,
Crown of gold on head he wore;
Messengers on either side,
Minstrels too, of mickle pride.
Henry swift from horse did spring,
Greeted fair that stranger king,   150
And that lady fair and free —
"Welcome be ye both to me!"
Thus to Westminster they go,
Lords and ladies fair also,
Trumpets sound a blast so gay
As to meat they take their way.
Knights, they served them with all speed,
More to tell there is no need.
After meat, right courteously,
Spake our lord, the King Henry,   160
To that king, there, at that same:
"Say, dear Sire, what is thy name?"
"Sire, men call me Corbaryng,
I of Antioch am king —"
Then he told our lord how he
Thro' a vision, set to sea:
"Sire, had it not been for this
I had brought more men, I wis,
And of vessels many more
That of victuals bare a store."   170
Asked our king the lady there:
"And thy name, thou maiden fair?"
"Cassidorien, without lie."
Thus she answered readily.
"Demoiselle, so bright and sheen
Wilt thou stay here as my queen?"
Quoth the maiden soft and still;
"I am at my father's will."
Then her father spake anon,
All the king's will should be done   180
And she should, with speed, be wed

As a queen, to royal bed;
But she prayed this courtesie
She be wedded privily.
Thus were they espoused that night,
At the feast danced many a knight,
Joy was made the court among —
With the morn a Mass was sung
Ere the Host they raised, I ween,
In a swoon she fell, the queen,   190
Wonder smote the folk, and dread —
To a chamber was she led,
Quoth: "This spell is laid on me
That the Host I may not see."
Corbaryng, the morrow's tide,
Sailed, nor longer would abide.
Henry dwelt with his fair queen,
Babes were born to them, I ween,
Two sons, and a daughter fair
As the book doth well declare,   200
Richard was the first, *sans* fail,
(He of whom I tell this tale)
John his brother, at that same,
Topyas, their sister's name.
Thus the twain this life they led
Till full fifteen years were sped.
On a day, before the Rood,
At the Mass, King Henry stood,
Came a lord of high degree,
"Sire," he quoth, "how may this be   210
That your wife, my lady-queen,
Dare not at the Mass be seen?
Give us leave to hold her here
So that she the Gospel hear,
Keep her still till Mass be said —
Thou shalt see a sight of dread!"
Then the king doth grant their will,
Said that they might hold her still:
"Nor for weal, nor yet for woe
From the kirk ne'er let her go!"   220
When the sacring bell they ring
For the canon to begin
From the kirk she would away —
But the Earl, he straight said: "Nay,
Lady, thou shalt here abide
Matters not what may betide."
By the hand she held anon
Her daughter and her young son, John,

Thro' the roof she took her flight
Openly, in all men's sight,   230
From the air John fell to ground,
Brake his thigh there in that stound.
With her daughter fled the queen,
Never more by men was seen.
Marvel on the king was laid
That she such an ending made,
For her love, who was served so,
No more would he come nor go,
His son Richard, by decree,
After him the king should be.   240

II

HOW RICHARD WON THE NAME OF CŒUR DE LION.

Now they dight them speedily
These three knights, to set to sea,
Hoisted sail, the wind was good,
Swift they crossed the salt sea flood,
Into Flanders did they go,
Richard, and his comrades two;
Took their way, with gladsome cheer,
Thro' strange lands, both far and near,
Till to Brindisi they came,
('T is a haven of great fame.)   10
There a goodly ship they found
Which was unto Cyprus bound,
The sail was raised, the ship was strong,
But the voyage, they deemed it long,
When 't was o'er, I understand,
They did in Famagusta land;
There they tarried forty days
Of that land to learn the ways.
Then once more they set to sea,
Came to Acre speedily,   20
Thence they passed to Macedon,
And the city, Babylon.
They would Cæsarea see —
Then would pass to Nineveh;
Came unto Jerusalem,
And the town of Bethlehem;
Saw the Sultan Turry's hold,
Ebuda did there behold,

And the Castle Orgelous,
And the city Aperrous;   30
To Jaffa go, and to Safrane,
To Tabaret, and eke Archane.
Thus they spied the Holy Land,
How to win it to their hand;
Homeward turned their face at last,
Into England fain had passed.
When they came o'er the great sea
To Almayne, those palmers three,
There they wrought, ere hence they go,
That which brought them mickle woe;
How it chanced I now will tell,   41
Lordings, listen to me well!
They had bought a goose for fare
In the tavern where they were;
Richard stirred the fire, I wit,
Thomas set the goose on spit,
Fulk d'Oyley, he trimmed the wood —
Very dear they bought that food!
When they well had dined that day
Came a minstrel on his way,   50
And he quoth: "Good men, be ye
Pleased to hear my minstrelsie?"
Richard bade him forth to go,
Words that turned to mickle woe,
For he laid that speech to mind,
Saying: "Ye be men unkind,
Ye shall rue, if so I may,
That ye gave me naught to-day,
Gentlemen should well entreat
Minstrels whom they chance to meet, 60
Of their meat and drink be free,
Fame is spread thro' minstrelsie!"
English, he the English knew
By their speech, and look, and hue;
On his road he went that day
Where the King of Almayne lay,
To the castle hath he gone,
With the porter spake anon:
"Go, nor wait for summoning,
Speak thus to thy lord the King: 70
"There be come unto thy land
Palmers three, a valiant band,
In Christendom the strongest they
And their names I'll tell straightway,

'T is King Richard, warrior grim,
Comrades twain he leads with him,
Sir Fulk d'Oyley, of renown,
And Sir Thomas of Multoun."
Sped the porter to the hall,
Told his lord these tidings all,   80
Glad, the king, he hearkened there
And by Heaven an oath he sware
He who brought to him this tale
For reward he should not fail.
Then his knights he bade straightway
To the city take their way:
"Take ye now these palmers three,
Bring them swiftly here to me."
Forth in haste those knights have gone
Unto Richard came anon,   90
Asked: "Who here at meat may be?"
Richard answered, fair and free:
"We be palmers three, no less,
Come from lands of heatheness,"
Spake the knights in answer there
"To the king ye needs must fare
Of your tidings is he fain —"
With the three they turn again;
When King Richard he did see,   99
"*Dieu me garde*," he quoth, "'t is he —
Yea, in sooth, my deadly foe,
Hence he shall not lightly go!"
Straight he doth of them demand,
"Say, what seek ye in my land?"
Quoth again: "With traitorous eye
Ye be come my lands to spy,
Treason would ye work on me!"
Quoth King Richard, readily,
"We be palmers, sooth to say,   109
From God's Land we pass this way."
Called the King on Richard's name,
Spake unto him words of shame:
"Now for king I know thee well,
These thy knights, tho' sooth to tell
Thou dost seem but ill bedight;
So I say it is but right
That thou in foul dungeon lie
Right and reason here have I!"
Richard quoth, with heart so free:
"Thou dost ill, so seemeth me,   120
Palmers passing on their way

Should go free, by night or day,
Nay, Sir King, for courtesie
Do us here no villainie,
For His Love Who thee hath bought
Let us go, and grieve us naught;
It may to your lot betide
In strange lands to wander wide."
But the king, he bade ere long
Shut them fast in prison strong.   130
Then the jailer at command
Took King Richard by the hand
And with him his comrades twain —
Food they might not taste again
Till the morrow waxed to prime.
The king's son, at that same time,
(Arthur was the prince's name,)
Thought to do King Richard shame,
(He was held throughout the land
For the strongest man of hand,)   140
To the jailer then quoth he:
"Let me now the prisoners see!"
Quoth the jailer, "At thy will
Thy command I will fulfil."
Swift he bringeth them anon,
And King Richard first hath gone,
The king's son, he spake forthright,
"Art thou Richard, that strong knight,
Whom men praise in every land?
Wilt a buffet from me stand,   150
And anon, as I shall live,
Thou shalt me a buffet give?"
Then King Richard, undismayed,
Hath with him this forward made,
And the king's son, proud and brave,
Such a blow to Richard gave
From his eyes, the fire, it sprung —
Richard deemed he did him wrong:
"By Saint Helena, I swear,
With the morn to pay thee fair!"   160
The king's son, he mocked him still,
Bade them give him, at his will,
Both of drink, and eke of meat,
Of the best that he might eat,
That he thirst nor hunger know
Lest o'er-feeble be his blow.
On the morrow when 't was day,
Richard rose, without delay,

And a fire he hath him dight,
Wax he took, so fair and white,   170
At the fire he waxed his hand
All about, I understand.
Came the king's son, free and bold,
As true man, his pledge to hold,
And before King Richard stood,
Spake to him, with eager mood:
"Richard, smite with all thy might
As thou wouldst be held true knight,
And if e'er I stoop or yield
May I never carry shield!"   180
'Neath his cheek his hand he laid,
(He who saw it soothly said,)
Flesh and skin were torn away;
In a swoon he fell that day,
For in twain it brake, the bone,
He fell dead as any stone!
To the king a knight then sped,
Bare to him these tidings dread:
"Richard, he hath slain thy son!"
"Woe is me! Now have I none!"   190
With that cry he fell to ground
As a man by woe fast bound,
Swooned for sorrow at their feet;
Knights, they raised him as was meet,
Saying: "Sire, turn from this thought,
Now 't is done, 't will help us naught!"
Then the king aloud did cry
To the knights who stood near by,
Saying: "I to hear am fain
In what manner he was slain!"   200
Silent stood they every one,
Yea, for sorrow speaketh none;
At their cry she came, the queen,
Cried: "Alas! What here hath been?
Why this sorrow, this despair?
Who hath brought ye all to care?"
"Dame," he quoth, "say, know'st thou
        naught?
Thy fair son to death is brought!
Since the day that I was born
No such grief my heart hath torn,   210
All to loss is turned my gain,
Yea, myself I fain had slain!"
When the queen, she understood,
Certes, she was well nigh wood,

With her nails her cheeks she tare
As one doth in madness fare,
Covered was her face with blood —
Rent the robe wherein she stood,
Cursed the day she first drew breath;
"Say, how was he done to death?"   220
Saith the king, "I'll tell to thee,
Here the knight who told it me,
Say the sooth," so spake the king,
"In what wise it chanced this thing,
If thou aught but truth shalt say
An ill death shalt die to-day!"
Then he doth the jailer call,
Bade him stand before them all,
Bear them witness here again
How the king's son had been slain.   230
He quoth: "Yesterday, at prime,
Came your son, in evil time,
To the prison door, to me;
Said, the palmers he would see,
Bade me fetch them forth to show: —
First of all did Richard go,
Straightway Arthur asked him there,
If to stand a blow he'ld dare
If so, as true knight in land,
He would take one from his hand.   240
Richard answered: 'By this light,
Smite at will, and do thy might!'
Arthur smote him such a blow
That he well nigh laid him low,
Saith, 'Now here I challenge thee
Such, at morn, to give to me.'
So they parted in this wise,
With the morn did Richard rise
And your son, again he came;
Richard met him at that same   250
As the forward 'twixt them lay,
Richard smote him, sooth to say,
Smote his cheek-bone there in twain —
Fell your son before him slain.
Here I swear I truly tell
In this wise his death, it fell."
Quoth the king with eager will:
"There in prison keep them still,
And in fetters bind with speed;
Trow me, for this evil deed,   260
In that he hath slain my son,

He shall now to death be done."
Forthwith doth the jailer go,
Swift his lord's command will do,
Meat that day the knights had naught,
Never drink to them was brought.
The king's daughter, that same day,
With her maids, in bower she lay,
Margery, she hight, that maid,
She her love on Richard laid;   270
At the midday, ere 't was noon,
To the prison hath she gone,
Taking with her maidens three —
"Jailer," quoth she, "let me see
These thy prisoners hastily."
Quoth the jailer, "Certainly."
Richard did he bring forthright,
Fair he greets that lady bright,
Saith to her with heart so free,
"Lady, what wilt thou with me?"   280
When her eyes on him she cast
Love of him hath gripped her fast,
And she quoth: "Save God above
O'er all things I do thee love!"
Richard answered in that stound.
"Nay! With wrong brought here to
        ground,
What may my love profit thee?
Captive I, as thou mayst see,
Now a second day hath gone
That of food I have had none!"   290
Then the maid, of great pitie,
Said this should amended be,
And she bade the jailer there
Meat and drink to him to bear,
And the irons from him take —
"Do thou this, for thine own sake,
And at eve, when supper's done,
Bring him to my bower anon,
A squire's vesture shall he wear,
I myself will keep him there,   300
By Christ, and by Saint Simon, thou
Shalt have guerdon fair, I trow!"
The jailer, he forgat it naught,
To her bower was Richard brought,
With the princess dwelt he still,
Of her favours had his fill,
Thus, until the seventh day,

Came and went he on his way.
Then hath spied on him a knight,
How he came to her by night,   310
To the king he spake with tongue:
"Shamed is now thy daughter young!"
And the king, he asked anon:
"Say, who now this deed hath done?"
"This that traitor Richard, he
Who hath thus dishonoured thee,
On my faith as Christian, know
I have seen him come and go!"
Then the king, he sighed full sore,
But to him he spake no more,   320
Swiftly did he send withal,
Did his council to him call,
Earls and barons, clerks also,
They should hear the words of woe.
Forth the messengers are gone —
Came the councillors anon,
It was on the fourteenth day
That they came, the tale doth say.
With one voice the king they greet,
Saith the tale, and fair entreat,   330
"Lords," he quoth, "be welcome all."
Forth they went unto the hall,
There the king his seat doth take
And without delay he spake —
"Lordings, I have bid ye come
That ye speak a traitor's doom,
Richard, who hath done this wrong
Lies now in my prison strong;"
Then he told them of his pain,
How his son by him was slain,   340
And his daughter brought to shame —
"I had killed him at this same
Save the law doth straitly say
That no man a king may slay."
Then out spake a baron bold:
"How came Richard in your hold,
Who so great a king is thought
That no man dare do him aught?"
Then he told them in what wise
He had come there, in disguise,   350
And two others with him came,
Noble lords, of knightly fame —
"I, suspecting them alway
Did them fast in prison lay."

Leave the king hath taken there,
Bade them to a hall repair,
And take counsel there alone,
Of what now might best be done.
Thus in speech they conned it o'er
For three days, I ween, and more.   360
Some had slain him willingly,
Some said, 't would unlawful be,
In this wise with jangling word
Could they come to no accord.
"Truly," said the wisest there,
"We his doom may not declare."
These the tidings that they tell
To their king, believe me well!
Swift a knight spake to the king:
"Vex thee not, Sire, for this thing,   370
Sooth, I wis, Sir Eldred, he
Soon shall tell what best may be,
Counsel ye right well he can,
He hath doomed full many a man."
Then the king, without delay,
Bade Sir Eldred come straightway,
He was brought before the king,
And he prayed him of this thing:
"How may I avengéd be
Of King Richard, tell to me!"   380
Quoth Sir Eldred, "Sooth to tell,
Thereon have I pondered well,
Ye wot well 't is 'gainst the law
Majesty to hang and draw,
This shall now my counsel be,
Take your lion speedily,
And withhold from him his meat
That for three days naught he eat,
Shut ye Richard in a hall,
Loose the lion on him withal,   390
In this wise he slain may be
And the law kept, verily,
When the lion thy foe hath slain
Hast thou fitting vengeance ta'en."
But the maid, she did espy
How he should, thro' treason, die,
Sent to call him speedily
That he warned thereof should be.
Came he to her bower straightway —
"Welcome, Love," she said that day, 400
"Know, my father doometh thee,

Three days hence thou slain shalt be,
In a chamber shut full close
They on thee a lion will loose,
Famishing, and hungered sore,
Then, I trow, thy life is o'er.
But, dear Love, (this wise she spake,)
Hence to-night our flight we'll take,
With us gold and treasure store
That may last us evermore."   410
Richard quoth: "Nay, nay, not so,
'T were unlawful thus to do,
So to fly, nor take our leave,
Loth were I the king to grieve.
For the lion care I naught,
How to slay him have I thought,
And by prime, on this third day
Thou shalt have his heart for prey."
Then he kerchieves prayed, of silk —
"Give me forty, white as milk,   420
To the prison bring them all
Ere the shades of evening fall."
When the hour had come, straightway
Went the maid upon her way,
And with her a noble knight, —
There they had a supper dight,
Richard bade his comrades two
With him to her supper go:
"And, Sir Jailer, come thou still,
For it is my lady's will."   430
That night were they glad and gay,
Then to chamber took their way,
Richard and that lady bright
Stayed together all that night.
At the morn, when it was day,
Richard bade her go her way;
"Nay," she quoth, "by God above
I shall die here with my love;
Here I will with thee abide
E'en tho' death should now betide,   440
Certes, hence I will not wend,
But will here await mine end."
Richard quoth: "Now, lady free,
Save thou swiftly go from me
Thou shalt surely grieve me sore
That I ne'er may love thee more."
Then again she answered: "Nay,
If so be, then Love, Good-day,

God, Who died upon the Tree,
Save thee, if His Will so be!"   450
Then the kerchieves hath he wound
Round his arms, full tightly bound,
For he surely hoped that day
With some wile the lion to slay;
But a kirtle did he wear
And the lion awaited there.
Then the jailer came anon,
Other two with him have gone,
With them lead the lion strong,
Claws had he both sharp and long,   460
Richard cried: "Help, Heaven's King!"
Swift the lion on him did spring,
Fain had torn him in that tide —
But King Richard sprang aside,
With his fist the lion he spurned
That the beast around he turned,
Famished was the lion *sans* fail,
Wrathful, bit at his own tail,
Then the wall he clawed that stead,
All about his paws he spread,   470
Roaring loud, with jaws gaped wide —
Richard saw right well that tide
What to do — he thrust full fast,
Down his throat his arm he passed,
Tore out with his hand the heart,
Lungs and liver rent apart,
On the ground the lion fell dead —
Scatheless all the king that stead;
Down he kneeléd in that place,   479
Gave God thanks for this, His Grace,
Shielding him from shame and harm —
Then he took the heart, yet warm,
Bare it swiftly to the hall,
'Fore the king and courtiers all;
Sat the king at meat that day,
Dukes and earls in great array,
On the board the salt it stood —
Richard pressed out all the blood,
Dipped the heart the salt within,
(All beheld who sat therein,)   490
Without bread the heart he ate.
Marvelled much the king thereat:
"Now it seemeth me, I wis,
This a fiend and no man is,
Who hath now my lion slain

And his heart from out him ta'en,
Of good will that heart did eat,
Men shall call him, as is meet,
Christened king of greatest fame,
Cœur-de-Lion shall be his name!"   500
Speak we no more of this thing,
Hearken how he did, the king,
Mournful doth he fare withal,
Caitiff he himself doth call,
Cursed the hour that he was born
To be thus of son forlorn,
And his daughter shamed to see,
While his lion slain should be.
Earls and barons came, I ween,
To her lord she hastes, the queen,   510
Asked of him what did him ail?
"Well ye wot," he quoth, "the tale,
If I now in mourning go
'T is for Richard, my strong foe,
Who such harm on me hath wrought
Yet may not to death be brought;
So I deem that from his hand
Ransom I may well demand,
'Gainst the Sacrament hath he
Shamed my daughter, verily,   520
From each church where priest shall sing,
Mass be said, or bell shall ring,
If two chalices there be
One of them shall be for me;
And if there be more than twain
I to have the half am fain.
When they bring me this as fee
Then shall Richard be set free."
Thus, he said it shall be done —
Then his lords assent anon,   530
And they call King Richard near
That the judgment he may hear.
Richard cometh to the hall,
Greets the king and barons all,
Quoth the king: "Know, verily,
This our judgment and decree,
Thou shalt ransom pay forthright
For thyself, and for each knight.
Every church throughout thy land
Shall pay tribute to my hand,   540
Where two chalices there be
One of them be brought to me,

And wherever there be more
I take half of all the store.
Thro' thy kingdom, mark it now,
I will have the half, I trow,
When thou this to me shalt pay
Thou hast leave to wend thy way,
And my daughter take with thee
That ye twain I no more see."   550
Richard quoth: "As thou hast said,
So our forward fast be made."
Then spake Richard, fair and free,
Said: "Who now will go for me,
Seek my chancellor straightway
That he here my ransom pay?
Whoso, faithful, comes again
Shall have guerdon for his pain."
Rose a knight so courteous there,
Said: "Thine errand I will bear."   560
Richard did a letter write,
(A skilled clerk did it indite,)
And therein he mention made
How the ransom should be paid.
"Greeting shall ye bear again
Unto my archbishops twain,
To my chancellor now say
That my letter he obey,
And if they in nowise fail
It shall mickle them avail."   570
Then he sealed the script that day —
The knight maketh no delay
But made ready speedily
For to sail across the sea.
When he to his goal was brought
On his task forgat he naught,
Swift to London did he go,
There the folk he found in woe,
With the letter, as I say,
To th' archbishops made his way,   580
Bade them swift the writing read —

"It was sent in mickle need."
There they read among them all
How the matter did befall,
How their king, betrayed to hate,
In Almayne did ransom wait:
"He hath slain the emperor's son,
And his daughter hath undone,
And hath killed his lion also —
All this harm he there did do."   590
Straight they bade their clerks to hie
To the churches, severally,
That their errand swift be wrought
And the treasure to them brought.
"Messenger," so spake they there,
"Here shalt dwell, and thus shalt fare;
Bishops five shall ride with thee,
And five barons, certainlie,
Other folk shalt have enow,
We shall fail thee not, I trow."   600
Of each kirk, both less and more,
Gather they the treasure store,
O'er the sea their way they take
That they may their offering make,
Thus unto the city fare,
To the king their greeting bear,
Quoth, as they themselves bethought:
"We have here the ransom brought,
Take it, as your will shall be,   609
And set these, your prisoners, free."
Quoth the king: "They have my leave,
I will them no longer grieve."
Takes his daughter by the hand,
Bids her straightway leave his land.
Then the queen, in that same hour
Called her daughter to her bower,
Saith, "Thou here shalt dwell with me
Till King Richard sends for thee,
As a king sends for his queen —
This the better rede, I ween."   620

SIR ORFEO

We read full oft, and find it writ,
As ancient clerks give us to wit,
The lays that harpers sung of old
Of many a diverse matter told.
Some sang of bliss; some heaviness;
And some of joy and gladsomeness.
Of treason some, and some of guile;
Of happenings strange that chanced
    awhile!
Of knightly deeds; of ribaldry;
And some they tell of Faërie.   10
But of all themes that men approve
Methinks the most they be of Love.
In Britain first these lays were wrought,
There were they made, and thence were
    brought.
They told of venturous deeds and days,
Whereof the Britons made their lays,
For, an they heard a story told
Of wondrous hap that chanced of old,
They took their harp withouten fail,
Made them a lay, and named the tale.
And of the deeds that thus befell   21
A part, not all, is mine to tell;
So hearken, lordings, true and leal,
The tale of Orfeo's woe and weal.

This Orfeo, he was king with crown,
A mighty lord of high renown,
A stalwart man, and hardy too,
Courteous and free of hand also.
His parents might their lineage trace
To Pluto, and to Juno's race,   30
Who, for their marvels manifold,
Were held as gods in days of old.
Now chief of all the arts that be
Sir Orfeo loved good minstrelsy,
He honoured much the harpers' skill,
And harboured them of right good
    will.
Himself upon the harp would play,
And set thereto his mind alway,
Till such his skill that, far or near,

No better harper might ye hear.   40
For never man of woman born,
Altho' for sorrow all forlorn,
But an he heard Sir Orfeo play
Forgot his heaviness straightway,
And deemed himself in Paradise
For joy of such sweet melodies.
In Traciens Orfeo held his court,
A city strong, a goodly fort,
And with him reigned his queen so fair,
Dame Heurodis, beyond compare   50
The fairest lady, so I read,
That ever ware this mortal weed;
So full of love and gentleness
That none might tell her goodliness.

It was the coming in of May,
When gay and gladsome is the day,
Vanished the chilly winter showers,
And every field is full of flowers,
When blossoms deck the bough so green,
And every heart is glad, I ween,   60
That Heurodis, the queen, was fain
To take unto her maidens twain,
And go forth on a morning tide
For pastime to an orchard side,
To hear the birds sing loud and low,
And watch the blossoms bud and blow.
And there they sat them down all three
Beneath a spreading elder tree;
And as they sat in shadows green
A slumber deep o'ertook the queen.   70
That sleep her maidens dare not break,
But let her lie, nor bade her wake;
And so she slept the morning through
Until the day to even drew.
But when she woke, ah me, the change!
Strange were her words, her actions
    strange;
She wrung her hands, and tare her face
Till that the blood ran down apace;
Her goodly robes she soon had torn,
As if of sense she were forlorn.   80

Affrighted were those maidens twain,
Back to the hall they ran amain,
And of their lady's woeful plight
They told each gallant squire and
     knight,
And aid to hold the queen they sought,
For sure they deemed her all distraught!
Forth run the knights, the ladies run,
Full sixty maids, if ever a one,
Swift to the orchard shade they hie,
And take the queen up speedily;   90
They bear her to her couch at last,
And there by force they hold her fast,
But she crieth what no man under-
     stands,
And will up and away from their holding
     hands.

Straight to the king they brought the
     word,
('T was the sorriest tidings he ever
     heard,)
Ten of his knights he called that hour,
And gat him to his lady's bower;
He looked on the queen right woefully,
And spake: "Sweet heart what aileth
     thee?   100
Wast ever wont to be so still,
And now thou criest wondrous shrill!
Thy flesh, but now so soft and white,
Hast torn with thy nails, a doleful sight!
Thy face, this morn so rosy red,
Is pale and wan, as thou wert dead;
Alack! and Alas! for thy fingers small,
Bloody they are, and white withal,
And thine eyes, so lovesome and shining
     clear,
Are e'en as a man's whose foe draws
     near.   110
Sweet heart, I prithee, hear my plaint,
Cease for a while thy sore complaint,
And say who hath wronged thee, when
     and how?
And if never a man may help thee
     now?"
Still was the queen for a little space,
While the bitter tears they flowed apace,

And she spake to the king with voice so
     drear:
"Alas, Sir Orfeo, lord most dear,
Since first the day we to wed were fain,
No word of wrath chanced between us
     twain,   120
But I, thy wife, have lovéd thee
E'en as my life, as thou hast me;
But now must we part, Ah woe the day!
Do what thou wilt, for I must away!"
"Alack," quoth the king: "forlorn am I,
Where goest thou, Sweeting, to whom,
     and why?
Whither thou goest I go with thee,
And where I may be shalt thou bide with
     me!"
"Nay, sir, nay, 't is an empty word,
For hearken and hear what hath chanced
     my lord: 130
As I lay but now by our orchard side,
And slumbered away the morning tide,
There came two gentle knights to me,
Armed at all points as knights should be,
And bade me come, nor make delay,
To speak with their lord the king
     straightway.
But I answered back, in queenly mood,
I might not, and would not if I could.
They turned them about, and fled
     amain,
And swift came the king with all his
     train,   140
A hundred knights, I wis, had he,
And a hundred maidens, fair to see;
And each one rode on a snow-white steed,
And each was clad in a snow-white
     weed,
Of all the folk that mine eyes have seen
They were the fairest folk, I ween.
The king ware a crown upon his head,
But it was not wrought of gold so red,
Nor of silver, but eke of a precious
     stone,
Bright as the noonday sun it shone.   150
And e'en as he came, without yea or
     nay,
Needs must I go with him straightway,

An I would or no, I must with him ride;
He gave me a palfrey by his side,
And he brought me unto his palace fair,
Builded and garnished beyond compare.
He showed me castles, and goodly
    towers,
Rivers and forests, meads with flowers,
And many a goodly steed and tall —
Then he turned again from his castle hall,
And brought me back to my orchard
    tree, 161
And spake in such wise as I tell to thee:
'Lady, to-morrow I bid thee be
Here, on this spot, 'neath this elder tree,
Hence shalt thou ride with me away,
To dwell at my court for ever and aye.
And if thou delayest to do my will
Or here, or there, it shall be thine ill;
For no man may help thee, or hold thee
    now,
Did they tear thee limb from limb, I
    trow; 170
For living or dying, or whole or torn,
Must thou ride with us to-morrow's
    morn!'"

"Alas!" cried the king: "now woe is me,
In sorry case methinks we be,
For liever were I to lose my life
Than thus to be robbed of my queen, my
    wife."
Counsel he craveth in this his need,
But no man knoweth a fitting rede.

.   .   .   .

'T is the morrow's dawn, and with cour-
    age high,
Sir Orfeo arms him fittingly, 180
And full a thousand knights with him
Are girded for combat stout and grim.
Forth with the queen they now will ride
To the elder tree by the orchard side,
And there in its shadow they take their
    stand,
And a shield-wall build on either hand,
And each man sweareth he here will stay,
And die, ere his queen be reft away.

Yet e'en as their lips might form the
    vow
The queen was gone, and no man knew
    how, 190
For the fairy folk, they have cast their
    spell,
And whither they bear her no man may
    tell!

Oh! then there was wailing, I ween, and
    woe,
To his chamber straight the king doth
    go,
And he casteth him down on the floor
    of stone,
And he maketh such dole, and such bit-
    ter moan,
That well nigh he wept his life away,
But counsel or aid was there none that
    day.
Then he bade his men come, one and all,
Earls, barons, and knights, to his council
    hall, 200
And they came — and he spake: "My
    lords so dear,
I take ye to witness before me here
That I give my high steward, and
    Seneschal,
The rule of my lands and kingdoms all;
I will have him stay in this my stead,
And rule the land, e'en as I were dead;
For since I have lost my wife, the queen,
The fairest lady this earth hath seen,
To dwell in the wilderness am I fain,
And look on no woman's face again, 210
But to spend my days, for evermore,
With the beasts of the field, in the wood-
    land hoar.
And when ye know that my days be
    done
Then come ye together, every one,
And choose you a king. — Now I go my
    way,
Deal with my goods as best ye may!"
Then a voice of weeping rose in the
    hall,
And a bitter cry from one and all,

And scarce might they speak, or old or
    young,
For fast-flowing tears that chained their
    tongue;   220
But they fell on their knees with one
    accord,
And they prayed, an so it might please
    their lord,
That he should not thus from his king-
    dom go —
"Go to," he quoth: "it must needs be
    so!"

Thus Sir Orfeo forth would fare,
Only a staff in his hand he bare,
Neither kirtle he took, nor hood,
Shirt, nor other vesture good,
But alway he took his harp in hand,
And gat him, barefoot, out of the land.
Never a man might with him go —   231
Alack! there was weeping, I ween, and
    woe,
When he who aforetime was king with
    crown
Passed, as a beggar, out of the town.
By woodland and moorland the king
    hath passed,
To the wilderness is he come at last,
There findeth he naught that his soul
    may please,
But ever he liveth in great misease.
He that was wrapt in fur withal
And slumbered soft 'neath purple and
    pall,   240
On the heather he now must rest his
    head,
With leaves and grass for a covering
    spread.
He that had castles, halls with towers,
Rivers, forests, fields with flowers,
Must make his bed 'neath the open sky
Though it snow and freeze right pierc-
    ingly.
Once knights and ladies, a goodly train,
To do him service were ever fain;
Now none are in waiting to please the
    king,

But the worms of the woodland coil and
    spring.   250
He that erstwhile might take his fill
Of food, or drink, as should be his will,
Now must he dig and delve all day
For the roots that may scarce his hunger
    stay.
In summer-time hath he fruit to eat,
The hedgerow berries, sour and sweet,
But in winter he liveth in sore misease,
On roots, and grasses, and bark of trees,
Till all his body was parched and dry,
And his limbs were twisted all awry;   260
Dear Lord, who may tell what sorrow
    sore
Sir Orfeo suffered, ten year, and more!
His beard, once black, is grey, I trow,
To his girdle clasp it hangeth low.
His harp, which was wont to be his glee,
He keepeth safe in a hollow tree,
And when the sun shone bright again
To take that harp he aye was fain,
And to temper the cords as should seem
    him good,
Till the music rang through the silent
    wood,   270
And all the beasts that in woodland
    dwell
For very joy at his feet they fell;
And all the birds in the forest free
Were fain to seek to the nearest tree,
And there on the branch they sat a-row
To hearken the melody sweet and low;
But when his harp he had laid aside
Nor beast nor bird would with him abide.

Oft-times, I ween, in the morning bright,
Sir Orfeo saw a fairer sight,   280
For he saw the king of the Fairies ride
A-hunting, down by the forest side;
With merry shout, and the horn's gay
    blast,
And the bay of the hounds the hunt
    swept past,
But never the quarry they ran to bay,
And he knew not whither they went
    alway.

In other fashion he 'ld come again,
With a warlike host in his royal train,
Full thousand riders richly dight,
Each armed as becometh a valiant
    knight,   290
Of steadfast countenance, tried and true;
Full many a banner above them flew,
As they rode with drawn sword, on war-
    fare bent,
But never he wist the way they went.
And then they would come in other
    guise:
Knights and ladies in joyous wise,
In quaint attire, as of days gone by,
Pacing a measure soberly,
To sound of tabor and pipe they pass,
Making sweet music, across the grass.
Again it chanced that he saw one day
Sixty ladies, who rode their way   302
Gracious and gay as the bird on the tree,
And never a knight in that company.
Falcon on hand those ladies ride,
On hawking bent, by the river side;
Full well they know it as right good
    haunt
Of mallard, of heron, and cormorant.
But now hath the waterfowl taken flight,
And each falcon chooseth his prey
    aright,   310
And never a one but hath slain its
    bird —
Then Sir Orfeo, laughing, spake this
    word:
"By faith, but those folk have goodly
    game,
I will get me thither, in Heaven's name,
Of old was I wont such sport to see —"
Thus he came to that goodly company,
And stayed his steps by a lady fair,
He looked on her face, and was well
    aware,
By all the tokens of truth, I ween,
That 't was Heurodis, his own sweet
    queen!   320
Each on the other to gaze was fain,
Yet never a word passed betwixt the
    twain,

But at sight of her lord in his sorry
    plight,
Who aforetime had been so fair a knight,
The tears welled forth, and flowed
    amain —
Then the ladies round they seized her
    rein,
By force must she ride with them away,
Nor with her lord might she longer stay.
"Alack!" quoth the king: "woe worth
    the day,
Thou sluggard, Death, why make de-
    lay?   330
Ah! wretched me that I live, I ween,
After the sight that mine eyes have seen!
Alas, that I needs must live my life
When I may not speak with my love,
    my wife!
And she dare not speak to her lord so
    true —
Now break my heart for ruth and rue!
I' faith," he quoth: "whate'er betide,
Whithersoe'er those ladies ride
That self-same way shall my footsteps
    fare,
For life, or death, I have little care!"   340
Then with staff in hand, and harp on
    back,
He gat him forth on the toilsome track,
Nor for stock nor for stone will he hold
    him still,
But goeth his way of right good will.
Thro' a cleft in the rock lies the Fairy
    way
And the king he follows as best he may;
Thro' the heart of the rock he needs
    must go,
Three miles and more, I would have ye
    know,
Till a country fair before him lay,   349
Bright with the sun of a summer's day;
Nor hill nor valley might there be seen
But level lands, and pastures green,
And the towers of a castle met his eye,
Rich and royal, and wondrous high.
The outer wall of that burg, I ween,
Was clear and shining, as crystal sheen,

And a hundred towers stood round
    about,
Of cunning fashion, and building stout.
Up from the moat sprang the buttress
    bold,   359
Arched and fashioned of good red gold.
The castle front was of carven stone,
All manner of beast might ye see
    thereon,
And the dwelling rooms within that hall
Of precious stones were fashioned all,
The meanest pillar ye might behold
Was covered all over with burnished
    gold.
Throughout that country 't was ever
    light,
For e'en when the hour was mirk mid-
    night
Those goodly jewels they shone, each one,
Bright as at midday the summer sun.
'T was past all speech, and beyond all
    thought,   371
The wondrous work that there was
    wrought,
Sir Orfeo deemed that at last his eyes
Beheld the proud palace of Paradise.
In at the gate rode the Fairy train,
And the king to follow them was full fain,
He knocketh loud at the portal high,
And the warder cometh speedily,
He asketh him where he fain would go?
"A harper am I" quoth Sir Orfeo;   380
"And methinks an thy lord would
    hearken me
I would solace his hours with min-
    strelsy."
With that the porter made no ado,
But gladly he let Sir Orfeo through.
The king looked round him, to left, to
    right,
And in sooth he beheld a fearsome sight;
For here lay folk whom men mourned as
    dead,
Who were hither brought when their
    lives were sped;
E'en as they passed so he saw them
    stand,

Headless, and limbless, on either hand.
There were bodies pierced by a javelin
    cast,   391
There were raving madmen fettered fast,
One sat erect on his warhorse good,
Another lay choked, as he ate his food.
Some floated, drowned, in the water's
    flow,
Shrivelled were some in the flame's
    fierce glow;
There were those who in childbed had
    lost their life,
Some as leman, and some as wife;
Men and women on every side
Lay as they sleep at slumbertide,   400
Each in such fashion as he might see
Had been carried from earth to Faërie.
And her, whom he loved beyond his life,
Dame Heurodis, his own sweet wife,
He saw, asleep 'neath an elder tree,
And knew by her raiment that it was
    she.
He looked his fill on these marvels all
And went his way to a kingly hall,
And he saw therein a goodly sight;
Beneath a canopy, rich and bright,   410
The king of the Fairies had his seat
With his queen beside him, fair and
    sweet,
Their crowns, their vesture, agleam with
    gold,
His eyes might scarcely the sight behold!
Sir Orfeo gazed for a little space,
Then he kneeled on his knees before the
    dais:
"O king," he said: "an it were thy will,
As minstrel I gladly would shew my
    skill,"
And the king he quoth: "Who mayest
    thou be
Who thus, unbidden, hast come to me?
I called thee not unto this my court, 421
No man of mine hath thee hither
    brought,
For never, I ween, since my reign began
Have I found so foolish and fey a man
Who found his way unto this my home,

Save that I bade him hither come!"
"Lord," quoth Sir Orfeo: "know for sure
That I am naught but a minstrel poor,
And e'en as the minstrel's manner is
I seek out castles and palaces;   430
Though never a welcome our portion be,
Yet needs must we proffer our min-
    strelsy!"
Then he took his harp, so sweet of tone,
And he sat him down before the throne,
And he tuned the strings, as well he
    knew,
And so sweet were the sounds that he
    from them drew,
That no man within the palace bound
But sped swift-foot as he heard the
    sound,
And down they lie around his feet,
The melody seemeth to them so sweet.
The king he hearkens, and holds him
    still,   441
Hearing the music of right good will,
And the gentle queen she was glad and
    gay,
Such comfort was their's from the min-
    strel's lay.
When he had finished his minstrelsy
Out spake the monarch of Faërie;
"Harper, right well hast thou played,
    I trow,
Whatever thou wilt thou may'st ask me
    now,
I am minded in royal wise to pay,
So what is thy will? Now harper say!"
Quoth Sir Orfeo: "Sire, I would pray
    of thee   451
One thing alone, that thou give to me
That lady fair, who is sleeping now
Beneath the shade of the elder bough!"
"Nay," quoth the king, "'t were an ill-
    matched pair
Did I send thee forth with that dame so
    fair,
For never a charm doth the lady lack,
And thou art withered, and lean, and
    black,   458
'T were a loathly thing, it seemeth me,

To send her forth in such company."
"Sire," quoth Sir Orfeo: "gentle king,
To my mind it seemeth a fouler thing
To belie a word, and forswear an oath —
Sire, thou didst promise, nothing loth,
That that which I asked I should have
    of thee,
And that promise thou need'st must keep
    to me!"
Then spake the king: "Since the thing
    be so
Take that lady fair by her hand, and go,
And may bliss and blessing with ye
    dwell!"
Then he kneeled adown, and thanked
    him well.   470

.   .   .   .

Sir Orfeo took his wife by the hand,
And he gat him swift from the Fairy land,
Out of the palace he took his way
By the self-same road he had come that
    day;
And never he stayed till again he stood
Before the walls of that city good
Where aforetime as king he ware the
    crown —
But no man knew him in all that town.
But a little way from the gate they go
Ere they come to a dwelling poor and low,
And Sir Orfeo deemed they would har-
    bour there,   481
For more would he know ere he 'ld
    further fare.
So he prayed, as a minstrel wan and
    worn,
They would shelter him and his wife
    till morn.
Then he asked his host who was ruler
    there?
And who was king of that country fair?
And the beggar answered him word for
    word,
And told him the tale as ye e'en have
    heard;
How ten years agone, in the month of
    May,   489

Their queen was by Fairies stolen away,
And, an exile, their king had wandered
  forth,
But none knew whither, or south, or
  north,
And the steward since then the land did
  hold —
And many another tale he told.
When the morrow came, and 't was high
  noontide,
The king bade his wife in the hut abide,
And he clad himself in the beggar's gown,
And, harp in hand, he sought the town,
And he gat him into that city good
That all men might see him an they
  would.   500
Earl, and baron, and lady bright,
Stared agape at the wondrous sight,
"Was ever," they cried, "such marvel
  known?
The man is by hair, as by moss, o'er-
  grown.
Look how his beard hangeth to his knee!
'T is e'en as he were a walking tree!"
Then as to the palace his way was set
In the city street the steward he met,
And he cried aloud: "Sir Steward, I pray
That thou have mercy on me this day;
I am a harper of heathennesse, 511
Help me in this my sore distress!"
And the steward he quoth: "Now come
  with me,
All that I have will I share with thee,
Every good harper is welcome here
For Sir Orfeo's sake, my lord most dear."
The steward he sat him down at the
  board,
With many a noble knight and lord,
All kinds of music had they, I trow, 519
Of trumpet and tabour, and harp enow,
In the hall was no lack of melody —
Sir Orfeo hearkened silently
And till all had done he held him still —
Then he took and tempered his harp with
  skill,
And I think me no tongue of man may
  say

How sweet was the music he made that
  day.
To hearken and hear was each one fain,
But the steward he gazed on the harp
  again,
And it seemed to him that he knew it
  well —
"Minstrel," he quoth: "I beseech thee
  tell   530
Whence had'st thou that harp, and who
  gave it thee?
I pray that thou truly answer me!"
"Lord," he quoth: "afar from here,
As I took my way through a desert drear.
I found, in a valley dark and grim,
A man by lions torn limb from limb,
Wolves gnawed his bones with teeth so
  sharp,
And beside the body I found this harp.
Full ten years ago it needs must be."
"Alas!" cried the steward: "now woe is
  me!"   540
'T was the corse of my lord Sir Orfeo!
Ah! wretched me, what shall I do?
Of so good a lord am I left forlorn,
Methinks 't were best I had ne'er been
  born!
Ah woe, that for him such lot was cast,
And so foul a death he must die at last!"
With that, the steward, he swooning fell,
But the lords they comforted him right
  well,
For no man so sad who draweth breath
But findeth healing at last in death.

. . . .

By all these tokens Sir Orfeo knew 551
A loyal man was his steward and true,
One who loved his lord, nor his pledge
  would break —
Then up he stood, and on this wise
  spake:
"Hearken, I pray thee, steward, my
  word,
Put case I were Orfeo now, thy lord,
Say I had suffered torments sore
In the wilderness full ten years and more,

That at last I had won my queen away
From the land where the Fairy king
    holds sway,   560
And that we had safely come, we twain,
Back to this city and burg again,
And my wife abode with a beggar poor
While I came again to my palace door,
In lowly guise, thus to test thee still,
And see if thou bore me right good
    will;
I wot, an I found thee so leal and true,
My coming again thou should'st never
    rue,
Verily, and indeed, without yea or nay,
The throne should be thine when I
    passed away!   570
But if news of my death had been joy to
    thee
Thou hadst passed from this house right
    speedily!"
Then never a man at the castle board
But knew that this was indeed their
    lord,
The steward right well his master knew,
Over and over the board he threw,
And low at Sir Orfeo's feet would fall —
And so do the lordings, one and all,
And they cry with one voice till the
    rafters ring: 579
"Thou art our lord, Sire, and our king!"
Blithe of his coming they were and gay,

To his chamber they led the king straight-
    way,
And they bathed him well, and trimmed
    his hair,
And clad him in royal raiment fair.
And then with solemn and stately train
They brought the queen to her burg
    again,
With all manner of music and min-
    strelsy;
I' faith there was joyous melody,
And the tears of joy they fell like rain
When the folk saw their king and queen
    again.   590

.   .   .   .

Now is Orfeo crowned once more, I wis,
With his lady and queen, Dame Heuro-
    dis,
And many a year they lived those two,
And after them ruled the steward so true.
Harpers in Britain, as I was told,
Heard how this marvel had chanced of
    old,
And thereof they made a lay so sweet,
And gave it the king's name, as was
    meet.
"*Sir Orfeo*," thus the title stood,
Good are the words, the music good —
Thus came Sir Orfeo out of his care, 601
God grant to us all as well to fare!

SIR TRISTREM

I was at Ercildoune,
With Thomas spake I there,
In mystic rede and rune
He told who Tristrem bare —
(He ware a royal crown —)
And who gave fostering fair,
A baron of renown
E'en as their elders were.
Thus, year by year,
Thomas, he told in town   10
What ventures were their share.

Of this sweet summer's day
In winter naught is seen,
The groves be waxen gray
That in their hour were green;
So doth this world alway
(So do I wot and ween),
Our sires be passed away
Who right good men had been
And so abide —   20
Of one I make my theme
Whose fame has waxen wide.

Roland would thole no wrong
Though Morgan ruled o'er all;
He brake his castles strong,
And levelled many a hall.
He smote his hosts among —
Loss did his foes befall,
And strife that duréd long. —
For peace did Morgan call,   30
Full sore his need,
Of fear was he the thrall
Lest death should be his meed.

For thus the strife began,
(I rede ye well 't was so)
Betwixt the Duke Morgan
And Roland, fiercest foe.
The land they overran,
And wrought the poor much woe,
They slew full many a man,   40
In strife they were not slow
But men of price;
The one was Duke Morgan,
The other Roland Riis.

Those knights, I ween, were wise,
A cov'nant made they there
To rest in peaceful guise
For seven years full fair.
The duke and Roland Riis
Thereto they steadfast sware.   50
Forthwith, as knights of prize
To England would they fare
And see with sight
Mark, who the royal crown ware,
And many a gallant knight.

To Mark the king they wend
With followers, famed in fight,
The venture to the end
They told him, fair and right.
He prayed them, as their friend,   60
Abide, both day and night,
In peace; thereto they lend
Their will, each gallant knight,
For act and deed.
To Tourney they invite
Full many, stout on steed.

A joyful man is he
Who will the Tourney cry;
Maidens his deeds shall see
As o'er the wall they lie.   70
They question fair and free:
"Who hath the mastery?"
Men say: "The best is he
The knight from Ermonie!"
Henceforth, in bower,
The chosen love is he
Of maiden Blancheflower.

That maiden, fair and bright,
She called her masters three,
And quoth: "That stranger knight   80
Full sore hath wrongéd me,
Methinks, by Magic's might —
A wondrous man is he
Thus through my heart to smite!
Wounded to death I be,
And that so soon!
Save he the wrong make right
My night is come ere noon!"

'T were hard his praise to mend,
That wise and stalwart wight,   90
Unto the wide world's end
Was never better knight,
Nor truer to his friend,
And Roland Riis he hight.
To battle did he wend,
And wounds he won in fight.
Full sore and fell;
Blancheflower, the maiden bright,
The tale she heard them tell.

And cried, "Ah, wellaway!"   100
When men sware it was so;
Her mistress did she pray
That she might straightway go
There, where the good knight lay,
She swooned for very woe;
He comforted the may,
And in that hour the two
Begat a son —
Whom men as Tristrem know
Where'er the tale doth run.   110

That oath the foeman sware
And to maintain had thought,
Duke Morgan brake his share,
Of truce would he have naught.
Rohant, of fealty fair,
A writing swift he wrought,
And bade to Roland bear;
His lord he there besought,
In this his need,
To help him as he ought,   120
Or all were lost indeed.

Then Roland Riis in woe
Prayed leave of Mark the king:
"Hence must I swiftly go
For men ill tidings bring;
A false and faithless foe
Seeketh my undoing —"
Blancheflower full soon must know,
Her hands the maid must wring
For sorrow sore: 130
"Myself to ruin I bring
For love I to thee bore!

"In shame I bide here still,
Thou sailest over sea —"
Quoth Roland: "Here I dwell
Save that thou wend with me!"
"To bide for me were ill,
Behold, and thou mayest see!
Steadfast my wish and will
From hence to fare with thee,   140
That I may find
Thy fair folk, frank and free,
Thy goodly land, and kind!"

They make them ready there,
No longer will they bide,
With banners floating fair
From haven forth they ride.
To Roland's castle fair
The winds their vessel guide.
Her sails adown they tear,   150
Forth from the ship they stride;
The knights, steel-clad,
In Roland's service tried,
To do his will were glad.

Swift Rohant's rede was sped:
"This maiden shall be our's,
With Roland Riis to wed,
And rule within these towers.
Fittest to share his bed,
Brightest in lady's bower,   160
None fairer e'er was bred
Than maiden Blancheflower,
That lady sweet!"
After love's richest dower
The parting followed fleet.

The folk, right well they know
How Morgan subtly wrought,
With wisdom, to and fro,
Among his men he sought.
His true knights, high and low,   170
Were to his summons brought;
With banners all a-row,
In weapons lacking naught;
That knight so bold,
As crownéd king he thought
To win him fame untold.

With folk on field arrayed,
Morgan his foe would bide,
Naught Roland's onslaught stayed,
Against him would he ride.   180
Sooth, 't was a mighty raid!
Sorrow befell each side,
With prowess proud displayed
Roland, he felled their pride.
'T was but with pain
Morgan escaped that tide,
Well nigh had he been slain!

The foemen came anew
Where Roland valiant stood,
The helms they hack and hew,   190
Thro' burnies wells the blood.
Then nigh to death there drew
Full many a hero good,
Of Roland men may rue
The death, by Holy Rood!
A hero bold,
His son, of valiant mood,
Payment full dearly told.

A rueful rede now hear
Of Roland Riis the knight,   200
Three hundred slew he there
With sword so keen and bright.
Of all who foemen were
None might him fell in fight.
In traitorous wise they fare,
And thus the death-blow smite,
With cruel guile
To death the hero dight —
Alas! Woe worth the while!

The steed his master bore   210
Dead, on his homeward way;
The folk marvelled the more
Who saw his knightly play.
They came with rueful lore
To Blancheflower straightway,
For her I sorrow sore —
On childbed, where she lay
In woe, was born
Sir Tristrem that same day —
She died ere morrow's morn.   220

A ring of richest hue
She ware, that lady free,
She gave it Rohant true
Her son's henceforth to be.
"Then grimy brother knew,
My father gave it me;
King Mark methinks shall rue
When he that same shall see,
And sorely weep!
As Roland lovéd thee   230
The ring for his son keep!"

The folk around her bed
Sadly their lady see, —
"Roland my lord is dead,
He speaks no more with me:" —
"Our lady too, is sped,
She dieth verily:
What do we in this stead?"
"As God wills, let it be
For good or ill." —   240
Right sad it was to see
Her lying cold and still.

Begotten thus, and born,
Was he, the child of woe;
Rohant was all forlorn
Nor wist what he might do.
His own true wife that morn
To childbed needs must go:
He sware that twins were born,
To joy was turned his woe —   250
Now shall ye list,
The child at court they know
As Tram before the Trist.

The duke was well content, —
His foe was slain alway;
His messengers he sent,
The folk he straight did pray,
To yield to his intent,
And to his word obey,   259
Yield town, and tower, and tent —
None might his word gainsay,
But all right soon
Unto his will had bent,
No king had better done.

Who gave rich jewels of gold?
Duke Morgan, he alone;
Ruthless of heart and cold,
To face him was there none.
Unto his counsel told
Was Rohant, true as stone,   270
In wisdom versed of old
By craft he held his own
His heart to hide,
Perished were blood and bone
If hope were laid aside!

Now Rohant, evermore,
Hides Tristrem, blithe is he,
The child of scholar's lore
Learneth full speedily;
By books he setteth store,   280
And studieth readily;
Glad hearts, in sooth, they bore
Who owed him fealty.
The lad, so bright,
His skill shewed readily
Against them when he might.

Now years full fifteen long
He hid, Rohant the true,
Tristrem, and every song
He taught him, old and new;　290
And laws of right and wrong,
And wise saws not a few;
The chase he followed long,
And to such skill he drew
I ween, that thus
Of venerie he knew
More than Manerius.

A ship of Norroway
Came to Sir Rohant's hold,
With hawks both white and gray,
And cloths full fair in fold;　301
So Tristrem heard men say —
For sport the lad so bold
Would twenty shillings pay
E'en as Sir Rohant told,
And ever taught;
The seamen to him sold
The fairest hawk they brought.

A chessboard by a chair
He saw, and fain would play;　310
The captain, debonair,
Quoth: "Child, what wilt thou lay?"
"Against this hawk so fair
Shillings two score, I say,
He who calls 'Mate' shall bear
The twain with him away." —
The captain bold,
With good will spake straightway:
"That cov'nant will I hold."

Their pledge in order lies,　320
To play they now begin;
They set the board in guise
A right long match to win.
The stakes they 'gan to rise —
Tristrem shewed guile therein,
He dealt as one full wise,
And gave as he might win,
The lad so brave;
The game's short space within
Six hawks he won, and gave.　330

Rohant would go on shore,
His sons he called away,
The fairest hawk he bore
Tristrem had won that day.
And with him he left more
Money, wherewith to play;
The captain roundly swore
Silver and gold to lay
In stake that stound —
Tristrem, he won alway　340
Of him a hundred pound.

Tristrem won all they laid;
A treason there they planned;
E'en as his master said
That even was at hand,
The while they sat and played
They gat them from the land.
Their sails the breezes fanned;
O'er waves they leap —
Blithely they leave the strand;　350
But Tristrem sore did weep.

They set his master free,
Gave boat, and eke an oar,
Crying: "Here is the sea,
And yonder be the shore,
Choose what thy lot shall be,
The which were wiser lore,
To sink, or sail; with me
The child, for evermore
Shall sail the flood."　360
Tristrem, he wept full sore;
The captain deemed it good.

Nine weeks, I ween, and more,
Those seamen sailed the flood,
Till anchor failed, and oar,
And storms their course with-
　　stood.
Tristrem, the blame he bore
For this, their mournful mood;
Small use the steersman's lore,
The waves they were so wood　370
With storm and wind —
To land their will was good
Might they a haven find.

To land they drew anigh,
A forest as it were,
The hills, they were full high,
The holts, they were full fair.
To shore right speedily
Tristrem the seamen bare,
His gains, his jewellery,   380
And bread, they gave him there,
The lad so mild —
In calm they thence did fare,
On shore they left the child.

The wind full fair did hold;
Alone on land was he,
His heart for fear grew cold
When he no ship might see.
His grief to Christ he told —
The Lord Who died on Tree —   390
"My plight, Dear Lord behold,
And guidance send to me
After Thy Will;
And of Thy Mercy free
Let me not come to ill!"

Thomas, he asks alway,
Who would of Tristrem hear
The tale aright must say,
And make each step full clear.
"Of a prince proud in play   400
Now hearken, lordings dear,
Who knoweth more alway
Let him shew counsel here
As courteous friend;
The tale to all men dear
Let each man praise at end."

The robe that wrapped him round
Tristrem from ship had brought,
'T was of a bliaunt brown,
The richest that was wrought.   410
So Thomas told in town —
Of that land he knew naught,
So, seemly, sat him down,
And ate as good he thought,
And then, anon,
The forest path he sought
Whenas his meal was done.

The track it was not light,
His prize with him he bore,
The hills of goodly height   420
He climbed, and holts so hoar.
The road it came in sight —
(Well knew he woodland lore!)
He struck the pathway right,
Two palmers there before
He saw, and quoth:
"Whence came ye to this shore?"
"Of England be we both."

Fearing they might him slay
He said he sought the king,   430
Money would gladly pay
(To each man ten shilling)
For guidance on the way,
Would they to palace bring —
They sware right gladly: "Yea,
By Heaven's Almighty King
'T were done right soon—"
Full wise his ordering,
Swiftly he had his boon.

Fair was the forest wide,   440
With game well plenishéd,
The court was nigh beside,
His guides toward it sped.
Tristrem saw huntsmen ride,
A leash of hounds they led;
A booty, in that tide
They bare, of harts well fed
Across their steed —
Tristrem they, in that stead,
Beheld, in goodly weed.   450

Quartered the beasts they bare, —
In simple wise they wrought
E'en as they cattle were
At Martinmas i-bought!
Tristrem, he haled them there,
Their ways full strange he thought,
And quoth: "Now saw I ne'er
Quarry in such wise brought
Of men's good will;
Of such craft I know naught,   460
Or else ye do full ill!"

Upstood a serjant bold,
And thus to Tristrem said:
"I wot our sires of old
On us this custom laid,
If other thou dost hold
There lies a beast unflayed,
Thy will in act be told,
Deal with it unafraid,
We are full fain   470
To see —" The huntsmen stayed
Their steeds, and gazed amain.

Tristrem, the breast he slit,
The tongue laid with the pride,
The hams, with skill, I wit,
He carved, and set aside.
The belly then he split
And laid it open wide,
With skilful strokes and fit,
He reft away the hide.   480
I wot and ween
The hart he trimmed that tide
As many since have been.

The first joint carven fair
The bowels he cast away,
The knee-joints sundered were,
In twain they severed lay.
Right well his part he bare —
The hounds they had their pay,
The numbles did he share   490
As all men saw that day;
Before their eyes
He cleft the spine alway,
The backbone cut crosswise.

The huntsman's share by right
The shoulder left shall be
With liver, heart and lights,
Which men do call *quirrie ;*
Hide for the hounds he dights,
And bids them all to see.   500
Now on the tree there lights
The raven for his fee
And sits a-row —
"Now, huntsmen, where be ye,
The prize in form to blow?"

The flesh on fork they bound,
And eke the gargilon;
A hunters' blast they wound
With cadence true and tone.
A messenger they found,   510
Bade seek the king alone,
And tell him, at that stound,
How all were fitly done
And homeward brought —
Then Mark the King with crown,
Right fair such tidings thought.

The merry blast they blew
Brought joy to many a heart,
None there such custom knew,
Up from the board they start.   520
"Forsooth, some huntsman new
Hath taught our men this art!
Methinks 't is fair and due
To others to impart
An unknown lore —"
Thus blithe were they of heart
Who came the king before.

Quoth Mark: "Where wast thou born?
Who art thou, *Bel ami ?* '
Tristrem, he spake that morn,   530
"Fair sire, in Hermonie
My father dwells, forlorn,
Rohant, by name is he,
Right skilful on the horn,
And king of Venerie
In all men's thought."
Mark deemed 't was verity,
Of Rohant he knew naught.

The king, he said no more,
But washed and gat to meat,   540
Bread lay each man before,
Enough they had to eat.
Whether they set most store
On ale, or red wine sweet,
At each one's will they bore
Great horns, or goblets meet
To fit their mood —
At will they kept their seat,
And rose when seemed them good.

A harper made a lay —   550
(Tristrem spake fair and free —)
The harper went his way:
"An thou can'st, better me!"
"An I do not this day
Wron'g have I done to thee!"
The harper quoth straightway:
"My harp I yield to thee
Of right good grace —"
Before the monarch's knee,
Tristrem must take his place.   560

Right gladsome were they all,
And marked his skill therein,
Each man throughout the hall
Were fain the child to win.
King Mark did Tristrem call,
That lad of royal kin,
Clad him in silken pall
And robe of fairest skin,
For raiment meet —
The royal bower within   570
He maketh music sweet.

Now Tristrem leave we there,
To Mark is he right dear —
Sorrow is Rohant's share,
No tidings may he hear;
Afar he needs must fare,
With sad and rueful cheer,
The pilgrim's staff he bare;
Through seven kingdoms drear
Tristrem he sought —   580
Riven the robes he ware,
His heart it failed him naught.

And still he naught might learn,
Rohant, that noble knight —
He wist not where to turn,
Bereft was he of might.
Men forced him then to earn
His bread, as labouring wight,
With hinds, on straw and fern
To lie throughout the night —   590
At dawn, I ween,
Those Palmers hove in sight
Whom Tristrem erst had seen.

The question ever new,
He asked, whate'er befell —
The lad the Palmers knew,
And where he now should dwell;
"His robe is of one hue,
Of bliaunt, sooth to tell,
His name is Tristrem true,   600
The meat he carveth well
The king before —"
For guidance did he tell
Ten shillings from his store:

"The same I'll give to ye,"
Quoth Rohant, "an ye may
Shew that same court to me."
The Palmers answered: "Yea."
Joyful at heart was he,
And paid them there straightway,   610
Of money round, in fee,
Ten shillings good that day,
And more, for gain —
Of Tristrem speedily
To hear, was he full fain.

Tristrem is his delight,
Of him he speaks alway —
The porter, in despite,
Quoth: "Churl, get thee away,
Or else I swift shall smite —   620
Why tarry here all day?"
He gave him there forthright
(The porter ne'er said Nay)
A ring in hand —
Wise man was he alway
Who first gave gifts in land!

Rohant, of hand so free,
He bade to pass the gate,
The ring was fair to see,
The gift were ill to mate.   630
The usher bade him flee:
"Churl, tempt thou not thy fate,
Broken thy head shall be,
And thou, ere it be late,
Trodden to ground —"
Rohant quoth: "Now let be,
And help me at this stound."

That man, so meek on mold,
Held forth another ring.
The usher took the gold,   640
('T were meeter for a king.)
Thus to the royal hold
He paid his entering,
And unto Tristrem bold
The usher would him bring,
And straightway brought —
Tristrem deemed wondering
A stranger him besought.

Tho' men had soothly sworn
The news he scarce might heed   650
That Rohant e'er had worn
So torn and rent a weed.
He prayed him fast that morn:
"Fair child, so God thee speed,
Wast thou not from me torn?
Hast thou forgot indeed?" —
Rohant again
He knew, and knelt with speed,
And clasped, and kissed, full fain.

"Father, now vex thee naught,   660
Right welcome shalt thou be,
By God, Who man hath bought,
Full hardly knew I thee!
With toil thou hast me sought,
To know that grieveth me —"
To Mark the word he brought:
"Wilt thou my father see
Here, in thy sight?
I'll robe him fittingly
As doth become a knight."   670

Tristrem, no more afraid,
Told Mark how he must fare,
How he with shipmen played,
How him from land they tare;
How storms their course delayed,
Brake oar and anchor there;
"My winnings then they laid
In hand, and bade me fare,
Set me on ground —
I climbed the holts so bare   680
Till I thy huntsmen found."

Rohant from bath did win;
A barber brought they there
Who shaved him, cheek and chin,
All snow-white was his hair.
In robe of costly skin
They garbed him, fresh and fair,
Rohant, of noble kin,
That raiment fitly ware
As knight so bold;   690
Who that had seen him there
Might for a prince him hold.

His tale in fitting wise
He told, though he came late;
Tristrem, in courtly guise,
To hall he led him straight.
Men quoth, none might devise
A fairer form or state
Than his they did despise,
And turn back from the gate   700
With beggar's fare —
Now no man bare him hate,
But bade him welcome there.

Water they asked straightway,
The cloth and board were spread,
With meats and drink alway,
And service, swiftly sped.
Tristrem they serve that day,
And Rohant — fitly fed,
They fain would go their way —   710
The king, with crownéd head,
He rose that tide —
An I have rightly read,
He set him by his side.

Rohant spake free and fair,
Thus was his tale begun:
"An ye wist who he were
Tristrem your love had won.
Your sister did him bear —"
(The king he heard anon)   720
"I owe him fealty fair,
By birth is he no son
To me, O King!
See, ere her race was run
Blancheflower gave me this ring!"

"When Roland Riis, the bold,
In strife did Morgan meet —"
Ere yet the tale was told
Rohant full sore did greet.
Mark saw that knight so old,   730
How fast the tears did fleet,
He took that ring of gold;
His sister's token meet
And sign, he knew,
Raised Tristrem to his feet,
With kiss, as kinsman true.

They kissed him, one and all,
Both lady fair and knight,
The servants there in hall,
And many a maiden bright.   740
Tristrem did Rohant call,
And prayed him there forthright:
"Sir, how did this befall,
How may I prove aright,
Nor doubt remain?
Tell me, for God's great Might,
How was my father slain?"

Rohant, he told anon
The venture, fierce and keen,
How battle had begun,   750
How erst the strife had been.
How Blancheflower, she was won,
The love the twain between:
"When Roland's race was run,
And Blancheflower dead, I ween,
Full sore afraid
Of Morgan, foe so keen,
My son thou wast, I said."

Tristrem, with kindling eye,
Before the king came he —   760
"Now into Ermonie
My heart, it draweth me;
Thither I fain would fly —
My leave I take of thee;
Morgan I will defy,
I slay him, or he me,
With good right hand —
Else none my face shall see
Again on England's strand!"

Woeful was Mark that day,   770
And heavily he sighed:
"Tristrem, I bid thee stay,
On English land abide.
Morgan is ill to slay,
His knights are men of pride;
Tho' thou be brave alway
Let others with thee ride
In rank and row —
Take Rohant at thy side,
Thy friends he best will know!"   780

To arms, the king, he bade
The folk throughout his land;
Tristrem, for better aid,
He knighted with his hand,
And gave him, fair arrayed,
The bravest of his band
To ride with him on raid
And by him true to stand
As staff and stay —
Yet, bound in sorrow's band,   790
No man might make him gay.

Nor would he dwell a night —
No more was there to say,
Ten hundred men of might
They rode with him away.
Rohant, that gallant knight,
Ready was he alway,
His castle hove in sight,
Upon the seventh day
Their goal they won;   800
His marshal did he pay —
Gave knighthood to each son.

His friends they were full fain,
(Small blame they won thereby!)
That he had come again
Thus, unto Ermonie.
Tidings were brought amain
That Morgan lay hard by,
Of that was Tristrem fain —
"With Morgan speak will I   810
And that with speed;
Too long we idle lie,
Myself must serve my need!"

Tristrem, that valiant knight,
Made ready as he swore,
Fifteen the tale of knights
Who rode with him, no more.
To court they came forthright —
(Men served their lord before,)
All deemed they saw with sight   820
Ten kings' sons pass the door,
And each, unsought,
The head of a wild boar
As goodly gift had brought.

(A thought to Rohant came,
And to his knights quoth he:
"As woman dowered with shame
Twofold, it were to me,
An harm to Tristrem came;
Ill guardians sure were we!   830
Now arm ye at this same,
My knights, and hasten ye
On swift steeds lithe,
Till that I Tristrem see
My heart shall ne'er be blithe!")

Tristrem would speech unfold —
"Sir King, God deal with thee
As I in love thee hold,
And thou hast dealt with me!"
Morgan made answer bold: 840
"I pray, my lord so free,
Or ban or bliss be told
Thine own the cost may be,
Thou daring knight!
Now make thou known to me
Thine errand, here forthright!"

"Amends! For father slain,
And theft of Ermonie!"
The Duke, he spake again:
"Certes, thou say'st no lie,   850
An thou for strife art fain,
'Amends!' thou well mayst cry!
Therefore, thou haughty swain,
I'll meet thee presently
In fitting guise;
Art thou come hastily
From Mark, thy kinsman wise?

"Thou shalt my will abide —
Thou fool, my wrath to dare!
Thy mother's shame to hide   860
She with her love must fare!
Now would'st thou come with pride;
Betake thee otherwhere!"
Tristrem, he spake that tide:
"In that, thou liest, I swear!
The truth I know —"
With a loaf Morgan there
At Tristrem dealt a blow.

Down to his breast amain
It gushed, the crimson blood;   870
His sword was bare for bane,
Nigh to the duke he stood;
He smote through bone and brain,
As one in murderous mood.
E'en as, with knightly train,
Came Rohant, friend so good,
In welcome aid —
All that their hand withstood
With life the forfeit paid.

As prisoner did they take   880
Baron, and earl, and knight,
I wot for Morgan's sake
Many were slain outright.
Many a shaft they shake —
Riven the shields so bright —
Many a head they brake —
Methinks, in sorry plight
Were found their foes —
From nones it was till night
Before the battle's close.   890

Thus Tristrem, fair of face,
Morgan the duke hath slain,
He gave his foes no grace
Till every hold were ta'en.
They yield in every place
Cities and towers amain,
The folk, they sought his grace,
No foeman did remain
Upon the land —
His father's slayer slain   900
All bowed them to his hand.

Two years he ruled that land,
And fitting laws did cry;
All bowed them to his hand, —
Almain, and Ermonie,
Both at his will did stand
Ready to do or die.
Rohant he gave command
And set him there on high,
E'en at his side —   910
"Rohant your cause shall try
And rule this land so wide."

"Rohant and his sons five
Shall hold this land of me,
The while he be alive
His shall it surely be —
What boots it more to strive?
Farewell, I bid to ye,
Southward my course I'll drive,
Mine uncle Mark to see   920
In life once more."
He turned, Tristrem the free,
His face to England's shore.

Goodly his furnishing,
And goodly his ships' fare;
Rohant he left as king
O'er all his winnings there.
Shipmen his barque did bring
Safely to England there.
There heard he new tidings   930
Such as, methinks, had ne'er
Come to his ear —
Weeping, the folk did fare
For Ireland's tribute drear.

Mark's tribute thus was told —
(Crowned king altho' he be,)
Three hundred pounds of gold
Must he lay down in fee —
Of silver, wrought and rolled,
Next year the sum must be;   940
When had past seasons three,
The same he 'ld pay —
The fourth, the tale was told
In noble bairus alway.

Tribute to fetch there came
Moraunt, the noble knight;
Far-spreading was his fame,
As giant, famed in fight.
Three hundred bairns, his claim,
His tribute they, by right.   950
Tristrem, as at that same,
Came to the shore by night
And there abode;
He of the ship had sight
As it in haven rode.

Mark, he was glad and gay
Tristrem once more to see,
Kissed him full oft that day,
Welcome in sooth was he.
Mark, he would tidings pray,   960
Know, how he had set free
His lands? — Tristrem did say;
"What may this gathering be,
So sore they greet?"
"Tristrem, I'll tell to thee
The truth, tho' all unsweet.

"The King of Ireland,
Tristrem, I am his thrall;
Too tight he strains the band,
With wrong 't was won withal.   970
Fain would I now withstand,
On him the blame must fall —"
"Thereto I set my hand,"
Tristrem spake in the hall,
Both loud and still. —
"Moraunt, tho' fierce withal,
Here shall not wreak his will!"

Mark gat him then to rede;
Counsel he prayed of this,
And said: "With wrongful deed   980
Tribute he claims amiss."
Tristrem quoth: "Take ye heed,
His mark he here shall miss!"
Quoth Mark the King, with speed:
"These bairns were never his
By law, or right —"
Quoth Tristrem: "That, I wis,
I will uphold as knight."

Throughout the royal hold
For tribute men made moan.   990
Tristrem, he bade withhold
Payment, in lofty tone.
On him the lot was told,
Otherwise was there none,
Never a man so bold,
Fashioned of flesh and bone,
Never a knight —
Who dare for wealth untold
Against Sir Moraunt fight.

Tristrem his way hath ta'en   1000
To Moraunt word to bring;
He spake in wrathful strain:
"Naught is to thee owing!"
Moraunt, he quoth again:
"Thou liest in this thing,
My body I were fain
To risk before the king
In battle's rage —"
He proffered him a ring;
Tristrem, he took the gage.   1010

They sailed the sea so wide,
Of barques they had but two —
Moraunt, his boat fast tied
But Tristrem let his go.
Moraunt upon him cried:
"Tristrem, why dost thou so?"
"Needs must one here abide
Tho' each find fitting foe,
And so, I wis,
Whoever hence may go   1020
May fit his need with this!"

Broad was the strand alway
Where they began their fight;
Of that was Moraunt gay,
Tristrem he held full light.
Sure ne'er was seen such fray! —
With blades of goodly might
Each would the other slay —
They hewed the helmets bright.
Now, for England   1030
He fights, Tristrem, the knight.
May God uphold his hand!

Moraunt, with all his might
He rode a rapid course
Against Tristrem the knight,
To bear him from his horse.
His lance was none too light —
The lion shield with force
He smote — Tristrem, forthright,
Pierced in his knightly course   1040
The dragon shield —
Moraunt the bold, perforce,
He bare down on the field.

Forthwith to foot he sprung,
And leapt upon his steed;
As ravening wolf he flung
Himself — Take ye good heed!
Tristrem his sword high swung —
Small dread he knew in need!
The sharp blade smote and stung —
Moraunt began to bleed.   1051
Right there, amain —
In Moraunt's greatest need
His steed's back brake in twain!

Then up he sprang again,
And cried: "Tristrem, alight!
Since thou my steed hast slain
Afoot we needs must fight!"
"Thereto am I full fain,"
Quoth Tristrem: "by God's Might!"
Together came the twain;   1061
On gleaming helms they smite,
And hew, and pierce,
Tristrem as valiant knight
Fought in that battle fierce.

The champion of Ireland
Smote Tristrem on the shield
That half fell from his hand
Riven upon the field.
Tristrem would him withstand,   1070
His sword he well could wield —
Thus with his trusty brand
Well nigh he forced to yield
Moraunt, the knight —
With wonder unconcealed
King Mark beheld that fight!

Moraunt to win was fain —
He fought as valiant knight;
That Tristrem should be slain
He strove, with all his might.   1080
Tristrem, he smote amain,
His sword brake in the fight,
And fast in Moraunt's brain
It held, a splinter bright —
His death he bore;
But through the thigh forthright.
Tristrem was wounded sore.

A word that smacked of pride
Spake Tristrem — thus quoth he:
"Ye folk of Ireland's side   1090
Your mirror may ye see!
He who will hither ride,
Such shall his portion be!"
With sorrow sore that tide
Moraunt, unto the sea
Weeping, they bare —
With joy Tristrem the free
To Mark the King did fare.

His sword, as offering due,
He to the altar bare;   1100
As Mark's near kinsman true
Tristrem was honoured there.
A covenant they drew
And stablish'd fast and fair;
As he had freed anew
The land, there he should bear
The rule one day,
If so he living were
When Mark had passed away.

Tho' Tristrem deemed it naught,   1110
Yet was he wounded sore;
Tho' healing salves they sought,
And drinks from distant shore,
Leeches no healing wrought,
His pain was aye the more —
To such pass was he brought
The foul smell no man bore,
From him they ran —
And none abode there more
Save Gouvernail, his man.   1120

Three years he lingering lay
Tristrem, (the True, he hight;)
No joy was his by day
Such pain he bare all night.
For dole is none that may
Behold him now with sight,
And each one, sooth to say,
Forsaketh now the knight,
From him they fare,
Each had done what he might,   1130
And had no further care.

At length upon a day
To Mark he did complain;
The counsel, sooth to say,
Was brief betwixt the twain:
"In grief have I been aye, —
My life brings little gain";
King Mark quoth: "Wellaway,
That I must see thy pain
Nor aid may bring!"   1140
Tristrem a ship, was fain
To pray from Mark the King.

"Uncle," he quoth: "I die,
From land will I away,
A ship forthwith will I,
My harp, whereon to play,
And food and drink thereby
To keep me, send alway —"
Tho' Mark would fain deny,
Tristrem they bare straightway   1150
To the sea strand —
Save Gouvernail that day
None fared with him from land.

The ship was ready there,
He craved Mark's benison;
From haven did he fare,
The town hight Carlion —
Nine weeks the salt waves bare
His vessel up and down,   1159
The wind blew fresh and fair —
They came unto a town,
Help was full nigh,
Develin hight that town
In Ireland, verily.

He ran before the wind —
Shipmen towards him bore,
His barque to boats they bind
And draw it to the shore.
There in the ship they find
A sick man wounded sore.   1170
He said; On shores unkind
Men wounded him, and bore
Him hither bound, —
None lingered with him more
So ill the stench they found.

Gouvernail quoth again:
"How call ye this sea strand?"
To answer were they fain
"Develîn is this land."
Tristrem to hear was fain,   1180
Swift did he understand;
Her brother had he slain
Who ruled within the land
In deadly fight;
To make him known were vain,
Tramtris, henceforth he hight.

Upon his barque that day
Gladness there was, and glee,
And every kind of lay
That harped or sung might be.   1190
Then to the queen said they,
(Sister to Moraunt she,)
How a man wounded lay,
A sorry sight to see
And full of care —
"A merry man were he
If but in health he were."

In Develîn her repair,
That lady sweet, the queen,
Fairest in vesture fair —   1200
In healing too, I ween,
Skill had she and to spare,
(That was on Tristrem seen;)
She brought him out of care
Though vain his search had been
By night and day —
She sent a plaister keen
That drew the stench away.

The morrow when 't was day
That dame of high degree   1210
She came where Tristrem lay
And asked who he might be?
"A merchant I, alway,
Hight Tramtris verily,
By pirates, sooth to say,
My comrades on the sea
Were slain — rich store
Of stuffs they took from me
And wounded me full sore."

He seemed a man to praise   1220
Tho' doleful wounds he bare,
Strange to their ears his lais,
(Men deemed them wondrous
       fair)
His harp, his lute always,
The chess board that he bare,
All filled them with amaze,
By Patrick good they sware
Never in all their days
The like were seen —
"A man of gentle ways   1230
In health had he but been!"

That lady of high kin
To search his wounds was bent,
Knowledge she fain would win,
Grimly he made lament.
(His bones brake through the skin
For anguish was he spent;)
They bare him to an inn,
A bath, with good intent,
Both soft and strong   1240
They made, that, well content,
Tristrem could walk ere long.

Soft salves to him they brought
And drinks both strong and sweet,
The cost they counted naught
So they brought healing fleet.
Oft to his harp they sought,
His pastimes they hold meet;
The queen his presence sought
And oft would him entreat   1250
To seek her bower,

With mirth and music sweet
To wile away an hour.

The king's own daughter dear —
Maiden Ysonde she hight —
Music was fain to hear
And Geste to read aright.
A teacher without peer,
Sir Tramtris bent his might
His skill to bring her near,   1260
And train both hand and sight,
Till, sooth to say,
In Ireland was no knight
Who durst with Ysonde play.

Ysonde men praise alway,
So fair, so bright, is she,
All clad in green and gray
With scarlet fittingly.
On earth is none who may
With her comparéd be   1270
Save Tramtris, who alway
Was lord of courtesie
And games on ground —
Tramtris would hence away
Since healéd was his wound.

Tramtris, on Irish ground
He dwelt, a twelvemonth clear,
Such tending good he found
Whole was he in that year.
He to the queen was bound
In service due and dear,
Ysonde, in glee and round
He trained, right sweet to hear;   1280
She knew each lay —
Then leave he prayed them here,
By ship he would away.

The wise queen, undismayed,
To Tramtris did she say:
"An ye a stranger aid
He passeth soon away!"   1290
His hire to him she paid
Silver and gold that day;
What he would, that the maid,
Ysonde, gave for his play;

Then, without fail,
He bade them both "Good-day,"
With him went Gouvernail.

Fair sails to mast they drew,
Both white and red as blood;
A favouring wind fresh blew,   1300
Towards Carlion they stood.
Now is he Tristrem true
And fareth over flood!
The ship the landsmen knew
It seemed to them right good,
The news was known —
(Of wrath in fear they stood
Since he had sailed alone!)

They ran and told the king
The ship was come again;   1310
I ween of no tiding
Was ever Mark so fain!
Straightway to town they bring
Tristrem with joyful train,
Full blithe was their meeting —
The king to hear was fain
There, at that stound,
"Tristrem, art whole again?
Cure for thy wound hast found?"

He told them all the tale   1320
Right strange unto their ear,
How she had blessed his bale
Who Moraunt held so dear,
And made him whole and hale —
All that he bade them hear.
Then Tristrem, without fail,
Of Ysonde, maiden dear,
Told tidings new —
"Fair is she without peer
In love is none so true."   1330

Mark did to Tristrem say:
"My land I yield to thee
To hold after my day —
Thine own it sure shall be
An thou bring me that may
That I her face may see."
This ever was his way,

Of Ysonde speaketh he,
How men should prize
Her grace and courtesie;   1340
In love was none so wise.

Thro' England far and wide
The barons them bethought
To quell Sir Tristrem's pride;
In cunning wise they wrought,
They prayed the king that tide
A queen for him be sought;
That Tristrem should abide
And claim hereafter naught,
Nor reign as king —   1350
He should, this was their thought,
Ysonde from Ireland bring.

"As blood upon the snow
So red and white her cheek,
A bride thus fair to show
Tristrem for thee shall seek."
Tristrem quoth: "Now I know
Thro' lies their spite they'ld wreak,
What never may be so
To ask is fools' bespeak!   1360
To wise man's mind
'T is folly all to seek
What man may never find!

"I bid ye cease your strife,
I heard a swallow sing,
Ye say, I'ld keep from wife
King Mark, since I'ld be king!
Then, since such talk be rife,
Bring ship and plenishing,
Ye see me not in life   1370
Save that to ye I bring
Ysonde the bright;
But find at my bidding,
Fifteen men, sons of knight."

The knights they chose that day,
All wary men, and wise,
Of lofty rank alway
Whom men might highest prize.
A ship with green and gray
And furs of varied dyes,   1380

With everything, I say,
Fitting to merchandise
In goodly store —
They set sail on this wise
For Ireland's distant shore.

His ship was richly found
With all the needful ware,
From Carlion was he bound,
Fitly he forth did fare.
They reared their gonfanoun,   1390
The wind blew fresh and fair,
They came to Develîn town,
A haven sought they there
As fit and best —
Gifts to the king they bare
And prayed his leave to rest.

Gifts for the king they brought,
And gifts they gave the queen,
For Ysonde took they thought,
(That do I wot and ween.)   1400
As they their vessel sought,
Who now at court had been,
(No fairer maid they thought
Had e'er on earth been seen
By mortal sight —)
The town and shore between
The folk were in full flight.

From Develîn they fled
Fast as their feet might fly;
Down to the shore they sped   1410
To drowning were they nigh;
All for a dragon dread —
"On ship-board!" was their cry,
The ships were dressed that stead,
Naught recked they, verily,
That he who slew
The dragon, his should be
Ysonde, as guerdon due.

Tristrem, right glad was he,   1419
He called his knights straightway;
"Which of ye all would be
The man to dare this fray?"
Each would the other see,

And for himself said nay;
" In sooth now woe is me! "
Sir Tristrem quoth that day:
" To aid, who can? "
Now hearken an ye may
Deeds of a valiant man.

From ship a steed he drew,   1430
The best that he had brought,
His armour, it was new,
Richly with gold inwrought.
His heart was staunch and true,
(In life it failed for naught,)
The country well he knew
Ere he the dragon sought,
And saw with eye
How Hell-fire, so he thought,
Did from the monster fly.   1440

Against that dragon dread
Tristrem he rode that tide,
Fierce as a lion he sped
The battle to abide.
With strong spear, at that stead,
He smote the dragon's side,
Naught was he furtheréd,
The spear point off did glide
With ne'er a dint,
That fearsome dragon's hide   1450
Was hard as any flint!

Tristrem thereof was woe,
Another spear took he,
Against his dragon foe
It brake in pieces three.
The dragon dealt a blow,
The good steed, slain was he;
Tristrem, I'ld have ye know,
He sprang beneath a tree,
To pray was fain —   1460
" Dear God in Trinity,
Let me not here be slain! "

On foot did Tristrem brave
Against that dragon fight,
Blows with his falchion gave
E'en as a doughty knight.

His lower jaw he clave
In twain, with stroke of might;
The dragon 'gainst him drave,
His breath, as fire alight   1470
Burning, he sent,
His arms that erst were bright
All scorched were they and rent.

Such fire he cast again
As burnt both shield and stone,
The good steed lieth slain,
His arms are burnt each one.
Tristrem, he cleft the brain,
And brake the fiend's back-bone —
Ne'er had he been so fain   1480
As when that fight was done.
Then more, to boot,
The fiend's tongue hath he ta'en
And shorn off at the root.

The tongue he safe would hide
And in his hose would bear;
Scarce had he gone ten stride
Ere speech had failed him there.
Needs must he here abide,
No further may he fare —   1490
The king's steward came that tide,
The head away he bare;
With guile he brought
That pledge to Ysonde fair
And vowed 't was dearly bought!

The steward had full fain
Won Ysonde, an he might —
The king, he quoth again,
Full fair had been that fight.
Ysonde to blind were vain,   1500
She fast denied his right;
There, where the foe was slain,
The queen and she, by night
They took their way,
And sought the valiant wight
Who could such monster slay.

" Think ye he did this deed
The steward? " quoth Ysonde; " Nay!
Look at yon gallant steed

He owned it ne'er a day.   1510
Look at this goodly weed,
'T was ne'er his, sooth to say!"
Further with haste they speed,
And found a man who lay
And breath scarce drew, —
Quoth they "So God us rede
This man the dragon slew!"

Betwixt his lips alway
Cordial they pour with care;
When speak Sir Tristrem may   1520
His tale he told them there:
"This dragon did I slay"
(Freely he spake and fair)
"The tongue I cut away,
Venom with me I bare —"
Straightway they look;
The queen, with craft and care,
Forthwith the tongue she took.

They quoth, his was the right,
The steward, he had lied;   1530
They asked him, would he fight
With him who claimed the bride?
Tristrem spake as a knight
The test he would abide.
So well his faith he plight
Ysonde, she laughed that tide.
Her gage he met,
His ship with all its pride
Pledge for his faith he set.

The queen asks who he is   1540
Who dared that fiend abide?
"Merchant am I, I wis,
My ship lies here beside.
Now hath the steward done this,
I will abate his pride
Ere that he Ysonde kiss!"
Against him would he ride
With all his might —
Ysonde, she softly sighed:
"Alas, wert thou but knight!"   1550

Their champion, day by day,
With fitting food they feed,

Until they deem he may
Adventure doughty deed.
His arms, full long were they,
His shoulders broad at need,
The wise queen, sooth to say,
To bathe would Tristrem lead
Such skill she knew, —
Herself she went with speed   1560
A strengthening drink to brew.

Now Ysonde, secretly,
Deemed that he Tramtris were,
His sword she fain would see,
Broken she finds it there.
Forth from a coffer, she
Draweth a piece with care
And fits it tremblingly —
The blade is whole and fair!
It fitteth right —   1570
Ysonde, in her despair
Would slay Tristrem the knight.

Ysonde by Tristrem stood,
Unsheathed she held the brand —
"Moraunt, my kinsman good,
He fell beneath thine hand,
For this thy red heart's blood
I 'ld see shed on this strand!" —
The queen deemed she were wood;
Smiling, with cup in hand,   1580
T'ward them she drew —
"Nay, thou shalt understand,
This wretch thy brother slew!

"Tristrem our foe is he,
That may not be denied,
The piece thou here may'st see
Thro' that mine uncle died,
It fitteth evenly,
See, I the twain have tried!"
Fain had she smitten free   1590
Sir Tristrem in that tide,
'T is sooth, I say,
He in the bath had died
Save for the queen that day.

Sir Tristrem smiling spake

To sweet Ysonde the bright;
"The chance was your's to take
The while I Tramtris hight;
Wroth are ye for the sake
Of Moraunt, noble knight,   1600
I no evasion make,
In battle and fair fight
I have him slain;
An he had had the might
So had he me, full fain!

"The while I Tramtris hight
I taught thee game and song;
Later, as best I might,
I spake thy praise with tongue
To Mark, the noble knight,   1610
Till he for thee did long!"
Thus sware he day and night,
And pledges set full strong
Their lands between,
That, for amends of wrong,
Ysonde should aye be queen.

Tristrem, he sware that thing,
(They said, so should it stand,)
That he should Ysonde bring,
(Thereto they set their hand)   1620
To Mark the noble king,
An he still bare command,
That she be made with ring
Queen of the English land.
The sooth to say
So did the forward stand
Ere yet they sailed away.

The steward denied his deed,
Hearing he Tristrem hight;
The king sware, God him speed,   1630
They both should have their
      right!
The steward took better rede
And sware he would not fight —
To Tristrem as his meed
They gave Ysonde the bright —
That they should bring
In ward that traitor knight
The maid besought the king.

Tristrem prayed land nor fee,
Only that maiden bright: 1640
For parting speedily
They trussed them, squire and knight.
Her mother, blithe was she,
She brewed a drink of might,
That love should waken free —
A maiden, Brengwain hight,
She gave the draught:
"See, on their bridal night
By king and queen 't is quaffed!"

Ysonde, the bright of hue,¡   1650
Is far out on the sea,
A wind against them blew,
No sail might hoisted be.
They rowed, those knights so true,
Tristrem, an oar took he
E'en as his turn fell due,
Nor one, against the three,
From toil would shrink —
Ysonde, the maiden free,
Bade Brengwain give them drink.   1660

The cup was richly wrought,
Of gold it was, the pin,
In all the world was naught
To match the drink therein.
Brengwain, she was distraught,
She to that flask did win
And to sweet Ysonde brought —
She bade Tristrem begin;
The sooth to say,
Each heart there found its twin   1670
Until their dying day.

A dog was at their side,
That was yclept Hodain,
The cup he licked that tide
When set down by Brengwain.
These three in love allied,
(Thereof were they full fain,)
Together must abide
In joy, and eke in pain,
Long as man's thought —   1680
In an ill hour they drain
The drink that ill was wrought.

Tristrem, each night he lay
Beside that lady sweet,
And found with her alway
Such solace as was meet.
In her bower, night and day,
Gaily the hours they fleet —
They dallied in love's play —
Brengwain doth well entreat   1690
For love the twain.
As sun in summer's heat
So waxed their love amain.

Two weeks thus bound to strand
No sail to mast they drew;
By favouring breezes fanned
Towards the shore they flew.
Mark hunted in the land —
A varlet whom he knew
He knighted with his hand   1700
For tidings good and true
That he did bring —
Ysonde, the fair of hue,
She wedded Mark the King.

Wedded with ring were they —
Of feasting speak I naught —
Then Brengwain, sooth to say,
Did as the three had thought;
(She took the drink that day
That was with magic fraught,)   1710
To Mark the King alway
In Ysonde's stead, was brought
Brengwain, that tide;
Till he his will had wrought
On her who lay beside.

When Mark had had his will
Ysonde her place would take;
A cup she bade them fill
That she her thirst might slake,
The drink she swift did spill;   1720
Small need for Tristrem's sake
To summon magic skill,
No man the bands might break
Betwixt the twain,
Nor clerk of wisdom make
Their true Love's secret plain.

They looked for joy alway,
Certes, it was not so!
Their dreams, they went astray,
Doubts fell betwixt the two.   1730
The one in languor lay;
The other fain would go;
Ysonde was blithe and gay
When Tristrem was in woe,
Such feint she made —
Ysonde, I'ld have ye know,
Brengwain full ill repaid.

She said: "I may be wroth,
She lay first with the king;
I vowed she should have cloth,   1740
Gold, and a rich wedding.
Tristrem and I for troth
Win shame and slandering —
Methinks 't were best for both
That maid to death to bring,
Secret and still —
Then, fearing naught the king,
Free, we may work our will."

The queen bade to her side
Two workmen, on a day;   1750
And told them at that tide
What was her will to say.
"I will ye slay and hide
Brengwain, that merry may!" —
She quoth: "Ye shall abide
In wealth for many a day.
Now go with speed,
Nor fear for lack of pay
An well ye do this deed."

Into a dark ravine   1760
They led the maiden good,
One drew his sword so keen,
And one behind her stood.
"Mercy," she cried, I ween,
And quoth: "By Christ on Rood,
What hath my trespass been,
Why would ye spill my blood?"
"The sooth to say,
Ysonde, that lady good
She sent us thee to slay."   1770

Then Brengwain secretly
Bade them to seek the queen:
"Greet well my sweet lady,
Say, I have faithful been;
White smocks had she and I,
But her's had lost its sheen,
When she by Mark should lie
I lent her mine all clean
And that she wore:
Against her, well I ween,   1780
Have I done nothing more."

The maid they would not slay
But gat them to the queen;
Ysonde, she asked alway
What passed the three between?
"She bade us soothly say:
'Since soiled your smock had been
When erst by Mark ye lay,
I lent ye mine all clean,
As well ye knew.'"   1790
Quoth Ysonde, quick and keen,
"Where is my maiden true?"

Ysonde in wrathful mood
Quoth: "Ye have killed Brengwain!"
She sware by Christ on Rood
Hanging should be their pain.
She proffered gifts so good
To bring that maid again:
They fetched her where she stood,
Then was Ysonde full fain   1800
And, sooth to say,
So true she found Brengwain
She loved her from that day.

Peace was betwixt them made,
And pardon given for ill —
Tristrem, all undismayed,
Of Ysonde had his will —
From Ireland's shore there strayed
A harper; to fulfil   1809
His thought, at court he stayed;
His harp was wrought with skill,
No man with sight
Had seen its like, and still
He bare it day and night.

The queen he loved her e'er —
The harp he hither brought
And in his bosom bare,
Full richly was it wrought.
He hid it aye with care
And drew it forth for naught.   1820
"Thy harp why wilt thou spare
If thou of skill hast aught
In lay or glee?"
"It cometh forth for naught
Save a right royal fee!"

Quoth Mark: "Now let me see,
Harp thou as best thou may,
And what thou askest me
That will I freely pay."
"Of right good will!" quoth he,   1830
And harped a merry lay.
"Sir King, by gift so free
Ysonde is mine to-day
With harp, I ween:
Foresworn art thou alway
Or else I take thy queen!"

Mark hath his council sworn
And asketh rede thereto:
"My manhood is foresworn
Or Ysonde must us fro'."   1840
Mark was of joy forlorn;
Ysonde, she fared in woe;
Tristrem, it chanced that morn,
Would to the woodland go
The deer to slay, —
Nor of the tale might know
Till Ysonde was away.

Tristrem in wrath I ween
He chode with Mark the King:
"Dost give gleemen thy queen?   1850
Hadst thou no other thing?"
His lute he there hath seen,
He took it by the ring;
Tristrem, he followed keen;
Ysonde to ship they bring
With joy and glee.
Tristrem began to sing,
She hearkened willingly.

He sang so sweet a strain
It wrought her mickle woe;   1860
For love her heart was fain,
Well nigh it brake in two.
The earl, he came amain
And many knights also,
He spake in tender strain: —
"Sweet heart, why mournest, so?
Tell me, I pray!"
Ysonde to land would go
Ere yet she sailed away.

"Within an hour this day   1870
Shall I be whole and sound,
I hear a minstrel play
Like Tristrem's rings his round."
"Curséd were he alway,
An he should here be found!
That minstrel for his lay
Shall have an hundred pound
This day of me,
An he with us be bound   1879
Since Love, thou lov'st his glee!"

To hear that music sweet
The queen was set on land;
Beside the waters fleet
The earl, he took her hand.
Tristrem, as minstrel meet,
A merry ruse had planned;
With ivory lute would greet
Their coming to the strand
Upon that stound.
Ysonde, on the sea sand   1890
Full soon was whole and sound.

Whole was Ysonde, and sound,
By virtue of that glee;
I wot the earl that stound
A joyful man was he.
Of pence two hundred pound
He gave Tristrem in fee.
To ship they now are bound,
In Ireland would they be,
Of heart full fain,   1900
The earl and his knights three
With Ysonde and Brengwain.

Tristrem, he took his steed,
And leapt thereon to ride;
The queen would have him lead
And take her at his side.
Tristrem was swift to heed —
The twain in woodland hide.
He scoffed: "Now in this need
Earl, have I lowered thy pride 1910
Without dispute —
Won by thy harp that tide
Thou'st lost her by my lute!"

Tristrem, he Ysonde bare
Into the woods away,
They found a bower fair
And fit for lovers' play.
Seven nights abode they there
Then took to court their way;
"Henceforth, Sir King,"   1920
Tristrem to Mark did say,
"Give minstrels other thing."

Now Meriadoc was one
Whom Tristrem trusted aye;
Much good he him had done, —
The twain together lay.
Tristrem to Ysonde won
By night, with her to play;
Wiser than he was none,
A board he took away   1930
From off her bower.
Ere he went on his way
Of snow there fell a shower.

So fast the snow did fall
That all the way was white.
Tristrem was woe withal
For sorrow and despite.
'Twixt bower, I ween, and hall
Narrow the road to sight
A chance did him befall   1940
As we find writ aright,
In hall he found
A straw wisp, and full tight
Around his feet he bound.

Meriadoc that night
He rose up, all unseen,
He took the path aright
That led him to the queen.
The board was loose to sight,
And there, in sooth, I ween,   1950
Of Tristrem's robe, the knight,
He found a piece of green
But lately tore —
Then Meriadoc, the keen,
It wondered him the more.

He told the king next morn
All he had seen with sight:
"Tristrem, traitor foresworn,
With Ysonde lay last night.
Counsel of need be born —   1960
Ask, Who shall be her knight
To shield her? Thou art sworn
The Cross to take forthright
If so ye may. —
'Tristrem, the noble knight.'
The queen herself will say!"

The king, he told the queen,
(They lay together there:)
"Lady, full soon, I ween,
On crusade must I fare;   1970
Say now, us twain between,
Who shall thee shield from care?"
"O'er all thy knights so keen,
Tristrem!" she answered there,
"None better can;
He hath my favour fair,
He is thy near kinsman!"

All that Mark to her told
At morn she told Brengwain;
"He sails on errand bold,   1980
Now may we be full fain!
Tristrem his court shall hold
Until he come again."
Brengwain did speech unfold:
"Thy deeds are known amain
And seen with sight —
Mark testeth thee again
In other wise to-night.

"Now watch thou well his will;
To wend with him thou pray,   1990
And if he love thee still
Bid Tristrem go his way.
Pray him to deal with skill;
Thy foe was Tristrem aye;
Thou fear'st he'll do thee ill
An so he holdeth sway
The land above —
Thou loved'st him ne'er a day
Save for his uncle's love!"

Ysonde, when came the night,   2000
Cried: "Mark, some pity show,
And deal with me aright,
Would'st leave me to my foe?
God knows, I, an I might,
From land with thee would go,
And slay Tristrem the knight,
Save that I love would show
To thee this day —
For men make feint to know
That Tristrem by me lay!"   2010

Mark, he was blithe and bold,
Faith in her word had he:
Him, who the tale had told,
He used despitefully.
Meriadoc, as of old
Spake: "Now thou let him be,
Their loves shalt thou behold
All for the love of me;
In sooth, I ween,
By wisdom thou shalt see   2020
The love the twain between."

Mark severed then the two,
Bade Tristrem go his way.
Ysonde was ne'er so woe
Nor Tristrem, sooth to say.
Tristrem was laid full low,
Ysonde herself would slay,
In sooth she mournéd so, —
And Tristrem, night and day;
In very deed,   2030
Each man may see alway
The life for love they lead.

Quoth Meriadoc: "I rede
Thou bid thy huntsmen ride
A fortnight full at need
To see thy forests wide;
Thyself the band shall lead;
Tristrem shall here abide,
And in the act and deed
Thou'lt take them at that tide.   2040
Here, in the tree,
I counsel thee to hide,
Thou shalt their feigning see."

Tristrem abode in town,
Ysonde was in her bower,
The streamlet bare adown
Light linden twigs that hour.
With rune he wrote them round —
Ysonde knew branch and flower —
She Tristrem's message found,   2050
With grace his prayer would dower,
His coming bide —
Next day, ere evening hour,
Tristrem was at her side!

Beneath the orchard's shade
They met, Ysonde and he,
Love's solace there they made
When they might win them free.
The dwarf a snare had laid,   2060
He watched them from a tree —
Anon, King Mark he prayed
To come, that he might see
Their deeds with sight —
"Thus, Sire, assured thou'lt be,
Thyself shalt prove me right."

His falsehood to fulfil
Forthwith he fain would greet
Tristrem (his thought was ill),
From Ysonde, lady sweet:
"The queen's wish I fulfil,   2070
As she did me entreat,
She prayeth thee of good will,
That thou would'st with her meet,
Both, face to face,
Tho' Mark be far, 't is meet
It be in secret place!"

Sir Tristrem him bethought:
"Master, my thanks to thee,
Since thou this word hast brought
My robe I give to thee.   2080
That thou hast failed in naught
Say to that lady free;
Her words I dearly bought
To Mark she slandered me,
That gentle may!
At morn she shall me see
In church, 't is sooth to say."

The dwarf he went his way,
To Mark he came full keen:
"By this robe judge ye may   2090
How well he loves the queen!
He trusteth me no way
In guise of go-between,
By seeming ye might say
Her face he ne'er had seen,
Before with sight —
And yet full sure I ween
He meeteth her to-night!"

King Mark hid in that tree —
The twain they met below;   2100
The shadow did he see
Tristrem, nor spake too low
That Ysonde warned should be,
And call Tristrem her foe —
"Here is no place for thee,
Hast no right here to go,
What doth thee bring?
Dead, would I fain thee know
Save that I love the king!

"My foe wast thou alway,   2110
Full sore thou wrongest me
With mockery night and day,
Mark scarce my face will see,
And threatens me to slay —
More courteous 't were in thee
To follow friendship's way
By God in Trinity!
Or I this tide
From this land must away
And seek Welsh deserts wide!"   2120

"Tristrem, tho', sooth to say,
I wish thee little good,
I slandered thee no day
That swear I, by God's rood!
Men said thou with me lay,
By that thine uncle stood —
Now get thee on thy way,
Thou ravest as one wood,
None save the man
Who had my maidenhood   2130
I love, or ever can!''

"Sweet Ysonde, hear my prayer,
Beseech the king for me,
If so thy will be fair,
That he would speak me free!
From land then will I fare,
No more my face he'll see —"
(Mark's heart was heavy there,
He hearkened from the tree
And thus he thought: 2140
"Guiltless, I ween, they were
In this vile slander brought.")

"Wrong 'gainst thee I deny,
Men said thou with me lay,
Yet, if for this I die
Thy message will I say.
Thine uncle's state is high,
Equip thee well he may —
I reck not if I lie
So that thou be away   2150
Of thine own will." —
Mark to himself did say:
"He shall abide here still."

Tristrem, his way would go,
And Ysonde too, I wis.
Never was Mark so woe,
Himself he heard all this,
In sorrow must he go
Till he might Tristrem kiss,
And hatred keen must know   2160
'Gainst him who spake amiss —
Then waked anew
At court their joy, with bliss
They welcome Tristrem true.

Now Ysonde hath her way,
Tristrem is Marshal hight —
Three years he wrought love's play
With Ysonde, lady bright.
None might the twain betray
So cunning was their sleight;   2170
But Meriadoc, he lay
In watch, both day and night,
With ill intent,
To ruin both queen and knight
Had he been well content!

A ruse he found alway,
Thus to the king said he:
"Their folly dureth aye,
'T was sooth I sware to thee.
Look now, upon one day   2180
Bid blood be let ye three,
And do as I shall say;
True token shall men see
And that right soon —
Bloody her couch shall be
Ere yet their will be done!"

Now have they bled the king,
Tristrem, and eke the queen;
After the blood-letting
They sweep the chamber clean.   2190
Meriadoc flour did bring,
Strewed it the beds between
That ne'er might pass a thing
But that its trace were seen
Clear to men's sight —
The thirty feet between
Tristrem he leapt that night.

Now Tristrem's will was this,
With Ysonde would he play,
They might not come to kiss   2200
So thick the flour it lay!
Tristrem, he leapt, I wis,
Full thirty feet alway,
But e'en as he did this
The bandage brake away
And fast he bled —
I wot ere dawn of day
He leapt from out her bed.

The thirty feet again
He leapt, I speak no lie —   2210
It hurt him sore, the vein,
Small wonder, verily.
Mark, he beheld the stain,
'T was plain unto the eye,
He spake unto Brengwain:
"Tristrem brake traitorously
The vow he plight."
The land he needs must fly
Out of his uncle's sight.

Tristrem was fled away,   2220
In land was no more seen;
At London, on a day,
Mark, he would purge the queen
Of guilt that on her lay —
A Bishop stood between;
With red-hot iron, they say,
She thought to make her clean
Of all they spake —
Ysonde was fain, I ween,
That doom on her to take.   2230

Men set the lists full fair,
At Westminster aright,
Hot irons would she bear
All for that valiant knight.
In weeds that beggars wear
Tristrem, he came that night,
(Of all the folk that were
None knew him then by sight
Who him had seen —)
E'en to sweet Ysonde bright,   2240
As pledged the twain between.

O'er Thames she needs must ride —
An arm 't is of the sea —
"E'en to the vessel's side
This man shall carry me:"
Tristrem bare her that tide
And with the queen fell he,
E'en by her naked side
As every man might see
Nor need to show —   2250
Her flesh above the knee
All bare the knights must know.

In flood they had him drowned,
Or worse, an that they may:
"Ye 'quite him ill this stound,"
The queen to them would say:
"He little meat hath found
Or drink, this many a day,
For weakness was he bound
To fall, the sooth to say,   2260
And very need —
Now give him gold, I pray,
That he bid me God-speed."

Gold did they give him there —
The judgment hath begun;
Ysonde doth soothly swear
That she no wrong hath done —
"But one to ship me bare,
These knights, they all looked on,
Whate'er his will then were   2270
Full nigh to me he won.
'T is sooth, this thing,
So nigh came never none
Saving my lord the king!"

Sweet Ysonde, she hath sworn
Her clean, that merry may,
Ready for her that morn
The iron they heat alway;
The knights, they stand forlorn
And for her safety pray —   2280
The iron she there hath borne —
Mark pardoned her that day
In word and deed —
And Meriadoc, they say,
Hath spoken traitorous rede.

Ysonde was spoken clean
In Meriadoc's despite,
Ne'er had she found, the queen,
Such favour in Mark's sight.
Tristrem, the true, I ween,   2290
To Wales he took his flight:
In battle hath he been,
Conflict he sought forthright
In sooth, I wis,
Solace he seeks in fight,
Ysonde he may not kiss.

In Wales the crown he bare
A king, hight Triamour,
He had a daughter fair
Men called her Blanche-flower.   2300
Urgain the giant there
Besieged him in his tower,
That maid he fain would bear
With him unto his bower
For that would fight —
Tristrem, with much honour,
Became of that king knight.

Urgain the land would hold
In wrongful guise alway;
Oft from his robber hold   2310
On Triamour he'ld prey.
This tale to Tristrem told
The king, one summer's day,
And quoth, he Wales shall hold
An that he win it may
Of lawful right —
Tristrem, none may say nay,
He won that land in fight.

Tristrem, he met Urgain—   2319
The twain in field would fight —
Ere they together ran
He spake as doughty knight:
"My brother true, Morgan,
Didst slay at meat, with might,
As I be valiant man
His death thou'lt rue to-night
Here, as my foe —"
Quoth Tristrem: "Here I plight
My word, thou'rt slain also!"

Twelve foot, the staff on strand   2330
Wherewith Urgain made play —
None shall his stroke withstand,
'T were strange if Tristrem may!
Full sharp was Tristrem's brand,
The staff it fell away,
And more, the giant's right hand
Was smitten off that day
In very deed —
Sir Tristrem, sooth to say,
He made the giant bleed!   2340

Urgain, with wrathful mien,
With his left hand he fought
Against his foeman keen;
A stroke, with danger fraught,
Fell on his helmet's sheen —
Tristrem to ground was brought
But up he sprang, I ween,
And aid from Heaven besought
Of God's great Might —
With brand for warfare wrought   2350
Fast he began to fight.

The giant, afar he stood,
Now had he lost his hand —
He fled as he were wood
To where his burg did stand.
Tristrem, in blood he trode,
He found the giant's right hand —
With that away he rode;
The giant, I understand
Healing had sought —   2360
Salves that would cure his hand
With him he swiftly brought.

Urgain, unfelled his pride,
After Sir Tristrem ran;
The folk from far and wide
Were gathered to a man.
Sir Tristrem thought that tide
"I'll take what take I can —"
On bridge did he abide,
Many their deeds did scan,   2370
They met for fray —
Urgain on Tristrem ran
With challenge grim alway.

Then strokes of mickle might
Were dealt the twain between;
That thro' the burnies bright
The blood of both was seen.
Tristrem fought as a knight —
Urgain, in anger keen
Dealt him a stroke un-light,   2380
His shield was cloven clean
In pieces two —
Tristrem, I wot and ween,
Had never been so woe!

Urgain, he smote amain,
The stroke, it went astray,
Tristrem, he struck again
And ran him through that day.
Urgain to spring was fain,
Dead 'neath the bridge he lay — 2390
"Tristrem the giant hath slain!"
The folk around they say
Both loud and still;
The king with joy that day
Gave Wales unto his will.

The king, a dog he brought
And gave to Tristrem true,
How fairly it was wrought
I would declare anew —
Softer than silk to thought, 2400
He was red, green, and blue,
They who the dog had sought
Much joy of him they knew
I wot alway;
His name was Petitcrewe,
Much praise of him they say.

The good King Triamour
That dog to Tristrem gave
Who from the giant's power
Him and his land did save. 2410
Tristrem was proved that hour
Courteous as he was brave,
To maiden Blancheflower
Wales for her own he gave
For aye, I ween,
The dog he sent o'er wave
To Ysonde, the sweet queen.

Now Ysonde, sooth to say,
Was of the dog full fain,
She sent him word straightway 2420
That he might come again;
Mark, he had heard alway
How Urgain had been slain,
And sent men on their way
To say that he was fain
Tristrem to see.
His coming he deemed gain
And kissed him fair and free.

King Mark did Tristrem call
And gave to him, I ween, 2430
Cities and castles, all
E'en as he steward had been.
Who then was blithe in hall
But Ysonde, the sweet queen?
Howe'er it might befall
The game was played between
Those lovers two —
They bare of love the mien —
Mark saw the thing was so.

Mark, he hath seen, I wis, 2440
The love the twain between,
Certes, the thought was his
Avengéd to have been.
Tristrem he called with this
And bade him take the queen,
And drave them forth, I wis,
No more they should be seen,
They must away —
Blither they ne'er had been
I wot, for many a day! 2450

Into a forest fair,
The twain, they fled that tide,
No dwelling have they there
Saving the woodland wide.
O'er hills and holts they fare,
Amid them they abide,
Ysonde of joy hath share,
And Tristrem, at her side;
I wot, full well,
Never before that tide 2460
In such bliss did they dwell!

Ysonde and Tristrem true
Are banished for their deed,
Hodain and Petitcrewe
The twain with them they lead.
An earth-house there they knew,
Thither they fare with speed;
He taught them, Tristrem true,
The beasts to take at need,
Nor be out-paced — 2470
In forest fastness freed
Tristrem with Hodain chased.

Tristrem wild beasts would slay
With Hodain, for their meat;
In an earth-house they lay,
There found they solace sweet,
Giants in a by-gone day
Wrought it in fashion meet —
Each even, sooth to say,
Thither they turned their feet,   2480
As best they might —
Thro' woodland boughs they greet
Changes of day and night.

In winter it was hot,
In summer it was cold,
Fair was that hidden grot,
The path to none they told.
No wine had they, I wot,
Nor good ale strong and old,
I trow it vexed them not   2490
They lacked for meat on mold,
Each had their will,
The loved one to behold,
Nor ever gaze their fill!

On a hill Tristrem stood,
Aforetime was he there,
He found a well right good,
Crystal its waters were.
Thereto in joyous mood
He came, with Ysonde fair;   2500
I wot this was their food,
On forest flesh they fare
With herbs, and grass —
In joy, all free from care,
Twelve months, save three weeks, pass.

Tristrem, ere dawn of day,
With Hodain forth would fare,
He found a beast of prey
Within a secret lair.
He slew that beast straightway   2510
And with him homeward bare —
Sweet Ysonde sleeping lay,
Tristrem, he laid him there
Beside the queen —
His brand, unsheathed and bare,
Was laid the twain between.

A hart to bay he ran
King Mark, that self-same day;
The track his huntsmen scan
And find a woodland way;   2520
Tristrem, in little span,
And Ysonde, sooth to say,
They find — sure no such man,
And none so fair a may,
E'er met their sight —
Between the twain there lay
A drawn sword, burnished bright.

The huntsmen went forthright,
Told Mark where they had been;
That lady and that knight   2530
Had Mark aforetime seen;
He knew them well by sight —
The sword, it lay between,
A sunbeam passing bright
It shone upon the queen
Thro' crevice small,
Upon her face so sheen —
It vexed the king withal.

His glove he set therein
To keep the sun away —   2540
King Mark, he woe must win,
And spake: "Ah, wellaway,
Two who would dwell in sin
Never in such wise lay!
Who live as loyal kin
Have no thought for love's play,
'T is sooth, I wis —"
The knights with one voice say:
"Pledge of their truth is this!"

Then wakened Tristrem true   2550
And Ysonde, fair and sheen,
The glove away they drew
And spake the twain between;
That it was Mark's they knew
And wist he there had been.
Their joy awakened new
To know he thus had seen
Them both with sight —
With that came knights so keen
To fetch the twain forthright.   2560

To court had come the twain
Who dwelt in woodland wide;
Mark kissed Ysonde again
And Tristrem, true and tried;
Forgiven was their pain,
Naught was to them denied;
Tristrem did office gain
Therein would he abide
As at that stound —
Hearken, who at this tide   2570
Would know of love the ground.

It fell the twain between
Upon a summer's day,
That Tristrem and the queen
Sought solace in love's play,
The dwarf the twain had seen,
To Mark he swift did say:
"Sir King, I surely ween
Thy wife is now away
With her true knight,   2580
Wend swiftly on thy way,
O'ertake them, an thou might."

King Mark, he swiftly ran;
His coming both might see,
Tristrem spake, woeful man,
"Sweet Ysonde, lost are we,
By naught that we may plan
The thing may hidden be,"
Ne'er was so sad a man
As Tristrem, verily,   2590
True knight and friend —
"For fear of death I flee,
In woe my way I wend.

"I flee, since death I dread,
I may not here abide,
In woe I seek this stead
The friendly forest side —"
A ring ere hence he sped
She gave him at that tide —
For fear of death he fled   2600
Unto the woodland wide
Forthwith I ween —
To seek him swift they ride,
Alone they found the queen.

Tristrem hath gone his way
As naught 'twixt them had been;
Therefore the knights they say
That Mark amiss had seen.
And straightway do they pray
That Mark forgive the queen —
Tristrem by Ysonde lay   2611
That night, in sooth I ween,
Good watch he kept —
Love's solace was between
The twain while others slept.

Tristrem hath fled away,
He cometh not again,
He sigheth, sooth to say,
For sorrow and for pain.
Tristrem, he fareth aye   2620
As one who would be slain,
Nor ceaseth, night and day,
Conflict to seek amain,
That knight so free —
He wandereth thro' Spain,
Of giants, he slew three.

Anon from Spain he fared,
Fain Rohant's sons to see,
Their joy they nowise spared,
Welcome to them was he.   2630
Long time with them he fared —
Good reason there should be,
Their land they fain had shared
With him who set them free
An 't were his thought —
He quoth: "My thanks have ye,
Of your land will I naught."

To Britain did he hie,
There was he the duke's knight,
The land in peace did lie   2640
That erst was full of fight.
The duke's lands, presently,
He won again with fight —
He gave him, 't is no lie,
His daughter fair and bright
There, in that land;
The maiden, she was hight
Ysonde, of the White Hand.

Tristrem, with love so strong,
He loved Ysonde the queen, 2650
Of Ysonde made a song
By Ysonde sung, I ween.
The maiden deemed a-wrong
That song of her had been —
Her yearning lasted long,
That hath her father seen,
Her will he knew —
Ysonde with hand of sheen
He offered Tristrem true.

Tristrem a wish doth hold 2660
Fast hidden in his thought;
"King Mark, mine uncle bold,
Great wrong on us hath brought,
I am to sorrow sold,
Thereto she me hath brought
Whose love was mine of old,
The book, it saith, with naught
Of lawful right —"
The maid henceforth he sought
For that she Ysonde hight. 2670

That was her heart's demand,
Her will would he obey —
True covenant and band
He bound with that fair may,
Ysonde of the White Hand
He wedded her that day —
At night, I understand,
As he would go his way
To bower and bed,
Tristrem's ring fell away 2680
As men him thither led.

Tristrem beheld the ring,
His heart was full of woe —
"Ysonde did no such thing,
She ne'er betrayed me so
Tho' Mark, her lord and king,
Force her with him to go —
My heart may no man bring
From her, as well I know,
The fair and free — 2690
Now severed are we two,
The sin, it rests on me!"

Tristrem, in bed he lay,
His heart was full of care;
He quoth: "Love's secret play
In sooth, I may not dare." —
He said the maiden nay,
If so her will it were —
She answered him straightway:
"Of that have thou no care, 2700
I'll hold me still,
Nor ask for foul or fair
Save as it be thy will."

Her father on a day
He gave them lands so wide,
Afar, upon the way,
The posts were set beside.
The duke's lands this side lay,
A giant's the other side —
No man durst there to stray, 2710
The giant would him abide
And challenge fight —
Lowered perforce his pride
Or king he were, or knight.

"Tristrem, I would thee rede
That thou, for love of me,
Pass not, for any need,
Beyond yon arm of sea.
Of Beliagog take heed,
A giant stern is he, 2720
Thou should'st him fear indeed
Since thou his brothers three
Hast slain in fight,
Urgain, Morgan, truly,
And Moraunt, noble knight.

"An thine hounds seek a hare
And from his lands come free,
So be thou debonaire
If his hounds come to thee."
The forest, it was fair 2730
With many an unknown tree,
Tristrem would thither fare
However it might be
His foe abide —
"That country will I see
What chance soe'er betide."

Tristrem would hunt the wood,
To chase a hart began,
There, where the boundary stood,
His hounds across it ran.   2740
Tho' black and broad the flood
He crossed it like a man,
The duke's word he withstood
But followed for a span
The further shore —
Then blew, as hunters can,
A blast, three notes and more.

Beliagog came that tide,
And asked who he might be?
"A-hunting here I ride   2750
As Tristrem men know me —"
"Who slew Moraunt with pride,
That Tristrem, art thou he?
Who Urgain too defied,
And slew? 'T were ill did we
Here kiss as kin,
That wrong shall righted be
Now thou my land art in!"

"I slew them, sooth to tell,
So hope I thee to slay,   2760
This forest will I fell
And build a burg straightway.
'T were merry here to dwell,
So here I think to stay —"
The giant heard full well
And waxed right wroth that day,
He scarce was wise —
In such wise did the fray
Betwixt the twain arise.

Then mighty spears and tried   2770
The giant to hurl began,
Sir Tristrem's life that tide
Had well nigh reached its span.
Betwixt hauberk and side

The dart methinks it ran —
Tristrem, he sprang aside,
Gave thanks, as valiant man
To God's great Might —
Tristrem, as best he can,
Now girdeth him for fight.   2780

Now Beliagog, the bold,
E'en as a fiend did fight,
As Thomas hath us told
He nigh had slain the knight.
By God's Will, there on mold,
His foot did he off-smite
Tristrem, to earth he rolled
That man of mickle might,
And loud he cried:
"Tristrem, now peace be plight,   2790
Take thou my lands so wide.

"Now hast thou vanquished me
In battle and in fight,
Fealty I swear to thee,
'Gainst thee have I no right."
His wealth he bade him see,
Tristrem, the noble knight,
And Tristrem spake him free —
His faith the giant did plight
That he full fain,   2800
Would build a bower bright
For Ysonde and Brengwain.

The giant led the way
Until a burg they found,
The water round it lay,
His fathers held that mound.
Tristrem the giant did pray
Strong walls to build around,
And Beliagog that day
Gave him of woodland ground   2810
Enough for all —
Ysonde, so fairly found,
He 'ld lead unto that hall.

(End of MS.)

AMIS AND AMILOUN

For love of God in Trinity
Ye who be gentle hearken me,
I pray ye, *par amour ;*
Hear what befell beyond the sea
To barons twain, of great bountie,
And men of high honour;
Their fathers, they were barons free,
And lordings come of high degree,
Renowned in town and tower;
The tale of these their children twain 10
Alike in pleasure and in pain
To hear is great dolour.

In weal and woe what was their lot,
And how their kinsmen knew them not,
Those children brave and fair;
(Courteous and good they were, forsooth,
And friends became from early youth,
E'en as in court they were.)
And how the twain they were dubbed
          knight,
And how together sware troth-plight, 20
And did as comrades fare;
The land from which those children
          came,
And how each one was called by name
I will to ye declare.

In Lombardie, I understand,
Of old it chanced, in that same land,
E'en as in Geste we read,
There dwelt two barons, brave and bold,
Who did as wives in wedlock hold
Two ladies, fair in weed. 30
And as it fell, those ladies fair
A son each to her lord did bear
Who doughty was in deed;
And true were they in everything,
And therefore Jesu, Heaven's King,
Requited them their meed.

The children's names as they were hight
In rhyme I will rehearse aright
And tell in tale to ye;
Begotten in the self-same night, 40
The self-same day they saw the light,
Forsooth and verily;
And the one baron's son, I wis,
They called him by his name, Amis,
When christened he should be;
The other was called Amiloun,
He was a child of great renown,
And came of high degree.

Those bairns, I trow, they well did
          thrive,
No fairer bairns were seen alive, 50
So courteous, true, and good;
Whenas their years they reckoned five
Then all their kin of them were blithe
So mild were they of mood;
When seven years were their's, I wis
That every man of them had bliss
Who saw them as they stood;
And when they were twelve winters old
Throughout the land all did them hold
Fairest of bone and blood. 60

Now in that time, I understand,
A duke was lord of that same land
Renowned in town and tower;
A message he sent speedily
To earl and baron, bond and free,
To ladies bright in bower,
A right rich feast he thought to make
And all for Our Lord Jesu's sake
Who is Our Saviour;
And many folk, the sooth to say, 70
He bade them come by a set day,
With mirth and great honour.

Those barons twain, who were so bold,
And these, their sons, of whom I told,
To court they came straightway,
When all were gathered, young and old,
Full many did the lads behold

Of lordings blithe and gay;
Saw them in body full of grace,
To all men's eyes alike in face,　　80
Well taught in Wisdom's way;
And all men sware that: "Verily,
Children so fair as these shall be
We saw not ere to-day!"

In all the court there was no wight
Nor earl nor baron, swain nor knight,
Were he or lieve or loth,
For that they were so like to sight,
And in their growth of equal height,
(I tell this on my troth —)　　90
Since that they were so like to see
Nor rich man there, nor poor might be,
Of those who saw them both,
Father nor mother of the two,
Who knew the one the other fro'
Save by their coat and cloth.

The rich duke, he his feast did hold
With earls, and many a baron bold,
As ye may list my lay,
A fourteen-night, as I was told,　　100
With meat and drink, merry on mold,
He bade his guests be gay;
For mirth they had, and melody,
And every kind of minstrelsy,
To show their skill alway;
Upon the fifteenth day they make
Ready, their homeward way to take,
With thanks their host they pay.

Then ere the lordings forth had gone
The duke of gracious mien, anon,　　110
He called to him that tide
These barons, proved in courtesie,
And prayed that they his friends should
　　be
And in his court abide;
And let their two sons, of goodwill,
Be of his house to serve him still,
And fare forth at his side;
And he as knight would dub the twain
And would them fittingly maintain
As lordings proud in pride.　　120

The barons answered him straightway,
And with their ladies spake that day
And made him answer fair,
And said, they were both glad and fain
That these their lovely children twain
In this his service were;
Blessing they gave their sons that day,
And Jesu, Heaven's King, did pray
To shield them both from care;
Full oft they thanked the duke that tide,
Then took their leave from thence to
　　ride　　131
And to their country fare.

.　　.　　.　　.　　.　　.

Thus were those children twain, I wis,
Childe Amiloun and Childe Amis,
Made free in court to feed,
A-hunting 'neath the boughs to ride,
O'er all the land their praise was cried
As worthiest in weed;
Such love each to the other bore
Were never children who loved more 140
Neither in word nor deed;
Betwixt the twain, in blood and bone,
A truer love was never shown,
In Geste as ye may read.

Thus on a day, these children bright,
Their troth each to the other plight,
While they might live and stand,
That both alike, by day and night,
In weal or woe, for wrong or right,
By free and friendly band,　　150
They'ld hold together in all need,
In word and work, in will and deed,
Where'er they were in land;
From that day forward ne'er to fail
Each other, aye for bliss or bale,
To that they set their hand.

Thus in the Geste as ye may hear
Within that land, those children dear
Did with the duke abide;　　159
The duke, he was both blithe and fain
Dear to him were those children twain
Who fared forth at his side.

When they were fifteen winters old
He dubbed them both, those bairns so
    bold,
As knights in that same tide,
And gave them all that they might need,
Horses and weapons, knightly weed,
As princes proud in pride.

That rich duke loved those lads so brave
All that they would he freely gave,   170
Steeds had they, white and brown;
Where'er they were to sojourn fain
The land, it spake but of those twain,
Were it in tower or town;
In whatsoever place they went,
Were it for joust or tournament,
Amis and Amiloun
The doughtiest were in every deed,
With shield and spear to ride on steed
They won them great renown.   180

The rich duke, he the twain did prize,
For that they wary were and wise,
Holden good knights to be,
Sir Amiloun, and Sir Amis,
He gave them office high, I wis,
In court for all to see;
Sir Amis, as I tell ye now,
Chief butler did he make, I trow,
Since he was fair and free;
Sir Amiloun, of his knights all   190
He made chief steward in his hall
To order his mesnie.

When thus into his service brought
To win them praise they spare them
    naught,
In courteous wise they fare;
With rich and poor so well they wrought
That they, I trow, in word and thought,
Well loved by many were,
For that they were so blithe of cheer
Throughout the land, both far and near,
All did their praise declare.   201
And the rich duke, an truth be told,
Above all men who lived on mold
Most love to them he bare.

The duke, for so I understand,
Had a chief steward o'er his land,
A doughty knight was he,
By envy urged, he, at this same,
Strove hard to bring them both to
    blame,
By guile and treachery;   210
For that they courteous were and good,
And high in the duke's favour stood,
He needs must envious be;
His lord with evil words he sought
And fain had shame upon them brought,
Such was his felonie.

Ere yet two years to end were brought
A messenger hath swiftly sought
Sir Amiloun in hall,
And said his parents twain were dead,
Father and mother, in that stead,   221
Must answer to God's call —
A sad man was the knight that day,
Unto the duke he took his way,
Told him what did befall,
How father brave, and mother fair,
Were dead, and he must homeward fare
And take his lands withal.

Then the duke rich, and fair to see,
He spake with kind words graciously,
And said: "So God me speed,   231
Sir Amiloun, thou hence shalt wend,
Ne'er grieved I so for any friend
Who left my court indeed!
But if the chance it falleth so
That thou shalt be in war or woe,
And of my help hast need,
Come thou thyself, or message send,
With all the force my land may lend
I'll aid thee in that deed."   240

Sir Amiloun was sad at heart
That he must from Sir Amis part,
On him was all his thought,
He with a goldsmith speech did hold,
And bade him make two cups of gold,
For pounds three hundred bought;
The twain they of one weight should be,

And of one fashion, verily, —
Full richly were they wrought; —
And both they were as like, I wis, 250
As Amiloun was like Amis,
Thereto there failéd naught.

Whenas Sir Amiloun was dight
He took his leave to wend forthright
And ride as swift might be,
Sir Amis was so full of care
For grief and woe, and sighing sare
That well nigh swoonéd he —
He sought the duke in dreary mood,
And prayed of him e'en as he stood,
Spake, "Sire, of charitie, 261
Now give me leave to wend thee fro',
Save I may with my brother go
My heart shall break in three!"

But the rich duke, so fair to see,
With courteous words, and graciouslie,
Answered without delay
And said: "Sir Amis, my good friend,
Now would ye both from this court
    wend?
Certes, I tell ye nay! 270
For an ye both should me forsake
Then all my sorrow should ye wake,
My joy were all away.
Thy brother seeks his lands this tide,
Thou on his way with him shalt ride
And come again to-day."

When they were ready forth to ride
The barons bold who should abide,
They busked them up and down;
Now hearken here, naught would I hide,
Those doughty knights who, at that
    tide, 281
Fared forth from out the town,
E'en as they rode, throughout the day,
Great mourning did they make alway
Amis and Amiloun,
And when they needs must part, the
    twain,
Then fair together on a plain
From horse they lighted down.

And when the twain on foot were 'light,
Sir Amiloun, that courteous knight, 290
Was likewise of good rede,
Thus to Sir Amis spake forthright:
"Brother, as we our troth once plight,
Alike in word and deed,
From that day forward, without fail,
To be of aid in bliss or bale,
And help in every need,
So brother, now be true to me,
And I will be as true to thee,
So God give me good speed! 300

"And brother, here I would thee warn
For His Sake, Who the Crown of Thorn
To save Mankind once wore,
Against thy lord ne'er be foresworn,
For if thou art, shalt be forlorn,
And lost for evermore!
But hold to truth and treason shun,
And think of me, Sir Amiloun,
Since parting lies before.
And brother, this I pray of thee 310
Shun the false steward's companie,
He'll do thee mischief sore!"

As thus they stood, those brethren
    bold,
Amiloun took those cups of gold,
Alike in everything,
And bade Sir Amis that he should
Choose whether of the twain he would
Without more parleying;
And quoth to him: "now dear, my
    brother,
Take thou the one, and I the other, 320
For God's Love, Heaven's King;
And let this cup ne'er go from thee,
But look on it, and think on me,
For Friendship's tokening!"

With sorrow sore they part, I wis,
With weeping eyes and many a kiss,
Those knights so fair and free,
To God each doth commend his friend,
Then sprang on steed his way to wend,
And rode thence speedily; 330

Sir Amiloun, he sought his land,
And brought straightway beneath his
    hand
All that his sire's should be,
Then with a lady fair he wed,
His bride with honour homeward led,
And much solemnity.

. . . .

Sir Amiloun now leave we here,
In his own land, with wife so dear,
(God grant them well to fare,)
And of Sir Amis will we tell,   340
Who came again, at court to dwell,
Then blithe of him they were;
For that he courteous was and good
Men blessed the sire, in bone and blood,
Who him begat and bare;
Save but the steward, who ever stroye,
Since hate and envy did him move,
To bring the knight to care.

Then as it chanced upon a day,
He met the steward on his way,   350
Who spake full courteouslie,
And quoth: "Sir Amis, thou art woe
In that thy brother hence must go,
Certes, 't is so with me,
But for his going cease to grieve,
If thou wilt now my rede believe
And let thy mourning be,
And wilt as comrade with me wend
I'll be to thee a better friend,
Than ever yet was he!"   360

He quoth: "Sir Amis, hear my prayer,
And brotherhood with me now swear,
Plight we our troth, we two;
Be true to me in word and deed,
And I shall be, so God me speed,
As true to thee also; "
Sir Amis quoth: "My troth I plight
Sir Amiloun, that gentle knight,
Ere that he hence must go,
And whiles that I in life shall be   370
That troth shall ne'er be broke by me,
Neither for weal nor woe!

"For by the truth that God doth send
I found him aye so good a friend
Since we each other knew,
For that to him my troth was plight,
Where'er he go, that gentle knight,
To him will I be true.
And if I now should be foresworn
And break my troth, I were forlorn,   380
And sore it should me rue.
But win me friends where'er I may
I ne'er shall change, by night or day,
This old friend for a new!"

The steward was of evil mood,
For wrath, I trow, he waxed nigh wood,
And spake without delay,
And sware by Him Who died on Rood:
"Thou traitor, of unnatural blood,
Shalt dearly buy this 'nay '";   390
And thus he spake: "Be warned by me,
A bitter foe I'll be to thee,
Henceforward, from this day!"
Sir Amis bold, he answered there,
"Sir, not a sloe for that I care,
Do all the ill ye may!"

'T was thus their quarrel rose that day,
In wrath upon their separate way
Those barons bold they go;   399
The steward ceased not day and night
Striving to shame that doughty knight
If chance the way should show.
In court together had they been
With wrathful cheer, and lowering mien,
For half a year or so,
And after that it chanced one while
The steward by treason and by guile
He wrought him mickle woe.

. . . .

Then on a time, 't is written fair,
The rich duke did a feast prepare   410
Seemly, in summer-tide,
And many a gentle guest there came,
Good meat and good drink, at that
    same,
Were served on every side;

Mickle the folk assembled all,
Of earl and baron, great and small,
And ladies proud in pride,
Nor greater joy on earth might be
Than in that hold of chivalrie
With bliss in bower to bide.   420

The duke, so doth the Geste declare,
He had a daughter passing fair,
Courteous and good was she,
When fifteen winters she had told
In all the land the people hold
Was none so fair to see;
Gentle she was, and *avenant*,
And by her name hight Belisant,
As ye may list from me;
Ladies and maidens bright in bower 430
They guarded her with great honour
And much solemnity.

The feast was held full fourteen-night,
With barons and with ladies bright,
And lords, full many a one,
And many a gentle knight was there,
And many a serjant, wise and ware,
To wait on every one;
Sir Amis, in that self-same hour,
As butler, he was deemed the flower, 440
So doth the true tale run;
The doughtiest in every deed,
The comeliest in every weed,
So, seemly, praise he won.

Then when the guests at the feast's
          end
Should from that lordly dwelling wend
E'en as in book we read,
That merry maid, she asked anon
Of these her maidens, every one,
Saying: "As God ye speed,   450
Say, who was held for bravest knight,
And seemliest in all men's sight,
And worthiest in weed?
Whose fame as fairest knight doth stand,
The most renowned throughout the
          land,
The doughtiest of deed?"

Her maidens answered her straightway,
And quoth: "Madame, we sure will say
The sooth in this same hour,
Of earl or baron, swain or knight,   460
The fairest man, and most of might,
And held in most honour,
Is the chief butler, Sir Amis,
The world hath not his peer, I wis,
Neither in town nor tower.
He is the doughtiest knight in deed,
He is the worthiest in weed,
Of praise he bears the flower!"

Then Belisant, that maid so fair,
When thus her maids the truth declare
As ye may hear from me,   471
Upon Sir Amis, gentle knight,
I wis, her love it now did light,
Yet in all secresy;
Where'er she saw him ride or go
Her heart was fain to break for woe
That speech there might not be,
Since she might not, by night or day,
Speak with that knight, the gentle may
Full oft wept bitterly.   480

That gentle maiden, young and fair,
Lay in love-languishing and care
Alike by night and day;
As in the tale I tell to ye
Since speech betwixt them might not be,
In bed sore sick she lay;
Her mother to her side did go,
Full fain was she her grief to know
And help her, if she may.
She answered her without debate   490
Her pain, it was so sore and great
Soon must she lie in clay.

That rich duke on a morn was fain,
With many a lording in his train,
As prince so proud in pride,
Without delay to dight him here
And go a-hunting of the deer, —
They busked them for to ride;
When as the lordings every one   499
From out that stately hold were gone,

(Here have I naught to hide —)
Sir Amis, so 't is sooth, that day
For that a sickness on him lay,
At home he would abide.

When as the lordings forth would go
With huntsmen keen, and bended bow,
To hunt 'neath greenwood tree,
Sir Amis, as the tale doth tell,
Was left behind, at home to dwell,
And guard what there should be.　510
That gentle knight was minded so
Into the garden fair to go,
For solace, verily;
Under a bough, I trow he lay
To listen to the birdling's lay —
In bliss, I trow, was he!

.　.　.　.　.　.　.　.

Now, gentles, list, and ye shall hear
How the duke's daughter, fair and dear,
Sore sick in bed she lay,
Her mother came with doleful mien,　520
With all her ladies, so I ween,
To solace that sweet may;
"Arise," she said: "my daughter fair,
And to the garden now repair
This seemly summer's day,
There shall ye list the birdlings' song,
Hearkening their joy and bliss, ere long
Thy care shall pass away."

Then up she rose, that lady bright,
And to the garden went forthright　530
With maidens fair and free,
And bright and fair the summer's day,
The sun shone as a flame alway
Seemly it was to see;
They heard the birds both great and small,
The nightingale's sweet notes withal
That gaily sang on tree,
But in such straits her heart was brought,
On pain of love was all her thought
She would nor game nor glee.　540

And so that maiden in her pride
Forth to the orchard went that tide
To ease her of her care,
Then straight Sir Amis did she see
There, as he lay beneath a tree,
To hear that song so fair;
Great bliss, I trow, that maid must know,
Her joy she could to no man shew,
Whenas she saw him there;　549
She thought she would for no man stay,
But straight to him would take her way
And say how she did fare.

Then was that maiden blithe of mood,
When she beheld him as she stood
She sought to him, the sweet;
Not for all good the world might hold
Would she fail with this knight so bold
In courteous wise to treat.
And even as that gentle knight　559
Beheld that maid, in bower so bright,
As she would with him meet,
Straightway towards her did he go,
With courteous mien and word also
He did the lady greet.

With that, the gentle maid, anon
She bade her ladies all begone,
Withdraw from her away,
And when the twain were left alone
She to Sir Amis made her moan,
And thus to him did say —　570
"Sir Knight, t'ward thee my heart is brought,
And on thy love is all my thought
Alike by night and day;
Save that thou wilt my lover be
I trow my heart shall break in three,
Nor longer live I may!

"Thou art," she quoth, "a gentle knight,
And I a maid in bower bright
And of high lineage born,
Alike by night and e'en by day　580
My heart is set on thee alway,
I am of joy forlorn;
Plight me thy troth thou wilt be true

Nor change thine old love for a new,
For none in this world born,
And I will plight my troth again
Till God or Death part us in twain
I ne'er will be foresworn."

That gentle knight then still he stood,
And very thoughtful waxed his mood,
He spake with heart so free: 591
"Lady, for Him Who died on Rood
As thou art come of gentle blood,
And this land's heir shalt be,
Bethink thee of thy great honour,
For son of king and emperour,
Were none too high for thee!
Certes, I deem thou dost not right
To set thy love on a poor knight
Who hath nor land nor fee.   600

"And if we should Love's game begin
And any man of this thy kin
Should chance the same to know,
Then all our joy and praise that day
For this, our sin, we'ld lose straightway,
And win God's Wrath also;
Should I dishonour thus my lord
Traitor were I, of all abhorred,
Nay, it may not be so!
Sweet Lady, do thou by my rede,   610
Think what should come of this, our
        deed,
I trow me, naught but woe!"

.   .   .   .

That maiden fair, of great renown,
Answered: "Sir Knight, hast shaven
        crown?
By God Who bought thee dear,
Or priest or parson shalt thou be,
Canon or monk, that thus to me
Dost preach in such wise here?
Thou never shouldst have been a knight
To company with maidens bright,   · 620
A Friar were thee more near!
Whoe'er he be who taught thee this
May have his lot in Hell, I wis,
Were he my brother dear!

"Alas! by Him Who hath us wrought
All this, thy preaching, helpeth naught
Withstand thou ne'er so long,
Save that my will thou doest here
Thou shalt pay this, my love, full dear,
With pains both sharp and strong,   630
My kerchief and my robe, anon,   ·
I'll tear, and swear that thou hast
        done
To me a mickle wrong;
I'll say that thou hast forced me now,
By law they'll hang thee then, I trow,
On gallows-tree, ere long!"

With that, the courteous knight stood
        still,
For in his heart he liked it ill,
To speak, I trow, was slow;
He thought, "If here I steadfast be   640
With this, her tongue, she'll ruin me
Ere yet I hence may go;
And if I do my lord this wrong
Drawn with wild horses swift and strong
The punishment I'll know!"
Full loth to do her will that day,
More loth to lose his life alway,
Ne'er had he known such woe.

And then he thought that, verily,
To grant her will should better be   650
Than life to lose alway, —
Thus to the maid made answering:
"For love of Christ, our Heavenly King,
Hearken to me to-day;
As thou art maiden good and true
Bethink how rape doth turn to rue
And bitter grief and gray,
But wait we for a seven-night,
And I, as true and courteous knight,
Will do as thou shalt pray."   660

Then answered him that maiden bright,
And sware: "By Jesu, Lord of Might,
Thou goest not thus from me,
But here and now thy troth shalt plight
That thou, as true and gentle knight
To tryst shalt faithful be!"

With that her will he granted there,
Troth-plight each to the other sware
With kisses verily;
Into her bower she went again,   670
Then was the maid so glad and fain
Past speech her joy should be.

.   .   .   .

Sir Amis tarried not, but straight
His lord's home-coming to await,
To hall he turned him there;
When from his hunting at that same
With many a noble lord he came
Unto that dwelling fair,
Then tidings of his daughter dear
He asked, they said that of good cheer
Was she, and free from care.   681
To eat in hall they brought that may,
And blithe and glad were all that day
And joyful hearts they bare.

Whenas the lords, without a lie,
Were set upon the daïs high
With ladies fair and sweet,
As prince who was full proud in pride
The duke was richly served that tide
With mirth and worship meet;   690
Whenas that maid of whom I spake
Among the maids her place must take
There, as she sat in seat,
Upon that courteous knight, Amis,
A thousand times she looked, I wis,
And did with eyes entreat.

Upon that gentle knight, Amis,
For evermore she gazed, I wis,
Nor would her glances spare;
The steward, with a traitorous eye   700
He did that maiden well espy
And of her mien was ware,
For by her glances did he see
That love betwixt the twain should
          be,
Sore was he grievéd there,
Bethought him how, within a while,
He might with treason and with guile
Bring both of them to care.

And thus, I wis, that merry may
She ate in hall, with joy and play,   710
For four days, or for five,
Whene'er Sir Amis she might see
Then was her heart from sorrow free,
She joyed to be alive,
Where'er he sat or stood in hall
Her eyes were fain on him to fall
With longing looks to strive;
The steward for envy he was fain
To bring much sorrow on the twain,
Now evil may he thrive!   720

.   .   .   .

That rich duke, now, as ye shall hear,
He rode a-hunting of the deer
And with him many a knight;
Then Belisant, that gentle may,
The chamber where Sir Amis lay
Thither she sought forthright.
The steward, as I read, that tide
Was in a chamber near beside,
He saw that maiden bright
As secretly her love she sought,   730
To spy upon the twain he thought,
Followed as swift he might.

Whenas the maiden came, anon,
She found Sir Amis there alone,
"Hail!" quoth the lady bright,
"Sir Amis," swiftly did she say,
"It is a seven-night to-day
That we our troth did plight,
And therefore am I come to thee
To know, as thou art fair and free,   740
And held for courteous knight,
Whether thou wilt me now forsake
Or wilt me now unto thee take
To hold, in truth and right?"

"Lady," then quoth the knight again,
"To wed with thee I were full fain
As thou with me would'st wive;
But an thy father heard men say
That with his daughter dear I lay
From land he would me drive.   750
If I were ruler of this land

And had more gold in this, my hand,
Than other kings full five
Right gladly would I wed with thee;
Certes, I but a poor man be;
Alas, that I'm alive!"

"Sir Knight," then quoth that maiden
    kind,
"Now by Saint Thomas, slain in Ynde,
Why dost thou say me Nay?
Thou ne'er shalt be so poor, I trow,   760
But riches I may find enow
Alike by night and day!"
That courteous knight no more de-
    layed,
But in his arms he took the maid
And kissed that gentle may;
They dealt with word and deed anon
Till he her maidenhood had won
Ere yet she went away.

And aye that steward did abide
In hiding, by the chamber side,   770
Their speech he hearkened there;
And thro' a hole, 't was none too wide,
He watched them both, at that same
    tide,
As they together were,
And as he saw the twain with sight,
Sir Amis, and that maiden bright,
The rich duke's daughter fair,
Then wroth was he, of angry mood,
And gat him thence, as he were wood,
Their counsel to declare.   780

Whenas the duke he homeward came
The steward he met him at that same
Their secret to betray;
"My lord, the Duke," he saith anon,
"Of thine own mischief, by Saint John,
I 'ld warn thee here to-day,
In this thy court thou hast a thief,
Who to my heart hath done sore grief,
Yea, shame it is to say;
Certes, he shall a traitor be, —   790
But now, by force and villainy,
He with thy daughter lay!"

The duke, his wrath it waxed to flame,
"Now who," he cried, "hath done this
    shame —
Tell me, with ne'er a lie?"
"Saint James," he quoth, "my witness
    be,
His name I'll truly tell to thee,
Now bid him hang on high;
It is thy butler, Sir Amis,
A traitor was he aye, I wis,   800
He with that maid did lie;
Myself I saw them, on my troth,
As I will prove before them both,
They shall me not deny!"

Then was the duke of wrathful mood;
To hall he ran, as he were wood,
For naught would he abide,
But with a falchion sharp and bright
Full fain would he Sir Amis smite,
The stroke, it went aside;   810
Sir Amis to a chamber fled,
And shut the door fast at that stead,
For fear his head would hide;
The duke, he smote so fierce a blow
That thro' the door the steel did go,
So wrathful he that tide.

And all who there around him stood
Besought the duke to calm his mood,
Both baron, earl, and swain,   819
He sware by Him Who died on Rood,
For all the world might hold of good
He 'ld have that traitor slain:
"Great honour hath he had from me,
And now a traitor vile shall be,
Hath with my daughter lain,
Not for the whole world's wealth, I
    trow,
The traitor shall escape me now,
But die by these hands twain!"

"Sire," quoth Sir Amis at the last,
"Let this, thy wrath, be overpast,   830
I pray, of Charitie,
If thou canst prove now, by Saint
    John,

That e'er such deed by me was done,
Then hang me high on tree!
If any man our harm hath sought,
And such a charge against us brought,
Then, whosoe'er he be,
He is a liar, shalt thou know —
As I will here in battle show,
And prove us quit and free!"   840

"Yea," quoth the duke, "and wilt thou
    so?
Say, dost thou dare to combat go
And make thee quit and clear?"
"Yea, certes, Sire," he answered free,
"And here my glove I give to thee,
His falsehood shall appear."
The steward answered back forthright,
And quoth: "Thou traitor, perjured
    knight,
Thou art attainted here,
Why, I myself have seen to-day   850
How that she in thy chamber lay,
Yourselves ye cannot clear!"

As thus the steward he said his say;
And thus Sir Amis answered, "Nay,
The thing it was not so."
The duke bade bring that maiden
    fair,
The steward did aye the same declare,
And sware: "'T was as I show!"
The maiden wept, her hands she wrung,
And ever on her mother hung,   860
Vowing it was not so.
Then quoth the duke: "Now, without
    fail,
Here shall we see the truth prevail
By combat 'twixt the two."

So 'twixt the twain they set the fight
For that day past a fourteen-night
For many a man to see;
The steward was of mickle might,
In all the court there was no knight
Would Amis' surety be;   870
The steward was so strong, I trow,
That sureties might he find enow,

Twenty at least they be;
Then quoth they all, that till that tide
Sir Amis should in prison bide
Lest he from thence should flee.

With that she spake, the maiden bright,
And sware by Jesu, Lord of Might,
That this were mickle wrong:
"Take ye my body for the knight,   880
And till the day he come for fight,
Hold me in prison strong;
And if the knight should flee away,
Nor durst abide the chance that day
That doth to fight belong,
Then, as the law is, deal with me,
And doom my body drawn to be,
And high on gallows hung!"

Then, with bold words, her mother still
Said she would be of right good will   890
His surety also;
That he fail not to keep the day
But as good knight and true alway
Should fight against his foe.
And thus those ladies fair and bright
Their lives for Amis, gentle knight,
As surety would forego,
With that, the lordings every one
Said, other hostage would they none,
The thing should aye be so.   900

.   .   .   .

When this was done, as now I say,
And pledges ta'en without delay,
And thus they granted were,
Sir Amis sorrowed night and day
For all his joy was fled away
And come was all his care;
For that the steward was so strong,
And had the right, and he the wrong,
When he accused him there;
For his own life, he held it naught,   910
But of the maid was all his thought,
Such sorrow no man bare.

For that he knew he needs must swear,
Ere that he should to battle fare,

An oath, on that same morn,
Praying that God should be his speed,
As he was guiltless of the deed
That was against him borne.
And then he thought, with ne'er a lie,
Rather would he be hanged on high
Than thus to be foresworn;   921
And oft he did to Jesu pray
That He should save them both that day
Nor let them be forlorn!

So it befell upon a day
He met the lady, and that may,
Beneath an orchard side;
"Sir Amis," quoth the lady there,
"Why dost thou go so full of care?
Tell me the truth this tide;   930
Now dread thee naught," she spake
          forthright,
"Against thy foeman now to fight,
Whether thou go, or ride,
So well I'll arm thee, foot and head,
That thou of no man shalt have dread,
But battle well abide."

"Madam," then quoth that gentle
          knight,
"For love of Jesu, Lord of Might,
Take to my words good heed;   939
Mine is the wrong, and his the right,
For that I be afraid to fight,
So God give me good speed,
For I must swear, nor else may be,
So help me God to victory
As he in word and deed
Is false — Therewith am I foresworn,
And am of life and soul forlorn,
Thereto I find no rede."

Then quoth the lady presentlie,   949
"None other way then, may there be
To bring that traitor down?"
"Yea, Lady," quoth he, "by Saint Giles,
There dwelleth distant many miles,
My brother Amiloun;
And if to him I now dare go,
Then, by Saint John, full well I know,

He wears of truth the crown,
An his own life should forfeit be,
His help he now would give to me,
And smite my foeman down."   960

"Sir Amis," did the lady say,
"Take leave to-morrow with the day,
And journey speedily,
And I will say that thou art gone
To thine own land, since thou anon
Thy parents fain would see.
When to thy brother com'st aright,
Pray him, as he be faithful knight,
And of great courtesie,
That he will here defend the right,   970
For thee against the steward fight
Who thinks to ruin us three."

. . . .

With morn Sir Amis busked him there,
And took his leave from thence to fare
And went upon his way,
For nothing would he slacken speed,
But, ruthless, forward spurred his steed,
Alike by night and day;
So fast he rode, and rested not,
The steed whereon he rode, I wot,   980
When far upon the way,
Was overpressed, and fell down dead, —
Sir Amis, brought in evil stead,
He cried, "Ah, wellaway!"

Then when the chance had fallen so
That he must needs on foot now go
Then, sorrowful, that knight,
He girt his skirts about him there,
And on his way began to fare
To hold what he had hight;   990
And all that day ran far and fast,
To a wild forest came at last,
Betwixt the day and night;
A slumber strong o'ercame him now,
Not for the whole world's wealth, I trow,
Further might fare that knight.

That courteous knight, so fair and free,
He laid him down beneath a tree,

And fell asleep that tide,
And all that night so still lay he,   1000
Till on the morrow men might see
Daylight on every side.
And that knight's brother, Amiloun,
Whom all men held of great renown
Thro' all that country side,
Dwelt, from the spot where Amis lay,
But half the journey of a day
As men might walk or ride.

.   .   .   .

Sir Amiloun, that gentle knight,
In slumber soft he lay that night,   1010
In dream it seemed him so,
That he Sir Amis needs must see
His brother troth-plight, verily,
Beset by many a foe;
For of a bear, both wild and wood,
And other beasts that with it stood
The onslaught must he know,
Alone, amidst them all he stood,
Nor found 'gainst them resistance good,
I trow, he was full woe!   1020

Whenas Sir Amiloun did wake,
Great sorrow he began to make,
His wife, he told her there,
How black beasts, so in dream he
     thought,
With wrath, his brother Amis sought
To slay, with mickle care;
"Certes," he quoth, "some man with
     wrong
Hath brought him into peril strong,
Of bliss shall he be bare";   1029
And then he quoth: "Forsooth, I wis,
I may know neither joy nor bliss
Till I wot how he fare!"

From bed he sprang up in that tide,
Nor longer would he there abide,
But dight him fair, anon, —
His mesnie, too, without delay,
Made ready for to ride straightway;
With him they fain had gone,
But that he bade them now to cease,

For love of Heaven to hold their peace,
Thus spake he to each one,   1041
And sware by Him Who made Mankind
That no companion there he'ld find,
But would go forth alone.

He robed him then in right rich weed,
And leapt astride upon his steed,
For naught would he abide;
His folk, he straight forbade them there
That none among them all should dare
After their lord to ride;   1050
So thro' the night he rode till day,
And came to where Sir Amis lay
All in that forest wide;
He saw, thro' weariness foregone,
A knight, who, sleeping, lay alone
And sought to him that tide.

With that, he called on him straight-
     way,
"Rise up, Sir Knight, for it is day
And time from hence to go!"
Sir Amis he beheld with sight,   1060
Straightway he knew that gentle knight
And he knew him also;
That courteous knight, Sir Amiloun,
From off his steed did light adown.
With that, they kissed the two:
"Brother," he quoth, "why liest thou
     here?
And why dost make such mournful
     cheer?
Say, who hath wrought thee woe?"

"Brother," Sir Amis answered there,
"In sooth such sorrow knew I ne'er
Since me my mother bore;   1071
Since thou didst from me go, I wis,
With joy, and eke with mickle bliss,
I served my lord before,
But now the steward, thro' sheer envy,
By guile, and eke by treachery,
Hath wrought me sorrow sore;
Save that thou help me in my need
Certes, I see none other rede,
My life must I give o'er!"   1080

"Brother," Sir Amiloun he said,
"What hath the steward 'gainst thee
laid?
Why thus hath done thee shame?"
"Certes, he doth by treason strive
From out mine office me to drive
And bring upon me blame," —
With that Sir Amis told him there
How that he, and that maiden fair,
In love together came,   1089
And how the steward did them betray,
And how the duke, he would him slay
In anger, at that same.

And how himself he needs must plight
His troth against the steward to fight
In battle fierce and strong,
And how, to save those ladies bright,
As surety, he ne'er a knight
Might find, the court among;
How ere he did to battle fare   1099
Needs must that he should falsely swear
Since he was in the wrong, —
"A man foresworn can never speed, —
Since I can find no better rede
'Alas!' may be my song!"

 . . . .

When thus Sir Amis told his tale
How the false steward should sure pre-
vail
O'er him, with evil mood,
Sir Amiloun, with words so bold,
Sware: "By the Lord Whom Judas sold,
Who died upon the Rood,   1110
Of this, his hope, he faileth now,
For I shall fight for thee, I trow,
Altho' he were well wood,
And if I meet him now aright,
With this, my brand, that is so bright
I'll shed his heart's best blood!

"But, Brother, this my weed take thou,
And in thy robes I'll clothe me now,
E'en as thyself I were,   1119
And I shall swear, So God me speed,
That I am guiltless of the deed

And plaint he 'gainst me bare." —
With that, those courteous knights, anon,
Each other's raiment did they on;
When they were ready there,
Quoth Amiloun: "Now by Saint Gile,
Thus we the traitor shall beguile
Who would thy ruin prepare.

"Brother," he quoth, "go home forth-
right
Unto my wife, that lady bright,   1130
And there with her remain;
And as thou art a gentle knight
Lie thou beside her every night
Until I come again;
Say, thou hast sent thy steed, I wis,
Unto thy brother Sir Amis,
Then will they be full fain,
They 'll deem that thou my-self shalt be
For none shall know thee now from me,
So like we be, we twain."   1140

And when he thus his word had plight
Sir Amiloun, that gentle knight,
He rode upon his way.
Sir Amis gat him home forthright
Unto his brother's lady bright
And made no more delay,
And said, how he had sent his steed
Unto his brother for his need
By a knight's hand that day.
And every man thought Sir Amis   1150
To be their very lord, I wis,
So like, the twain, were they.

And when Sir Amis spake full fair
And told them now of all his care
Full well the thing did go,
For great or little, verily,
All men who there in court should be
They deemed it had been so.
When it was come unto the night
Sir Amis and that lady bright   1160
To bed they fain would go;
When side by side the twain were laid
Sir Amis drew his shining blade
And laid it 'twixt the two.

The lady looked on him alway,
And wrathful gleamed her eyes of gray,
She deemed her lord were wood,
And, "Sir," she asked, "why dost thou so?
Thus wert thou never wont to do   1169
Who now hath changed thy mood?"
"Lady," he answered, "verily
I be sick of a malady
That doth infect my blood,
And all my bones so sore they be
Thy flesh may not be touched by me
For all of this world's good!"

And thus, I wis, that faithful knight
He kept him for a fourteen-night,
As lord and prince in pride,
And he forgat not every night   1180
Betwixt him and that lady bright
His sword to lay beside;
The lady deemed 't was rightly done
For that her lord, Sir Amilon,
He was sore sick that tide;
Therefore she thought to hold her still
And speak no word, but this, his will,
She would in peace abide.

. . . .

Now Lordings, hear, and I shall say
How Amiloun, he went his way,   1190
And would for nothing spare;
He spurred his steed by night and day
As hero stout and stiff alway
To court he swift doth fare;
The self-same day, withouten let,
That was afore for battle set
Sir Amis was not there,
They take those ladies by the hand,
The judgment now they needs must stand,
With tears and sighing sare.   1200

The steward mounts his steed that tide,
With shield and spear would combat bide
He boasteth loud alway;
Before the duke he spurs his steed
And saith, "Now, Sire, as God me speed

Hearken to what I pray, —
This traitor, he hath fled the land,
And if he now were nigh at hand
He should be hanged to-day,   1209
Therefore 't is meet that judgment turn
Against his sureties, that they burn
E'en as the law doth say."

That rich duke, moved by anger there,
He bade them take those ladies fair
And lead them forth beside,
A great fire then he bade them make,
Therewith should they a barrel take
To burn them there, inside;
Then, as they looked upon the field,
They saw a knight with spear and shield   1220
Come pricking in his pride,
With that each one he cried, "I wis,
Yonder comes hastening Sir Amis —"
They should his coming bide.

Sir Amiloun no stone doth heed,
But o'er them all he spurred with speed
The duke seeks hastily,
"My lord, the Duke," he saith, "for shame,
Set free these ladies at this same,
For good and true they be,   1230
And hither am I come to-day
To save them both, if so I may,
From bond to set them free;
Certes, a mickle wrong it were
To make a roast of ladies fair,
'T were naught but crueltie!"

I trow it pleased those ladies well,
Their joy they might to no man tell
Their care was all away;   1239
And sithen, as ye now may know,
The twain did to their chamber go
And made no more delay,
But richly did they arm that knight
With helm, and plate, and byrnie bright,
His tiring, it was gay;
When he was mounted on his steed

That God the knight should save and
    speed,
Full many a man did pray.

.   .   .   .

As he came riding from the town,   1249
There came a voice from Heaven adown
That no man heard save he,
And saith: "Thou knight, Sir Amilon,
The God Who died the Rood upon
Doth message send by me;
An thou this combat fight withal
A venture strange shall thee befall
And that within years three,
For ere these three years they be gone
Leper so foul was never none
As thou thyself shalt be.   1260

"And since thou art good knight and free
Jesu this word hath sent by me
To warn thee now anon,
So foul a wretch thou shalt be sure,
Such grief and poverty endure,
As fell, I trow, to none;
O'er all the world, both far and near,
Thy best friends, whom thou held most
    dear,
They shall thy presence shun;   1269
Yea, e'en thy wife and all thy kin
Shall flee the place that thou art in,
Forsake thee every one!"

That knight stood still as any stone;
Those words he hearkened every one
That were so drear and dread;
He knew not what were best to do,
To flee, or to the combat go,
His heart was e'en as lead;
He thought: "If I confess my name
Then is my brother put to shame,
His life in sorrow fled, —   1281
Certes," he quoth, "for fear of care
To keep my troth I will not spare,
The Will of God be sped!"

And all the folk, they deemed, I wis,
That this knight he was Sir Amis,

Who came to fight indeed, —
He, and the steward, as I say,
Before the justice brought were they
To swear for this their deed,   1290
Before the folk, the steward, he,
Sware that his word no lie should be,
God help him at his need!
Sir Amiloun, he steadfast sware
He ne'er e'en kissed that maiden fair,
Our Lady be his speed!

When they had sworn, as thus I told,
To fight were fain those barons bold
And busked them for to ride,   1299
And young and old, all folk that day,
They straightly unto God did pray
He would Sir Amis guide!
On steeds that were both stiff and
    strong
They met, their spears, so sharp and
    long,
Were shivered on each side;
Then each man drew his sword so good
Together hew, as they were wood,
For naught would they abide.

Those champions, who were fierce to
    sight,
With falchion fell begin to fight,   1310
As madmen hack and hew,
Hard on each other's helm they smite
With strokes so strong, and of such
    might
That fire from out them flew;
So hard they smote on head and side
That from their deadly wounds and wide
Blood wells in crimson hue;
From morning-tide till noon were past
The combat did betwixt them last,
Fiercer their anger grew.   1320

Sir Amiloun, as flame of fire,
Sought for his foe with fierce desire
And smote with might and main,
His blow, it glanced aside that stead
And smote the good steed on the head,
Scattered was all the brain;

The steed fell dead upon the ground
Then was the steward, in that stound,
Fearful lest he be slain;
Sir Amiloun adown doth light,   1330
Afoot he seeks the steward forthright
Raising him up again.

"Now rise up, Steward," the knight did
        say,
"Thou needs must fight afoot to-day
Since thou hast lost thy steed;
By Saint John, he were craven knight
Who with a fallen man would fight
Who thus were brought in need"; —
That courteous knight, so free and fair,
The steward by hand he taketh there,
Saying: "So God me speed,   1341
Since that afoot thou needs must go
I'll fight with thee afoot also:
Other were falsehood's rede!"

The steward, and that man of might,
Anon together met in fight
With brands both bright and bare;
So fierce a fight they then began
The blood from out their armour ran
For nothing would they spare;   1350
The steward his shoulder smote that tide,
And made a wound both deep and wide
A grisley gash it were,
And thro' that wound, as ye may hear,
That knight was known with rueful
        cheer,
When he was come to care.

Wroth was Sir Amiloun and wood,
Seeing his armour red with blood
That erst was white as swan,   1359
Then, with his falchion sharp and bright,
He smote in wrath a blow of might
As hero bold, anon,
That even from the shoulder blade
Down to the breast a wound it made
Sheer thro' the heart hath gone; —
With that the steward fell down dead,
Sir Amiloun smote off his head
Thanked God the fight was won!

Then all the lordings, men of might,
Or lesser folk, who saw that sight   1370
Were filled with joy that tide,
The head upon a spear they bare
And to the town they gat them there
For nothing would abide;
From town to meet the knight they came
In fair procession, at that same,
Seemly, from either side,
The victor to the tower they led
With mickle honour at that stead
As a prince proud in pride.   1380

When to the hall they came, I wis,
All in that palace deemed Amis,
He stood their face before, —
"Sir Amis," quoth the duke anon
Before the lordings every one,
"What I forbade of yore
I grant thee now, that gentle may,
My daughter, dearly bought to-day
With grisley wounds and sore;   1389
Therefore I freely grant thee here
My land, with this my daughter dear
To hold for evermore."

Then glad and blithe that courteous
        knight,
And thanked the duke with all his might,
Full glad was he, and fain;
In all the court was none, I ween,
Who wist what his true name had been
Who saved those ladies twain.
Then leeches to their will they found
Who handled these, his wounds, and
        bound,   1400
And made him whole again,
And all were joyful in that hold,
To God gave thanks a thousand-fold
In that the steward was slain.

Sir Amiloun, he dight him there
And said that he from thence would fare
And get him on his way,
And tell his friends, both less and more,
And all who friendship to him bore
How he had sped that day;   1410

The duke, he granted leave that tide,
And proffered knights with him to ride,
But he made answer, Nay,
No man he thought with him to take
But swiftly did him ready make
And rode from thence away.

Thus on his way he went alone
For never man with him had gone
Or were he knight or swain,   1419
That knight, so brave in blood and bone,
He stayed for neither stock nor stone,
Till he came home again.
Sir Amis, as I now shall say,
Waited his coming every day,
Up in the forest plain,
There Amiloun and he they meet,
With joy he doth Sir Amis greet,
Tells how the steward he'd slain;

And saith how he should wed for meed
That gentle maid, in goodly weed,
Who was so fair of face.   1431
Down from his steed he sprang anon,
The other's raiment each does on
As erst in that same place,
"Brother," he quoth, "now go thy
        way —"
And taught him all that he should say
Within a little space.
Sir Amis, he hath joy untold
And thanked him there a thousand-fold,
Who shewed him so much grace.   1440

And as they needs must part, the twain,
Sir Amis thanked him oft again
For this, his right good deed:
"Brother," he saith, "an it should be
That care or woe befalleth thee
And of my help hast need,
Send thou thy messenger nor spare,
Be sure that I shall fail thee ne'er,
As God shall be my speed,
For be thy peril ne'er so strong   1450
I'll be thy help, for right or wrong,
If life I lose for meed!"

.   .   .   .

With that they part asunder there, —
Sir Amiloun, that knight so fair,
Went homeward in that tide
Unto his wife, who scarce was kind,
Welcome he from his friends did find
As a prince proud in pride;
And when it came unto the night
And he, with this, his lady bright,   1460
In bed lay, side by side,
Within his arms with many a kiss
He clasped her close, in joy and bliss,
For nothing would abide.

His wife, she was full fain to know
For what cause he had acted so
For this last fourteen-night,
And laid his sword betwixt them two
That she durst not, for weal or woe,
Touch him, her lord, aright?   1470
With that, Sir Amiloun, he knew
That Amis, as a knight so true,
Had kept the troth he plight;
"Lady," he quoth, "I now will say
And tell the truth to thee alway —
Betray me to no wight!"

With that the lady straitly prayed
For love of Him, Who this world
        made,
To tell her how it were;   1479
Without delay, that gallant knight,
The truth he told to her forthright
How he to court did fare,
And how he slew the steward strong
Who would, by treason and by wrong,
His brother bring to care;
And how Sir Amis, courteous knight,
Had lain beside her every night
While he afar did fare.

The lady wrathful waxed that tide
And angrily her lord did chide,   1490
Words waxed betwixt the two;
She quoth: "With wrong, and not with
        right
Now hast thou slain a gentle knight,
I wot thou ill didst do."

"Lady," he quoth, "by Heaven's King,
I did it for no other thing
Only to save from woe
My brother; and were I in need
I hope he'ld give his life for meed
If he might help me so!"   1500

And thus, as now the Geste doth say,
Sir Amis, he was glad and gay,
To court went speedily;
And when he thither came again
By earl and baron, knight and swain,
Honoured, I trow, was he;
The rich duke took him by the hand,
And gave him seizin of his land
That his for aye it be;
Sithen, with joy upon a day   1510
He wed with Belisant, the may,
And true and kind was she.

A seemly folk, and great, withal,
Came to that bridal, there in hall,
Whenas he wed that flower,
And earls and barons, many a score,
With other lordings, less and more,
And ladies bright in bower;
A royal feast they there did hold
Of earls and many a baron bold   1520
With joy and great honour;
Throughout that land, from east to
    west,
Amis was held of knights the best,
For praise elect in tower.

.   .   .   .

And then, within a two years' space,
Unto the twain there chanced a grace
By God's hand was it told,
For the rich duke, he needs must die,
With him his lady low did lie
Buried in clay so cold;   1530
Then men Sir Amis, fair and free,
As duke, and lord, in majesty
O'er all that land did hold,
Two bairns begat he on his wife,
No fairer children e'er saw life
As in the Geste 't is told.

So was that knight of great renown,
The lord of many a tower and town,
A mighty duke was he,
While this, his brother Amiloun,   1540
In grief and care was brought adown
Who erst was fair and free;
For as the Angel had foretold
No fouler leper did one hold
Within the world than he,
In Geste to read it is sore ruth,
What grief he had for this his truth
Ere years had passed but three.

For ere three years had come to end
He wist not whither he might wend —
Such woe was his, alway;   1551
For all who erst his friends had stood,
And most of all his kinsmen good
As foes they turned away;
Yea, and his wife, as I say truth,
By day and night she wrought him ruth
More than they all, i' fay.
When this hard lot befell the knight
A man in a more friendless plight
Were not on earth that day.   1560

A wicked shrew she was, his wife,
She pierced his heart, as with a knife,
With words so sharp and keen,
She quoth: "Thou caitiff wretch, in strife
The steward he wrongful lost his life
As may by thee be seen,
Therefore, by Saint Denys of France,
This evil sore to thee doth chance,
Pity were sin, I ween!"   1569
Then oft his hands for woe he wrung
Vowing that he hath lived too long
Whose life but loss hath been!

Alas! Alas! that gentle knight
Who whilom was so fair to sight
And suffered so much woe,
That from his wife, so fair and bright,
From his own chamber, of a night
Was bidden forth to go!
And in his own hall, in the day,   1579
From the high board was turned away

For it was ordered so,
At the board's end he ate, to wit,
For no man would beside him sit,
Sore sorrow must he know.

When but six months had passed withal
That he had eaten thus in hall
And had good nourishing,
His lady's anger waxed full strong,
She deemed that he had lived too long,
No lie I here do bring —   1590
"Now thro' the land there runs this
        word,
I feed a leper at my board,
He is so foul a thing
My kin these tidings sore displease,
No longer shall he sit at ease,
By Jesu, Heaven's King!"

She summoned him upon a day,
"Sir, it doth chance," so did she say,
"'T is truth, I swear to thee,   1599
That thou dost eat too long in hall,
Thy presence doth displease us all,
My kin be wroth with me!"
The knight, he wept, and spake so
        still:
"Now send me where it be thy will
That no man shall me see,
And I from thee no more will pray
Than meat for but one meal a day,
For holy charitie!"

That lady then, for her lord's sake,
She bade that men should timber take,
For nothing would she stay,   1611
Without the gates, but half a mile,
She bade them build a lodge that
        while,
That stood beside the way,
And when that lodge, I trow, was
        wrought
With him, of all his wealth, he brought
But his gold cup away;
When he was in his lodge alone
To God in Heaven he made his moan,
Gave thanks to Him alway.   1620

When he within that lodge was dight
In all the court there was no knight
Would do him service there
Save but one child, who with him came,
Childe Owen, did they call his name,
Who wept for this, his care;
The child was true, of good renown,
And sister's son to Amiloun,
He spake with words full fair,
Saying he would beside him stand   1630
Nor cease to serve him, foot and hand,
While that in life he were.

.   .   .   .

The child, who was so fair and bold,
As Owen was his name first told,
He came of noble blood,
When he was twelve years old withal
Then Amoraunt his name they call,
Courteous was he, and good,
Beside his lord each night he lay
And fetched from out the hall each day
What they should have for food;   1641
And when each man made mirth and
        song
For his lord's sake, he sat among
Them all in dreary mood.

Thus Amoraunt, as I now say,
To court he cometh every day,
Nor stayed for all they strive,
For all, that he should come away
And leave the leper, straitly pray,
Then should he better thrive.   1650
He answered them in gentle mood,
Swearing by Him Who died on Rood
And suffered Wounds full five,
That for the whole world's wealth to take
His lord he never would forsake
Whiles that he were alive.

When as the twelvemonth's end did fall
And Amoraunt came to the hall
Their food to take, one day,
The lady, she waxed wroth anon   1660
And bade her servants every one
To drive that child away;

She sware by Him Whom Judas sold,
That tho' for hunger and for cold
Stark dead her lord, he lay,
Nor meat nor drink, nor anything
To succour him should any bring
From her, from that same day.

The child, his hands he wrung, the twain,
And, weeping, gat him home again 1670
With mickle grief and care,
His lord, he did him straightway pray
And bade him tell without delay
What thus had grieved him there?
He answered him, and said also;
"I wis I well may be in woe,
And grief and sorrow bear,
Thy wife hath sworn in evil mood
That she no more will give us food,
Alas! how shall we fare?" 1680

"God help me!" quoth that gentle
    knight;
"Whilom was I a man of might,
To deal out meat and cloth,
And now I am so foul to see
That every man who looks on me
The sight of me doth loathe!
Now son," he saith, "thy weeping
    stay,
Tho' these be tidings ill to-day,
I tell thee by my troth,
Certes none other rede I know 1690
Than that to beg our bread we go,
So it behoves us both."

The morrow soon as it was light
The child, and eke that gentle knight,
Made ready to be gone,
And forth they journeyed in that stead
As needs they must, to beg their bread,
Since they of meat had none.
So long they journeyed up and down
They came unto a market town, 1700
A five mile further on;
Weeping, they go from street to street,
For love of God they pray for meat,
Much grief they knew anon.

In that same time, I understand,
Great plenty was throughout the land
Both meat and drink had they;
The folk, they were of hand right free,
And brought unto them willingly
Of everything that day, 1710
Since they the man a leper see,
And the child passing fair to be,
Pity upon them lay,
They brought enow of all their good,
Then was the boy right blithe of mood,
And let his weeping stay.

The good knight's foot, it waxed so sore
That he, I trow, might walk no more
For all of this world's good, 1719
To the town's end the lad him bare
And straight a hut he built him there
That by the highway stood;
And as the country folk, each day,
To market bound, must pass that way,
They gat from them their food,
And Amoraunt oft went to town
And meat and drink begged up and down
When most in need they stood.

Thus in the Geste 't is writ to see
That here they dwelt for years full three
The lad and he, also, 1731
In poverty and care they live
On what the country folk may give
As thus they come and go;
But it fell out in the fourth year
That corn began to wax full dear,
Hunger stalked to and fro,
Was neither young nor old, I trow,
Who meat and drink would give them
    now,
Then want they needs must know. 1740

Oft Amoraunt to town hath gone
But meat and drink there found he none,
Neither of man nor wife,
And when the twain they were alone
Then ruefully they made their moan,
Weary were they of life;
Amiloun's wife, the sooth to say,

Within that land she dwelt alway
Of miles but distant five,
And lived in joy both night and day
While he in care and sorrow lay,   1751
Now evil may she thrive!

One day, as thus they sat alone,
That gentle knight, he made his moan,
Spake to the child that tide,
And saith: "Now must thou go, my son,
And seek my lady swift anon,
Who dwelleth here beside,
Pray her, by Him Who died on Rood,
She grant me now, of all my good,   1760
An ass, whereon to ride,
Forth from the land we now will fare
And beg our bread with grief and care
Nor longer here abide."

Then Amoraunt, to court went he,
Before that lady fair to see,
With courteous speech alway:
"Lady," he quoth, "with good intent,
My lord a message by me sent,
For walk no more he may,   1770
He prayeth thee, in humble mood,
This much to grant of all his good,
An ass to ride to-day;
Then forth from out this land we 'll fare,
And come again I trow me, ne'er,
Tho' hunger should us slay."

The lady quoth she were full fain
To send unto them asses twain
If they from hence would fare,
Afar, in distant lands remain —   1780
"Nay, certes, Lady, ne'er again
Thou seest us —" he sware.
The lady, she was blithe and glad,
An ass she bade them give the lad,
And said in anger there:
"Now ye from out my land shall go,
God grant that it may fall out so
That I behold ye ne'er!"

The lad, he would no longer bide,
But swift his ass he did bestride   1790

And gat him home again,
And told his lord in that same tide
All that his lady, in her pride,
Did shamelessly maintain;
He set the knight upon the ass,
Forth from the city gate they pass
Thereof were they full fain,
Through many a country, up and down,
They begged their meat from town to
     town,
Alike in wind and rain.   1800

By God's Will, o'er that land, ere long,
The famine waxed so grim and strong
As they went far and wide,
That they for hunger were nigh dead,
They had not half their fill of bread,
The twain were sorely tried,
Then quoth the knight upon a day:
"We needs must sell our ass away,
'T is our sole wealth this tide,
Save this, my goodly cup of gold,   1810
And certes, that shall ne'er be sold,
Tho' I for hunger died!"

Amoraunt, and the good knight, there,
With rueful cheer, in grief and care,
With morn, upon a day,
They gat them to a market-town,
And when the knight had lighted down,
With never more delay,
Amoraunt, to the town he sped,
And this, their ass, with him he led,
Five shillings, did men pay;   1821
And on that money lived they long,
The whiles the dearth, it waxed full
     strong,
Nor more might get alway.

And when that ass they now had sold,
For shillings five, as here I told,
There they abode days three,
Amoraunt, he waxed strong, I ween,
Of winters had he told fifteen,
Courteous, and fair, and free,   1830
For this, his lord, he well did care,
Upon his back he set him there,

Forth from the town went he,
And thus, for half a year and more,
To seek his meat the knight he bore,
Now blesséd shall he be!

Thus Amoraunt waxed strong and stout,
And thus he bare his lord about
As read in Geste ye may,   1839
Then winter came, so hard and strong
That oft, "Alas!" must be their song,
For deep the country lay;
The roads in mud were deep, that tide,
And oft-times did they slip and slide,
And fall down in the clay;
True was the lad, and kind of blood,
And served his lord in gentle mood,
Nor thought to go his way.

Thus Amoraunt, as now I say,   1849
He served his lord by night and day
And on his back still bore,
But "Wellaway" was oft his cry,
So deep in mire the land did lie
His bones they waxed full sore,
And all their money, it was gone,
Till but twelve pence was left alone,
Therewith, so runs my lore,
The twain, a hand-cart did they buy,
So that the knight therein might lie,
He might not bear him more.   1860

Thus the lad pushed Sir Amiloun
Thro' many a country, up and down,
As ye may understand,
Till to a town they came, I wis,
Wherein that baron, Sir Amis,
Was duke and lord in land,
Then straitly did he pray, the knight,
"Bear me to the duke's court forth-
      right,
Good lad, 't is my command,
He is a man of gentle mood,   1870
And there, I ween, we 'll get some good,
Thro' grace of God's own Hand.

"But hearken to me now, dear son,
And for His Love, Who this world won,

As thou art fair and free,
See thou tell no man, at this same,
Whither I go, or whence I came,
Or what my name shall be."
The lad, he heard and answered, "Nay,"
Forthwith to court he took his way
As ye may hear from me,   1881
Before the other beggars then
He pushed his cart thro' mire and fen,
Great dole it was to see!

And it befell that self-same day
As now I tell, in this my Lay,
It was mid-winter tide,
And the rich duke now at the same
With joy and bliss from church he came
As lord and prince in pride;   1890
When he came to his castle-gate
The beggars all who stood thereat
They drew them on one side,
And with his knights and serjaunts all
He passed into his noble hall
In joy and bliss to bide.

As in king's court, 't is law, I know,
The trumpets for the meat 'gan blow,
To board they went so bold,
When all were set in order there   1900
Then in due time they served them
      fair
As men most blithe on mold;
And that rich duke, no lie I tell,
E'en as a prince they served him well
With right rich cups of gold,
While he who brought him to that state,
He lay shut out, without the gate,
A-hungered sore, and cold.

Forth from the gate a knight there
      came,
With him a serjaunt at that same,   1910
To field they passed anear,
And thro' the Grace of God on high
On Amiloun he cast his eye
Saw him of loathly cheer,
Sithen, they Amoraunt behold,
And very fair the lad they hold,

As ye in Geste may hear;
Then said they both that, by Saint John,
In all the court they knew of none
For beauty half his peer! 1920

That good knight straight to him did go
And courteously was fain to know,
As ye may understand,
Whither he went, and whence he came,
And why he stood there at that same,
And whom he served in land?
He answered: "Sir, so God me save
Here am I but mine own lord's knave
Who lieth in God's Hand,
As thou be knight of gentle blood 1930
I pray thee, that to us some good
Be done, at thy command!"

With that the good knight asked him fair
If he would leave the leper there
And service with him take?
And promised him, by sweet Saint John,
To serve the duke in court anon,
And rich he would him make.
The lad, he answered, mild of mood,
And sware, by Him Who died on Rood,
Whiles he might walk and wake, 1941
That, might he win this whole world's
good,
This, his dear lord, by whom he stood,
He never would forsake!

The good man deemed him mad to be,
Or fool to a wise man was he,
Who was of wit forlorn;
Or else his lord, so foul to eye,
Had been a man of station high
Of noble lineage born; 1950
Therefore he thought no more to say,
But back to hall he took his way,
Spake to the duke that morn:
"My lord," he said, "now hearken me,
The best jest, by my loyalty,
Shalt hear, since thou wert born!"

Then the rich duke bade him anon
To tell before them every one

His tale, without delay —
"Now, Sire," he said, "by sweet Saint
John, 1960
Without this gate I now had gone
Intent on this my play,
Of poor men many, at thy door,
Both old and young, both less or more,
There I beheld them stay,
And midst the men who there did stand,
The foulest thing in any land,
A leper, there he lay.

"That leper in a cart doth lie,
He is so feeble, verily, 1970
On foot he may not go,
A naked lad by him doth stay,
No fairer child, the sooth to say,
In this world do I know.
In Christendom, I trow, there be
No fairer lad to-day than he
That any land can show;
And yet the greatest fool he is
With whom I ever spake, I wis,
Here in this world below." 1980

The rich duke answered him straight-
way,
"What folly, tell me, did he say,
How is he mad of mood?"
"Now, Sire," he said, "I bade him part
From this, the leper in the cart,
By whom but now he stood,
And in thy service should he be,
I proffered him both land and fee,
Enough of this world's good.
He answered me straightway with *No*,
He from his lord would never go, 1991
Therefore I hold him wood."

Then quoth the duke: "Perchance of yore
His lord, who now doth suffer sore,
Hath holpen him in need;
Or of his blood the boy was born;
Or he an oath, may be, hath sworn
With him his life to lead.
Or stranger he, or of his blood, 1999
That lad," he said, "is true and good,

As God, He shall me speed,
I'ld speak with him ere hence they go,
Since he such steadfast truth doth
    show,
I would requite his meed."

With that the duke, in Geste 't is told,
He called to him a squire so bold,
    And spake as he was fain:
"Take thou," he quoth, "my cup of
    gold,
As full of wine as thou may'st hold,
Within these, thy hands twain;   2010
Forth to the gate the cup now bear,
A leper shalt thou seek out there,
    He lieth in a wain;
This wine, now, by Saint Martin, say,
He and his page shall drink straight-
    way, —
My cup, bring thou again."

The squire, he took the cup that stead,
And to the castle gate he sped,
    The cup brimfull he bare,
And to the leper straight did say: 2020
"This cup of wine, my lord to-day
Sends, drink it if ye dare."
The leper took his cup of gold,
'T was fashioned in the self-same mould,
    E'en as the duke's it were,
And the rich wine therein did pour
Till both alike, nor less, nor more,
    Of wine had equal share.

The squire gazed those cups upon,
The leper's and his lord's, anon,   2030
    E'en as he stood before,
And never in that moment he
Could say which should the better be
    So like the guise they wore;
Back to the hall he ran that day,
And, "Certes, Sire," he straight did
    say,
"Hast lost good deeds of yore,
Here a good deed was wasted now,
He is a richer man than thou,
I swear thy face before!"   2040

With that the rich duke answered,
    "Nay,
That may not be, by night or day,
    Against the law it were!"
The squire again he answered, "Yea,
A traitor is he, by my fay,
    Who should to judgment fare,
For when I brought him this, thy wine,
A gold cup he drew forth, so fine,
Thine own, methought it were,   2049
Thro' all the world, by sweet Saint John,
So wise a man there shall be none,
    Who could discern the pair!"

"Certes," Sir Amis quoth anon,
"In all the world, of cups were none
    So like in everything,
Save mine, and his, my brother's true,
The twain were wrought for us anew,
    At this, our severing;
If it be so, then, so I ween,
Sir Amiloun, he slain hath been,   2060
    An here no lie ye bring,
If any stole his cup away
Then I myself that thief shall slay
    By Jesu, Heaven's King!"

Then from his seat he sprang, the lord,
And, like a madman, drew his sword,
    Urged on by wrath and wrake,
Straight to the castle gate he ran
In all the world there was no man
Who might him overtake;   2070
He saw the leper in the wain,
And gripped him fast with his hands
    twain,
And soused him in the lake,
And smote him e'en as he were wood,
And all who there about him stood,
    Great dole began to make.

"Traitor," then quoth the duke so bold,
"Say, whence had'st thou that cup of
    gold;
How didst thou come thereto?   2079
For now, by Him Whom Judas sold,
My brother did that same cup hold,

Whenas he went me fro'."
"Yea, certes, Sire, so doth it stand,
'T was his, while he in his own land
Abode, now is it so
As certainly, while I be here,
That it is mine, I bought it dear,
And have a right thereto!"

With that the duke waxed fierce of mood,
There was no man who by him stood
Durst lay upon him hand,   2091
But with his foot he spurned him there,
And smote him, as he frenzied were,
With this, his naked brand.
The leper fast by feet he made,
And in the slough and mire he laid,
For naught would he withstand,
But cried: "Thief, shalt be slain straight-
        way,
Save of the cup the truth dost say
How came it in thine hand?"   2100

Amoraunt stood the folk among,
Saw how his lord with woe and wrong
So ruefully was dight,
A hardy lad and strong was he,
He gripped the duke right manfully,
With arms he held him tight,
And saith: "Sire, of discourteous mind
Art thou, and in thy deeds unkind,
To slay this gentle knight,
For he the day may rue full sore   2110
That for thy sake such wounds he bore,
And saved thy life in fight!

"For he Sir Amiloun is hight,
Who whilom was a noble knight
Alike to ride or go,
Now must he thole sore pain and loss,
May God Who died upon the Cross
Bring him from out his woe!
For thy sake he of bliss is bare, —
Full ill didst thou repay him there,
Breaking his bones in two!   2121
He helped thee at thy sorest need,
Full ill dost thou repay his meed,
Alas, why dost thou so?"

Whenas Sir Amis heard, forthright,
He turned him swiftly to the knight
With never more delay,
Clasped him within his arms that tide,
And often-times, "Alas!" he cried,
His song was "Wellaway!"   2130
He looked upon his shoulder bare,
The grisley wound he saw it there
As Amoraunt did say,
Therewith fell swooning to the ground,
And oft he cried "Alas!" that stound,
That e'er he saw this day!

"Alas!" he cried, "my joy is gone,
Unkinder blood was never none,
I wot not what to do!
For he that saved my life of yore,   2140
With scorn did I requite him sore,
And wrought him mickle woe!
Brother," he cried, "of charitie,
This wicked deed forgive it me,
That I did smite thee so!"
Then swift he gave forgiveness fair,
And many times he kissed him there
While fast the tears they flow.

Then was Sir Amis glad and fain,
For very joy he wept again   2150
And seized his brother there,
He took him in his arms withal
And carried him into the hall,
None other might him bear;
Within the hall his wife, she stood,
She deemed her lord were surely wood,
And ran, that lady fair,
Crying: "Now, Sire, what is thy
        thought?
Why hast this leper hither brought?
For Christ's sake now declare!"   2160

"Oh, wife!" he cried, "by sweet Saint
        John,
Such woe ne'er lay my heart upon
As thou must know to-day,
In all the world so good a knight
Was none, yet sore I did him smite,
Well nigh I did him slay!

It is my brother Amiloun,
Who now by grief is cast adown,
Who erst was knight so gay!"
Swooning, that lady fell to ground,   2170
Weeping, she wrung her hands that
        stound,
And oft "Alas!" did say.

Tho' he was leper foul, I wis,
That lady straightway did him kiss,
For nothing would she spare,
And oft-times she "Alas!" did cry,
That such hard fate on him should
        lie,
To live in woe and care,
Into her bower she did him lead,
And cast aside his beggar's weed,   2180
And bathed his body bare;
Then to a bed the knight they brought
Covered with clothes so richly wrought,
Right glad of him they were.

And thus, as now the Geste doth say,
Twelvemonths he in her chamber lay
For true they were and kind,
And ne'er denied him with a "Nay,"
Whate'er he asked, by night or day,
It tarried not behind,   2190
He every meat and drink must share
That men at board before them bare,
They kept him aye in mind;
And after this a twelvemonth's space
God granted them a wondrous Grace,
As in the Geste we find.

For it befell upon a night
The duke, Sir Amis, that good knight,
In slumber as he lay,   2199
An angel bright he saw that stead,
From Heaven, stand before his bed
Who thus to him did say:
An he would rise on Christmas Morn,
E'en at the hour that Christ was born
And his two children slay,
Anoint his brother with their blood,
By grace of God, Who aye is good,
His ill were turned away.

And thus he thought that, for nights
        three,
That angel bright he sure did see,   2210
Who warned him evermore,
And said, an he did as he hight,
His brother were as fair a knight,
As e'er he was before.
Sir Amis, he was blithe that day,
Yet for his children grieved alway,
Fairer no woman bore,
Full loth was he his bairns to kill,
More loth to fail his brother still
Who was so true of yore.   2220

To Amiloun, too, did it seem,
An angel warned him in a dream,
And did to him declare,
An Amis had his children slain
The virtue of their heart's blood twain
Might cleanse him from his care.
With morn Sir Amis went his way,
And sought his brother as he lay
And asked how he did fare?   2229
And Amiloun quoth low and still:
" Brother, I here abide God's Will,
My hope, it lieth there!"

Then, as they sat together there
Spake of adventures as it were,
Those knights so fair and free,
Sir Amiloun quoth at that tide:
"Brother, I naught from thee would
        hide
But tell thee privilie,
As in a dream I saw last night
An Angel come from Heaven bright,
Forsooth, he said to me,   2241
The blood of these, thy children twain,
Might make me whole and clean again,
From sorrow set me free."

Then thought the duke that, sooth to
        say,
These children young, the twain to slay
It were a deadly sin, —
And then, by Heaven's King, he thought,
An Amiloun from grief were brought,

He'ld risk the wrong therein; 2250
So it befell, on Christmas Night,
What time that Jesu, Lord of Might,
Was born, to save men's kin,
That all the men in court who were,
They dight them, forth to church to fare
With joy, for this world's win.

When all were ready forth to fare
The duke bade all men who were there
To church to wend straightway,
And, as they all his friends should be,
Of great or small, none, verily, 2261
Should there in chamber stay;
He quoth, that he himself that night
Would guard his brother, the true knight,
Who was so good alway.
To say him "Nay," I trow, was none,
To church the household went anon,
The duke at home did stay.

The duke, with care he did espy
The keys of this the nursery, 2270
Ere that they should be gone;
And privily he watched them there,
And of the place he was aware
Where they had laid them down.
When all men thus to church did go,
Sir Amis, as the Geste doth show,
He there was left alone;
He took a candle, burning bright,
And to the keys he went forthright,
Bare them away anon. 2280

With that alone, with no delay,
He to the chamber made his way
Where these, his children, were;
Beheld them both, as in that stead
They lay together in the bed,
Sleeping together there,
And thus unto himself did say:
"By Saint John, it were ill to slay
What God hath wrought so fair!"
His knife, he drew it forth that tide,
For very grief he turned aside, 2291
And wept for sorrow sare!

Awhile he wept there as he stood,
Anon he changed again his mood,
And saith without delay:
"My brother was so true and good,
From grisley wounds he shed his blood
For love of me that day;
Then why should I my children spare
To bring my brother out of care? 2300
O certes!" he quoth, "nay!
To help my brother in his need,
Maid Mary grant that well I speed,
God prosper me alway!"

No longer lingering, as he stood,
He grasped the knife in dreary mood,
And took the children two,
And, since he would not spill their blood,
Over a basin fair and good,
Their throats, he slit them thro'. 2310
And when the two he thus had slain
He laid them back in bed again,
Small marvel he were woe!
Covered them, that by none 't were seen
That any man with them had been,
From chamber forth did go.

When from the chamber he had gone,
The door, behind him shut, anon,
Fast as it had been aye,
The keys he laid beneath a stone, 2320
Thinking that men would deem, each one,
That they had gone astray.
Straight to his brother did he go,
Quoth to that man so full of woe,
By dawn of Christmas Day:
"Here have I brought my children's blood,
I trust that it may do thee good,
So did the Angel say!"

"Brother," Sir Amiloun did say,
"Didst thou indeed thy children slay?
Alas! Why didst thou so?" 2331
He wept, and cried: "Ah! Wellaway!
Liever had I till Judgment Day
Lived thus in pain and woe!"

Then quoth Sir Amis: "Be thou still,
Thro' Jesu, an it be His Will,
I bairns again may know,
For my sake thou of bliss art bare,
I wis, to bring thee out of care,
To death I'ld freely go!"   2340

He took the life-blood, red and bright,
Anointed there that gentle knight,
Who erst was fair and hale,
And then in bed he did him lay
And wrapt him warm and soft alway
Nor coverings rich did fail;
"Brother," he quoth, "now lie thou still
And fall asleep, now, as God's Will
The Angel told in tale;
And well I trust, with ne'er a lie,   2350
That Jesu, King of Heaven High,
Shall bring thee out of bale."

Sir Amis let him lie alone
And to his chamber went anon
As ye in Geste may hear,
And for the bairns whom he had slain
To God in Heaven he did complain,
Praying, with rueful cheer,
That he be saved from shame that day
Thro' Mary Mother, who alway   2360
Was to his heart full dear.
And Jesu Christ, in his sore need,
To that knight's prayer He gave good
          heed,
As ye in Geste may hear.

The morrow, soon as it was day,
Homeward she came, that lady gay,
With knights in train, I trow,
They sought the keys where they should
          lie,
And might no trace of them descry,
Woeful were they enow;   2370
The duke, he bade their mourning cease,
And prayed them all to hold their peace,
And quiet keep them now,
He had the keys, his wife alone
Should thither go, beside them, none,
That did he surely vow.

Anon, his wife he prayed her hear,
And quoth to her: "My love so dear,
Prithee be glad of mood,   2379
By Him Who for mankind was born
Our children have I slain this morn,
Who were so fair and good,
For that in dream I saw, by night,
An Angel come from Heaven's height,
Who told me, by their blood
My brother should be freed from pain,
For his sake did I slay the twain
To help him, as I should."

Then was that lady full of woe,
Seeing her lord in sorrow go   2390
She comforted him there:
"Oh! dearest life," thus did she say,
"God, He can give us bairns alway,
Of them have thou no care,
For if it were mine own heart's blood,
An it might do thy brother good,
My life I would not spare;
Our eyes alone our bairns shall see,
To-morrow shall they buried be,
As natural death it were."   2400

Thus did that lady, fair and bright,
Comfort her lord with all her might,
As ye may understand;
With that, the twain, they go their way,
Sought Amiloun, there, where he lay
Who erst was free of hand;
When Amiloun, he woke anon,
Behold, his foulness all was gone,
Thro' grace of God's Command!
And then was he as fair a knight   2410
As ever he was seen by sight
Since he was born in land!

With that full blithe and glad they were,
Their joy they might to none declare,
They thanked God oft, that day,
And then, as here the Geste doth shew,
They swiftly to the chamber go
Wherein the children lay,
Without a wound the bairns they found,
With ne'er a scar, but whole and sound,

The twain, they lie, and play!   2421
They wept for joy as there they stood,
Gave thanks to God in humble mood,
Their care was all away.

. . . .

When Amiloun was whole and fair
And all his strength had waxen there,
And he might go and ride,
Amoraunt, as a squire so bold,
Of gladsome cheer he then did hold
To serve his lord beside;   2430
Then quoth the knight upon a day
That homeward would he take his way,
Speak with his wife that tide,
For that she so had helped his need
He thought to well requite her deed,
Nor longer there abide.

Sir Amis, then, with swift intent,
For many a valiant knight he sent,
Who doughty were in deed,   2439
Five hundred knights, both true and keen,
And many a baron more, I ween,
On palfrey and on steed,
And night and day they, at that same,
Rode swift, till to his land they came
There was he lord indeed;
A knight of that same country there
He had espoused that lady fair
As now in Geste we read.

And thus in Geste as now I say,
Home came her lord the self-same day
They would the bridal hold,
To castle rode without delay,
Anon began a sorry play
Among those barons bold;
A messenger to run was fain
Crying, her lord was come again
As fairest man on mold!
The lady, she waxed pale and wan,
And there was many a mournful man
Among them, young and old!   2460

Sir Amiloun, and Sir Amis,
With many a baron bold, I wis,

And knights and squires withal,
With helmet, and with habergeoun,
And with their sword blades bright and brown,
They gat them to the hall,
And all whom they within it caught
With many a mighty stroke they sought,
Yea, were they great or small,
And glad and blithe they were that day
Whoso alive might flee away,   2471
Such bridal did befall!

And thus, when they had vengeance ta'en,
And brown and black to flee were fain
From out that hall, anon,
Amiloun, for his lady's sake,
A great lodge there he bade them make
Builded of lime and stone,
Within it was that lady led,
On bread and water was she fed,
Till her life-days were done.   2481
In such wise died that lady — He
Who mourns her fate, a knave must be
As ye have heard, each one!

Then Amiloun sent speedily
To earls and barons, bond and free,
All who were frank and fair,
And where they came, he seized in hand
. . . . . er all this land,
. . . . d kin wav'e'er;   2490
. . . hen he thus had done, I wis,
. . . his, his brother Sir Amis,
. . . k again did fare;
T. . . in much oy and little strife,
Toge. . er did they lead their life
Till called of God they were.

Anon those courteous barons twain
To build an Abbey were they fain
Endow it well also,
In Lombardy, till Judgment-Day   2500
Mass for their souls to sing alway
And for their parents' too.

The same day died those knights so
    brave,
Were laid together in one grave,
    As men to-day shall show;

For this, their steadfast truth, I wis,
They have reward in Heavenly Bliss
    That ne'er an end shall know!
          Amen, Amen.

SIR LAUNFAL

In the days when Arthur bold
Rule in English land did hold
    Such a feat befell
That men set it in a Lay,
Hight "*Sir Launfal*," e'en to-day
    Ye may know it well.
Doughty Arthur did some while,
Hold his court in fair Carlisle,
    And, in solace fair,
Valiant knights with him were found,
Heroes of the Table Round,   11
    Better knights were ne'er.

Perceval, and good Gawain,
Gaheries, and Agravain,
    Lancelot du Lake;
Kay the seneschal, Ywain,
Who in fiercest fight on plain
    Stern defence could make;
King Banboort, King Bors, his mate,
(Of the twain the praise was great)
    None their peer might find;   2?
Sir Galafr , Sir Launfale, —
    Of this last a noble
Here I'ld bring to mind.

Arthur had a knight, I ween,
(Many a year at court he'd bee
    Launfal, was he hight;
Gift nor largesse did e spare
Gold and silver, raiment fair,
    Gave to squire and knight.   30
For his gifts and bounty free
Steward unto the king was he
    Fourteen years, forthright;
Nay, of all the Table Round
None so free of hand was found
    Both by day and night.

Then it chanced, in the tenth year,
Merlin, who was Arthur's seer,
    Bade the king to ride
Unto Ryon, Ireland's king,   40
Thence his daughter fair to bring,
    Gwennore, as his bride.
Arthur brought her home, I wot,
But Sir Launfal liked her not,
    Nor his comrades tried,
Such repute the lady bare
Lovers had she, and to spare,
    Her good lord beside.

They were wedded, so men say,
On the Feast of Whitsunday, —   50
    Many a prince of pride,
And more folk than man may tell
To that bridal came as well
    From lands far and wide.
Each who in that hall was set
Bishop was, or Baronet
    (Naught in heart I'ld hide —)
Tho' men sat not equal there
Service rich and good they bare
    Certes, to each side.   60

When the lords had eaten all,
And the cloths were drawn in hall,
    E'en as ye may hear,
Butlers bare, with one accord,
Wine to each and every lord
    Yea, with gladsome cheer.
Then the queen gave gifts so fair,
Gold and silver, jewels rare,
    Courtesy to show;   69
To each knight gave brooch or ring,
To Sir Launfal ne'er a thing,
    Grief he needs must know.

Came the wedding-feast to end,
Launfal fain his way would wend,
Prayed leave of the king.
Said: "The news but now is sped
How my father lieth dead,
To his burying
I would go" — The king so free,
Quoth: "Launfal, wilt go from me   80
Take for thy spending;
And my sister's sons, the two,
I will bid with thee to go,
Homeward thee to bring."

Launfal, on his journey bound,
Took leave of the Table Round,
Went his way, I ween,
Till to Karlion he came,
And the mayor's house, at that same,
Who his man had been —   90
Stood the mayor without, that tide,
Saw his master gently ride,
Knights with him doth bring.
Forth he goes the knight to greet, —
"Sir, I bid thee welcome meet,
Say, how fares our king?"

Launfal spake in answer there:
"Ne'er a man doth better fare,
Else were ruth the more —
But Sir Mayor, without leasing,   100
I be parted from the king,
And that rues me sore;
None beneath me, nor above,
For the sake of Arthur's love
Owes me honour more.
Sir, I prithee, of thy grace,
May I here have dwelling-place,
We were friends of yore?"

Straight the mayor him bethought,
And a fitting answer sought   110
Thus to him 'gan say:
"Seven knights would dwell with me,
Here to-day they sure shall be,
Of little Britain they —"
Launfal turned him with a smile,
Knightly scorn he gave for guile,

Saith to his knights twain:
"Who a lord of little fame
Thinks to serve, he, of that same
Service should be fain!"   120

Launfal on his way would ride,
Quoth the Mayor: "My lord, abide —"
(In this wise he spake —)
"Turn ye by mine orchard side,
I have where, in joy and pride,
Ye your home may make."
Launfal, he anon alights,
Thinking there, with his two knights,
For awhile to dwell;
Right and left his wealth he cast   130
Till, ere the first year was past,
In great debt he fell.

So it chanced at Pentecost,
Such time as the Holy Ghost
Did on men alight,
That Sir Hugh, and eke Sir John,
Took their leave, for to be gone
From Launfal, the knight;
Saying: "Sir, our robes be rent,
And thy treasure all be spent,   140
We be evil dight."
Quoth Sir Launfal, fair and free,
"Tell none of my povertie,
Prithee, by God's Might."

Spake the gallant knights straight-
      way,
They would ne'er his plight betray
All this world to win.
So they left him at that same,
Straight to Glastonbury came,
Arthur lay therein.   150
When he saw those knights draw nigh
Swift towards them did he hie
They were of his kin;
But the self-same robes they ware
As when they from court did fare,
Torn they were, and thin.

Of ill-will, the queen quoth there:
"Say, how doth the proud knight fare

May he armour wield?"   159
Quoth the good knights: "Lady, yea,
Well he fares, as good men may,
Heaven be his shield!"
Good the tidings that they bring
To the queen, and eke the king,
Of Launfal the bold
And they quoth: "He loved us so
That when we were fain to go
He would us withhold;

"But there came a rainy day
When Sir Launfal went his way   170
Hunting thro' holts hoar,
In our old robes did we ride,
So we went our way that tide
As we came of yore."
Arthur was right glad of mood
That it well with Launfal stood —
Grieved was queen Gwennore —
She desired with all her might
He should have, by day and night,
Pain and sorrow sore.   180

Came the feast of Trinitie,
Which, with great solemnitie
Men in Karlion hold;
Earls and barons, many a knight,
Burgess good, and lady bright,
Flock there, young and old;
But Launfal, the knight so free,
Might not of that gathering be,
For his lack of gold;
To the feast the mayor was bent,   190
His fair daughter straightway went
To the knight so bold;

Prayed him dine with her that day —
"Demoiselle," quoth Launfal, "nay,
Thereto I lack heart;
For the three days that be gone
Meat and drink have I had none,
This my sorry part;
I had fain heard Mass to-day,
Hose and shoes I lacked alway,   200
Linen clean and white.
Thus for want of clothing fair

In the feast I may not share
That doth me despite.

"This one thing I pray of thee,
Saddle, bridle, lend to me
That I forth may ride,
Solace would I find withal,
In a meadow, 'neath the wall,
In this undern-tide."   210
Launfal, then, he girt his steed,
Squire nor page had he at need,
Humbly did he ride;
His horse threw him in the fen,
Mocked he was of many men,
Yea, on every side.

On his horse he sprang again,
And, to chase his longings fain,
Rode towards the west;
Sultry waxed that undern-tide,   220
He, dismounting, would abide
'Neath a fair forest;
And, because the day was hot,
He would fold his cloak, I wot,
Sat him down to rest.
Sat thus in simplicitie
'Neath the shadow of a tree
Where it liked him best.

As he sat, and sorrowed sore,   229
Forth there came, from holts so hoar,
Maidens twain that day;
Silk of Inde their kirtles were,
Tightly laced, and fitting fair,
Never maids more gay;
Velvet were their mantles green
Bordered well with gold, I ween,
Lined with fur so gray;
On each gracious head was set,
Wrought of gold, a coronet,
Set with gems alway.   240

White their skin as snow on down,
Red their cheeks, their eyes were
      brown,
(None such have I seen —)
One, a basin all of gold

Bare, the other maid did hold
Towel of silken sheen.
Bright their kerchiefs were to see
With gold thread in broiderie —
Launfal 'gan to sigh —
O'er the turf to him they came   250
He would, rising, at that same
Greet them courteously:

"God be with ye, maidens bright!"
"Fair befall thee, noble knight,
Know, Dame Triamour
Bids thee come and speak with her
An it were thy will, fair Sir,
In this very hour."
Launfal answered, courteously,
He would come right willingly —   260
White were they as flour.
In the forest glade on high
He a fair tent did espie,
Merrie was that bower.

That fair tent was wrought, I wis,
All of work of Sarsynys,
Crystal was each ball;
Over all an eagle stood,
Wrought of red gold, rich and good,
And enamelled all;   270
For his eyes carbuncles bright —
As the moon that shines at night
Did the beams fair fall;
Alexander, monarch great,
Arthur, in his richest state,
Lacked such gem withal!

And in that pavilion
Lay the maid of Oleron,
Triamour, she hight;
King, her sire, of Faërie,   280
All the West, at his decree
Owned him man of might.
In that tent a couch withal
Found he, decked with purple pall,
Seemly 't was to sight,
Therein lay that gentle maid
Who Sir Launfal thither bade,
Lovesome lady bright.

For the heat she cast aside
Covering, to her waist that tide   290
Well nigh was she bare;
White as lily-flower in May,
Or as snow on winter's day —
He knew none so fair —
Yea, the red rose, newly-blown,
Pale against her cheek had shewn,
This to say I dare.
Bright her hair as threads of gold,
None her rich attire had told,
Thought had known it ne'er.   300

Quoth she: "Launfal, hark to me,
All my joy I'ld leave for thee,
Be my paramour;
For in Christendom is none
Whom I love, save thee alone,
King nor Emperour."
Launfal looked on that sweet maid,
All his love on her he laid,
Kissed her in that hour.
Down he sat him at her side,   310
Saying: "Sweet, whate'er betide
I am in thy power."

Quoth she: "Gentle knight, and free,
All thy state is known to me
Prithee, shame thee not;
Wilt thou me as true love take,
Other maids for me forsake,
Rich shall be thy lot.
For a purse I'll give thee here
Wrought of silk and gold so clear   320
With fair figures three;
Oft as thou thy hand within
Puttest, thou a mark shalt win
Wheresoe'er thou be.

"Yea, and more my gifts shall be,
With my steed, I'll give to thee
Geoffrey, mine own knave;
Of mine arms, a penoncel,
With three ermines painted well,
From thy lance to wave.   330
And in war and Tourney, know
Thou shalt ne'er be harmed by blow,

I my knight will save!"
Then he quoth, the gentle knight:
"Gramercie, my lady bright,
No more shield I'll crave."

Up she sat, the lady fair,
Bade her maidens bring her there
Water, for her hand;
This they did, nor made delay,   340
Set the board, and served straightway
Supper at command.
Dainties had they, fair and fine,
Pyement, claret, Rhenish wine,
Else great wonder were —
Thus they supped, the day was sped,
Then anon they sought their bed,
Knight and lady fair.

Scarce for joy they slept that night,
Till dawn came, and morning light,   350
Then she bade him rise,
Spake to him: "Sir Knight, art fain
E'er to speak with me again
Guard 'gainst prying eyes.
Secretly, I'll come to thee
In a place where none may see
Still as any stone."
Blithe and glad was Launfal then,
Joyful, he, above all men,
Kissed that maid anon.   360

"But of one thing warnéd be,
Ne'er, tho' profit 't were to thee,
Boast of me shalt make;
If thou doest, I thee warn
Thou shalt be of love forlorn —"
Thus the lady spake.
Launfal prayed her leave to go —
Geoffrey fain his skill would show
Brought the knight his steed,
Launfal straight the steed bestrode,   370
Back to Karlion he rode,
Poor was still his weed.

Glad at heart, his lady's will
Fain to do, he held him still,
All that undern-tide;

Thro' the burg came riding men,
Harnessed well, in number ten,
Sumpter steeds they ride.
Some with silver, some with gold,
(This for Launfal did they hold   380
Fit gear to provide,)
Raiment rich, and armour bright —
Then thy ask: "Launfal, the knight,
Where doth he abide?"

Silk of Inde the ten they ware,
Geoffrey, he behind did fare
On Blaunchard, the white;
In the market place one stood,
Quoth: "Where goeth all this good,
Tell us, gentle wight?"   390
Geoffrey spake: "As gift so fair
We this store to Launfal bear
Who in dolour rides —"
Quoth the boy: "He lives in need,
Men of him take little heed,
With the mayor he bides."

At the mayor's door they light,
Proffer to the noble knight
All the gifts they bear;
The mayor saw their goodliness,   400
Knew Sir Launfal's nobleness,
Shame o'ertook him there.
Quoth: "Sir Knight, of Charitie,
Prithee eat to-day with me,
As yestre'en it were
To the feast with thee I'ld ride,
Solace had been ours that tide
But thou forth didst fare."

"Nay, Sir Mayor, God pardon thee,
While I dwelt in povertie   410
Ne'er didst bid me dine,
Now my friends have sent to me
Greater store in gold and fee
Than was ever thine!"
Shamed, the mayor, he went his
    way,
Launfal did on fair array,
Purple, furred with white;
All the debts he ever made

Geoffrey hath the tale repaid
As was fit and right.   420

Launfal held rich feast that stead,
Fifty poor guests well he fed
Who were in ill plight;
Gave to fifty, each a steed,
Gave to fifty, goodly weed,
Were they squire or knight.
Fifty priests, I trow, he paid,
Fifty prisoners he made
From their bondage free,
Fifty jesters clothed he then,   430
Honour did to many men
Tho' of far countrie.

Lords of Karlion that tide
Bid a Tournament be cried
All for Launfal's love,
And for Blaunchard, his good steed,
All to wit how he might speed
And his valour prove.
When the day at last they see
That the jousts should ridden be   440
Forth to field they move,
Trumpeters a shrill blast blow,
All the lords ride out a-row
From the burg above.

Thus the Tourney fair was set,
Each doth on the other whet
Swords, and maces both,
So doth Fortune shifting run,
Some lose steeds, and some have
                                 won,
Knights were wondrous wroth;   450
Since the Table Round begun
Better Tourney was there none
That I say for sooth.
Many lords of Karlion town
On that field were smitten down,
Certes, without oath.

The constable of Karlion
Did upon Sir Launfal run
Nor would more abide —
He smote Launfal, Launfal him,   460

Stern, I trow, the strokes and grim,
Smitten on each side.
Launfal of his foe was ware,
From his steed he did him bear
To the ground that tide.
As the constable lay low,
Geoffrey leapt to saddle-bow,
From the field would ride.

Chester's earl beheld with eye,
Wroth he was, to madness nigh,   470
Rode on Launfal good.
On the helm he smote withal
That the crest adown must fall,
(So the French tale stood —)
Launfal was of mickle might,
From his steed he did alight,
Laid his foemen low;
Then there came, the knight about,
Of Welsh knights so great a rout
None their tale might know.   480

Shields were shattered then withal,
Shivered spears in splinters fall,
Yea, in rear and van;
Launfal and his steed of pride
Bare to earth, I ween, that tide
Many a gallant man.
So the Tourney's prize by right
Gave they to Launfal the knight,
Nor had need of oath.
Many a lord, I trow, that day   490
To the mayor's house took their way
With him, little loth.

Then that noble knight and bold
Royal feast and rich did hold,
E'en for fourteen-night;
Earls and barons in that hall
Service seemly found withal,
Royally were dight.
Every day fair Triamour   499
Sought her love, Sir Launfal's, bower,
Fell the shades of night;
But of all men in that place
Two alone might see her fare,
Geoffrey, and her knight.

Lived a knight in Lombardie,
Jealous of Sir Launfal he,
Valentine he hight.
Of Sir Launfal he heard tell
How he jousted wondrous well
Man of mickle might.   510
Valentine was strong, I ween,
Measured well of foot fifteen,
Deemed himself good knight;
Launfal he to test was fain,
In fair field to meet, they twain,
Or for joust or fight.

Valentine, he sat in hall,
Bade a messenger to call,
Said: "Needs must thou wend —
Unto Launfal, that good knight,   520
Who is held of such great might
I'll to Britain send.
Say, for love of his ladie,
If of gentle birth she be,
Courteous, fair, and free,
Would he keep his armour bright
Nor be deemed a coward knight,
He must joust with me."

Fain to do his lord's command
Sailed the messenger from land,   530
Fair the wind at will;
O'er the water came anon,
To Sir Launfal hath he gone
Spake with words so still,
Quoth: "Sir Valentine, my lord,
Who right skilful is with sword
Sent me unto thee,
Praying, for thy true love's sake
Thou a spear with him wilt break —"
Launfal laughed out free.   540

Quoth, as he was gentle knight
That same day, a fourteen-night,
He would 'gainst him ride —
For the tidings he did bring
Gave the messenger a ring,
Horse, and robe of pride.
Launfal kissed fair Triamour,
(Brightest maiden she in bower)

Prayed her leave to ride —
Then she quoth, that maiden dear,   550
"Of thy foeman have no fear,
He shall fall that tide."

None would Launfal with him lead
Saving Geoffrey, and his steed,
Blaunchard, so they three
Took to ship, the wind was good,
Swift they crossed the salt sea flood,
Came to Lombardie.
And when he had crossed the tide
Where the joust he needs must ride,   560
E'en in Atalie,
Valentine had there great host,
Launfal he hath lowered their boast,
With small companie.

When Sir Launfal, armed aright,
Sprang upon his charger white,
Spear and shield did hold,
All who saw his armour bright
Quoth that ne'er so fair a knight
Did their eyes behold.   570
Then they rode a joust so well
That their lances shivered fell
Shattered on the field,
At the second joust alway
Launfal's helm, the tale doth say,
To the spear did yield.

Laughed his foeman, and made
          game,
Launfal ne'er had felt such shame
Nay, tho' fierce the fight.
Geoffrey proved him good at need,   580
Leapt upon his master's steed,
(No man saw that sight —)
Ere the knights again had met
Launfal's helm on head he set,
Laced it fair and tight.
Launfal, he was glad and gay,
Geoffrey well he thanked that day
For his deed of might.

Valentine, he smote so well,
Launfal's shield adown it fell   590

Even at that stound;
Geoffrey, he that shield hath ta'en,
Given it to his lord again
Ere it came to ground.
Launfal, he was blithe and gay,
The third joust he rode straightway,
Showed his valour there;
Smote his foeman in that stead,
Horse and man, they both fell dead,
Grisley wounds they bare.   600

But of Atalie, the men,
Were full wroth with Launfal then
Since their knight was dead,
Sware that he should surely die
Ere he passed from Lombardie,
Hanged, and drawn that stead.
Launfal drew his falchion bright,
Smote them low, as dew falls light,
In a little space;
When he thus their lords had slain   610
He to Britain's shores again
Joyful set his face.

Thus to Arthur news they bring,
All the truth they tell the king
Of Launfal, his fame,
Then a script the king would send
Bidding Launfal to him wend
When Saint John's Feast came;
For the king a feast would hold
Of his earls and barons bold,   620
Lordings great and less,
Launfal should be steward in hall,
And the guests should order all
And give fair largesse.

Launfal straight his leave did pray
From his love, to go his way
The king's feast to lead.
Mirth he found and praise that hour,
Ladies, who were bright in bower,
Knights, right good at need.   630
Forty days the feast so high
Held they rich and royally,
Truth I tell to ye, —
Came the forty days to end,

Then the lords their way would wend,
Each to his countrie.

After meat it chanced Gawain,
Gaheries, and Agravain,
And Launfal, the knight,
Went to dance upon the green   640
'Neath the tower where lay the queen
And her ladies bright.
Launfal led the dance withal,
(For largesse, in hold and hall
Men, they loved him so;)
The queen lay, the dance would see,
Spake: "There danceth Launfal free,
I to him will go!

"He of all the knights I see
Seemeth fairest unto me,   650
Never had he wife,
An it be for good or ill
I will ask of him his will,
Whom I love as life!"
Maids she chose, a companie,
Of the fairest she might see
Sixty-five they were,
Thus they went their way forth-
            right —
To disport them with the knights
Courteously they fare.   660

Thus the queen her place hath ta'en
Twixt Launfal, and good Gawain, —
And her ladies bright
Followed her full speedily,
Yea, 't was fair the dance to see
Each maid with a knight.
Minstrels well the fiddle play,
Cithole, too, and trumpet gay,
As 't was fit and right.
So they sported, sooth to say,   670
After meat, the summer's day,
Till 't was nigh to night.

When the dance was done, I ween,
Nigh to Launfal drew the queen,
Spake thus in his ear:
"Know for certain, gentle knight,

I have loved thee, day and night,
More than seven year;
Save thy love be given to me
I shall die for love of thee,   680
Launfal, leman dear!"
Quoth the good knight at that same:
"Traitor ne'er shall be my name,
Heaven help me here!"

Quoth the queen: "Thou coward, fie!
Fain I were men hanged thee high
Would thou ne'er wast born!
That thou livest, grieveth me,
Scorning women, all scorn thee,
Art of love forlorn!"   690
Sore abashed, the knight so bold
Speech no longer might withold,
Spake the queen before:
"I have loved a maid more bright
Than thou e'er hast seen with sight
Seven years and more.

"Lowest maiden of her train
Fitter were as queen to reign
Than thou e'er hast been!"
Very wroth, the queen, that day   700
With her maidens went her way
To her bower, I ween;
Laid her down upon her bed,
Sware she was full sick that stead,
Sware, as she might thrive,
She'ld on Launfal vengeance wreak,
All the land of him should speak
Ere days waxed to five!

From the chase doth Arthur ride,
Blithe and gay was he that tide   710
To his bower went he —
Then the queen on him did cry:
"Save thou 'venge me I shall die,
My heart breaks in three!
I to Launfal spake, my king,
And he prayed a shameful thing,
Would my leman be.
When I would not, boast he made
Of his love, whose loathliest maid
Fairer were than me!"   720

Then King Arthur, he waxed wroth,
And by God he sware an oath
Launfal would he slay;
Bade his doughty men, forthright
Take Launfal, and that good knight,
Hang and draw straightway.
Sought they for that knight anon —
To his chamber had he gone,
Fain was he to play,
But his love, she came no more,   730
As she warned him once of yore
So it fell alway.

Then his purse he did behold
Which was ever full of gold,
When of gold was need;
Ne'er a piece was there that day,
Geoffrey, he had ridden away
On Blaunchard, his steed.
All the good that he had won
Passed, as snow beneath the sun,   740
So the tale doth read;
E'en his harness, shining white,
Had become as black as night —
Launfal, in his need

Spake: "Alas! how may it be
That I live apart from thee
Sweetest Triamour?
Of all wealth am I forlorn,
And, far worse, from thee am torn
Brightest maid in bower!"   750
Then he smote him on the head,
Cursed the mouth that spake, that stead,
Yea, he sorrowed sore,
And for very grief that stound
Fell a-swooning to the ground —
Then of knights came four,

Laid the knight in bands straightway
(Double waxed his woe that day)
Led him to the king —
Arthur quoth, with anger moved,   760
"Heark to me, thou traitor proved,
Why make such boasting?
Fairer than my wife, didst say
Thy love's loathliest maid alway

Foul the lie, I trow!
And ere that wert fain the queen
Should thy paramour have been —
All too proud art thou!"

Quoth the knight, in eager mood,
As before the king he stood: 770
"'T is the queen doth lie!
Never since I saw the light
I besought her, day nor night,
Of such treacherie;
But she quoth, no man was I,
Woman's love, it passed me by,
Maids would naught of me —
And I answered her, and said,
I held my love's loathliest maid
Fitter queen to be!   780

"Certes, lordings, this is so,
I am ready here to do
All the court shall say —"
Saith the story, at that same,
Twelve good knights together came,
Judgment sought straightway,
And they spake themselves between,
How right well they knew the queen,
This was aye her way —
"Of her ever went the word   790
She loved others than her lord,
None shall that gainsay."

On the queen, and not the knight,
Should the blame be laid by right,
Thereof was he free;
And might he his lady bring,
She of whom he spake this thing,
And her maids should be
Brighter than the queen in hue,
Launfal should be holden true,   800
Free from felonie;
But, save he his love might show,
A thief's death he needs must know,
And be hanged on tree.

This, then, was their counselling:
Launfal should his true love bring,
His life on it lay —

Quoth the queen, with ne'er a lie:
"If she fairer prove than I,
Blind these eyes of gray!"   810
Thus the wager fast was bound,
Launfal hath two sureties found,
Noble knights were they —
Perceval and good Gawain,
They were sureties, the twain,
Till a certain day.

This they sware, my faith I plight,
In a year, and fourteen night,
He his love must bring —
Sorrow sore, and bitter care   820
Then, I ween, were Launfal's share
He his hands did wring;
Yea, so heavy was his woe,
All his life henceforth must know
Naught but mourning drear,
Glad his head to forfeit he —
Full of woe all men must be
Who these tidings hear.

Draweth nigh th' appointed day —
With his sureties he, straightway,   830
'Fore the king must go.
Arthur spake: "Thy love now
        bring —"
Launfal answered, sorrowing,
"It may not be so."
Arthur bade his lords forthright
Sit in judgment on the knight,
Speak his doom straightway;
Spake the earl of Cornwall free,
(Leader of the council he)
Boldly said him "Nay,"   840

"Mickle shame on us would light
An we doomed this gentle knight,
Fair is he, and free,
This my lords, shall be my rede,
We our king shall better lead,
Launfal hence shall flee."
As they council hold that tide
Maidens thro' the city ride,
Ten, right fair to see;
Yea, so fair were they, and bright,   850

That the loathliest to sight
Well a queen might be.

Quoth Gawain, that knight so dear:
"Brother, be of better cheer,
See thy true love ride!"
Launfal answered him: "I wis,
None of these my true love is,
Comrade true and tried!"
To the castle are they gone,
At the gate they 'light anon,   860
To the king they win,
Bade him in all haste prepare
For their dame a chamber fair,
Maid of royal kin.

"Who is she?" King Arthur said —
"Ye shall wit well" spake the maid,
"Hither doth she ride."
Arthur bade prepare that hour
For that maid the fairest bower
In his palace wide;   870
Then his barons straightway bade
That the doom be not delayed
Of that traitor's pride.
But the barons quoth forthright:
"Till we see those maidens bright
Must our judgment bide."

A new tale they weave also,
Part of weal, and part of woe,
To appease their lord;   879
Some would judge Launfal, the knight,
Some would speak him free by right,
Diverse was their word.
Maidens ten again they see,
Fairer than the first they be,
As they'ld doom the knight —
Each one rode a mule of Spain,
Saddle, bridle, of Champagne,
Harness, gleaming bright.

Clothed they were in silk of Tyre —
Each man yearned their fair attire   890
Better to behold;
Gawain quoth, that courteous knight:
"Launfal see, thy lady bright

Freeth thee from hold!"
Launfal quoth right drearily:
"Strangers one and all they be,
They, and all their race."
To the hall the maids forthright
Ride, and at the daïs alight,
'Fore King Arthur's face.   900

King and queen they gracious greet;
One maid spake, in fashion meet,
To the king that hour:
"Deck thy hall and hang the wall
Eke with purple and with pall
For fair Triamour!"
Arthur answered them forthright,
"Welcome be ye maidens bright,
Yea, in Christ's own Name."
Lancelot du Lake he bade   910
To her fellows lead each maid
Courteous, at that same.

Then the queen, with thought of
        guile,
Fearing Launfal, in a while,
Should be spoken free
Thro' his love, who thither came,
Cried on Arthur at that same;
"Sire, 't were courtesie,
And for honour fit and right
To avenge me of that knight   920
Who set shame on me!
Launfal should'st thou nowise spare,
Fain thy lords were thee to snare,
Dear to them is he!"

As the queen spake on this wise,
Lo! before the baron's eyes
Rode a demoiselle,
On a palfrey white and tall,
Never such was seen withal,
That I know right well, —   930
Light was she as bird on bough
In all fashion fair enow
A king's hall to grace,
Bright as blossom blowing meet,
Gray her eyes, her smile was sweet,
Very fair her face.

Red her cheeks as rose is red,
And the hair upon her head
As gold thread was bright;
And her crown ye might behold   940
Of rich stones, and ruddy gold,
Gleaming in the light.
Clad was she in purple pall,
Slight of form, in waist full small,
Seemly to men's sight;
And her mantle, fair and wide,
Showed, turned back on either side,
Fur of ermine white.

Rich her saddle was, I ween,
With its skirts of velvet green   950
Painted cunningly;
And a border all of bells,
Of pure gold, and nothing else
That a man might see,
Front and back, each saddle-bow
Was with eastern gems a-glow,
Gay exceedingly;
And her palfrey trappings bare
That were worth an earldom fair
E'en in Lombardie.   960

Hawk on hand the lady rode,
Soft and slow her steed, it trode,
All might well behold;
Thus thro' Karlion did she ride,
Two white greyhounds, at her side,
Collars bare of gold;
Launfal saw that lady's face,
Raised his voice, and in that place
Cried on young and old;
"Now may ye my true love see,   970
Who may, an she gracious be,
Set me free from hold!"

Rode that lady to the hall
Where the queen, and maidens all,
Sat beside the king;
Swift to aid fair Triamour
All her maidens, in that hour,
To her stirrup spring.
Straight her cloak she cast aside
That the better in that tide,   980

Men her form might see,
Arthur would her gracious greet,
And she spake, in answer meet,
Words both fair and free.

Stood the queen, and maidens all,
They, that lady fair and tall,
Fain would see with sight;
All their beauty was fordone,
As the moon before the sun
Fades with morning light.   990
Quoth she then unto the king:
"Sire, I come but for one thing,
E'en to save my knight.
Ne'er had he such traitorous thought
That he the queen's love besought,
Ne'er by day nor night!

"Therefore, Sire, take heed to this,
Tho' he prayed not, she, I wis,
Fain his love would be;
He refuséd her, and said   1000
That his true love's lowest maid
Fairer were than she!"
Arthur spake: "It needs no oath,
All can see that, by my troth,
Fairer far ye be!"
To the queen the lady stept,
But a breath her brow hath swept,
Blind for aye is she.

To her steed she leapt straightway,
Quoth: "I bid ye all Good-day,"   1010
No more would she bide.
From the forest Geoffrey sped,
Launfal's steed with him he led
To his master's side.
On his back he sprang, the knight,
Tarried not, but thought forthright
With his love to ride.
And the maidens, every one,
With their dame their way have gone
In great joy and pride.   1020

Rode the lady thro' Carlisle,
Far, unto a goodly isle,
Oleron, 't was hight,

And each year, as falls that day,
Launfal's steed ye may hear neigh,
Yea, and see with sight!
He who fain a joust would see,
Keep from rust his harness free,
Or in field would fight,
Needeth not to further ride,   1030
Jousts enow he'll find that tide
With Launfal, the knight.

Thus Launfal, who erst was found
Good knight of the Table Round,

Passed to Faërie;
None in this land saw him more,
Nor of him have better lore
Than I tell to ye;
Thomas Chester made this tale
Of the good knight, Sir Launfale,
Famed for chivalrie;   1041
Jesu Christ, we pray thee here,
With Marie, Thy Mother dear,
Send us blessings free!
              Amen.

SIR AMADACE

THEN the good knight and his steward
              true
They sat them down, and counsel drew
Alike from far and near;
Quoth the steward: "Sir ye owe yet more
Than your lands have yielded heretofore
E'en for this seven year,
Of whom ye can, I beseech you pray
He give you grace to a further day;
Then call your household here,
And put away many of your men,   10
And keep but one where ye now keep ten
Tho' they be ne'er so dear."

Sir Amadace quoth: "'Twere long, to wit,
Ere I of all these, my debts, were quit
Altho' I naught might spend,
Did I dwell the while where I was born
I were held of every man in scorn
Who now have many a friend!
Accursèd of all men should I be   19
Since I of their goods had been so free
That they erst while did lend.
Or I must hold them by fear and threat
Lest that which was theirs again they
              get
Thus made I a sorry end!

"I will take unto me another rede,
And another counsel, in this my need,

Hid sorrow is better than seen!
But now good Steward, as thou hold'st
              me dear,
Of my plight so sore let no man hear,
Hide it us twain between!   30
My land in pledge for seven years set,
To the worth of all that I be in debt,
So shall I be freed, I ween!
For out of this land I think to wend
The while I have silver and gold to spend
Till of debt I be quit full clean.

"But certes ere yet afar I fare
My goods in right royal wise I'll share
To aid me thou shalt not fail: 39
Rich gifts will I give at each man's desire
To noble knight and to humble squire,
The poor shall his portion hail.
For some there be, an they knew my
              woe,
Who were even fain that it should be
              so,
And naught would better my bale,
So courteous a man was never born
Who should 'scape from every breath of
              scorn
When each man had told his tale!"

Sir Amadace, so the tale doth say,
Would get him forth, as fell the day, 50

From his country in that stound,
But first full rich were the gifts he gave
Alike to squire and knight so brave,
Of steed and hawk and hound.
Thereafter, so doth it run, my tale,
He made him ready withouten fail
And to his woe he found,
When he upon his way would wend,
Naught in his coffers had he to spend
But barely forty pound! 60

Thus as I tell ye Sir Amadace
Gat him forth on his way apace
As fast as ever he might,
He rode thro' a wood right cheerily
Till he came to a chapel of stone and tree
Wherein there burnt a light;
He bade his servant thither speed,
And take of that light therein good heed
And tidings bear forthright.
The servant, he hasted to do his will, 70
But the stench of the chapel, he liked it
ill,
Withstand it no man might!

His hood he drew over mouth and nose,
And came to the chapel door full close,
Tidings he fain would hear:
He turned his eye to a pane of glass
To see what marvels within might pass,
And lo! there stood a bier,
Around it candles, a goodly store,
A woman watcher, and no man more, 80
Christ, she was sad of cheer!
To tarry there was he no-wise fain,
Back to his master he sped again
And told him the tale so drear.

He quoth: "At yon chapel have I been,
A wondrous sight I there have seen,
My heart is heavy as lead;
There standeth a bier, of lights great
store,
There sitteth a woman, and no man
more,
Bitter the tears she shed! 90
So evil a savour there was alway

That certes never before to-day
Have I been so sore bestead!
By grace of the palfrey that I bestride
But short while did I in that stress
abide,
I trow I had soon been dead!"

Sir Amadace bade his squire to fare:
"Ask thou of the woman what doth she
there,
True tidings bring to me!"
The squire he gat to the chapel wall, 100
And e'en as he said he saw withal,
It vexed him right bitterly:
But his nostrils were smitten with such
a smell
He might there in no-wise longer dwell,
Back to his lord went he,
And quoth: "Good Master, by your
leave,
Altho' I be loath your heart to grieve
Naught may ye know thro' me!

"A bier and candles, and nothing more,
A woman watching, and weeping sore,
Christ, she hath mickle care! 111
She sigheth sore, and her hands doth
wring,
And ever she calls on Heaven's King
How long must he lie there?
She saith: 'Dear God, why must this
be,
This sorrow that I needs must see,
Why should he so foully fare?'
She saith she will leave him not alone
Till she lieth dead on that floor of stone
For the love that to him she bare." 120

Sir Amadace hearkened, and spurred his
steed,
To the chapel door he came with speed,
And hastily did alight;
As his squire had said, so he found it
truth,
'T was the wickedest whiff he had smelt,
i-sooth,
Yet in went that gallant knight,

And he quoth: "Dame, God's mercy be
      with thee."
She answered: "Sir, welcome may ye
      be,"
Greeting she gave aright.
He quoth: "Say, Lady, what dost thou
      here,   130
Watching this dead corpse on this bier
Thus lonely throughout the night?"

She saith: "Sir, my place is at his side
For in sooth none other will here abide,
He was my husband dear."
Sir Amadace quoth: "I like it not,
'T will be your death, so God me wot,
He lieth o'er long on bier!
But say, what manner of man was he?"
"Sir, a merchant of good degree   140
In this city; every year
Of rent had he full three hundred pound,
Of ready money, good and round,
And for debt he lieth here!"

Sir Amadace quoth: "By the Holy
      Rood,
In what manner hath he so spent his
      good
That thus it be all away?"
"Sir, on knights, and squires, and offi-
      cers,
And lordings great who were his peers,
He gave them gifts alway.   150
Right royal feast he loved to make;
The poor folk, too, for Christ's dear sake,
He fed them every day;
Who to his door should come anon
And for love of God would pray a boon
He ne'er would say him nay.

"Yet in sooth he wrought as doth a fool,
For he clad more men at every Yule
Than ever a noble knight!   159
His meat he thought in no wise to spare,
The board in his hall was never bare
With fair cloth richly dight;
And if I said that he did amiss,
He sware 'God would all repay,' I wis,

And made of my words full light.
To so much had he pledged his name
I dare not say for very shame
How sorry was his plight!

"And then came death — Ah, woe is
      me!
My lord and I must sundered be,   170
He left me sorrow sore!
When the neighbours heard that sick he
      lay
They came in haste, nor made delay,
Of their goods they asked the store:
All that was ever his or mine,
House or oxen, sheep or swine,
Forthwith from me they tore.
My marriage portion then I sold,
And all the pennies in payment told,
And yet he owed still more!   180

"For when my quittance thus was told
Yet thirty pounds of good red gold
As debt remained alway,
To a merchant of this city good
Who fared afar by field and flood
Nor came till dead he lay.
Soon as he knew my sorry fare
He came as grim as any bear
The burial rites to stay:
He sware dogs should his body draw   190
And on the field his bones should gnaw —
Drear is my lot alway!

"These sixteen weeks I have sat me here
Guarding this dead corpse on the bier
With candles burning bright,
And so I think to do alway
Till death shall take me hence away
By Mary, Maid of might!"
Sir Amadace asked the merchant's name
Who thus had done her grievous shame,—
She told him how he hight.   201
He quoth: "God's Power may well
      avail
To comfort thee, and cure thy bale,
I bid thee, Dame, good-night!"
                    Fytte

Sir Amadace on his palfrey leapt,
Nor might forbear, but sorely wept,
On his deeds he him bethought:
He quoth: "He who lieth those walls
    within
Of a truth he and I might well be kin
For right so have I wrought!" 210
He told his squire how the merchant
    hight,
And said: "In his house I will lie to-
    night
By Christ Who dear me bought!
Go, look that the supper be ordered fair
With royal meats, and dainties rare,
Of spices spare thou naught!"

Soon as the squire he heard the tale
To seek the merchant he did not fail
And made ready for the knight.
Sir Amadace came with valiant show
But in his heart was mickle woe, 221
Hastily down he light,
He gat him into a chamber there,
And robed him in raiment rich and rare,
Set torches burning bright;
Forthwith he bade his squire to go
And pray his host, and his wife also,
To sup with him that night.

Straightway the squire he went his way,
And came to the merchant without delay,
His errand told anon: 231
The host right joyfully he sware:
"By Christ Whom Mary Maid did bear,
Thy lord's will shall be done!"
The board was set, and the cloth was laid,
The meal with dainties fair displayed,
Thus to the daïs they won;
Sir Amadace sat, and made good cheer,
But he thought of the dead man on the
    bier,
Full sadly he mused thereon. 240

He quoth: "As I rode my way, I trow,
I saw a sight which I think on now
It grieveth me evermore,
In a lonely chapel beside the way

All on a bier a body lay,
With a woman weeping sore."
"Yea," quoth his host, "God give him
    woe,
And all such wastrels as he also,
He wrought me ill of yore; 249
He lieth there with my thirty pound
Of honest money, red gold and round,
I shall see it never more!"

Quoth the knight: "I will tell thee a
    better rede
Forgive, e'en as God has forgiven, his
    deed,
And merit thou sure shalt have;
Think thou how God ordained for thee
A better lot than this man might see,
Let the corse be laid in grave!"
Then he sware: "By Jesu, Mary's Son,
That body its rest shall ne'er have won
Till I have the price I crave; 261
Let the woman die, as well as he,
Dogs shall gnaw their bones, as I fain
    would see,
Wastrel was he, and knave!"

When Sir Amadace heard what the mer-
    chant sware
He bade his steward in haste to fare,
Great kindness he did that day:
He said: "Go fetch me thirty pound
Of ready money good and round,
Nor tarry upon the way." 270
The steward, he held it for little skill,
Yet needs must he do his master's will,
Now hearken, for well ye may!
Full thirty pound the knight paid him
    there,
Then bade them the wine cup around to
    bear,
And prayed his host be gay.

Sir Amadace quoth: "Sir Host, now
    tell,
Doth he owe thee more?" "Nay, God
    keep thee well,
Thou hast paid me all, Sir Knight."

Then he quoth: "So far as ten pound will
    take   280
That will I do for the dead man's sake,
So far shall he have his right;
Mass for his soul shall they say and sing,
His body to Christian burial bring,
That shalt thou see with sight.
Bishop and priest shalt thou aye entreat
That to-morrow they eat with me at
    meat,
And see that the feast be dight."

Whenever it came to dawning time
Then all the bells began to chime   290
To bring that soul from stress;
All the religious, every one,
Towards that dead corpse are they gone
With many a rich burgess.
Thirty the priests who that day did sing,
And that gentle knight, he gave a ring
At every Mass, no less.
And then, when the service was done,
    full soon
He prayed them to eat with him at noon
Great, and small, in gentleness.   300

The host, by a pillar he took his stand
And men drew nigh him on either hand
To wit what he would say —
He said: "Sirs, of late there hath lain
    here
The corpse of a man upon a bier,
Ye know the cause alway;
Hither a royal knight he rode,
Of all the money the dead man owed
Hath he made me ready pay;   309
Then from his coffer he bade them bring
Ten pounds, with many a goodly ring
For his burying here to-day.

"In his name, and in that of the Dead,
    't is meet
I bid ye to-day with him to eat
All of ye who be here."
As Sir Amadace prayed so did they all,
Of meat and drink took their fill withal,
Rich wine and food full dear.

But Sir Amadace spared to sit adown,
He served the poor folk of that town,
They lay to his heart anear.   321
When they had eaten their fill withal
Sir Amadace took his leave of all,
It seemed, of right good cheer.

When all the folk thus had had their fill
They saddled his palfrey at his will
And brought it before the door;
Sir Amadace, he was ready dight,
But he knew not where he should lie that
    night,
Of money had he no more!   330
Small wonder if he were sad at heart
When from all his goods he thus must
    part,
In sooth it was sorry lore!
Then, e'en as a courteous knight became,
He prayed leave of the master of noblest
    name,
So gentles were wont of yore!

And scarcely the knight had gone his way
When every man would have his say
Ere he had passed the gate;   339
Some said: "This money was lightly won
When thus like water he lets it run,
And spendeth both morn and late."
Some said: "He was born in a lucky day
Who might win a penny of that man's
    pay!"
Little they knew his state!
Lo! how they misjudged that gentle
    knight
Who had spent even more than he justly
    might,
Sorrow was now his mate!

At the six-mile stone he drew his rein
Where a cross, it parted the way in
    twain,   350
And he quoth, Sir Amadace,
To his faithful steward, ('t was him full
    loth,)
To his sumpterman, and his squires
    both,

And said: "Now by Christ, His Grace,
Good Sirs, I pray ye do not grieve
But now must ye take from me your
    leave
Yourselves, ye know my case;
No man will I longer with me lead
When I have no silver that man to feed
Or clothe, in any place!"   360

Never a man was so hard of heart
But when he thus from his lord must
    part,
He made mourning, loud and low.
Sir Amadace quoth: "Nay, have no
    care,
For ye shall find masters everywhere,
I wot well it shall be so.
And God of His mercy, I give ye rede,
May send me counsel in this my need,
And bring me clean out of woe;
Merry of heart shall I once more be,
Then a welcome glad shall ye have from
    me,   371
That would I have ye know."

He quoth to his servants in that stound:
"The worst steed here is worth full ten
    pound,
That shall ye have anon;
Sumpterman, steward, squire and knave,
Each of you all for his own shall have
The horse that he rides upon,
Saddle, and bridle, and other gear,
Altho' I bought it never so dear,   380
I give it ye, by Saint John!
God keep ye all good men, I trow!
To the keeping of Christ I commit ye
    now —"
So they left him, every one.

Thus all his men they went their way
And the knight, in sorrow he rode that
    day,
All by himself alone.
Through the forest thick the road led
    right,
Down from his palfrey would he alight

And, mournful, he made his moan,   390
When he thought of his lands, so fair
    and good,
His towns and castles that stately stood,
How all were set on loan;
And how he was now so sore bestead
That for poverty he afar had fled,
For folly must thus atone.

Then in sorrow he spake, Sir Amadas:
"A man that of good but little has,
Men set him lightly by;
When I had three hundred pound of
    rent   400
Two hundred I spent in that intent
Of such forethought was I!
The while I such household had at hand
Men held me a noble lord in land,
And gave to me honour high.
But now may the wise man dwell at
    home
While fools are forced afar to roam,
And Christ wot, so may I!"

He said: "Sweet Jesu, Who died on
    Rood,
Who shed for me Thy Precious Blood,
And all this world hath won,   411
I pray that I come not in the sight
Of any who knew me afore as knight,
Save I prosper, 'neath moon and sun.
And grant that I win unto me again
Those who their way from me have
    ta'en,
Who have loyal service done.
Or else, Lord, I humbly pray of Thee
That Death may come swiftly unto me,
And my race betimes be run.   420

"For want of wit, so it seemeth me,
Out of the land I needs must flee,
From friendship I find small grace:
Thro' naught save good will and kindli-
    ness
Have I brought myself to this sorry
    stress —"
Thus prayed Sir Amadace:

And he quoth: "Lord Jesu, Who died on
 Tree,
I pray Thee Thy succour send now to
 me
Speedily, in this place;   429
For if but a measure of help thou send
I wot of that measure I fain would lend,
Nor turn from the poor my face!"

Thus he rode thro' the forest ways alone
And deemed that no man might hear his
 moan,
For no man was there in sight;
Yet sudden a horseman was at his side,
And spake to him hastily in that tide,
Thereof was he sore affright:
The horseman, he rode a milk-white
 steed,
And milk-white, I ween, was all his weed
He seemed a full gallant knight. 441
Tho' Sir Amadace was to sorrow brought
In courtesy was he lacking naught,
Greeting he gave aright.

Quoth the White Knight: "Say, Friend,
 shalt thou be he
Who maketh his moan thus bitterly,
With sad and sorry cheer?"
Sir Amadace, he made answer, "Nay!"
Quoth the knight: "That availeth thee
 naught alway,
This long while have I been here; 450
I rede thee to mourn not in such wise,
He who falls, by the grace of God may
 rise,
For His help is ever near.
Riches are but a loan, I wot,
Which thou hast, and again thou hast it
 not,
Thou shalt find full many a peer!

"Now think thou on Him Who died on
 Rood,
Who shed for the world His Precious
 Blood,
For thee, and for mankind all;
The man who giveth in fashion free 460

To his fellow of high, or of low, degree
Shall reap his reward withal;
He who ever dealeth in customs kind
A courteous man, forsooth, shall find
Who shall his need forestall.
Repent thee of naught that thou hast
 done,
For God, He Who shapeth moon and
 sun,
Shall yet repay thee all.

"Say, would'st thou love him o'er
 everything
Who should thee out of thy sorrow
 bring, 470
And set thee free from care?
To the land of a king art thou full
 near
Who hath no treasure so close and dear
As his daughter young and fair:
He hath sworn to no man her hand to
 yield
Save to him whom men reckon the first
 in field,
Who the prize of the joust shall bear,
Now I hold thee well for the goodliest
 knight
That ever mine eyes have seen with sight
Of all men who harness wear. 480

"Thou shalt ride to the joust in such fair
 array
As ever a knight of worship may,
But thou needs must go alone:
Thou shalt say: the folk who set forth
 with thee
Were drowned in a tempest upon the
 sea,
Thou hast lost them every one.
Rich gifts shalt thou scatter with open
 hand,
And shalt win thee the nobles of the
 land,
I would have thee spare for none;
See thou be fair of speech and free 490
Till thou draw a following unto thee,
From me is their payment won!"

He quoth: "Be thou free of hand alway,
The cost of thy household will I pay
Tho' it count ten thousand head:
For mickle honour thy deeds shall crown,
Fair fields and forests, tower and town,
That lady shalt thou wed!
And when thou hast won thy friends to
    thee
Then look thou again my face to see, 500
I will seek thee in that stead.
But a covenant make ere hence I fare
That thou wilt freely with me share
In such wise as thou hast sped!"

Then answered him fair, Sir Amadace:
"An thou hast power, by God's good
    grace,
In this wise to comfort me,
Thou shalt find me in all things true and
    leal,
All that I have will I fairly deal
In twain, 'twixt me and thee."   510
The   White   Knight   quoth: "Now
    Friend, Farewell,
The blessing of God upon thee dwell,
And work with thee verily."
Sir Amadace answered: "Friend, God
    speed,
I trow thou shalt find me in act and deed
True as a man may be!"
       Fytte

Sir Amadace came to the salt sea strand,
And lo! ships lay broken upon the sand,
A marvel it was to see!
Wreckage lay scattered here and there,
Knights in armour and minevère,   521
And strong steeds white and gray.
Riches and goods in every guise
That the heart of man might well devise
Cast up by the waters lay;
Chests and coffers of gold and good,
Scattered among the wreckage stood,
No man had borne aught away!

Sir Amadace robed himself with speed
In a web of gold, a goodly weed,   530

Better there might not be;
He chose him a steed whereon to ride,
A better methinks, might none bestride,
Who jousting were fain to see.
This chance befell him beside a tower,
Thereafter he won to him great honour
Within that fair citie.
The king beheld that goodly knight,
He, and his daughter fair and bright,
The prize of the joust was she.   540

The king to his daughter quoth that
    tide:
"Lo! yonder a gallant knight doth ride."
Messengers took he there,
His body-squire, and of good knights
    three,
And saith: "Go, see who yon man may be
And whence he did hither fare.
Tell him his goods shall be held in hand
Wholly as he shall here command,
For that shall he have no care.   549
If he asketh aught that ye well may do
Say ye that your will is good thereto,
If hither in peace he fare."

The messengers came to the salt sea
    strand,
They took Sir Amadace by the hand,
Tidings of him they pray:
"Our lord, the king, us hath hither sent
To welcome your coming with good
    intent
An ye your will shall say.
He saith, your goods shall be held in
    hand
Wholly as ye shall here command,   560
No lie do we speak to-day.
Whatsoever ye will that the king's men
    do
Ye have but to give them command
    thereto
For service right glad and gay."

Quoth Sir Amadace: "I was a prince of
    pride,
And I had bethought me at this tide,

At the tourney here to be:
I was victualled well with meat and
    wine,
With gallant steeds and harness fine,
And good knights, verily,   570
But such a storm did upon us break
That my goodly ships are gone to wreck,
As ye yourselves may see.
Of gold and silver have I enow,
But the men who sailed with me, I trow,
Not one is left to me."

Sir Amadace on his gallant steed
Anon to the castle gates they lead,
And told the king his case;
The king, he quoth: "Thou art welcome
    here,   580
I rede thee to be of joyful cheer,
Thank Jesu for His Grace!
So fierce a tempest hast thou been in,
'T was a right fair hap that thou
    should'st win
To shelter in this place.
But of all the men I have seen, I trow,
None have come so near to my heart as
    thou
Who art fair of speech and face."

Thereon the king, for that good knight's
    sake,
A cry through the city bade them make,
And stablished it by decree,   591
That all who a master were fain to find
Of knight or squire, of knave or hind,
Each man in his degree,
Should get him unto Sir Amadace,
Who found himself in such sorry case,
His men had been drowned at sea.
He would give them payment as much
    and more
As any master had done before,
An they would with him be.   600

The gentlemen all who heard that cry
They gat them to him right hastily,
Of his service were they fain,
So when the Tourney abroad was cried

There was no lord on either side
With half such gallant train!
There did he win to him great renown
In field and meadow, tower and town,
Castles he held again;
A hundred steeds and more he won,   610
One half he gave to the King anon,
Parting his prize in twain.

Thence to the palace the knights would
    fare,
Thither they went, and would not spare,
As fast as they might ride;
The King made that knight full noble
    cheer,
And saith: "Now welcome my friend so
    dear,
Ye be come in a happy tide!"
He called him his daughter so fair and
    sweet,
And they sat them down to the board at
    meat,   620
The knight by the maiden's side;
Each on the other to gaze was fain,
The love-light was kindled betwixt the
    twain,
True lovers were they and tried!

Then the king, he led Sir Amadace
Aside with him for a little space,
And thus to him did say:
"Sir Knight, I have but one daughter
    fair,
Of all my lands shall she be the heir,
She ate with thee to-day: 630
An thou be a man who would wed a
    wife,
I swear to thee truly by my life,
I will give thee that gentle may;
And another gift I will with her give,
The half of my kingdom while I live,
And the whole when I be away!"

"Gramercy, Sire!" quoth Sir Amadace:
He thanked the king for his royal grace,
And for his gifts so good.
Thereafter, so the tale doth say,   640

They made forthwith to the kirk their
    way,
He wedded her, by the Rood!
Of gold he gave freely in that stound,
Largesse of silver, many a pound,
As on their way they rode;
Then they sat them down to feast in hall
Full many a lord and lady, all
Who were of gentle blood.

Thus came Sir Amadace forth of woe,
God grant us His grace, that we find it
    so —   650
Great feasting did they make!
The revel lasted a good fortnight,
With meat and drink the board was
    dight,
Nor spears they spared to break;
A year and a half with that lady fair
He dwelt, and a son unto him she bare,
Great mirth made for his sake!
Now listen, lordings, and ye shall hear
How there came to him his comrade
    dear,
His share of all to take.   660

He came in raiment so sheen and fair,
Even as he an angel were,
Clad was he all in white:
The porter his errand fain would know,—
He quoth: "Do thou to thy master go
And bear my words aright;
Go quickly, and if he ask aught of me,
Whence I be come, and of what countrie,
Say, I ride all in white;
And say that we twain have together
    been,   670
Methinks, he aforetime my face hath
    seen,
If he be a loyal knight!"

The porter, he sped to the castle hall,
Full soon he had sought out his lord
    withal,
And he hailed him thus anon:
"Lord, lord, there be come the fairest
    knight

Whom ever mine eyes have seen with
    sight,
Beneath or sun or moon,
White as the snow his gallant steed,
White as the snow his knightly weed,
He asketh of thee no boon,   681
He saith that ye have together been —
I trow who aforetime his face hath seen
Shall know him again eftsoon!"

"Is he come?" quoth the knight, "my
    comrade dear,
I trow me he is right welcome here,
As behoveth him well to be!
Now one and all, here I make command
That ye do to this knight, with foot and
    hand,
Such service as due to me!"   690
Sir Amadace straight to the portal drew,
And with him she went, his lady true,
Who was right fair to see;
And she made him welcome with right
    good cheer,
For the friends of her lord to her heart
    were dear,
Blesséd such wives as she!

Who should stable his charger then?
Knight, squire, yeoman, nor serving
    men,
No one with him he brought: 699
Gentlemen gladly would take his steed,
Knights would him fain to his chamber
    lead,
Thereof would he have naught.
He saith: "Nay, certes, the sooth to tell,
Here will I eat, nor drink, nor dwell,
By Christ, Who dear me bought!
But now shalt thou deal thy goods in
    two,
Give me my portion, and let me go,
If I be worthy aught!"

Then quoth Sir Amadace fair and free:
"For the love of God, let such words be,
They grieve my heart full sore,   711
For we may not part in equal share

Our lands that lie so broad and fair,
In a fortnight's space, and more!
But let us dwell together here,
E'en as we twain were brethren dear,
And thine the treasure store!
'T were well the rest should not parted
    be,
But we hold it all as due to thee,
Methinks 't were the better lore!"   720

The White Knight quoth: "Keep thy
    lands so wide,
Thy towers, and castles, on every side,
Of these do I covet none:
Keep thou thy woods, thy waters clear,
Thy fields and forests far and near,
Thy rings with sparkling stone;
Thy silver and thy gold so red,
I trow they may stand me in no stead,
I swear it by Saint John!   729
But upon thy faith, and without strife,
Give me half thy child, and half thy wife,
To fare with me anon!"

Then Sir Amadace cried with woeful
    cheer:
"Alas, that I won this lady dear,
Or aught of this world's good!
For the love of Him Who died on tree,
Whatsoever thou wilt, that do with me,
By Him Who died on Rood!
Yea, take all the goods that here I have
With thee, but her life I prithee save!"
The knight, he understood,   741
And he sware: "By God, Who dear me
    bought,
Of other things I will have naught
Of all thy worldly good!

"Think thou on the covenant that we
    made
In the wood, when thou wast so sore
    dismayed,
How thou didst speak me fair!" —
Sir Amadace quoth: "'T is truth alway,
But methinks should I now my lady
    slay

A deadly sin it were!"   750
The lady fair, right well she knew
How the matter stood betwixt the two,
She stayed her weeping there —
And spake: "As thou art a loyal knight
Thy covenant shalt thou keep aright,
Nor for love of me forbear!"

Then bravely she spake, that lady
    bright,
"Thou shalt keep thy faith with this
    goodly knight,
By the Blessèd Trinity;
Ye made a covenant true and fast,   760
Look it be holden to the last,
By Him Who died on Tree!
If the Will of Christ must needs be so
Take me, and part me here in two,
My lord art thou verily!
God forbid that for true love's sake
A scorn of thy name in the land I make,
And falsehood of fealty!"

Steadfast she stood, and fair of face,
Nor shed a tear, a little space,   770
Then quoth that lady dear:
"Fetch me my little son so fair
Whom a while since I of my body bare,
Lay him my heart anear." —
"Now," quoth the White Knight:
    "answer me,
Which of the twain shall more precious
    be?"
He saith: "My wife so dear!"
"Then since thou lovest her the best
Thou shalt part her in twain at my
    behest,
Her flesh asunder shear!"   780

Then when Sir Amadace needs must see
That never a better lot might be
He fared as he were wood;
And all the men who were in that hall
Swooning for sorrow adown they fall,
Who erst by their master stood:
They made ready a board whereon to lie,
She kissed her lord full tenderly,

And signed her with Holy Rood.   789
Then meekly she laid her down in place,
And they drew a cloth across her face,
That lady mild of mood!

Quoth the White Knight: "I would not
    do thee wrong,
The goods which of right unto thee be-
    long,
Thou shalt part them at thy will:" —
Then answered Sir Amadace fair and free:
"E'en as thou sayest, so shall it be,
Thy wish would I fulfil."
Sir Amadace lifted his sword alway
To smite the lady who lowly lay —   800
Quoth the White Knight: "Peace, be
    still!"
He lifted the lady and child so fair,
And gave them again to Sir Amadace
    there,
And quoth, "That were little skill!

"I blame thee little, by this my troth,
If to slay such lady thou wert full loth,
Tho' it were thy pledge to save:
But now shalt thou know I was e'en as
    glad
When thou gavest all that ever thou had
My body to lay in grave!   810
Unburied, I lay, doomed the hounds to
    feed,
First thirty pounds didst thou pay at
    need,
Then all that thou didst have.
I prayed God to bring thee forth from
    care
Who hadst made thyself of goods so bare,
Mine honour and name to save!

"Now, farewell," he said: "my comrade
    dear,
For no longer may I linger here
Nor speak with thee at will:
But see thou cherish her as thy life   820
Who had given her body withouten
    strife
Thy covenant to fulfil!"

With that he swift from their sight did
    pass
As dew it melteth from off the grass,
And the twain abode there still;
Then down they knelt them upon their
    knee,
And gave thanks to God, and to Mary
    free,
Who had guarded them from ill!

Thus Sir Amadace, and his gentle wife,
With joy and bliss they passed their life
Unto their dying day.   831
I wot there be ladies not a few
To-day, who had been to their lord as
    true,
Yet some would have said him nay!
But whoso serveth right faithfully
Our Lord, and His Mother Maid Marīē
Of him would I soothly say,
Tho' like misfortune at times befall
Yet God shall grant Him his will withal,
And lead him in Heaven's way.   840

His messengers then that good knight
    sent,
Far and near thro' the land they went
E'en to his own countrīē,
Till all unto whom his lands he sold,
Field or forest, town or hold,
Were bought out rightfully.
His steward and those who to him were
    dear
He sent, and called them again anear,
And dowered with gold and fee,
That they with him their days might
    spend   850
Evermore, unto their life's end,
In gladness and peace to be.

And then it chanced, at God's good will,
The king died, and the knight abode
    there still,
As ye shall understand:
And now was he lord of town and tower,
They came to his bidding in that hour
The knights throughout the land:

They crowned Sir Amadace on that
    day
With golden crown, in royal array,   860
And bowed to his command. —

Now pray we One God, in Persons
    Three,
To gladden and comfort this companie,
And keep us safe in His Hand!

YWAIN AND GAWAIN

THE WINNING OF THE LADY OF THE FOUNTAIN[1]

THEN went Sir Ywain to his inn,
His men he ready found therein,
Unto a squire then did he say:
"My palfrey saddle now straightway,
The same do by my strongest steed,
And take with thee my richest weed;
At yonder gate I forth will ride,
Without the town I will abide.
Now hie thee swiftly unto me,
I go a journey, speedily,   10
My palfrey thou again shalt bring,
And speak no word of this same thing —
If me again thou fain would'st see,
Let none know of this secresy,
If any man would fain be told,
See that thou, loyal, promise hold."
"Yea, sir," he quoth, "with right good-
    will,
All that thou biddest, I'll fulfil,
And at your own will shall ye ride,
Thro' me, ye shall of none be spied."   20

Forth did he go then, Sir Ywain,
He thinketh, ere he come again,
To 'venge his cousin, an he might —
The squire, he hath his harness dight,
He followed aye his master's rede,
Brought him his harness and his steed.
When Ywain was without the town
He from his palfrey lighted down,
Robed him, as fitting, in his weed,
And leapt upon his goodly steed,   30
Into the country rode forthright,

[1] *Ywain and Gawain*, ed. Schleich, ll. 565–1266.

Until the day drew nigh to night.
He rode by many a mountain high,
Desert, and plain, he passed them by,
Until he to that pathway came
Which he must needs take, at that
    same,
Then was he sure that he should see
The fountain, and the wondrous tree.
The castle he beheld at last,
Thither he hied him fair and fast,   40
More courtesy, and honour fair,
I trow me, were his portion there
And comforts more, by manifold,
Than Colgrevance in sooth had told;
Within that tower he lodged, I wot,
Better than e'er had been his lot.

At morn he rode forth on the street,
And with the churl right soon did
    meet
Who should direct him on his way —
He crossed himself, the sooth to say,   50
Twenty times, in a little span,
Such marvel had he of that man,
He wondered much so foul a wight
E'er on this earth had seen the light.
Then to the well he rode, swift pace,
Down he alighted in that place,
The basin would he take anon,
Water he cast upon the stone;
Full soon there followed, without fail,
Both wind and thunder, rain and hail, 60
When ceased the storm, he straight did
    see
The birds alight upon that tree,
They sang as sweetly on the bough
As they had done afore, I trow.

And then, full soon, he saw a knight,
Coming as swift as bird in flight,
With semblance stern, and wrathful cheer,
And hastily he drew anear.
To speak of love they thought no more
For each the other hated sore,⁣ 70
They drive together on the field,
Riven full soon is each knight's shield,
Shivered to haft, their spears they fell,
But each knight kept his seat full well.
Then forth they drew their swords so keen,
Dealt doughty strokes, the twain between.
To pieces have they hewn each shield,
The fragments fly full far afield;
They smite the helms with wrath and ire,
At every stroke outbursts the fire;⁣ 80
Buffets right good they give, indeed,
But neither stirs from off his steed —
Boldly, the twain, they shew their might,
I trow it was no feint, their fight!
As from their hauberks men might know —
The blood did from their bodies flow,
Each on the other smote so fast
No long time might such battle last.
Hauberks were broken, helmets riven,
Strong strokes, and stiff, I trow, were given;⁣ 90
Yet on their steeds they fought always
The battle was the more to praise.
Sir Ywain, at the last, doth show,
Valiant, his might against his foe,
So eagerly he smote him there
Helmet and head, he cleft them fair,
The knight was well-nigh slain, indeed,
Flight was, he knew, the better rede,
And fast he fled, with might and main,
And fast he followed, Sir Ywain;⁣ 100
But he might not his flight o'ertake,
Therefore great mourning did he make,
Yet followed stoutly where he fled,
Full fain to take him, quick, or dead.

So to the city followed he
And ne'er a living man did see;
Both, to the castle-gate they win —
Ywain would swiftly pass therein;
At either entry hung, I wis,
Full straitly wrought, a portcullis,⁣ 110
With iron and steel 't was shod full well
Fitting right closely where it fell.
There-under, was a blade so keen
That sore misliked the knight, I ween —
His horse's foot, it touched thereon,
The portcullis, it fell anon,
Before the hinder saddle-bow,
Saddle, and steed, it smote them thro'
The spurs from off his heels it shore —
Sir Ywain, he must mourn him sore,⁣ 120
But, ere he could have passed them quite,
The other gate, it closed full tight.
'T was of God's Grace it chancéd so
That tho' it cut his steed in two,
And smote the spurs from either heel
Yet he himself no harm did feel.
Betwixt the gates he's captive now, —
Much mourning did he make, I trow,
And much bemoaned his evil plight⁣ 129
And that he'd thus escaped, the knight.
As in a trap he stood, withal,
He heard behind him, in a wall,
A doorway open, fair and well,
Thereout there came a demoiselle,
The door behind her fast did make
And gracious words to him she spake.
"Sir, by Saint Michael," thus quoth she,
"Here hast thou evil hostelry,
Dead art thou, dost thou here remain,
For this, my lord, whom thou hast slain,⁣ 140
For sooth it is, thou didst him slay, —
My lady mourneth sore alway,
Yea, and his household, every one,
Full many a foeman there hast won.
Yea, for thy bane they be full bold,
Thou comest not from out this hold,
They shall not fail for very might, —
Slay thee they will, in open fight."

He quoth: "By God, Who gave me
    breath
Numbers shall ne'er do me to death. 150
Their hands on me they ne'er shall
    lay —"
"Nay, certes," quoth she, "an I may,
For tho' thou be full straitly stead
Methinks, in no wise art adread;
And Sir," she quoth: "I owe to thee
Service and honour fair and free;
Long time ago, I needs must bring,
When young, a message to the King
Such wisdom had I not, or wit,   160
As doth a maiden well befit,
And from the time I did alight
At court, was none so courteous knight
Who unto me would then take heed,
Save thou alone, God give thee meed!
Great honour didst thou do to me
And I shall now repay it thee.
Tho' seldom I thee saw, I trow,
By birth, King Urien's son art thou,
And men shall thee, Sir Ywain, call;
Of me thou may'st be sure withal,   170
Wilt thou my counsel follow still
No man shall do thee harm or ill;
My ring I here will leave with thee,
(But at my asking yield it me,)
When thou be brought from out thy
    pain
Then shalt thou give it me again.
For as the bark doth shield the tree,
E'en so my ring shall shelter thee,
When on thy hand thou bear the stone
Of mischief men shall do thee none. 180
For this same stone, it hath such might
That no man shall of thee have sight."
Now wit ye well, that Sir Ywain,
Of these her words, he was full fain;
In at the door she hath him led,
And set him down upon her bed,
A noble quilt, it lay thereon,
Richer, I trow, was never none,
She said, if he would aught, anon,
That, at his liking, should be done; 190
He said to eat was he full fain;
She went, and swiftly came again,

A roasted capon brought she soon,
With a clean cloth, and bread thereon,
A jar of rich wine too, she bore,
And cup, wherein the wine to pour.
With right good cheer he drank and
    ate,
I trow, his need thereof was great.
When he had drunk, and eaten well,
A noise, upon his ears it fell,   200
Men sought for him, they would him
    slay,
Fain to avenge their lord were they,
Ere that the corpse in earth was laid —
The demoiselle, she to him said:
"Thy foemen seek to slay thee now,
But whoso comes or goes, do thou
Of them be in no wise adread,
But stir thou not from out this stead;
Within this chamber seek they will, 209
But on this couch here hold thee still,
And of them all thou shalt make light.
But when they bear the corpse forth-
    right
Unto the kirk, upon the bier,
Forsooth, a sorry cry shalt hear,
Then shall they make a doleful din,
Then shall they seek thee oft herein,
But look thou be of heart full light,
Never of thee shall they have sight,
Here shalt thou be, maugre their beard,
And therefore be nowise afeard;   220
Thy foes shall be e'en as the blind,
Seeking before thee, and behind,
On every side shalt thou be sought. —
Now must I go, but fear thee naught,
I'll do as shall be good for thee
Tho' ill thereof should come to me."

Then to the portal forth she gat,
Full many men she found thereat,
Well armed they were, and were full fain
Sir Ywain to have caught, and slain. 230
Half of his steed they found that day
Where dead within the gate it lay,
But of the knight there found they
    naught.
There mickle grief had they unsought,

Of door or window, was there none
Thro' which he might away have gone.
They quoth, that there he needs must be
Unless in witchcraft skilled were he,
Or nigromancy well had known,
Or else on wings away had flown.   240
Thus, hastily, they gat them all,
And sought him in the maiden's hall,
In chambers high, where naught did hide,
In cellars deep, on every side;
Ywain, of that was well aware,
Still on the couch he held him there,
No man amid them all who might
Come nigh, a blow thereon to smite.
But all about they smote so fast   249
That they their weapons brake at last,
And great their sorrow, and their woe,
That they their vengeance must forego.
They went their way with doleful cheer,
And soon thereafter came the bier,
A lady followed, milk-white, fair,
None with her beauty might compare,
She wrung her hands, out-burst the blood,
For sorrow was she well nigh wood;
Her locks so fair she tare eft-soon,
And oft she fell adown in swoon,   260
In doleful tone she mourned her loss —
The holy water, and the Cross
Men bare before that train anon;
There followed many a mother's son,
Before the corpse a knight bestrode
The dead man's steed, a charger good,
In all his harness well arrayed,
With spear and shield fitly displayed.
The cry, Sir Ywain heard it there,
The dole of this, the lady fair,   270
None might surpass her grief and woe
When thus her lord to grave must go,
The priests and monks, in fit degree,
They do the service solemnly.

Lunete, she stood within the throng
Until Sir Ywain deemed it long,
Then from the crowd she goes again,
Swiftly she seeketh Sir Ywain,

She quoth: "How goes it Sir, with thee?
I trust thou well advised shalt be?"   280
"Certes," he quoth, "thou speakest well,
Abashed was I the sooth to tell";
He quoth: "Leman, I pray of thee
If it in any wise may be,
That I may look a little space
Thro' hole or window, in this place,
For wondrous fain" he quoth, "am I
To see your lady, verily."
That maid, she soon undid withal,
A little wicket in the wall,   290
There of that dame he gat a sight:
Aloud she cried on God's great Might:
"Have mercy on his sins, I pray,
For in no land there lived alway
A knight who was so fair as he,
And none such may there ever be —
Thro' the wide world, beneath the sun,
So fair, so courteous, was there none!
God grant thee grace, that so thou may
Dwell with His Son, in endless day.   300
So generous liveth none on land,
Nor none so doughty of their hand." —
When thus her speech to end was brought
Swooning, oft-times she fell, distraught.

Now let we that fair lady be,
Of Ywain speak we presently, —
Love, that so mickle is of might,
With sore wounds doth Sir Ywain smite,
That wheresoe'er he ride, or go,
She hath his heart who was his foe.   310
His heart is surely set, I ween,
Where he himself dare not be seen;
Thus, sorely longing, bideth he,
Hoping his lot may bettered be.
All men who at that burial were
Their leave take of that lady fair,
And to their home they all be gone —
The lady have they left alone,
She with her waiting-maid doth dwell.
And others, whom she loveth well.   320
Then her lament began anew
For sorrow paled her skin and hue,

For his soul's health her beads she
　　told —
She took a psalter all of gold,
To say the psalms she swift began
And took no heed to any man.
Sir Ywain woeful was indeed,
For little hope had he to speed,　　328
He quoth: "Here am I much to blame
Since I love them who would me shame,
But yet I wrought her woe, 't is true,
Since I it was her lord who slew;
Nor know I how I may begin,
With trick or wile, her love to win;
Slender that lady is, and small,
Her eyes be clear as crystal all,
Certes, no man on earth that be
Could tell her beauties fittingly."
Thus was Sir Ywain sore bestead,
From Reason's path aside was led　　340
To set his love on one, who 'ld see
Him brought to death right willingly;
He said, he 'ld have that dame to wife
Or in that cause would lose his life.

Thus doth he sit and think amain:
The maiden comes to him again,
She said: "How hast thou fared to-day
Since that from thee I went away?"
Soon did she see him wan and pale
And knew right well what did him ail,
She quoth: "I know what would thy
　　heart,　　351
To hinder it were ne'er my part,
Certes, I 'll help thee out of ward
And bring thee to a sure reward, —"
He quoth: "Now Lady, certainly,
Hence will I steal not, privily,
But I will go in full day-light
So that I be in all men's sight,
Openly, and on every side —
What matters it what may betide?　　360
But as a man I hence will fare." —
Then answered him that maiden fair:
"Sir, thou shalt hence in honour go,
And goodly succour shalt thou know,
But Sir, abide here patiently
Until I come again to thee."

Soothly she knew his heart's intent,
And therefore 't was she wisely went
Unto the lady fair and bright,
For unto her she freely might　　370
Say all that was within her will,
For that she was her mistress still,
Keeper, and counsellor full dear —
To her she spake as ye shall hear
In counsel good betwixt the twain —
"Madam, to marvel am I fain
That ye thus grieve, and sorrow sore;
For God's sake, give your mourning
　　o'er,
Bethink ye now of this one thing,　　379
How that he comes, Arthur the King,
Bethink ye of that message well
That late the sauvage Demoiselle
Did in her letter to ye send —
Alas! Who shall ye now defend,
Your land, and all your folk, I pray
Since ye will not your weeping stay?
Ah! madam, now take heed to me,
You have no knight in this countrie
Who durst his body risk at need
Upon the chance of doughty deed,　　390
Nor who should dare withstand the
　　boast
Of Arthur, and his goodly host.
Yet if none dare the king withstand
Then ye, for certain lose your land!"

The lady understood full well
Why in this wise her counsel fell,
She bade her swiftly leave her there,
And that she should in no wise dare
To speak with her such words again —
Her heart, for grief, to break was
　　fain.　　400
She quoth: "Now get thee hence away!"
The maiden thus began to say:
"Madam, 't is often women's mood
To blame those who give counsel good."
She went her way, dismayed for
　　naught, —
And then the lady her bethought
The maid, in sooth, had said no wrong,
And so she sat, and pondered long.

In study thus she sat alone:
The maiden, she returned anon, — 410
"Madam," she said, "a child ye be,
Yourself may ye harm easily,
Chastise your heart, Madam, I pray,
Great shame it doth to ye alway,
Thus sore to weep and make great cry,
Think thou on all thy chivalry;
Dost deem that all thy knighthood's
     flower
Died with their lord, in that same hour,
And were with him put under mold?
Nay, God forbid such tale were told, 420
For better knights than he shall be!"
"By Heaven's Queen, thou liest!"
     quoth she;
"Now tell me, if so be thou can,
Where shall be found such valiant man
As he was, who was wed with me?"
"Yea, can I, an thou promise free
And give me full assurance here
That thou shalt hold me none less dear!"
She quoth: "Now be thou sure alway
That for no word that thou canst say 430
Will I wax wrathful against thee —"
"Madam," she said, "now answer me,
I'll tell a secret in thine ear,
And no one save we twain shall hear.
Say, if two knights be in the field,
Mounted on steed, with spear and
     shield,
And one be by the other slain
Which is the better of the twain?"
She quoth: "Now he who wins the fight!"
"Yea," saith the maiden, "ye be right;
The knight who lives shall braver be 441
Than was your lord, since slain was he.
Your lord, he fled from out the place,
The other knight, he gave him chase,
And followed him e'en to his hold —
Here may ye wit that he was bold."
The lady quoth: "Thou doest shame
Here before me to speak his name,
Thou sayest neither sooth nor right,
Now get thee swiftly from my sight!"
The maiden said: "So may it be, 451
And yet but now ye promised me

Ye would in no wise me miscall —"
With that she gat her from the hall,
And hastily she went again
Unto her bower, to Sir Ywain.
The lady pondered thro' the night
How she in no wise knew a knight
To keep her land, as guardian stout,
Against King Arthur and his rout. 460
Then she began herself to shame,
And in her heart she took much blame,
'Gainst herself brought reproaches
     strong —
She quoth: "I trow, I did her wrong,
Now doth she deem I never more
Will love her, as I did afore;
I'll love her well, in grateful mood,
For all she said was for my good."

With morning light the maiden rose,
And soon unto the chamber goes, 470
There did she find that fair ladie
Hanging her head full drearily,
There, where she left her, yestere'en —
Then, in such wise she spake, I ween,
E'en as she spake the day before —
Thus spake the dame: "It rues me
     sore
That I miscalled thee yesterday,
Amends I'll make, if so I may,
For of that knight I fain would hear,
Who is he? Say, whence came he here?
I trow I spake too hastily, 481
I'll do as thou shalt counsel me.
Now, ere thou leave, tell me aright
If he be gently born, this knight?"
"Madam," she saith, "I swear to thee,
Of better birth shall no man be,
The fairest man ye shall him find
Of all men born of Adam's kind."
"To know his name I sure were fain —"
"Lady," she quoth, "it is Ywain — 490
And gentler knight was never none,
Unto King Urien is he son."
Content she was to hear that thing,
That he was son unto a king:
"Now bring him here into my sight
Sometime 'twixt this, and the third night,

Or earlier; if it so might be,
I am full fain that knight to see.
Nay, bring him, if thou canst, to-
   night —"
"Madam," she quoth, "that were not
   light,   500
His dwelling further is away
Than one may journey in a day,
But I have a swift-footed page
Who'll do that journey in a stage
And bring him here to-morrow night."
The lady quoth: "See, if he might
To-morrow eve be here again —"
"Yea, he shall speed with might and
   main."
"Bid him to hasten on his way,
I will his service well repay,   510
A higher post shall be his boon
An so he do his errand soon."
"Madam," she quoth, "my word I
   plight
To have him here ere the third night;
The while unto your council send,
And ask them who shall ye defend,
Your well, your castle, and your land,
Against King Arthur, and his band,
For of them all I trow is none
Who such a battle will not shun.   520
Then shall ye say: 'I needs must take
A lord to do what ye forsake —'
Ye needs must have some noble knight
Who will and may defend your right,
And say: were death your lot alway
Ye would but do as they shall say.
Blithe shall they be of this, your speech,
And thank ye oft-times, all and each."
The lady quoth: "By God's great Might
I'll talk with them this very night, 530
Methinks too long thou here dost stay,
Send forth thy messenger straightway."

Then was the lady glad and gay,
She did all that her maid did say;
Unto her council sent anon,
And bade them come there, every one.
The maid to play her part was fain,
A bath made ready for Ywain,

Clad him right well in scarlet fold,
Well furred, and trimmed with fret of
   gold;   540
A girdle rich she brought him there,
Of silk enwrought with stones so fair.
She told him all that he should do,
When he was come that lady to,
And thus, when he was ready dight,
She to her mistress went forthright,
And said, he came, her messenger —
She swiftly spake: "Now, let me hear,
As thou would'st thrive, comes he
   straightway?"   549
"Madam," she quoth, "without delay
I'll bring him swiftly to ye here —"
Then quoth the dame, with gladsome
   cheer:
"Go, bring him hither privily
That none may know, save thou and I."
With that the maiden went again,
Swiftly she came to Sir Ywain,
She quoth: "Sir, as I bliss may win,
My lady knows thou art within,
To come before her be thou bold, 559
And keep in mind what I have told."
Then by the hand she took the knight,
And led him to the bower forthright,
Before her lady — sooth to tell
Her coming, it rejoiced her well.
Sir Ywain feared much at that same,
When he unto the chamber came,
The chamber floor, and all the bed,
With cloth of gold was overspread,
For peerless knight she doth him take,
But never word to him she spake. 570
For fear, he fain aback would draw,
The maiden laughed, when this she
   saw,
And quoth: "Now ill befall that knight
Who hath of such a lady sight,
And to her dare not shew his mind!
Come forth, Sir Knight, and courage
   find,
Fear not my lady smiteth thee,
She loves thee well, and guilelessly,
Do thou to her for mercy cry,
And for thy sake, e'en so will I, 580

That she forgive thee, in this stead,
For Salados, le Roux, now dead,
That was her lord, whom thou hast
    slain —"
Upon his knees fell Sir Ywain,
"Madam, I yield me to your will,
Do with me as shall please ye still,
E'en if I might, I would not flee —"
She quoth: "Now, wherefore should
    that be?
If I to death should do thee now,
Small profit 't were to me, I trow.   590
But since so humble thou shalt be,
And in such wise be come to me,
And thus hath put thee in my grace,
I here forgive thee in this place.
Sit down," she said, "and tell me here
Wherefore dost shew such gracious
    cheer?"
"Madam," he quoth, "with but one
    look,
My heart erstwhile thou captive took,
Since first thou camest to my sight
Have I thee loved, with all my might;
Other than thee, my lady fair,   601
Hath in my love nor part, nor share,
And for thy love prepared am I
Faithful to live, or faithful die."
She quoth: "Now durst thou undertake,
In this, my land, true peace to make,
And steadfast to uphold my rights
Against King Arthur, and his knights?"
He quoth: "Yea, surely, as I thrive,
'Gainst him, or any man alive!"   610
Such counsel had she ta'en ere this,
She quoth: "Now are we friends, I wis."
Her lords to counsel her were fain
To take a lord to her again.

Swiftly she went unto the hall,
Assembled were her barons all,
There did they hold their parliament
That she should wed, by their assent.
She quoth: "Sirs, ye with one accord,
Have said, I needs must have a lord   620
My lands to govern and defend —
Say now, whereto your rede doth tend?"

"Madam," they quoth: "your will now
    do,
And we will all assent thereto."
Straightway the lady went again
Unto her bower, to Sir Ywain,
She quoth: "By God, this vow I make,
None other lord than thee to take,
If I thee left, that were not right,   629
King's son art thou, and noble knight."

Now has the maid done as she thought
Sir Ywain out of anger brought,
The lady led him to the hall,
Before him rose the barons all,
And all men said, with certainty,
"This knight shall wed with our Lady."
And soothly said, themselves between,
So fair a man they ne'er had seen —
"So fair is he in hall and bower
He seemeth well an emperour,   640
We would that these twain were troth-
    plight
And wedded, aye, this very night."
She sat her down, that lady fair,
And bade them all keep silence there,
And bade her steward somewhat say
Ere that from court men went away.
The steward said: "Sirs, understand,
That war doth threaten this, our land,
King Arthur, he be ready dight
To come within this fourteen-night,   650
He thinketh, with his knights, the king,
This land within his power to bring;
They know full well that he be dead
Who once was ruler in this stead,
None have we here weapons to wield,
No man our land boldly to shield,
Women may ne'er maintain their power,
They need a lord, and governour.
Therefore our lady needs must wed,
E'en hastily, for very dread,   660
But to no lord her will is bent
Save that it be with your consent."
The lords, a-row, to counsel fell,
They deemed that he had spoken well,
And with one voice assent they make
That at her will a lord she take.

Therewith the lady spake forthright:
"What think ye now of this same
    knight?
He proffers here, in every wise
To serve me, as I may devise,   670
And certes, sirs, the sooth to say,
I saw him never ere to-day.
But, so I trow the tidings run,
Unto King Urien is he son;
He cometh of high parentage,
Most doughty he, in vassalage,
Wary, and wise, and courteous he,
And fain his wife he 'ld have me be.
Nevertheless, I trow, he might   679
Have chosen better, 't were his right!"
Then with one voice the barons said:
"Madam, we hold us well repaid,
But hasten ye, if so ye may,
That ye be wed this very day."

And prayer from every side they make
That she be pleased the knight to take.

Then soon unto the kirk they went,
And wedded were, with full consent;
Full solemnly was wedded there
Ywain, to Alundyne, the fair, —   690
Duke's daughter of Landuit, she —
Else should her country wasted be.
The marriage did they celebrate
Among their barons, all in state,
And mickle mirth they made that day,
And feasting fair, with rich array —
Rejoicing great they made that stead,
And all forgotten is the dead.
Of him, sometime their lord so free, 699
They say, this knight is worth the three.
And that they love him mickle more
Than him, who was their lord before.

SYR PERCYVELLE OF GALLES

DEAR Lords, listen now to me,
Hearken words but two or three
Of a hero fair and free,
    Who was fierce in fight;
His right name was Percyvelle,
He was fostered on the fell,
Drank the water of the well
    Yet was valiant wight.
Of a nobleman the son,
Who, since that he first begun,   10
Goodly praise and worship won
    When he was made knight.
In the good King Arthur's hall
He was best beloved of all,
Percyvelle they did him call
    Whoso reads aright.

Who the tale aright can read
Knows him one of doughty deed,
A stiff knight upon a steed,
    Wielding weapons bold;   20
Therefore did the King Arthour
Do unto him great honour,

Gave his sister Acheflour
    For to have and hold
As his wife, to his life's end;
And with her broad lands to spend,
For right well the knight he kenned
    Gave her to his hold.
And of goodly gifts full share
Gave he with his sister there,   30
(As it pleased the twain full fair,)
    With her, robes in fold.

There he gave him robes in fold,
And broad lands of wood and wold
With a store of goods untold
    That the maid he take;
To the kirk the knight did ride
There to wed that gentle bride
For rich gifts and lands so wide
    And for her own sake;   40
Sithen, without more debate,
Was the bridal held in state
For her sake who, as her mate,
    This good knight would take;

Afterward, withouten let,
A great jousting there was set,
And of all the knights he met
  None would he forsake.

None would he forsake that stead,
Not the Black Knight, nor the Red, 50
None who there against him sped
  With or shaft or shield;
There he did as noble knight,
Who well holdeth what he hight,
And full well he proved his might,
  All to him must yield;
There full sixty shafts I say
Brake Syr Percyvelle that day, —
On the wall his bride, she lay,
  Watched him weapons wield. 60
Tho' the Red Knight, he had sworn,
From his saddle is he borne,
And, well nigh of life forlorn,
  Lieth on the field.

As he lay there on the wold
Many a man must him behold
Who, thro' shield and armour's hold,
  'Stonied was that tide;
All men marvelled who were there,
Whether great or small they were, 70
That thus Percyvelle should dare
  Doleful dints abide;
There was no man, great or small,
No, not one amongst them all,
Who on grass dare risk a fall
  And would 'gainst him ride;
There Syr Percyvelle that day
Bare the tourney's prize away,
Homeward did he take his way,
  Blithe was she, his bride! 80

But tho' blithe the bride, and gay
That her lord had won the day
Yet the Red Knight sick he lay
  Wounded by his hand;
Therefore goodly gifts he plight
That, an he recover might,
And again by day or night,
  In the field might stand,

That he'ld quit him of the blow
Which he from his hand must know, 90
Nor his travail fruitless go,
  Nor be told in land
That Syr Percyvelle, in field,
Thus had shamed him under shield —
Payment full for that he'ld yield
  If in life he stand!

Now in life they be, the two,
But the Red Knight naught may do
To bring scathe upon his foe
  Till the harm befell; 100
As it chanced, there fell no strife
Till that Percyvelle, in life,
Had a son by his young wife,
  After him to dwell;
And whenas that child was born
He bade call him on the morn
By the name his sire had worn,
  Even Percyvelle;
Then the knight was fain to make
Feast for this, his young son's sake, 110
Thus without delay they spake
  And of jousting tell.

Now of jousting do they tell,
And they say, Syr Percyvelle,
In the field he thinks to dwell
  As he aye has done;
There a jousting great they set
E'en of all the knights they met
For he would his son should get
  That same fame anon; 120
When thereof the Red Knight heard
Blithe was he of that same word,
Armed him swift with shield and sword,
  Thither hath he gone;
'Gainst Syr Percyvelle would ride
With broad shield and shaft that tide,
There his vow he would abide,
  Mastery maketh moan!

Mastery, it hath made moan —
Percyvelle right well hath done 130
For the love of his young son,
  On the opening day,

Ere the Red Knight thither won
Percyvelle smote many a one,
Duke, earl, knight, and eke baron
  Vanquished in the play;
Honour had he won for dower, —
Came the Red Knight in that hour
But, "Woe worth false armour"
  Percyvelle may say!   140
There Syr Percyvelle was slain —
That the Red Knight was full fain
In his heart, I will maintain,
  When he went his way!

When he went upon his way,
Then no man durst aught to say
Were it earnest, were it play,
  For to bid him bide;
Since that he had slain right there
The best champion that was e'er,   150
With full many a wound so sare,
  'Stonied all that tide;
Then no better rede had they
Than the knight to lowly lay,
As men must the dead alway,
  And in earth must hide:
She who was but now his wife
Sorely might she rue her life,
Such a lord to lose in strife,
  She ailed not for pride.   160

Now is Percyvelle, the knight,
Slain in battle and in fight,
And her word that lady plight,
  Keep it if she may,
That ne'er, so her vow doth run,
She will dwell with her young son
Where such deeds of arms were
        done,
  Nor by night, nor day.
In the woodland shall he be,
Where, forsooth, he naught shall see 170
But the green and leafy tree,
  And the groves so gray;
Never shall his mind be bent
Nor on joust nor tournament,
But in the wild wood content,
  He with beasts shall play!

There with wild beasts should he play —
Thus her leave she took straightway,
Both of king and lord that day,
  Gat her to the wood;   180
Left behind her bower and hall,
But one maid she took withal,
Who should answer to her call,
  When in need she stood;
Other goods would she have naught,
But a flock of goats she brought,
For their milk might serve, she thought,
  For their livelihood;
And of all her lord's fair gear
Naught she beareth with her here   190
Save a little Scottish spear,
  Serve her son it should.

And when her young son should go
In the woodland to and fro',
That same spear, I'ld have ye know,
  She gave him one day;
"Mother sweet," then straight quoth
        he,
"Say, what may this strange thing be,
Which ye now have given me,
  What its name, I pray?"   200
Then she spake, that fair ladie,
"Son," she quoth, "now hearken me,
This a doughty dart shall be
  Found in woodland way."
Then the child was pleased at heart
That she gave to him this dart,
Therewith he made many smart
  In the woodland gay.

Thus amid the woodland glade
Dart in hand, the lad, he strayed,   210
Underneath the wild wood's shade,
  Throve there mightily,
And with this, his spear, would slay
Of wild beasts and other prey
All that he might bear away,
  Goodly lad was he;
Small birds too, he shot them there,
Many a hart and hind so fair
Homeward to his mother bare,
  Never lack had she.   220

So well did he learn to shoot,
There was no beast went afoot,
But in flight might find small boot,
    Run them down would he!

All the prey he marked, it fell —
Thus he grew and throve right well,
Was a strong lad, sooth to tell,
    Tho' his years were few;
Fifteen winters, yea, and more,
Dwelt he in those holts so hoar,   230
Naught of nurture nor of lore
    From his mother knew;
Till it fell upon a day,
That to him she thus did say:
"Sweet son, now I rede thee pray
    To God's Son so true,
By His aid to prosper thee,
So that, by His Majesty,
Thou a good man well may'st be
    And long life thy due!"   240

"Mother sweet," then answered he,
"Say, what kind of god is He
Whom thou now hast bidden me
    In this wise to pray?"
"Son, 't is the great God of Heaven,"
So she spake, "within days seven
Hath He made both Earth and Heaven,
    Ere closed the sixth day."
"By great God," his answer ran,
"An I may but meet that man,   250
Then, with all the craft I can,
    I to Him will pray!"
Thus then, did he live and wait,
E'en within his mother's gate,
For the great God lay in wait,
    Find Him if he may!

Then, as thro' holts hoar he fled,
So the chance befell that stead,
That three knights toward him sped,
    Of King Arthur's inn;   260
One, King Urien's son, Ywain,
And with him was good Gawain,
And Sir Kay rode with the twain,
    All were of his kin;

Thus in raiment rich they ride,
But the lad had naught that tide
Wherewith he his bones might hide,
    Saving a goat's skin;
Burly was he, broad to see,
On each side a skin had he,   270
Of the same his hood should be
    Even to his chin.

The hood came but to his chin,
And the flesh was turned within,
The lad's wit, it was full thin
    When he should say aught;
And the knights were all in green,
Such as he had never seen,
Well he deemed that they had been
    The great God he sought;   280
And he spake: "Which of ye three
Shall in sooth the great God be,
Who, my mother told to me,
    Hath this wide world wrought?"
Straight made answer Sir Gawain,
Fair and courteous spake again:
"Son, so Christ to me be fain,
    Such shall we be naught."

Then he quoth, the foolish child,
Who had come from woodland wild,   290
To Gawain the meek and mild,
    Soft of speech and fair:
"I shall slay ye now all three
Save ye straightway tell to me
What things ye shall surely be,
    Since no Gods ye were?"
Swift he answered him, Sir Kay,
"Yea, and then who should we say
Were our slayer here to-day
    In this woodland bare?"   300
At Kay's words he waxed full wroth,
Save a great buck 'twixt them both
Stood, I trow me, little loth,
    Had he slain him there.

But Gawain, he quoth to Kay:
"Thy proud words shall us betray,
I would win this child with play,
    Would'st thou hold thee still."

"Sweet son," in this wise spake
  he,
"Knights, I trow we be, all three,   310
With King Arthur dwelling free
  Who waits on the hill."
Quoth then Percyvelle, so light,
He who was in goatskin dight:
"Will King Arthur make me knight,
  An I seek him still?"
Then Sir Gawain answered there:
"That to say, I do not dare,
To the king I rede thee fare,
  Ask of him his will."   320

Thus to know King Arthur's will,
Where he tarried stayed they still,
And the child he hastened, till
  To his home he came.
As he sped him thro' the wood,
There he saw a full fair stud
Both of colts and mares so good,
  But not one was tame;
And he said: "Now, by Saint John,
Such beasts as I now see yon,   330
Such the knights did ride upon,
  Knew I but their name!
But as I may thrive, or thee,
E'en the biggest that I see
It shall shortly carry me
  Home unto my dame!"

"When I come unto my dame
An I find her, at this same,
She will tell to me the name
  Of this stranger thing."   340
Then, I trow, the biggest mare
Swiftly did he run down there,
Quoth: "I trow thou shalt me bear
  With morn, to the King."
Saddle-gear the lad did lack,
Sprang upon the horse's back,
She bare him the homeward track,
  Failed him for no thing.
Then his mother, woe-begone,
Wist not what to do anon,   350
When she saw her youthful son
  A steed with him bring.

Horse she saw him homeward bring;
And she wist well by that thing
What is in-born out will spring
  Spite of wiles she sought.
Swift she spake, the fair ladie:
"That this dole I needs must dree,
For the love of thy body
  That I dear have bought!"   360
"Dear son," so she spake him fair,
"Much unrest for thee I bear,
What wilt do with this same mare
  That thou home hast brought?"
But the boy was blithe and gay
When he heard his mother say
This, the brood-mare's name alway,
  Of naught else he thought.

Now he calleth her a mare,
E'en as did his mother ere,   370
Such he deemed all horses were,
  And were named, i' fay;
"Mother, on yon hill I've been,
There three knights I now have seen,
And with them have spoke, I ween,
  These words did I say:
I have promised them all three,
That I with their king will be,
Such an one shall he make me
  As they be to-day."   380
Thus he sware by God's great Might:
"I shall keep the words I plight,
Save the king shall make me knight
  Him with morn I'll slay."

Spake the mother full of woe,
For her son she grievéd so
That she thought she death should
  know,
  Knelt down on her knee:
"Son, hast ta'en to thee this rede,
Thou wilt turn to knightly deed,   390
Now where'er strange fate may lead,
  This I counsel thee;
Morn is furthermost Yule-day,
And thou say'st thou wilt away
To make thee knight, if so thou may,
  So hast told to me;

Dost of nurture little know,
Now in all things measure show
If in hall or bower thou go,
　And of hand be free." 400

Then she quoth, the lady bright:
"Where thou meetest with a knight
Doff thy hood to him forthright,
　Greet him courteously; "
"Mother sweet," he answered then,
"Saw I never any men,
If a knight I now should ken
　Tell the sign whereby?"
Then she showed him miniver,
For such robes she had by her, 410
"Son, where thou shalt see such fur
　On their hoods to lie."
"By Great God," then answered he,
"Where that I a knight may see
Mother, as thou biddest me,
　Even so do I."

All that night till it was day
He beside his mother lay,
With the morn he would away,
　May what will betide; 420
Bridle had he never none,
In its stead, he naught hath won,
But a withy took anon
　This, his steed, to guide;
Then his mother took a ring,
Bade the same again to bring:
"This shall be our tokening
　Here I'll thee abide."
Ring and spear he taketh there,
Springeth up astride the mare, 430
From the mother who him bare
　Forth the lad doth ride.

Fytte II

On his way, as he did ride,
Stood a hall, his way beside,
"Now for aught that may betide
　Here within will I."
Without let within he strode,
Found a broad board set with food,
A well plenished fire of wood

Burning bright thereby. 440
And a manger too, he found,
Therein corn, it lay, unground,
To the same his mare he bound
　E'en with his withy.
Said: "My mother counselled me
That I should of measure be,
Half of all that here I see
　I shall let it lie."

Thus the corn, he parts it fair,
One half gives unto his mare, 450
To the board betakes him there
　Well assured that tide;
Found a loaf of bread so fine,
And a pitcher, full of wine,
And a mess, whereon to dine,
　With a knife beside.
All the meat he findeth there
With his hands, in even share
He doth part — "One half the fare
　Shall for other bide." 460
And the one half eateth he,
Could he more of measure be?
He of hand would fain be free,
　Tho' he had no pride!

Tho' the lad he had no pride,
Further did he go that tide
To a chamber there beside
　Wonders more to see;
Clothing rich he there found spread,
Slept a lady there, on bed, — 470
Quoth: "A token that we wed
　Shalt thou leave with me."
Then he kissed her, that sweet thing,
From her finger took a ring,
His own mother's tokening
　Left her there in fee.
Then he went forth to his mare,
The short spear he with him bare,
Leapt aloft as he was ere,
　On his way rides he. 480

Now upon his way rides he,
Marvels more full fain to see,
And a knight he needs must be

With no more delay.
He came where the king should be,
Served of the first mess was he,
And to him, right hastily,
   Doth he make his way;
Hindrance brooked not, nor debate,
E'en at wicket, door, or gate,   490
Gat in swift, nor thought to wait,
   Masterful, that day;
E'en at his first entering,
This, his mare, no lie I sing,
Kissed the forehead of the king,
   Came so close alway.

Startled was the king, I trow,
And his hands, he raised them now,
Turned aside from off his brow
   Muzzle of the mare;   500
And he quoth: "Fair child, and free,
Stand thou still, aside of me,
Say from whence thou now shalt be,
   And thy will declare?"
Quoth the fool to Arthur mild:
"I be mine own mother's child
Come from out the woodland wild
   Unto Arthur fair;
Yesterday I saw knights three,
Such an one make thou of me   510
Here, on this my mare by thee,
   Ere thy meat thou share."

Out then spake Sir Gawain free,
Carver to the king was he,
Saith: "Forsooth, no lie this be,
   I was one, i' fay.
Child, now take thou my blessing
For thy fearless following,
Here in sooth hast found the king
   Who makes knights alway."   520
Then quoth Percyvelle the free:
"Now, if this King Arthur be,
Look a knight he make of me
   Even as I say:"
Tho' he were uncouthly dight,
He sware: "By God's mickle Might,
Save the king shall make me knight,
   Here I shall him slay."

All who heard him, young and old,
Marvelling, the king behold   530
That he suffer words so bold
   From so foul a wight;
Stayed his horse the king beside —
Arthur looked on him that tide,
Then for sorrow sore he sighed
   As he saw that sight;
Tears fell from his eyes apace,
Following each the other's trace,
Quoth the king: "Alas, this place
   Knew me, day, or night —   540
That without him I should be
Living, who was like to thee,
Who so seemly art to see
   An thou wert well dight!"

Quoth the king: "Wert better dight,
Thou wert like unto a knight,
Whom I loved with all my might
   Whiles he was in life;
And so well he wrought my will,
In all ways of knightly skill,   550
That my sister, of goodwill,
   Gave I him for wife.
For him must I make my moan,
He, now fifteen years agone,
By a thief to death was done
   For a little strife;
Sithen am I that man's foe,
For to wreak upon him woe,
Death thro' me he may not know
   He in crafts is rife!"   560

Quoth: "His crafts they be so rife
There is no man now in life
Who, with sword, or spear, or knife,
   'Gainst him may avail,
Save but Percyvelle's young son;
An he knew what he had done,
The book saith, he might anon
   'Venge his father's bale," —
The lad deemed too long he stayed
Ere that he a knight was made,   570
That he e'er a father had,
   Knowledge did him fail;
Thus his meaning less should be

When unto the king said he:
"Sir, now let thy chattering be,
   I heed not such tale."

Quoth: "I think not here to stand,
Nor thy chatter understand,
Make me knight with this, thy hand,
   If it may be done." 580
Courteously, the king, he hight
That he now would dub him knight
If that he adown would light
   Eat with him at noon;
Saw the king his face so free,
Evermore he trowed that he,
This child, of a sooth should be
   Percyvelle's own son;
And it ran in the king's mood,
Acheflour, his sister good, 590
How she gat her to the wood
   With her boy alone.

This boy, he came from the wood,
Evil knew he not, nor good,
And the king, he understood,
   He was a wild wight;
So he spake him fair withal —
Then he lighted down in hall,
Bound his mare among them all,
   To the board was dight; 600
But, ere that he might begin,
Or unto the meat might win,
'Mid them all, the hall within,
   Came he, the Red Knight;
Pricking on a blood-red steed,
Blood-red too, was all his weed,
Fain to mock them all at need
   With crafts, as he might.

With his crafts began to call,
Loudly hailed them recreants all, — 610
King and knights within that wall
   At the board they bide;
Roughly took the cup in hand
That before the king did stand,
None withstood him, all that band
   Deemed him mad that tide;
Portion full of wine it bare,

The Red Knight, he drank it there,
And the cup was very fair
   All of red gold tried. 620
In his hand, as there it stood,
Took he up that cup so good,
Left them sitting at their food,
   And from thence did ride.

As from them he rode away,
He who made this tale doth say
The grief that on Arthur lay
   Never tongue might tell;
"Ah, dear God!" the king, he said,
"Thou Who all this wide world made,
Shall this man be ever stayed, 631
   Yon fiend forced to dwell?
Five years has he, in this way,
Borne my cup from me away,
And my good knight did he slay,
   E'en Syr Percyvelle.
Sithen, has he taken three,
And from hence he rideth free
Ere that I may harness me
   Him in field to fell!" 640

"Peter!" Percyvelle doth cry,
"Strike that knight adown will I,
And thy cup bring presently,
   Wilt thou make me knight."
"As I be true king," said he,
"I will make a knight of thee
If again thou bringest me
   This, my cup so bright."
Up he rose, I trow, the king,
To his chamber hastening, 650
Thence good armour would he bring
   That the lad be dight;
Ere the armour down was cast,
Percyvelle from hall had passed,
On his track he followed fast
   Whom he thought to fight.

With his foe he goes to fight,
He none other wise was dight
But in goatskins three, to sight,
   As a fool he were; 660
Cried: "Man, on thy mare now hear,

Bring again now the king's gear,
Or I'll smite thee with my spear,
  And make thee less fair!"
After the Red Knight would ride
Boldly, would for naught abide,
Quoth: "A knight I'll be this tide,
  Of thine armour heir!"
And he sware by Christ's sore Pain:
"Save thou bring this cup again   670
With my dart thou shalt be slain,
  Cast down from thy mare!"
When the knight beheld him so,
Fool he deemed who was his foe
Since that he had called it so,
  This his steed, a mare.

Thus to see him well with sight
He his vizor raised forthright,
To behold how he was dight
  Whose words sense did lack;   680
Quoth: "An I reach thee, thou fool,
I will cast thee in the pool,
E'en for all the Feast of Yule,
  As thou wert a sack!"
Then quoth Percyvelle the free:
"Fool or no, whate'er I be,
This I trow, we soon shall see
  Whose brows shall be black!"
There his skill the lad would try,
At the knight a dart let fly,   690
Smote him full there in the eye,
  Came out at the back!

For the blow that he must bear,
From the saddle shaken there,
Who the sooth will hearken fair,
  The Red Knight was slain!
On the hill he fell down dead,
While his steed, at will it fled,
Percyvelle quoth in that stead:
  "Art a lazy swain!"   700
Quoth the child in that same tide:
"Would'st thou here my coming bide,
I to catch thy mare will ride,
  Bring her thee again;
Then I trow we twain with might,
Will as men together fight,

Each of us as he were knight
  Till the one be slain."

Now the Red Knight lieth slain,
Left for dead upon the plain,   710
And the boy doth ride amain,
  After his good steed;
But 't was swifter than the mare,
For naught else it had to bear
But the harness, fast and fair
  Fled, from rider freed;
Big with foal the mare that tide,
Of stout make was she beside,
Little power to run when tried,
  Nor pursue with speed;   720
The lad saw how it should be,
Swift adown to foot sprang he,
And the right way hastily
  Ran, as he had need.

Thus, fleet-foot, the lad he fled,
On his way he surely sped,
Caught, strong - hand, the steed that
    stead,
  Brought it to the knight;
"Now a fell foe shalt thou be,
Wilt not steal away from me,   730
Now I pray thou dealest free
  Blows, as fits a knight!
See, thy mare I bring thee here,
Mickle of thy other gear,
Mount, as when thou first anear
  Came, an thou wilt fight!"
Speechless still the knight he lay,
He was dead, what could he say?
The child knew no better way
  Than adown to light.   740

Percyvelle adown is light,
Of his arms would spoil the knight,
But he might not find aright,
  How was laced the weed;
Armed was he from head to heel
In iron harness, and in steel;
The lad knew not how to deal,
  Aid himself in need;
Quoth: "My mother counselled me

When my dart should broken be, 750
From the iron burn the tree,
　Fire is now my need."
Thus he seeks a flint straightway,
His fire-iron he takes that day,
And with never more delay
　He a spark hath freed.

Kindles there a flame, I trow,
Mid the bushes seeking now,
Swift he gathers branch and bough,
　That a fire would make; 760
There a great blaze doth he light,
Thinks therein to burn the knight,
Since he knew no better sleight
　This, his gear, to take.
Now Sir Gawain, he was dight,
Followed fast to see the fight
'Twixt the lad, and the Red Knight,
　All for the boy's sake;
Found the Red Knight where he fell,
Slain was he by Percyvelle, 770
And a fire, that burnt right well,
　Birch and oak did make!

Of these twain the fire alway,
Great the brands and black, that day;
"With this fire what wilt thou, say?"
　Quoth he, soft and still.
"Peter!" quoth the boy also,
"An I thus the knight might know,
From his iron I'll burn him so,
　Right here, on the hill." 780
Answered him the good Gawain:
"Since the Red Knight thou hast
　　slain,
To disarm him am I fain,
　Wilt thou hold thee still."
Then Sir Gawain down did light,
Took his harness from the knight,
On the child the same did dight,
　E'en at his own will.

In his armour doth he stand,
Takes the knight's neck in his hand, 790
Casts him on the burning brand
　There to feed the flame;

Then quoth Percyvelle in boast:
"Lie thou still therein and roast,
I keep nothing of thy cost,
　Naught that from thee came."
Burns the knight, and none doth heed,
Clad the boy is in his weed,
And hath leapt upon his steed,
　Well-pleased, at that same; 800
He looked downward at his feet,
Saw his gear so fair and meet,
"Men may me as knight entreat,
　Call me by that name!"

Quoth Gawain the boy unto:
"From this hill I rede we go,
Hast done what thou willed to do,
　Near it draws to night."
Quoth the lad: "Dost trow this thing,
That unto thy lord and king, 810
I myself again will bring
　This, his gold so bright?
Nay, so I may thrive, or thee,
I'm as great a lord as he,
Ne'er to-day he maketh me,
　Any way a knight!
Take thou now the cup so fair,
And thyself the present bear,
Forth in land I'll further fare
　Ere from steed I light." 820

Neither would the lad alight,
Nor would wend with that good
　　knight,
Forth he rideth all the night,
　So proud was he then;
Till at morn, on the fourth day,
With a witch met, so men say,
And his horse and fair array,
　She right well might ken;
And she deemed that it had been 829
The Red Knight, whom she had seen
In those arms afore, I ween,
　Such steed spurred he then;
Swiftly she to him would hie,
Quoth: "In sooth I tell no lie,
Men said, thou didst surely die,
　Slain by Arthur's men!

"Of my men one but now came
From yon hill, and at that same,
Where thou see'st the fierce fire flame,
   Said that thou wast there!"   840
Percyvelle he sat stone still,
Answer made he none, until
She had spoken all her will,
   Never word spake there:
"I on yonder hill have been,
Nothing else I there have seen,
But goat-skins, naught else, I ween,
   Than such worthless fare."
"My son, tho' thou there wast slain,
And thine armour from thee ta'en,   850
I could make thee whole again,
   Hale, as thou wert e'er."

Then by that wist Percyvelle
It had servéd him right well
That wild fire he made on fell,
   When the knight was slain;
And he deemed 't were well that she
In that self-same place should be;
That old witch on spear bare he
   To the fire again;   860
There in mickle wrath and ire
Cast the witch into the fire:
"With the son thou didst desire
   Lie ye still, ye twain."
Thus the lad, he left them there,
And upon his way did fare,
Such-like deeds to do and dare,
   Was the child full fain.

Came he by a forest side,
There ten men, he saw them ride,   870
Quoth: "For aught that may betide
   With them would I be."
When the ten they saw him, they
Deemed him the Red Knight alway,
Who would seek them all to slay,
   Fast they turned to flee;
Since he so was clad that stead,
For their life from him they fled,
Aye the faster that they sped
   Faster followed he.   880
Till he knew one for a knight,

Of the miniver had sight,
Put his vizor up forthright:
   "Sir, God look on thee!"

Quoth the child: "God look on thee!"
Quoth the knight: "Well may'st thou
   be,
Ah! Lord God, now well is me
   That I live this day!"
By his face right well he thought
The Red Knight it should be naught,
Who as foeman had them sought,   891
   Boldly there did stay;
For it seemed him by the sight
That the lad had slain the knight
In whose armour he was dight,
   Rode his steed alway;
Soon the knight, he spoke again,
And to thank the child was fain;
"Thou the fiercest foe hast slain
   Who beset me aye!"   900

Quoth then Percyvelle the free,
Saith: "Now wherefore did ye flee
All of ye when ye saw me
   Riding here anigh?"
Then he spake, that agéd knight,
Who was past his day of might,
Nor with any man might fight,
   Answered, loud and high,
Saying: "These nine children here
They be all my sons so dear   910
Since to lose them I must fear
   For that cause fled I,
For we deemed that it had been
The Red Knight we now had seen,
He had slain us all, I ween,
   With great cruelty.

"Without mercy he were fain
One and all of us were slain,
To my sons he'd envy ta'en
   Most of any men: 920
Fifteen years agone, 't is true,
That same thief my brother slew
And hath set himself anew
   For to slay us then;

Fearing lest my sons should know
When they should to manhood grow,
And should slay him as their foe
 Where they might him ken.
Had I been in that same stead
When he smote my brother dead,   930
I had never eaten bread,
 Till I'd burned him then!"

"Burned," quoth Percyvelle, "he is,
I sped better than I wist," —
As the last word he must list
 Blither waxed the knight;
By his hall their road it fell,
Strait he prayed that Percyvelle
There awhile with them should dwell,
 And abide that night.   940
Well it should his guest befall —
So he brought him to the ball,
Spake him fair, that he withal
 From his steed should light;
Then, the steed in stable set,
To the hall the lad doth get,
And, with never further let,
 They for meat are dight.

Meat and drink for them were dight,
Men were there to serve aright,   950
And the lad found with the knight,
 Enow, to his hand.
As at meat they sat, and ate,
Came the porter from the gate,
Said, a man without did wait,
 From the Maiden-Land;
Saith: "Sir, he doth pray of thee
Meat and drink for charitie,
For a messenger is be,
 Nor for long may stand."   960
The knight bade him come within,
For he said: "It is no sin
That the man who meat may win
 Fill the traveller's hand."

Came the traveller at that stead,
By the porter thither led,
Hailed the knight who sat at bread
 On the daïs on high.

And the knight, he asked him there
Courteously, whose man he were?   970
And how far he thought to fare?
 "Tell me without lie."
"From the Lady Lufamour
Am I sent to King Arthour,
That he lend, for his honour
 To her grief an eye;
There hath come a Soudan bold,
Ta'en her lands, slain young and
 old,
And besieged her in her hold,
 Plagues her ceaselessly!   980

"Saith, at peace he'll leave her ne'er —
Since the maid is wondrous fair,
And hath mickle wealth for share,
 He doth work her woe.
Thus in grief she leads her life,
All her men he fells in strife,
Vows he'll have her for his wife,
 And she will not so;
By that Soudan's hand, I ween,
Slain have sire and uncle been,   990
Slain hath she her brothers seen,
 He is her worst foe!
He so closely her hath sought
To one castle is she brought,
From those walls he yieldeth naught,
 Ere he come her to.

"Saith, he will her favours know —
Liever she to death would go
Than that he, her bitterest foe,
 Wed her as his wife!   1000
But he is so valiant wight,
All his foes he slays forthright,
And no man may with him fight,
 Tho' his fame were rife!"
Then quoth Percyvelle: "I pray
Thou wilt show to me the way,
Thither, as the road it lay,
 Without any strife!
Might I with that Soudan meet,
Who a maid doth so entreat,   1010
He full soon his death should meet,
 I remain in life!"

But the messenger, he sware,
He should bide there where he were:
"To King Arthur will I fare,
  There mine errand say.
Mickle sorrow me betide
If I longer here abide,
But from hence I now will ride
  Swiftly as I may."   1020
When the lad in this wise spake,
Prayer to him the knight doth make,
His nine sons with him to take,
  But he saith him "Nay."
Yet so fair his speech shall be
That he taketh of them three,
In his fellowship to be,
  Blither then were they.

Of their errand blithe they were,
Busked them, on their way to fare,   1030
Mickle mirth then made they there,
  Little their amend!
He had ridden but a while,
Scarce the mountenance of a mile,
He bethought him of a guile
  They the worse did wend!
They with him to fare were fain —
Otherwise thought their chieftain,
Sendeth ever one again
  Back, at each mile's end,   1040
Till they one and all were gone —
Then he rideth on alone
Spurring over stock and stone
  Where no man him kenned.

Known of no man would he be;
Ever further rideth he
'Midst a strange folk, verilie,
  Valiant deeds to do;
Now, I trow, hath Percyvelle
With two uncles spoken well,   1050
Nor might one the other tell,
  Or his true name know;
Now upon the way he's set
That shall lead him, without let,
Till the Soudan he has met,
  Blacked his brows with blow.
Percyvelle no more I'll sing,

On his way God shall him bring —
Unto Arthur now, the king,
  Thither will we go.   1060

On our way we'll go anon —
To Caërbedd the king has gone,
Mourning doth he make and moan,
  He doth sigh full sore;
Woe its will on him doth wreak,
And his heart is waxen weak
For he deems that he shall speak
  With Percyvelle no more.
As abed he lieth there
Came the messenger, who bare   1070
Letters from the lady fair,
  Stood the king before;
Arthur might not stand that day,
Read the script as there he lay:
"This thy message," doth he say,
  "Answered is before."

Quoth: "Thine answer dost thou see,
He who sick and sore may be
Scarce may fare afar, that he
  In the field may fight!"   1080
Cried the messenger withal,
Quoth: "Woe worth this wicked hall,
Why did I not turn at call,
  Go back with that knight?"
"What knight was that?" quoth the
      king;
"Whom thou meanest in this thing,
In my land is no lording
  Worthy name of knight!"
Quoth the messenger straightway:
"This his name he would not say,   1090
Fain were I to know alway
  What the lad, he hight.

"This much had I from that knight,
He 'His mother's son' was hight,
In what manner he was dight
  Now I shall ye tell;
Worthy wight was he to see,
Burly, bold of body he,
Blood-stained arms should, verilie,
  Tale of battle tell;   1100

He bestrode a blood-red steed,
Aketoun, and other weed,
All of that same hue indeed,
   They became him well!"
Then he gave command, the king,
Horse and armour forth to bring:
"May I trow thy chattering,
   That was Percyvelle!"

For the love of Percyvelle
They to horse and armour fell,   1110
There would they no longer dwell,
   Forth to fare were fain:
Fast they ride upon their way,
They were sore afeard that day
Ere they come unto the fray
 · That he should be slain;
Arthur with him taketh three
Knights, the fourth himself shall be,
Now so swiftly rideth he
   Follow may no swain.   1120
Now the king is on his way,
Let him come whene'er he may
I will seek now in my play
   Percyvelle again.

Seek we Percyvelle again, —
He hath passed out on the plain,
Over moorland, and mountain
   Seeketh Maiden-Land;
Till toward the eventide
Warriors bold he saw abide,   1130
With pavilions pitched in pride
   Round a city stand;
Hunting was the Soudan then,
He had left there many men,
Twenty score, an ye would ken,
   Should the gates command;
Ten score, while the day was light,
And eleven, through the night,
All of them were armed aright,
   Weapons in their hand.   1140

There with weapons in their hand
They would fight e'en as they stand,
Sitting, lying, all that band,
   Eleven score of men;

Riding as one rides a race,
Ere he wist, in little space,
Thro' the thickest press, apace,
   Rode he 'mongst them then;
Started up a soldier bold,
Of his bridle layeth hold,   1150
Said that he would fain be told
   Of his errand then;
Said he: "I be come here fain
For to see a proud Soudain,
He, i' faith, shall soon be slain
   If I might him ken!

"If to know that man I may,
Then at morn, when dawns the day,
Fast together shall we play
   With our weapons tried!"   1160
When they heard that he, in fray,
Thought their Soudan for to slay
Each one fell on him that day,
   There to make him bide;
When he saw he thus was stayed,
Him, who hand on bridle laid,
Rode he down, and undismayed,
   There, the gate beside,
Thrust with spear about him there,
And his point through many bare,   1170
There was no man who might dare
   Face the lad that tide.

Who in town the tidings tell
Say, beneath his feet they fell,
That bold body, Percyvelle
   Sped, his foes to still;
Thought, 't was small speed with his
     spear,
Tho' it shore thro' many sheer,
Folk enow he found them here,
   Had of fight his fill;   1180
From the hour of middle night,
Even till the morning light,
Were they ne'er so wild, or wight,
   He wrought at his will;
And he dealt thus with his brand,
There was none might 'gainst him stand,
Half a blow take from his hand
   Struck with such good-will.

Now he striketh them, I ween,
Till the Paynim's heads are seen   1190
Hop as hailstones on the green,
   Round about the grass;
Thus he dealt them many a blow,
Till the dawn began to show
He had laid their lives full low,
   All who there would pass;
When his foes thus slain should be
Very weary then was he,
This I tell ye verilie,
   He but cared the less,   1200
An he living were, or dead,
So he found him in such stead
He might peaceful lay his head,
   Surety find in stress.

There he found no surety
Save what 'neath the wall should be,
There a fair place chooseth he,
   And adown did light;
There he laid him down that tide,
And the steed stood him beside,   1210
For the foal was fain to bide,
   Wearied with the fight.
On the morn, when it was day,
On the wall the watchman lay,
Saw signs of an ugly fray
   On the plain there dight;
Yet more marvel should there be,
Living man was none to see, —
Then they call that fair ladie
   To behold that sight.   1220

Comes the lady to that sight;
Lufamour, that maiden bright,
Mounts the wall, that from the height,
   She may see the field;
Heads and helmets, many a one,
(Trow me, lie I tell ye none,)
There they lay the grass upon,
   With them many a shield;
'T was a marvel great they thought,
Who had such a wonder wrought   1230
In such wise to death had brought
   All that folk on field,
And within the gate came ne'er

For to tell what men they were,
Tho' they knew the maid was there
   Fair reward to yield.

Their reward she fain would pay —
Forth in haste they go their way
If on field they find them aye
   Who had done this deed.   1240
'Neath their hand they looked around,
Saw a mickle steed that stound,
Blood-stained knight who lay on ground
   By a blood-red steed;
Then she quoth, that lady bright:
"Yonder doth there lie a knight,
Who has surely been in fight
   If I right may read;
Either hath that man been slain,
Or to slumber is he fain,   1250
Or he is in battle ta'en,
   Blood-stained is his weed."

Quoth she: "Blood-stained is his weed,
Even so his goodly steed,
Such knight in this land, indeed,
   Did I never see;
What may he be, if he rise?
He is tall as there he lies,
And well made in every wise
   As a man may be."   1260
Then she called her chamberlain,
Who by name hight fair Hatlayne,
The courtesy of good Gawain
   In hall practised he;
Then she bade him go his way —
"If yon knight he live alway,
Bid him come to me straightway,
   Pray him courteously."

Now to pray him as he can
'Neath the wall he swiftly ran,   1270
Warily he waked the man,
   But the steed stood still;
As the tale was told to me
Down he kneeléd on his knee,
Mildly hailed the knight so free,
   Spake him soft and still;
"This my lady, Lufamour,

She awaits thee in her bower,
Prayeth thee, for thine honour
   Come, if so thou will."   1280
When he heard her message there
Up he rose with him to fare,
That man, who a stout heart bare,
   Would her prayer fulfil.

Now her prayer to fulfil
Followed he her servant's will,
Went his way with him, until
   To that maid came he;
Very blithe that maiden bright
When she saw that lad with sight,   1290
For she trowed that he was wight,
   Asked him fair and free —
Of that lad she asks alway,
(Tho' he fain had said her nay,)
If he wist who did them slay
   Who her foes should be?
Quoth he: "None of them I sought,
I had with the Soudan fought,
To a stand they had me brought,
   Slain they were by me."   1300

Quoth he: "There they needs must
     stay!"
Lufamour, that lady gay,
By his words she knew straightway
   That the lad was wight;
And the maid was blithe that stound
That she such an aid had found
'Gainst the Soudan, who was bound
   With them all to fight;
Straight she looked upon him there,
Thought him meet her land to share
If on field he won her fair   1311
   With mastery and might;
Then they stabled there his steed,
And himself to hall they lead,
For delaying was no need,
   They to dine are dight.

Set the lad on daïs fair,
And with richest dainties there,
'T is no lie I now declare,
   Serve him speedily;   1320

Sat him on a chair of gold
By the mildest maid on mold,
And the fairest to behold,
   As at meat sat she;
There she made him semblance good,
As they fell there to their food,
Skilfully she soothed his mood
   At meat, mirthfully;
That for this, her sake, I trow,
He doth undertake, and vow,   1330
He will slay the Soudan now,
   And that speedily.

Quoth he: "Without any let
When I have the Soudan met,
A sad stroke on him I'll set
   That his pride shall spill."
Quoth the lady fair and free:
"Who my foeman's bane shall be
He shall have my land and me,
   Rule us as he will."   1340
There his meal had been but small
When word came unto the hall
Saying, many men withal
   Harnessed were on hill.
Woeful for their fellows slain
They the city nigh had ta'en,
Men within the hold amain
   Tolled the bell with will.

Now they toll the common bell;
Word is come to Percyvelle   1350
He no longer there would dwell,
   Leapt from daïs that day.
Lust for fighting did he know,
Crying: "Kinsmen, now I go
All yon men I'll lay them low
   Ere I cease to slay!"
Then she kissed him without let,
On his head the helm she set,
To the stable did he get
   Where his steed did stay.   1360
There were none with him to fare
For no man from thence he'ld spare,
Forth he rides, and hastes him
     there
   To the thickest fray.

To the press he came apace
Riding as one rides a race,
All the folk before his face
  They of strength had none;
Tho' to take him fain they were
Yet their blows, they harmed him
      ne'er,   1370
'T was as they had smitten there
  On a right hard stone;
Were they weak, or were they wight,
All on whom his brand did smite
Felled their bodies were forthright
  Better fate had none;
And I wot so swift he sped
Ere the sun was high o'er head
He that folk had smitten dead
  Left in life not one.   1380

When they all were slain, then he
Looked around him, fain to see
If anigh him more should be
  Who would with him fight;
As he, hardy, did behold,
Lo, he saw far off on wold,
Four knights under shield so bold
  Thither ride aright;
The first should King Arthur be,
Then Ywain, flower of chivalry,   1390
And Gawain, be made them three,
  Kay, the fourth was hight;
Percyvelle, he spake full fair:
"Now to yonder four I'll fare,
If the Soudan shall be there
  Do, as I am plight."

Now to hold the troth he plight
'Gainst the four he rideth right,
On the wall, the lady bright
  Lay, and did behold,   1400
How these many men he'd slain,
Sithen, turned his steed again
'Gainst four knights doth ride amain
  Further on the wold;
Then I trow she was full woe
When she saw him further go
And to seek four knights as foe
  Shield and shaft uphold;

Mickle men and stern they ride,   1409
And right well she deemed that tide
That with bale they'd make him bide
  Who was her strong hold.

Tho' he was her surest hold
Yet that maid must needs behold
How he rideth forth on wold
  'Gainst the four amain;
Then King Arthur quoth forthright:
"Hither comes a valiant knight
Who, because he seeketh fight,
  Forth to ride is fain;   1420
If to fight he fares anon
And we four should strive 'gainst one,
Little fame we then had won
  If he soon were slain."
Fast the four, they forward ride,
And the lot they cast that tide,
Sought who first the joust should bide,
  That fell to Gawain.

When unto Gawain it fell
Thus to ride 'gainst Percyvelle,   1430
Then the chance it pleased him well,
  From them did he fare;
Ever nearer as he drew,
Ever better then he knew
Of the arms and steed the hue
  That the lad he bare;
"Ah! dear God," quoth Gawain free,
"Now what may this venture be?
An I slay him, or he me,
  Sorry fate it were!   1440
We be sisters' sons, we twain,
Were one by the other slain
He who lives might mourn amain
  That he born was e'er!"

Of his skill no proof he showed
Sir Gawain, as there he rode,
Drew his rein, and there abode
  To himself quoth low:
"Now an unwise man I be
Thus to vex me foolishly;   1450
None shall aye so hardy be
  But his peer may know;

Percyvelle, he slew that knight,
Yet another, e'en as wight,
May in that same gear be dight,
  Taken all him fro'
If my kinsman I should spare
And his gear another ware
Who should overcome me there
  That would work me woe!   1460

"That would work me mickle woe —
Now, as I on earth may go
It shall ne'er befall me so
  If I right may read;
One shaft shall I send, to wit,
And will seek first blow to hit,
Then shall I know, by my wit,
  Who doth wear that weed."
No word more he saith that tide
But together swift they ride,   1470
Men, who joust were bold to bide
  And stiff knights on steed;
Strong and stalwart steeds had they,
And their shields failed not that day,
But their spears brake in that fray,
  As behoved them need.

Spears, that erst were whole, they
    brake, —
With that, Percyvelle, he spake,
In this wise a tale would make
  That on his tongue lay;   1480
Saith: "My way I wide have gone,
Yet, I trow me, such Soudan,
I' faith, saw I never none,
  Ne'er by night or day:
I have slain, if I thee ken,
Twenty score of these, thy men,
Yet of all whom I slew then
  Deemed it but a play,
'Gainst the dint I took from thee,
Ne'er such debt was owed by me,   1490
Two for one, my pay shall be
  If so be I may!"

Then he answered, Sir Gawain,
(Sooth it is, be ye certain
Of that same was he full fain

Where in field they fight;)
For, by these, his words so wild
Of a fool, the knight so mild
Wist full well it was the child
  Percyvelle, the wight —   1500
Quoth: "No Soudan now I be,
But that same man, certainly,
Who thy body aided thee
  First in arms to dight;
Thy stout heart I praise alway
Tho' thy words were rough to-day,
And my name, the sooth to say
  Is Gawain, the knight!"

Quoth he: "Who will read aright   1509
Knows me for Gawain the knight."
Then the twain, they ceased to fight,
  As good friends of old;
Quoth: "Bethink thee, when thy foe
Thou wast fain in fire to throw
To disarm thou didst not know
  This, his body cold"; —
Then was Percyvelle the free
Joyful, as he well might be,
For he wist well it was he
  By this token told;   1520
Then, as Gawain did him pray,
He his vizor raised straightway
With good cheer they kissed that day
  Those two barons bold.

Now they kiss, the barons twain,
Sithen talked, as they were fain,
Then, by them he draweth rein,
  Arthur, king, and knight;
Then, as they afore had done,
Gave he thanks to God anon.   1530
Mickle mirth, I trow, they won,
  That they met aright;
Sithen, without more delay,
To the castle made their way
And with them he rides that day
  Percyvelle the wight;
Ready was the porter there,
Thro' the gate the knights they fare,
Blither heart no lady bare
  Than Lufamour, the bright!   1540

"Succour great thou dost me send,
This my castle to defend
If the Soudan 'gainst me wend
 Who is my worst foe!"
Then they set their steeds in stall
And the king wends to the hall,
His knights follow him withal
 Since 't was fitting so,
Ready was their meal that day,
And thereto they take their way   1550
With the king, the lady gay,
 And the knights also.

Welcome good she gave her guest,
Rich meats proffered of the best,
Dearest drinks at their behest
 Brought for them, I ween,
Ate and drank with mirth on mold,
Sithen talked, and tales they told
Of deeds that were wrought of old
 Both the king and queen;   1560
And the first thing, did she pray
Of King Arthur, he would say
Of child Percyvelle alway
 What his life had been?
Lufamour, she wondered sore,
That he arms so bravely bore,
Yet knew naught of knightly lore
 As she well had seen.

She had seen, with this same child,
Naught but words and works so
  wild,   1570
Marvelled much, that lady mild,
 Of his folly there;
Then hath Arthur shewn, that stead,
How that Percyvelle was bred
From the first, till he was led
 Forth, on field to fare;
How his father, slain was he,
And his mother fain would flee,
Dwell alone 'neath woodland tree,
 None her flight to share;   1580
"There he dwelt for fifteen year,
Had for fellow the wild deer,
Little need ye wonder here
 That so wild he were!"

When he told this tale withal
To that lady fair in hall
Gracious words had he at call
 For them everyone;
Then quoth Percyvelle, the wight:
"If I be not yet a knight   1590
Thou shalt keep thy promise plight
 Thou would'st make me one!"
Then the king he answered so:
"Other deeds thou needs must do,
'Gainst the Soudan shalt thou go,
 Thus thy spurs be won!"
Then quoth Percyvelle the free:
"Soon as I the Soudan see,
Even so, I swear to thee,
 Shall the deed be done!"   1600

"As I sware," so doth he say,
"That I would the Soudan slay,
I will work as best I may
 That word to maintain."
That day did they no more deed,
Those knights, worthy under weed,
Busked them there, to bed to speed
 Great and small were fain;
Till ere morn hath waxen high
Comes the Soudan with a cry   1610
All his folk, he found them lie,
 They'd been put to pain;
Soon he asked who was the knight
Who had slain his men with might
And in life had left the fight,
 Mastery to gain?

Now to win the mastery
To the castle doth he cry
If one were with heart so high
 Fain with him to fight?   1620
Man for man to challenge fain:
"Tho' he all his folk hath slain,
He shall find Gollrotherame
 Meet him as is right;
But this forward I demand,
That thereto ye set your hand,
He who shall the better stand,
 Prove the most of might,
That he slay his foe this tide,

He the land, both broad and wide,   1630
Holds, and taketh for his bride
  Lufamour, the bright!"

And that same, the King Arthour,
And the lady Lufamour,
All who were within that tower
  Granted readily;
They called Percyvelle the wight,
And the king there dubbed him knight
Tho' he little knew in sight
  Stout of heart was he;   1640
Bade him that he be to praise,
Gentle, and of courteous ways,
And Syr Percyvelle the Gallays,
  Should his title be.
Thus the king, in Maiden-land,
Dubbed him knight with his own
    hand,
Bade him firm 'gainst foe to stand,
  Plague him ceaselessly.

Little peace he took that same,
'Gainst the Soudan swift he came,   1650
Who hight Gollerotherame,
  And was fell in fight;
In the field so broad and wide
No more carping made that tide
But together soon they ride
  With their shafts aright;
Then the Soudan, strong in weed,
Percyvelle bare from his steed,
Two land's length, I trow, indeed,
  With mastery and might;   1660
On the earth the Soudan lay,
And his steed, it fled away,
Jesting, Percyvelle doth say:
  "Hast the troth I plight!

"I thee plight a blow, I trow,
And methinks, thou hast it now,
Were it so, 't would please me, thou
  Ne'er of this should mend!"
O'er the Soudan did he stay,
As upon the ground he lay,   1670
Held him down to earth alway
  E'en with his spear-end.

Fain he had his foeman slain,
E'en that miscreant Soudane,
But no way could find again,
  Had small skill to wend;
Then he thinks, the lad so bold,
Of wild works he wrought of old,
"Had I now a fire on wold
  Burning were thine end!"   1680

Quoth: "I 'ld burn thee here forthright,
Then thou should'st have no more might
'Gainst a woman aye to fight,
  I would teach thee fair!"
Quoth the good Gawain that day:
"Thou could'st, didst thou know the
    way,
And would'st light from steed alway
  Overcome him there."
Light of mood, the boy, and gay,
Thinks on other thing straightway.   1690
Quoth: "A *steed*, now didst thou say?
  I deemed this a *mare!*"
In the stead there, as he stood,
Little recked for ill or good,
Swiftly did he change his mood
  Slacked his spear point there.

When he up his spear had ta'en,
With that, Gollerotherame,
This same miscreant Soudane,
  Sprang upon his feet,   1700
Forth his sword then draweth he,
Strikes at Percyvelle the free,
And the boy scarce skilled should be
  These, his wiles, to meet;
But the steed, at his own will,
Saw the sword, and stayed not still,
Leapt aside upon a hill,
  Five strides maketh fleet;
Even as he sprang there-by,
Then the Soudan raised a cry,   1710
Waked the boy full suddenly
  From his musings sweet.

He in musing deep did stay,
All his dreams then fled away,
Lighted down without delay

'Gainst him for to go;
Quoth: "I trow, hast taught to me
How I best may deal with thee."
Swift, his sword then draweth he,
   Struck hard at his foe;   1720
Thro' the neck-bone shore the blade,
Mouthpiece, gorget, useless laid,
And the Soudan's head he made
   Fly the body fro'.
Then he strode, the knight so good,
To his steed, as there it stood,
That fair maiden mild of mood,
   Much mirth might she know.

Very mirthful he, that tide,
To the castle did he ride,   1730
Boldly there did he abide
   With that maiden bright;
Joyful were they everyone
That the Soudan was undone,
And he had the woman won
   By mastery and might.
Said of Percyvelle, that he
Worthy was a king to be,
Since he kept full faithfully
   That which he had hight.   1740
There was nothing more to say
But, on the appointed day,
He wed Lufamour, the may,
   Percyvelle, the wight.

Now has Percyvelle the wight
Wedded Lufamour, the bright,
King hath he become of right
   Of that land so wide;
Then King Arthur, on a day,
Thought no longer there to stay,   1750
Took leave of the lady gay
   And from thence would ride;
Percyvelle there leaveth he
King of all that land to be
Since with ring, the knight so free,
   Wed that maid as bride.
Sithen, on th' appointed day,
Rode the king upon his way,
As for certain sooth I say,
   Nor would more abide.   1760

Now doth Percyvelle abide
There, within those boroughs wide,
For her sake who was his bride,
   Wedded there with ring;
Well he wielded rule in land,
All men bowed them to his hand,
At his will the folk, they stand,
   Know him for their king;
Thus within that burg, right well,
Till the twelvemonth's end, it fell,   1770
With his true love did he dwell,
   Thought of ne'er a thing,
Thought not how his mother, she,
Dwelt beneath the greenwood tree,
How her drink should water be
   That from well doth spring.

Drinks spring-water from the well,
Eats of herbs, no lie I tell,
With none other thing doth dwell
   In the holts so sere;   1780
Till it chanced upon a day
As within his bed he lay,
To himself he 'gan to say
   Soft, with sigh and tear:
"Last Yule day, methinks it were,
I on wild ways forth did fare,
Left my mother man-less there
   In the woodland drear —"
To himself then sayeth he:
"Blithe, I ween, I ne'er may be   1790
Till I may my mother see,
   Or of her may hear."

Now to wot how she doth fare
That good knight doth armour bear,
Nor would longer linger there
   Spite of aught they say;
Up he rose within that hall,
Took his leave of one and all,
Both of great and eke of small,
   Forth would go his way,   1800
Tho' she doth him straight entreat,
Lufamour, his true love sweet,
While the days of Yule fast fleet
   He with her should stay,
He denied her of that thing,

But a priest he bade them bring,
Bade a Mass for him to sing,
  Rode forth that same day.

Now from thence the knight doth
    ride,
Never man he wist that tide   1810
Whitherward he thought to ride
  His grief to amend;
Forth he rideth all alone,
Goeth from them everyone,
None might know where he is gone
  Or might with him wend;
Forward doth he take his way,
'T is the certain sooth I say,
Till a road he found alway
  By a forest end.   1820
Then he heard, the road anigh,
As it were a woman's cry
Praying Mary mild, on high,
  She would succour send.

Praying Mary, mild of mood,
She would send her succour good —
As he came there thro' the wood
  He a marvel found;
For a lady, fair to see,
Stood fast bounden to a tree,   1830
'T is the sooth I say to ye,
  Hand and foot were bound;
When her plight he thus did know
Fain was he to ask her who
He should be, who served her so,
  As he thus had found?
Saith she: "Sir, 't is the Black Knight,
He who is my lord by right,
Who in this wise hath me dight
  Brought me to this stound."   1840

Quoth she: "Here he left me bound
For a fault that he hath found,
Yet I warrant thee this stound,
  Evil did I none!
For it chanced e'en as I say,
That upon my bed I lay
As it were the last Yule-Day,
  Now a twelvemonth gone,

Were he knight, or were he king,
One in jest hath done this thing,   1850
He with me exchanged a ring,
  Richer had I none!
That man did I never see
Who made this exchange with me,
But I wot, whoe'er he be,
  He the better won!"

Quoth: "The better doth he own,
For such virtue in a stone,
In this world I ne'er have known,
  Set within a ring,   1860
For the man who doth it wear,
Or upon his body bear,
Never blow may harm him there,
  Or to death him bring."
Percyvelle wist without fail,
When he heard that lady's tale,
He had brought her into bale
  When he changed her ring;
Straightway to her speaketh he,
To that lady fair and free: 1870
"I shall loose thee from that tree
  By my faith as king!"

Percyvelle was king and knight,
Well he held what he had hight,
And he loosed that lady bright,
  Who stood bound to tree;
Down she sat, the lady fair,
Percyvelle beside her there,
Wayworn, since he far did fare,
  Fain to rest was he;   1880
Deemed he well might rest that tide,
Yet short leisure might he bide,
As he lay, the dame beside,
  His head on her knee,
She waked Percyvelle the wight,
Bade him flee with all his might:
"Yonder cometh the Black Knight,
  Slain thou sure shalt be!"

Quoth she: "Sir, thou sure shalt die,
This I tell thee certainly,   1890
Yonder, see, he draweth nigh
  Who shall slay us two."

But the knight he answered free:
"Thou but now didst say to me
That no dint my death should be,
  Nor should work me woe."
Then his helm on head he set,
But, ere he to horse might get,
The Black Knight with him hath met,
  Hailed him as his foe;   1900
Quoth he: "How? What dost thou
    here?
Would'st thou then thy playmate cheer?
For this shalt thou pay full dear
  Ere I hence shall go!"

Quoth the knight: "Ere hence I go,
I shall surely slay ye two,
And the like of ye also,
  Fair reward to yield!"
Then quoth Percyvelle the free:
"Now, methinks, we soon shall see 1910
Who of us shall worthy be
  To be slain in field!"
No word more they spake that tide,
But right soon together ride,
As men who would war abide,
  Stiff, with shaft and shield.
And Syr Percyvelle, the wight,
He hath borne down the Black Knight,
Then, I trow, the lady bright
  Succoured him on field;   1920

His best succour did she wield,
Save she there had been his shield,
He had sure been slain on field,
  Swift and certainly;
For as Percyvelle the keen
Fain the Black Knight's bane had been
Came the lady in between,
  And did "Mercy!" cry;
For her sake did he forbear,
And he made the Black Knight swear
To forgive that lady fair,   1931
  Put his ill-will by;
And, himself, he sware that day
That he ne'er beside her lay,
Wronged her not in any way
  That were villainy!

"Villainy I did her ne'er,
When I saw her sleeping there,
Then I kissed that lady fair,
  That to own, I'm fain!   1940
From her hand I took a ring,
And I left her slumbering,
And the truth of that same thing
  Will I here maintain!"
That naught else had chanced, that,
    he
Sware by Jesu, verilie,
For that same, right readily,
  Here would he be slain!
"Ready is the ring, I trow,
If mine own wilt give me now,   1950
Of that same exchange, I vow,
  Shall I be full fain!"

Quoth: "Mine own I'll gladly take —"
In this wise the Black Knight spake:
"No denial will I make
  Thou too late shalt be!
Swift that ring did I demand,
Drew it there from off her hand,
To the lord of this same land,
  Bare it speedily!   1960
Mourning sore, that ring I bare,
To a good man took it there,
No more stalwart giant shall fare
  On this earth than he!
There is neither knight nor king
Who durst ask from him that ring,
But that same to death he'll bring,
  Hot his wrath shall be!"

"Be he hot, or be he cold —"
Thus spake Percyvelle the bold,   1970
(For the tale that knight had told
  He waxed wroth that day;)
Quoth: "On gallows high may he
Hang, who gives this ring to thee
Ere mine own thou bringest me,
  Which thou gav'st away!
If none other way there be
Then right soon shalt tell to me
What like man, in sooth, is he
  Who is strong in fray?   1980

I to speak no more be fain,
I must win it back again,
Lost thy share in these rings twain
   Tho' more precious they!"

Quoth: "Had they more precious
     been —"
Quoth the knight in wrath, I ween,
"That with small delay be seen,
   What like man is he,
If to keep thy word thou dare,
Percyvelle of Galays, fare   1990
To yon lofty palace, there
   Should he surely be;
Thy ring with that giant grim,
(Bright the stone, and nothing dim,)
There, forsooth, shalt find with him,
   Given it was by me.
In that hold, or eke without, —
Or, perchance, he rides about, —
But of thee he'll have small doubt
   As thou sure shalt see!"   2000

Quoth the knight: "Thou sure shalt see,
That I tell thee certainlie," —
On his way then rideth he
   Wondrous swift that tide;
Stood the giant in his hold
Who was lord o'er wood and wold,
Saw Syr Percyvelle the bold
   O'er his land to ride;
On his porter calls, I ween,
Saith: "Now say, what may this mean?
For a bold man have I seen   2011
   O'er my lands to ride.
Reach me down my plaything there,
And against him will I fare,
Better lot at Rome he'ld share
   As I thrive, this tide!"

An he thrive, or vanquished be,
Club of iron taketh he,
And 'gainst Percyvelle the free,
   Goes his way forthright,   2020
Weighty blows that club should deal,
That a knight full well should feel,
For the head, well wrought of steel,

Twelve stone weighed aright;
Bound the staff with iron band,
And with ten stones of the land,
One was set behind his hand,
   Was for holding dight;
Three and twenty, fully told,
Ill might any man on mold,   2030
As the tale it now is told,
   'Gainst such weapon fight!

Thus, to smite each other down,
Met they on a moorland brown,
A full mile from any town,
   'Neath their shield so bold;
Then he quoth, the giant wight,
Soon as he beheld that knight:
"Mahoun, praiséd be thy might!"
   Did him well behold;   2040
"Art thou he, now tell me true,
Who Gollerotherame slew,
Other brother ne'er I knew
   Than himself, of old?"
Then quoth Percyvelle the free:
"Thro' God's Grace, I'll so serve thee,
And such giants as ye be
   Slay them all on fold!"

Such a fight was seldom seen,
For the dale it rang, I ween,   2050
With the dints that passed between
   These two, when they met;
The giant, with his weapon fell,
Fain had smitten Percyvelle,
Bending low, he swerved full well,
   And a stroke swift set;
The giant's blow, it went astray,
Hard as flint the club alway,
Ere the staff he well might stay,
   Or his strength might let,   2060
In the earth the club, it stood,
To the midmost of the wood,
Percyvelle, the hero good,
   Forth his sword would get.

Forth he drew his sword that day,
Smote the giant without delay,
Nigh unto his neck alway

Even as he stood,
Strikes his hand off with a blow,
His left foot doth cleave also,   2070
Dealt such dints upon his foe,
  Nighed him as he would;
Percyvelle he quoth: "I ween,
Had thy weapon smaller been
Better luck thy hand had seen,
  Thou hadst done some good;
Now, I trow, that ne'er again
Shall thy club from earth be ta'en,
Or thy way thou ridest fain,
  Ne'er, upon the Rood!"   2080

Quoth he: "By the Holy Rood,
As in evil aye thou stood,
Of thy foot thou get'st no good,
  Save that hop thou may!"
Then his club aside he laid,
Smote the hero undismayed,
In the neck, with knife's sharp blade,
  Near enow were they.
Wrathful at the blow, I ween,
The giant's hand he smote off clean,
As none had aforetime been,   2091
  Both hands were away!
Then his head from off him drave —
He was a discourteous knave
Thus a giant's beard to shave,
  I forsooth, may say!

Then, as I the sooth may say,
Left the giant where he lay
And rode forth upon his way
  To the fortress-hold;   2100
When he saw his lord was dead,
Then the porter swiftly sped,
From the knight, the keys, that stead,
  Would he not withhold;
Percyvelle, ere other thing,
Prayed the porter of the ring,
Thereof, could he tidings bring?
  And straightway he told,
Showed him straightway to the kist,
Where the treasure was, he wist,   2110
Bade him take there, as he list,
  All he would of gold.

Percyvelle, from treasure hold
Speedy, turned out all the gold,
There, before him on the mold,
  Fell the ring he sought;
Stood the porter at his side,
Saw the ring from coffer glide,
And he quoth: "Woe worth the tide
  That same ring was wrought!"   2120
Percyvelle, he answered free,
Asked him why, and wherefore, he
Banned that ring so bitterly,
  What was in his thought?
Then the porter answered fair,
By his loyalty he sware:
"I the truth will here declare
  And delay for naught."

Quoth: "The truth I tell to thee,
The knight whose this ring should
    be   2130
As a present gave it free,
  And hath hither brought;
He, forsooth, my master there,
Took the gift with favour fair,
Lord of this land was he e'er,
  For his marvels wrought.
Dwelling nigh, there chanced to be
At that time, a fair ladie,
And my lord, right loyally,
  Loved her, as I thought;   2140
So it chanced upon a day
As in sooth I now shall say,
That my lord went forth to play,
  And her love besought.

" Now the lady doth he pray
His true love to be alway,
Pleading straitly, that he may
  Of her favoured be;
As his first prayer he would bring,
He would proffer her the ring,   2150
When she saw that tokening,
  Sore dismayed was she;
Wept, and wailed, and cried amain:
'Traitor, thou my son hast slain,
And the ring from him hast ta'en
  That was given by me!'

Then her clothes from off her tare,
Gat her to the woodland there,
Witless doth that lady fare,
    This the cause shall be!   2160

"Even for such cause as this
Is the lady mad, I wis,
Wild within the wood she is
    Ever since that tide;
Fain would I her succour be,
But whene'er she seeth me
From me swiftly doth she flee,
    Will for naught abide."
Quoth Syr Percyvelle that day:
"Now will I without delay   2170
Strive to make that lady stay,
    But I will not ride;
But afoot I now will go,
An that lady shall me know
I may bring her out of woe,
    For her son she'll bide!"

Quoth: "For this, her son, she'll bide,
But ahorse I will not ride
Till that lady I have spied,
    Speed as best I may;   2180
With none armour that may be,"
Quoth the knight: "I'll cover me,
Till that I my mother see,
    Or by night or day;
But the self-same garb I ware
When from her I forth did fare,
That, I think again to bear
    After other play;
And I trow that never more
Come I from the holts so hore   2190
Till her lot, who once me bore,
    I again may say."

"This for sooth I think to say." —
With that would he go his way,
With the morn, at dawn of day,
    Forth the knight did fare;
All his harness left within,
Did on him a coat of skin,
To the woodland forth did win
    'Mid the holts so bare;   2200

Seven days long in vain he sought,
Of his mother found he naught,
Nor of meat or drink he thought,
    He was full of care;
On the ninth day it befell
That he came unto a well
Nigh where he was wont to dwell,
    And refresh him there.

He had drunk his fill that tide,
Further thought to wander wide,   2210
When he saw, close to his side,
    That same lady free;
But, whenas she saw him there,
She with threats would 'gainst him fare,
And swift answer did she dare
    E'en that fair ladie;
She began to call and cry,
Saying: "Such a son had I!"
Then his heart for joy beat high,
    Blithe, I trow, was he;   2220
As he came to her anear,
So that she his voice might hear,
Spake he: "Sweet my mother dear,
    Bide ye there for me!"

By that time so nigh was he
That she might in no wise flee,
This I tell ye certainly,
    She must needs abide;
Sprang on him in wrath so keen,
That of very truth, I ween,   2230
Had her strength but greater been
    He were slain that tide;
But the stronger was he e'er,
Up he took his mother there,
On his back the lady bare,
    Pure, I trow, his pride.
To the castle gate that day
Hastens he, the nearest way,
And the porter without stay,
    Opens to him wide.   2240

Bare his mother in that day, —
He who made the tale doth say
With what robes they had alway
    Wrapped her warmly there;

There the lord a drink had wrought,
And that same the porter brought,
For none other had he thought
　Save that lady fair.
Then, for so the tale they tell,
With a spoon they fed her well,　　2250
And asleep she swiftly fell
　As I now declare;
And the lady sleeping lay
Three nights, and three days, alway
Doth the porter with her stay
　Wakes and watches there.

Thus the porter watched her there,
Loyal love to her he bare,
Till at last the lady fair
　Wakened, so I ween;　　2260
Then distraught was she no more,
But herself in such wise bore
As one hale, who ne'er of yore,
　Otherwise had been;
Then they kneeléd down, the three,
Gave God thanks on bended knee

That men thus His grace should see
　As on them was seen.
Sithen, go they on their way,
And a rich bath make straightway,　　2270
For that lady, robed her gay,
　Both in gray and green.

Percyvelle without delay,
'T is the sooth to ye I say,
Took his mother, and his way
　Homeward rideth he;
Then great lords, and his sweet queen,
Welcomed him with joy, I ween,
When they him in life had seen
　Blithe they well may be.　　2280
Then he fared to Holy Land,
Cities won with his strong hand,
There was slain, I understand,
　This his end should be!
Jesu Christ, high Heaven's King,
Who is Lord of everything,
Grant to us His dear blessing,
　Amen, for charitie.

SIR LANCELOT[1]

THE MAID OF ASCOLOT

(*Sir Lancelot would ride secretly to a
　Tournament.*)
AN earl, he dwelt there at that tide,
The lord of Ascolot he hight,
Thither Sir Lancelot would ride,
Craving a shelter for the night.
They welcomed him with fitting pride,
A supper rich for him they dight;
His name from all he fain would hide
Saying, he was a stranger knight.

Of sons the earl he had but two,
And those two newly knighted were —
At that time was the custom so　　11
That, when young knights their shield
　would bear,

Throughout the first year must they
　show
One hue alone, whate'er that were,
Or red, or yellow, white, or blue —
Thus of young knights the fashion fair.

Then, as they sat at meat, forthright
Sir Lancelot his host did pray:
"Sir, is there here a youthful knight
Who fain were for the Tourney's fray?"
"I have two sons, dear to my sight,　　21
But one, he lieth sick to-day,
An he a comrade found, 't were right
The other sought the field alway."

"Sir, an thy son will thither ride,
His company I'll keep withal;
There will I battle at his side,

And help him there, lest harm befall."
"Thy courtesy thou can'st not hide;
Good knight art thou, 't is plain to all,
Now till to-morrow here abide,   31
My son shall ride with thee from hall."

"Fain would I ask ye one thing more,
I ask it here for better speed,
Say, have ye armour here in store
That I might borrow for my need?"
"My son, he lies in sickness sore,
Take ye his harness and his steed,
Brethren they 'ld deem ye, an ye wore,
The twain of ye, the same red weed."

The earl, he had a daughter sweet,   41
Fain was she Lancelot to see,
(Her face was red as blossom meet,
Or flower in field that springeth free.)
Gladly she sat by him at meat,
In sooth, a noble knight was he!
Yet swift her tears adown they fleet,
Fast set on him her heart shall be.

Up rose that maiden fair and still,
And to her bower she went in woe,   50
Adown upon her couch she fell,
Her heart, it well nigh brake in two.
Sir Lancelot, he wist her will —
(The signs of love he well doth know,)
He called her brother soft and still,
And to her chamber swift they go.

He sat him, for that maiden's sake,
Down on the bed whereon she lay,
In courteous wise to her he spake —
(He fain will comfort, an he may,)   60
Then in her arms she doth him take
And these the words she soft doth
          say:
"Sir, save that ye the medicine make,
No leech may save my life to-day!"

"Lady, I prithee cease to fret,
And do thyself for me no ill,
My heart elsewhere is steadfast set,
My love lies not within my will.

Yet naught on earth henceforth will let
Me from thy service, loud or still,   70
Another time when we have met
Thou mayest better speak thy fill."

"Then, since I may no better fare,
As thou be valiant knight, and free,
I pray thee in this Tourney bear
Some sign of mine, that men may
          see."
"Lady, the sleeve thou now dost wear
I'll take it for the love of thee,
So much I did for lady ne'er
Save her, who most hath lovéd me!"   80

Then, on the morrow, when 't was day,
They dined, and made them ready there,
Then gat them forth upon their way
In guise as tho' they brethren were —
(*Then follows the account of the Tour-
nament, in which Lancelot greatly
distinguishes himself, but is badly
wounded. The Maiden of Ascolot and
her aunt tend him carefully. Meanwhile
Arthur, who suspects the winner of the
Tourney to be Lancelot, sends Gawain
in search of him.*)
Then from the king, and from the queen,
Sir Gawain took his leave that tide,
Of all his comrades too, I ween,
And busks himself, with mickle pride.
To Ascolot, by wood-ways green,
He hastes as fast as he may ride,   90
Till he Sir Lancelot hath seen
Nor night, nor day, would he abide.

By that, Sir Lancelot, whole again,
Made ready on his way to go,
Leave of the folk hath courteous ta'en —
The maiden wept for grief and woe:
"Sir, if your will thereto were fain,
Since I of ye no more may know,
I pray that I some gift may gain   99
To look on, when my tears fast flow."

Lancelot spake, with heart so free —
(The maiden's grief would he amend —)

"Mine armour will I leave with thee,
And in thy brother's hence will wend.
Look that thou long not after me,
No space within these walls to spend
Have I, yet short the time shall be
Before I either come or send."

Sir Lancelot, he fain would ride,
And on his way he went forthright, —
Sir Gawain came within that tide   111
And tidings asked of such a knight.
They welcomed him with mickle pride,
And supper for him richly dight,
The truth they have small care to
   hide —
"He left but now for fourteen night."

Sir Gawain courteous mien doth make,
He sat him down, that maid anear,
And told of Lancelot du Lake,
How in the world was none his peer. 120
The maid, of Lancelot she spake,
Said, how he to her heart was dear:
"Yea, for his love he doth me take,
His armour might I show you here."

"Sweet Demoiselle," he saith anon,
"Right glad am I the thing be so,
For such a lover hast thou won
That this world may no better show.
Of lady fair there liveth none   129
For wealth or beauty famed, that tho'
Her heart were hard as steel or stone
With love for him it would not glow.

"But, Demoiselle, I'ld ask of thee
That thou his shield to me would'st
   show,
That if Sir Lancelot's it be
By its device I well may know."
That maiden was both frank and free,
She led him to a chamber new,
Lancelot's shield she bade him see,
And all his armour forth she drew. 140

Sir Gawain turned him swift about,
And to the maiden gaily spake:

"Lady," he quoth, "without a doubt
He is Sir Lancelot du Lake!
And Lady, that a knight so stout
Should ye for true-love truly take
Rejoiceth me, within, without,
I am your servant, for his sake!"

With that sweet maid he spake the night
All that he had in heart to say, 150
Till that his bed for him they dight
Much mirth he made, and gladsome play.
He took his leave of earl and knight
At morrow morn, when dawned the day,
Bade "Farewell," to that maiden bright,
And gat him forth upon his way.

He wist not where to seek that knight,
Nor whither Lancelot would ride,
For when he once was out of sight
He wist right well his tracks to hide. 160
He takes the road he knows aright,
To Arthur's court he needs no guide,
Welcome he was to king and knight,
As hero courteous, true, and tried.

Then it befell upon a tide
The king and queen together spake,
(Sir Gawain standing at their side,)
Each to the other plaint doth make
How long they must with sorrow bide
His coming, Lancelot du Lake, 170
Of Arthur's court abased the pride,
And sore the sighing, for his sake.

"Certes, an Lancelot did live
So long from court he ne'er would be —"
Swiftly Gawain doth answer give:
"Nay, nay, no marvel 't is to me,
The fairest lady that doth live
Chosen unto his love hath he,
Gladness to every man 't would give
An he so fair a sight might see!" 180

King Arthur, he was glad that day,
Such tidings deemed he passing fair;
Then of Gawain he straight did pray
He would the maiden's name declare.

"Earl's daughter she," (so doth he say,)
"Of Ascolot, I well did fare
Within that burg so blithe and gay,
Lancelot's shield she shewed me there."

The queen, she spake no word that
    day,
She gat her to her bower with speed, 190
And prone upon her couch she lay,
Nay, well nigh mad was she, indeed.
"Alas," she cried, and "Wellaway!
That ever life on land I lead,
Now have I lost, I trow for aye,
The best knight who e'er spurred a
    steed!"

The ladies who about her stood,
And all her secrets well might know,
They bade her be of comfort good,
And to no man her sorrow show. 200
They made her bed with sorry mood,
And on her couch they laid her low,
Ever she wept, as she were wood, —
Full sore they mourn their lady's woe.

The queen thus sick for sorrow lay,
Never her grief might solace know,
Until it chanced, upon a day,
Sir Lionel and Sir Hector go
Forth to the forest, blithe and gay,
'Neath leafy branch, where sweet
    flowers blow, 210
And as they rode the woodland way
Sir Lancelot himself doth show.

Small wonder they were glad, the twain,
When they their master saw with sight,
Upon their knees to fall are fain,
Give thanks to God, for this, His Might.
'T was joy to see, and gladsome gain,
The meeting with that noble knight,
Nor can he question swift refrain: 219
"How fares it with my Lady bright?"

Straightway the knights they answer
    free:
"The queen, she lies in sickness sore,

'T is dole enow to hear, and see,
Such mickle grief ne'er lady bore.
The king, a sorry man is he
Since that to court ye come no more,
He saith, that dead ye sure must be,
So do the courtiers, less, and more.

"Were it your will with us to fare,
And speak a little with the queen, 230
Methinks that blithe henceforth she
    were
An she but once your face had seen.
The king, he goes in grief and care,
And so doth all the court, I ween,
They deem no more in life ye were
Since ye from court o'er long have been."

He granteth them their prayer that day,
Saith, he will homeward with them ride,
Forsooth, those knights were glad and
    gay
And busked them there with mickle
    pride. 240
Straight to the court they take their way,
Nor day nor night they would abide,
Both king and court were blithe alway
Whenas they heard the news that tide.

The king, he stands on tower so high,
And by him standeth Sir Gawain,
When Lancelot they saw with eye
Were never men on mold so fain!
Whenas the gates he drew anigh
They ran there-out, with might and
    main, 250
Gave welcome glad, both low and high,
And kissed him, king, and knight, and
    swain.

The king him to a chamber led,
Close in his arms he did him fold,
And set him on a goodly bed
That covered was with cloth of gold.
No man, to serve him at that stead
But strove, with labour manifold.
With joy and gladness was he sped —
Then all his deeds to them he told. 260

Of days in court he dwelt full three
But never spake word with the queen,
So fain the folk were him to see,
The king, and all the court, I ween.
That lady, fair as flower on tree,
She wept her love, so long unseen,
Ever her tears they flow so free
Fain would she hide her mournful
    mien.

Then did it chance upon a day
The king, he would a-hunting ride, 270
In forest fair he maketh gay
And all his knights are at his side.
Sir Lancelot, in bed he lay,
Fain was he with the queen to bide,
Thus to her bower he takes his way
And greeteth her in knightly pride.

He kissed that lady fair and sheen,
And greeted her with gladsome glee,
And all her ladies too, I ween,
For joy, the tears flow fast and free. 280
"Ah, wellaway!" thus sighed the queen,
"Sir Lancelot, that I thee see,
The love that was us two between
That now it thus should severed be!

"Alas, Sir Lancelot du Lake,
That thou hast all my heart in hold,
And now would'st the earl's daughter
    take
Of Ascolot, so was it told.
Now for her love thou wilt forsake
Thy doughty deeds, thy ventures bold,
So must I woeful weep and wake 291
Till this, my heart, in clay be cold!

"But, Lancelot, I beseech thee here,
Since that of needs it must be so,
That no man from thy lips shall hear
The love that was betwixt us two!
And never hold that maid so dear
That ye should knightly deeds forego,
Such tidings were to me full drear —
Henceforth I needs must walk in
    woe!" 300

Then Lancelot, so still he stood,
His heart was heavy as a stone,
So sorrowful it waxed, his mood,
For ruth his joy was all foregone.
"Madam," he said, "by Holy Rood,
What is the meaning of thy moan?
By Him Who bought me with His
    Blood
Of all these tidings knew I none.

"But by these words it seemeth me
That ye were fain I were away, 310
In sooth no more ye shall me see,
My Lady fair, have ye Good-day!"
Forth from the chamber goeth he,
In sooth grief o'er his heart held sway;
The queen, she fell in swoonings three,
Fain had she slain herself straightway.

The knight his chamber sought with
    speed
There, where his harness ready lay,
He armed himself in knightly weed,
Small joy was in his heart that day. 320
As sparks from glowing embers freed,
(Yet sorely grieving, sooth to say —)
He sprang forth on his goodly steed,
And to the forest went his way.

(*Here follows the death by poison of Mador
de la Porte, and the accusation of the
queen.*)
Now leave we Lancelot to dwell
In hermit cell, in forest green,
And forthwith of a venture tell
That came to Arthur, king so keen.
With Gawain would he counsel well,
Full sore their mourning for the queen,
So on a morn, as chance befell, 331
The two met in a tower, I ween.

And as they there in converse stood
How best the thing might ordered be,
The river fast beneath them flowed,
And on the water, there they see
A little boat, and passing good,
That with the current floated free,

No fairer sail was seen on flood,
No better boat was wrought of tree. 340

Whenas King Arthur saw that sight
He wondered of the hangings fair
Wherewith the boat was all bedight,
So rich the coverture it bare.
All arched above with cloth so bright
Shining as gold, it saileth there —
Then quoth Gawain, that gentle knight:
"This boat in costly wise doth fare!"

"Forsooth," the king in answer spake:
"Such boat I never saw before, 350
I rede our way we thither take
Some venture surely lies in store.
Be it within of such-like make
As 't is without, or may be more,
An oath I 'ld dare thereof to take
Its wonders be not swiftly o'er!"

Arthur the king, and good Gawain,
Forth from the tower adown have
gone.
They to the boat to haste are fain,
Swiftly they go, those two alone. 360
They came as it hath harbour ta'en,
And, sooth to say, they gaze anon,
Then doth he raise the cloth, Gawain,
That hides the boat, and steps thereon.

When they were in, on either side
Richly arrayed it was to see,
A fair couch in the midst they spied
Whereon a king might bedded be.
Then with their hand they draw aside
The coverture, right hastily, 370
Its folds, a maiden's corpse they hide,
Fairest of women once was she.

Then to Gawain he spake, the king,
"I trow Death here a wrong hath
wrought,
In that he hath so fair a thing
Forth from the world untimely brought.
Her beauty passeth everything,
Tidings of her I fain had sought,

Who might she be, this sweet darling?
And where her life to end was brought."

His eyes Sir Gawain on her cast, 381
Beheld her face with heart so free,
And well he knew her at the last,
The Maid of Ascolot was she.
(Whom he ere-while had wooed full
fast,
His love would fain have had her be,
His proffered love she from her cast
For Lancelot's alone was she.)

Thus to the king he spake, Gawain:
"Dost mind thee of a certain day 390
How with the queen we stood, we twain,
And made together jest and play?
I of a maid to tell was fain
Whom Lancelot loved well — Now say?"
"Forsooth," the king he spake again.
"Now thou dost mind me of it, yea!"

"Then, Sire, forsooth," Gawain doth
say:
"This is the maid whereof I spake,
O'er all the world, I trow, alway
She loved Sir Lancelot du Lake." 400
"Then sure," King Arthur spake
straightway,
"Her death it rues me for his sake,
Your words the cause full well betray
For grief and love her heart it brake."

Forthwith Gawain, the gentle knight,
About that maiden fair he sought,
A purse he found, so richly dight,
With gold and pearls 't was all in-
wrought.
Empty at first it seemed to sight,
But when into his hand 't was brought,
A letter lay therein, so light, 411
Fain would they know if it told aught.

The writing eager to behold
Sir Gawain took it to the king,
Bade him that letter swift unfold,
Thereto he made small dallying, —

Within he found the story told
From first to last, without leasing,
'T was but that tale both new and old
How Love a maid to death may bring.

"Unto the king, and all his knights   421
Who to the Table Round belong,
Who courteous be, of valiant might,
Stable and steadfast, true, and strong;
Most worshipful in fairest fight,
Most helpful where men most have
    wrong,
The Maid of Ascolot, aright
Would greeting send, with truest tongue.

"Thus to ye all my plaint I make,
Bemoan the wrong that hath been
    wrought,   430
Yet I would not ye undertake
To mend the ill, 't would profit naught.
This would I say, for this, your sake,
That tho' men thro' the wide world
    sought
Your like doth neither walk nor wake,
For deeds with courage courteous
    wrought.

"Wherefore to ye it shall be shown
How I, in sooth, for many a day
Such loyal love, and true, have known
That Death hath fetched me hence
    away.   440
But would ye know for whom alone,
I thus so long in languor lay
I'll tarry not the truth to own,
Denial profits naught to-day.

"And would I now rehearse the tale
For whom I suffered all this woe,
I say, Death wrought on me this
    bale
For the best knight this earth may
    know!
In doughty dints he doth not fail,
Such royal mien may no man show,   450
So churlish yet, 'neath silk, or mail,
Have I found neither friend nor foe!

"Of foe, or friend, the sooth to say,
So harsh in deed was never none,
His gentleness was all away,
Such churlish manners he put on.
For ne'er so straitly might I pray,
Kneeling, with tears and rueful moan,
To win his love, but he said 'Nay,'
Vowing of leman he 'ld have none.   460

"Therefore, my lords, for this, his sake,
Grief to my heart I took and care,
Till Death at last did me o'er-take,
Forth from this life it did me bear.
Thus for true love my heart I brake,
And of my bliss was stripped all bare,
For sake of Lancelot du Lake,
An ye would know what knight it
    were!"

Arthur, I ween, that noble king,   469
He read the script, and knew the name,
And quoth to Gawain, marvelling:
"Lancelot here hath been to blame;
Men shall account as evil thing
That soileth much his knightly fame,
That love this maid to death did bring —
That he denied her doth him shame!"

Then to the king he quoth, Gawain:
"I did but jest the other day
When I said Lancelot was fain
To take for love that gentle may,   480
His love, it seeketh higher gain,
Know ye it is but truth I say,
A lowly love he doth disdain,
He will some lady great and gay."

"Sir Gawain," quoth King Arthur there:
"Now say, what here shall be thy
    rede,
How deal we with this maiden fair?"
Sir Gawain quoth: "So God me speed,
Methinks 't were well we should her
    bear,
(An so it were your will indeed,)   490
Within the town, for burial care
In noble wise, as is her meed."

The king, he gave assent withal;
Sir Gawain called men, hastily,
Straightway, unto the palace hall
They bare that maiden tenderly.
The king, he told his barons all,
Whether of high or low degree,
How she a prey to death did fall ·
Since Lancelot's she might not be.   500

Sir Gawain straightway went his way
Unto the queen, and thus he spake:
"Madam," he quoth, "I trow alway
I wronged Sir Lancelot du Lake;
I did but jest the other day
When we together sport did make,
In that I said he idle lay
For the fair Maid of Ascolot's sake.

"Of Ascolot, that maiden free,
I said she was his love, I trow,   510
That I so jested rueth me,
For all the truth I know it now.
He loved her not, that may we see,
She lieth dead — as snow on bough
So white — and writing there shall be
With plaint of Lancelot enow!"

The queen was wroth as winter wind,
And to Sir Gawain thus began:
"Forsooth, Sir, thou wert too unkind
Thus to make jest of any man.   520
'T were best to keep it in thy mind,
Or yea, or nay, howe'er it ran,
Thy courtesy, it lagged behind
When first thine idle jests began!

"Much hast thou harmed thy knightly
     fame
In wronging thus so good a knight,
I trow he never wrought *thee* shame,
Therefore thou hadst the lesser right
To jest unseemly with his name,
Behind his back, out of his sight,   530
And Sir, thou know'st not, at this
     same,
What harm may spring from words so
     light!

"I deemed thee steadfast knight, and
     true,
The mirror of all courtesie,
Methinks, hast got thee manners new,
Which all be turned to villainy!
'Gainst other knights thine envy grew,
Therefore didst jest thus recklessly,
Who honoured thee, it may them rue —
Now get thee from my companie."   540

Sir Gawain swiftly went his way,
He saw the queen was angered sore,
No more he thought to her to say,
Deeming she 'ld hate him ever more.
The queen, she cried: "Ah, wellaway!"
Wringing her hands, she wept full
     sore,
"Most wretched I, I well may say,
Of all whom ever mother bore!

"My heart, alas, why wert so wood
To trow that Lancelot du Lake   550
So fickle were, so false of mood,
That other love than thee he 'ld take?
Nay, certés, all of this world's good
He had despiséd for thy sake,
And naught that knight, by field or
     flood,
Might tempt, his vows to thee to
     break."
(*The end of the episode is missing.*)

THE DEATH OF ARTHUR

SINCE Brutus out of Troy was brought,
And Britain for his kingdom won,
Such wonders ne'er before were wrought
Of mortal man beneath the sun.
By eventide there lived there naught,
Who erst was clad in flesh and bone,
Than Arthur, and two knights he
     brought
Thither, and Mordred, they alone.

Lucain the butler was one knight,
I trow his wounds were sore to see,   10

His brother, in the self-same plight,
Sir Bedivere, right sick was he.
Arthur, he spake these words forthright:
"That traitor slain by us shall be!"
With fell intent, their spears gripped
    tight,
They ran together manfully.

Smitten is Mordred thro' the breast,
The spear e'en thro' the back-bone shore,
Needs must he yield to death's behest,
Word hath he spoken never more.   20
Yet, dying, on his foe he prest,
And dealt the king a wound full sore,
Right to the head, thro' helm and crest,
Thrice hath he swooned, that blow
    before.

Sir Lucain and Sir Bedivere
Upheld the king betwixt them twain,
They get them forth with sorry cheer,
Their comrades on the field lie slain.
That doughty king, their lord so dear,
His strength for wounds it ebbed amain,
A chapel to that place was near,   31
No better shelter might they gain.

All night they in the chapel lay
Beside the sea, so did I hear,
To Mary Mother crying aye
With woeful voice, and many a tear.
To Jesu Christ they piteous pray,
Beseech Him for His Name so dear
To lead his soul in the right way
That Heaven's Bliss he lose not here. 40

Then from the mount, Sir Lucain good
Saw folk, who to the field drew nigh,
Bold barons they, of bone and blood,
Their thoughts were bent on robbery.
Of besant, brooch, and baldric good
They took all that they might espy —
Back to the king again he would,
Thinking to warn him hastily.

He spake to Arthur soft and still,
With rueful cheer, in voice full low: 50

"Sire, I have been on yonder hill
There many folk, they come and go,
Whether they will us good or ill
I know not, be they friend or foe
I rede, an so it be your will,
We busk us, to some town to go."

"Sir Lucain, good thy rede I hold,
Now lift me up, while life doth last —"
The knight he in his arms did fold,
With all his strength he held him fast.   60
Wounded to death, that monarch bold
Swooning, his weight on him hath cast,—
Sir Lucain did the king uphold,
His heart within him brake at last.

Half-swooning, as I tell ye here,
The king beside an altar stood,
Sir Lucain, whom he held full dear,
Lay dead, and weltering in his blood.
His brother, bold Sir Bedivere,
I trow he was of mournful mood,   70
For grief the corpse he might not near,
But ever wept, as he were wood.

The king, he turned him as he stood,
And spake to him, in words so keen:
"Excalibur, my sword so good,
(A better brand was never seen,)
Go, cast it in the salt sea flood,
Then shalt thou marvels see, I ween.
Now hie thee swift, by Holy Rood,
And tell me all that thou hast seen."   80

The knight, he was both fair and
    free,
To save that sword had he been fain,
He thought, "Who shall the better be
If none this weapon see again?
Were I to cast it in the sea,
Then were I mad, that seemeth plain —"
He hid the blade beneath a tree
And gat him to his lord again.

"What saw'st thou there?" then said the
    king,
"Now tell me if thou canst, anon."   90

"Certes," he quoth: "never a thing
Save waters deep, and wild waves wan."
"Ah! thou hast failed me!" cried the
    king;
"Why didst thou so, thou faithless man?
Far other tidings must thou bring!"
Straightway Sir Bedivere he ran —

He thought the sword he still might hide
And cast the scabbard in the flood, —
"If any venture then betide
Thereby shall I see tokens good."   100
From hand he let the scabbard glide,
And there awhile on land he stood,
Back to the king he went that tide,
Said, "Sire, 't is done, by Holy Rood."

"And saw'st thou any marvel fair?"
"Nay, certes, Sire, there saw I naught."
"Ah! traitor false," cried Arthur there,
"Now twice on me hast treason wrought.
The punishment shalt surely bear,
Bold tho' thou art, 't were dearly
    bought!"   110
The knight cried: "Lord, thy wrath
    now spare," —
And swift the sword again he sought.

Needs must the knight obey at last,
To the good sword he went his way,
Into the sea the blade he cast,
A marvel great he saw that day.
A hand from out the water, fast
Hath caught the blade, with deftest
    play
Brandished it high, then swift it passed
E'en as the lightning's gleam, away.   120

Swift to the king he hastened there,
And quoth: "Liege Lord, I saw a hand,
Forth from the waves it came all bare,
And brandished thrice that goodly
    brand."
"Now help me, that I thither fare —"
He led his lord down to the strand,
A goodly ship, with ladies fair,
And richly found, had put to land.

The ladies, who were frank and free,
Welcomed the king with courteous
    tongue,   130
And one, who fairest was to see,
Wept sore the while her hands she
    wrung;
"Brother," she said; "Ah! woe is me,
Thy wounds lack leechcraft over-long;
I wot that sorely grieveth me,
Methinks thy pains be all too strong!"

The knight, he raised a bitter moan,
As sick and sore, on land he stood:
"Ah! why dost leave me thus alone?
Whither dost go, my lord so good?"   140
The king, he spake in mournful tone,
"I will a little o'er this flood,
Unto the Vale of Avalone,
There shall my wounds find healing
    good."

Whenas the ship from land was brought,
The knight, he saw that barque no
    more —
Throughout the forest land he sought,
The hills so high, he passed them o'er,
For this, his life, he careth naugth,
Faring all night in sorrow sore,   150
At daybreak he hath found, fair wrought,
A chapel 'twixt two holts so hoar.

Thither he straight hath ta'en his
    way —
There doth he see a wondrous sight,
Upon the ground a hermit lay
Before a tomb, all newly dight.
Covered it was with marble gray,
And with rich letters graven aright,
And on a hearse in fair array
Full hundred tapers, all alight.   160

Then of the hermit was he fain
To ask who might be buried there?
The hermit answered him again,
He wist not rightly who it were; —
"At midnight came a goodly train
Of ladies, but I knew them ne'er,

Bearing on bier a body slain,
Full piteous were the wounds it bare. 168

"They proffered me of Besants bright,
Methinks, more than a hundred pound,
And bade me pray, both day and night,
For him, whose tomb thou here hast
        found,
That Christ's dear Mother, of her might,
Should help his soul, as at this stound," —
The knight the letters read aright,
For sorrow fell he to the ground.

"Hermit, in sooth," so did he cry,
"Now of my lord am I forlorn,

Arthur, my king, he here doth lie,
The best prince e'er in Britain born. 180
Give me thy habit presently,
For Him Who ware the Crown of Thorn,
That I within these walls may lie
And pray for him both night and morn."

That holy hermit said not Nay —
(Sometime Archbishop had he been,
By Mordred was he driven away
And found a home in forest green.)
Christ Jesu did he thank that day
That he Sir Bedivere had seen,   190
Right welcome was he there to stay —
The twain, they dwelt in peace, I ween.

TALES

THE FOX AND THE WOLF

A fox came forth from out the wood,
A-hungered sore, in search of food,
Never in all his life before
Had hunger plagued him half so sore.
He went by neither road nor street,
For loth he was with folk to meet,
Liever he were one hen to see
Than fifty women, tho' fair they be!
Over the fields he sped full fast,
Till that he came to a wall at last,   10
Within the wall a house there stood;
The fox he hastened in eager mood,
For he thought his hunger there to still
With meat or drink, as should be his will.
Looking about him on every side
With swifter pace the fox, he hied,
Until he came to the wall of stone,
And some thereof was overthrown,
And the wall was broken all along,
But locked was the one gate stout and strong.   20
At the nearest breach that the fox might win
Over he leapt, and gat him in.
When he was in he laughed, I trow,
And of his coming made sport enow,
For that he had entered and asked no leave
Either of bailiff, or yet of grieve!
To an open door he crept so soft,
There sat the hens in a row aloft,
Five there were, which doth make a flock,
And there in the midst there sat one cock.   30
The cock, he had perched him far on high,
And two of the hens they sat him nigh.

"Fox," quoth the cock: " what dost thou there?
Get thee from hence, Christ give thee care!
Oft to our hens hast thou done foul shame,
Be gone, I bid thee, in Heaven's Name!"
Then answered the fox: "Sir Chanticleer,
Fly thou adown, and come anear,
Ne'er have I done thee aught but good,
To thy hens have I sometime let their blood,   40
Sick they were 'neath the ribs, I wot,
Short span of life had been then their lot
Save that their veins should opened be,
And that have I done, for charity!
I have but drawn from their veins the blood,
And Chanticleer, it would do thee good,
Thou, too, hast that sickness beneath the spleen,
Scarce ten days more shalt thou live, I ween,
Thy life-days all shall pass with speed
Save that thou follow this my rede,   50
I will let thee blood beneath the breast,
Else soon must thou bid to thee the priest!"
"Get hence," quoth the cock: "shame be to thee,
Thou hast wronged our kin right woefully,
Get thee away, ere thou doest worse,
And here I call on thee Heaven's curse!
For an I came down, in Heaven's Name,
I were assuréd of bitter shame.

But an he wist, our Cellarer,
That thou hadst dared to enter here, 60
For sure he were on thy track ere long,
With pikes, and stones, and staves so
    strong,
All thy bones he would swiftly break,
And thus our vengeance upon thee
    take!"

The fox was still, he spake no more,
But now was he athirst full sore,
I ween the thirst it vexed him more
Than e'er the hunger had done afore;
All around him he prowled and sought
Until by hap his wanderings brought 70
Him nigh to a well of water clear,
Of cunning fashion, as ye shall hear.
Two buckets there at the well he
    found,
The one was down to the water wound,
And when men wound it up to the
    brink
The other bucket adown would sink.
The fox knew naught how the matter
    lay,
Into the bucket he leapt straightway,
For so he thought him his fill to drink —
But swift the bucket began to sink; 80
Too late the fox himself bethought,
And saw how he in a snare was caught,
But tho' he bethought himself enow
It helped him naught in this need, I
    trow!
Down must he go, he was held fast
    there,
Trapped he was in a cunning snare,
Had he known, it had been his will
To leave that bucket hanging still!
What with sorrow, and what with dread,
All his thirst, it hath from him sped. 90
Thus at last he came to the ground,
Water, enow, I ween, he found,
But tho' 't was there, he little drank,
For it seemed to him that the water
    stank
Since against his will he was there down
    thrust —

"Woe worth," quoth the fox: "desire
    and lust,
That knoweth not measure unto his
    meat, —
Were I not minded o'ermuch to eat
This shame had never my portion been,
But the lust of my mouth was over
    keen, 100
He who to thieving doth set his hand,
Ill is his portion in every land!
Here am I caught in trap and gin,
Methinks some devil brought me herein,
I was wont to be wise, but now I see
My race is run, here 's an end of me!"

The fox he wept, and made loud lament:
There came a wolf on like errand bent,
Out of the woodland deep he sped,
For he, too, was sore a-hungeréd, 110
Nothing throughout the night he found
To still his hunger at that stound.
He came to the well where the fox made
    moan,
And knew him again by his voice alone,
For that he had long his neighbour been,
And gossip unto his bairns, I ween.
Adown by the brink of the well he sat,
Quoth the wolf aloud: "What now is
    that?
Whose voice is that in the well I hear,
Art thou baptizéd my comrade dear? 120
Mock me not, but I prithee tell
Who now hath put thee adown the
    well?"
The fox, he knew him well for his kin,
And straight by his coming did counsel
    win,
And sought some wile that success might
    crown,
To bring himself up, and the wolf adown.
Quoth the fox in answer: "Who cometh
    here,
I ween it be Sigrim's voice I hear?"
"That is sooth:" quoth the wolf with
    speed,
"But who shalt thou be? So God give
    thee rede!" 130

"Aye," quoth the fox: "now hearken
    me,
In no single word will I lie to thee;
I am Reynard, thy friend of old,
And had'st thou afore-time thy coming
    told
Then in very sooth had I prayed for
    thee,
As boon, that thou should'st come here
    to me!"
" To thee ?" quoth the wolf, " I prithee
    tell,
What should I do there, in the well?"
Quoth the fox: "Nay, nay, thou art un-
    wise,
Here is the bliss of Paradise,   140
Here in plenty I ever fare
Free from trouble, and free from care,
Here be meat and drink enow,
And bliss that fadeth not, I trow,
Hunger herein shall ye never know,
Nor sorrow, nor any kind of woe,
Of every good is there plenty here —"
The wolf he laughed those words to hear:
"God give thee rede, art thou dead,
    i-troth,   149
Or yet of this world?" the wolf he quoth.
He spake again: "When dids't thou die?
And what art thou doing there, verily?
There are scarce passéd days but three
Since thou and thy wife ye supped with
    me,
Ye, and your children, small and great,
Ye all together with me ate."
"Yea," quoth the fox: "thou sayest
    sooth,
God be thanked, yet now hear the truth,
Now have I made a right fitting end, 159
Naught do I owe thee for that, my friend;
For all this world hath of good or gain
To dwell therein am I no more fain,
Why should I again to this world fare?
Therein is naught but woe and care!
In sin and uncleanness my life I past,
Here many a joy to my lot is cast,
Here be both sheep and goats, I ween!"
The wolf was vexed by hunger keen,

'T was over-long since he last might eat,
And when he thus heard him speak of
    meat   170
Right fain was he then to share the food;
"Ah!" quoth the wolf: "my comrade
    good,
Many a meal hast thou ta'en from me,
Let me, I pray thee, come down to thee!
And all, I promise, shall be forgiven —"
"Yea," quoth the fox: "an thou first
    wert shriven,
If all thy sins thou would'st now forsake,
And thyself to a better life betake,
Then would I in such wise pray for thee
That thou shouldest come adown to
    me!"   180
The wolf he quoth: "An that be so
To whom may I for confession go?
Here in this place be none alive
Who in this stress my sins could shrive;
Oft hast thou been my comrade dear,
Wilt thou now my confession hear?
And all my life will I truly tell —"
"Nay," quoth the fox: " that were not
    well."
Quoth the wolf: "For mercy I pray once
    more,
For in sooth I be a-hungeréd sore,   190
I wot to-night am I dead indeed
Save thou find counsel in this my need!
For the love of Christ do thou be my
    priest!" —
The wolf, he bowed adown his breast,
In sob and sighing forth he brake —
"Wilt thou," quoth the fox: "confession
    make,
One by one thy misdeeds unfold
That never a sin remain untold?"
"Yea," quoth the wolf: "that shall be
    my will —
All my life-days have I done ill,   200
Upon me lieth the widow's curse,
Therefore, I ween, do I fare the worse.
A thousand sheep have I torn and bit-
    ten,
And more, if the tale thereof were
    written!

Thereof do I now repent me sore —
Say, Master, needs must I tell thee
    more?"
"Yea," quoth the fox: "all must thou
    say,
Otherwise must thou forfeit pay."
"Friend," quoth the wolf: "forgive it
    me,
Oft have I spoken ill of thee,   210
Men said of thee when thou wert on
    life
That thou hadst ill dealings with my
    wife;
One time to watch ye was I fain,
In bed together I found ye twain.
Often times was I nigh to ye,
How ye fared together I needs must see,
I deemed, as many another doth,
That what I saw with mine eyes was
    sooth,
Therefore to me thou wast full loath —
Dear Gossip, I prithee, be not wroth!"
"Wolf," the fox quoth to him alway : 221
"All thou hast done before this day,
Be it in word, or deed, or will,
In each and every kind of ill,
All I forgive thee at this need."
"Now," quoth the wolf: "may Christ
    thee speed,
Now at last am I clean in life,
Little I reck for child or wife,
But tell me now what I needs must do,
And how I may come thy bliss unto?"
"Do?" quoth the fox: "that shalt thou
    hear,   231
See'st thou a bucket hang anear?
There is the entrance to Paradise,
Leap thou therein, an thou be wise,
So shalt thou be with me anon —"
Quoth the wolf: "That is lightly done!"
He sprang therein, and his weight 'gan
    tell,
(Of that the fox had advised him well)
The wolf he sank, the fox he rose,
Sorrow and fear the wolf he knows, 240
When he came mid-way adown the pit
The fox on the upward way he met;

"Friend," quoth the wolf: "what dost
    thou now?
What hast thou in mind? Where goest
    thou?"
"Whither I go?" the fox he said,
"I will up! so God give me aid!
Go thou down to thy meed withal,
Methinks thine earnings shall be but
    small!
Therefore am I both glad and blithe 249
That thou be shriven and clean of life,
A fitting knell I'll bid them ring,
And Mass for thy soul I'll have them
    sing!"

.   .   .   .

That wretch in the well he nothing
    found
Save water, by hunger he fast was
    bound,
At a banquet cold he needs must feed,
Frogs the dough for his bread must
    knead.
Down in the well the wolf, he stood,
Mad for hunger, I ween, his mood,
He cursed him roundly who brought
    him there,
The fox thereof had little care.   260
Nigh to a house it stood, the well,
Where many good Friars, I ween, did
    dwell,
And when it came that the night was
    done,
And the brethren must needs arise, each
    one,
To say their Mattins, and Morning-
    song,
One Friar was there, the rest among,
Who should them all from their sleep
    awake,
When they to the Chapel their way
    should take;
He bade them arise by one and one,
And come to the House-song, every
    one.   270
That same Friar he was hight Ailmer,
He was their Master-Cellarer,

It chanced he was gripped by thirst full
    strong
Ere yet they had finished their morning-
    song,
All alone to the well he went,
To quench his thirst was the brother
    bent;
He came to the well, and would water
    wind,
Heavy the weight he needs must find,
The friar he drew with all his might
Until that the wolf he hove in sight, 280
When he saw the wolf in the bucket sit,
He cried: "The Devil is in the pit!"
To the well the brethren hied each one

Well armed with pike, and staff, and
    stone,
Each with his weapon was not slack,
Woe worth him who a tool did lack!
They drew the wolf up e'en to the
    ground,
Many a foeman the wretch there found,
Fain would they chase the wolf that day,
Hunt him with hounds, and beat alway,
Fell and fiercely they smote him there,
Stung him with staves, and pierced with
    spear, 292
The fox betrayed him with guile, I wis,
For in sooth he found no kind of bliss,
Nor pardon for all he had done amiss!

THE LAND OF COCKAIGNE

FAR in the sea, and west of Spain,
There lieth a land, i-hight Cockaigne;
Beneath high Heaven there lies, I wis,
No land in goodness like to this!
Tho' Paradise be fair and bright
Cockaigne is e'en a gladder sight;
Paradise, what doth it bear
But trees, and grass, and flowerets
    fair?
Of joy and pleasure no lack is known,
But no meat is there save fruit alone: 10
In hall or bower is naught, for sure,
To quench the thirst, save water pure!
Two men only, I rede thee well,
Elias and Enoch, there may dwell;
Lonely I ween, their lot, and sore,
Who of comrades may have no more!

In Cockaigne is meat and drink,
Free from sorrow, care, and stint,
The meat is choice, the drink is clear,
At every meal throughout the year. 20
I say for sooth, this wide world round,
Its peer may nowhere else be found,
'Neath Heaven there is no land, I wis,
Of such abounding joy and bliss!

There is many a goodly sight,
'T is ever day, there falls no night,
There is no quarrel, there is no strife;
There is no death, but endless life;
There is no lack of wealth, nor cloth;
Nor man nor woman there waxeth
    wroth; 30
There is no serpent, wolf, nor fox,
Horse nor gelding, cow nor ox;
There is no goat, nor swine, nor sheep,
Never a steading, so God me keep!
Neither stallions, nor mares for brood,
The land is full of other good.
There is no fly, nor flea, nor louse,
In cloth nor bedding, town, nor house;
There is no thunder, sleet, nor hail,
No vile earth-worm, nor e'en a snail! 40
There is no storm, no rain, no wind;
There is no man nor woman blind;
But all is gladness, joy, and glee,
Oh! Well is him who there may be!

There be rivers great and fine,
Of oil, milk, honey, and eke of wine,
Water, it serveth naught, I ween,
Save for washing, and to be seen:

There be fruits of all kinds, I trow,
There is solace, and joy enow!   50

There is a right fair Friary,
Both of the White Friars, and the Grey;
There, I ween, be bowers and halls,
All of pasties be the walls,
Of flesh, of fish, of choicest meat,
The daintiest that a man may eat.
Of floury cakes the shingles all
On church and cloister, bower and hall;
The pinnacles be of plump puddings
Meet for princes, and eke for kings!   60
A man thereof may eat his fill,
Free from sorrow, of right good will;
All is common to young and old,
To stout and valiant, meek and bold.

There is a cloister fair and light,
Broad and long, a seemly sight:
The pillars of that cloister tall
Are wrought of crystal clear withal;
With every base and capital
Of jasper green, and of red coral.   70
In the meadow there is a tree,
Very pleasant it is to see,
The roots are ginger and spices good,
The branches all of liquorice wood,
Of choicest mace it is, the flower,
Cinnamon, the bark, of sweet odour,
Of gilly-flower cloves the fruit, I ween. —
No lack of cabobs there is seen —
Roses red, methinks, there be,
And snow-white lilies, fair to see,   80
That fade not either by day or night,
Methinks it should be a goodly sight!

.   .   .   .

Four be the wells in that Friary,
Of treacle one, and of healing whey,
Of balsam, and of spicéd wine,
Ever running, fair and fine,
With their streams to enrich the
        mould —
There be precious stones and gold;
There be pearl and sapphire rare,
Carbuncle red, and crystal fair.   90

Emerald, jacinth, chrysoprase,
Beryl, onyx, and eke topaze,
Amethyst, and chrysolite,
Chalcydone, and malachite.
Of birds 't were ill to count the tale,
Throstle, thrush, and nightingale;
Woodpeckers green, and larks there be,
And of all birds great company,
That never slack, but use their might
In merry song, both day and night.   100

And yet I do you more to wit —
Roasted geese upon the spit
Fly to that abbey, so God wot,
Crying, "Geese, all hot, all hot!"
Garlick they bring in plenty there,
Right so as cunning cooks prepare;
The laverocks too, I say for sooth,
Fly adown to each man's mouth,
Stewed they are, and right well done,   109
Stuffed with cloves, and with cinnamon.
Of any drink that there be, at will
Every man may take his fill.
When the friars they go to Mass
All the windows that be of glass
Turn themselves to crystal bright
That the brethren may have more light.
When the Masses all be said,
And the books aside are laid,
The crystal turns to glass once more,
Even as it had been afore.   120

.   .   .   .

Whoso will come that land unto
Sorry penance must he do;
Seven years long, in filth and grime
Must he wade, and all the time
Therein be plunged, up to the chin —
So shall he to that land win!
Lordings good, I 'ld have ye know,
Never shall ye thither go
Save that first ye take this chance,
And fulfil this sore penance,   130
So may ye this fair land gain,
And may never turn again.
Pray we God it so may be!
Amen, Amen, by Charity!

THE SEVEN SAGES OF ROME

Tale II

THE Emperor rose at dawn of day
And bade them bring his son straightway,
And hang the lad, ere it was long,
Upon a gallows high and strong.
The knights and townsfolk, high and low,
Much pity for the boy they show
That he should thus to death be dight,
And all of wrong, with naught of right. ·
A-horse came Master Bausillas,
Who the lad's master soothly was,   10
His pupil sore bestead must see,
Heavy at heart, I trow, was he.
To gallows-tree the lad must fare,
The Master rode in grief and care;
Unto the palace-gate he came,
His horse he leaveth at that same,
Fast doth he hie him to the hall —
The Emperor sits 'mid courtiers all —
Greeting he gave, the Master good;   19
The monarch spake, in mournful mood:
"To evil end may'st thou be brought
Who thus my son hast evil taught!"
Quoth Master Bausillas straightway:
"Why are ye vexed Sire? Tell me pray,
Ye who of old were meek and mild
Now wrongfully would slay your child!"
The Emperor, without more ado,
Quoth: " Flatterer, I'll slay thee too!
My son I gave unto thy care
To learn his book, in fashion fair,   30
Ill customs have ye taught him here,
For such ye sure shall pay full dear.
My son is reft of speech withal —
The Devil take ye, each and all!
With that he fain had forced my wife —
Therefore shall no man save his life;
But sure to death I'll have them done
Who should have better taught my son!"
"Nay, Sire," quoth Master Bausillas:
"That were great wrong, saving your
          grace,   40

Say that your son had vexed your wife
Were that a cause to take his life?"
Quoth he: "I found my wife forlorn,
Her face and raiment rent and torn,
If one be ta'en in act and deed
Of other witness is small need."
The Master quoth: "Sire, have a care,
Trow not a step-dame's tale tho' fair,
Her bolt is all too swiftly shot,
Rather for ill than good, I wot!   50
If thou for her shalt slay thy son
Such payment may'st thou well have
          won
As fell unto that knight so true
Who once his faithful greyhound slew."
To hear that tale the Emperor prayed —
Straightway the Master answer made:
"Sire, while that I may tell my tale
Thy son may suffer mickle bale,
Thus were my travail all for naught —
I pray that he be hither brought,   60
Give him respite, and, without fail,
I'll tell to ye a wondrous tale."
The Emperor quoth: "I grant the
          boon."
A sergeant went his way right soon,
And brought the lad into the hall
Before his sire, and courtiers all;
Obeisance fitting doth he make
To all, yet never word he spake.
The Emperor quoth: " Now this thy tale
Set forth, Bausillas, without fail."   70

He quoth: "Sire, in this same citie,
Upon a Feast of Trinitie,
A tournament men fain would hold
For many a noble knight, and bold,
On meadow green, with knightly play —
And it befell on that same day
The knight I speak of, at that stound,
At home had left his good greyhound.
His manor by that meadow stood
Encircled by the river's flood,   80

And very ancient was each wall
By hole and cranny pierced withal.
The knight had wed a lady fair,
A goodly child she to him bare;
Cherished he was by nurses three,
One gave him suck, it seemeth me;
One washed and bathed him as 't was
    need,
Bedded, and dressed in goodly weed;
The third she washed his sheets full oft,
And rocked the babe to slumber soft. 90
The dóg, of whom but now I told, *
A right good hound it was, and bold,
Therewith had he been trained so well
For naught that knight his dog would
    sell.
The knight then, armed in fitting weed,
Full soon had leapt upon his steed,
With shield on arm, and shaft in hand,
To joust with knights of that same
    land,
Full soon unto the field he came —
His gentle lady, at that same, 100
Beheld him from the turret stair,
Full fain to see the tourney fair.
The nurses said they too would go
And look upon the knightly show,
The three they gat forth from the hall —
Setting the cradle 'neath a wall
Wherein the child fast sleeping lay,
The three they went to see the play
E'en from a secret place beside. —
Now hearken what befell that tide. —
An adder lurked within that wall, 111
It heard the sound of hoof-beats fall,
And creeping forth the cause to know
Beheld the child who lay below.
Down to the ground it made its way,
Intent, the child forthwith to slay.
The greyhound wandering thereabout
Saw where the snake crept stealthy out,
The adder did he swift assail,
Taking it tightly by the tail, 120
But soon the adder bit him sore
So that he dare keep hold no more.
Loosed from his jaws, the adder crept
To where the babe in cradle slept,

Full fain was he the child to sting —
Once more the hound did on him spring,
Amid the back he held him tight,
Shook him on high with all his might,
Betwixt the adder and the hound
The cradle fell unto the ground, 130
They over-turned it in the fray
So that the child face downward lay;
The four posts held it o'er the child,
Unharmed was he, and undefiled.
The adder bit the greyhound there
On side, on back, yea, everywhere;
The adder bleeds, e'en so the hound,
Fierce was the fight they fought that
    stound!
At last the dog the snake doth kill,
Tare him to pieces at his will; 140
When they had done, then all around
With blood was dyed and stained the
    ground.

" The tournament to end is brought,
The knights, I trow, they stay for naught,
Each takes his harness as he may
And swiftly goes the homeward way.
The nurses to the hall they go,
Great was their grief, and great their
    woe;
The cradle with the child they found
O'erturned, it stood upon the ground; 150
They deemed the child were dead, i' fay,
Therefore they looked not where it lay,
But all about they saw the blood —
Such was their woe they waxed nigh
    wood!
Great sorrow had they in their heart —
The greyhound howled for bitter smart,
They deemed he had waxed wood and
    wild,
And, in his madness, slain the child.
The lady oft in swoon did fall
There, 'mid her maidens in the hall: 160
'Alas,' she said, 'that I was born
Now my fair child from me is torn!'
The knight came home at that same
    tide
And all his men were at his side,

He saw them sorrow evermore,
For the child's sake they wept full sore.
The knight he asked what ailed them
          there?
The tale they swift to him declare,
The lady said: 'Sir, this your hound
Our child hath eaten on this ground, 170
Save that thou here shalt take his life
I'll slay myself with this, my knife.'
The knight, he went without delay;
The good dog met him on the way,
To fawn upon his lord was fain
Barking the while, for very pain,
To run about he might not cease,
The venom gave him little peace.
With wagging tail fawned on his lord —
The knight in haste drew forth his
          sword,   180
Upon the back-bone smote the hound,
Clave him asunder to the ground.
The greyhound good, he lieth dead —
The knight unto the cradle sped,
Wherein the infant peaceful slept
The while the women sorely wept.
The knight, he found the adder dead,
And torn to pieces in that stead,
With blood of snake, and blood of
          hound,   189
Stained were the cradle and the ground.
The cradle turned, the child they see
Alive, and marvel mightily —
They saw the hound, the snake had
          slain —
The knight, he sorroweth amain,
His grief, I trow, was grim and great:
'Sorrow,' he quoth, 'shall be his mate
Right certainly, and without fail,
Who hearkeneth to a woman's tale!
Alas!' he quoth 'for so did I!'
With that he mourned, and made great
          cry,   200
He called his household less and more,
And showed to them his sorrow sore,
How that his child was hale and sound,
But he had slain his faithful hound
All for his valour, and good deed,
In that he trowed his lady's rede.

'Alas,' he quoth, 'in slaying thee
Myself must rue it bitterly,
Good knights and true I'll teach each
          one
The counsel of their wives to shun,   210
He sat him down in dole so drear,
And bade a groom take off his gear,
His garments gay aside did throw,
And barefoot all, he forth would go.
He took no leave of wife nor child
But gat him to the woodland wild,
In forest far from men would be
That no man might his sorrow see,
And suffered many a sorry stound
For grief of this, his good greyhound. 220
Thus, thro' the counsel of his wife,
In woe henceforth he passed his life.
Sir Emperor, so may ye share
Sorrow and shame, dishonour bear,
If ye should slay, against all right,
Your son, as did his hound the knight,
O'er hasty he, of ruthless deed,
And of his wife he wrought the rede."

The Emperor sware: "By Jesu free,
Such fortune ne'er shall fall to me,   230
And Master, here I soothly say
My son, he shall not die to-day!"
"Yea Sire," quoth Master Bausillas:
Follow my counsel in this case,
For all the world shall him despise
Who trusts his wife, nor heeds the
          wise."
The Emperor quoth: "Ye rightly say,
I will not do what she doth pray."
His son he back to prison sent,
Upon his way the Master went.   240

Tale XI

When all from out the hall had gone
The Emperor sought his bower anon,
The Empress did he find therein
Sorry of cheer, of mournful mien;
"Lady," he quoth: "what aileth thee?"
She answered: "Sire, 't is naught to
          thee,

Wilt not avenge me of my foe,
Therefore I think from thee to go
Unto my kin, who hold me dear,
And never more to come thee near,   250
Liever were I to wend my way
Than dwell in dole by night and day!"
He answered: "Have I done amiss
Speak, and I'll right the wrong, I wis!"
She quoth: "It profits naught, by Heaven,
Thy ruin shall be thy Masters seven,
To whom thou lendest ear alway
Aye sparing him who shall thee slay.
To thee may well befall such thing
As fell to Herod's lot, the king,   260
Who lost his sight for evil rede
'T were well if thou this tale wouldst heed!"
"Lady," he quoth: "I pray of thee
That self-same tale now tell to me."
"Yea Sire," she said: "with right good cheer
God send thee grace to rightly hear!"

"Once Sire, there lived in high estate
An Emperor of honour great,
Herod, I trow, that monarch's name,
A mighty prince of noble fame;   270
And seven clerks had he always
Like these, whom ye for wisdom praise,
And whatsoe'er was in his thought
After their rede he ever wrought.
The seven clerks, they made decree,
Stablished a custom, wrongfully,
That who so dreamed in any night,
And gat him to the clerks, forthright,
Bringing with him a crown of gold,
And to the clerks his vision told,   280
That they thereto would take intent,
And tell him what the dream had meant.
And some was false, and some was true,
Yet many folk to them they drew,
Burghers, and peasants, high and low,
The meaning of their dream would know.
And nobles came from divers lands
Each brought a besant in his hand —

They wrought this craft for many a day
Till richer than their lord were they.   290

"The Emperor, upon a day,
Thought he would wend him forth to play,
Out of the gate he fain would ride
With him his men on either side,
Sudden he waxed blind as a stone —
Unto his clerks he sent anon,
And asked them what had made him blind?
But ne'er a reason might they find;   298
For four-score days they asked respite,
Within that time they hoped they might,
By lore of books, find reason why
Their lord waxed blind thus suddenly.
The Emperor gat him home again —
The clerks, they wrought with mickle pain
Within their books the cause to find
Why thus the Emperor was blind.

"The clerks soon after on a day,
Met with an old man in the way,
To him they now recount their tale,
And he quoth: 'Masters, without fail,   310
No man may help ye, more or less,
Saving a child, who's fatherless,
True counsel shall he give to ye,
But I wot not where he may be.'
The Masters would no longer bide,
To seek that child they forth would ride,
And some rode East, and some rode West,
Where'er they thought to find him best,
A fortnight thus they fruitless ride,
Seeking the child on every side.   320
At last their way led thro' a town
Where children sported up and down,
They saw one boy who smote another,
Calling him 'Blockhead, Devil's Brother,
Thou art a son of Devil's blood,
Evil dost work, and never good,
Fatherless blockhead, I thee call!'
Thereto agreed the children all.

Two of the Masters right well heard 329
The children's striving, word by word;
Then Merlin saw he was espied,
And straitly sware his fellows lied,
He saith: 'Now here two clerks I see,
In many a place they seek for me,
To Rome, methinks, they 'ld have me
    go
Judgment on certain points to show.'
The Masters came unto that child,
And spake to him in accents mild:
'Child, tell us what shall be thy name?'
'Merlin,' he answered at that same. 340
With that, a goodman of that land
Came with a besant in his hand
To Merlin gave it presently —
He quoth: 'Full hasty Sir, shalt be
The meaning of thy dream to know
That may full well misfortune show;
But since thou profferest such meed
Ready am I thy dream to read.
There, in thy midden, didst thou see
A well spring forth with waters free, 350
And of that water sweet, I think,
Thou, and thy neighbours oft did drink.
This is the meaning. — In that mould
Shalt find a hoard of good red gold,
Which in thy midden hid doth lie,
Thither we 'll go, the truth to try.'
Then with that man they all would go,
For all were fain the truth to know;
Their way unto the place they made —
The child bade bring forth pick and
    spade, 360
A hole they delved, deep in the ground,
There, as he said, a hoard they found,
For good red gold the hole did fill,
The good-man bade take at their will,
His fellow towns-men, all and each
With that same treasure were made
    rich;
The Masters took gold at their will,
But Merlin, he refused it still.
To Rome their way the Masters make,
The little lad with them they take; 370
Then, as they went upon their way,
They asked the child if he could say

Or any certain reason find
Wherefore the Emperor was blind?
Merlin he quoth: 'Assuredly,
I well can tell the reason why —'
Then were the Masters blithe and gay,
Swiftly to Rome they took their way,
And ere the term was at an end
Safely to court their way they wend. 380
Then to the Emperor thus they say:
'Sir, we be come on this set day.'
He saith: 'An answer do ye bring?'
'Nay, Sire' they quoth, 'by Heaven's
    King,
But Sire, a child we here have brought
Who well may tell ye all your thought.'
The Emperor said: 'Ye surety stand
For this, upon your life and land?'
'Yea, Sire,' they said, 'our all we 'll
    stake
That he an answer true shall make.' 390
The Emperor quoth: 'Tell, if thou may.'
The child spake: 'Swiftly go thy way
Unto thy chamber, there, aright,
I 'll say why thou hast lost thy sight.'
Into his chamber went anon
The Emperor, and his clerks each one,
Upon his bed he sat him there
And bade the child the truth declare.
Quoth Merlin to the Emperor: 399
'Beneath thy bed, in this same bower,
Beneath the ground, yea, deep adown,
Lieth a boiling calderon,
That bubbles sevenfold, day and night,
And Sire, that has thee reft of sight,
For while these bubbles boiling rise
The sight is banished from thine eyes;
But might a man those bubbles stay
Thine eyes were fair and bright alway.'

" The Emperor marvelled much at this,
And bade them move his bed, I wis, 410
Full deep they diggéd at that same
Until they to the caldron came,
The seven bubbles boiling see,
And know the lad spake veritie.
Then quoth the Emperor straightway:
'Child, I will do thy will alway,

Some reason canst thou find, I ween,
Of what this calderon may mean?'
The child quoth: 'Yea Sire, without
    doubt,
But bid thy Masters stay without,   420
The tale to end then shall ye know.'
The Emperor bade them forth to go,
No man of them might longer stay —
The child began his tale straightway;
'Those seven bubbles shall ye know
Thy seven Masters soothly show,
For they have stablished customs new
The which ye shall full sorely rue.
If any man dream, night or day,
That they shall come to them straight-
    way,   430
And bring a besant in that stead
That so their dream be rightly read.
The dream at will they read alway
And thus thy clerks the folk betray,
And for this sin, Sire, do I find,
Thou of thine eyes be waxen blind.'
The Emperor quoth: 'If it be so
Tell me what it were best to do?'
The lad quoth: 'Sire, I trow 't were best
By one of them the truth to test,   440
If ye the oldest Master slay
The largest bubble sure shall stay.'

The Emperor bade his men off-smite
The oldest Master's head, forthright,
And even as that deed was done
The largest bubble ceased anon.
With that the Emperor, straightway,
Bade men the Masters all to slay;
Then cold and calm the water grew,   449
And joy henceforth the Emperor knew,
Merlin, he washed his eyes that tide,
Then could he see to walk and ride:
The Emperor thus regained his sight,
His seven Masters lost their might.

"Sir, so they blind thee, and beguile,
Thy Masters seven, with cunning wile,
For if thou follow this their rede
An evil road they will thee lead,
As Herod, for his trusting came
Well nigh unto an end of shame."   460
The Emperor quoth: "Nay, Lady fair,
Such shame shall never be my share,
Sooner shall they to death be dight!"
"Certes," she quoth, "there art thou
    right!"
"Lady, I pledge me in this stead
To-morrow shall my son be dead,
And none shall free him from his bale."
Here endeth the eleventh tale.

PROVERBIAL AND DIDACTIC

PRECEPTS OF ALFRED

THERE sat, in the town of Seaford,
Full many a thane and lord,
Earls were there, proud in might,
And each one a gallant knight.
There Aelfric, the earl, I saw,
A wise man he, in their law;
And Alfred, too, might ye see,
Shepherd of England he,
Of English men was he king,
And of England was he darling.　　10
His folk would he teach right well
As now ye may hear me tell,
Good counsel he gave, wise rede
How they their lives should lead.

I

Alfred, he ruled England
As king, with his strong right hand,
He was king, he was clerk as well —
God's Word he loved right well.
Very wise was he in rede,
And wary, too, in his deed:　　20
Wisest was he of men
Who dwelt in England then.

II

Quoth Alfred, England's king,
For Englishmen's profiting:
"An ye, my folk so dear,
The words of your lord would hear,
Guide ye aright he could
And teach ye things wise and good —
How ye in this world may share
Worship and honour fair,　　30
And yet save your soul, I wis,
And get ye to Christ in bliss."
(Wise was the counselling
Spoken by Alfred the king —)
"Mildly I'ld 'monish here
Ye all, my friends so dear,

(Both rich and poor are ye,
Yet all ye my folk shall be,)
I would that all men here
Our Lord Christ fitly fear,　　40
Love Him, withouten strife,
For He is the Lord of Life;
He is One God in Three,
Good o'er all Goodness He —
Joy, o'er all Joyfulness —
Bliss, o'er all earthly Bliss.
A Man among men shall He be,
The mildest of Masters He;
As Father, this folk He'll guide,
As Comforter, Help provide,　　50
Righteous His Governing —
And so Mighty is He as King
That lack He shall never know —
Nor shall he his will forego
Who fitting honour alway
To God in this world doth pay."

III

Thus quoth Alfred the king,
For Englishmen's profiting:
"His crown may no king wear
'Neath Christ, nor rule fitly bear,　　60
Save that he learnéd be
In book-lore, cunningly,
So that his wits, all five,
May thro' his knowledge thrive.
In letters he versed must be,
That he himself may see
How he his land should school,
And hold it in lawful rule."

IV

Thus quoth Alfred the king:
"The earl and the atheling　　70
Under the king they be,
To rule the land lawfully.

The clerk, I ween, and the knight,
Judgment shall give aright,
Equal to poor and rich,
The judgment, for all and each.
For e'en as a man doth sow
That crop, I ween, must he mow,
And each man's doom to his door
Returneth, evermore."   80

V

Thus quoth Alfred the king:
"The knight shall this service bring,
To stand upon watch and ward
Wary, the land to guard;
With hunger and harness prest,
That so the Church may have rest,
And the churl abide in peace
To gather his land's increase.
In such wise to sow his seed,
In such wise to mow his mead,   90
In such wise his plough to drive,
That all men therefrom may thrive.
This is the law of the knight —
See that he hold it aright!"

VI

Thus quoth Alfred the king:
"The man who in youth doth bring
Good will to his fostering,
Is fain to learn wisdom and wit,
And the lore that in books be writ,
I trow in old age, that he   100
A right good teacher shall be.
But he who in youth doth prove
That for learning he hath small
        love,
Careth naught for wisdom and wit,
And the lore that in books be writ;
That which he lacked in his youth
His old age shall rue, for sooth.
For old age cometh apace,
And sickness he needs must face,
And his hopes, that full high had
        been,   110
To loss are they turned, I ween.
In such wise do they him betray,
In such wise vanish away."

VII

Thus quoth Alfred the king:
"Weal is a worthless thing
Save Wisdom with it it bring;
For tho' a man have and hold
Seventy acres, all told,
And tho' those acres were sown
With good red gold alone,   120
And that gold should grow, I ween,
As groweth the grass so green,
That man shall, for all his share
Of wealth, none the better fare,
Save friends for himself he win
Ere ever his toil begin;
For naught but a stone is gold
Save a wise man have it in hold."

VIII

Thus quoth Alfred the king:
"Youth, be thou 'ware of this thing; 130
Yield not to sorrowing
Tho' the lot that to thee may fall
Pleasure thee not at all;
And tho' thou shalt hold far less
Than the goods thou would'st fain
        possess.
For God may give, an He will,
Good, in the stead of Ill,
Weal in the stead of Woe —
Well is he who doth find it so."

IX

Thus quoth Alfred the king,   140
For Englishmen's profiting: —
"A hard task it is to row
When the salt sea doth 'gainst thee flow;
So is it to labour and toil
If ill fortune thine efforts foil.
He who, in the days of his youth,
So striveth that he, in truth,
May win this world's wealth alway
And so, in his old age, may
Rest, and enjoy his ease,   150
And eke, with his goods' increase,
Serve God, ere he hence shall go,
His toil he doth well bestow!"

X

Thus quoth Alfred the king:
"Full many shall think a thing
In which be small profiting;
A man counteth on length of days
But ill Fate him full oft betrays,
For even as he doth find
His life be most to his mind, 160
That life is he forced to leave
Altho' he full sore may grieve.
For there groweth no herb so good
In meadow, I ween, nor wood,
That the life of a man it may
Prolong to an endless day.
And no man the hour doth know
When he from this world must go;
None knoweth the way of his end,
Or whither he hence shall wend. 170
The Lord of all Power, I wot,
He casteth and ruleth, our lot,
And God, He alone, doth know
When we from this life must go."

XI

Thus quoth Alfred the king,
For every man's profiting:
"If so be that thou silver and gold,
And the wealth of this world, shalt hold,
Beware lest it so betide
That thy profiting turn to pride. 180
'T is not from thy sire thou dost own
Thy wealth, 't is from God a loan,
In the hour that His Will is so
Therefrom must we surely go;
This life of ours must we quit
And all that we hold, to wit,
And our foes shall seize and hold
What once to our lot was told,
The treasure we needs must leave —
For us shall they little grieve!" 190

XII

Thus quoth Alfred the king:
"See not over much trust thou bring
In the tide that floweth fair —
If treasure shall be thy share,

If thou hast money, and more,
Of gold and silver a store,
Yet all may crumble to naught,
To dust may thy wealth be brought —
God liveth, nor waxeth old —
Many a man, for his gold, 200
Hath won him God's Wrath alway,
And for his silver, such pay
That his soul he at last hath lost —
In such wise must he pay the cost
That 't were better for him, I ween,
If born he had never been."

XIII

Thus quoth Alfred the king:
"My folk, give me hearkening;
Since yours it shall be, the need,
I will give unto ye good rede. 210
Wit and Wisdom, believe me well,
Do all other things excel,
He safe and secure may sit
Who for comrades hath Wisdom and
Wit.
For tho' riches may flit away
His Wisdom shall with him stay,
And never that man shall perish
Who Wisdom as friend shall cherish,
But harm shall he from him hold
The while his life-days be told." 220

XIV

Thus quoth Alfred the king:
"An thou goest sorrowing
Then speak it not loud nor low,
But whisper thy saddle-bow,
And ride thence singing away —
So that the folk may say,
(Who little thy thoughts can tell,)
'This life, it pleaseth him well!'
For if sorrow draw to thee near
And thy foeman thereof shall hear 230
Tho' he pity thee much to thy face
To thy back he will mock thee apace.
Thy grief to a man may'st tell
Who in sooth may wish thee full well,
While another will hear thee complain
And wish thee as much woe again!

Thy sorrow hide well in thine heart
For so it shall bring thee less smart;
The servant should never be told   239
What the master's heart doth hold."

XV

Thus quoth Alfred the king,
For the husband's profiting:
"An thou seekest a wife, beware;
Choose her not for her face so fair,
Nor for gold, nor for other thing
That she unto thee may bring.
But mark well what her ways may be
For needs must she shew them thee;
He who chooseth wealth, I trow,
Oft findeth evil enow;   250
And oft, with a face full fair,
Hath he frailty for his share.
Woe to him who an evil wife
Bringeth to share his life,
I ween he shall little thrive
In his time, who shall evil wive.
For she worketh him here on earth
Sorrow in place of mirth;
And many a man doth sing   259
When his bride he doth homeward bring,
Did he know what he brought, in
          truth,
He had wept, for sorrow and ruth!"

XVI

Thus quoth Alfred the king,
For the husband's profiting:
"See thou be never so mad,
Tho' the wine-cup make thee glad,
As to tell thy wife, loud or still,
All that is in thy will.
For if it should so fall out
That thy foemen were round about,   270
And that thou had'st made her wroth
With thy words, then, by my troth,
Never, for living thing,
Thou could'st her to silence bring,
Upbraid thee, she would alway,
Thine ill fortune to all display.
Word-mad is woman, I ween,
Her tongue aye too swift hath been,

And rule it, she never may
Tho' such were her will alway!"   280

XVII

Thus quoth Alfred the king,
For the husband's profiting:
"Leisure and pride, alway,
Oft lead a young wife astray;
So that oft she the thing hath done
That were better if left undone.
And yet, I think me, 't were light
Vice and evil to put to flight,
Were she willing to toil and sweat,
And her hand to labour set;   290
Tho' 't is ill to bow, in the end
The tree breaks that will not bend.
The cat learneth to mouse, I ween,
Where the mother her guide hath
          been.
But woe to the man who shall let
His wife the mastery get!
For never shall he be heard,
Nor be lord o'er his will and word;
With him shall she sternly deal,
To his woe, and not to his weal,   300
Of gladness is he forlorn
Whom his wife doth hold in scorn;
As an apple is fair to see
When the taste thereof sour shall be,
So with woman it doth befall —
She is fair in her father's hall,
Sweet to a man's embrace —
And yet she doth bring disgrace.
So full many men there be
Who a-horse be goodly to see,   310
Yet as friends are worth naught to
          thee —
Haughty are they upon steed,
And worthless in hour of need."

XVIII

Thus quoth Alfred the king:
"I rede thee for profiting
That thou be not too swift to heed
Thy wife's counsel, nor follow her rede;
For so that she wroth may be
For word or deed, verily,

She weepeth for angry mood 320
More oft than for reason good.
She maketh plaint, loud, and still,
But that she may have her will;
She weepeth some other while
Because she would thee beguile;
Solomon saith indeed
That women give evil rede,
Would'st thou her counsel follow
She bringeth thee swift to sorrow.
And as the old song doth say: 330
'Bubbles rise swift, and swift pass
away';
And 't was said by the folk of old:
'Women's counsel is counsel cold.'
And that man doth come to ill
Who is led by a woman's will.
But that a good woman, God wot,
Is a good thing, I doubt it not;
Well for him, who, from out all other,
Shall choose her, and ne'er another."

XIX

Thus quoth Alfred the king, 340
For every man's profiting:
"Full many a man, in thought,
Hath that which small good hath
wrought,
That he hath a friend for his share
In the man who speaketh him fair; —
To his face, he doth give him praise,
To his back, he maligneth his ways.
But his wealth, an the truth be
told,
A man may the longer hold
If he ever to trust be slow 350
Where speech doth more swiftly flow.
Then believe not everything
Which thou hearest men to sing,
For of soft speech many shall be
Who would lightly do ill to thee;
Nor canst thou lightly conceive
In what wise he will thee deceive."

XX

Thus quoth Alfred the king,
For every man's profiting:

"By wise saws a man waxeth wise; 360
With himself, too, his wisdom lies,
For by falsehood, he winneth hate,
And by ill deeds, a worthless state.
For the grasping hand alway
The head must oft forfeit pay.
Keep thee from falsehood's rede,
And shun every evil deed,
And so, where'er thou shalt dwell,
The folk, they shall love thee well.
And of thy neighbour take heed, 370
For he may be good at need.
If to market or church thou shalt fare
Make to thee friends everywhere;
Whether rich, whether poor, they be,
Of all alike, verily.
Then steadfast and sure thy seat
For abiding, an seem thee meet,
Or secure shalt thou journey still
Thro' the land, an it be thy will."

XXI

Thus quoth Alfred the king. 380
For every man's profiting:
"The wealth that this world hath
brought
I ween, it shall turn to naught,
And the treasure a man doth hold
Shall melt into muck and mould.
And our life shall be swiftly past,
But a little space shall it last.
For e'en an it did betide
That a man ruled the world so wide
Yea, and all joys might win 390
Of the joys that be here within,
Yet neither for gladness nor gold
His life might he longer hold,
But all must be forfeited
When but a few years be sped.
And then shall this earthly bliss
Be turnéd to bale I wis,
Save that we bend us still
To follow and work Christ's Will.
Now bethink us, and take good heed 400
Our life in such wise to lead
As Christ in His Word doth tell;
For so may we hope full well

To be honoured by Him alway.
For thus doth Solomon say:
'The man who doth well below
Hereafter reward shall know.'
He leaveth his life behind,
And fareth, reward to find."

XXII

Thus quoth Alfred the king,   410
For every man's profiting:
"I rede thee be ne'er so bold
As to wrangle against a scold;
Nor chide 'gainst a foolish tale
For error shall aye prevail.
And ne'er, an thou wouldst not rue,
Begin to tell tidings new;
And at every freeman's board
Be thou sparing of thy word.
The wise man his task hath done   420
With few words, and may much have
        won;
A fool's bolt full soon is shot, —
And I hold him a fool, God wot,
Who sayeth all in his will
When his profit were to be still.
A tongue breaketh bones full oft
Tho' itself be boneless and soft!"

XXIII

Thus quoth Alfred the king:
"The wise child bliss shall bring

To his father; if so it be   430
That a bairn be born to thee,
The while he be young and small
Teach him good customs all;
Then, as he shall wax, and grow,
He shall turn his mind thereunto;
And the better shall be his worth
The while he abide on earth.
But if thou shalt let him go
In this world, to and fro,
Ever, both loud and still,   440
Working but his own will,
Then as the years o'er him roll
Thou shalt him no more control
Than thou rulest death; I trow,
That shall bring thee grief enow —
Oft shall he thy word transgress,
And bring thee to heaviness.
'T were better for thee, I ween,
That born he had never been;
For better an unborn child   450
Than a son unruly and wild.
The man who the rod doth spare
And letteth his young child fare
In such wise that it beareth the rule,
And he may not teach it, nor school,
When he cometh to years so hoar
Methinks he shall rue it sore!"

        Amen.

Expliciunt Dicta Regis Alfredi.

THE PROVERBS OF HENDYNGE

Who would learn of Wisdom's rede
Let him take to Hendynge heed,
Marcolf's son was he;
Laws and customs, not a few,
Did he teach to many a shrew,
As his wise should be.

Jesu Christ, Our Help in thrall,
Who hath died to save us all
Nailéd to the Tree,
Teach us Wisdom's way to wend   10

That we serve thee to the end,
Amen, par Charitie.
"Good beginning maketh good ending,"
        quoth Hendynge.

Wit and Wisdom learn full fain,
See none other thee restrain,
Be in Wisdom free;
Better walk in Wisdom's way
Than go clad in rich array
Wheresoe'er thou be.   20

"Wit and Wisdom be a good garri-
son,"
        quoth Hendynge.

Here on earth is ne'er a man,
Let him try as try he can,
If he bide at home,
Who such knowledge may attain
As that man, for learning fain,
Who afar doth roam.
"So many Folk, so many Fashions," 29
        quoth Hendynge.

Tho' the child be dear, I wis
An it doeth aught amiss,
Spare the rod for naught;
An its way it goeth free,
Willy, nilly, it shall be
But a good-for-naught.
"Lief child behoveth lore,"
        quoth Hendynge.

Wisdom thou shalt win to thee
From what thou dost hear and see   40
Man, in this thy youth,
Thou in age shalt surely follow,
Both at eve, and on the morrow,
Thine it is, in sooth.
"What thou young dost hold, thou shalt
    lose not old,"
        quoth Hendynge.

If thou list a sin to do,
And thy thoughts be turned thereto,
Good 't is to refrain;
For when heat be overcome,   50
And thy wit again hast won,
Thou shalt count it gain.
"Let lust overgo, liking shall follow,"
        quoth Hendynge.

Art thou light of thought withal,
That thou should'st thro' weakness
    fall
In a wicked sin,
Be that fault so rarely told
That in sin thou grow not old,

Nor shalt die therein.   60
"Better be eye-sore than blind,"
        quoth Hendynge.

Men may teach a simple child
Teachable of mood, and mild,
With but little lore;
But an ye would further go
Pain and trouble shall ye know
Ere ye teach him more.
"The simple son is taught right soon,"
        quoth Hendynge.

Would'st from fleshly lusts be free   71
Thou must fight, and swiftly flee
Both with eye and heart.
Fleshly lust, it bringeth shame,
What the Body thinketh game
Makes the Soul to smart.
"He fights well who flees well,"
        quoth Hendynge.

Wise men ne'er of words are free,
For they will begin no glee   80
Ere they tune their pipe;
Fools be fools, as may be seen
By their words, they speak them
    green,
Ere that they be ripe.
"A Fool's bolt is soon shot,"
        quoth Hendynge.

See thou ne'er thy foeman tell
Shame or loss that thee befell,
Nor thy care nor woe;
He will try, an so he may,   90
Both by night, and eke by day
One woe to make two.
"Tell never thy foe if thy foot acheth,"
        quoth Hendynge.

Hast of bread and ale no lack
Put it not all in thy sack,
Deal it freely out;
If thy meals dost freely share
Then where men have meat to spare,

Thou go'st not without. 100
"Better an apple given than eaten,"
                    quoth Hendynge.

Yet, the while I lived on earth,
I have deemed of little worth
Wine from other's store;
That which I may call mine own,
Wine and water, stock and stone,
That doth please me more.
"Best be our own Brand," 109
                    quoth Hendynge.

If thou lackest meat or cloth
Be not for that cause too wroth
Tho' thy debtor stay;
He that still hath his good plough
And of worldly good enow,
Knoweth no care alway.
"Good-less is greedy,"
                    quoth Hendynge.

Art thou rich in house and hold
Be not thou for that too bold, 120
Nor wax wood and wild;
Measure shew in everything,
That shall sure a blessing bring,
Be thou meek and mild.
"Full cup needs steady hand,"
                    quoth Hendynge.

If an old man thou shalt be
Take no young maid unto thee
For to be thy spouse,
Tho' thou shew her love, I trow, 130
She shall flout thee oft enow
E'en in thine own house.
"Oft a man doth sing
When he home doth bring
His young wife;
Did he know what he brought
He had wept, methought,
The rest of his life,"
                    quoth Hendynge.

Tho' thou thinkest much, withal, 140
Guard thy tongue as with a wall,

Speak not all thy rede;
He who swallows down his speech
Ere unto his lips it reach,
Findeth friends at need.
"The tongue breaketh bone, tho' itself
    it hath none,"
                    quoth Hendynge.

Many a knave, I trow, there be,
Who, if men but little fee
Give him, wrath doth show, 150
I say: 'He doth well by me
Who doth give a little fee
When he naught doth owe.'
"Who little doth give is fain I should
    live,"
                    quoth Hendynge.

If it please thee to do ill
When the world is at thy will,
Then of this take heed,
If from thine estate thou fall
That which thou hast brewed withal, 160
Shalt thou drink at need.
"The better thou be, the better thee
    be-see,"
                    quoth Hendynge.

Tho', forsooth, 't would please thee
    well
In a goodly house to dwell
Thou must need abide;
Best within a hut to be
Till thou feel that thou art free
From all taint of pride.
"Neath a bush may ye hide, and the
    storm abide," [1] 170
                    quoth Hendynge.

No man wretched do I hold
Tho' unto his lot be told
That which makes him smart;
When man goeth most in fear
God, I trow, the prayer shall hear
Offered from true heart.

[1] Cf. Scotch proverb. "He 'll gae daft on a horse that 's prood on a ponie."

"When Bale is highest, Boot is nigh-
    est,"
             quoth Hendynge.

Draw thy hand back with all speed 180
When they do thee an ill deed,
Whom didst help with store;
So that child withdraws his hand
From the fire, and from the brand,
Who was burnt afore.
"A burnt child dreads the fire,"
             quoth Hendynge.

To some men I've lent my cloth
Who have made me feel right wroth
Ere it came again; 190
He that served me so, i-fay,
Tho' such loan right oft he pray,
He shall lose his pain!
"Seldom comes loan laughing home,"
             quoth Hendynge.

If thou trust to borrowing
Thou shalt lack for many a thing,
Tho' thou like it ne'er;
But if thou thine own hast won
All thy woe is overcome, 200
Thou hast no more care.
"A man's ain is his ain, another's, but
    blame,"
             quoth Hendynge.

This world's love I hold not dear,
Little reck I who may hear
What I speak on high;
Well I see that oft one brother
Careth little for the other,
Be he out of eye.
"Far from eye, far from heart," 210
             quoth Hendynge.

That man who betrayeth me
And of my goods maketh free
His own fame to win,
For the veriest cur I take
Who at board the bread shall break
His own hall within.

"Of unbought hide ye may make thongs
    wide,"
             quoth Hendynge.

Many say: "An rich I were 220
No man should with me compare
For my gifts so free;
But when he much goods hath gotten,
This free hand is all forgotten,
And laid under knee.
"He is free of his horse who never had
    none,"
             quoth Hendynge.

Many a man of poor estate
Doth his daughter lightly mate
Nor is better sped, 230
Who, if he a wise man were,
Might, with but a little care,
Have her better wed.
"Lightly won is lightly held,"
             quoth Hendynge.

Riches, hard to get they be,
And their going ill to see,
Wise man, think on this;
All too dear is bought the ware
That may never, free from care, 240
Please man's heart, I wis.
"Dear is bought the honey that is licked
    off the thorn,"
             quoth Hendynge.

Ye who fain would cross the flood
If the wind be wild and wood
Bide ye quiet and still;
Bide thee still, if so thou may,
Thou shalt have, another day,
Weather to thy will. 249
"He abideth well who waiteth well,"
             quoth Hendynge.

But an ill hap his shall be
Who a-ship shall set to sea
When the wind is wood;
Be he come unto the deep
He may wring his hands and weep

In right dreary mood.
"Rashness oft rueth,"
                quoth Hendynge.

Trow ye well, an evil man   260
May do wonders, an he can,
All the world affright;
Yet he fares as doth the knave
Whom men with a trusty stave
Ever smartly smite.
"Tho' the thief master be he hangs
    highest on tree,"
                quoth Hendynge.

Wicked man, and wicked wife,
If they led a sinful life,
Ever evil wrought,   270
Never they such road might wend
But they needs must, at the end,
Show their inmost thought.
"An ill-spun web aye ravels out,"
                quoth Hendynge.

Better is the rich man sped
Who doth a good woman wed
Tho' her purse be bare,
Than to bring into his house
A proud maiden for his spouse   280
Who is false as fair.
"For land and name many wed them to
    shame,"
                quoth Hendynge.

Let no man trust child or wife
When he needs must leave this life,

Nigh to death be brought;
When his bones be laid in mold
They will take to them his gold,
Of his soul reck naught.
"Friendless is the dead,"   290
                quoth Hendynge.

When the glutton finds good ale
He to drink it shall not fail,
And for naught will stay —
Drink he will with one and all —
Seeks his home when night doth
    fall,
Lies dead by the way.
"Drink less alway, and go home by
    day,"
                quoth Hendynge.

Rich and poor, and young and old, 300
While that wit to you is told,
Seek ye your soul's bliss;
For when ye shall hope the best
To rejoice in peace and rest
The tree falls, I wis.
"Hope of long life beguiles many good-
    wife,"
                quoth Hendynge.

Mickle sooth he spake, Hendynge —
Jesu Christ, of Heaven the King
Us to gladness bring;   310
And for His sweet Mother's love,
Who doth sit in Heaven above
Grant us good ending. Amen.

THE SACRILEGIOUS CAROLLERS [1]

FULL ill shall it be in churchyard to dance,
This same will I show ye by sore mischance —
And this tale, so I swear to thee, is truth,
Yea, as Gospel lore, so shall it be sooth —
And it happened here, in this very land,
Yea, here in this England, I understand;

[1] From Robert of Brunne's *Handlyng Synne.*

In the days of a king men called Edward
It befell, this chance that was wondrous hard.

For so it fell out, on a Christmas Night,
That twelve foolish folk would a carol dight,   10
Yea, in fashion mad, as in strife it were,
To the town of Colbek they needs must fare;
Therein was a church which was fair and great,
To St. Magnus the Martyr 't was dedicate,
With St. Buckcestre joined, for she, I ween,
Had sister unto St. Magnus been.
The dancers' names, they be written all,
Of some shall ye learn how men did them call —
Gerlew, was he hight, the leader, 't was he
Set the time of their dance, and made the glee;   20
And maidens twain were that band within,
Merswynde were they called, and Wybessyn.
Thus to Colbek the dancers their way had ta'en
To seek the priest's daughter they there were fain;
The priest was hight Robert — he had a son,
And as I have read, he was named Ayone,
And his sister, she whom the band did crave
To join in the Carol, was known as Ave.
Then counsel the dancers held withal
Who that maiden forth from the house should call,   30
The council, I trow, they were of one mind
They would send Wybessyne, and maid Merswynde.
Straightway went the women, and brought her out,
To carol with them the churchyard about.
Bevis was the dancer who led the ring,
While Gerlew, he wrote what they all should sing,
And this was the carol the dancers sung
As men found it writ in the Latin tongue —
"Equitabat Bevo per silvam frondosam,
Ducebat secum Merswyndam formosam —   40
Quid stamus, cur non imus?"
"Bevis he rode thro' the leafy glade,
He led with him Merswynde, the lovely maid —
Why stand we here? Why go we not?"
This the carol that Gerlew wrote, I wot.

So sang they in the churchyard there,
Nor fear for their folly in heart they bare,
But they sang till the Mattins all were done,
And 't was time for the Mass to be begun;
The priest, he vested him for the Mass,   50
But never a whit they danced the less,

As they began, so they danced alway,
Nor e'en for the Mass did they think to stay.
The priest at the altar, he needs must hear
The noise, and the dance, that were all too near;
From the altar down stepped the priest so good,
And without the door, 'neath the porch, he stood,
And he quoth: "In God's Name, now take ye heed,
I forbid ye all, longer to do such deed,
But in fashion seemly now draw anear,   60
And come into the church, the Mass to hear.
Of Christian folk shall ye keep the law,
Nor longer carol — have Christ in awe,
And worship Him now with all your might
Who once of a Virgin was born this night."
But for all his bidding they stayed them naught,
But danced on ever, as was their thought.
The priest for that was full sorely grieved,
And he prayed to God, on Whom he believed,
That, for Magnus the Martyr, since in his name   70
The church was founded, to guard His fame,
And such vengeance upon the dancers send
Ere yet they might forth from the churchyard wend,
That their song, and their carol, should ever last
Until that the twelvemonth be overpast —
(But I trow, in Latin the writing bore
Not "a twelvemonth" only, but "evermore.")
Thus on each one singly the curse he laid
The while that, dancing, they merry made.
And soon as the words from his lips had passed   80
The hands of the dancers were locked full fast,
That never a man, for spell, or wonder,
For a twelvemonth might part their clasp asunder.

The priest went home when the Mass was done,
And straightway hath bidden Ayone, his son,
His sister Ave, without more delay,
Forthwith from the Carol to bring that day.
But all too late he the words had said,
For the curse on them all was straitly laid!
Ayone, he did after his father's rede,   90
And unto that Carol he went with speed,
His sister he fast by the arm did take
When lo! the arm from the body brake!
All wondered that marvel to behold,
But a greater marvel shall now be told,
For altho' the arm in his hand he bore,
The body, it danced on ever more,

And neither the body, nor e'en the arm,
Shed a drop of blood, were it cold, or warm,
But muscle and bone were as dry to see 100
As a stick that is broken from a tree.
Ayone, he would back to his father fare,
And a sorry present he brought him there:
"Look, Father," he quoth, "see I bring thee here
Her arm who was once thy daughter dear,
Who was, of aforetime, my sister Ave —
I went thither intent the maid to save,
But thy curse hath fallen, as may be seen,
On thy very flesh and blood, I ween!
All too bitter thy curse, and all too soon — 110
Thou didst pray for vengeance, thou hast thy boon!"
Small need to ask me if sorrow sore
Fell on the priest, and on many more!

The priest who had cursed thus that evil dance,
On himself, and his folk there fell mischance;
He hath taken his daughter's arm, forlorn,
And hath buried it on the morrow's morn —
But the very next day, that arm of Ave,
He hath found it lying above the grave!
Once more was it buried, the self-same day, 120
On the morrow, without the grave it lay;
A third time the arm, it was buried low,
And again the ground it forth did throw.
The priest, he dare bury that arm no more,
For the dread of God's Vengeance oppressed him sore,
But into the church did he bear that arm
In dread, and in doubting of further harm,
Ordaining that it in such place should be
That all men with eye might the marvel see.
The dancers who carolled there in that band, 130
Thro' the whole year round, hand fast in hand,
Forth from that place might they never go,
For no man might lead them the churchyard fro';
Where first in the curse's fetters bound,
In that self-same spot did they dance their round,
Nor pain nor weariness did they know,
Such as falls to folk who too far shall go.
They stayed them not, or for meat, or drink;
And never they slept, not a passing wink;
Were it day, were it night, they noted none, 140
For they knew not whether 't was come, or gone;
Neither frost nor snow, neither hail nor rain,
Neither cold nor heat it might bring them pain.

Their hair nor their nails, ne'er a whit they grew,
Nor faded their clothes, and changed in hue;
Thunder nor lightning, it vexed them not,
God's Mercy, it sheltered them well, I wot,
They sang aye the song that the woe had wrought —
"Why stand we? Why go we naught?"
I trow ne'er a man should living be   150
Who such marvel were not full fain to see.
The Emperor, Henry, he came from Rome,
He was fain to behold this dance of doom,
But when he had seen it, full bitterly
Did he weep, to behold such misery;
He bade his carpenters build full fast
A roof that should shelter them from the blast,
But all in vain was the work they wrought,
For unto an end might it ne'er be brought,
That which they builded within one day   160
At dawn of another, on ground it lay,
Once, twice, a third time, the roof they wrought,
But for all their making it came to naught,
From the cold they should never covered be
Till in Christ's own time they should Mercy see.
And that time of Grace came, by God's great Might,
At the twelvemonth end, on that same Yule night,
At the self-same hour that the dance was banned,
At that very hour they loosed their hand;
At the self-same hour that the curse he spake   170
At that very hour the ring it brake;
Then, e'en in the twinkling of an eye,
Straight to the church did the dancers fly,
And all, on the pavement they fell adown,
And lay as men dead, or in a swoon.
Three days did they lie, as still as stone,
And never they moved, nor in flesh nor bone,
And then when the three days' course was run
To life hath God brought them, every one,
Upright they sat them, and all men heard   180
How to Robert the priest they spake this word:
"'T is thou art the author and cause withal
Of the penance long which did on us fall,
The maker thou wert of our travail sore
That full many a man hath marvelled o'er,
And by travail too shalt thou find thine end,
For soon to thy long home shalt thou wend!"

Then rose they up, on the self-same day,
Save Ave, she, lifeless, beside them lay —

Her father and brother great mourning made, 190
And wonder and dread on all men were laid,
Her soul, they deemed it was safe that stead,
But they needs must mourn o'er the body dead.
I trow that the first by her side to lie
Was her father, the priest, in veritie.
The arm that had once belonged to Ave,
Since it ne'er might lie quiet in the grave,
The Emperor bade that a shrine be made
Therein, in the church, should it be displayed,
That all men might look thereupon, and see, 200
And think of the dance and its penaltie.

Those men that had carolled, a godless band,
Thro' the whole year long, hand fast locked in hand,
Tho' at last their ring, it asunder brake,
Yet the world it still of that wonder spake,
For e'en as they, springing, the carol led,
So, dancing, from land to land they sped;
As aforetime they never might be unbound
So together they never might now be found,
For never, I trow, an it were but twain, 210
To one place, at one time, they came again!

To the court of Rome four, methinks, did go,
Ever hopping and springing to and fro',
With leaps and bounds did they get them thither,
But never, I trow, did they come together;
Their clothes ware not out, and their nails ne'er grew;
Their hair waxed not long, nor hath changed in hue;
Nor cure might they find for their sore complaint
At the shrine, so 't is said, of any Saint,
Save but at S. Edith's, the virgin pure, 220
There they say that S. Theodrich found a cure,
On Our Lady's day, in a Lenten tide,
E'en as he slumbered, her tomb beside,
He found there the medicine he sore did crave
At S. Edith's, the holy virgin's, grave.
Now Bruno, the bishop of S. Toulous,
He hath written this tale so marvellous,
Sithen, did he win him a greater fame,
For as Leo, the Pope, all men know his name.
Even there, at the court of Rome, to wit, 230
In the chronicles shall ye find it writ.
And in many places beyond the sea
It is better known than in this countrie,
And therefore the saying, it goes abroad,

"The nearer the church, the further from God."
And in different wise the tale doth fare,
For some for a fiction that same declare,
While in other places they hold it dear,
And the marvel be ever fain to hear.
But the tale doth examples twain rehearse: 240
For first, 't is a warning against a curse;
And again, it should teach ye to fear this thing,
In church, or in churchyard, to dance and sing;
Still less shall ye do it against the will
Of the priest, if he bid ye cease, be still!

THE DEBATE OF THE BODY AND THE SOUL

It chanced, as on a winter's night,
I drowsing lay, ere dawn of day,
Methought I saw a wondrous sight —
Upon a bier a Body lay,
That erst had been a haughty knight,
Who God would neither praise nor pray;
Now was he reft of this life's light,
His Spirit, freed, must hence away.

But ere that Spirit far would roam
It turned, and, by the bier it stood,   10
Beheld the Body, erst its home,
In sorrowful and dreary mood:
"Ah, wellaway!" it made its moan —
"Woe worth thy flesh, woe worth thy blood,
Thou wretched Body, now alone
Dost lie, who wast so wild, and wood!

"Thou that wast wont afield to ride,
On warlike steed, 'mid courtly crowd,
Of stature tall, in garment wide,
E'en as a lion fierce and proud,   20
Where now is all thy mickle pride,
Thy boastful speech, ere-while so loud?
Thou liest bare, hast naught beside
One garment poor, and that a shroud!

"Where be thy castles, where thy towers,
Thy chambers and thy stately halls?

Whose walls were painted fair with
      flowers —
And where thy rich apparel all?
Where be thy couches, where thy bowers?
Thy sendals, and thy costly palls?   30
Sorrow awaiteth thee as dower,
With morn thy fate shall thee befall.

"Where now are all thy goodly weeds?
The sumpter-mules that bare thy bed?
Thy palfreys, and thy noble steeds,
By hand of goodly pages led?
The hawks that thou wast wont to feed?
The hounds that swift behind thee sped?
Methinks God bringeth thee to need   39
Since all thy friends be from thee fled!

"Where be thy cooks who served thee
      well,
And dainty meats did aye prepare,
With fragrant spices sweet to smell?
Methinks thou wast aye full of care
To make that flesh with fatness swell
Which now shall be the foul worm's fare,
Henceforth, methinks, the pains of Hell
For gluttony shall be thy share!

"For God thee in His image cast,
And dowered thee with wit and skill,   50

But in thy choosing was I last,
Didst follow aye thy wilful will!"
"No wisdom had I in the past,
I wist not what was good or ill,
But in dumb folly holden fast
All thy behests did I fulfil.

" To serve and please thee was I bent,
Alike at even and at morn,
Ever I sought for thy content,   59
E'en from the time that thou wast born:
Thou who to judge my deeds wast lent,
Why didst thou not thy comrade warn?
Thou sawest me on folly bent,
Now of thyself art thou forlorn!"

The Soul it quoth: "Body, lie still,
Who now hath taught thee all this wit?
Thou chidest me with words at will
Tho' swollen as by viper bit!
Thinkest thou, wretch, that tho' thou fill
With that foul flesh of thine a pit   70
Of all the deeds thou wrought of ill
That thou so lightly shalt be quit?

" Thinkest thou peace with God to win
Whenas thou liest low in clay? —
Tho' thou be rotted bone and skin,
And blown upon the blast away,
Yet shalt thou come with joint and limb
Again to me on Judgment Day,
We twain to God's high court must win
Together take our bitter pay!   80

" Yea, tho' to teach thee I had thought
Full soon to Evil didst thou speed,
Thou with thy teeth the bridle caught,
Naught of my counsel wouldst thou heed.
To sin and sorrow hast thou sought,
To evil custom, lawless deed,
Tho' to withstand thee still I fought
Thou hearkened'st but thy Body's rede!

" Whenas I thought to tame and teach
Of what was ill, and what was good, 90
Of Christ and kirk would'st hear no
    speech,

Didst start and shy, as wild and wood!
Enow I then might pray and preach,
But ne'er a jot might turn thy mood,
To God thy knowledge ne'er might
    reach,
Thou didst what in thy heart first stood.

" I bade think on thy soul's sore stress,
On Matins, Mass, and Evensong,
Thou said'st: 't was naught but idleness,
Must follow first the busy throng.   100
To water, wood, and field would'st
    press,
Or sped to court, to judge a-wrong,
Saving for pride, or gain, no less,
Small good hast done thy whole life long!

" Now may the wild beasts seek their
    den,
And lie in peace 'neath linden tree,
The wild fowl fly by field and fen,
Since Death hath cleft the heart in thee.
Thine ear is deaf, naught canst thou ken,
Thy mouth is dumb, thou canst not see,
And tho' thou fiercely grin, yet men 111
Shrink from the evil smell of thee!

" There is no lady bright of blee,
Tho' late for praise she deemed thee
    meet,
Who now would lie a night by thee,
Tho' men might richly her entreat.
Unseemly art thou now to see,
Uncomely all for kisses sweet,
Thou hast no friend who would not flee
Didst thou come stalking down the
    street!"   120

The Body quoth: "Now this I say,
Soul, thou hast done me wrong, I wis,
When thou the blame on me dost lay
That thou, thro' me, hast lost thy
    bliss.
Where have I fared, by wood or way,
Or sat, or stood, or wrought amiss,
When I beyond thy glance did stray?
Well dost thou know the truth of this!

" Whether I journeyed up or down,
I bare thee aye, as on my back,   130
Whenas I fared from town to town
Why led'st thou me to ruin and wrack?
Were I to speech or action bound
Counsel from thee I did not lack,
Truth to men's ears my plaint shall
    crown
Tho' now I lie so blue and black!

" The while thou wast my comrade dear
Naught did I lack of fit and meet,
Then might I speak, and see, and hear,
Might come and go, and drink and eat. 140
Changed for the worse is now my cheer,
Since thou afar from me didst fleet,
Now dumb and deaf I lie on bier,
And fettered fast in hands and feet.

" Fain had I been a silly sheep,
Dumb as a neat, or e'en as swine,
To eat and drink and lie and sleep,
No cause had I then to repine!
Of cattle never count they keep,
Of water naught they know, nor wine,
Ne'er shall they lie in Hell-pit deep! 151
No wisdom had I save but thine!"

The Soul it quoth: "Yea, without doubt
Thou barest me, Body, aye with thee,
Had'st need thereto! — I was without
Hand or foot, it seemeth me!
Yet as thou bore me thus about
For action was I never free,
Must follow aye thy guidance stout,
Needs must, where never choice may
    be!   160

" Alike of woman born and bred
Body, I think me, were we two,
Together fostered fair and fed
Till thou could'st somewhat speak and
    go.
For love, right softly thee I led,
I was full loth to cause thee woe,
The loss of thee I needs must dread,
Other save thee I ne'er might know.

" When thou wast young, a little space
Thou didst my will, in childish wise, 170
For awe of friends, didst thou lack
    grace
With rod thy faults they would chastise.
But when hadst thriven and grown
    apace,
Desire beset thee in such guise,
Didst learn of rest and leisure's grace,
And wrought as thy will might devise.

" I saw thee fair in flesh and blood,
And all my love to thee addrest,
That thou should'st thrive, that seemed
    me good,
The while I joyed in peace and rest. 180
And so thou waxed of wilful mood,
Drear were thy deeds, and all unblest,
Small profit mine, an I withstood,
I, whom thou barest in thy breast!

" To riot in lust and gluttony,
In pride and wicked covetousness,
To hate and strive in black envy
'Gainst God in Heaven, and all of His;
Ever in discontent to lie
With waste and want — no jot of this 190
But I must now full dearly buy —
Full sore I now must greet, I wis!

" What should us both at last befall
Times and enow I warning gave,
But idle tales didst deem them all
Tho' thou saw'st kinsfolk laid in grave.
What the world bade, that didst thou all,
All that thy flesh of thee might crave
I bare — madness did me befall,
I made thee master, I was slave!"   200

"Nay, Soul, I ween it profits naught
Not so I ween thy debt is paid,
For all too worthily wast wrought
To say that thrall of thee I made.
Never in life to ill I sought —
In theft or robbery undismayed, —
But first from thee it came, the thought,
Forfeit is by the loser paid!

"How might I know or wrong or right,
What I should take, and what should
    shun,   210
Save thou didst set it in my sight,
Thou who alone hadst wisdom won?
If thou against my will didst fight,
And bid me for misdeed make moan,
Thereafter did I strive with might
To do what pleasured me alone!

"Ah! would to Christ in very sooth
Hadst plagued with hunger, thirst, and
    cold,
And warned me rashness led to ruth
When in ill-doing I waxed o'erbold!   220
That which I had begun in youth,
I held that same as I grew old,
Didst let me ravage North and South,
Ever I had my will on wold!

"Thou shouldest for neither life nor land,
Nor profit that thou here couldst win,
Have suffered me to lend a hand
To that which turns to shame or sin.
But thou wast easy to withstand,
Thy wit and wisdom, I found thin   230
And yielding, e'en as hazel-wand,
To mend I never might begin!

"To sin thou knewest I aye inclined,
Forsooth with man 't is ever so!
On this poor world I set my mind,
Followed the Fiend who is our foe.
Thou should'st have striven my will to
    bind,
When I mis-wrought have done me woe,
As when the blind doth lead the blind
We both in ditch are fallen low!"   240

But then the Soul 'gan weep full sore,
And sighed "Ah, Body, Alas! Alas!
My love I set on thee of yore
Since all my pains *sans* profit pass!
Feigning to love me ever-more
Thou madest for me a cap of glass,
I did on which thy heart set store,
Traitor to me thou wert, Alas!

"Who may more cunning treason do,
Or know more skilful web to wind   250
Than he his lord trusts all things to,
Without, within, as faithful hind?
For since that thou could'st come and go
I strove to serve with all my mind
That ease and pleasure thou might
    know —
And now my ruin in thee I find!

"The Fiend of Hell, who e'er doth try
To snare mankind, his plots he laid,
Dwelt in us twain, methinks, as spy,
When to good deeds I thee had prayed,
The World he took to company   261
Who many a soul hath aye betrayed,
With Flesh to folly brought thee nigh,
Thy course both wild and witless made!

"Whene'er I bade thee shrift to make,
Forsake thy sin for ever and aye,
To fast, do penance, early wake,
The Fiend forbade thee that straight-
    way!
Thus soon didst thou thy bliss forsake
Ever in grief and pain to stay,   270
I counselled joy and bliss to take,
Thus should'st thou live for many a
    day!

"And when I bade thee leave thy pride,
Thy many meats, thy harness stout,
The World stood ever at thy side
And bade thee all my warnings flout,
And garb thy Flesh in rich robes wide,
Not as a beggar, in a clout,
And high on warlike steed to ride
With knightly comrades in and out!   280

"And when I bade thee early rise
And me, thy Soul, in safety keep,
Thou said'st it pleased thee in no wise
To lose thy merry morning sleep!
And now ye summon your assize,
Ye traitors three, I needs must weep,
Ye load me now with your emprise,
E'en as a butcher doth the sheep

"For when three traitors at one tale
Together be against me sworn,   290
Ye make my words of none avail,
Of plea, methinks, am I forlorn!
Ye lead me on by down and dale,
E'en as an ox is led by horn,
Unto the spot that brings him bale
Whenas his life is from him torn!

"For love I followed all thy will,
And thus to mine own death I drew,
Through serving thee, my servant still,
Who fickle wast, and aye untrue.   300
Thou didst the deed, I hid the ill,
That it was evil well we knew,
Therefore our fate must we fulfil
In pain, and shame, and sorrow new!

"Tho' all the men now under moon
To sit on Judgment seat were brought
Of all the shame that shall be done
To us, not half were in their thought!
It profits us nor bede nor boon,
And all our wit availeth naught,   310
The hounds of Hell, they come full soon,
Way of escape in vain were sought!"

But when that Body saw the Ghost
Such doleful moan, and mourning make,
It quoth: "Alas, my life is lost,
Since I have lived but for Sin's sake!
'T were better that my day had past
Ere yet to life I might awake,
Then had I been in cold clay cast,
Or lain and rotted in a lake!   320

"For then, methinks, I naught had
    learned
Of what was ill, and what was good,
And ne'er towards the wrong had
    yearned,
Nor suffered pain in wrathful mood.
No saint with this our prayer hath
    turned
To Him Who bought us with His Blood,
That when in Hell-fire we be burned
He do us mercy, by His Rood!"

"Nay, Body, now it is too late,
It boots thee naught to pray or preach,
For now the hearse is at the gate,   331
And now thy tongue hath ceased from
    speech.
One pang of torture to abate
Exceeds the skill of wisest leech,
Together must we gang our gait
Where God's forgiveness may not reach!

"But hadst thou turned a willing ear
The while that life to us was lent,
And as the hour of death drew near
Been shrived, the Devil's power were
    spent.   340
Hadst thou but dropt a rueful tear,
To mend thy life thy will had bent,
Then were we free from fright or fear,
And God His bliss to us had sent.

"Tho' all the men that be on life
Were priests, and Mass for thee would
    sing,
And every maid, and every wife,
A widow, hands for grief to wring —
And every one, methinks, were five,   349
And in this world five-fold each thing,
We ne'er might hope ourselves to shrive,
And none to bliss us twain might bring!

"Body, no longer may I dwell,
Nor linger here to speak with thee,
The hounds of Hell, I hear them yell,
And devils, more than man may see,
They come to carry me to Hell,
I may in no wise from them flee,   358
With flesh and bone, I rede thee well,
At Doomsday shalt thou come to me!"

And scarce the Soul had spake this word,
(Who wist right well where it must go,)
When in there rushed a hideous horde,
Full thousand devils, all a-row.
With talons sharp the Soul they clawed
In woe their grip it needs must know,
A sorry sight it did afford
Whenas they haled it to and fro.

For they were rugged, rough, and tailed,
With hunches huge upon their back, 370
Long were their claws, and sharply
    nailed,
And ne'er a limb such gear did lack!
On all sides was the Soul assailed
By many a devil, foul and black,
Its prayers for mercy naught availed,
For Christ His vengeance would not
    slack.

And some, the cheeks and jaws they tare,
And molten lead therein they poured,
To drink thereof they prayed him fair
The while they spread it all abroad. 380
At last there came a devil there,
Master of all, he seemed, and lord,
A red-hot coulter did he bear,
And pierced the heart, as with a sword.

Then glowing glaves, methinks, they set
To back, and breast, and to each side,
The points, within his heart they met
And made him wounds both deep and
    wide.
They quoth: "Full well we'll plague thee
    yet,   389
Thou heart that wast so full of pride,
That which was promised shalt thou get,
And more, and worse, shall thee betide!"

They said that goodly weeds to wear
That were the thing he loved the best,
In quenchless cope they robed him there,
All burning bright — with mocking jest!
With red-hot clasps that gleamed a-flare
They fitted it to back and breast,
A helmet that was none too fair
Anon upon his head they prest.   400

Then forth they brought, with mickle
    pride,
A curséd devil, as a foal,
That gnashed, and gaped, with jaws full
    wide,
Where-from both smoke and flame did
    roll.

The saddle that he should bestride
Of sharp pikes, pointed, bare its toll,
Jagged as a hedge whereon to ride,
And all was glowing as a coal!

Upon that saddle he was slung,
As one who should to Tourney fare, 410
A hundred devils on him hung,
And, ruthless, dragged him here and
    there.
With fiery spears his flesh they stung,
Anon with hooks they catch and tear,
At every blow the sparks they sprung,
As when men forge a red-hot share.

Thus in this wise a course he rode
Upon that sharp and fiery seat,
Then down they cast him, as a toad,
With hounds of Hell he needs must meet!
They sprung from out those pits so
    broad,   421
As he to Hell-ward set his feet,
And underfoot the Soul they trod
Till blood-drops marked each foot-step
    fleet.

Anon his horn they bade him blow,
On Hanston and on Bevis cry,
The hounds that he was wont to know,
To bay they brought him speedily —
A hundred devils on a row   429
Drew him with ropes, he fain would fly,
Natheless they brought him to that glow
That marked Hell's portals, verily!

When to that grisley goal they won
The fiends, they set up such a yell,
The earth, it open'd wide anon,
Smother and smoke thereout did well;
With stench of pitch, and eke brim-
    stone,
Men five miles off might know the smell;
Ah, Lord! That man is woe-begone
Who to his share one tithe may tell! 440

But when the Soul had come so nigh
And knew its goal, it cried in woe,

And quoth: "Thou Christ, Who sit'st on
          high,
Upon Thy sheep now mercy shew!
Didst Thou not shape me, verily?
Thy creature was I here below,
E'en as those souls who sit thee nigh,
To whom Thou dost such favour shew!

" Thou knowest all things, eve and morn,
Why wrought'st Thou me for bale alway,
That I should thus be tugged and torn,
While others have such goodly pay? 452
They that are doomed to be forlorn,
Wretches Thou mightest cast away,
Why dost thou let them e'er be born
To give the Fiend such goodly prey?"

The fiends against him clamoured high:
"Wretch, it availeth thee no more
To raise to Christ thy piteous cry
Or Mary Mother to implore;   460
For thou hast lost their company
Since thou hast served us well of yore,
Thou needs must find such hostelry
As those who well have learned our lore!"

The foul fiends all, as they were fain,
Anon upon the soul they fell,
And cast it down, with might and main,
Into the deepest pit of Hell.

The sun's light shall he seek in vain, 469
Where he hath sunken must he dwell,
The earth hath closed o'er him again,
The dungeon gates are locked full well!

(*He who beheld that vision sore
Lo! he speaketh somewhat more!*)

When they had borne that evil load
Unto Hell's gates, ere dawn of day,
On every hair a drop it stood
For very dread as there I lay.
To Jesus Christ, with humble mood, 479
My soul it yearned, and fain would pray,
As when the Foul Fiend's noisome brood
Were come to carry me away!

I thanked Him Who His Blood did spill
On Rood, and torment for us bore,
Who shieldeth me from many an ill
Which for my sins had lain in store.
All sinful souls I rede them still
To shrive them, and do penance sore,
Never may sin a measure fill   489
But that Christ's mercy shall be more!

(Christ His Grace to him impart
Who with hand this tale hath writ,
That he serve with perfect heart
Father, Son, and Spirit!)

THE OWL AND NIGHTINGALE

In summertide it so befell
I found me in a hidden dell,
Where strife did 'twixt two birds pre-
          vail,
Even an Owl and Nightingale.
Their plaint was shrill, and sharp, and
          strong,
Whiles was it soft, then loud, their song;
Each with the other waxed right wroth,
And each her evil mood poured forth;
Each on the other's customs cried,   9
And said the worst she knew that tide;

And each one 'gainst the other's song
There made complaint both loud and
          long.

The Nightingale was first with speech,
Ensconced was she within a beech,
And perched upon a fair green bough,
While all about were flowers enow;
For very thick it grew, the hedge,
With blades of grass mixed, and green
          sedge,
The gladder for that fair green bough

Skilful her song, and sweet, I trow, 20
Yea, one had deemed, those notes to
    hear,
That harp and pipe were hidden near;
Rather it seemed it came, each note,
From harp, or pipe, than from bird's
    throat.

There stood an old stump near beside,
There the Owl sung her song that tide,
With ivy was it over-grown,
Unto the Owl 't was house and home.

The Nightingale the Owl saw well,
Scornful her glances on her fell, 30
She thought right evil of that Owl,
(Men deem it aye loathly, and foul —)
"Monster," she quoth; "hence shalt
    thou flee,
I am the worse for seeing thee,
I trow thine evil cry, and strong,
Doth force me oft to cease my song;
My tongue doth fail, my courage flee,
When thus I know thee close to me,
Liefer am I to spit than sing, 39
Thy hooting doth such loathing bring!"

The Owl sat still, for eve drew nigh,
Nor longer would withold reply,
Her heart it swelled to hear that tale,
Well nigh her breath for wrath did fail.
She spake a word ere it was long:
"How? Thinkest thou to blame my
    song?
What, dost thou deem I cannot sing
Since trill nor run I skilful string?
I trow full oft thou dost me blame
And heapest on me scorn and shame; 50
Nay, an my foot had hold of thee, —
May chance betide that so it be! —
And thou wert down from off thy bough,
Wouldst sing another song, I trow!"

The Nightingale made answer there:
"An I may keep me fast and fair,
And shield me with the open bough,
I care not for thy threats, I trow.

So I may hold my hedge alway,
I little care what thou may'st say. 60
I wot small mercy dost thou tell
To those who may not shield them
    well,
Dost show thy wrath, and evil spite
To all small birds, when hast the might.
All kinds of fowl, they loath thee sore,
And drive thee hence, their flocks before:
'Gainst thee they shriek, 'gainst thee
    they cry,
And ever close behind thee fly.
The very titmouse, tho' she be
Right small, would tear thee willingly!
Yea, thou art loathly to behold, 71
Thine ugliness is manifold;
Thy body short, thy neck so small,
Greater thy head than thou withal;
Thine eyes be black, and broad to see,
As with burnt wood they painted be;
Thou starest, as wert fain to bite
Those whom thy claws would sharply
    smite.
Thy bill is hooked, and sharp withal,
Yea, like unto a crooked awl; 80
With that thou clackest oft, and long,
And that alone shall be thy song.
Fain art to threaten this, my flesh,
Would'st catch and hold me in a mesh,
As I to frogs were kin, I wit,
Who hidden 'neath the mill-wheel sit,
But snails and mice, and vermin small,
These be thy kin, thy right withal.
Dost hide by day, by night dost fly,
A monster art thou, verily, 90
Loathsome thou art too, and unclean,
As by thy nest is clearly seen,
And by thine owlets, right foul brood
Be they, and fed on right foul food."

. . . .

These words she spake, the Nightingale,
And having ended thus her tale,
She sang so loud, and shrill, and sharp,
'T was e'en as tho' one twanged a harp.
The Owl, she hearkened well that cry,
And ever downward turned her eye, 100

So puffed and swollen was she seen,
As she had gulped a frog, I ween,
For that she wist the song should be
Against her sung, in mockery.
Natheless, swift answer would she try;
"Why dost not in the open fly,
And see which of us twain shall be
Brightest of hue, most fair to see?"
"Nay, all too sharp thy claws, I trow,
I would not they should hold me now,
So swift and strong thy clutch doth fall,
E'en as a tongs it grips withal,   112
Didst think, as doth thy like alway,
Thou could'st with fair words me
    betray?
I follow not thy rede, I wis,
Thy counsel fain would lead amiss,
Forsooth, it bringeth shame on thee,
Discovered is thy treachery!
Nay, shield thy treason from the light,
And hide thy wrong beneath the right;
Wilt thou indulge thine evil spleen,   121
Then look thou that it be not seen!
For treason is with hate received
If it be open, and perceived.
Thy guile, it naught may profit thee
Since I be ware, and well may flee;
It helps thee naught that thou hast
    might,
I, with my wiles, may better fight
Than thou may'st do, with all thy
    strength,
I have, alike in breadth and length,   130
Here on my bough good harbourage,
'Well fights, who flies well,' saith the
    sage!
But put we to this strife an end,
It profits naught such words to spend,
And a right judgment now to win
With fair and peaceful words begin.
Though we be not of one accord
'T were better far with gentle word,
Without discord, and without fight,
To plead our cause with sooth and
    right.   140
Let each of us say what she will,
In words well chosen, and with skill."

Then quoth the Owl: "Who shall be
    fain
To judge aright betwixt us twain?"
"I trow well," quoth the Nightingale
"Hereof shall be no lengthy tale,
For Master Nichole, of Guildford,
Right wise shall be, of skilful word,
In judgment wary he, and wise,
No vice finds favour in his eyes,   150
He'll know right well, in this our song,
Who singeth right, who singeth wrong,
And he can sever from the right
The wrong, the darkness from the light."

The Owl awhile had her bethought
Before this answer forth she brought:
"I'll grant that he our judge shall be;
Tho' one-while passionate were he,
And loved the Nightingale withal,
And other song-birds that be small,   160
I trow his passions now be cooled,
And he by thee will not be fooled
In such wise that, for olden love,
He put me down, and thee above.
Ne'er shalt thou please him so, I wis,
That he for thee shall judge amiss.
Of wisdom ripe, of steadfast rede,
To ill advice he'll ne'er take heed;
Now hath he no more lust for play,
But sure will take the rightful way."   170

Ready the Nightingale; (I trow
Had learned her lesson well enow —)
"Owl," quoth she then, "now say me
    sooth,
Why dost thou as a monster doeth?
Thou sing'st by night, and not by day,
And all thy song is 'Wellaway,'
I trow thy song, it bringeth fear
To all men who its fashion hear;
Thou to thy mate dost shriek and yell
In grisley wise, the sooth to tell.   180
Wise men, or fools, awaked from sleep,
They deem thou sing'st not, but dost
    weep.
Thou fly'st by night, and not by day —
Thereof I marvel, and well may,

For everything that shunneth right
Loveth the darkness, hateth light;
And every one who loves misdeed
Seeketh the darkness for his need.
A wise word, tho' perchance unclean,
Is in men's mouths full oft, I ween, 190
King Alfred, he hath written, Owl,
'*A man shuns those who know him foul.*'
I trow e'en so with thee it is,
Thou fliest aye by night, I wis.
Another thing with thee is seen,
By night thine eyes be bright and keen,
By day-light shalt thou be stark blind,
Thou see'st neither bough nor rind;
Art blind, or well nigh blind, by day —
Thereby in parable men say: 200
Right so the evil man doth wend
Who seeth naught to a good end,
And is so full of evil guile
That no man may escape his wile.
Right well the dark way doth he know,
And from the light aside doth go.
And even so thy kin doth fare,
For light, I trow, have they no care."

The Owl had hearkened over long,
Her wrath by now had waxed full strong,
She quoth: "Thou *Nightingale* would'st
    be, 211
Chatterer, were fit name for thee!
Forsooth, too many tales dost tell,
A splint would suit thy tongue right well!
Thou deemest thou hast won the day;
Now shalt thou let me have my say,
Shalt hold thee still, and let me speak,
I will my vengeance on thee wreak.
Now list how I'll defend me well
And truly, nor long tale will tell. 220
Thou say'st I hide my head by day —
Thereto I think not to say Nay,
But hearken, and I'll tell to thee
Both why, and wherefore, this shall be.
I have a bill both stiff and strong,
And right good claws, both sharp and
    long,
As suiteth well unto hawk's kin —
Pleasure and practice lie herein

That I may nature follow free —
No man for that lays blame on me, 230
Therefore in me it may be seen
That I by nature be right keen.
Thus to the small birds loath am I,
Who low by ground or thicket fly,
They cry and shriek behind my back,
Follow in flocks upon my track;
It pleaseth me to be at rest,
And hold me still upon my nest,
I trow no whit the better I
To chafe and chatter, verily, 240
And scold them in foul words withal,
Herdsmen each other so miscall.
With shrews I have no lust to chide,
My way, it lieth from them wide.
A wise man judgeth thus alway,
And he full oft that same doth say:
'Men should not with the foolish chide
Nor with the oven yawn full wide,'
And I have some-time heard it tell
How Alfred spake, wisely, and well: 250
'*Look that thy way thou never hold
Where men be wont to strive and scold —
Let fools chide, and the wise men go —*'
And I be wise, and do also.
And Alfred spake, some other tide,
A word well known, both far and wide:
'*Who mixeth with a fool, I ween,
He cometh never from him clean.*'
Dost think the hawk the worse shall
    be
When marsh-crows scold him angrily,
And follow on his track in might 261
As they were fain with him to fight?
The hawk good counsel takes thereby,
He goes his way, and lets them cry.
But now thou say'st another thing;
Dost tell me that I cannot sing,
My song shall naught but wailing be,
Grisley to hear, in veritie.
That is not true, full oft I sing
Full loud, my voice doth clearly ring,
All songs thine ear as grisley strike 271
That be not to thy piping like.
My voice is bold, not weak to hear,
As a great horn it ringeth clear;

But thine is like a feeble pipe,
Blown thro' a reed, green, and unripe.
Better I sing than thou at best,
As Irish priest thou chatterest;
I sing at eve, when day is sped,
I sing when men should seek their bed,
I sing again when 't is midnight,   281
And so my song is fitly dight
Whenas I see to rise afar
The daybreak, or the morning star.
Thus with my throat much good I win,
And men much profit find therein.
But thou dost sing the live-long night
From even, to the morning light,
And dost repeat that self-same song
Unceasing, thro' the whole night long.
Dost crow thy wretched cry alway   291
That never ceaseth, night nor day,
But with thy pipe, I trow thee well,
Dost din men's ears, who near thee dwell,
Until thy song doth worthless grow
And men no joy therein may know.
For mirth, I ween, so long may last
That all its pleasure be o'erpast;
And harp and pipe, and birdling's song
Mislike men, if they last o'er long.   300
Nor shall thy song so joyful be
But one shall deem it misery
If he must hearken 'gainst his will —
So shall thy song be wasted still.
Alfred, he spake the sooth indeed,
As one in book right well may read:
'*All things may lose their goodliness
Thro' lack of measure, and excess.*'
With pleasure thou may'st satiate,
And over-fullness breedeth hate;   310
Each joy to weariness shall tend
If it continue without end,
Save one, that is God's Kingdom meet,
Ever the same, and ever sweet;
Take without ceasing from that store,
'T is ever full, and running o'er,
God's Kingdom is a wonder sure
That aye shall spend, and aye endure.

"Thou puttest on me other shame;
Thou say'st, I in mine eyes be lame;   320

Thou say'st, in that I fly by night
'T is that I cannot see in light.
Thou liest! It may well be seen
That I have sight both good and keen,
For there be never duskiness
In which I e'er may see the less.
Thou deem'st, I cannot see with eye
Therefore by day I do not fly;
The hare all day shall hidden be
Natheless the hare right well can see,
And should hounds chance to run his
    way   331
Full swift he flies from them away;
And many a narrow path doth take,
And many a twist and turn doth make,
And fares with many a bound and leap,
So to the groves his way doth keep.
For both his eyes so never he
Would do, if that he might not see.
Well as the hare I see, methinks,
Tho' thro' the day I sit, and blink.   340
The valiant man, who beareth shield,
And, near and far, doth fare afield,
Thro' many a land his way doth take
And doth by night good progress make;
Follow these valiant men will I,
And with their band by night will fly."

The Nightingale, within her thought
She pondered this, and long she sought
What she thereafter best might say,
Since she in no wise might gainsay   350
That which the Owl had said, indeed,
For that she spake both right, and
    rede.
In sooth she deemed she so had sped,
Their speech to such a point had led,
She needs must fear right ill to fare
Nor true and fitting answer bear.
Natheless, she spake out valiantly
For he is wise, who, hardily,
Doth make good face against his foe,   359
Nor cause thro' cowardice doth forego.
For they wax bold, an thou shalt flee,
Who 'ld fly didst thou fight valiantly,
For, if he see thee bold, straightway,
Your boar 's a barrow pig, i' fay!

And therefore, tho' full sore afraid,
The Nightingale a brave show made.
She quoth: "Now, Owl, I prithee say,
Why sing in winter, 'Wellaway'?
Thou sing'st as doth a hen in snow,
All that she singeth is for woe; 370
In winter thou dost cry, and wail,
In summer-time thy song doth fail.
'T is for foul envy thou, alway,
With other birds wilt not be gay.
For jealousy dost burn, I wis,
Whenas our bale be turned to bliss;
Thou dost as evil men do still,
All gladness is against thy will;
To frown, and grudge, that is their way,
Whenas that other men be gay. 380
The envious would ever spy
Salt tears in this, his neighbour's, eye,
Nor recks he tho' their flocks shall fare
In wild confusion, head, and hair.
So is thy custom, at this tide,
For, when the snow lies thick and wide
And every man goes sorrowing,
Then thou from eve to morn dost sing.
But I, with me I bring all bliss,
My song rejoiceth all, I wis, 390
Men bless the day they hear my voice,
And at my coming all rejoice.
Blossom and leaf again are seen
On bough of tree, on meadow green;
The lily beauteous doth blow
To welcome me, I'ld have ye know,
And by her fairness doth invite
That I, to her, shall wing my flight.
The rose, that blusheth red, I trow,
And springeth from the thorney bough,
She biddeth me to sing alway 401
For love of her, a roundelay.
And so I do, by night, by day,
The more I sing, the more I may.
And thus I please them with my song,
That, natheless, lasteth not o'erlong,
For when I see that men be glad
Naught would I do to make them sad,
When I have done what hither brought
My flight, I fare, by wisdom taught. 410
For when man thinketh on the sheaf,

And yellow hues come on the leaf,
I say, Farewell, and hence I go —
Naught do I reck of winter's woe,
For when hard times I needs must see
I get me home right speedily.
Thus love and thanks I ever know,
In that I come, and that I go.
Once I have done my work, then say,
Why should I bide, and wherefore? Nay,
I hold him no wise man, indeed, 421
Who lingers where there is no need!"

The Owl in silence sat, and heard,
And held in heart word after word,
And then bethought her how she might
An answer give, both fit and right;
For every man must take good heed
When he, 'gainst trick of word must
    plead.
"Thou askest me," she quoth, "this
    thing,
Why I, in winter cry and sing — 430
It is with men a custom good,
From the beginning hath it stood,
That each good man should, with his
    friend,
From time to time, in gladness spend
Some hours with him, in house, and
    board,
With gracious speech, and gracious word,
And specially at Christ's own Feast,
When rich and poor, greatest, and least,
Their Antiphon sing, night and day —
I fain would help them, an I may, 440
My mind is set on other thing
Than just to play, or eke, to sing,
And, answer were I fain to find,
I have one ready to my mind;
For summer-tide is all too fair,
And man full oft misdoeth there;
For Purity he careth naught,
On Lust, I trow, is all his thought,

.   .   .   .

"And thou thyself art there among,
In that of Lust is all thy song, 450

.   .   .   .

"And when thine hour of passion's o'er
I trow thy song is heard no more.

. . . .

"Now art thou ta'en, what thinkest
    thou?
Art rightly overcome, I trow!"

"Nay, Nay," she quoth, the Nightin-
    gale,
"Now shalt thou hear another tale,
Not yet our speech fore-judged shall be,
Now hold thee still, and list to me;
With but one word I'll swiftly teach
How all of naught it is, thy speech!" 460
"That were not right," the Owl then
    said,
"Thou at thy will thy plaint hast made,
And I have answered even so —
Now, ere we both to judgment go,
Here I set forth my cause 'gainst thee,
Thou, in thy turn, shalt speak 'gainst me,
And answer me, if so thou might!
But tell me now, thou wretched wight,
If thou hast any merit still   469
Save that thy throat be loud, and shrill?
No good art thou for anything,
Naught dost thou know, save chattering,
For small thou art, and weak shalt be,
Thy plumage nothing is to see,
What good I pray, dost do 'mid men?
No more than doth a wretched wren!
In thee men find none other good
Save that thou criest in the wood,
And if thy song be past and gone
Of other wisdom hast thou none.   480
King Alfred said, a wise man he,
And well he spake, for true it be:
'There is no man who, for his song,
Is loved or cherished over-long,
For he is but a worthless thing
Who knoweth naught, save how to sing,'
And thou art but a thing of naught,
Nor, save thy chatter, hast thou aught;
Of dim and dull hue art, withal,
Naught but a little sooty ball!   490

. . . .

"What dost thou eat, save only lice?
Spiders thou lovest, and foul flies,
And worms, if such thou mayest find
In crevices of bark, and rind.
But true and good my service is,
I watch men's dwellings well, I wis,
And men, they deem my service good,
For that I help them with their food.
The mouse I take in barn withal,
And eke in church, when dusk doth
    fall;   500
For dear to me shall be Christ's House,
Gladly I cleanse it from the mouse,
And never shall there come thereto
Vermin, if I my will may do.
And if it so shall please me well
To 'void the place where men may dwell,
I have within the wood a tree,
Thick and well-clad its boughs shall be,
And ivy green doth it o'er grow,
Ever the same that tree shall show; 510
Its hue, I trow, is never lost,
Whether it be or snow or frost;
Therein I have a sure stronghold,
In winter warm, in summer cold,
My house stands ever bright and green
When of thy dwelling naught is seen."

The Nightingale herself bethought,
Good counsel to her aid she brought,
Seeking 'mid hard and tough, I trow,
Until her rede seemed good enow,   520
And she an answer fit had found
To do her service at this stound.
"Owl," thus she quoth, "fain would'st
    thou know
If I another skill may show
Save to sing sweet in summer-tide,
And bliss to spread both far and wide.
Why ask what further skill be mine?
Better my one than all of thine —
Better one song from me to win
Than all the songs of all thy kin — 530
Hearken, and hear wherefore — I wot
Man, he was born but to this lot
That he should come to Heaven's bliss,
Which is but song and mirth, I wis,

And every man doth strive thereto
Who aught of good doth know, or do.
Therefore in Holy Church men sing,
And clerks their skill in music bring
That men be minded by their song
Whither they go, and thereto long;   540
That men shall of true bliss be fain,
And thereof think, thereto attain,
Since by the church good proof is given
How glad shall be the bliss of Heaven.
Thus clerks, and monks, and canons all,
Who dwell within this holy wall,
Rise from their couches at midnight,
And sing a song of Heaven's light;
And priests, throughout the land they
          sing,   549
Whenas the light of day doth spring;
And I, I help as best I may
And sing with them both night and day.
And thus for me more joy they know,
For me their song doth swifter flow,
So do I warn men for their good
That they should be of blithesome mood,
And thus I bid them seek alway
That self-same song that lasts for aye.
Now, Owl, thou well mayst sit and blink,
Here is no chatter, so I think,   560
Ready am I afar to fare
And from the Pope my judgment bear.
Yet, natheless, shalt a little stay
And hear what I have yet to say,
Nor shalt thou, for this English land,
My words with any truth withstand.

. . . .

"Thou deemest me the worse for this
That but one craft I know, I wis,

. . . .

"Cast thou thy crafts together, still
The mine shall be the better skill.   570
The hounds the fox to death can drive,
The cat can save himself alive
Tho' never trick he know save one —
The fox, such good trick knoweth none
Altho' he hath full many a wile,
And deems each hound he may beguile.

The fox knows secret paths enow —
The cat, he hangeth on the bough
So that the hound doth go astray,
And turneth oft another way.   580
The fox, he thro' the hedge doth crawl,
And from his first path bend withal,
Full oft he doth such cunning show
The dogs the scent no longer know,
Nor know whether, upon the track
'T were best to go afore, or back.
Thus doth the fox his wiles expend
That to his earth he, at the end,
Hath safely come, — yet, sooth to tell,
Altho' his tricks may serve him well, 590
Spite of his wiles, at last he'll be
Robbed of his red coat, verily.
The cat, he knows but one trick still,
Whether he fly by fen, or hill,
He knows right well to climb, alway,
So can he ward his coat of gray.
Thus my one craft, I say to thee,
Better than all thy twelve shall be!"

"Abide, abide," the Owl did cry,
"Thy plaint, it leans to treachery,   600
Thou glozest so thy words alway
That men shall deem thou sooth dost say.
Abide, abide, I'll answer thee
So that all men shall truly see
That here dost much, and greatly, lie,
I'll show thine untruth, verily.
Thou say'st, that by thy song, Mankind
Be taught their way from hence to find
Up to the song that lasts for aye —
In sooth I wonder, and well may,   610
Thou darest to lie thus openly —
Dost think that thou, so easily,
Shalt bring to Heaven's bliss by song?
Nay, nay, they needs must find ere long
That, with sore tears and weeping, they
Must for their sins still pardon pray
Ere they may hope that bliss to find —
I rede men that they bear in mind
Rather to weep, than thus to sing,   619
An they would fain see Heaven's King.
For there be no man void of sin,
Therefore needs must, ere hence he win,

That he with grief and tears entreat
He find that sour, that erst was sweet —
Thereto I'll help him as I may
Therefore I sing no empty lay;
My song is all with longing blent,
At whiles it turneth to lament,
That man bethink him well, I wis,   629
And mourn what he hath done amiss,
Thus would I urge him by my song
To groan for this, his guilt, and wrong.
If here would'st take to arguing
Better I weep than thou dost sing,
If right shall go ahead of wrong
Better my mourning than thy song.
And tho' some men be truly good,
And pure in heart, of righteous mood,
Natheless they yearn from hence to go —
That they be here, it brings them woe, 640
Tho' they themselves be saved, I ween,
Here have they naught but sorrow keen;
For other's sins they weep alway,
Ever for them Christ's Mercy pray.
Thus in both ways I help enow,
And two-fold aid I give, I trow;
The good I urge to yearning strong,
His longing quickens at my song,
And I the sinful help also,
Teaching, his way doth lead to woe. 650

.   .   .   .

" But thou dost sing of lustfulness,
Man finds in thee no holiness.

.   .   .   .

" Why dost not seek some other land
Where folk in greater need shall stand?
In Ireland thou dost never sing,
To Scotland ne'er thy flight dost wing,
Why dost not fare to Norroway,
Or sing to men of Galloway?
For there be men who little know
Of how a song should sweetly flow;   660
Why to their priests dost thou not sing
And knowledge of thy trilling bring?
Couldst teach them by thy voice, I
          wis,
How angels sing in Heavenly bliss.

Nay, as a useless well dost do
That springeth by a streamlet's flow,
The down it leaveth parched and dry
And, useless, runs the waters by.
But I, both North and South I roam,
In every land I be at home,   670
Both far and near, both East and West,
I do mine office with the best,
And warn men by my voice to heed
Lest thy false song should them mislead.
I warn them well, by this my song,
That they in sin dwell not o'erlong;
I pray them cease their sin alway
Nor that they should themselves betray;
Better by far bemoan them here
Than be the mate of Devils drear!   680

.   .   .   .

" Once didst thou sing, 't is sooth indeed,
In lady's bower, and fain would lead
That dame a secret love to know —
There didst thou sing both loud and low,
Wouldst lead her to a deed of shame
And wrong against her wifely fame.
Her lord was well aware that time,
And cunning snare of gin, and lime,
He set to catch thee there withal,
Full soon into the trap didst fall;   690
Taken thou wast in cunning snare
Fast by the foot it held thee there.
This was thy doom, and this the law,
Wild horses should thy body draw.
Seek, if thou wilt, by evil rede
Or wife, or maiden, to mislead,
Such profit shalt thou win, by hap,
That thou shalt dangle from a trap!"

The Nightingale, at this same word,   699
With knightly art of spear and sword,
An she were man, were fain to fight,
So hath she done as best she might,
And wise, did ward her with her tongue,
" Who speaks well, fights well," saith the
          song,
Thus, in her tongue her trust she laid:
" ' Who speaks well, fights well,' Alfred
          said;

Wouldst shame me by this tale? I trow
Thereof the lord had grief enow;
He was so jealous of his wife
That he would not, for very life,　710
That with another man she spake,
It went full nigh his heart to break.
He locked her in a bower ere long,
That builded was full sure and strong,
I but took pity on her woe,
And sorrow for her lot would show;
Fain would I please her with my song,
Early I sang, and late, and long.
Therefore the knight with me was wroth,
For envy, I to him was loath,　720
He thought on me to wreak his shame,
But all was turnéd to his blame.
Henry the King thereof had dole,
(Jesu have mercy on his soul!)
He set his ban upon the knight
Who thus had sinned against the right
In such a good king's land and state,
For envy sheer, and foulest hate,
A little bird did cruelly snare
And, limb from limb, asunder tear.　730
'T was to the honour of my kin,
Thereby the knight small joy did win,
He gave for me an hundred pound —
Thereof my birds, much joy they found,
Such bliss was theirs, and sheer delight,
They blithely sang, as well they might,
Since I was so avenged, I hold
My speech henceforth shall be more bold,
Since Fate thus once hath dealt with
　　me,
Ever the blither shall I be.　740
Now may I sing both loud and low,
No man may wrath against me show.
But thou, thou miserable ghost,
I wot that ne'er a nook thou knowest,
No hollow bush to hide, withal,
Where no man's grasp on thee shall fall.
Master, and servant, children, be
All of one mind to worry thee,
If they may see thee sit alone
Swift do they take to them a stone,　750
With turf, and stones on thee they fall,
Thy bones are fain to break withal.

If thou to death be smitten, or shot,
Then first art thou of use, I wot,
Men hang thee then upon a stick
And with thy feathers, foul and thick,
And with thy claws that erstwhile fore,
Guardest the wheat, from the barn door.
Tho' thou art naught as flesh and blood
Thou art as scare-crow very good!　760
And when men would their new seeds
　　sow,
Sparrow, nor goldfinch, rook, nor crow,
Never to come anigh will dare
If so thy body hangeth there.
And so the tree shall surely blow,
And the young seeds shall spring and
　　grow,
And never bird comes there among
If thou shalt be above them hung.
Thy life is vile and foully sped,
Thou art no use, save thou be dead.　770
So shalt thou know, of surety,
Thy features all right grisley be
The while thou livest, when dost see
That when thou, dead, hanged high
　　shalt be,
They dread of thee the very sight
Those birds, who cried upon thy flight.
I trow with reason men be wroth
'Gainst thee, thy song to them is loath,
Early and late, I trow, thy song
Is ever of man's loss and wrong,　780
Men well may dread to hear thy cry, —
Thou singest ere some man shall die;
Ever thy song, it bodeth woe —
A man shall loss of riches know;
Perchance a friend shall ruined be;
Perchance his house burnt presently;
Or thieves, or foemen, steal by night;
Or murrain shall his cattle smite;
The folk shall suffer scarcity;
Or wife bereft of husband be;　790
Ever foretellest misery —
Ever of harm to man dost sing,
Sorrow and poverty dost bring;
In very sooth thou singest ne'er
Save when thou would'st some ill
　　declare.

That thou be shunned by all, 't is meet,
And that men should thee pelt, and beat
With sticks, and stones, with turf, and
    clout,
So that thou findest no way out.
Woe to the herald who shall ne'er   800
A message save of evil, bear,
Who ever bringeth tidings ill,
Whose speech is but of mischief still;
Yea, God with him full wroth shall be,
And all who wear such livery!"
The Owl, she tarried not o'erlong,
But gave an answer sharp and strong:
"What?" so she quoth, "shalt cowléd be
That thus thou cursest laity?   809
Priest's office here thou fain wouldst do
Say, hast thou been ordained thereto?
I know not if thou Mass canst sing
But loud enow thy curses ring!
'T is but for thine old jealousy
That thus thou layest blame on me.
Here is an answer good alway;
'Draw to thee!' doth the carter say;
Wouldst here reproach me with insight,
For knowledge deep, and secret might?
For, in good sooth, I be full wise,   820
And know what in the future lies,
For I of war and famine know;
Whether a man live long, or no;
I know what wife shall widowed be;
What land shall waste and violence see;
Who breathes on gallows his last breath,
Or dies some other evil death;
When men shall forth to battle fare
The victor I could well declare;   829
I know when pest shall smite the kine;
I know when deer for hunger pine;
Right well I know which tree shall blow;
Right well I know if corn shall grow;
I know which house with fire shall burn;
Who from his foe in flight shall turn;
I know when seas o'er-whelm the ship;
I know when frost and snow shall grip;
And yet I trow I know e'en more —
Well am I learnéd in book-lore,
And of the Gospels know I well   840
Far more than I can rightly tell;

For I full oft to churches turn
And much of wisdom there I learn.
Of Symbols I the meaning know,
And many another thing also;
If ill to any man befell
And I its coming may foretell,
Full oft, for this, my mickle wit,
Right sad and sorrowful I sit.
For when I see that woe and ill   850
Draw near, I must bemoan me still.
I would that men thereof take heed
And find aforetime fitting rede.
Alfred in wisdom spake this word —
He well may ponder who hath heard —
'The ill that thou canst well foresee
Of half its strength it robbed shall be.'
Tho' hard the dints, their force is less
If I keep me in wariness,
And all in vain the shaft shall wing   860
If thou hast seen it leave the string.
For thou right well may'st turn aside
And flee, if thou its course hast spied.
And if disgrace a man befall
Should he reproach me therewithal?
Tho' I afore his harm have seen
It was not caused by me I ween.
So dost thou see one who is blind,
Who the straight path may nowise
    find,
Shall follow a false road withal   870
Till in the ditch and mire he fall.
Dost ween because the harm I see
It therefore falls more speedily?
E'en so it fareth with my wit
The while upon my bough I sit
I know, and see, with sight full clear,
That harm to some man draweth near;
Shall he, who naught thereof may know
Reproach me, if the thing be so?
Shall he the mischief lay to me   880
Because I wiser am than he?
But when I see that grief and pain
Be nigh to man, I sore complain,
And pray that he himself may guard
For that misfortune's ways be hard.
But tho' I mourn, both loud and still,
All that betides is thro' God's Will.

Then why should men blame me, for-
    sooth,
In that I warn them of the truth?
For tho' I warn throughout the year 890
Evil to them is not more near,
But for this reason do I sing
That they may understand this thing,
That some misfortune draweth nigh
Whenas they hear me hoot and cry.
For no man so assured hath been
But that he well may dread, I ween,
That harm shall sometime him befall
Altho' he see it not withal.
King Alfred, very well he spake, 900
(And men his words as Gospel take)
That each man shall the better speed
The better that he taketh heed,
And trusts to none his wealth, I trow,
In haste, tho' folk he have enow.
No heat there be but cold may grow;
No white so pure but stain may know;
Nothing so dear but may wax loath;
No gladness but may make men wroth;
But all that ever was, I wis, 910
Is fleeting, as is this world's bliss.
Here may'st thou know full speedily
That thou dost speak but giddily,
All that thou sayest for my shame
It turneth ever to thy blame,
Go as it may, it chances yet
Thou fallest to thine own onset;
The words thou dost against me spend
Turn to mine honour in the end,
Nay, better must thy plaint begin 920
If aught but shame dost think to win!"
The Nightingale, she sat, and sighed,
Right woeful was she at that tide,
For that the Owl spake in this wise
And laid her speech in such like guise.
Good counsel to her heart she laid
Pondering what she thereafter said,
Natheless, her part she understood —
"What, Owl," she quoth, "say, art thou
    wood?
Of secret wisdom speakest aye, 930
Thou know'st not whence it comes
    alway

Save that in witchcraft it hath share;
Thereof, thou wretch, should'st well
    beware,
If thou midst men in peace would'st be
Else from the land thou need'st must flee,
For all who in such dealings share
From days of yore accursèd were
By priest, and such thou yet shalt be —
From witchcraft ne'er hast set thee free.
In such wise did I speak but now 940
And thou didst ask of me, I trow,
In mockery, if 'cowled' I were,
That ban, it reacheth everywhere,
And tho' no priest in land were seen,
A cursèd wretch thou still hadst been.
For every child shall call thee foul,
Each man, 'A miserable owl,' —
Yea, I have heard, and sooth it be,
That men be star-wise, verily,
And thus may future things foretell, 950
Thou sayest what is known full well.
But, wretch, what know'st thou of a star
Save that thou see'st it from afar?
So doth full many a beast and man
Who of such knowledge nothing can;
An ape may well a book behold
And turn its leaves, its pages fold,
But for all that he knows no more
Nor first, nor last, of clerkly lore; 959
And thus, tho' thou the stars shalt see
Never the wiser shalt thou be.
Again, foul thing, thou chidest me,
And dost reproach me wrathfully,
Saying, that by my song alway
Wives learn their husbands to betray.
Thou liest, I wis, thou wretched thing,
Shame did I ne'er on marriage bring;
But sooth it is I sing alway
For ladies sweet, and maidens gay.
And sooth it is of love I sing, 970
For marriage many a wife doth bring
To give to this, her husband true,
A love that ne'er her lover knew.
And maidens well such love may choose
That they their honour never lose,
But love with rightful love that same
Who hath the right their love to claim;

Such love I teach, such love they learn,
Thereto my song their heart doth turn."

.   .   .   .

The Owl rejoiced at such a tale,   980
But yet bethought the Nightingale,
Tho' she at first the sooth would say,
At last had somewhat gone astray.
She quoth: "Now, of a sooth, I find
That maidens' weal be in thy mind,
Dost cherish them, and guard them well
And art full fain their praise to tell,
Ladies full often turn to me,
And let me oft their sorrow see.

.   .   .   .

"For there be husbands manifold   990
Who know not how a wife to hold,
If others speak with her, I trow,
He deems she'll break her marriage vow;
Nay, to behold if she but dare
Another man, or speak him fair,
He shuts her in with lock and key,
Thereby shall vows oft broken be,
For oft by wrong shall she be brought
To do what ne'er was in her thought.
Woe to him who so swift shall speak   1000
That his wife shall such vengeance
        wreak!
Thereof the ladies' plaint shall be
Full oft, and sore it troubleth me,
My heart, I trow, for grief is fain
To break, when I behold their pain,
With them I needs must weep full sore,
And pray Christ's Mercy evermore,
To aid that lady ere too late,
And send to her a better mate.
Another tale I'ld now begin: 1010
And thou shalt ne'er, to save thy skin,
With answer fit o'er this prevail
But thy contention here shall fail.
Many a merchant, many a knight,
Doth love, and hold his wife, aright,
And many a bondsman, even so —
The good wife, she the same shall do,
And serves her lord, by bed and board,
With gentle deed, and gentle word,

And ever seeks in service true   1020
The thing that to her lord is due.
Full oft it doth her lord befall
To fare afield, when need doth call,
Then is that good wife sad at heart
In that she from her lord must part;
She sits, and sigheth evermore,
For woe her heart is grieved full sore,
And, all for this her dear lord's sake,
Watcheth by day, by night doth wake,
And very long it seems, the while,   1030
Each step, she deemeth it a mile.
When others sleep her couch about,
I, alone, hearken there without;
And, since I know her mournful mood,
At night I sing, for this, her good,
And of my song, for this, her sake,
Sometime a lamentation make,
Thus, in her sorrow take a share
Therefore she gives me welcome fair.
Thus do I help her all I may   1040
For that she treads the rightful way.
But thou hast shamed me bitterly,
My heart thereof shall heavy be,
So that, in sooth, I scarce may speak
But yet my wrath I needs must wreak.
Thou sayest, that I to man be loth,
That every man is with me wroth;
With sticks and stones doth threaten me,
Beats me, and tears me, willingly;
And when at last I shall be slain   1050
To take and hang me they be fain,
That I may scare the pie and crow
From off the furrows where they sow.
Say it were sooth, I do them good,
And for their profit shed my blood,
I die, and serve them at that same —
Wherefore to thee the greater blame;
When thou art dead, shrivelled and dry,
Thy death helps no man, verily!
In sooth, I know not how it might   1060
For thou art but a wretched wight!
But tho' my life be shot away
Good service may I do alway,
For men may set me on a stick
There, where the wood grows close and
        thick,

And thus may draw unto their snare
The little birds, and catch them there.
And so thro' me it doth befall
Man findeth roast for food withal —
But thou, thou ne'er, alive or dead, 1070
To profit man didst stand in stead,
I know not why dost rear thy brood
Alive, or dead, thou art no good!"

The Nightingale heard well enow
And hopped upon the leafy bough;
Higher she perched than she did ere —
"Owl," so she quoth, "now be thou
    ware,
With thee I think to plead no more
For thou hast lost the rightful lore,
Thou criest, thou to man art loth, 1080
That every man with thee is wroth;
That with thy cry, and with thy yell,
Thou art accurst, thou knowest well.
Thou say'st that grooms take thee in
    snare,
High on a rod they hang thee there,
They tear thee, and in pieces shake,
And some a scare-crow of thee make.
Methinks, that thou hast lost the game,
Thou criest aloud of thine own shame,
Methinks, dost play into mine hand 1090
Crying thy shame throughout the land."
When she had said this word, I trow,
She sat her on a leafy bough
And lifted up her voice on high
And sang so shrill, so piercingly,
That far and near men heard her song —
Anon, unto that tree they throng,
Thrush, throstle, wood-hatch, song-birds
    all, 1098
Of fowls, I trow, both great and small,
For that they deemed the Nightingale
The Owl had vanquished, without fail,
Therefore they cried and sang, I wis,
Among the boughs with mickle bliss.
E'en so men heap upon him shame
Who, playing dice, hath lost the game.
The Owl the clamour heard withal:
"Would'st thou," she cried, "an army
    call?

And would'st thou, wretch, against me
    fight?
Nay, nay, thereto hast thou no might.
Why dost thou call them here to thee?
Methinks, would'st lead them against
    me, 1111
But thou shalt know, ere hence thou go,
How my kin guard them 'gainst a foe,
All they whose bills be strong and
    hooked,
All they whose claws be sharp and
    crooked,
All they be of my kin, indeed,
All they will come to me at need.
The very cock, who well can fight, 1118
Should hold with me, I trow, of right,
We both have voices loud and strong,
And both, by night we sing our song;
Should I my loudest cry 'gainst thee
The stronger army mine should be.
'Pride goeth aye before a fall';
A turf were more than worth ye all!
And ere the day be turned to eve
I'ld not a quill upon ye leave.
But 't was our forward fast and true
Ere yet to thither-ward we drew,
That we should other daysman seek
Who judgment fair 'twixt us should
    speak, 1131
And now would'st from that forward
    shrink —
The judgment all too hard dost think!
Never thou durst that doom abide
So would'st thou, wretch, now fight and
    chide.
But would ye all my counsel take
Ere hue and cry 'gainst ye I make,
Then ye our strife would now let be,
And from this place would swiftly flee
For, by the claws of which I boast, 1140
If ye should now await my host,
Ye soon another song shall sing,
And curse all strife and quarrelling,
For none so keen shall be this tide,
I trow, mine onslaught to abide."
The Owl, she spake right valiantly,
Tho' she would not, so speedily,

After her army straightway fare,   1148
Yet would she, natheless, answer there
The Nightingale with fitting word —
For many a man, with spear and sword,
Hath little strength, or e'en with shield,
But yet may well upon the field,
With valiant words, so brave appear
He makes his foe to sweat for fear.
The wren, who sang well, at that same,
In morning-tide, she thither came,
To help the Nightingale withal;
For tho' her voice, it was but small,
Her notes were very clear and shrill,   1160
And many songs had she at will;
The wren for wise men ever hold,
Tho' she were born upon the wold,
Yet among men had she been taught,
And all her lore from them she brought,
And she might speak where'er she would,
Before the King, if so she should.
"Listen," she quoth, "the word I'll take,
What, think ye here the peace to break,
And do unto the King such shame?   1170
Yet is he neither dead nor lame,
And harm and shaming shall ye win
An ye break peace his land within.
Let be, and make your peace, I pray,
And to your judgment go straightway,
And take the verdict on your plea
E'en as ye sware it so should be."
"That will I," quoth the Nightingale,
"Yet, Wren, I go not for thy tale
But all for sake of lawfulness;   1180
I would not, of unrighteousness
Be at the ending overcome —
In sooth, I fear for no man's doom,
But I have said, and hold for truth,
That Master Nichole, who, in sooth,
Is wise, should judge between us two,
And still I deem he so will do.
But say, where shall we find him now?"
The Wren sat on a linden bough;
"What, know ye not," quoth she, "his
     home?   1190
He dwelleth sure at Portesholme,

In Dorset that same town shall be
Beside an inlet of the sea.
There judgment doth he deal aright,
And many wise saws doth indite,
And thro' his mouth, and thro' his hand,
Bettered we be to Scottish land.
Easy it is to seek his face
For he hath but one dwelling-place.
I trow that doth the bishops shame,   1200
And every man who of his name
Hath heard, and knoweth of his deed —
Why seek they not from him good rede
That he among them oft shall be
To teach them wisdom, verily,
Find him a place, and goodly rent,
That so his time with them be spent?"

"Certes," the Owl quoth, "that is so,
And these rich men much wrong they
     do
When they a good man leave aside —
(Who is in wisdom true and tried —)
And office give to whom they will   1212
Unheeding, and neglect him still.
But with their kin are they more free,
And children office-holders be,
Ill judgment on their wit they pass,
As sheweth Master Nicholas.
But let us now unto him fare
For judgment swift awaits us there."
"That do we," quoth the Nightingale,
"But who shall now rehearse our tale,
And set it forth ere judgment fall?"   1222
"That," quoth the Owl, "I'll do withal,
For our debate, in order fair,
Word after word, I will declare,
And if thou think'st I speak amiss
Then shalt thou check my tale, I wis."
Then with these words away they flew
Alone, nor followers with them drew;
To Portesholme, I trow, they came,   1230
But how they farèd at that same
That can I you in no wise tell,
I know no more of what befell.
          Explicit.

A BESTIARY

THE LION

I

THE Lion from a hill doth hear
If the huntsman draws anear,
Or thro' his scent so keen,
Knoweth him nigh, I ween;
By which-ever way he will
Wend to the dale from hill,
His foot-prints, at that same tide,
Behind him he well doth hide,
His tail doth with dust o'erlay
The track that would mark his way,   10
Either with dust or with dew,
That no man may him pursue.
Thus he goeth adown to his den
Where he hideth him well from men.

II

And another custom is his;
Whene'er he is born, I wis,
All still the lion doth keep,
And stirs not, as if in sleep,
Till that the sunshine's ray
Doth three times upon him play,   20
Then his sire doth cause him to wake
With the roaring he doth make.

III

A third custom the lion doth keep;
When he lieth adown to sleep,
Never, in his repose,
The lids of his eyes he'll close.

Significatio

I

The hill that is very high,
Is Heaven, assuredly,
And the Lion, our Lord shall be —
Above, in Heaven, is He,   30
Whenas it seemed Him well
Here upon earth to dwell,

The Fiend might not know, I wis,
Tho' all huntsman's craft were his,
How He came down that tide,
Nor how He Himself did hide,
Or unto that Maiden came —
Mary, I trow, her name —
From whom He took human frame.

II, III

When Our Lord for us did die,   40
And willed in the grave to lie,
In a cave so still He lay
Till it came unto the Third day;
With His Father's help, that stead,
He rose again from the dead;
To Life eternal thus
'T is His will to waken us.
As a shepherd his flock doth keep
Is He Shepherd, we, His sheep,
He will shield us from all ill   50
If His word we hearken still
And in no way forsake His will.

THE EAGLE

OF the Eagle I'll speak this stead,
As in book I his ways have read,
How he casts old age away,
And reneweth his youth that day:
When he feels of his limbs the weight,
And his beak, it is none too straight,
And weak hath become his flight,
And dimmed of his eyes the sight,
Thus doth he renew his might.
He seeks a well flowing aye,   10
That springeth by night and day,
Thereover doth upward fly,
Till he seeth the heaven high;
Thro' the skies both six and seven,
Till he cometh unto the heaven,
And his way so high hath won
That he cometh e'en to the sun,

And the heat doth stay his flight,
His eyes maketh once more bright.
Scorched are his feathers all,   20
And downward he needs must fall,
E'en to the well's deep ground,
Where he waxeth both whole and sound,
And cometh forth all anew,
Save his beak, which is yet untrue.
Tho' his limbs, they be waxen strong,
If his beak, it be twisted wrong,
Then may he not find him food
That doeth him any good.
Therewith doth he seek a stone,   30
And pecketh full hard thereon,
Pecks, till his beak once more
To its right shape he doth restore,
Sithen, with a straightened bill
Doth he get him meat at his will.

Significatio

Like an Eagle be ye men,
Listen now to me,
Old in sin ye've waxen then
Ere ye Christian be;
Thus is he renewed, each man,   40
When he goes to kirk,
Ere that think thereof he can
These, his eyes, be mirk.
There he Satan must forsake,
And each sinful deed,
And to Jesu Christ betake,
He shall be his meed.
Doth on Jesus Christ believe,
Priestly lore doth learn,
So the mist his eyes shall leave,   50
Ere he thence shall turn.
All his hope to God doth run,
Learns His Love so true,
This, I trow, shall be the Sun
Gives him light anew!
Naked, falls he to the font,
There renewed is he,
But a little doth he want,
That I'll tell to ye;
All untutored yet his mouth,   60
Paternoster, Creed,

Fare he North, or fare he South,
He to know doth need.
Teach his mouth in humble mood
God to praise and pray,
Thus to win his soul's true food
Thro' God's Grace alway.

THE SERPENT

I

A worm thro' the world doth go,
Full well men that same they know,
Adder, by name is he —
Thus he renewed shall be;
When his strength, it begins to break,
And old age doth him overtake,
He fasteth, for days full ten,
Till his skin, it loosens then,
He is lean, and weak also,
And scarce on his way may go.   10
Crippled, he creeps on his way,
And thus doth his craft display;
A stone with a hole seeks he,
And narrow that hole must be,
Thro' the hole he his way doth find,
But his skin, he leaves behind,
In the flesh he comes forth that day;
Water-ward makes his way,
As he drinketh there, to wit,
He the venom forth doth spit   20
That bred in his breast hath been
From his birth-time, so I ween,
And when he his fill hath ta'en
Then is he renewed again.

II

When the Adder hath shed his skin,
Is of poison purged within,
If a naked man he spy
Then he will not go anigh,
But fast from his face will flee
As if he a fire should see.   30
If a clothéd man he behold,
Straightway he waxeth bold,
And reareth him up on high,
To harm him readily,

To harm him, or e'en to slay,
Is he ready, if so he may.
And save the man valiant be,
And defend himself worthily,
With the Worm is fain to fight,
And doth him attack forthright,   40
'Gainst the Adder defence shall wield,
And make of his body shield,
In this wise to shield his head —
For his limbs he hath little dread —
Scarce his life he may hold that stead.

Significatio

Ye Christian men know now
What ye each to Christ did vow,
There, at the kirk door fair,
Such time as ye christened were.
Thou didst vow to believe His saw,   50
And to love His holy law,
To hold with heart and hand
To Holy Church's command,
If thou hast broken this vow
Then feeble and failing thou,
And forfeit, I trow, thy share
In the endless Life, and fair.
Art waxen too old for Bliss
As this Worm of the world it is!
Thou must, so I tell thee true,   60
Like the Adder, thyself renew,
Thou hast need thereof no less —
Confirm thee in steadfastness,
In virtue, and all good deed,
And help the poor man in need,
Whenever they meet with thee.
Think not thou shalt worthy be
To walk with thy head on high,
And thy glances toward the sky;
As ye walk among men, be seen   70
Gentle, and mild of mien,
And I rede thee, beware of pride,
And all other vice beside;
And see that thou ever pray
Alike by night and by day,
That Mercy may be thy meed,
And pardon for thy misdeed.
This life, it betokens withal

The path that the Adder doth crawl,
And this is the hole in the stone   80
Thro' which thou must pass anon;
Thou must free thee from this, thy sin,
As the Worm he doth from his skin,
Then unto God's house draw near;
The Gospel thou there shalt hear
To the soul is refreshing drink,
And the quenching of sin, I think.
The tale of thy sins alway
To the priest in shrift shalt say,
Thus the filth from thy breast be
        cast,   90
And the covenant holden fast,
In this thine heart aright
Which thou didst aforetime plight.
Thus shalt thou be young and new;
To thy forward be thou true,
And the Devil, he needs thee not,
He may do thee no harm, I wot,
He shall flee from before thee there
As the Worm from him that is bare.
With the clothed man the Adder is
        bold,   100
And the Devil on sins hath hold;
And the man who is sinful yet
With his wiles doth he oft beset.
For ever against mankind
Hatred he bears in mind
If leave unto him be given
From Him, yea, Our Lord in Heaven,
To do to us mischief sore
As he did to our sires of yore.
So put we our body in bale,   110
To the soul shall it much avail;
What was given us from on high
Let us hold it worthily.

THE ANT

THE Ant is mighty, tho' small,
And mickle her toil withal,
In summer, and weather soft,
In such wise as we see full oft.
In the harvest-time we see
How she goeth openly,

And runneth to and fro,
And rest doth she seldom know,
But food doth she fetch to her mind
Where'er she the same may find,   10
And gathers whereon to feed
Whether of wood or of weed;
Corn and grass doth she gather free
Where'er she the same may see;
Such store in her hold hath laid
As later shall be her aid.
When the winter snows lie deep
She into her cave may creep,
And the winter may harm her not
Who meat in her hole hath got   20
Whereby she may live, I wot!
Thus she layeth up a store
Ere the fitting time be o'er,
So well doth she know her lore.
But wheat above all the rest
Is the corn that she liketh best,
For that will the seed forsake
Of the which but now I spake.
But the barley she leaveth there,
And never about will bear,   30
She shuns it, and shakes the same,
E'en as she held it shame.
In the Ant is a marvel seen
More than a man doth ween,
The corn that she bears, forthright
The grain she in twain will bite,
Lest it sprout, and be spoilt for meat
Ere she willeth the same to eat.

Significatio

The Ant, she doth teach us still
For our meat to toil and till,   40
This our livelihood to gain,
The while we on earth remain.
For when we must wend our way
Then cometh our winter's day,
We shall hunger and hardship bear
Save that we here were 'ware.
Do we as the Ant doth here, —
Then I tell ye true,
On that day of Doom so drear
We shall never rue.   50

Seek we our life's Food, I wis,
Then we sure may be
As the Ant in winter is,
Never lack to see.
As the Ant doth barley shun
When she takes the wheat,
With the Old Law ye have done,
Find the New Law sweet!
As the corn she bears for food
She in twain doth break,   60
So the Law bids us do good,
Bids us sin forsake;
Gives us earthly rules so good,
Heavenly laws also,
Yet I ween that different food
Soul and Body know;
Our Lord Christ, He bade us aye
On His law to feed,
Now, and on the last great Day,
When we be in need.   70

THE HART

The Hart, it hath customs twain
From which we ensamples gain;
Thus we read in the book withal
That men *Physiology* call.
He doth drag the Adder from stone,
With his nose pulls it up anon,
From stone, or from stock also
When thereunder it fain would go.
Swift doth he swallow the Worm,
Thereafter he sore doth burn,   10
For the poisonous thing that tide
To heat doth it turn inside.
Then with cunning, he fareth fleet
Where floweth the water sweet,
And he drinketh it at his will
Till thereof he hath ta'en his fill,
And the venom hath no more power
To harm him, from that same hour.
But then doth he cast his horn,
Either in thicket or thorn,   20
Thus the wild Deer renews his
        youth
So have I learned for truth.

Significatio

Thus men, they the poison draw
From our elders, who brake the Law,
Thro' the Serpent, thereby Mankind
Have envy and strife in mind,
Be lustful, and covetous,
Lascivious and gluttonous,
And haughty, and proud in mien —
This is the poison I mean.   30
Full oft do we burn in mood,
And fare as if we were wood,
And whenever we thus do burn
It behoveth us swift to turn
And haste to Christ's living well,
That we may not go to Hell.
If His Teaching, we drink it in,
It will quench in our heart each sin.
Let us cast away pride that stead,
As the Hart his horns doth shed,   40
And to God-ward renew us thus
That Salvation be sure for us.

A practice have hart and hind,
That we all ought to bear in mind;
They be all of the self-same mood, —
If they go forth in search of food
And over the water fare
None leaveth his comrade there,
But one, he in front doth swim,
And the others, they all follow him,   50
Whether he swim or wade —
At need each the other doth aid,
The one doth his shinbone lay
On the other's loin alway;
If he who the train doth lead
For weariness slacks his speed,
The others, they come anear,
And help him to take good cheer,
Bear him, from watery ground,
To the shore, all hale and sound,   60
Thus aid in his need he found.
This custom is mid'st them seen
Tho' a hundred in herd they've
    been.

Significatio

From the Hart this lesson we win
Ne'er to help another to sin,
But each one to love the other
E'en as he were his brother;
With his friend to steadfast fare
And his burthen with him to share,
And help him, in case of need,   70
For this, God, He giveth meed.
Heaven's Kingdom we sure shall see
If to others we helpful be.
Thus Our Dear Lord's law should we
Lovingly fulfil,
Mickle need, I trow, have we
To obey His Will.

THE FOX

A WILD beast there is, I trow,
That knoweth of wiles enow,
For her cunning and craft, the fame,
Fox, do men call her name.
To the husbandman is she loth
For the harmful deeds she doth,
The cock and the capon good
She seizeth them both for food;
The gander and goose will take,
By neck or by beak fast make   10
And carry them off to her lair.
Thus men to her hatred bear,
And men alike, and fowl,
After her cry and howl.
Now hearken ye to a wonder
That this beast, she doth for hunger;
In the field to a furrow she'll go,
And therein she lieth low,
Where the plough thro' the earth did
    cleave,   19
Thus the birds would she fain deceive.
And she stirreth not in that stead,
But lieth as she were dead
For a good part of the day,
And scarce draweth breath alway.
The raven he sees, I wot,
Thinks a corse lieth there to rot,

And other birds come with speed
Thinking thereon to feed,
Safely, and without dread,
For they deem that the beast be dead.
On the Fox's fur they peck — 31
When she feeleth them on her back,
Then she leapeth up straightway
And swiftly doth them repay,
For these, the pecks of their beak,
She a vengeance ill doth wreak,
And teareth them all, I ween,
With her fangs so sharp and keen,
And when she hath eaten her fill
Then she goeth her way at will. 40

Significatio

Methinks that qualities twain
We find in this beast again,
Prudent and wise is she —
So the Devil and bad men be,
For subtle the Devil's way,
As he would in no wise betray,
Maketh feint he would harm us not,
Yet leads us to sin, I wot.
Bids us do of the Flesh the will,
And eat and drink our fill, 50
And in our amusement, there
He prepareth for us a snare.
He pecketh the Fox's fell
Who idle tales doth tell,
And his flesh he, I trow, doth rend
Who himself to sin doth lend;
And the Devil these pecks alway·
Doth with shame and disgrace repay,
For his sinful work and deed
Into darkest Hell doth lead. 60
The Fiend like the Fox shall be,
Full of guile and deceit is he;
Men like to the Fox in name
Be worthy of naught but shame;
He who good words and fair doth find
But hath evil thoughts in mind,
Is both Fiend and Fox, I wis —
Nor the Book it doth lie in this,
For a false Fox Herod we know,
What time Christ on earth did go 70

He said he 'ld believe His word,
Yet he purposed to slay Our Lord.

THE SPIDER

SOME things created they be
And now in the world we see,
That be loathly and loathsome all,
And yet we believe withal
That every living thing
May to man a lesson bring.
The Spider, she spins with speed,
To the house roof, as she hath need,
This, her means of life at last
To beam, or to eave makes fast. 10
From old hath she had this skill
This, her web, to cast at will,
In her wise to weave aright
Until she the same hath dight.
With that, she doth go her way,
In her hole doth hidden stay,
And, watching, in wait doth lie,
Till thitherward fares a fly,
And, fallen therein at last,
In the web it struggles fast 20
Striving itself to free;
Then she runneth rapidly,
For ever ready is she.
She comes anon to the net,
Takes the fly in the trap she set,
To bite it sharply is fain,
So doth she become its bane.
She slays it, and drinks its blood,
Nor doeth it other good,
Then when she her fill hath ta'en 30
Into hiding she goes again.

Significatio

This creature betokens alway
The man who would others betray,
Whether in stead or in stall,
In market, or moat, or hall,
In open or secret guise,
Or in any other wise.
To bite his neighbour he sought

Who hath bale upon him brought;
Methinks he doth drink his blood   40
Who maketh him sad of mood;
And he eateth his neighbour still
When he worketh upon him ill.

THE WHALE

THE Whale is a fish, I wis,
None greater in sea there is,
So that thou sure would'st say,
Did'st thou see it float alway,
That the same must an island be,
Girdled about by the sea.
That fish is so huge, the tide
That it hungers it gapeth wide,
From his throat comes a scent so fair
Earth hath naught may therewith com-
    pare,   10
Other fishes to him draw nigh,
For it pleaseth them mightily.
Thus into his mouth they swim,
For they know not the guile of him;
The whale shuts his jaws straightway,
Sucks them in without more delay,
'T is the small fish he doth deceive,
The greater, he needs must leave.
He dwells in the deep sea ground,
And liveth there hale and sound,   20
Until it shall chance that there be
A storm that stirs up the sea.
When summer and winter strive,
There may he no longer thrive;
So troubled the sea, its ground,
He may not abide that stound,
But doth rise up, and lieth still
While the weather it is so ill.
The sailors, in tempest's strife,   29
Who dread death, and are fain for life,
Looking round them, this fish they see,
And they deem it an isle to be,
Then joy in their hearts they know,
And toward it they swiftly row,
Their ship do they fasten there
And up on its back they fare,
With tinder and steel, and stone,

They make them a fire anon,   38
They warm them, and eat and drink —
The Whale, feeling the fire, doth sink,
And soon doth he dive to the ground,
And all, without wound, are drowned.

Significatio

The Devil is mighty in wile,
(So witches have craft and guile,)
He maketh men hunger and thirst
With sinful desires accurst,
And draweth to him with his breath
(Whoso follows him, findeth death —)
They who love but little the law;
The great he may never draw,   50
The great, those who true have been
In body and soul, I mean.
He who lists to the Devil's lore
At long last he shall rue it sore;
He who fastens his hope on him
Must him follow to Hell's depths dim.

THE SIRENS

I WOULD have ye know, in the sea
Full many a marvel there be,
There is one is y'clept Mermaid,
That is like to a maiden made
In body, and eke in breast,
But it is not so with the rest;
From the navel down is she
Other than man to see,
But the form of a fish doth show
With fins that from out her grow.   10
This wonder her home doth keep
In treacherous parts of the deep,
And there, on the whirlpool's brink,
She maketh the ship to sink,
And doth scathe to the sailor bring.
Merrily doth she sing,
And many voices hath she,
Diverse and shrill they be,
And evil are all verilie;
For the shipmen forget to steer   20
Whenever her voice they hear,

But a slumber doth them o'ertake,
They sleep, and too late they wake,
The ship sinks with its folk, I ween,
And never again is seen.
But he who is wise and ware
Will turn again from her snare,
And oft he escapeth still
From the breast that would do him ill.
Of the marvel he hath been told —   30
Now this creature strange to behold,
Half man, and half fish, it is
Some lesson for us, I wis.

Significatio

Now in many a man, I ween,
The meaning of this is seen,
Without, do they show lamb's-skin,
But they be very wolves within;
They speak full righteouslie,
But their deeds, they wicked be;
Their deeds, they accord but ill   40
With what their mouth speaketh still.
Thus two-fold, I trow, their mood,
They are ready to swear by the Rood,
By the Sun, and eke by the Moon,
And yet do they lie eftsoon.
Thus with what they sing and they say
Do they many a man betray,
Of thy goods by treason take toll,
And by lying, destroy thy soul.

THE ELEPHANT

In Ynde ye may Elephants see,
Big and burly in body they be,
Together they herd on the wold,
As sheep that come forth from the fold.
And of young they beget and rear
But one, tho' three hundred year
In this world to their lot were set
No more would they aye beget.
One thing have they most in thought,
That they ne'er to a fall be brought,   10
Since they be lacking the power
To rise again in that hour.

(How this beast his rest doth take
When he wanders wide,
Since he is of monstrous make
Hear me tell this tide.)
He doth seek to himself a tree,
That shall strong and steadfast be,
And against the trunk doth lean
When weary with walking, I ween.   20
When the hunter this doth know,
Who a trap will set,
Seeing where the beast doth go
This his rest to get,
Then the tree doth he saw away,
In such wise as best he may,
His work he with care doth hide
And makes him a place that tide
Wherein he may watch and see
If the beast, he deceived shall be.   30
Then cometh the monster, I ween,
On his side 'gainst the tree doth
lean,
In the shade of the tree so tall,
Doth he sleep, and together they fall.
If none other near him be stayed
Then he crieth and calleth for aid,
And rueful, I ween his cries —
He hopeth with help to rise,
One cometh who nigh is at hand,
And hopeth to make him stand,   40
With all his might tho' he tries,
He stirs him no whit as he lies.
Naught can he do, nor another,
They can only cry with their brother.
Tho' they shake him, a goodly band,
Deeming to make him stand,
Yet for the help of them all
He may not arise from his fall.
Then they trumpet so loud and fast,
Like a bell, or of horns the blast,   50
And for this, their mickle cry,
A youngling comes hastily,
And stooping adown that tide
His trunk he puts 'neath his side,
With the help of all the band
He makes him again to stand,
Thus he 'scapeth the hunter's snare
In such wise as I now declare.

Thus Adam, he fell thro' a tree,
Our first father, and so fell we;   60
Moses fain would him raise again,
But he might in no wise attain,
Nor after him prophets all
Could make him arise from his fall,
And stand once more as he stood
The heir to all Heavenly good.
With sorrow and sighing they thought
How succour might best be brought,
And with one voice they raised a cry
That pierced unto Heaven high,   70
And their calling and care did bring
To their aid Christ, Our Heavenly King.
Who is greatest in Heaven, withal
Became Man, and on earth was small,
His Passion He bare for us,
And going 'neath Adam thus
Raised him up, and Mankind with
          him,
Who had fallen to Hell's depths dim.

THE TURTLE DOVE

In the book of the Turtle Dove
We find it writ in rhyme,
How, loyal to one true love
She keepeth her whole life time.
If she once hath found a mate,
Never will she stray,
Wives from her may pattern take
As I now will say;
By her mate she sits at night,
Thro' the day they fly,   10
Whoso saith they part in flight,
I say, he doth lie.
But and if her mate be dead,
Widowed then is she,
Lone she flies and fares that stead,
Will none other's be.
So she sitteth alone for aye,
Her old love awaiteth she,
In her heart bears him night and day,
E'en as he alive should be.   20

List, each loyal man, this lore,
Oft upon it muse,
This, our Soul, at the kirk door
Christ for mate did choose.
Of our Soul the Spouse is He,
Love Him with your might,
Never from Him severed be
Or by day or night.
Tho' from out our sight He fare
Be we to Him true,   30
Take no other lord, and ne'er
Change old love for new;
But believe He lives to reign
High on Heaven's Throne,
And that He will come again,
And by us be known;
Judgment upon man to tell
By Doom diverse given,
Those He hates shall pass to Hell,
Those He loves, to Heaven!   40

THE PANTHER

The Panther, a wild beast is he,
On earth is none fairer to see,
For black is his hue, I wot,
Marked over with many a spot,
Round as a wheel, and white,
That becometh him well to sight.
And where'er he his life doth lead
He on other beasts doth feed;
He taketh the best at will
And eats of the meat his fill,   10
Then still in his lair he keeps,
And for three days long he sleeps,
Then, when the third day is o'er,
He doth rise, and will loudly roar;
From his throat there cometh a scent,
With his voice it abroad is sent,
That balsam doth far exceed
In sweetness, (so runneth my rede,)
Or all things of perfume fair
Whether moist or dry they were.   20
For the sweetness his breath hath stored,

Whenever he walks abroad,
Wherever he wander, or stay,
The beasts, they draw near alway,
And follow him up on the wold
For the sweetness whereof I have told;
Save the Dragon, that stirs not out
While the Panther, he roams about,
But stays in his lair that stead
As if he for fright were dead.   30

Significatio

Now this beast of which I have told
For a token of Christ I hold,
Fairer is He than men,
As a star is fairer than fen;
And He showed man His love full well
When He won him by Holy spell,
And lay alone in a hole
When for us He would share Death's
      dole.
Three days did He lie alone,
Dead in blood, and in flesh, and bone,
Then He rose up, and cried, I wis,   41
Of Hell's torment, and Heaven's Bliss,
And rising to Heaven's fair host
Dwells with Father, and Holy Ghost.
With man left He so sweet a smell,
'T is the lore of His Holy Spell,

Whereby we may follow His way,
With the Godhead abide for aye.
And the Dragon, our foe is he;
Where the sound of God's word shall be
He stirs not, nor nigh may draw   51
To him who doth love God's law.

THE DOVE

WITH the Dove we good customs find
That by us should be borne in mind,
Seven qualities good hath she
Which may well our ensample be.
The Dove hath in her no gall;
Be we simple and soft withal.
Nor her living as thief doth win;
Hold we robbery for a sin.
She lives not on worms but on seed;
On Christ's lore we all should feed.   10
To other birds is she a mother;
So ought we to be to each other.
As a moan and a groan her song;
So should we confess our wrong.
She in water the hawk doth see;
Warned in Book of the Fiend are we.
In the rock doth she make her nest;
In Christ's Mercy our hope should
      rest.

RELIGIOUS AND LYRICAL

HYMN OF SAINT GODRIC

HOLY MARY, thou Virgin clean,
Mother of Jesu, the Nazarene,
Me, thy Goderic, help alway,
Shield, accept me, when I pray,
That eternally with thee
In God's Kingdom I may be.

Holy Mary, in Christ's Bower
Pearl of Maids, of Mothers Flower,
All my sins wash thou away,
Reign within my heart to-day,   10
Bring me to God's Bliss with thee,
God Himself for aye to see!

ORMULUM

DEDICATION

Now, Brother Walter, brother mine
After the flesh, in sooth,
And brother mine in Christendom
Thro' Baptism, and thro' truth,
And Brother mine in God's own House
In the third wise thou art,
Since in the self-same rule of life
We two have sworn our part —
And that we do as Canons live
Saint Austin's rule fulfil —   10
After thy bidding have I done,
And have performed thy will,
And turned into the English tongue
The Gospel's holy lore,
After such little wit as God
Hath given me in store.
For that thou thoughtest it might well
To mickle profit turn,
If English folk, for love of Christ,
Were fain the same to learn.   20
And follow it, its hest fulfil,
In word, and deed, and thought,
And therefore didst thou much desire
This work by me be wrought.
And now, behold, 't is done for thee
As Christ His Help did lend,
'T were fitting that we both thank
    Christ

That now 't is brought to end.
In sooth, well nigh the Gospels all
In book I've gathered here   30
That in the Mass-book may be found
For Mass, throughout the year;
And after every Gospel text
Its meaning may ye read,
That one may to the folk make clear
That which their soul doth need;
And yet, beside this, more enow
I've added thereunto
Of that which all Christ's Holy Folk
Shall both believe and do —   40
And I have set here, in this book,
Amid the Gospels still,
All of myself, full many a word,
The rhythm and rhyme to fill.
But thou shalt find that these, my words,
Where'er they added be,
Shall help the man who readeth it
To understand, and see
In better wise how he, in sooth,
The Gospel Words should hear —   50
Therefore I trow thou should'st permit
The words I've written here,
Where'er such words, in Gospel lore,
May not by thee be found —
For whoso must, to simple folk,
The Gospel lore expound,
His words, to words of Holy Writ,

Full oft he addeth still,
And I might not, with Gospel Words,
My verses fitly fill; 60
And therefore doth it chance that I
Should find the need, oft-time,
To add unto the Gospel Words
To fill my verse and rhyme.
To thee I now entrust this book
As charge and duty high,
That thou right well thro' it should'st
look,
The verses search and try,
That ne'er in all this book shall be
A word 'gainst Christ's Own Lore, 70
A word the folk may not believe
And practise evermore.
They shall be trodden underfoot,
And cast out utterly, —
(This is the doom of that foul flock
Who blind thro' malice be, —)
Who blame the thing that they should
praise
Thro' pride and envy drear;
Methinks, they shall judge scornfully
Our labour, Brother dear! 80
For all such folk the work shall hold
Useless and idle all,
And this not thro' their skill, thro' pride
And envy shall befall.
Here it behoves us pray to God
That He forgive their sin,
And that we love Him well, for Whom
We did this work begin.
And give Him thanks that it be brought
By this His aid, to end, 90
For it may help all, who thereto
A willing ear shall lend,
And love its lore, and follow it
In thought and word, and deed —
And when, hereafter, any man
To write this book doth need,
I bid him to set down aright
Whate'er the book doth hold,
And follow closely all that I,
In this first copy, told. 100
With all such rhyme as here is set,
The words in number right,

And that he look right well that he
The letters double write;
For everywhere throughout this book
He'll find 't is written so —
Let him mark well that so he write,
For naught else may he do
In English, would he write it right,
That shall he soothly know! 110
And if a man should ask me why
I thought this deed to do,
I did it for this cause, because
Man's bliss for evermore
Doth hang upon this thing, that he
The Gospel's Holy Lore
With all his might should follow right
In thought, and word, and deed,
For all on earth to follow this,
The Christian's Faith, have need, 120
As they be taught, in deed and truth,
Of Holy Gospel Lore —
And therefore whoso learneth it,
And doth it, evermore,
He at his end shall worthy be
To God's salvation reach —
And therefore have I turnéd it
Into the English speech,
For that I would, right joyfully,
That English people all 130
Who with their ears shall hearken it,
In heart believe it all,
They, with their tongue, should tell it
forth,
After its precepts do,
So that their soul, thro' Christian Faith,
Come God's Salvation to.
For if they thus its teaching hear,
And walk its ways within,
I shall have helped them, by Christ's
Grace,
Eternal Bliss to win. 140
And I shall have, for this my toil,
A good reward, I wis,
In that I here, for love of God,
And hope of Heavenly Bliss,
Have done this into English speech,
Men's souls to profit win —
And if they now reject my work

'T is counted them for sin.
But I, I shall have earned thereby
The Grace of Christ indeed,   150
In that I wrought for them this book
To help their soul's true need;
Altho' they may, thro' sinful pride,
Refuse my words to read!

Now *Gospel* is in English writ
Good Word, or *Tidings Good*,
Good Errand, insomuch as it
Thro' Holy Writers stood,
All wrought and written in a Book
Of how Christ came to earth,   160
And how, for Mankind's need, True God
As Man had here His Birth.
Of how Mankind, thro' this, His Death,
Was freed from bonds of Hell,
How He assuredly rose from Death
The Third Day — doth it tell.
How he thereafter did ascend
Surely to Heaven high,
And shall hereafter come again
All folk to judge and try,   170
And payment mete to every man
Fair, after his own deed —
That which of such good bringeth word
Good Tidings are indeed.
Therefore, I trow, the Gospel we
Good Message well may call,
And men may in the Gospel books
Right good deeds find withal;
Kindness, that Our Lord Jesus Christ
Hath done for us on earth,   180
When that He came to Man, for us
As Man had here His Birth.

For this good deed for us He did
The Lord Christ, here below,
In that He did True Man become
To free Mankind from woe —
Another kindness hath He done
Lord Christ, for this our good,
In that He was, for all men's need,
Baptized in Jordan's flood;   190
Since He would water, for our use
In Baptism, sanctify,

Therefore was He Himself baptized
In water, verily.
A Third good hath He done for us,
The Lord Christ, in that He
Hath yielded up His Life for us
Of right good will, and free,
To suffer Death upon the Cross,
Guiltless, and without stain,   200
To free Mankind, by this, His Death,
From out the Devil's chain.
The Fourth good that He did for us,
The Lord Christ, will I tell,
'T was thro' His Holy Soul's descent
From Cross to Shades of Hell;
To draw out from the pains of Hell
The good souls, every one,
Who in this life had pleased Him well,
And righteously had done.   210
The Fifth good He hath done for us,
The Lord Christ, will I say,
'T was in that, for our good, He rose
From Death, on that Third Day,
And let th' Apostles see Him well
In human Flesh, and kind,
For that He would the Truth implant
And fasten in their mind,
That He, in very Truth and Deed,
Did from the Dead arise   220
In that same Flesh, which to the Cross
Was nailed before their eyes.
Since He would fasten and implant
That Truth within their heart,
His Presence to th' Apostles He
On earth did oft impart
Within the space of forty days
Since that He rose, I wis —
The Sixth good He hath done for us,
The Lord Christ, it is this —   230
That He ascended, for our good,
Again to Heaven's Bliss,
Thereafter sent the Holy Ghost
To His Disciple's band
To comfort, and embolden them
The Devil to withstand;
To give them Wisdom, that aright
His Holy Lore they know,
And good desire, and fitting might,

Patient to suffer woe,   240
All for the Love of God, and ne'er
To win them earthly gain —
A Seventh good, I trow, Our Lord
To do for us is fain,
In that, on Doomsday, He to us
Heaven's Bliss shall open throw,
If it so chance we worthy be
God's Mercy for to know.

And thus to us hath Our Lord Christ
A Sevenfold goodness shown   250
In that He unto us hath come,
As Man on Earth was known.
Now, in that Holy Book that as
Apocalypse we know,
Thro' teaching of the Holy Ghost,
Saint John to us doth show
That up in Heaven he saw a Book,
With Seven Seals beset,
And so fast closed that never one
Was found to ope it yet,   260
Save but the Holy Lamb of God,
Whom he saw there, in Heaven, —
And this, I trow, the token of
Those Seals, in number Seven —
The Sevenfold favours, that, for us,
Christ thro' His Coming won,
That never by no man, I trow,
Those Seals should be undone
Save by God's Lamb, Who came to us —
And thereby are we shown   270
Angel nor man there ne'er shall be
Nor any creature known,
Who of Himself could ever show
Such goodness sevenfold
To Man, that he might loose Mankind
From out of Hell's dark hold
Nor give him might, that Heaven's Bliss
Shall to his share be told!

But even as the Lamb of God
By this, His Might alone,   280
With little toil hath light, I trow,
Those Seven Seals undone,
Thus, even so, did Our Lord Christ,
By this, His Might alone, —

(With Father and with Holy Ghost
As One God only known —)
Even so did He right easily,
By this, His Might and Power,
Upon Mankind, Himself alone,
A Sevenfold goodness shower.   290
So that He lightly might Mankind
From bonds of Hell set free
And give Mankind Desire and Love,
Power, Wisdom, Will, that we
May persevere in serving God,
And Heaven's Bliss may win;
And therefore is that goodness shown
The Gospel Book within,
This Sevenfold kindness that Our Lord
Hath shown us evermore —   300
Thus it behoves all Christian Folk
To follow Gospel Lore,
And therefore have I rendered it
In English, as 't is spoke,
For that I would, right joyfully,
That all our English folk
With ear should hearken to its rede,
In heart believe it aye,
And with their tongue should tell it
     forth,
By deeds their Faith display;   310
And thus their souls, thro' Christian
     Faith,
With Heaven's Bliss fulfil —
Now God Almighty give us Power,
Desire, and Wit, and Will,
To follow from this English Book
All holy lore, I wis,
That so at last we worthy be
To taste of Heaven's Bliss!
          Amen, Amen, Amen.
And I, who did this English write   320
For English men withal,
I, men, when they did christen me,
As *Orm*, they did me call;
And here I, Orm, right earnestly,
With mouth and heart, would pray
That Christian men, who hear this
     book,
Or read its words alway,
I would beseech them, one and all,

This prayer for me to pray —   329
"The Brother who, in English tongue,
First hath this writing wrought,

May he, for this his work's reward,
To Heavenly Bliss be brought!"
                                                    Amen.

A GOOD ORISOUN OF OUR LADIE

CHRIST's dear Mother, Mary mild,
Light of life, Maid undefiled,
Low I bow and bend the knee,
Mine heart's blood I offer thee.
Thou my soul's light, mine heart's bliss,
Life, and hope, and health, I wis,
I thy praise sing, day and night,
Honouring thee with all my might.
Thou hast helped me passing well,
Brought my soul from out of Hell   10
E'en to Heaven — so thanks I give,
Lady dear, the while I live.
Christian men should worship here,
Sing thy praise with gladsome cheer,
Since thou, freed from Satan's hand,
Brought them to the Angel's land;
So we owe thee, lady sweet,
Our heart's love, and worship meet.
Fairest, blest o'er women thou,
Dearest to God's Heart, I trow;   20
Maidens worship thee alone,
Flower of Maids, before God's throne.
None on earth be like to thee,
None in Heaven thy peer shall be;
High thy throne o'er Cherubim,
Christ thou see'st 'mid Seraphim;
'Fore thee angels merry sing,
Music make, with carolling,
In thy presence glad to be,
Never sad thy face to see.   30
None thy bliss may understand —
Heaven lies within thine hand,
Of thy friends thou makest Kings;
Royal robes, and golden rings
Thou dost give — and rest full fair,
Safe from sorrow, death, or care.
There in bliss bloom, red and white,
Blossoms frost nor snow may smite,
Ever fresh, in summer glad —
There no man is weak or sad;   40

There they rest who served thee here,
Kept their lives from evil clear,
Free from sorrow, toil, or tears,
Groans of Hell ne'er vex their ears.
There they quaff, from cups of gold,
Draughts of life, with bliss untold.
Never heart of man may reach,
Never tongue may tell with speech,
What their share of Heaven's delight
Who have served thee day and night!
White the robes thine household wear,
Crown of gold doth each one bear;   52
White as lily, red as rose,
Glad the songs that each one knows!
In each crown the gems gleam fair;
Never wish is thwarted there;
Christ their King, their Queen art thou;
Wind nor rain may vex them now. —
Endless day they have for night,
Song for sorrow, peace for fight.   60
Theirs is bliss without annoy,
Game and gladness, endless joy, —
Lady dear, too long the day
Till thou fetchest us away!
Perfect joy we ne'er may know
Till thy bliss thou dost us show.
Chosen Maid, God's Mother dear,
Earth hath never seen thy peer,
Mother thou, and Maid confest,
Holy, high, in Angel's rest!   70
Saints and angels ever sing,
Hailing thee of life the spring;
Mercy aye is found in thee,
None who trusts thee lost shall be.
Save thy Son, all things above,
In my heart, I do thee love!
Heaven fulfilled is with thy bliss,
Earth with this, thy gentleness;
Such thy grace, thy mercy free,
None lack help who cry to thee!   80

Mercy dost refuse to none
Tho' he wrong 'gainst thee have done.
Holy Queen of Heaven, I pray,
Thou wilt list my bede to-day, —
"Lady, by that greeting fair
Gabriel from on high did bear,
For the Sake of Jesu's Blood
Shed for us on Holy Rood,
Mother's pain, and sorrow sore,
When thou stood'st His Cross before, 90
Make me clean, without, within,
That I be not lost thro' sin.
The foul fiend, and all his train
Banish, keep me free from stain;
From thy love I'll ne'er depart,
Thou my life, my safety, art;
For thy love I toil and sigh,
For thy love thy thrall am I;
For thy love forswore, I wis,   99
All things dear — think thou on this!
Sore I rue what grieveth thee,
For Christ's Five Wounds, pity me!
Save for that, I know full well,
I shall burn in fires of Hell.
Silent, all my deeds didst see,
Where, and what, yet bore with me;
Hadst thou 'venged thee of my sin
Paradise I ne'er might win.
Since thou, merciful, didst spare,
Pardon full I hope to share,   110
Ne'er in pains of Hell to fall
Since I yield me here thy thrall.
Thine I am, and thine will be —
On God's Mercy, and on thee,
Rests my life — For thee I long
With desire exceeding strong!
Without thee no joy I know —
Be thou near when hence I go,
Show thy love at my last breath,
Shield my soul from lasting death.   120
Would I thrive? Look well to me,
No weal cometh save thro' thee.
With vile sins my soul is bound,
Healing in thine hand is found;
Thee I trust, next to thy Son,
For His Name, my life, as loan

Grant me, keep the fiend away,
Lest of Hell I be the prey.
For the best rule thou my days,
If I thrive, be thine the praise;   130
Never sinner didst forsake
Who did true repentance make.
Lightly could'st my grief allay,
Grant me more than I could pray,
Thou could'st still my sorrow now
When I, weeping, lowly bow;
Nothing fair in me to see,
Nothing fit to offer thee,
Wash me, clothe me, at this tide,
Thro' thy mercy, spreading wide.   140
Small thine honour if I fall,
Great the Devil's joy withal,
He doth grudge thee worship fair
And the bliss thy servants share.
Well thou know'st he hateth me
Most, because I honour thee!
Watch me, ward me, so I pray,
From his toils, from error's way;
An thou dost, thou 'lt grant, I wis,
Portion fair of Heavenly bliss.   150
Sinning much, I'll much repent,
Shrive me, pray as penitent,
Yea, while life and health be mine
Ever servant true of thine
At thy feet I'll lie, and grieve,
Till my misdeeds thou forgive.
Life, and love, and heart's blood, thine,
Lady, I dare claim thee mine.
Have thou praise on Heaven and earth,
And the joy that 'seems thy worth.   160
Do thou, of Christ's Charitie,
Love and blessing give to me;
Keep my body pure alway —
God in mercy grant, I pray,
I may see thee throned in bliss; —
And my friends may be, I wis,
Better for this Lay I sung
Here to-day, in English tongue.
Mary, for thy holiness,
Bring this monk to joyfulness   170
Who this song hath made of thee,
Christ's dear Mother, Saint Marie!"
                              Amen.

A LOVE RUNE

A Maid of Christ did me entreat
To weave for her a rhyme of love,
That she might learn, in fashion meet,
On whom 't were best to set her love.
Where truth were sure with truth to meet,
And best a woman's choice approve —
I'll not deny that maiden sweet,
But teach her, as my heart doth move.

"Maiden, here may'st thou well behold
How this world's love full fast doth flee,
Beset by frailties manifold,   11
Fickle, and false, it faileth thee.
Thy wooers, but awhile so bold,
Have passed, as wind that bloweth free,
Beneath the clay they now lie cold
As meadow-grass, they withered be.

"There is no man, I trow, alive,
Who steadfast here on earth may be,
With sorrow must he ever strive,
In peace or rest small share hath he. 20
Swift at the goal doth he arrive,
His life-days fleet so speedily,
And Death from this world shall him drive
When he doth live most joyfully.

"No man so rich, no man so free,
But taketh soon from hence his way,
Nor shall he find safe warranty
In gold nor silver, green, nor gray.
None so swift-foot his death to flee,
And guard his life, e'en for a day;   30
Thus is this world, as ye may see,
A shadow, that fast fleets away.

"Its fashion shall ye changing find,
The one doth come, the other go,
He now doth lead who lagged behind,
Who once was friend is now your foe.
Forsooth, he doth as doth the blind
Who sets his heart on this world's show,
Ye'll see it do as doth the wind   39
That e'er from shifting point doth blow.

"Think not that love shall here abide.
Dost trust? 'T is to thy grief, I trow,
Be sure it swift from thee shall glide
Unsound, as reeds that wavering bow.
Froward it is at every tide,
While it endures, 't is grief enow;
At end, no man so true and tried
But he shall fall, as leaf from bough.

"Man's love endureth but a stound,   49
Now doth he love, — now is he sad, —
He cometh, — none his place have
        found, —
Now is he wroth, — now is he glad!
Here one-while, then afar he's bound,
He loves, ere love return hath had,
But never true hath he been found,
Who trusteth him methinks is mad.

"If one be rich in this world's weal,
His heart, it none the less doth ache,
Dreading that thieves shall stealthy
        steal   59
He thro' the night doth watch and wake.
He ponders how he best may deal
To guard, and full assurance make;
What profits all to help or heal
When Death the whole will from him
        take?

"Where now is Paris? Helen, where?
Beauteous they were, and bright and
        gay;
Where Amadace and Idoine fair?
Tristrem and Isoude, where be they? 68
Hector, who shield did dauntless bear,
And Cæsar, who o'er worlds held sway?
As shaft from bow-string fast doth fare
So from this world they've passed away.

"I trow 't is as they ne'er had been,
Yet men of them have wonders told,
And still are fain to hear, I ween,
Their pains and sorrows manifold.

What they in life had said and seen —
But now their heat is turned to cold,
Thus hath this world aye faithless been,
Vainly ye think its joys to hold.   80

"Yea, tho' as rich a man he were
As Henry, now our king, shall be,
And fair as Absalom was fair,
Whose equal earth shall never see;
Yet soon his pride from him doth fare —
(A herring were too dear a fee —)
Maiden, wouldst have of love thy share
True lover will I show to thee.

"Ah! Maiden sweet, an thou but knew
The virtues all that in Him be,   90
So fair He is, so bright of hue,
Of gladsome cheer, and mild is He.
Delight of Love, in Truth most true,
In Wisdom wise, of Heart most free,
Forsooth, thy deed thou ne'er shalt rue
If to His power thou yieldest thee.

"Richest of men is He on land
So far as men may speak with mouth,
The folk, they bow them to His Hand,
To East, to West, to North, to South.
Henry, the King of Engelland,   101
His vassal is, to Him he boweth;
Maiden, He bids thee understand
That Friendship fair to thee He voweth.

"He will with thee nor folk, nor steed,
Nor green, nor gray, nor raiment fair,
Of all such gear He hath no need
For riches hath He and to spare.
If thou wouldst proffer Him indeed
Thy love, wert fain His Love to share,
He 'ld wrap thee in such royal weed   111
As never King nor Kaiser ware!

"What speakest thou of house or hold,
Such as was raised by Solomon?
Of jasper, sapphire, purest gold,
And many another precious stone?
Fairer His dwelling, hundredfold,
Than aught that man hath seen, or known,

He will its gates to thee unfold
If thou wilt Him for True-love own.   120

"On a foundation sure withal
'T is set, that may not yield nor fail,
No sapper undermines that wall,
No foeman may its towers assail.
All ills are healed within that hall,
And endless bliss doth there prevail;
For thee this hold is destined all,
Thou know'st not of its joys the tale!

"There friend from friend ne'er goes his
        way,   129
None may be robbed of this, his right,
Nor hate nor wrath therein may stay
But pride and envy take their flight.
And all shall with the angels play
In concord sweet, in Heavenly light;
Do they not well, sweet Maiden, say,
Who such a Lord shall love aright?

"And never man His face shall see
E'en as He is, enthroned in Might,
But all with bliss fulfilled shall be
Beholding Him, Our Lord, with sight.
To look on Him is joy and glee,   141
For He is Day, that knows not Night,
Methinks, sweet Maid, right blest is she
Who hath her home with such a Knight!

"He set a treasure in thy power
Better than gold, or raiment fair,
And bade thee lock it in thy bower,
He 'ld have thee guard it with all care.
'Gainst thieves, 'gainst robbers, every
        hour,
Needs must thou wakeful be, and ware,
Sweeter thou art than any flower   151
The while thou dost it scatheless bear.

"A gem it is, from far 't was brought,
Better is none 'neath Heaven's ground,
Chosen o'er all that be in thought
The wounds of love it maketh sound.
Ah! Happy she who so hath wrought
To guard it well at every stound,

For an that gem be lost, for naught
May it again by her be found! 160

"Of this same stone wouldst know the
     name?
I trow, 't is calléd 'Maidenhood,'
A precious gem it is, its fame
O'er other jewels high hath stood.
'T will bring thee, Maiden, free of
     shame
To Paradise, of gladsome mood,
Whilst for thine own that gem dost
     claim
Sweeter art thou than spices good.

"Nay, speakest thou of any stone
That be in virtue rich, or grace, 170
Of amethyst, of chalcedone,
Of lectorie, or e'en topace,
Of jasper, sapphire, of sardone,
Emerald, beryl, chrysoprace,
Above all other precious stone
This one is prized, in every place.

"Sweet Maiden, as I thee have told,
This precious gem that thou dost
     bear
Is better, yea, an hundredfold,
Than all these, tho' their hues be fair.
For set it is in Heavenly gold, 181
Of love hath fulness, and to spare,
All may right well that jewel behold,
In Heaven's bower it shineth fair.

"Maiden, didst pray me in thy rede
To choose for thee a lover, so
To do thy will I'll take good heed
And choose for thee the best I know.
Methinks, he doth an evil deed
Who, when his choice doth lie 'twixt two,
Shall choose the worse, and without
     need 191
Shall let the better from him go.

"This rhyme, sweet Maid, to thee I
     send,
'T is open, and unsealed alway,
Prithee, unroll it to the end,
And learn by heart what it doth say.
Thine ear unto its lesson lend,
And teach it other maids, I pray,
Whoso doth pains to learn it spend
Shall profit much, by night and day. 200

"So when thou sittest, languishing,
This written rhyme then take to thee,
And with sweet voice its verses sing,
And do what writ therein shall be.
Thy Love, He sendeth thee greeting,
May God Almighty be with thee,
And thee unto His Bridal bring
In Heaven, where His Throne shall be!

"And give to him a good ending
Who this same rhyme hath writ for
     thee. 210
               Amen."

A HYMN TO THE VIRGIN

To one that is so fair and bright,
     Velut maris stella,
Brighter than the noonday light,
     Parens et puella,
To her I cry: "See thou to me,
Sweet lady, pray thy son for me,
     tam pia,
So that I may come to thee,
     Maria!

"Thou in care art counsel best, 10
     Felix fecundata,
To the weary art thou rest,
     Mater honorata!
Pray thou Him with mildest mood,
Who for us hath shed His Blood
     in cruce,
That by Him at last we're stood
     in luce.

" All this world it was forlorn,
   Eva peccatrice, 20
Till Our Lord as Man was born,
   di te, genitrice,
With *Ave,* it passed away
Darkest night, and dawned the day,
   Salutis,
From thee sprang the well alway,
   Virtutis.

" Lady, flower of everything,
   Rosa sine spina,
Who bare Jesu, Heavenly King, 30
   Gratia divina,
Thou o'er all dost bear the prize,

Lady, Queen of Paradise,
   electa,
Mother-maid, our prayers arise,
   es effecta!

" Well He knows He is thy Son,
   Ventrem quem portasti,
He will not deny thy boon,
   Parvum quem lactasti; 40
Good and gracious as He is,
He hath brought us unto Bliss,
   Superni,
And the pit hath closed, I wis,
   Inferni! "

         Explicit cantus iste.

A SONG ON THE PASSION

SUMMER's come, and winter gone,
Longer wax the days,
And the birdlings every one,
Joyful songs they raise,
Yet by care I'm straitly bound
Spite of joy that may be found
   in land,
    All for a Child
    That is so mild
     of Hand. 10

Fair that Child, and wondrous kind,
Mighty is His thought,
Thro' the woods and hills to find
Me, he straitly sought;
And at last He findeth me
Thro' an apple from a tree
   fast bound,
    He brake ere long
    The bands so strong,
     with Wound. 20

That Child, Who was so fair and free,
To me bent Him low,
Sold unto the Jews for me,
Naught of Him they know,
But they quoth: "Now here shall we

Nail Him high upon a tree
   on hill,
    Yet ere that same
    We'll do Him shame
     at will." 30

Jesus, is that fair Child's Name,
King of every land,
Of this King have they made game,
Smitten Him with hand,
Fain to try Him; on the tree
Gave Him wounds, yea, two and three
   full sore,
    And therewithal
    A drink of gall
     they bore. 40

Death He bare on the Rood tree
For the life of all,
Otherwise no help might be,
We to Hell must fall,
And the fires of Hell must meet,
That, I trow, were never sweet
   withal;
    Nor might us save
    Tower, castle brave,
     nor hall. 50

Maid and Mother, there she stood,
Mary, full of grace,
From her eyes, the tears of blood
Fell fast in that place,
As the tears of blood ran free
Changed in flesh and blood was she,
   and face,
  Her Son was drawn
  As deer is torn
    in chace!   60

Death He bare as Man, for men,
High upon the Rood,
All our sins He washed them then
With His Holy Blood,
With that flood adown did 'light,
Brake the gates of Hell forthright;

  From hold
He led, I wis,
Those who were His
  of old.   70

Thus He rose on the Third Day,
Sat Him on His throne,
Comes again on Judgment Day
And our doom makes known.
Ever may he groan and greet,
Who his death in sin doth meet;
  Jesus,
  As to the skies
  Thou did'st arise,
    Raise us!   80
      Amen.

QUIA AMORE LANGUEO

As thro' a vale, in restless mind,
I sought by mountain and by mead,
A true-love for my need to find,
Unto a hill then took I heed;
A voice I heard — (there did I speed —)
That spake in dolour and in woe:
"Behold My Sides, how sore they
  bleed!
Quia Amore langueo!"

Upon this hill I saw a tree,
Beneath, there sat a Man alone,   10
Wounded from Head to Foot was He,
I saw His Heart's Blood run adown.
Well fitted He to wear a Crown,
Such gracious mien He sure did show;
I asked His grief, He spake anon:
"Quia Amore langueo!

"I am True Love, that false was
  ne'er,
I loved Man's Soul, my sister, so,
That, eager all with her to share,
Forth from My Kingdom did I go;   20
I wrought for her a palace fair —

She fled, I followed, loving so
That I this piteous pain did bear —
Quia Amore langueo!

"My fair Love, and My Spouse so bright
From stripes I saved; she smote Me sore;
Her robe I wrought of Grace and Light,
Behold My Vesture crimsoned o'er!
And yet love-longing waxed the more —
Sweet are the stripes I bare, and lo!   30
The troth I pledged I ne'er forswore —
Quia Amore langueo!

"Of Bliss her crown, and Mine of Thorn;
The Bower her portion, Mine the Tree;
Worship I brought her, she, but Scorn;
Honour I gave, she, Villanie.
Love paid for Love is easy fee,
Her Hate ne'er made my Love her foe;
Ask Me no more why this should be —
Quia Amore langueo!   40

"Look well upon My Hands, O man!
These Gloves as gift from her were
  brought,

They be not white, but red, and wan,
Blood's broiderie My Spouse hath
    wrought!
I doff them not, nor loose for aught,
They woo her still where'er she go,
These Hands for her so friendly fought —
Quia Amore langueo!

"Marvel not, man, tho' I sit still; 49
See, Love hath shod Me wondrous strait,
Buckled My Feet, as was her will,
With sharpest Nails — (Thou well
    may'st wait!)
My Love thereof made no debate,
My Members would I open throw,
My Body, to her heart as mate —
Quia Amore langueo!

"Within My Side I made her nest,
Look in, how wet a Wound is here!
Here as in chamber may she rest,
Together shall we slumber here. 60
Here may she wash her white and
    clear,
Here is the charm for all her woe,
Come when she will she shall have
    cheer —
Quia Amore langueo!

"Lo! I abide and wait her will,
I'll sue the more she sayeth Nay;
If ruthless she, I'll press her still;
If dangerous, I will her pray.
But if she weep, with no delay
Mine arms out-spread I'll round her
    throw, 70
Cry once, 'I come!' Now, Soul, assay!
Quia Amore langueo!

"Set on a hill, as watch-tower high,
I watch the vale, my spouse to see,
She runs away, yet cometh nigh,
Out of My sight she may not flee.
Some wait their prey, to make her flee,
I run before, and chase her foe,
Return my spouse again to me,
Quia Amore langueo! 80

"Behold! my Love, let us go play;
My garden beareth apples fine,
I shall thee clothe in rich array,
Feed thee with honey, milk, and wine —
Behold! My Love, let us go dine —
Within My scrip thy food is — Lo!
Tarry thou not fair Spouse of Mine —
Quia Amore langueo!

"If thou be foul, I'll cleanse the stain;
If thou be sick, I will thee heal; 90
Comfort thee if thou should'st com-
    plain;
Fair Love, dost fear with Me to deal?
Foundest thou ever love so leal?
What wilt thou, Soul, that I shall do?
With force I may not make appeal —
Quia Amore langueo!

"What shall I do now with My Spouse
But wait her will with gentleness
Till she look forth from out her house
Of Worldly Love? Yet Mine she is —
Her couch is made, her pillow bliss, 101
Her chamber chosen — Since 't is so,
Look on me, Love, in kindliness —
Quia Amore langueo!

"My Love is in her chamber, peace!
Make ye no noise, but let her sleep,
Vex not of this, My Babe, the ease,
I were full loth My Child should weep!
Nay, on My Breast I will her keep —
Marvel not tho' I tend her so — 110
My Side had ne'er been pierced so deep
Save, *Quia Amore langueo!*

"Nay, would'st thou set thy love on
    high?
My Love is more than thine may be;
In joy, in sorrow, I am nigh,
Would'st thou but once, Love, look on
    Me!
I would not that thy food should be
But children's meat, nay, Love, not so!
I'll prove thee with adversitie,
Quia Amore langueo! 120

"Nay, wax not weary, Mine own Wife,
'T were ill to live at ease alway,
In tribulation and in strife
I reign with but the surer sway.

In Weal and Woe I am thy stay,
Mine own Wife, bide, nor from Me go,
Death bringeth thee thy meed alway —
Quia Amore langueo!"

FILIUS REGIS MORTUUS EST

As reason ruled my reckless mind,
And on wild ways as forth I went,
A city grave I chanced to find,
To turn thereto was mine intent;
I met a Maid, a Mother kind,
With sobs and sighing well nigh spent,
She wept, she wailed, so sore she pined,
Her hair and face with hands she rent.
Herself she did full sore torment,
Body, and bosom, without rest   10
She tare, and cried aye as she went:
"*Filius Regis mortuus est!*"

"The King's Son" so she cried: "is
    dead,
The joy on which my life was stayed,
To see my Son, how sore He bled,
It cuts my heart as knife's sharp blade!
My Son, Whom at my breast I fed,
Soft lapped, with songs to sleep hath
    laid,
To see Him thus His life-blood shed   19
Makes me, His mother, sore dismayed; —
I am both mother, wife, and maid,
Have no more sons to suck my breast,
Thus my grief's debt may ne'er be
    paid —
Filius Regis mortuus est!

"Thus *Filius Regis*, mine own Child,
Hangs on the Cross, I needs must see
How He was wounded, and defiled
With spear and spitting, piteouslie!
I cried on Him as I were wild: 29
'My dear sweet Son, say see'st Thou me
Thy mother dear?' With looks so mild
He spake: 'Mourn not, let sorrow be,
I shall be thine, and come to thee —'

He spake, I swooned, by grief opprest,
Son mine! Son mine! On rough Rood
    Tree
Filius Regis mortuus est!

"He died! He died! Who was my bliss —
I seeing, swooned, and cried, 'Alas!'
Small wonder if I mourn like this,
My Father, Brother, Spouse, He was!
My Mother, Succour, all that is,   41
All orphaned on my way I pass,
Of Spouse and Brother robbed, I wis,
A thing forlorn, that nothing has —
Gabriel hailed me '*full of Grace,*'
Nay, '*full of Sorrow*' had been best,
The tears, they trickle down my face —
Filius Regis mortuus est!"

She said: "I looked up to my Child,
Cried on the Jews to hang, ere long,   50
Mother by Son, the Undefiled —
Oh Death! Oh Death! Dost do me
    wrong,
My Babe dost slay, Who ne'er was wild,
My slaying tarries over long,
Thou Murderer, why art thou mild
To me, who would to Death belong?
Dost pain my Son with torment strong,
The mother pain, at her behest,
Alas! I sing a sorry song —
Filius Regis mortuus est!   60

"Oh Earth! 'gainst thee complaint, I
    make
That thou didst drink His guiltless
    Blood;
Stone, why didst thou thy hardness
    slake

To Mortar, that the Cross firm stood?
The earth, the stone, Himself did make —
Ye yield ye servants to the Rood
To slay your Lord — an truth ye spake
He did ye never harm, but good!
Meek was He ever, mild of mood,
Ye pierce Him as He were a beast,   70
Alas! my Babe, my life's true Food —
Filius Regis mortuus est!

"Thou Tree, thou Cross, how durst thou
        be
Gallows, to hang thy Maker so?
His Sire, to Him I cry 'gainst thee
Who on His Son hast worked this woe!
Not cause, but help, that slain is He!
Mercy ye trees! Ye be my foe,
Had ye but made a Rood for me   79
To hang by Him, 't were fitting so —
What may I say? Where shall I go?
The Tree hath hanged a King, a Priest!
Of all kings none His peer I know,
Filius Regis mortuus est!

"Ye creatures cruel, Iron, Steel, sharp
        Thorn,
How dare ye thus your best Friend slay?
The Holiest Child that e'er was born
Did wounds and torment on Him lay!
With spear and nails His Flesh have torn;
Spear! the smith's hand why didst not
        stay,   90
That ground thy blade so sharp this morn
That to His Heart didst cleave a way?
I cry on thee both night and day,
A Maiden's Son to death didst wrest,
Forlorn, I wring my hands alway,
Filius Regis mortuus est!

"Thou Scourge, thus made of toughest
        skin,
Knotted and jagged, I cry on thee,
Didst beat my Babe, Who ne'er knew
        sin,   99
Why smotest Him, and spared'st me?
Did He not make thee? Wherefore then
His flesh should thus so mangled be

That ne'er a spot should mercy win
But Flesh and Blood must follow thee?
Didst mar what was so fair to see —
Yet o'er thee shall He win conquest —
Father of Heaven in pity see,
Filius Regis mortuus est!

"Thou Wretch, who proffered Him the gall
For drink, thou didst torment Him
        more;   110
Here down upon my knees I fall
God's judgment on thee now implore!
Upon ye Jews, the first of all,
Ye would Him not, His Flesh ye tore
With these, the tools on which I call,
Ye made them thus to grieve Him sore!
Ye Jews He made, and to restore
Was born as Man, but ye have drest
His Cross! Unhappy who ye bore!
Filius Regis mortuus est!   120

"O ye false Jews! why did ye thus?
Why did ye slay your Saviour so?
When He in judgment sits o'er us
To shun His Wrath where will ye go?
All creatures else were piteous,
The Sun, the Clouds, for this, His Woe
Their mourning made, discourteous
Ye mocking words did 'gainst Him throw!
Temple, and tower, 'neath earthquake's
        throe   129
They shook, to bear ye on earth's breast,
The sun no light to ye would show —
Filius Regis mortuus est!

"Now *mortuus est* mine own fair Lord,
Death doth mine own dear Child deface;
Now thro' this world I walk abroad
E'en as a wretch that wanteth grace;
My grief I fain would thus record,
No more may I behold His Face!
The weary way from Calvary-ward
Weeping, and wailing, thus I trace.   140
If any love me, lend a place
Where I may weep my fill, and rest,
My Son for that will grant ye Grace —
Filius Regis mortuus est!"

LYRICS [1]

ALISOUN

MARCH is yielding to April,
Leaf and flower afresh they spring,
Little birdlings at their will
In their wise do sing.
I in love and longing go
For the sweetest maid I know,
She can bring me out of woe,
I to her am bound.
A happy chance doth me betide,
Methinks that Heaven my choice did
    guide   10
From other maids to turn aside,
And light on Alisoun!

Oh! Her hair is fair to see,
Black her eyes 'neath dusky brow,
Sweetly doth she smile on me,
Slight is she, I trow.
An it were her will to take
This poor heart, and me to make
Her true love, I'ld life forsake,
Dying, fall adown!   20
A happy chance doth me betide,
Methinks that Heaven my choice did
    guide
From other maids to turn aside,
And light on Alisoun!

Thro' the night I watch and wake
So my cheeks wax pale withal,
Lady, all for thy sweet sake
I be longing's thrall!
In this world I know is none
Fit to sing her praise, not one, —   30
White her throat as throat of swan,
Fairest maid in town.
A happy chance doth me betide,
Methinks that Heaven my choice did
    guide
From other maids to turn aside,
And light on Alisoun!

[1] Böddeker, *Alt Englische Dichtungen*, MS. Harl. 2253.

Weary as the sleepless tide,
All for-worn with wooer's woe,
Lest Fate rob me of my bride,
Lo! I yearning go.   40
Better languish for a day,
Than in mourning go alway,
Fairest maid, in gear so gay,
Listen to my rune!
A happy chance doth me betide,
Methinks that Heaven my choice did
    guide
From other maids to turn aside,
And light on Alisoun!

A SPRING SONG

LENT is come with Love to town,
With blossom, and with birdling's rune,
That all gladness bringeth —
Daisies blow on down and dale,
Sweetly trills the nightingale,
Each her glad song singeth.
The Throstle-cock doth loudly cry,
Past is winter's misery
When the woodruff springeth;
Yea, so glad the birdlings be   10
When they Winter's waning see,
That the woodland ringeth!

Now the rose is clad in red;
On the light twigs overhead
Leaves unfold at will;
And the moon doth shew her light,
Fair the lily blossoms white,
The fennel by the rill.
Wooing, preens himself the drake;
Man and maid, they merry make   20
Where the stream runs still.
But the sad, he moaneth aye,
I be one of those to-day,
Love doth like me ill!

Now the moon sends forth her light,
As the seemly sunbeams bright

When the birds sing gay;
Dank, the dew on down it lies;
Lovers in their secret wise
Speak their Yea, or Nay.   30
'Neath the clod the worm doth woo,
And the maidens proudly go,
Fair to see are they!
If I lack the love of one
Of this joy will I have none
But will, outlawed, stray!

WINTER SONG

WINTER wakeneth all my care,
Now the boughs be waxen bare,
Oft I sigh, and mourn full sair
When it cometh in my thought
How this world's joy doth go to naught!

Now it is, and now 't is not,
As it ne'er had been, I wot,
Many a man this word hath got:
"Naught endureth save God's Will —"
That we must die doth please us ill.   10

What afore was fresh and green
Now doth fade and fail, I ween,
Jesu, let Thine Help be seen,
Shield us all from Hell —
For where I go I may not know,
Nor how long I here may dwell!

LOVE–LONGING

WHEN I see the blossoms spring,
Hear the birds' sweet song,
Yearning thought, and love-longing
Thro' my heart they throng.
All set on a love so new —
Love so sweet, and love so true
Gladdens all my song.
For in very truth, I wis,
All my joy, and all my bliss,
Go with Him along!   10

When myself I, wondering, stand,
And with eye do see
How they pierced Him, Foot and Hand,
With sharp nailés three;
And all bloody was His Brow —
There was naught of Him, I trow,
That from pain was free.
Well, ah! well, should'st thou, my heart,
For His love have bitter smart,
Sigh, and sorry be!   20

Jesu mild, I Thee implore,
Grant me strength and might,
That, with ceaseless yearning sore,
I love Thee aright.
Pain may suffer willingly
For thy gentle Son, Mary,
Lady free and bright.
Maiden thou, and Mother mild,
For the love of This thy Child,
Grant us Heaven's light.   30

Woe is me! Could I to-day
Turn to Him my thought,
Take Him for my love alway
Who us dearly bought;
Wide and deep His Wounds they were,
Long and sore the Pains He bare —
(We of love know naught!)
By the Blood that flowed that tide
From His piercéd Hands and Side,
Us from Woe He brought!   40

Jesu, Lord, so mild and sweet,
Here I sing to Thee,
Yea, full oft I would Thee greet,
Pray Thee piteouslie,
Grant that I may sin forsake,
In this world atonement make,
And from wrong be free, —
And when this, our life, shall end,
And from hence we needs must wend,
Take us unto Thee!   50

RELIGIOUS POEMS [1]

THE SWEETNESS OF JESUS

LORD CHRIST, might I Thy Sweetness
see,
Thy Grace to me wouldst truly show,
Bitter all earthly love should be,
Thy Love alone I fain would know.
Teach Thou this lesson, Lord, to me,
To long in such wise here below
That all my heart be set on Thee,
And all my yearning t'ward Thee flow.

My Lord of love most worthy is
To souls who may Him soothly see,   10
To love Him rightly were true bliss,
The King of Love y-clept is He.
By chains of true love wrought, I wis,
Fast bound to Him I fain would be,
That so my heart be wholly His, —
For none save Him rejoiceth me!

If for love shewn I love my kin,
Why, then, it seemeth to my thought,
I should of right with Him begin
Whose Love hath fashioned me of
naught.   20
His Likeness set my soul within —
This goodly world for me hath
wrought —
As Father, seeks my love to win,
And me for heir of Heaven hath bought.

A Mother's love to me He gave
Who, ere my birth, to me took heed,
That babe in Baptism's font did lave
Who erst was soiled thro' Adam's deed.
Rich Food and nourishment He gave,
For with His Flesh He did me feed,   30
A better Food no man may crave —
To lasting Life He doth me lead.

Brother and Sister is He still
For that He spake and taught this lore;

1 From the Vernon MS.

That they who do His Father's Will
His Brethren are they, evermore.
He chose mankind this lot to fill —
I set my trust on Him therefore,
That He will keep me safe from ill
And heal me from His Mercy's store.   40

His Love surpasseth, so I wis,
All earthly love that may be here,
My spouse, both God and Man He is,
I earth-born wretch, must hold Him
dear!
For Heaven and Earth be wholly His —
A mighty Lord is He to fear —
His title is the King of Bliss —
To Him I fain would draw me near.

Yea, for His Love I needs must long   49
Since He hath mine so dearly bought,
When I had sinned, and wrought Him
wrong,
From Heaven to Earth my soul He
sought.
As Man, was born mankind among,
And all His glory held for naught;
He strove with prayer and crying strong
Ere me again to bliss He brought.

When I was thrall, to make me free
His Love from Heaven to Earth Him
led,
Naught but my love He asked in fee,
For me His Life with Death was
wed.   60
When with my foe He fought for me
Wounded He was, and sorely bled;
His precious Blood, as on the Tree
He hung, for me was freely shed.

Blood-stained He was, and stripped all
bare
Who sometime was all fair to see;
His Heart with spear was piercèd there,
His wide Wounds gaped full piteously.

He gave His Life, and naught would
    spare,
That all my guilt should ransomed be; 70
Thus I his suffering fain would share
And hold His Death most dear to me.

For grief my heart must break in twain
If to His Love I take good heed,
The cause was I of all His pain,
He suffered sore for my misdeed.
That I eternal life should gain
He died as Man — such is man's meed,
Then, when He willed to live again,
He rose as God, in very deed.   80

To Heaven He passed with mickle
    bliss, —
Vanquished, the fiends before Him
    quail,
His banner o'er me floats, I wis,
Whene'er my foes would me assail.
My heart must needs be wholly His,
For He as Friend shall never fail,
Nor asked He more than simply this:
Troth of true Love, for sore Travail.

Thus did my Lord my battle fight,
And for my sake was wounded sore,   90
To win my love to Death was dight,
What favour might He shew me more?
To pay Him doth surpass my might,
I can but love Him evermore,
And do His Will, and deal aright,
E'en as He taught in lovesome lore.

His Bidding faithful to fulfil
That were, methinks, both fit and
    kind,
By day and night to work His Will
And bear Him ever in my mind.   100
But ghostly foes they work me ill
E'en as frail flesh doth make me blind;
I needs must crave His Mercy still,
For better aid I may not find.

None other help is left to me,
I to His Mercy me betake,

Who with His Flesh hath made me free,
And me, poor wretch, His Child would
    make.
I pray my Lord, of Charitie,
That He this sinner ne'er forsake,   110
But give me grace from sin to flee
And in His Love my longing slake.

Sweet Jesu, grant me only this,
Take thought of me when hence I wend,
Keep me in steadfast truth, I wis,
From foul fiends shield me and befriend.
Forgive what I have done amiss,
From pains of Hell my soul defend,
And lead me, Lord, unto Thy Bliss   119
To dwell with Thee, World without end!
                   Amen.

PRAYER AT THE ELEVATION

WELCOME, Lord, in form of Bread,
Thou the Living, Thou the Dead,
Jesu, Thee we name!
Thou, One God in Persons Three,
Lord, have Mercy upon me,
Shield me here from shame!

Thou the Sole-Begotten Son,
With the Spirit, Three in One,
Crownéd King art Thou!
Man of more than mortal Might,   10
God of God, and Light of Light,
Born of Mary now!

Jesu, hail! we worship Thee!
Fairest Blossom on Life's tree,
Hail! Thy message fair!
Hail! the Fruit, and hail! the Flower,
Be our Saviour in this hour,
Lord of Earth and Air!

Hail! Thou King of Life and Light!   19
Hail! Thou Man of Deathless Might,
Prince enthroned and crowned!
Hail! Thou Mighty Conqueror!
Hail! be Thou the Governor
Of this wide world round!

Holy Flesh, and Holy Blood,
God and Man, be Thou our Food,
Jesu, King of Kings!
Hail! Thou Born of Maiden mild,
Very God and very Child,
Maker of all things!   30

Hail! thou Rose upon the Bough,
Here as Man we hail Thee now,
For us wert Thou dead!
Hail! Thou God of endless Might,
Son of God, in Glory bright,
Hail! in form of Bread! Amen.

ORISON TO THE FIVE JOYS OF OUR LADY

MARY MOTHER, hail to thee!
Maid and Mother, think on me
For thy mickle might;
Mary, Maiden meek and mild,
From mischance keep me thy child,
And harm, by day and night. *Ave.*

Mary, Maid withouten peer,
This my orison now hear
Tho' I merit naught;
Unto thee I cry and call,   10
Thou, who art the flower of all,
Keep me in thy thought! *Ave.*

Mother thou, and Maid alway,
By that first joy here I pray
Born of Gabriel's rede,
That it keep me day and night
From the devil and his might,
Shield me from misdeed! *Ave.*

For thy joy when God was born,
Lady, leave me not forlorn   20
Whom thy Son bought dear!
Grant that this my prayer to-day
Stand me in good stead alway,
To me lend thine ear! *Ave.*

For thy joy when Christ, Alive

Rose, as God, with wide Wounds Five,
On the Paschal Day,
Pray thy Son, O Mother mild!
That He keep from ill His child,
E'en as well He may! *Ave.*   30

For thy joy at His Ascent
When to Heaven again He went,
Help me, Maid of might!
Be my shield, and be my spear,
That no evil one draw near
Keep me day and night. *Ave.*

For thy joy at thy last end
When thou didst to Heaven wend
Gladness to fulfil;
To that rest, O! Maiden pure,   40
Which for ever shall endure,
Bring me, at thy will! *Ave.*

A MIRACLE OF OUR LADY

WHOSO loves Our Lady aye
She his love will well repay,
Whether life or death his share;
Gracious is she, e'en as fair
As this tale doth truly tell
Which in Paris once befell.

In that city, long ago,
A poor child went to and fro;
As a beggar, would he win
Food and drink for this, his kin,   10
Father, mother, up and down
Begged his way throughout the town.

With his mouth his bread he won,
Other craft the boy had none,
Save his voice so sweet and clear,
All men joyed his song to hear;
With his notes that rang so sweet
He gat food from street to street,
All men hearkened readily
The Antiphon of Our Ladie.   20

And men called the song, I wis,
"*Alma Mater Redemptoris.*"

Would ye now its meaning hear,
"Hail the Saviour's Mother dear!
Gate of Heaven, Star of the Sea,
Save the souls that trust in thee."
On that song men set great store
As he sang from door to door.

But so sweetly rang the song
All the Jews waxed wroth ere long;   30
Till it chanced, one Saturday,
That his road thro' Jewry lay,
Loud he sang the song, and clear,
Well he loved the words to hear,
To the Jews 't was loath alway —
So they thought the child to slay.

One, on evil purpose bent,
Bade him enter, well content;
Seized the child, and with a knife,
Cut his throat, and took his life.   40
Ill the deed, and foul the wrong,
Yet it might not stay the song,
Even when that deed was done
Way to silence him was none!

Then the Jew, full sore afraid
Lest his malice be displayed,
Down a sewer-hole, full nigh,
Thrust the corpse right secretly;
Down the hole the child he threw,
Yet the song burst forth anew;   50
Lustily it rang, the cry
Of a boy's voice, clear and high.
All men heard, both far and near,
Piercing rang the notes, and clear.

The child's mother, patiently,
Till the noontide sun was high,
Waited, that he homeward bare
Food and drink, with them to share.
Noontide came, and noontide passed,
And the mother, sore aghast,   60
In dismay, thro' every street
Sought, where she her boy might meet.

When she came to Jewery
Lo! his voice rang sweet and high,

Clearer as she nigher drew —
Where he was right well she knew.
Then she prayed her child to see —
But the Jew spake, verily,
No such child was there alway —
Yet she ceaséd not to pray —   70
Quoth her boy was there indeed —
Still the Jew denied her rede.

Said the woman: "Thou art wrong,
He is here, I hear his song."
Still the Jew he steadfast sware
No such child had passed by there.
None the less all men might hear
How the song rang loud and clear,
And the longer, louder grew,
Far and near his voice they knew.   80

On her way she went anon,
Hath to mayor and bailiff gone,
Saith: the Jew he did her wrong,
Stole her child for this his song.
Prayeth of them law and right,
That her son be brought to sight;
Prays the mayor, of Charitie
From his bonds her boy to free.

Then she tells, the folk among,
How she lived by this, his song —   90
The mayor pitied her withal,
Did the folk together call,
Told them of the mother's plight,
Quoth, he would do law and right,
Bade the folk with him to wend
To bring the matter to an end.

They came with clamour loud and
         noise,
Yet o'er all they heard the voice,
As an angel's, to their ear
Loud it rang, so sweet and clear,   100
The mayor forced the door forthright
Bade them bring the boy to sight.
No more might the Jew refuse,
Otherwise himself excuse,
But confessed his deed of wrong —
Brought to judgment by a song!

The mayor to seek the boy was bound —
In the sewer the corpse they found,
Drownéd deep in filth — straightway
Forth 't was drawn to light of day. 110
Filth and grime the corpse besmear,
Slit the throat from ear to ear, —
Ere the folk would wend their way
For his crime the Jew must pay.

Then the Bishop, verily,
Came, this wonder fain to see,
In his presence, loud and clear,
Sang the child, for all to hear.
With his hand the Bishop sought
To the throat, and forth he brought 120
A lily flower, so glistening white
Fairer none had seen with sight,
On its leaves, in gold, I wis,
"Alma Mater Redemptoris!"

As the lily forth they take
Of that song an end they make,
These sweet notes are heard no more,
'T was a dumb, dead corpse they bore.
Then in guise most solemn, all
As the Bishop bade, withal, 130
Through the town the corpse they bare
(He himself would with them fare,)
With priest and clerk, who well could
    sing,
While the bells he bade them ring;
With lighted torch, and incense sweet
To that corpse do honour meet.
To the Minster came they then,
Did as meet for all dead men,
Sang a Mass of Requiem fair —
Soon they stood astonied there 140
Rose the corpse the clerks among,
"Salve Sancta Parens," sung.

The child, as men right well might
    see,
Well had loved Our Sweet Ladie,
Here she honoured him, I wis,
And his soul she brought to bliss.
So I rede that every man
Do her service, as he can,

Yield her love, as best he may,
She that love will well repay, 150
Mary Maid, by this, thy might,
Bring us safe to Heaven so bright!

AGAINST MY WILL I TAKE MY LEAVE

Now lords and ladies, blithe and bold,
To bless your name I fain were bound,
I thank ye all a thousand-fold,
And pray God keep ye whole and sound.
Where'er ye fare, on grass or ground,
I pray He cause ye not to grieve,
For friendship fair I here have found, —
Against my will I take my leave.

For friendship fair, for gifts so good,
For meat and drink, in great plentie, 10
The Lord Who suffered on the Rood
Keep all this comely companie.
On sea or land, where'er ye be,
I pray He cause ye not to grieve,
So well have ye entreated me —
Against my will I take my leave.

Against my will I needs must wend
Nor longer make abiding here,
For everything must have an end,
And friends may not be ever near. 20
Hold we each other ne'er so dear
Notice to quit we all receive,
And when we busk us for our bier
Against our will we take our leave.

Depart we must, I know not when,
Nor know I whither we must fare,
But this is aye within our ken
Each man, or bliss, or bale, shall share.
Therefore I rede ye all, beware,
Nor deem fair words ill works retrieve, 30
That so our soul we forfeit there
When that of life we take our leave.

When this our life our form hath left
Our body, shrouded, lieth low,

Our riches all from us be reft
And cold earth on our corpse they throw.
Where are the friends who thee may
    know?
Say now, who shall thy soul relieve?
I rede thee, man, ere hence thou go
Prepare thee well to take thy leave.   40

Be ready for what may befall
Lest suddenly the summons smite,
Thou know'st not when thy Lord may
    call,
Look that thy lamp be burning bright.
Believe me well, save thou have light
Thy Lord shall thee right ill receive,
And drive thee hence from out His Sight
For all too late didst take thy leave.

Christ, Whom a Virgin Mother bore,
Now grant us grace to serve Him so   50
That we may come His Face before
When from this world we needs must go,
Amend the ill that here we do
While that to clay we cling and cleave,
And make our peace with friend and
    foe
So in good time to take our leave.

Now Fare-ye-well, ye good men all,
And Fare-ye-well, both young and old,
And Fare-ye-well, both great and small,
I thank ye all a thousand-fold.   60
I wot that good were richly told
If from mine hand ye might receive;
Christ shelter ye from care so cold
For now 't is time to take my leave.

DEO GRATIAS

In a church this chance befell,
Bells to morning Mass did ring,
Sure it pleased me wondrous well
So I tarried, lingering.
Saw a clerk a book forth bring,
Pointed well in many a place,
Swift he sought what he should sing:
All was *Deo Gratias.*

All the cantors in the choir
With one voice the words they cry,   10
Sweet the sound — I drew me nigher,
Called a priest full privily;
Said: "Sir, of thy courtesy
Prithee, grant me now this grace,
Say what meaneth this, and why
Ye sing *Deo Gratias?*"

All in silk that clerk was clad,
O'er a lectern leanéd he,
Spake a word that made me glad
Saying: "Son, now hearken me;   20
Father, Son in Trinitie,
Holy Spirit, Fount of Grace,
God we praise, so oft as we
Sing our *Deo Gratias.*

"Sure, to thank Him are we bound
With such wit as man may win,
Sorrowful the wide world round
Till He crept into our kin.
Virgin womb He lay within —
Mary Maiden, full of grace;   30
Shed His Blood for all men's sin —
Therefore — *Deo Gratias.*"

Quoth the priest: "Son, by thy leave
I must now mine office say,
Nor for this I prithee grieve,
Thou hast heard the truth alway.
Wherefore now we priests must pray,
Holy Church must offer Mass
In Christ's Honour, day by day,
Saying, *Deo Gratias.*"   40

From the church my way I went,
On that word was all my thought,
Said it o'er and o'er, intent,
Praying, I forgat there naught.
Tho' from bliss my lot were brought
'T were small help to cry, Alas!
In God's Name, whate'er be wrought,
Say I, *Deo Gratias.*

Mend what thou hast done amiss,
Do the right, from fear be freed,   50

Be thy lot or bale, or bliss,
Sure, thy patience winneth meed,
An a gentle life thou lead,
Kindness show in every case,
Thank thy God if well thou speed,
Saying, *Deo Gratias.*

Should God on thee gifts bestow
More than other two or three,
Then I rede thee, rule thou so
That men may speak well of thee.   60
Shun all pride, from boasting flee,
Lest thy virtues sin deface,
Keep thee courteous, pure, and free,
Think on *Deo Gratias.*

Should men bid thee office bear,
Set thee in a place of might,
See thou givest judgment fair,
Rob thou no man of his right.
Art thou valiant, fierce in fight,
See thou none for envy chase;   70
Fear thy God by day and night,
Think on *Deo Gratias.*

If this word in heart we bear,
And in love and loyalty lend,
We thro' Christ may claim a share
In the joy that knows no end.
When from out this world we wend
To His Palace we may pass,
With His Saints to sing *sans* end
Blissful, *Deo Gratias.*   80

MANE NOBISCUM, DOMINE

One summer, ere Ascension fell,
'T was Evensong, and eke Sunday,
Long in devotion did I dwell,
And earnestly for peace did pray.
A text I heard that pleased me aye,
Written it was in words but three,
And thus it runneth, sooth to say,
"*Mane nobiscum, Domine!*"

Now what this word doth rightly mean
In English tongue that will I tell,   10

If we in conscience keep us clean
"*Deign Thou, Our Lord, with us to dwell.*"
The foul Fiend's power do Thou fell
Who died for us upon the Tree,
Whether things fall out ill or well,
Mane nobiscum, Domine!

When Thou from death had'st risen,
      anon,
In Palmer's guise Thy way wouldst go,
Thou met'st with pilgrims making moan,
But Who Thou wert, they might not
      know.   20
Then Cleophas this word also
Spake: "Night is nigh as we may see,
The light of day is waxing low,
Mane nobiscum, Domine!"

Abide with us Our Father dear,
Thy dwelling is in Heaven's Bliss,
Thy Name by us be hallowed here
That we Thy Kingdom may not miss.
In Heaven Thy Will fulfilléd is,
And that it so on earth may be   30
Guide us aright — to teach us this
Mane nobiscum, Domine!

Our daily bread, our natural food,
Dear Lord, we pray Thee, for us dight,
Our debts, do Thou our God so good,
Forgive us, of Thy mickle Might.
So shall we those, with heart so light,
Forgive, who in our debt may be;
Then, lest we rule us not aright,
Mane nobiscum, Domine!   40

Dwell with us, lest we suffer loss,
Let no temptation lead astray,
But if we sin, then by Thy Cross
Mercy and pardon would we pray.
With all the meekness that we may
We cry, low kneeling on our knee,
"When men our corpse on bier shall lay
Mane nobiscum, Domine!"

Lord, dwell with us in all our need,
For without Thee we have no might   50

To raise our hands, or tell our bede,
Nor wit nor wealth may cleanse our
    sight.
What snare soe'er may hold us tight
Safe are we, an we cry to Thee,
In all our need, by day and night,
Mane nobiscum, Domine!

He dwelleth with thee, have no fear
For evil chance that may befall,
Or for the fiend who lurketh near
To rob us of our bliss withal.   60
Save we be 'neath Thy ruling here
Our flesh is frail, we cannot flee,
Then keep our path from cumbrance
    clear —
Mane nobiscum, Domine!

Dwell with us, Lord of Love and Peace,
And make Thy home our hearts within,
That we in Charity increase,
And keep us clean from deadly sin.
Grant us Thy Smile, O Lord, to win,
For Mary's sake, that Maiden free — 70
In every work that we begin,
Mane nobiscum, Domine!

Mane nobiscum, Domine!
Without Thee we were surely naught,
What Joy or Bliss else may there be
For those whom Thou so dear hast
    bought?
In word and will, in heart and thought,
We here beseech the Trinitie:
"When we from out this world be
    brought
Mane nobiscum, Domine!"   80

TRUTH IS EVER BEST

Whoso would him well advise
Of this sad world's way, I ween,
He must needs, forsooth, despise
Falsehood foul, that wrought hath
    been.
Certes, some day shall be seen
How our toil doth miss its quest,

When Good and Ill be judged, I ween,
We shall find that Truth is best.

Truth is best for king and knight —
Certes, he who runs may read,   10
Ladies all, so fair and bright,
Truth should love in act and deed.
Merchant-men, in goodly weed,
Who to buy and sell are prest,
Should from falsehood foul be freed,
Follow Truth, 't is ever best.

Verily, I dare to say,
Man nor woman here shall be
But would fain, if but they may,
Have in life prosperity;   20
And at death would presently
Come to Heaven's eternal rest —
None those goodly courts shall see
Who held not here that Truth was best.

Truth shall judge us all one day,
Righteously, and without wrong,
Then must we both see, and say,
We withstood him overlong.
Therefore lordings, stout and strong,
Judge betimes at Truth's behest;   30
For God's Love, all men among,
Truth uphold, as aye the best.

Therefore keep this in your mind,
Whoso dealeth with the law,
Ne'er with Falsehood's feints unkind
Stifle right, nor Truth withdraw.
Nay, of Falsehood stand in awe,
Tho' ye be for Truth opprest,
For Christ's Sake, let no gold draw
Thee aside — since Truth is best.   40

Would we rule us all with Truth,
Make Him aye our Governour,
Sin nor Sloth should work us ruth,
We should be of Knighthood flower.
Truth in strife shall aye have power,
Greatest, when most hardly pressed,
Stand we faithful in that hour
Vowing, Truth is ever best.

Truth was sometime here our Lord,
Virtue reigned with Him as Queen,   50
Spain and Britain this record,
Other lands have witness been
That we honour due, I ween,
Did them, bade them here to rest,
Falsehood ne'er with them was seen,
Truth they loved — 't was ever best.

Would we now let Truth again
O'er us crown and sceptre bear,
Other lands should yield full fain
Fealty and homage fair.   60
Boldly this I would declare,
Falsehood foul should stand confest,
None, from prince to page would
    dare
War with Truth, that aye is best.

Falsehood well may reign awhile
When maintained by Avarice,
Greed at last shall him beguile
Tho' in wisdom he be nice.
Falsehood, he hath had his price
In the North, and eke in West,   70
Hunt him, as the cat hunts mice,
He who chooseth Truth doth best.

SALVE, SANCTA PARENS !

Hail, lovely Lady, leman bright,
Mighty Mother, and Maiden mild,
Who bare within thy body bright
At once thy Maker, and thy Child,
And yet wert Maiden undefiled —
Rose and Root of true reverence,
Wit and Wisdom unbeguiled,
Salve, Sancta Parens !

Hail for the joy when Gabriel,
Chieftain chosen in chastitie,   10
Low on his knees before thee fell,
And spake with great solemnitie:
"Hail full of grace, God is with thee,
Thou shalt conceive without offence,
For all time blessèd shalt thou be —
Salve, Sancta Parens !"

Hail, Empress high of Heaven and Hell!
When of that angel's tidings fair
Elisabeth didst speed to tell
Right joyful was the meeting there.   20
He leapt for joy, the babe she bare,
For John of Jesus was *gaudens*,
Thus Queen, to thee I make my prayer,
Salve, Sancta Parens !

Hail, Maiden, hope of men forlorn;
In Eastern skies there shone a Star,
To Bethlehem, when thy Babe was born,
It led three kings from lands afar.
Rich offerings for thy Child they bare
Of gold, and myrrh, and frankincense,
To thee I sing, as I did ere,   31
Salve, Sancta Parens !

Hail, Woman crowned with Weal and
    Woe,
Whenas the Passion-tide drew nigh
And dole and dread thy Son must
    know
That Man be saved eternally;
When, on His Resurrection Day
He saw thee erst in His Presence,
In gracious wise He spake alway:
"*Salve, Sancta Parens !"*   40

"Hail, holy Mother!" Sooth to say
Thus spake Our Lord, in fashion
    meet,
To Mary, and then went His Way,
Nor did henceforth Our Lady greet.
And Holy Church, she knoweth why,
As clerks declare it in sequence,
It draweth me to thee, Mary —
Salve, Sancta Parens !

Hail, crownèd Queen of Heaven and Hell!
Hail, true Love to the Trinitie!   50
Thou Darling dear, dight us to dwell
In Paradise, that fair citie.
Princess *sans* peer, of thy pitie,
Put us in peace when we pass hence,
That we may sing with joy to thee,
Salve, Sancta Parens !

CAROLS

Rejoice, all ye who be here present,
Omnes de Saba venient.

Out of the East a star shone bright,
To three kings hath it given light,
Who travelled far by day and night
To seek the Lord, Who all hath sent —
Rejoice, all ye who be here present,
Omnes de Saba venient.

Thereof King Herod needs must hear,
How three kings drew his land anear,
Seeking a Child Who had no peer,   11
And after them he straightway sent —
Rejoice, all ye who be here present,
Omnes de Saba venient.

He spake, King Herod, to those kings
three:
"If so be that Child ye are fain to see,
Pass on, yet come again to me
And tell if your labour be well spent —"
Rejoice, all ye who be here present,
Omnes de Saba venient.   20

Then forth they went by the starry
gleam
Till they came to gladsome Bethlehem,
And a goodly Babe, forsooth, they deem
Him Who His Blood for us hath spent.
Rejoice, all ye who be here present,
Omnes de Saba venient.

Balthasar, he kneeléd first adown,
And he cried:"Hail King of high renown,
Thou of all kings dost bear the Crown,
Therefore have gold for Thy Present!"
Rejoice, all ye who be here present, 31
Omnes de Saba venient.

Melchior, he knelt, that king so good,
And he quoth: "All hail to Thy high
Priesthood,

Take incense as gift to Thy true Man-
hood,
For. here I brought it with good
intent —"
Rejoice, all ye who be here present,
Omnes de Saba venient.

But Jaspar, he kneeléd in that stead,
And quoth: "Hail Lord, for Knighthood
sped   40
I offer myrrh to Thy true Godhead,
For Thou art He Who all hath sent!"
Rejoice, all ye who be here present,
Omnes de Saba venient.

Now lords and ladies in rich array
Lift up your hearts on this Holy
Day,
And to God the Son here let us pray,
Who once for us on Rood was rent —
Rejoice, all ye who be here present,
Omnes de Saba venient.   50

Mater, ora filium,
Ut post hoc exilium
Nobis donet gaudium
Beatorum omnium !

"Who this Babe, O! Maiden fair,
Thou within thine arm dost bear?"
"'T is a King's Son, mark Him well,
Who in highest Heaven doth dwell!"
        Mater, ora filium, etc. —

"Man for Father had He none,   10
Save Himself, Yea, God alone,
Fain to save Mankind forlorn
Of a maiden was He born."
        Mater, ora filium, —

"Kings their homage free have told,
Frankincense, and myrrh, and gold,

To my Son, of aweful Might,
King of Heaven, and Lord of Light."
        Mater, ora filium, —

"Maiden, do thou pray for us   20
To thy gentle Son Jesus,
That He grant us of His grace
In His Heaven to find a place!
        Mater, ora filium," —

Make we merry in hall and bower,
To-day was born Our Saviour!

To-day hath God, of His Mercie
Sent His Son with man to be,
To dwell with us in veritie,
        God that is Our Saviour!

To-day in Bethlehem did befall
A Child was born in ox's stall,
Who needs must die to save us all,   9
        God that is Our Saviour!

To-day there spake an angel bright
To shepherds three, who watched by
        night,
And bade them take their way forth-
        right
        To God, that is Our Saviour!

Therefore, 't is meet we kneel to-day
And Christ Who died on Cross we
        pray
To shew His Grace to us alway,
        God that is Our Saviour!

All of a Rose, a lovely Rose,
All of a Rose I sing a song.

Hearken to me both old and young,
How from its root a Rose-tree sprung,
Of fairer rose no song was sung,
        Never, in any king's land!

Branches six had that Rose, I ween,
Those branches were both bright and
        sheen,   8
That Rose is Mary, Heaven's Queen —
        From her breast a Flower sprung!

The first Branch was of wondrous might,
When It sprang forth on Christmas
        night
A star shone over Bethlehem bright,
        Far and wide its beams flung.

The second Branch was of great honour,
It came adown from Heaven's tower,
Blesséd shall be that goodly Flower,
        Break It shall the Fiend's band.

The third Branch, wide afar it spread;
To Mary, in her lowly bed,   20
Three kings Its beams have safely led,
        Branch and Flower to show!

The fourth Branch sprang adown to
        Hell
The foul Fiend's boast to surely quell,
That never soul therein should dwell —
        Blest be the day, and land!

The fifth Branch was right fair to see,
It sprang to Heaven, both top and tree,
There shall It dwell, our Boon to be,
        Yet rest in priest's hand.   30

The sixth Branch, it shall, bye and
        bye,
Be the Five Joys of Maid Marie, —
Now Christ save all this companie,
        That long life we may know!

Pray for us to the Prince of Peace,
Amice Christi, Johannes!

To thee, who wast Christ's own darling
Man and maid alike, I bring
My homage, and from heart I 'ld sing,
Amice Christi, Johannes!

For that he was so pure a maid
On Christ's Own Breast asleep he laid,
God's secrets were to him displayed —
Amice Christi, Johannes!   10

When Christ to Pilate's house was
    brought
This virgin Knight forsook Him naught,
To die with Him was all his thought —
Amice Christi, Johannes!

Christ's Mother in his care was laid,
Fit mate a maiden for a Maid,
Now pray we to him for his aid —
Amice Christi, Johannes!

What shall I sing but Hoy!
When the jolly shepherd made so much joy?

The shepherd upon a hill he sat,
He ware his tabard and his hat,
He had tarbox, pipe, and flageolet,
And his name was Jolly, Jolly, Wat,
For he was a good herd-boy —
    ut Hoy!
In his pipe he made so much joy,
    What shall I sing but Hoy?   10

The shepherd down on the hill was laid,
His dog was fast to his girdle made —
In a little while he was sore dismayed,
"Gloria in Excelsis!" to him was said —
    ut Hoy!
In his pipe —
    What shall I sing —

The shepherd high on the hillside stood,
The sheep, they flocked round the
    shepherd good,
With his hand he raised from his brow
    the hood,   20
He saw a star as red as blood —
    ut Hoy!
In his pipe —
    What shall I sing —

"Now Farewell Mall, and Will, Fare-
    well,
Now keep ye still, and guard ye well,
Until I come my news to tell,
And Will, ring evermore thy bell — "
    ut Hoy!
In his pipe —   30
    What shall I sing —

"Now must I go where Christ is born,
Farewell, I come again with morn,
Dog, keep the sheep from out the corn,
And gird ye well when I blow my horn — "
    ut Hoy!
In his pipe —
    What shall I sing —

To Bethlehem now Wat hath sped,
His sweat ran down, so fast he fled,   40
Jesus doth lowly hide His Head,
'Twixt ox and ass he makes His bed —
    ut Hoy!
In his pipe —
    What shall I sing —

The shepherd said: "I go forthright
To see that strange and wondrous sight,
Where angels sing from Heaven's
    height,
And yonder star doth shine so bright."
    ut Hoy!   50
In his pipe —
    What shall I sing —

"Jesu, my pipe I give to Thee,
Robe, tarbox, scrip, I offer free, —
Home to my fellows now I flee,
The sheep, methinks, have need of me."
    ut Hoy!
In his pipe —
    What shall I sing —

"Now Farewell Wat, my herdsman
    true — "   60
"What, lady, so my name ye knew?
Lull ye my Lord to sleep anew,
And Joseph, now Good-day to you — "

ut Hoy!
In his pipe —
What shall I sing —

"Now dance and sing full well I may,
For at Christ's Birth was I to-day,
Home to my mates I'll take my way,
Christ bring us all to bliss I pray."   70
ut Hoy!
In his pipe he made so much joy,
What shall I sing but Hoy?

This very night
I saw a sight,
A star as bright
As any day;
And hearkened long
A Maiden's song,
Lulley, by-by,
Lully, lulley.

A lovely Lady sat and sung,
Thus to her Babe did say: 10
"My Son, my Lord, my Dear Dar-
ling,
Why liest thus in hay?
Mine own dear Son,
Whence art Thou come?
Art very God, I-fay,
Yet none the less
I will not cease
To sing, *by, by, lully, lulley.*"
This very night —

Then spake the Babe that was so young,
And thus methinks He said: 21
"Yea, I am known in Heaven as
King,
Tho' now in manger laid.
And angels bright
Round me shall light,
E'en now they wing their way;
In that fair sight
Shall ye delight,
And sing, *by, by, lully, lulley.*"   29
This very night —

"Jesu my Son, of Heaven the King,
Why liest Thou here in stall,
And why hast Thou no fair bedding
Spread in some rich king's hall?
Methinks of right
The Lord of Might
Should lie in fair array;
But none the less
I will not cease
To sing, *by, by, lully, lulley.*"   40
This very night —

"O! Mary Mother, queen of Bliss,
Methinks it were ill done
If I should seek the kings, I wis
'T is they should hither run.
But you shall see
Kings crownéd three
Come here on the twelfth day —
For this behest
Give Me your breast,   50
And sing, *by, by, lully, lulley.*"
This very night —

"Jesu, my Son, I pray Thee say,
As Thou art to me dear,
How may I please Thee best alway,
And make Thee right good cheer?
For all Thy Will
I would fulfil,
Thou knowest it well, I-fay,
Rock Thee, perchance,   60
Or may-be, dance,
And sing, *by, by, lully, lulley.*"
This very night —

"Now Mary, Mother, heark to Me,
Take thou Me up aloft,
And in thine arms soft cradle Me,
And dance Me now full oft;
And lap Me warm,
That, free from harm,
Secure I rest alway,   70
And if I weep,
And will not sleep,
Then sing, *by, by, lully, lulley.*"
This very night —

"Jesu, my Son, high Heaven's King,
If so Thy Will it were,
Grant me my will in this one thing
As seemeth fit and fair;
And all men still
Who can, and will,   80
Make merry on this Day,
To Bliss them bring,
And I will sing,
Lully, by, by, lully, lulley."

This very night
I saw a sight,
A star as bright
As any day;
And hearkened long
A Maiden's song,   90
Lulley, by-by,
Lully, lulley.

LYRICS BY RICHARD ROLLE OF HAMPOLE

I

JESU! For us didst hang on Rood,
For Love Thou gavest Thine Heart's
        Blood,
Love made of Thee our soul's True Food,
Thy Love has brought us to all good.

Jesu, my Love! Of Heart so free,
All this didst do for love of me,
What shall I for this offer Thee?
Naught dost Thou crave but love from me.

Jesu! My God, my Lord, my King,
Would'st have of me none other thing 10
Save but true love, and heart's longing,
And tears of love, and true mourning.

Jesu! My Love, my Joy, my Light,
I would thee love as is Thy right,
Grant me to love with all my might
And mourn for Thee by day and night.

Jesu! Grant me such love of Thee
That all my thought on Thee may be,
Turn Thou Thine eyes, I pray, on me,
And graciously my sorrow see!   20

Jesu! Thy Love is all my thought,
Of other things I reck me naught
Save what I have against Thee wrought
And Thou hast me so dearly bought!

II

Jesu! Forsooth naught doth me move
In all this world both far and near,
With longing sore, and with true love,
Save Thou, my Lord, and Love so dear!

Jesu! True love I owe to Thee   29
Who on the Cross didst show, that tide,
The Crown of Thorns, the sharp Nails
        three,
The cruel Spear that pierced Thy Side.

Jesu! Of Love the pledge I see,
Thine Arms are spread to clasp me close,
Thine Head is bowed for kisses free,
Thy cloven Side, thine Heart's Love
        shows!

Lord Jesu! When I think of Thee,
And look upon Thy Cross aright,
Thy Body stained with Blood I see, 39
Lord, pierce my heart with that sad sight!

Jesu! Thy Mother by Thee stood,
Her tears of love full fast must flow,
To see Thy Wounds, Thy Holy Blood,
Her heart it sore oppressed with woe.

Jesu! Love made Thy Tears to fall,
'T was Love that made Thy Blood to flow,
For Love wast scourged and smitten all,
For Love Thy Life Thou didst forego.

Mary, I pray, as thou art free,
A part of this thy grief I'ld bear,   50
That I may sorrow here with thee,
And bliss with thee hereafter share!

THE FIVE JOYS OF THE VIRGIN MARY [1]

FULL many a man a song doth find
For her who gladdens all mankind
    And once was born on earth;
Yet, tho' all men who speak with tongue
Should sound her praise in joyous song,
    Still more should be her worth!

Angels on high their voices raise,
As Queen of Heaven show forth her
        praise,
    And find in her their bliss;
Earth doth her as Our Lady own,   10
And throughout Hell her power is known,
    For Empress there she is.

The cause of all this dignity,
Her pureness and humility,
    And God's Almighty Grace,
Whereby she bare high Heaven's King;
So men may worthy worship bring
    To her, in every place.

All that is on, or under, mold
How might they now from her withhold
    The reverence that is meet,   21
When He, Who rules the world alway
Himself doth homage to her pay
    As this, His mother sweet?

And many a virgin now doth fare
Who doth God in her spirit bear
    And in her holy thought,
But she, who never man had known,
In deed, and not in thought alone,
    Her God to birth hath brought.   30

Of her, from whom God flesh did take
A fitting song how might I make

Whose life so foul hath been?
Yet Sister, thou dost bid me sing,
And in one song together bring
    These, her Five Joys, I ween.

That such a song be made by me
Who an unlearnéd man shall be,
    In sooth, I dare not say,
I trust me to Our Lady still,   40
And make it as shall be her will
    To teach me that same Lay.

As in our Creed we well may see
Her joys so manifold they be,
    None may them rightly tell,
Such joy she hath thro' her dear Son,
As never by mankind was won,
    No tongue may speak the spell.

Four Joys, they were her portion here
Thro' Grace of Him, her Son so dear,   50
    The Gospel bids us know,
And all from that same Fount of bliss
Whereof she now doth joy, I wis,
    As streams from well they flow.

The well of Paradise, I ween,
Hath of this same a token been
    With its fair rivers four,
That watered all that goodly ground,
And never mortal man hath found
    The measure of its store.   60

This well is God Himself, made Man,
And all her joys from Him they ran,
    In four-fold fashion sped;
First when she did her Child conceive,
And Gabriel must high Heaven leave
    As messenger, that stead,

[1] William of Shoreham.

To bring her tidings great that morn
How Christ of her would fain be born
　　Man's guilt to wipe away,
To bring mankind from out of Hell — 70
What heart may think, or tongue may tell
　　The joy she felt that day?

In Nazareth, that goodly town,
There Gabriel, he 'lighted down,
　　"*Ave Maria!*" his cry,
He gave that maiden greeting fair,
And unto her a gift he bare
　　From God in Heaven high.

In her would God His dwelling make,
There flesh and blood of her to take　80
　　E'en as the angel said;
Nor she a man should know, I trow,
Nor break in any wise her vow,
　　But still abide a maid.

Saint John the Baptist knew that same,
Whenas she to his mother came,
　　Sprang when he heard her voice;
Elizabeth knew well that tide
How the babe moved beneath her side,
　　And there would fain rejoice.　90

More cause, Our Lady, then had she,
Joyous and blithe I ween, to be,
　　Without or pride or boast,
For well she knew the truth, I wot,
And wist full well He was begot
　　Of God the Holy Ghost.

And Joseph dealt as man so mild,
For that he wist she was with child
　　Alone he 'ld go his way,
He would not that she should be slain,
Nor by the law be judged, and ta'en, 101
　　And stoned with stones alway.

And Joseph, he was blithe that night
Whenas there came an angel bright
　　To give assurance still;
And blither far was she, that may,
For she was comforted all day
　　With angels, at her will.

To this First Joy, of which I speak,
We count her joy of forty weeks　110
　　The while she went with child;
Within her womb, as at that same,
The unicorn, He waxed full tame,
　　That erstwhile was so wild.

The Second Joy, it was her lot
When Jesus, He was born, I wot,
　　Upon the Christmas night,
With never sorrow, never sore —
And so shall never woman more
　　Who is for child-birth dight.　120

For e'en as she did first conceive,
Nor sin its stain upon her leave,
　　From fleshly lust was freed;
Therefore her Child, to birth He won
As thro' the glass doth pass the sun
　　Nor opening doth need.

In swaddling bands she did Him dight,
As it shall be for children right,
　　And gave Him suck anon;
Tho' He was born in dark of night　130
Yet was there never lack of light
　　For Heaven itself looked on.

In beam of light an angel came
Into the field of Bethlehem,
　　The shepherd-folk among,
The tidings of Christ's Birth he bore —
Therewith came singing many more,
　　Of angels a great throng.

I trow those words he spake full well
"*Gratia plena*," Gabriel,　140
　　That meaneth, "full of Grace;"
They sang of glory great above,
And peace our portion, for her love,
　　The angels in that place.

The ox and ass, amid the straw,
Whereas they their Creator saw
　　There, 'mid their food to lie,
Altho' unknowing beasts were they
Yet they rejoiced in their own way,
　　And language, verilie.　150

And when it came to the eighth day
He did the Jewish law obey,
   Was circumcised aright,
Jesus, they called His name that morn,
As angels, ere that He was born,
   Had said He should be hight.

Mary with mickle joy espied
Three Kings, as they did thither ride
   From Eastern lands afar,
Gold, frankincense, and myrrh, they
   bring,   160
Since He was Lord, of kings the King,
   As tokened by the Star.

When He was offered fittingly
Within the *templo Domini*
   E'en as the law did say,
The old man, Simeon, on high
He spake of Him a prophecy
   As in his arms He lay.

When He had but twelve winters told,
Seated among the masters old,   170
   Altho' He softly spake,
Men held it for a marvel fair,
To all the clerks who questioned there
   An answer could He make.

Thus virtue crowned His Childhood's
   hour,
And so He waxed to Manhood's power,
   In Jordan's stream, aright
He was baptized; from Heaven above
The Father spake, in form of Dove
   The Holy Ghost did 'light.   180

And to this Joy we count them all,
The joys, that to her lot did fall
   Of this, her Child, so good,
E'en from the day that He was born
To save mankind that was forlorn
   Until He died on Rood.

A Third Joy must Our Lady's be
When she the Risen Christ did see
   From Death's hard bondage wend,

From out the grave wherein He lay   190
As it befell on the third day
   After His Life did end.

What joy of Him might she have more
After such grief and suffering sore
   As she had seen with eye,
Than thus in life her Son to see,
And know He aye alive should be
   And never more might die?

That He was Life, and Strength, and
   Might,
That did He show on Easter night   200
   Ere darkness passed away,
And all the Earth, I trow, did quake,
And Heaven above did joyful make
   His Resurrection Day!

For thence came angels, white in weed,
Who said that Christ was Risen indeed,
   She saw that they spake true;
That in the grave no more He lay —
Lest any should their word gainsay
   The stone they overthrew.   210

By these, His Manhood's deeds, she
   knew
"Dominus tecum" to be true,
   As erst the angel said,
That is to say "God is with thee,"
And here in truth and verity
   The Godhead was displayed.

Nor was she lonely in her bliss,
But shared it with her friends, I wis
   It was so much the more ;   219
For gladness sure doth seem more fair
When with our friends the same we share
   After we've sorrowed sore.

Ah! blithe I trow they well may be
Their Living Lord again to see,
   Amid them had He been!
First showed Himself, for our relief,
To her, of penitents the chief,
   To Mary Magdalene;

To Peter next, then unto all —
Thomas of Ynde, to doubt a thrall,   230
   His Wounds hath felt that stound,
And handling flesh, and bone, and blood,
He cried aloud, as there he stood,
   "My Lord I here have found!"

Our Lord made answer swift, I ween:
"Thou dost believe since thou hast seen
   And touched Me as I stand;
My Blessing, Thomas, here I leave
To those who, seeing not, believe,
   Nor crave to touch with hand!"   240

And to this Joy I count as well
All other joys whereof they tell
   Body or soul's content,
From this, Christ's Resurrection Day,
Till His Ascension came alway
   When forty days were spent.

The Fourth Joy, as I now will tell,
Upon the Holy Thursday fell
   Upon a mountain high,
Jesus she saw, Who was her Son,   250
And flesh and blood from her had won,
   Ta'en up into the sky.

All joy, I trow, was hers that tide
When she our kinsman thus espied,
   Jesus, her own dear Son,
Thus rise into high Heaven's bliss,
A worthy home to make, I wis,
   Where she might dwell anon.

Yet were it not enough, I ween,
That this, her place, prepared had been
   Thus high in Heavenly bliss,   261
But also ours, there is none other,
For that He is so kind a Brother
   As we believe, I wis!

Nor doth He will a long delay,
But we to Him shall go our way
   Whenas we hence shall win,
Save that to Him we be unkind,
And bear not this, His Love, in mind,
   But grieve Him by our sin.   270

Yet is He mild, and spareth some —
As He went hence, so shall He come
   On Doomsday, with great light,
To try of every man his deed,
And then, according to his meed,
   Judgment to give aright.

There is no better counsel here
Than thus to be Christ's comrades dear
   In Heavenly Bliss, for aye,   279
From stain of sin we needs must flee,
And pray God, and Our sweet Ladie,
   To be our help, alway.

Her power shall ne'er the lesser be,
Above all others blest is she,
   Be they, or wife, or maid,
As this, the Gospel telleth us,
"*Benedicta tu in mulieribus*,"
   Elizabeth, she said.

And all her joys at Pentecost,
And other joys, both least and most,   290
   That did on earth befall,
Since Christ's Ascension, with that same,
Until her own Assumption came,
   I here include them all.

The Fifth Joy of Our Lady dear
No tongue of man may speak it here,
   Thereof no more descry,
Save that the glorious Bride, at last,
From out this world in glory passed
   With sweetest melody.   300

Unknown to man the mode, for sure,
The office of her sepulture
   Was all in heavenly wise,
And duller man to heavenly speech
Than beast, that man were fain to teach
   Reason, in human wise.

Therefore thereof is nothing writ,
For man thereof knows naught, to wit,
   So lofty is the theme;
But Holy Church right well doth know
To feel of death no mortal throe   311
   Doth such a life beseem.

We find it writ that angels bright
Do at a good man's death alight
   Who here on earth doth lie,
From Holy Writ we apprehend
That God Himself, He would descend
   Whenas she came to die.

Thereby, I trow, we well may wit,
Tho' there be naught in Holy Writ,   320
   That Christ Himself was there,
And Heaven's host with Him that day,
Our Lady sweet to lead away
   Lest fiends to touch her dare.

Thus, brethren dear, did she ascend,
With soul and body heavenward wend,
   For Christ is true, and kind,
That flesh wherefrom He Flesh did take
Should it its grave 'mid others make
   Nor greater honour find?   330

So I dare say, and with good right,
That all the Court of Heaven did 'light
   When she from hence would fare,
And Christ Himself, He came that day,
Body and soul He bare away
   His dwelling-place to share.

There doth she reign as Queen, *sans*
   end,
I pray her grace to us she send
   Who these her joys now tell;
I trust from sin she'll keep us still,   340
For He is fain to do her will
   Who is of joy the well.

For of her womb the Fruit is He
Whereby the angels nourished be,
   Who is our holy Food;
Elizabeth hath spoken this —
"*Et benedictus fructus ventris
   Tui, Jesus*" the good!

Now this my song to end is brought,
As thou, my Sister, hast besought,   350
   And as I best might speed;
To Heaven's Queen now pray and
   sing,
That us from pain and loss she bring,
   E'en in our utmost need.
                Amen.

(*Oretis pro anima Willelmi de Schoreham,
   quondam vicarii de Chart, iuxta Ledes.*)

NOTES

NOTES

HISTORICAL

LAYAMON. The translations are based upon Sir Frederic Madden's edition (2 vols., 1847). A special interest attaches to Layamon's work, both from the point of view of language and of subject-matter. It marks the transition point from Anglo-Saxon to English, and is therefore one of the very earliest monuments of English literature, in the strict sense of the term. Ostensibly a translation of the French *Brut*, by Wace, it is fully twice as long as that work, and contains much material absent from it. This is particularly remarkable in the Arthurian section; the account of the founding of the Round Table, and of Arthur's Dream, given in the text, are peculiar to Layamon; Wace simply says that Arthur founded the Round Table *"Dont Bretons dient moult fables,"* but gives us no idea of the character of these "fables." He makes no allusion to Arthur's dream, yet this latter must have been a well-established tradition, for it appears in the romances in a form different from that here given. In a previous volume, *Romance, Vision, and Satire*, I have translated the version found in the Old English *Morte Arthure*, where Arthur's fate is foreshadowed under the symbolism of Fortune's Wheel, in which form it was taken over by the prose romances. Layamon's version of the fall of the rooftree, if less elaborate, is even more vivid and picturesque, and possesses the additional feature, absent from the romances, that Gawain is associated with his uncle's downfall, which of course corresponds with the facts, both in pseudo-history and romance. There can be little doubt that there was a popular tradition asserting that Arthur's fate was foretold to him through a dream, but whether Layamon represents the original form of that tradition we cannot say. Nor is it easy to decide whence he drew his additional material; there are three theories as to his immediate source, all of which are possible: (*a*) He may have used a later, and much enlarged "Wace" text, differing from that of the manuscripts preserved to us. (*b*) He may have used an intermediate chronicle, based upon Wace, but incorporating insular traditions unknown to the French writer. Such, for example, might have been the *Brutus* of Martin of Rochester, referred to in a manuscript of Robert de Borron's *Merlin*. That such a chronicle did really exist seems to be proved by the latter part of the Modena *Perceval*, where we find lines and passages derived from Wace in juxtaposition with details found only in Layamon. (*c*) That Layamon, living on the borders of Wales, was familiar with, and utilized, popular tradition, orally transmitted, especially tradition connected with Arthur; (*b*) and (*c*) are not exclusive of each other, and may both have been operating causes. I should be more inclined to accept the conjunction of these two than to postulate the existence of a "Wace" version which has now completely disappeared. There is a large field for research work here, and, in any case, the literary merit of Layamon's chronicle is so great, he is so genuine a poet and patriot, that his work must always possess an interest and fascination for the student of English literature.

ROBERT OF GLOUCESTER. Translated from the edition by W. A. Wright, *Rolls Series* (1886–87). The author of this chronicle must not be confounded with the famous Robert, Earl of Gloucester, who was so generous a patron of literature in the twelfth century. He was probably a monk of the Abbey of Gloucester, a foundation which played no unimportant rôle in the collection and dissemination of English legendary literature. The writer probably lived towards the end of the thirteenth century, and, while familiar with the works of earlier chroniclers, is also drawing upon his own personal experiences. A discussion of the sources employed will be found in Mr. Wright's Introduction. The chronicle, which breathes a genuine spirit of patriotism, may be considered as the earliest attempt to supply the demand, on the part of the rising English middle class, for a popular history of their own land.

ROBERT OF BRUNNE. Translated from the edition by Dr. Furnivall, *Rolls Series* (1887). The extract given explains clearly the aim, and gives all the information we possess as to the personality, of the writer. The chronicle is of interest, also, from the literary point of view, as indicating the development of a movement for the provision of a popular literature in a form that could be readily understood. Robert of Brunne was also the author of a lengthy treatise of a didactic character, *Handlyng Synne,* from which an excerpt is given later on. The chronicle is a later work, and was written in the first half of the fourteenth century, concluding with the year 1338.

BARBOUR'S BRUCE. From the edition by Skeat. *Early English Text Society* (Extra Series, vols. XI, XXI, XXIX). This poem, while the events recorded cannot be said to be generally lacking in historical foundation, is yet so strongly colored by romantic and popular tradition, that its general character is that rather of a *Chanson de Geste,* in the strict sense of that term, than of a chronicle proper. At the same time it is much less of a fiction than is the poem of *Richard Cœur de Lion,* and it has therefore been included in the historical section.

LAMENT FOR KING EDWARD I. Taken from *Alt-Englische Dichtungen des MS. Harl. 2253* (Böddeker), a work to which fuller reference will be made later. On account of its genuine historical character it has seemed best to include this poem with the historical selections rather than with the lyrics drawn from the same source. The author is unknown.

LEGENDARY

The Legendaries form a very important group in English mediæval literature; designed for purposes of edification the *Lives of the Saints* were at first confined to independent poems, more or less romantic, and popular, in form. Gradually the demand for a collection which could be utilized for readings on Sundays and festivals, suitable for church or monastic use, caused these originally independent stories to be brought together in one or more authoritative collections. Of these, two, in especial, have been preserved; the Southern, which was the work mainly of the monks of Gloucester, the Northern, of those of Durham. Dr. Horstmann, who has devoted himself to the study of these texts, considers that the completion of these Legendaries must

have been the work of many decades and much collaboration; that during the progress of the work the manuscripts were widely circulated, and augmented by additions on the part of other monastic communities, so that the versions preserved to us vary considerably in content and arrangement. The translations of the lives of *Saint Dunstan* and *Saint Thomas* are based on Mätzner (*Alt-Englische Sprach-Proben*); that of *Saint Brandan,* on Horstmann's edition (*Early English Text Society,* vol. 87). The *Saint Brandan* text may be studied also in connection with the *Imrama,* or *Wonder-Voyages* literature, of which it is a very famous example.

SAINT CECILIA, belonging to the Northern group, is taken from *Alt-Englische Legenden,* Horstmann (Heilbronn, 1881); that of *Saint Eustace* (*Placidas*), which represents the popular and independent form of these legends, from the same source.

OWAIN MILES, from the edition by Turnbull and Laing (Edinburgh, 1837). This poem occupies much the same position as that of *Placidas :* both are popular versions of a story which, in a more extended form, was later on incorporated in the official Legendaries. The story of Saint Patrick's Purgatory, and the revelation of its marvels to a knight of King Stephen's reign, was exceedingly popular in the Middle Ages. The earliest version is the Latin text of Henry of Saltry (1140), which was copied by various writers and finally rendered into French verse by Marie de France. There are three distinct Middle English versions: one, in the rhyming couplets of Marie's translation, from which extracts are given in Turnbull and Laing's edition of our poem; the version of the Southern Legendary, which has been twice published by Dr. Horstmann, from different manuscripts, first in *Alt-Englische Legenden* (Paderborn, 1875), and later in the volume of the *Early English Text Society,* referred to above. Finally, there is the version of our poem, which, from its rarity, as well as its intrinsic interest, seemed worthy to be included in this volume. The first part, dealing with the torments of Purgatory, is somewhat "banal," and full of repetition, but the visit to Paradise presents many points of interest. The origin of the whole story merits a more detailed and careful study than it has as yet received; I am inclined to think that it preserves a "Mystery" tradition of peculiar interest.

ROMANCES

KING HORN. From the edition by Mac-Knight (*Early English Text Society*, vol. 14). This romance possesses peculiar interest for English readers, as it probably represents a genuine historic tradition. The incidents and topography have been the subject of much discussion by scholars, and while different theories of "provenance" have been suggested there is a general consensus of opinion that the story has a real foundation in fact. Two other versions exist: the Anglo-Norman *Horn et Rimenild*, the authorship of which presents some interesting problems; and *Horn Childe*, a later English form. The relation of the three versions is fully discussed by J. Hall, in his edition of our poem, with the result that he decides that they are independent forms of the same traditional theme.

HAVELOK THE DANE. From the edition by Skeat (*Early English Text Society*, Extra Series, vol. IV). In this poem, again, we have the echo of probably genuine historic events. The close connection with the town of Grimsby renders it particularly interesting to English readers. A full discussion of the poem and its probable source will be found in *History of English Literature*, W. H. Schofield, pp. 266–71. We have so few remains of what may be called genuine "English" romance that this and the preceding poem are, perhaps, of more value than others which possess higher literary merit.

ARTHUR AND MERLIN. From the edition by Kölbing (*Alt-Englische Bibliothek*, vol. IV, Leipzig, 1890). The exact source of this poem remains to be determined; in its general lines it follows closely the version of the prose, or vulgate, *Merlin*, but is much less detailed. Kölbing was of opinion that it is by the same hand as *King Alisaunder* and *Richard Cœur de Lion*, and in the introduction to his edition gives the grounds for this opinion. One of his reasons is the writer's frequent reference to the seasons of the year and their effect upon men. I have given translations of these passages, to which no parallel exists in the original *Merlin*, but in so far as they may be held to be evidences of authorship it is well to remember that such a love of, and reference to, Nature, in her varying aspects, is a distinct characteristic of English mediæval poetry. (Cf., for example, *Sir Gawain and the Green Knight;* Malory's translation abounds in similar passages.) It may be remembered, too, that Arthur is "*der Meienbaere Mann*," and there is reason to believe that much of Arthurian material and tradition finds its ultimate root in nature cults. Kölbing may quite possibly be in the right, but his arguments must be used with caution.

RICHARD CŒUR DE LION. From the edition by Weber (*Metrical Romances*, vol. II). This poem is a curious combination of genuine historical fact and romantic fiction. It is partly based upon traditions of the House of Anjou. One of the early counts was wedded, so the chronicles relate, to a lady of surpassing beauty and demoniac origin, who disappeared in the dramatic manner related in the poem. The uncontrollable temper possessed by the members of the Angevin family was held by them to be an inheritance from this demon ancestress; Richard himself was in the habit of saying, "We came from the Devil, and we go to the Devil." No hint of diabolical origin is, however, attached to Richard's mother, Elinor of Aquitaine. The story of his encounter with the lion was probably a mere invention in order to provide a picturesque explanation for his title. Love-affairs between captive knights and the daughters of their jailers, heathen or Christian, were doubtless of frequent occurrence in the times of the crusades, and the popular story of Gilbert à Becket and his Saracen bride may well have suggested later imitations.

SIR ORFEO. From the critical edition by Zielke (Breslau, 1880). This charming presentation of a classical theme in the guise of a mediæval fairy-tale is particularly interesting as a specimen of the *lais*, which preceded, and in some instances (as, for example, the *Tristan*) no doubt formed the basis of, the later and more elaborate chivalric romances. Arthurian literature abounds in references to such *lais*. The immediate source of our poem appears to have been a French version, now lost, but to which allusions are not infrequent in mediæval romance.

SIR TRISTREM. From Kölbing's edition (*Die Nordische und die Englische Version der Tristan Sage*, Heilbronn, 1883). This poem is a translation of the famous *Tristan* of Thomas, fragments of which alone remain. The English version is distinctly inferior in literary merit both to its original and to the parallel German translation of Gottfried von Strasbourg; but the abrupt and vivid style is not without a charm of its own, and the importance of the subject-matter is such that it has seemed worth while to give the text in its entirety. Students should refer to M. Bédier's edition of Thomas for information on the question of the "content" of the original poem, and the relation in which the existing translations stand towards their source. The passage given previously from Robert of Brunne is of interest here; it is curious that both Thomas and his translator, Gottfried von Strasbourg, express themselves in similar terms; the first asserting that no one tells the story according to Bréri, who knew "*les gestes et les cuntes, De tuz les reis, de tuz les cuntes Ki orent esté en Bretaingne,*" while the German poet asserts that while many have read the story of Tristan but few have read it aright. The origin and growth of the *Tristan* tradition present a fascinating problem which still awaits solution.

AMIS AND AMILOUN. From the edition by Kölbing (*Alt-Englische Bibliothek*, 1884). The story of these two devoted friends has had a remarkable and most varied career. It makes its first appearance in the Latin poem of Radulfus Tortarius, written probably in the last decade of the eleventh century. The heroes were next adopted as paladins of Charlemagne, and became the subjects of a *Chanson de Geste;* here they are slain by the Saracens, and buried in the church of Mortara, in Lombardy, where their tombs were long a favorite object of pilgrimage. The next stage was that of an Anglo-Norman *Roman d'Aventure,* from which source the poem translated in our text is derived. Hofmann, in his edition of the *Chanson de Geste,* gives a list of no fewer than twenty-one versions and translations of the story; as he justly remarks, it is one of the most famous and widely spread of all the mediæval tales — "in the five centuries 1100-1600, it made its way from Italy to England, from Spain to Iceland." It may be doubted whether any other story can show such a record.

SIR LAUNFAL. From the edition by Erling (1883). This poem, an amplification of the *lai* of *Lanval,* by Marie de France, is by Thomas Chester, who may possibly also be the author of the poem *Sir Libeaus Desconus,* which deals with the adventures of Gawain's son. It thus, originally, belongs to the same category as *Sir Orfeo,* both being representatives of the Breton *lai* which formed the groundwork for much of the later mediæval romance. The theme of our poem, the love of a fairy for a mortal, and their separation in consequence of the knight's neglect to observe the conditions imposed by his "other-world" mistress, was remarkably popular; we have more than one *lai* of a similar character. As a folk-tale theme it retains its vitality to the present day, and may be met with in most collections of folk- or fairy- tales.

SIR AMADACE. From the editions by Weber (*Metrical Romances*) and Robson (*Three English Metrical Romances,* Camden Society, 1842). Both the manuscripts of this charming poem are defective, and they differ a good deal verbally, so I have thought it well to use both for the purposes of this translation. The main theme of the poem is identical with that of *Amis and Amiloun,* i.e., the rigid fidelity of the hero, even under the most trying circumstances, to the obligations imposed by friendship and gratitude; but here the theme is combined with another of widespread popularity, that of *The Grateful Dead,* a story found in one form or another all over the world. The two themes are most ingeniously combined and worked out, and the romance, both on account of its subject-matter and the skill with which it is composed, seemed worth giving in its entirety.

YWAIN AND GAWAIN. From the edition by Schleich (1887). This poem was probably written in the early part of the fourteenth century, and is a translation of the *Chevalier au Lion,* or *Yvain,* of Chrétien de Troyes, held by many scholars to be the best of that author's works. The story is a good story, but the main interest of the poem is critical, and lies in the problem of its relation alike to its immediate source and to the other versions of the tale. While on the whole the poet is undoubtedly translating from Chrétien, he, from time to time, diverges from his source in a manner which indicates a familiarity with other, in some points, superior, versions of the story.

SYR PERCYVELLE OF GALLES. From the edition by Halliwell (*The Thornton Romances,* Camden Society, 1844). This romance is of special interest, as it gives us a version of the *Perceval* story in folk-tale form, and entirely independent of the Grail theme with which it is, as a rule, combined. The position to be assigned to this poem in the evolution of the *Perceval* story is a point much debated by scholars. Does it represent a genuine early and popular form of the tale, or is it, on the contrary, merely an abridgment, with certain folk-tale additions, of the poem of Chrétien de Troyes? The late M. Gaston Paris held the first view, and considered the *Syr Percyvelle* to represent the original form of the story. German scholars, who, like Professors Foerster and Golther, maintain the overwhelming importance of the works of Chrétien as sources of Arthurian tradition, hold the second. There is, however, no doubt that, carefully analyzed, the poem presents a surprising proportion of primitive features, — features, in many instances, absent from the French work. Dr. Griffith, who has published an exhaustive study of the poem, is of opinion that it is a popular "minstrel" version of a folk-tale current in the northwest of England, and adduces strong evidence in support of this theory. Dr. Brugger, who is the most competent of modern German Arthurian critics, also maintains its primitive and independent character. Alike from its charm as a tale, and its importance as a member of the *Perceval* group, it has seemed well to give the poem in its entirety.

SIR LANCELOT. From the edition of the Harleian *Morte Arthure*, by Bruce (*Early English Text Society*, Extra Series, vol. LXXXVIII). This version of the Arthurian legend is of great interest, not only on account of its literary merit, which is considerable, but also for the position which it occupies in the evolution of the Arthurian cycle. It was largely used by Malory in the concluding section of his work; for example, the final interview between Lancelot and Guenevere, of which there is no trace in the original French *Lancelot*, has been borrowed from this poem. There are correspondences in the arrangement of subject-matter between the prose compilation, the Harleian poem, and the Italian *Chantari di Lancilotto*, preserved in a manuscript of the Laurentiana Library in Florence, which can hardly be accidental. The ultimate sources of our English Arthurian literature have not yet been satisfactorily determined, and the *Morte Arthure* poems of the Thornton and Harleian manuscripts are of special interest in this connection.

TALES

THE SEVEN SAGES OF ROME. From the edition by Campbell (*The Seven Sages of Rome*, Boston, 1907). Probably no collection of tales has ever been so popular or so widely diffused as that known by the name of *The Seven Sages*, or *Seven Wise Masters*. Professor Campbell, in an exhaustive Introduction to his edition, records no fewer than eight Oriental and forty European versions, all differing, more or less, in their content. Thus, while the framework was practically fixed, the tales might be altered, or transferred from one speaker to another, at the will of the compiler. Many of them are of a character little edifying to modern readers; the two chosen as specimens have been selected, that of the dog, as an early form of a persistently popular tale, that of Merlin, as an interesting variant of an important theme.

THE FOX AND THE WOLF. From Mätzner (*Alt-Englische Sprach-Proben*). This story is a specimen of the numerous *Beast* tales which were extremely popular in the Middle Ages, and finally led to the compilation of the *Thier-Epos*, or *Romance of Reynard the Fox*, a popular satire on the social and religious conditions of the time. Our story is found in the epic, but may well have had an independent source. It is an amusing tale, well and picturesquely told.

THE LAND OF COCKAYGNE. From Mätzner (*Alt-Englische Sprach-Proben*). The idea of a purely material Paradise seems to have been very popular in the Middle Ages. In this particular poem we have the theme treated as the vehicle for a satire of a somewhat broad character, upon the religious life.

PROVERBIAL AND DIDACTIC

THE PRECEPTS OF ALFRED. From the edition by Morris (*Early English Text Society*, vol. 49, 1872). These precepts (which seems a more correct term than the frequently applied proverbs) testify to the reputation for wisdom enjoyed by Alfred; he might, indeed, be termed the English Solomon. The poem of *The Owl and Nightingale*, given in the text, is an interesting illustration of this, both disputants quoting sayings of Alfred in support of their argument. These little poems are exceedingly charming, showing alike a sense of humor and no inconsiderable knowledge of human nature. They deserve to be more generally known than is the case at present.

PROVERBS OF HENDYNGE. From Böddeker (*Alt-Englische Dichtungen*, 1878). This collection, which is really proverbial in character, is especially interesting in view of the fact that the putative author, Hendynge, is said to be "Marcolf's son," thus connecting the work with the famous *Dialogues of Salomon and Marcolf*, extremely popular in the Middle Ages. Nothing is known of the compiler; the work is later than the *Precepts of Alfred*, but contains much genuine old proverbial matter.

THE SACRILEGIOUS CAROLLERS. From the edition by Furnivall (*Early English Text Society*, vols. 119, 123). This curious title is the literal translation of the original, *Manuel des Péchiez*, by William of Waddington, a lengthy treatise on the Seven Deadly Sins, illustrated by tales setting forth the punishment incurred by the different classes of sinners. We have already given the Introduction to Robert of Brunne's Chronicle; the *Handlyng Synne* was composed some thirty years previously (*c.* 1303), and is not a mere translation of the French, as Robert has considerably enlarged the collection of tales; there are almost as many again in the English as in the French. These illustrative tales are of varying value, and some would certainly not appeal to modern readers. The example given in the text has more than one claim to notice; it is obviously based upon an old tradition, and, while a good story in itself, it also finds interesting parallels in mediæval romance, where we have more than one instance of knights joining inadvertently in a 'Carole,' and finding themselves unable to stop. Both the prose *Lancelot* and *Méraugis de Portlesguez* contain an adventure of this description. Cf. "The Caroles in Mediæval Romance," J. L. Weston (*The Quest*, April, 1911).

THE DEBATE OF THE BODY AND THE SOUL. From Mätzner (*Alt-Englische Sprach-Proben*). The source of the English popular poems on this subject appears to be the detailed Latin dialogues, current in the twelfth century. The theme, however, was known earlier, as there exists an Anglo-Saxon version in the famous *Exeter Book* (tenth century), and also in a manuscript of Worcester Cathedral. There are several Middle English versions, the one here given being the most poetical; and also French and Spanish texts. In fact, this was one of the most popular themes for a mediæval writer whose aim was that of edification.

THE OWL AND NIGHTINGALE. From the edition by Wells (Boston, 1907). This poem is another example of the popular "Debate" literature, but more secular in tone. We know

nothing of the author, who may, perhaps, be the Master Nicholas to whom the disputants agree to refer the subject of their debate.

A BESTIARY. From the edition by Morris (*Early English Text Society*, vol. 49). This curious example of the lore of the Middle Ages is a translation from the Latin *Physiologus* of Theobaldus, but the English version differs somewhat from the original, as it omits the description of the Centaur, and adds that of the Dove, which concludes the text. The Latin descriptions are not all in the same meter, but each adheres to the same style throughout; the sudden changes, which I have endeavored to reproduce faithfully, are a peculiarity of the English version. The curious analogies and interpretations of the *Bestiary* are met with so frequently in mediæval sermons and religious art that its inclusion in a volume of this character appeared to be desirable.

RELIGIOUS AND LYRICAL

HYMN OF SAINT GODRIC. From Zupitza (*Englische Studien*, vol. XI). This charming little lyric is traditionally supposed to have been taught to Saint Godric, a monk of Whitby, by the Blessed Virgin herself. Cf. W. H. Schofield, *History of English Literature*, p. 436, where the story is given in detail. We possess two other fragmentary poems, by the same author.

ORMULUM. From the revised edition by Holt (1878). This work shares with Layamon's *Brut* the interest of being one of the earliest monuments of our language, in its period of transition from Anglo-Saxon to English. The two works, though practically contemporary, were written in different parts of England, and represent different dialects. Layamon wrote on the borders of Herefordshire (West Midland dialect); Orm's dialect, on the other hand, shows a strong intermixture of Scandinavian forms, and is probably of Anglian provenance. The writer very possibly belonged to the Augustinian Monastery of Peterboro'. It is interesting to compare this introduction with that of Layamon; the two are singularly alike in their genuine simplicity and desire to be of service to their fellows, without any thought of personal fame or reward; to be remembered in the prayers of their readers is all they ask.

A GOOD ORISOUN OF OUR LADIE. From the edition by Morris (*Early English Text Society*, vol. 34). This poem, written by an unknown hand at the beginning of the thirteenth century, shows the author to have been a poet of no mean order; his picturesque imagery, combined with a mystical fervor, recalls the style of the Rossettis, brother and sister. It is a poem that deserves to be included in any representative collection of English verse.

A LOVE RUNE. From the edition by Morris (*Early English Text Society*, vol. 49). The dedication of this poem runs: "*Incipit quidam cantus quem composuit frater Thomas de Hales, de ordine fratrum minorum, ad instanciam cujusdam puelle Deo dicate.*" Nothing more is known of the writer, who, from the internal evidence, must have been a man well read in the popular literature of his time. The poem is interesting both for its intrinsic merit and on account of its numerous allusions. It is well known to students of English literature.

A HYMN TO THE VIRGIN, and A SONG ON THE PASSION. From the same collection as above (*Early English Text Society*, vol. 49). These poems are given as good examples of the religious poetry of the time; the authorship is unknown.

QUIA AMORE LANGUEO, and FILIUS REGIS MORTUUS EST. From the edition by Furnivall (*Early English Text Society*, vol. 15). In each case the poems have been printed from two manuscripts in parallel columns, the translation in the text is from MS. Lambeth, 853, which gives the better version. The authorship of these two fine poems is unknown; they are found in the manuscripts as part of a series of "Complaints" (the liturgical term "Reproaches" would probably be better), but are decidedly superior to the rest of the poems. *Quia Amore Langueo* has been included in *The Oxford Book of English Verse*, but I have not met with the *Filius Regis* elsewhere, and its claim to attention as a poignant and pathetic piece of verse seemed to demand its inclusion here.

LYRICS FROM THE HARLEIAN MS. 2253. These poems are taken from Böddeker's edition (*Alt-Englische Dichtungen des MS. Harl. 2253*). This is one of our most valuable miscellaneous collections of English mediæval literature. Before the invention of printing had rendered the acquisition of books a comparatively easy matter, men of literary tastes were compelled to make their own collections of such works, in prose and verse, as appealed to them personally. Sometimes these collections seem to have been the work of one hand; in other cases the manuscript was a family heritage, receiving additions in each generation. The value of such collections to the modern student is inestimable. To them, in many cases, we owe the knowledge of important works which, but for the care and industry of the compilers of these collections, would have been lost to posterity. Thus the Auchinleck MS. has preserved for us *Sir Tristrem*, the Thornton, *Syr Percyvelle;* both works of extreme importance for the criticism of the romantic cycles to which they belong. The Harleian MS. is especially valuable for its lyrical selections, forty in number, many of which are not found elsewhere.

POEMS FROM THE VERNON MS. From the edition by Horstmann, and Furnivall, for the *Early English Text Society: Minor Poems of the Vernon MS.*, vols. 98, 117. The principal characteristic of this important MS. is the presence of a large number of lyrics with Latin refrains, several of which are given above. They are very charming and well worth knowing. The general character of the Vernon poems is religious.

CAROLS FROM THE HILL MS. From the edition by Fluegel (*Anglia*, XXVI). The Hill MS. is extremely miscellaneous in character, being the commonplace book of a merchant of the City of London in the sixteenth century; the contents include lists of civic dignitaries, secular pieces, and a specially good collection of carols, many of which are not found elsewhere. I have chosen those which seemed to me the most poetical for inclusion here. A larger selection from the same source will be found in *Old English Carols*, J. L. Weston (Nutt, London, 1911).

LYRICS BY RICHARD ROLLE. From the edition by Horstmann (*Early Yorkshire Writers, 1895*). Rolle was a well-known religious writer of the fourteenth century; probably born at Thornton in Yorkshire, he became at an early age a hermit at Hampole, in the same county, whence he is generally known as Richard Rolle of Hampole. His works, which are fairly voluminous, are marked by a genuine mystic fervor, the prose treatises being superior to the poems in this respect. He was long supposed to have been the author of a lengthy didactic work, *The Prick of Conscience*, but recent criticism has thrown doubt on this attribution.

THE FIVE JOYS OF THE VIRGIN MARY. From the edition by Konrath (*Early English Text Society*, Extra Series, vol. LXXXVI). The dialect of the poems is Kentish, and the author, of whom nothing further is known, was, apparently, a native of Shoreham in Kent, and sometime Vicar of Chart, a living appropriated by Walter Reynolds, Archbishop of Canterbury, to the Augustinian Priory and Convent of Leeds, Kent. The poems, seven in all (of which one is attributed to Robert Grossetête, Bishop of Lincoln, and may be a translation from the Latin of that prelate), are of a didactic character, and evidently composed with a view to edification and instruction. They deal with such subjects as *The Seven Sacraments; The Seven Deadly Sins; The Ten Commandments; Creation and Fall of Man;* thus differing from the writings of Richard Rolle, which are strongly personal in character, expressions of the relation of the Soul to God. William of Shoreham was evidently an expert theologian, and master of his subject, but hardly a poet of distinction. The poem in the text was selected as being shorter and less didactic in tone, while the colophon left no doubt as to the authorship.

ADDITIONAL NOTES

For the information of students unfamiliar with the subject it may be well to say that, of the principal manuscript groups referred to as sources, the Harleian and the Cotton are in the British Museum; The Douce, Digby, Laud, Vernon, and Hill, at Oxford. The Auchinleck MS. is in the Advocates' Library, Advocates' Hall, Edinburgh.

BIOGRAPHICAL

Biographical data concerning the poets of this period unfortunately are both rare and incomplete. Thus, concerning Layamon, Orm, Robert of Brunne, we know just what they tell us in the passages given in the text, and no more; i.e., we know their position in life, where they lived, and why they wrote, but beyond that, even their date has to be determined by internal evidence. We have the name of Thomas of Hales, and we know where William of Shoreham lived; Richard Rolle is really the only writer concerning whom we have anything like full details. With regard to the authorship of the romances, we are in even worse case; we have one name, Thomas Chester; for the rest we know neither their names, their date, nor the sources upon which they drew. These are all questions of internal evidence and critical hypothesis.

BIBLIOGRAPHY

BIBLIOGRAPHY

GENERAL WORKS OF REFERENCE

FOR the student of Early English literature the best general collection of material is to be found in the series of texts published by the *Early English Text Society*. They are issued in two series, Original and Extra, distinguished from each other by the numerals, the Original texts bearing Arabic figures, the Extra, Roman numerals. Volumes of both are issued annually, the Original series dating from 1864, the Extra, from 1867. Certain of the texts have been reëdited in the light of later knowledge, and the editors are all scholars of reputation. The Series is published by Kegan Paul, Trench, Trübner & Co., London; and by Henry Frowde, Oxford University Press, Oxford and London. It has been largely used in the preparation of this volume.

The two first volumes of Messrs. Macmillan's HISTORY OF ENGLISH LITERATURE, *English Literature from the Beginning to the Norman Conquest* (Stopford Brooke), and *English Literature from the Norman Conquest to Chaucer* (W. H. Schofield), cover the same period; the latter, in especial, will be found a good book of reference.

Mätzner's ALT-ENGLISCHE SPRACH-PROBEN (2 vols., Berlin, 1867) contains a very useful selection of Middle English texts, with good Notes, and Glossary.

A TREASURY OF ENGLISH LITERATURE. Kate Warren (Constable, London, 1906). This is an anthology covering the ground from the beginning of Anglo-Saxon literature, in the seventh to the eighteenth century, with an introductory essay by Mr. Stopford Brooke, whose *Primer of English Literature* it was designed to illustrate. The compiler is a Lecturer in English Language and Literature, attached to the London University, and the texts chosen have been used by her to illustrate her lectures. They are given in the original, with translation in footnotes, but, naturally, the extent of the scheme has necessitated their being very restricted in length. The book, however, may be very useful as a lecturer's manual.

HISTORICAL

GENERAL

SOURCES AND LITERATURE OF ENGLISH HISTORY. C. Gross (London and New York).

THE ARTHURIAN MATERIAL IN THE CHRONICLES. R. Huntingdon Fletcher (Harvard Studies, Boston, 1906). Though specially devoted to the Arthurian pseudo-history, this work contains a description and discussion of the various chronicles, and is a most useful book of reference.

SPECIAL

LAYAMON'S BRUT. Ed. by Sir Frederic Madden, 2 vols. (London, 1847).

THE ROLLS SERIES, for *Robert of Gloucester*, and *Robert Brunne*. This series contains critical editions of all the principal British Chronicles.

LAYAMON, VERSUCH UEBER SEINE QUELLEN. Imelmann (Berlin, 1906). A study on the immediate source of Layamon, which the writer decides must have been of French origin.

THE LEGEND OF SIR PERCEVAL. J. L. Weston (vol. II, chap. XII). A discussion of the *Mort Artus* section of the Modena *Perceval*, which is a prose rendering of a metrical chronicle apparently occupying the intermediate position between Wace and Layamon.

LEGENDARY

EARLY ENGLISH TEXT SOCIETY, vol. 87, for the Southern Legendaries, printed by Dr. Horstmann from the Laud MS. 108 (Bodleian Lib.); Mätzner, ALT-ENGLISCHE SPRACH-

PROBEN, gives the Lives of *Saint Thomas* and *Saint Dunstan* from MS. B. M. Harleian, 2277; these are the two principal manuscript collections of the Southern group.

ALT-ENGLISCHE LEGENDEN. Horstmann (Heilbronn, 1881), gives the Northern group from MSS. Harleian, 4196, and Cotton, Tiberius, E. VII (both B. M.).

ALT-ENGLISCHE LEGENDEN. Horstmann (Paderborn, 1875), contains the pseudo-Gospels of the *Nativity* and *Childhood* of Our Lord, from the Northern Legendary, and *Barlaam and Josaphat*, and the *Purgatory of Saint Patrick* from the Southern.

The *Saint Brandan* text, included here, from the Southern legendary, really belongs to a somewhat different category; it is a noted example of the *Imram* or *Wonder-Voyage*, a theme extremely popular in all literatures.

THE BOOK OF WONDER-VOYAGES. J. Jacobs (Nutt, London, 1896), contains a very good collection of these stories, drawn from different literatures, with interesting notes on the sources by various scholars. In his notes to *The Voyage of Maelduin*, the late Mr. Alfred Nutt remarked that this was probably the original source of the *Voyage of Saint Brandan*, "a Christian adaptation of the theme immensely popular throughout the Middle Ages. Thanks to it the Irish seamen's legends became part of the literature common to all Western Christendom. As late as the fifteenth century the Isles of the Blessed Brandan were being sought for by adventurous seamen, and Columbus himself was probably influenced by the tale."

THE VOYAGE OF BRAN SON OF FEBAL TO THE LAND OF THE LIVING. Kuno Meyer and Alfred Nutt (London, Grimm Library, vols. IV and VI), is an Irish pre-Christian version of the same theme, and may, not improbably, have suggested the name of our monk.

OWAIN MILES. Ed. from the unique MS. Auchinleck, Advocates' Library, Edinburgh, by Turnbull and Laing (Edinburgh, 1837); the edition was limited to thirty-two copies, and is now difficult to procure. I am indebted to Professor Ker for the loan of his copy.

THE PURGATORY OF SAINT PATRICK, in its final "legendary" form, will be found in Horstmann's edition of the Southern Legendary, and also in the Paderborn volume mentioned above.

ROMANCES

GENERAL

EPIC AND ROMANCE. W. P. Ker (2d ed. London, Macmillan, 1908). An excellent Introduction to the general study of this literature.

ANCIENT ENGLISH METRICAL ROMANCES. Ritson (3 vols., 1802), contains the text of thirteen metrical romances, some of which have not been reprinted.

METRICAL ROMANCES. Weber (3 vols., 1810), contains ten romances, other than those published by Ritson.

SYR GAWAYNE. Sir Frederic Madden (for Bannatyne Club, 1849). A collection of romances dealing with that hero; a very fine volume, and now difficult to procure.

THREE ENGLISH METRICAL ROMANCES. Robson (from the Irland MS. for Camden Society, 1842), contains *Sir Amadace*.

THE THORNTON ROMANCES. Ed. Halliwell (Camden Society, 1844), contains *Syr Percyvelle of Galles*.

ALT-ENGLISCHE BIBLIOTHEK. Ed. Kölbing, contains critical editions of English metrical romances.

SPECIAL

KING HORN. (Three manuscripts: Cambridge, Gg.; Harleian, 2253; Laud, 108.) Ed. Ritson, *Ancient Metrical Romances; Early English Text Society*, vol. 14 (MacKnight, Editor of E. E. T. S.); Wissmann, 1881; J. Hall, Oxford, 1901. This last is a critical edition, with full Introduction, and discussion of previous editions and literature.

Mätzner, ALT-ENGLISCHE SPRACH-PROBEN, vol. I.

The Anglo-Norman, HORN ET RIMENILD, was published by F. Michel (Bannatyne Club, 1845), and reëdited by Brede and Stengel (1881). HORN CHILDE is printed by Hall at the end of his edition.

THE STORY OF HORN AND RIMENILD. W. H. Schofield (*Modern Language Association of America*, 1903), contains a discussion on the sources and topography of the legend.

HAVELOK THE DANE. (Unique MS. Laud, 108, Bodleian.) Ed. by Sir Frederic Madden (Roxburghe Club, 1828); by Skeat, *Early English Text Society* (Extra Series, vol. IV), and reëdited in 1902; Holthausen, 1901.

ARTHUR AND MERLIN. (Unique MS. Auchinleck, Advocates' Library, Edinburgh.) Ed. Turnbull (Abbotsford Club, 1838); Kölbing (*Alt-Englische Bibliothek*, vol. IV, Leipzig, 1890). A later version of this poem exists in four manuscripts, incomplete in each case, and is printed by Kölbing in the same volume. The vulgate *Merlin*, which represents the ultimate source of the poem, is accessible in Dr. Sommer's edition (London, Nutt, 1894).

RICHARD CŒUR DE LION. (Five manuscripts, all incomplete; Caius Coll. Cambridge; Auchinleck; Douce; Harleian, 4690, and one in the possession of the Marquis of Stafford.) Ed. by Weber from the Caius MS., *Metrical Romances* (vol. II); and by Turnbull and Laing, from the Auchinleck, in their edition of *Owain Miles*.

SIR ORFEO. (Three manuscripts: Auchinleck; Ashmolean, 61, Bodleian Lib.; and Harleian, 3810.) Ed. from the Harleian by Ritson, *Ancient English Metrical Romances*; from the Auchinleck by Laing (1822); finally by Zielke, in a critical edition based on all the manuscripts (Breslau, 1880).

SIR TRISTREM. (Unique MS. Auchinleck.) Ed. by Scott (1804); Kölbing, *Die Nordische und die Englische Version der Tristan Sage* (Heilbronn, 1883); MacNeil, *Scottish Text Society* (1886). The Norse translation of Thomas's poem is contained in the first volume of Kölbing's edition; the German translation, *Tristan und Isolde*, by Gottfried von Strasbourg, has been several times published; the most accessible form is that by Bechstein, *Deutsche Classiker Des Mittelalters* (3 vols.). An abridged prose translation by J. L. Weston will be found in No. II of *Arthurian Romances* (Nutt, London, 1899). For a discussion of these different versions, their relation to the original, and the probable source of Thomas's poem, the student should consult M. Joseph Bédier's edition of Thomas, *Le Roman de Tristan* (*Société des Anciens Textes Français*, 2 vols., Paris, 1902, 1905).

AMIS AND AMILOUN. (Four manuscripts: Auchinleck; Douce; Harleian, 2386; and one belonging to the Duke of Sutherland.) Ed. Weber, *Metrical Romances*, and Kölbing, *Alt-Englische Bibliothek* (1884). *Amis et Amile*, Hofmann (Erlangen, 1882), contains the Latin text, and the *Chanson de Geste*, with a full bibliography; and *Les Épopées Françaises* (L. Gautier), also contains *Chanson de Geste* and bibliography.

SIR LAUNFAL. (Unique MS. Caligula, A. II.) Ed. Ritson, *Ancient English Metrical Romances*; Halliwell (Shakspeare Society, 1845); and Erling (1883). Cf. also *Englische Studien* (vol. XVIII). The *lai* of *Lanval*, of which the poem is an amplified version, will be found in Warnke's edition of the works of Marie de France (2d edition, 1901); a prose rendering is given in *Four Lais of Marie de France*, J. L. Weston (*Arthurian Romances*, No. III, Nutt, London, 1900). For a discussion of the variants of this popular theme, cf. *The Lays of Graelent and Lanval*, W. Schofield (*Modern Language Association of America*, 1900).

SIR AMADACE. (Two manuscripts, both defective at commencement: Auchinleck, and Irland.) Ed. from the Auchinleck by Weber, *Metrical Romances*; from the Irland by Robson, *Three Early English Metrical Romances* (Camden Society, 1842). Cf. also, *The Grateful Dead*, G. H. Perrould (*Folk-Lore Society*, extra vol., 1907), where a detailed discussion and comparison of the central theme will be found. This work is interesting and valuable as throwing light upon the sources of many mediæval chivalric tales.

YWAIN AND GAWAIN. (Unique MS. B. M. Cotton, Galba, E. IX.) Ed. Ritson, *Ancient English Metrical Romances*, and Schleich (1887). The poem of Chrétien de Troyes, of which this is a translation, will be found in Professor Foerster's edition of Chrétien's works (vol. II, 1887); the German version, by Hartmann von Aue, in *Deutscher Classiker des Mittelalters* (1888); the Welsh, in Mr. Alfred Nutt's edition of the *Mabinogion* (London, 1902). A discussion of the English poem and its relation to the other versions will be found in vol. I of *The Modern Language Quarterly* ("Ywain and Gawain," J. L. Weston). On the formation of the poem, *Legend of Sir Lancelot*, J. L. Weston. (Chap. v, "The Position of Chrétien de Troyes in the Arthurian Cycle").

SYR PERCYVELLE OF GALLES. (Unique MS. Thornton, Library of Lincoln Cathedral.) Ed. Halliwell (Camden Society, 1844); and by W. Morris (1895). A very full discussion of this poem, its sources, and relation to other versions of the *Perceval* story, will be found in *Sir Perceval of Galles*, by R. H. Griffith (University of Chicago Press, 1911). Cf. also a review of the above work by J. L. Weston, *Romania*, 1911, and *The Legend of Sir Perceval*, J. L. Weston (vol. I, chaps. II and III).

INDEXES

INDEX OF FIRST LINES

INDEX OF TITLES

Child's ?????? .... 9, 41, 60, 61.
36... ?, ??

King Arthur + King Cornwall - Child 30.

The Boy and the Mantle - Child, 29.

The Marriage of Gawen, Child, 31.